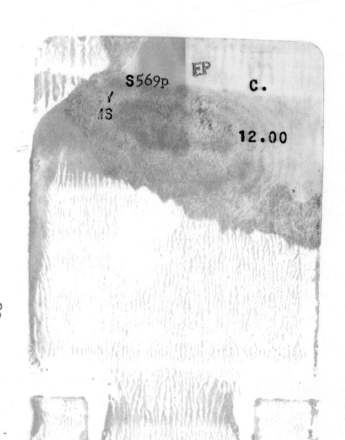

THE POEMS OF
Sir Philip Sidney

Oxford University Press, Amen House, London, E.C.4

GLASGOW NEW YORK TORONTO MELBOURNE WELLINGTON
BOMBAY CALCUTTA MADRAS KARACHI LAHORE DACCA
CAPE TOWN SALISBURY NAIROBI IBADAN ACCRA
KUALA LUMPUR HONG KONG

SIR PHILIP SIDNEY

Aged 22, from the portrait at Warwick Castle

THE POEMS OF
Sir Philip Sidney

EDITED BY

WILLIAM A. RINGLER, Jr.

OXFORD
AT THE CLARENDON PRESS
1962

To the Memory of
ROBERT KILBURN ROOT

PREFACE

THE poems of Sir Philip Sidney have hitherto been available only in texts containing varying degrees of corruption, because he did not himself supervise their publication and his holograph originals have disappeared. Therefore the primary purpose of the present edition is to determine the original wording of his poems in accordance with the received principles of textual criticism. More than a hundred manuscripts and early prints containing his poems have been analysed, only a small proportion of which were either used by or even known to previous editors. The relationships of all the known substantive texts have been established, the sequence of authorial revisions has been determined, and the corruptions of scribes and early printers have been removed to produce texts of the poems in a form that it is hoped Sidney himself would have approved.

In addition the Introduction gives an account of Sidney's literary career, his sources, his programme for reforming English letters, and his numerous technical innovations. The Commentary provides information about the date and circumstances of composition or revision of each group of poems, and explanatory comment for each poem. In gathering material for the notes I have done a good deal of independent investigation and have also tried to make a thorough survey of all the published scholarship on Sidney's poetry; but I have not tried to make the notes by any means variorum, and have passed over in silence a number of published comments which in my judgement appeared to be manifestly wrong or unsupported by adequate evidence.

Free time to work on this edition was made available by leaves of absence from Princeton University and Washington University. I began the collection of material in British and other libraries with the aid of a John Simon Guggenheim fellowship, and completed the collection with a renewal of that fellowship. In between I worked at the Folger Shakespeare Library with the aid of a fellowship from that institution and a grant from the American Philosophical Society, and I completed the preparation of the printer's copy while research associate at the Henry E. Huntington Library. Microfilms of almost all the manuscript and printed textual sources are in the Washington

University Library, purchased from funds made available by a university research grant. To these institutions and their officers I tender my heartiest thanks.

I also owe thanks for many courtesies to the librarians and staff members of most of the chief libraries of England and the United States. I owe special debts of gratitude for permission to examine and quote from items in their collections to the librarians and governing bodies of the British Museum, the Public Record Office, Somerset House, the Lambeth Palace Library, the Bodleian Library, the libraries of Corpus Christi College, Jesus College, The Queen's College, and Wadham College, Oxford; the Cambridge University Library, and the libraries of St. John's College and Trinity College, Cambridge; the University of Edinburgh Library and the National Library of Scotland; Marsh's Library, the library of Trinity College, Dublin, and the library of the Representative Body of the Church of Ireland; the Bibliothèque de l'Université de France; the Folger Shakespeare, the Henry E. Huntington, the New York Public, the Newberry, and the Pierpont Morgan libraries; and the university libraries of Chicago, Harvard, Princeton, and Washington University. I am also indebted for access to the private collections of the Duke of Norfolk, Mr. T. Cottrell-Dormer, and the late Dr. A. S. W. Rosenbach. I am particularly indebted to three individuals: Viscount De L'Isle and Dudley, who gave me access to the Sidney treasures at Penshurst, especially the Davies manuscript of the *Psalms;* Dr. B. E. Juel-Jensen, who allowed me to collate his manuscript of the *Psalms* and to print its unique version of the Countess of Pembroke's poem to her brother; and most of all Mr. Arthur A. Houghton, Jr., who when he learned that I could not get permission to quote from the Briton manuscript that provided the decisive evidence for determining the relationships of the *Astrophil and Stella* texts, purchased the manuscript and put it at my disposal, and most recently gave me access to and permission to quote from the newly discovered Helmingham Hall manuscript of the *Old Arcadia* and *Lady of May* of which he is now the owner.

This edition is built upon the labours of many others. My obligations are first to the anonymous scribes and compositors who first preserved Sidney's texts, next to the scholars and editors who have preceded me, and finally to my friends and associates who have provided information and have criticized my work. My earliest debts are to Fulke Greville and Matthew Gwinne for their editing of the

1590 *Arcadia*, to the Countess of Pembroke and Hugh Sanford for
their editing of the 1593 edition and the 1598 collected works, to
the anonymous corrector of the 1613 edition for his intelligent con-
jectural emendations, and to Thomas Newman for making *Astrophil
and Stella* available even though in a corrupt text. The later editors
from whom I have profited most are William Gray, the Reverend
Alexander B. Grosart, A. W. Pollard, Albert Feuillerat, Mona
Wilson, and Michel Poirier, and I have been greatly aided by R. W.
Zandvoort's analysis of the two versions of the *Arcadia*.

I have tried to acknowledge all specific items of indebtedness in
the notes, but my obligations are so numerous that there are probably
several persons whom I have failed to mention. I hope those who
are not named will accept my thanks and my apologies. To certain
individuals more general acknowledgement is due. First to my
teachers (many of whom alas are no longer living), especially Asher
E. Hinds who first introduced me to Sidney, Hoyt H. Hudson and
Charles G. Osgood who acquainted me with things Elizabethan,
and Robert K. Root who both by precept and example tried to
teach me what a scholar ought to be. To many others I am obliged
for various items of information and advice that are not specified
in the notes: Robert J. Barry, Jr., A. M. Buchan, John Buxton, Miss
Cornelia C. Coulter, John Crow, Charles W. Eckert, Gwynne B.
Evans, F. S. Ferguson, Miss Helen Gardner, W. S. Howell, Miss
Ruth Hughey, G. K. Hunter, W. A. Jackson, Miss Kathrine Koller,
Saul Levin, George Russell, Walter F. Staton, Jr., Frederick W.
Sternfeld, Allan Stevenson, A. H. Travis, Bernard M. Wagner, and
Franklin B. Williams, Jr.

I am also especially indebted for personal assistance to a number
of Sidney scholars. When I first began to collect materials for this
edition William H. Bond put at my disposal his dissertation on
Sidney and gave me leads to two important manuscripts; Ephim G.
Fogel kept me acquainted with his own researches and gave me many
items of information; Robert L. Montgomery, Jr., read and com-
mented on many of my notes; and J. C. A. Rathmell, who is prepar-
ing an edition of the Countess of Pembroke's version of the *Psalms*,
checked my descriptions of the manuscripts and pointed out some
omissions in my remarks on the later Psalms translated by the Coun-
tess, and also called to my attention some peculiarities in the read-
ings of F that led me to re-examine the textual evidence and to dis-
cover that PS 27–150 of F were transcribed from A. I owe most to

Miss Jean Robertson, who is herself preparing a critical edition of
the two versions of the *Arcadia* and whose complete collation of all
the prose provided information to reinforce my classification of the
manuscripts. I am not certain that she agrees with my classification
of Ph, and the latest communication I have had from her indicates
that I am in error in assuming that the Countess of Pembroke con-
sulted Cm when she edited 93; she suggests instead that the Coun-
tess used another now lost transcript of G rather than Cm itself.
Finally I am grateful to the readers and officers of the Clarendon
Press for their advice and technical assistance and their patience
during my long struggle with the proofs, and most of all to my wife
for her long-enduring and cheerful assistance and encouragement.

After the text of this edition was in page-proof a hitherto un-
recorded manuscript of the *Old Arcadia* and *Lady of May* was sold
at Sotheby's on 6 June 1961 (lot 21). Miss Jean Robertson, who
examined the manuscript before it was sold, sent me a description of
it, and three months later the purchaser, Mr. Arthur A. Houghton,
Jr., allowed me to examine the original in New York. The manu-
script came from Helmingham Hall, Suffolk, and the initials 'S L T'
on the binding indicate that it belonged to Sir Lionel Tollemache
(1562–1612), the first baronet. It originally consisted of 160 ff., the
first and last leaves blank and the intervening leaves numbered 1–158,
written throughout in a single late sixteenth-century secretary hand,
on paper with watermarks similar to Briquet's Nos. 8077–82 which
appear in other documents dated 1561–1602. Ff. 1–152^v originally
contained the complete text of the *Old Arcadia*, untitled, but ff. 25
and 33–44 are now wanting, causing the loss of lines 50–134 of OA 9
and all of OA 15–24; ff. 153^r–154^r are blank; ff. 154^v–158^r contain
The Lady of May, untitled and beginning 'her most excellente ma^{tie}
walkinge in wansted garden', and ending 'Plauditamus & Valeamus'.
     Miss Robertson in her preliminary examination of the manuscript
found that its *Old Arcadia* text shares a number of agreements in
error with both Je and Qu, but that it agrees in error with Qu in other
places where Je has the correct reading; she therefore concluded
that it and Qu must both be independent transcripts of a lost original
(Z), and that Z and Je are both independent transcripts of another
lost original X (see stemma on p. 380). My own examination of the
manuscript merely served to confirm Miss Robertson's findings. It
clearly derives from T rather than from P because it preserves the

errors peculiar to T in OA **3**. 6, **7**. 60, **10**. 7, &c. (see p. 367). Like Je and Qu it also derives from T¹, the earliest preserved version of T, because it contains the discussion of quantitative verse at the end of the First Eclogues (see pp. 389–90), which is otherwise preserved only in Je-Qu and was deleted in T²; because it contains the earlier text of OA 28, which was revised in T³; and because it contains the name 'Hippa' in OA 29, which was changed to 'Cosma' in T⁴. Like Je–Qu it omits OA **31**. 25 and **67**. 31–33; and like Qu it contains a 114-line version of OA 62 that omits lines 25–26, 29–36, and 71–92 (Je omits lines 25–26, 29–36, and 69–70, has 71–86 written in the margin, and wants all the following lines because of missing leaves). This indicates that OA 62 in T¹ probably contained 124 lines (rather than 130 lines as I suggested on p. 369) and that lines 87–92 were probably added in T². The manuscript also contains the side-note to OA 13 otherwise preserved only in Je–Qu–St, and the scansion patterns for all eight quantitative poems otherwise preserved completely only in St (see p. 367). The text of the manuscript appears to be somewhat less accurate than Je, but considerably more accurate than Qu. Since Je is defective in a number of places the manuscript will be of value for determining the earliest state of the *Old Arcadia* text; but its readings will not in any way change the present critical text, whose object is to reconstruct the final version of Sidney's poems. I have not been able to insert its variant readings in the apparatus, because to do so would have required resetting the entire apparatus to the *Arcadia* poems and repaging the whole volume.

Hitherto the only known substantive text of *The Lady of May* was that printed at the end of the 1598 *Arcadia*. Though the new manuscript version is carelessly written with many errors, it also corrects a number of manifest errors in 98 and contains some evidently authentic phrases that 98 omitted. Thus for 98's 'sleepish' (Feuillerat's reprint, ii. 334. 35) the manuscript correctly reads 'sheepish', and for 98's 'yet thus much I concerne of them, that I must euen giue vp what my conscience doth find' (ii. 335. 29–30) it reads 'yet this muche my capacitie doth conceave of him that I muste geue vp from the Botome of my stomack what my conscience doth fynde'. Both texts agree, probably in error, in assigning LM 3 to Espilus alone (see p. 363). The manuscript concludes with a speech, wanting in 98, in which Rombus presents the Queen with a chain of agates and tells her of the loyal service of 'mʳ Roberte of wanstead' (the Earl of Leicester), who 'so states the case that he is fowlly commaculated wth the papisticall enormitie'. It is therefore a substantive text of fundamental importance. With the generous permission of Mr. Houghton I have listed on p. 5 its variant readings in the three *Lady of May* poems.

W. A. R.

Washington University
St. Louis

CONTENTS

INTRODUCTION

In the second decade of the seventeenth century the newly formed Bodleian Library was decorated with a series of portraits of the great writers of all ages. In the section devoted to the arts (what is now the western range of the upper reading room) the portraits began with Homer, who as the greatest of the ancients was given the place of honour over the doorway, and continued in chronological order along both walls to the western window, where the place of honour as the greatest of the moderns was given to Sir Philip Sidney.[1] Chaucer, in company with Dante and Petrarch on the side wall, was the only other English poet represented. There is abundant evidence to show that the pre-eminence accorded Sidney in this series of portraits was by no means an eccentricity of the Bodleian authorities, because for more than a century after his death he continued to be the most admired and the most read writer of his generation. Part of his reputation stemmed from the charm of his personality and his fame as a soldier; but even when we restrict our examination to the impact of his literary works alone we find that he was more frequently praised as a writer, both at home and abroad, than either Spenser or Shakespeare, Ben Jonson or Donne. Seventeenth-century readers called for three editions of Spenser's collected works and four of Shakespeare's, but for nine of Sidney's; and in the earlier part of the seventeenth century his *Arcadia* was translated into French, German, Dutch, and Italian, long before any other Elizabethan literary works were printed in a European vernacular.

Contemporary popularity is no certain index to enduring excellence, and we today give other Elizabethans the place of pre-eminence; but Sidney at the very least still deserves a position near by, and that not merely for his historical importance. Though his *Arcadia* will no longer hold children from play and old men from the chimney corner, it is still the most interesting work of Elizabethan prose fiction; his *Defence of Poesy* remains, as a literary composition,

---

[1] J. N. L. Myres and E. Clive Rouse, 'Further Notes on the Painted Frieze', *Bodleian Library Record*, v (1956), 294–5. The portraits were plastered over in 1830, and that of Sidney was not uncovered until 1954; but visitors to the Bodleian are still unable to see him in his place of eminence, because his portrait is now hidden behind a new wall that was built to enclose a book lift.

the most perfect example of renaissance criticism; and now that his poems are available in more accurate texts it is hoped that they may come to be regarded more highly by those who appreciate excellence of craftsmanship and are interested in experiencing emotion controlled by intellect.

The Making of the Poet

Sidney was born at Penshurst in Kent on 30 November 1554.[1] King Philip was his godfather; he was the prospective heir of his childless uncles, who became the earls of Leicester and Warwick, two of the most influential noblemen in the kingdom; and his father, Sir Henry, who from 1559 onwards was Lord President of the Marches of Wales and who in addition served three times as Lord Deputy of Ireland, was one of the most able and most respected of Queen Elizabeth's administrators. As the eldest son he was expected to follow in the footsteps of his father and his uncles, so he was trained from infancy for a career as a statesman and a soldier. It apparently was no part of his family's plans or his own that he should also achieve eminence as a writer. His father 'had some sight in good letters and in histories and armories, and would discourse verie well in all things';[2] but there is no evidence that he had any special interest in fiction or poetry. His mother's taste in literature may be judged from some verses she once copied:

> If not for to spede thou think a pain
> will not the thing that thou maeist not attain
> for thou and none other art Cause of thy Lett
> if that which thou mayest not thou craue to Gett.[3]

When Philip had completed his seventh year his parents put him in charge of a tutor[4] who taught him to write an Italianate hand and instructed him in the rudiments of Latin grammar and French. Just before his tenth birthday he entered the third form of the newly established Shrewsbury School, on the same day as Fulke Greville

---

[1] Unless otherwise noted, biographical details are from M. W. Wallace, *The Life of Sir Philip Sidney*, 1915. References for quotations of Sidney's prose writings are to the volume and page of his *Complete Works*, ed. Albert Feuillerat, 4 vols., 1912–26.

[2] Edmund Molyneux in Holinshed's *Chronicles*, 1587, Ireland, p. 152.

[3] Written in her own hand in a blank leaf of a copy of Halle's *Union of Lancastre and Yorke*, 1550, now in the Folger Library; attributed to Hermes in Ho, f. 83.

[4] Thomas Moffet, *Nobilis*, ed. Heltzel and Hudson, 1940, p. 71.

who became his life-long friend. Two years later his father wrote him a letter of advice on his studies and his conduct:

Let your first action be the lifting up of your mind to Almighty God by hearty prayer. . . . Mark the sense and the matter of that you do read, as well as the words; so shall you both enrich your tongue with words and your wit with matter. . . . Be courteous of gesture and affable to all men, with diversity of reverence according to the dignity of the person. . . . Give yourself to be merry. . . . But let your mirth be ever void of all scurrility and biting words to any man. . . . Above all things tell no untruth; no, not in trifles. . . . Study and endeavour yourself to be virtuously occupied. So shall you make such a habit of well-doing in you as you shall not know to do evil, though you would. Remember, my son, the noble blood you are descended of by your mother's side; and think that only by virtuous life and good action you may be an ornament to that illustrious family.

At Shrewsbury for three years he read Calvin's Catechism, Caesar, Cicero, Livy, Sallust, Cato, Horace, Ovid, Terence, and Virgil. He also continued his study of French, and got some knowledge of Greek from Clenardus's grammar and reading parts of the New Testament, Xenophon's *Cyropaedia*, and Isocrates. He composed the usual Latin exercises, and learned the rules of scansion from Rudolphus Gualterus's *De Syllabarum et Carminum ratione*. He later wrote workmanlike Latin prose in letters to his continental friends; but he was insufficiently interested in Latin versifying to continue it after it was no longer required as a schoolboy task.

The remarkably competent headmaster, Thomas Ashton, had been a fellow of St. John's College, Cambridge, when Ascham, Cheke, and Watson were in residence.[1] In ten years he built Shrewsbury School from almost nothing to one of the finest schools in the kingdom. Later he entered the service of the first Earl of Essex, and also served the Crown on missions requiring both judgement and tact. He prepared abstracts of Cicero and Vives to aid his pupils in their study of Latin, and gained considerable reputation for his Whitsuntide productions of religious plays. In 1566 his play was about Julian the Apostate. In the same year Sidney paid a brief visit to Oxford, in company with Mr. Ashton and Thomas Wilson, author of *The Arte of Rhetorike*, where his uncle the Earl of Leicester, Chancellor of the University, received the Queen. There he witnessed the usual academic exercises, and three plays—*Marcus*

[1] J. B. Oldham, *Headmasters of Shrewsbury School*, 1937, p. 10.

Geminus, James Calfhill's *Progne*, and Richard Edwards's *Palamon and Arcyte*. But he apparently was unimpressed by the school and university drama, for he later wrote that of all the comedies and tragedies he had seen in England, none observed rules either 'of honest civilitie, nor skilfull Poetrie, excepting *Gorboduck*', and even that was faulty because it failed to observe the unities of place and time (iii. 38). On his return journey to school he gave 12*d*. to a blind harper near Stratford on Avon; but it was on some other occasion that his heart was 'mooved more then with a Trumpet' at hearing the crude old song of Percy and Douglas sung by a 'blinde Crowder, with no rougher voyce, then rude stile' (iii. 24).

In February 1568 he entered Christ Church, Oxford, where he boarded with the Dean, Dr. Thomas Cooper,[1] who had been chosen Vice-Chancellor through the influence of the Earl of Leicester. Cooper had been master of Magdalen College School, where he had prepared his great *Thesaurus*, the most complete and authoritative Latin–English dictionary of the century; but by this time he had become more involved in theology and administrative affairs than in classical scholarship. Sidney's tutor was Thomas Thornton, an accomplished Latinist and theologian who in later years twice served as Vice-Chancellor of the University. Thornton often befriended poor scholars of promise, and at this time was supporting in his own lodgings the young historian William Camden. Both at school and at the University Sidney was placed under the care of men who were staunch Protestants, and competent in practical affairs as well as in learning.

Undergraduates were expected to read with their tutors, attend public lectures, and dispute in the schools. All lectures and disputations were in Latin. One of his contemporaries, Richard Carew of Antony, who later translated Tasso and wrote the *Survey of Cornwall*, records that in 1569 he was 'called to dispute extempore . . . with the matchless Sir Philip Sidney in the presence of the Earls of Leicester, Warwick and divers other great personages'. As the favoured nephew of the Chancellor, Sidney was probably given many special privileges; but since he was always a serious student, we may assume that he performed most of the required exercises. The prescribed subjects were grammar, rhetoric, and dialectic. The authors read for grammar were Priscian or Linacre and Cicero, Horace, or Virgil; for rhetoric Cicero or Aristotle; and for dialectic Porphyry or Aristotle.

[1] *HMC De L'Isle*, i. 244.

Sidney did not appreciate the minute attention paid to Latin style, and later referred to Ciceronianism as 'the cheife abuse of Oxford, *Qui dum verba sectantur, res ipsas negligunt*' (iii. 132). His own undergraduate letters to Sir William Cecil, though not technically Ciceronian in style, are unhappily exercises in saying nothing prettily. Yet the most valuable product of his studies and disputations in Oxford was the thorough training he received in logic and formal classical rhetoric. He learned the principles of invention, the various formulas for disposition, and the many varieties of schemes and tropes. His easy command of all the possible configurations of language distinguishes his own later compositions from those of earlier Tudor writers who had not yet completely absorbed the academic discipline of rhetoric. At the end of the century John Hoskyns illustrated a handbook on composition with examples from the *Arcadia*, because it exemplified 'all the figures of rhetoric and the art of the best English'. His feeling for structure, one of the characteristic merits of his poetry, was developed through these early studies. In addition he thoroughly mastered the contents of Cicero's writings, and through them gained a knowledge of Roman literary, moral, and political ideas. He also studied several Greek and Roman historians, and some of the philosophers, especially Aristotle, whose *Ethics* and *Politics* he read in Latin translations, and the first two books of whose *Rhetoric* he translated into English at this or a later time.

Since the main business of Oxford was to train young men for the service of the Church, the University produced many preachers and theologians, but few men of letters. The only students of Sidney's time who later achieved recognition for their English writings were George Pettie of his own college and John Lyly of Magdalen; but there is no evidence that he became particularly acquainted with them as undergraduates, and he later harshly criticized their prose style. The chief literary light of Christ Church was Canon James Calfhill, Professor of Divinity, whose Latin tragedy *Progne* had been performed during the Queen's visit in 1566. He was a competent Latin versifier whose pen was always at command to lament the death of an important person or celebrate the advent of a distinguished visitor. The only member of the college at this time known to have written English verse besides Sidney was John Badger, superior bedel of divinity, who contributed a few formless lines to the Kenilworth entertainment of 1575. The attitude of most of Sidney's contemporaries in the University toward fiction and poetry is exemplified by Nathaniel Baxter, who lamented that we neglect the Bible,

> And spende our time in tryfling toyes, to our perpetuall shame:
> We do delight in Matchevile his cruell pollecie,
> And reade the booke of Arthurs knights being full of Papistrye.
> And Guy of Warwicke, Scoggins gests, and Gargantua,
> The court of Venus, Howleglasse, Legenda Aurea.[1]

In the spring of 1571 a severe visitation of the plague caused a suspension of all University exercises, and Sidney in his sixteenth year left Oxford without taking a degree. After some time at Reading, he perhaps spent the remainder of the year with his parents, who were residing at Lambeth and in London in close proximity to the Court.[2] Then in May 1572 he was licensed to travel abroad with three servants and four horses, 'for attaining the knowledge of foreign languages'.

His uncle the Earl of Leicester gave him a letter to Sir Francis Walsingham, the English ambassador at Paris, introducing him as 'young and raw' and one who 'no doubt shall find those countries and the demeanours of the people somewhat strange unto him'. He spent three months in Paris, but left after the horrors of the St. Bartholomew massacre and never again set foot in France. He then went by way of Heidelberg to Frankfort, where he remained until the spring of 1573. During the summer he travelled through Heidelberg and Strasbourg to the Imperial Court in Vienna, whence in September he took a side trip to Hungary. From November 1573 until the beginning of August 1574 he was in Italy, staying most of the time in Venice and Padua, but also taking a circular tour through Florence and Genoa. He then returned to Vienna where, after a brief excursion into Poland, he remained for the winter. In the spring of 1575 he travelled on a wide arc through Prague, Dresden, and Heidelberg to Strasbourg. He then proceeded to Antwerp, where, after an absence of three years, he sailed for England.

Sidney already had an excellent command of French, which he probably perfected during his stay at Paris; and he also kept up his Latin, the international medium of diplomatic and learned com-

---

[1] In the preface to his translation of the *Sermons, of Calvine . . . upon the Prophet Jonas*, 1578, B3. Years later Baxter claimed that he had been Sidney's tutor (*Sir Philip Sydneys Ourania*, 1606, N1ᵛ); but he appears to have been a student of Magdalen rather than Christ Church, and did not get his M.A. until 1577—though Dr. Cooper may have brought him from Magdalen to Christ Church.   [2] *HMC De L'Isle*, i. 246.

munication, by writing and conversation and by studying the familiar epistles of Cicero. His chief servant was Lodowick Bryskett, who had been born in England of Italian parents, and it was probably under his tutelage that he learned Italian during his nine-month stay in Italy. During the following winter in Vienna he became a close friend of the diplomat Edward Wotton, who had lived for several years among the Spanish residents of Naples. It may have been with his assistance that he acquired the reading knowledge of Spanish that his later writings show he possessed. But though he spent almost two years in the German states of the Empire, he never could bring himself to learn the language, which he considered harsh and unpleasant (iii. 84).

But the learning of languages was by no means the only object of his travels. Some years later, when his younger brother Robert was sent on a tour of the Continent, he wrote him a letter of advice:

> Your purpose is being a Gentleman borne, to furnish your selfe with the knowledge of such thinges, as maie be serviceable to your Countrie, and fitt for your calling . . . the knowledge of all leagues, betwixt Prince, and Prince, the topograficall descripcion of eache Countrie . . . howe stored with shippes, howe with Revenewe, howe with fortificacions and Garrisons, howe the People warlicklie trayned or kept under . . . their religions, pollicies, lawes, bringing upp of their children, disipline both for Warr, and Peace (iii. 125–6).

He appears to have followed his own advice, and to have devoted his major energies to meeting important people and to gaining a knowledge of the political, economic, and religious conditions in the countries he visited.

During his first winter in Frankfort he lived in the house of the learned printer and French Huguenot refugee Andrew Wechel, where he met the elderly statesman Hubert Languet, a Burgundian in the service of the Elector of Saxony. Languet, an ardent disciple of Melanchthon, recognized the eighteen-year-old Sidney's worth and saw in him, because of his abilities and family connexions, a means for involving England in the active support of the Protestant parties of the Continent. He therefore gave him his companionship, advised him on the course of his travels, and provided him with letters of introduction to statesmen and scholars throughout Europe. Though he may have originally cultivated Sidney's acquaintance for his future usefulness as an ally of the Protestant cause, he soon developed a warm personal affection for him. Sidney reciprocated his affection, acknowledged that he had acted as a father to him (iii. 102), and later paid high tribute to the value he set upon his friendship:

> Languet, the shepheard best swift Ister knewe,
> For clerkly reed, and hating what is naught,
> For faithfull hart, cleane hands, and mouth as true:
> With his sweet skill my skilless youth he drewe,
>   To have a feeling taste of him that sitts
>   Beyond the heaven, far more beyond your witts.
>
>   .   .   .
>
> With old true tales he woont mine eares to fill,
>   How sheepheards did of yore, how now they thrive,
>   Spoiling their flock, or while twixt them they strive.
>
>   (OA **66**. 23–35)

Partly through his own inclinations and partly through the influence of Languet, the people whose acquaintance he made were almost all Protestants. Even in Italy he appears to have associated more with the few Italian Protestants like Cesare Carafa and the French and German members of the foreign colony than with the native Catholics.[1] He sought first of all to know statesmen, military leaders, and princes whose acquaintance would be valuable to him in his future political career—men like Lewis of Nassau, brother of William of Orange, and Count Hannau, a nobleman of the Empire. But he also had an eager intellectual curiosity, and enjoyed the company of scholars and professional men of all kinds. At Paris he met briefly the educational reformer Ramus (Pierre de la Ramee); at Heidelberg he struck up an acquaintance with a fellow traveller, the scholar-printer Stephanus (Henri Estienne); at Strasbourg he called upon the humanist educator Sturmius (Johann Sturm); and in Vienna he became a friend of the botanist Clusius (Charles de L'Ecluse) and the Emperor's physician Crato (Johann Crafft von Crafftheim). But there is no evidence that he sought or made the acquaintance of Ronsard, Tasso, or any of the other prominent poets of the time.

The main subjects of his letters from the Continent are people and politics, though he also made some references to books and reading. He prepared himself for his journey to Hungary by reading Pietro Bizari's *Historia della Guerra Fatta in Ungheria* (iii. 95). In Venice he read Contarini's *La Republica e i Magistrati di Vinegia*, the standard work on the government of the city; Ruscelli's *Imprese Illustri*, a sort of Who's Who providing information about the leading families of Italy; and collections of letters by Paolo Manuzio and others as a

---

[1] John Buxton, *Sir Philip Sidney and the English Renaissance*, 1954, p. 68.

help in learning Italian (iii. 83). At Venice he also studied astronomy and a little music (iii. 80), and while in Vienna he practised horsemanship and read the standard books on the subject (iii. 3 and 133). He considered continuing his study of Greek, in order to read Aristotle's *Politics* in the original (iii. 84); he tried to buy Amyot's French translation of Plutarch's *Morals* (iii. 81); and he became acquainted with Machiavelli's *Prince* (iii. 90).

Years later, after Sidney had become known as a poet, his servant Bryskett wrote that they scaled the Alps and Apennines 'still with the Muses sporting';[1] but there is no other evidence that he read the poets and romancers of France and Italy at this time. Even the professional statesman Languet would quote Petrarch on occasion; but Sidney never mentioned a vernacular poet. His letters contain schoolboy tags from Horace and Terence, but the only indications of his reading in more modern poetry are his transmitting some Latin verse by an anonymous Frenchman to a physician in Poland (iii. 102), and his once quoting Buchanan's dedication to his Latin paraphrase of the Psalms (iii. 90). If he had any interest in vernacular poetry, he kept it to himself. His known interests can be judged by the books his continental friends dedicated to him. In 1576 Stephanus dedicated his edition of the Greek New Testament, the following year Banosius dedicated his edition of Ramus's *Commentariorum de Religione Christiana Libri*, and in 1581 Clusius dedicated his translation of Monardes's *Simplicium Medicamentorum ex Novo Orbe Delatorum . . . Historiae Liber Tertius*. The men who knew him best on the Continent thought of him as a young man interested in learning and religion; they did not think of him as a future poet.

Early in June 1575 Sidney, now in his twentieth year, returned to England with his friend Edward Wotton. He went first to London, and then probably joined Queen Elizabeth's progress at Kenilworth, where his uncle the Earl of Leicester entertained the Queen for most of the month of July, and where his parents[2] and his sister Mary, now a young lady of fourteen, were members of the royal party. There were elaborate pageants and recitations for which some of the most prominent professional poets of the time—Ferrers, Gascoigne, and Hunnis—had been engaged to compose verses in praise of the Queen. Judging from the descriptions that have come down to us, the most entertaining performances were the low-comedy antics of the rustics in their bride-ale and morris dance, and in their Hock-

---

[1] *A pastorall Aeglogue* [1587], line 90.   [2] *HMC De L'Isle*, i. 426.

Tuesday mock combat led by the Coventry mason and ballad lover Captain Cox. The spectacles devised by the professionals may have been impressive in their elaborateness, but their verses were neither interesting nor even competent.

In August Sidney visited Shrewsbury with his father, who was on his way to Ireland for what turned out to be a three-year term as Lord Deputy. During the autumn and winter he remained in the vicinity of the Court, taking care of his father's interests and learning the complex system of influence peddling by which the government was run. By the following spring he had succeeded his father as Cupbearer to the Queen,[1] an honourable sinecure which gave him a ceremonial position at Court. In the late summer and early autumn of 1576 he visited his father in Ireland, and returned to Court for the winter.

During these months of attendance at Court he had no duties of consequence and so found time hanging heavily upon his hands. His sister Mary was also in attendance upon the Queen and Sidney, who had been away at school and on his travels for ten years, now had his first opportunity for becoming really acquainted with her. They had many interests in common; she admired, almost worshipped, her brilliant older brother, and he had a profound affection for her. If she had kept a diary like Dorothy Wordsworth, we might have seen evidence of his developing interest in literature; as it is we can only speculate that, in addition to continuing his more serious studies in history and philosophy, to pass the idle hours he may have read with her the popular fiction of the day—*An Æthiopian Historie written in Greeke by Heliodorus*, translated by Thomas Underdown; the *Golden Ass* of Apuleius, translated by William Adlington; Sannazaro's *Arcadia* in Italian; one or more of the many books of *Amadís de Gaul*, probably in a French translation; and Montemayor's *Diana* and its continuations in Spanish.[2]

Finally, in February 1577, the Queen gave Sidney something to do by appointing him ambassador to the German Emperor Rudolph II,

---

[1] His first acquittance for the fee of the office, dated 10 May 1576, is in the Folger Library.

[2] These works became the principal sources of his *Arcadia*. John Hoskyns in 1599 was the first to point out that 'for the webb (as it were) of his storie hee followed three *Heliodorus* in greeke, *Sanazarus Arcadia* in Itallian, and *Diana* de montemaior in spanish'. Robert Southey in 1807 appears to have been the first to indicate a connexion with the *Amadís*. The possible derivation of the trial scene and denouement of the *Old Arcadia* from Book X of Apuleius has not previously been noticed.

the Elector Palatine Louis VI, and his brother Prince Casimir to convey her condolences for the recent deaths of their fathers. Though outwardly his embassy was merely ceremonial, he also had instructions to collect information about the attitude of the princes of the Empire toward the formation of a Protestant protective league. With half a dozen other courtiers and their servants, including his friend Greville and Sir Henry Lee, he proceeded in leisurely fashion, taking almost four months for the journey to Prague and return. On the way he had his portrait painted and had several copies made. One copy, now at Longleat, bears a couplet presentation inscription which may be his earliest datable verse (PP 3).

The Emperor he found 'extreemely Spaniolated' and the Elector Palatine non-commital on the subject of a Protestant league; but the Elector's younger brother, Prince Casimir, who gave him to understand that he had a powerful personal following among the princes and soldiers in Germany, was enthusiastically in favour of action against the Catholic powers providing he could find someone to pay his mercenaries. Sidney had audience with the Princes Palatine at Heidelberg, and when he left them the Court poet Melissus (Paul Schede) addressed him as 'Sydnee Musarum inclite cultibus'.[1] This is the earliest reference we have to his interest in poetry. Melissus, though primarily a neo-Latin poet, was also concerned with improving the vernacular literature of his country and had translated part of the French Protestant Psalter of Marot and Beza into German. He was also interested in the theories of the Pléiade; admired Baïf, Jodelle, and Ronsard; and wrote many of the kinds of poems that Sidney himself later essayed in the *Arcadia* (epithalamia, echo poems, sonnets). The two men maintained a correspondence for several years.[2]

While on the Continent Sidney received additional instructions to visit the Prince of Orange in order to stand proxy for the Earl of Leicester at the christening of the Prince's second daughter, for which purpose Edward Dyer was also dispatched from England. The meeting with Orange provided opportunity for more political conversations, in which the Prince proposed that Queen Elizabeth, in return for special trading privileges, enter into a treaty of alliance for the protection of Holland and Zealand.

When Sidney returned to England in June his friends enthusiastically praised the success of his embassy. Walsingham wrote:

---

[1] Buxton, p. 91. [2] *Cal. SPD 1581–90*, p. 307.

'There hathe not ben any Gentleman, I am sure these many Yeres, that hathe gon throughe so honorable a Charge with as great Comendacions as he.' But the aggressive policy that Walsingham, Leicester, and Sidney favoured was not the one that Queen Elizabeth wished to follow. She wanted to avoid war and to postpone an open break with Spain for as long as possible. Immediately upon Sidney's return she dispatched the veteran negotiator Daniel Rogers to Orange to reject his offer of a treaty of alliance; and shortly afterwards she sent Robert Beale, Clerk of the Privy Council, to the German princes to persuade them to form a Protestant league without any commitments from England. Beale discovered that Casimir did not have as strong a following as he pretended, and found that the German princes would not take any concerted action for the cause of Protestantism because of their doctrinal differences.[1] It appears that Sidney was too optimistic in his report of the possibilities for an alliance of German princes, and too enthusiastic in pressing for the involvement of England in defence of the Protestant states of the Continent. Though his friends praised his conduct of the embassy, the Queen does not seem to have been impressed, and Sidney received no further official employment for eight years.

He continued to pay attendance at Court, though not as regularly as heretofore because, aside from the usual social festivities, he found little to occupy his time. In the autumn of 1577 he composed a discourse on Irish affairs in defence of his father's policies (iii. 46–50). In the spring of the following year he composed a playlet, *The Lady of May*, for the entertainment of the Queen. About the same time he considered serving against Spain in the Netherlands, but the Queen would not allow him to accept a foreign military command. Yet, though he had no opportunity to perform heroic deeds or have a part in decisions of state, he was like his own Philisides 'thought of good hope' (iv. 313), and attracted the attention of all by his intellectual attainments and his personal charm. When the Queen stopped near Cambridge on her summer progress, Gabriel Harvey prepared a volume of verse commending the most prominent members of her Court—the Earl of Leicester, Lord Burghley, the Earl of Oxford, Sir Christopher Hatton, and Master Philip Sidney. This was distinguished company for a young man of twenty-three. Harvey praised Sidney for his embassy, for the attention he had received from learned men, and for his virtues of heart and

---

[1] Conyers Read, *Mr Secretary Walsingham*, i. 347–8 and 300–1.

mind; but he especially praised him as the perfect pattern of a courtier—

> Et quia, si quisquam est magis, et minus Aulicus altro,
> Tu visus sociis Aulicus esse magis.[1]

Early in 1579 Sidney and his father were hosts to Prince Casimir when he visited England. During the summer he wrote, probably at the Earl of Leicester's request, a letter to the Queen (iii. 51–60) arguing against the proposal that she marry the French Catholic Duke of Anjou, a proposal which she then appeared to favour. William Stubbes, who about the same time published a pamphlet against the proposed marriage, for his temerity had the hand with which he had written it cut off by the public executioner. But Sidney as a courtier was privileged to advise his sovereign, and allowed his letter to be seen only in manuscript; there is no evidence that the Queen showed any signs of displeasure against him. In November he probably took part in a tournament celebrating the anniversary of her accession,[2] and on New Year's day he exchanged gifts with her, which indicates that he retained the royal favour.

But he much preferred to withdraw from Court, to 'read and dispute somewhere in an inn with a few University men'.[3] He had a continuous curiosity in things of the mind and studied chemistry under John Dee with his friend Dyer,[4] listened to Nicholas Hilliard explain technicalities of the painter's craft,[5] and pored over maps to follow the attempts of Frobisher to find gold and the north-west passage in the New World.[6] While he had been abroad on his embassy in 1577, his sister Mary had married the Earl of Pembroke. Thereafter, when Sidney visited London he stayed at the Earl's residence Baynard's Castle more often than he stayed at Leicester House, and he also frequently visited his sister at her country home at Wilton near Salisbury—he was there in August, September, and December 1577, for most of the spring and summer of 1580, and probably on many other occasions. But he chafed at his lack of official employment, and complained that his mind was beginning 'to lose its strength, and to relax without any reluctance. For to what

---

[1] *Gratulationum Valdinensium Libri Quatuor*, 1578, K4.   [2] See note to AS 41.
[3] Moffet, p. 83.   [4] Moffet, p. 75.
[5] *A Treatise Concerning the Arte of Limning*, Walpole Society, i (1912), 27.
[6] In 1582 Richard Hakluyt dedicated to Sidney his first publication, *Divers voiages touching the discoverie of America*, which contained a map of the New World separately inscribed to him by Michael Lok.

purpose would our thoughts be directed by various kinds of know-
ledge, unless room be afforded for putting it into practice, so that
public advantage may be the result, which in a corrupt age we cannot
hope for.'[1] So having no opportunity for an active political or military
career, in his 'idlest times' he 'slipt into the title of a Poet' (iii. 3),
and sought in literature the outlet that his energies were denied in
public affairs.

Influences and Sources

When Sidney turned from politics to poetry he continued to be an
opponent of things as they were, and denied an opportunity to strike
against the foes of his religion abroad he waged a vigorous campaign
against the artistic ineptitude of his countrymen. But where he had
been frustrated as a statesman, he was successful in literature. The
early blossoming of Tudor poetry in the works of Skelton, Wyatt,
Surrey, and their lesser contemporaries had withered without fruit,
so that for almost thirty years after the reign of Henry VIII very little
verse worth preservation had been produced in England. When in
his *Defence of Poesy* Sidney surveyed the earlier literature of his own
country he could find only three works that had 'poeticall sinnewes
in them' (iii. 37)—the writings of Chaucer, *The Mirror for Magis-
trates*, and the Earl of Surrey's lyrics (with which he probably
included those of Wyatt and of the anonymous authors in Tottel's
Songes and Sonettes). But these had not beaten paths that he wished
to follow, so that, aside from a few experiments with the Surreyan
form of the sonnet and the adaptation of some verse forms from
Wyatt and some images from Chaucer and Skelton, he made no
use of the earlier English poets.

He also resolutely ignored the works of his contemporaries, the
Eglogs Epytaphs and Sonettes of Barnaby Googe, the *Arbor of
Amitie* and *Newe Sonets* of Thomas Howell (who was a dependant
of his sister), the songs of Richard Edwards, William Hunnis, and
others in *The Paradyse of daynty devises*, and even the more com-
petent productions of George Turberville and George Gascoigne.
These men cast their verses in lumbering fourteener couplets,
poulter's measure, or sixain stanzas; wrote diffusely without grace
of phrase; and knew no rhythm but the mechanical iambic. They
had no discernible influence upon Sidney.

[1] Letter to Languet, 1 Mar. 1578 (iii. 119), translated by Pears, p. 143.

The two best-known poets of Queen Elizabeth's court, Thomas Sackville, Lord Buckhurst, and Edward de Vere, Earl of Oxford, do not appear to have been his personal friends. Lord Buckhurst had contributed the 'Induction' and the tragedy of Buckingham to the 1563 *Mirror for Magistrates* and had collaborated with Thomas Norton in composing *Gorboduc*, but he wrote no poetry after the early 1560's and made no more than an occasional appearance at Court in the 1570's. Sidney knew and admired his published writings, but did not choose to imitate his Chaucerian Virgilianism. The Earl of Oxford, patron of Lyly and a company of players, had some of his poems printed in the *Paradyse of daynty devises* in 1578, and circulated a few others in manuscript. Sidney came in contact with him at various courtly functions and probably knew his poetry; but they belonged to opposed factions, and after the affair of the tennis court in the summer of 1579, when the Earl called him 'puppy' and Sidney sought a duel, they were bitter personal enemies. Oxford's lyrics were written in the conventional Tudor forms and Sidney had nothing to learn from him.

The personal acquaintances most likely to have influenced him as a poet were Thomas Drant, Daniel Rogers, Fulke Greville, Edward Dyer, and Edmund Spenser. Drant, a popular London and Court preacher who had translated Horace's *Satires*, *Epistles*, and *Ars Poetica* into fourteeners, had sought Sidney's attention as early as 1576.[1] He had been at Cambridge after the time of Ascham and Watson, and had formulated a set of rules for the application of quantitative principles to English verse which he gave to Sidney (see p. 391). None of Drant's own quantitative experiments survive, and since he died early in 1578 his acquaintance with Sidney was brief; but he may have been one of the first to turn his attention toward the creation of a new English poetry.

Another associate was the diplomat Daniel Rogers, who had been sent to the Continent by the Queen to follow up the political conversations Sidney had begun on his embassy in 1577. Rogers was a Latin poet of considerable industry, and an extensive manuscript collection of elegies, epigrams, odes, and epistles, which he probably transcribed in his own hand in 1579 or 1580, is in the library of the Marquis of Hertford.[2] Three of his poems are addressed to Sidney: one on his travels, another on his picture, and a third written from

---

[1] See the adulatory references in his *Praesul*, [1576], F3–4.
[2] *HMC Fourth Report*, 1874, pp. 252–4.

Ghent in January 1579. Rogers spent most of his time on the Continent and probably first became acquainted with Sidney when he delivered letters to him in March 1578. He remained in England during the latter part of 1579 and the early part of 1580, and Harvey writing to Spenser in May 1580 asked him to show his verses to Sidney, Dyer, and Rogers. I have not seen the poems of Rogers and so do not know to what extent he may have influenced Sidney; from the description of them in the Report of the Historical Manuscripts Commission they appear to be mainly commendations of persons and descriptions of places, which were not kinds that interested Sidney.

One of his closest friends, who formed with Sidney and Dyer the 'happy blessed Trinitie' of OP 6, was Fulke Greville. Sidney and Greville had been schoolmates at Shrewsbury, renewed their friendship after Sidney returned from his three-year continental tour, and travelled together on the embassy of 1577; but their intimacy was later interrupted because for considerable periods of time in 1578, 1579, and 1580 Greville was in the Netherlands, travelling on the Continent, and in Ireland.[1] The title-page of his posthumously published *Workes* states that they were 'Written in his Youth, and familiar Exercise with Sir Philip Sidney'; but other evidence proves that his plays and treatises were all written after Sidney's death, and that only some of the shorter poems to Caelica could have been written while he was alive.[2] Since some of Greville's poems to Caelica are ironical commentaries on certain of the poems to Stella and on occasion echo phrases or take over images from Sidney,[3]

---

[1] He was in the Netherlands with Walsingham from 15 June to 7 Oct. 1578; in Feb. 1579 he left England for a tour of the Continent of unknown duration but had certainly returned by the end of the year; in Mar. 1580 he was preparing to sail with the Irish fleet, he served as messenger between the Admiral and Sir William Pelham in Ireland during the summer, and was back in England by September. The Spenser–Harvey correspondence from Oct. 1579 to May 1580 frequently mentions Sidney and Dyer but never refers to Greville, which suggests that at that time he was not a member of the literary group at Leicester House.

[2] G. A. Wilkes, 'The Sequence of the Writings of Fulke Greville, Lord Brooke', *SP* lvi (1959), 489–503.

[3] See Geoffrey Bullough's judicious listing of the similarities in his notes to Greville's *Poems and Dramas*, 1938. J. M. Purcell, *PMLA* l (1935), 413–22, attempted to prove that 'parallelisms occur in similarly numbered poems' of the first forty sonnets of each sequence, and that Sidney and Greville in consultation 'suggested topics for sonnets, and then wrote upon these subjects'; but his evidence does not support his hypothesis, because most of the supposed parallels he cites are of the 'salmons in both' variety. The direction of influence appears to be from Sidney to Greville rather than the other way around. See OP **7.** 45 and note.

and since Greville was never mentioned by contemporaries as a poet in conjunction with Sidney, he probably did not begin to write poetry until 1582 or later, after Sidney himself had already composed most of his own original poems.

Sidney's most intimate friend during the time he was composing most of his own poetry, and the only person whose name was linked with his as a poet by contemporaries,[1] was the courtier Edward Dyer, some eleven years his senior, who was also the confidential adviser of his father and his uncle the Earl of Leicester. Dyer never collected or published his verses, and only a handful preserved in manuscript anthologies survive.[2] None of his compositions in quantitative verse, mentioned by Spenser, have been identified; he wrote one Surreyan sonnet (CS 16a), to which Sidney wrote a reply; but his other poems are in the common metrical forms of the time— poulter's measure, fourteeners, pentameter couplets, or sixain stanzas. His verse is somewhat old fashioned, more in the style of Tottel's *Songes and Sonettes* than in that of the new poetry of Sidney and Spenser. Though Sidney valued Dyer's friendship, it is clear that he had nothing to learn about poetry from him.

The only one of his early associates who could have led Sidney along the paths of a new poetry was Edmund Spenser; but there is no good evidence that he met Spenser before the autumn of 1579, by which time he had completed many, perhaps most, of his *Arcadia* poems, and the two men do not appear to have become intimately acquainted. Spenser had received his M.A. from Cambridge in 1576, had acted as secretary to the Bishop of Rochester in 1578, and sometime in 1579 had received marks of favour and possibly employment from the Earl of Leicester. By April 1579, if we can depend

---

[1] In 1579 Spenser wrote of Sidney and Dyer's experiments with quantitative verse; in 1580 Harvey called them 'our very Castor and Pollux' for poetry; in 1581 Charles de L'Ecluse dedicated a book to them jointly and mentioned their friendship; about the same time Abraham Fraunce, Sidney's protégé, dedicated his *Shepherds Logic* to Dyer, and to the same manuscript appended a comparison of the logic of Aristotle and Ramus which he dedicated to Sidney; in 1582 Thomas Watson expressed the hope that his *Ekatompathia* might find a place in the bookchests of Sidney and Dyer, whom he considered the arbiters of literary excellence at Court; and in 1586 Geoffrey Whitney wrote a poem hailing Sidney as the successor of Surrey in improving English poetry, which Sidney modestly insisted should be addressed to Dyer instead. On the other hand, there are no extant references to Greville as a poet before 1589.

[2] R. M. Sargent, *At the Court of Queen Elizabeth*, 1935, printed 14 poems attributed to Dyer, and B. M. Wagner, *RES* xi (1935), 466–71, added 3 others; but no more than 8 of these can be confidently accepted as his. The one poem for which he is best known, 'My mind to me a kingdom is', is almost certainly not of his composition.

upon the date of E. K.'s prefatory epistle, Spenser had arranged the twelve eclogues of his *Shepheardes Calender* in order. He at first intended to dedicate them to the Earl of Leicester, but by October he had begun to wonder whether they were not 'too base for his excellent Lordship', and when they were printed in December he entitled them 'to the Noble and Vertuous Gentleman most worthy of all titles both of learning and chevalrie M. Philip Sidney'. That this dedication to Sidney was a last-minute decision is indicated not only by Spenser's letter to Harvey of the preceding October, but also by the lines 'To his Booke' calling his patron 'the president Of noblesse and of chevalree', which bear internal evidence of having been originally composed for the Earl of Leicester.[1]

Therefore the earliest indication of Spenser's acquaintance with Sidney comes from his first letter to Harvey dated from Leicester House in October 1579. In this he said:

As for the twoo worthy Gentlemen, Master Sidney, and Master Dyer, they have me, I thanke them, in some use of familiaritie.... And nowe they have proclaimed in their αρείῳ πάγῳ, a generall surceasing and silence of balde Rymers, and also of the verie beste to: in steade whereof, they have by authoritie of their whole Senate, prescribed certaine Lawes and rules of Quantities of English sillables, for English Verse: having had thereof already greate practise, and drawen mee to their faction.

Spenser returned to the subject of quantitative versifying in his second letter to Harvey, written from Westminster in April 1580, in which he included some of his own elegiacs, and exhorted Harvey:

I would hartily wish, you would either send me the Rules and Precepts of Arte, which you observe in Quantities, or else followe mine, that M. Philip Sidney gave me, being the very same which M. Drant devised, but enlarged with M. Sidneys own judgement, and augmented with my Observations.

But some time before this second letter was written Sidney had left the Court to visit his sister at Wilton, where he probably remained through the summer, and in August Spenser himself sailed for Ireland. Thus the two men had only occasional opportunities for meeting one another during a period of less than six months.

[1] See my note in *Renaissance News* xiv (1961), 159–61.

Sidney may have rewarded Spenser for the dedication of the *Shepheardes Calender* by using his influence to get him appointed as secretary to Lord Grey in Ireland, and he probably also encouraged him in his writing. When Spenser published his *Faerie Queene* ten years later, he said in a dedicatory poem to the Countess of Pembroke that her brother was the one

> Who first my Muse did lift out of the flore,
> To sing his sweet delights in lowlie laies,

and W. L. in a commendatory poem said that when Sidney read Spenser's pastorals he persuaded him to undertake a greater work in praise of the Queen. But despite Spenser's later statements of indebtedness to Sidney, which were in part motivated by a desire to gain the patronage of his sister, there is very little evidence of Sidney's direct influence upon his poetry. Sidney was not responsible for Spenser's writing pastorals, because the *Shepheardes Calender* was almost completed before they became acquainted. For a short time, inspired by Sidney's example, Spenser essayed some of the same poetical experiments by composing a Surreyan sonnet,[1] adding a sestina to his 'August' eclogue, and writing some English quantitative elegiacs and iambics. In his sestina, where Sidney had reproduced the form with precise accuracy, Spenser varied from it considerably and apparently did not understand the principle by which the end words were repeated in successive stanzas; and despite his protestation that his quantitative verses 'varied not one inch' from Sidney's formulation of 'Maister Drants Rules', the plain fact is that they will not scan by those rules.[2] Since it is clear that Spenser had only a vague and inaccurate notion of what Sidney was trying to accomplish in his own poetry, we must conclude that the two men never

---

[1] This was later printed as *Amoretti* 8, but it also appears in four manuscript anthologies (Bodleian MS. Rawl. Poet. 85, British Museum MS. Harley 7392, Cambridge University MS. Dd. 5. 75, and British Museum MS. Sloane 1446), the first three of which draw most of their texts from courtly poetry of the late 1570's and 1580's; it is attributed to 'Mr Dier' in the first and earliest of these manuscripts and is anonymous in the others. Further evidence of its early circulation among members of the Sidney circle is Greville's imitation of it in *Caelica* 3.

[2] The only principle Spenser follows consistently is to apply the Latin rule of position to English syllables; his natural quantities are both arbitrary and self-contradictory. In his elegiacs 'See' and 'me' are long (Sidney considers them short), but 'yee' and 'he' are short; and the first syllables of 'Lovers' and 'Moother' are long (Sidney counts them short), but the first syllable of 'bloodie' is short. His iambics, even though he gains freedom by making them 'licentiate', contain similar inconsistencies, and Harvey's harsh criticisms of them are completely justified.

became well acquainted and never had any really serious discussions of the technicalities of their craft.

Neither did Sidney, except once in OA 66, appear to have been influenced by Spenser. He later paid him a generous compliment, saying that he 'hath much poetry in his eclogues'; but, he continued, 'that same framing of his style to an old and outworn language I dare not allow' (iii. 37). Diction was not the only matter on which they disagreed. Spenser subscribed to the notion that poetry is 'poured into the witte by a certaine ἐνθουσιασμὸς and celestiall inspiration'; Sidney observed wryly,

> Some do I heare of poets' furie tell,
> But (God wot) wot not what they meane by it.   (AS 74)

Spenser followed entirely different paths in devising new stanza forms and rhythms; Sidney eschewed 'allegory's curious frame' which Spenser considered essential to the highest poetry. How widely they differed can be seen in their independent handling of a similar device, the singing match in 'August' and OA 7, where Spenser concentrates on the song and Sidney on the contest, so that the one produces a musical composition and the other constructs a dramatic incident. Their greatest mutual influence was to encourage each other to be themselves.

So Sidney, looking at the English poetry of his own time and before, found it inadequate, and found none of his countrymen suitable guides to aid him in making it better. He perhaps first turned to the poetry he had earliest known, that of Rome, and dissatisfied with the dull monotony of the accentual iambics produced by his contemporaries, wondered whether English verse could be written in the rhythms used by Virgil and Horace. In this, according to Spenser, he was first influenced by Thomas Drant. Since Drant died in April 1578, Sidney's earliest imperfect attempts to follow his 'rules', probably OA 31 and 34 and CS 5, must have been made before that time. His later quantitative poems show superior skill in applying the rules, and his comments in the *Defence of Poesy* (iii. 44) indicate that he continued to be interested in the possibilities of artificial versifying at least until 1581 or 1582. That he took it seriously is indicated by the fact that the quantitative poems in the *Old Arcadia* are assigned only to the princes Pyrocles and Musidorus and to Philisides, who is Sidney himself. But eventually he must have become dissatisfied with the experiment, for in the *New Arcadia* he held it up to gentle ridicule by having the clownish Dametas compose a humorous hexameter (OP 2).

He also, probably from the very beginning, used the established English accentual metres; but in these too he depended most heavily upon the classics for forms, themes, and images, especially in his pastorals.[1] For further models of the poetic art he turned to Spain and Italy. Like other well-read gentlemen of the renaissance he was acquainted with the poems of Petrarch, both the *Rime* and *Trionfi*. He had also read Sannazaro's *Arcadia*, which provided him with the title for his own romance and a few verse forms; and his study of music in Venice had given him some knowledge of contemporary Italian art song—madrigals (OA 52 and 55), villanellas (CS 27), and other forms (CS 3, 4, 6, and 26). I am not certain of what other Italian poets he had read. In Spanish he was well acquainted with the more than 150 poems in the *Diana* of Montemayor and the continuations of Alonso Pérez and Gil Polo.

It has been generally assumed that he was widely read in French poetry,[2] but there is no conclusive evidence of his having read any French poems other than the *Semaine* of the Protestant du Bartas and the metaphrase of the Psalms by Marot and Beza, and he does not appear to have made use of these until 1582 and later. He had probably heard of the programme of the Pléiade, but there is no certain evidence to prove his direct acquaintance with works of the Catholic Ronsard and du Bellay. It may be that his reading of French literature was guided more by his Protestant sympathies than by aesthetic considerations.

The tracing of sources is more difficult in Sidney than in almost any other Elizabethan poet, because he did not write, as did so many of his contemporaries, with source books open before him, but from a mind well stored with reading that he had thoroughly assimilated and made his own. He prided himself on being 'no pick-purse of another's wit' (AS 74) and, except for his avowed translations, he

---

[1] The Latin poets he knew best were Ovid, Virgil, and Horace, in that order. He was also acquainted with the plays of Terence and Seneca, perhaps Juvenal and Persius, the fables of Phaedrus, and the later Cato. He was the first Englishman to translate Catullus, and the first to show a knowledge of the *Anacreontea*, which he probably read in Stephanus's Latin translation. I have found no certain evidence of his first-hand acquaintance with Propertius or Tibullus, or with the earlier Greek poets. Aside from Alciati and Buchanan, I am also uncertain of the extent of his reading in the neo-Latins.

[2] See Sir Sidney Lee's *Elizabethan Sonnets* and *The French Renaissance in England*, Janet Scott's *Les Sonnets Élisabéthains*, A. W. Osborn's *Sidney en France*, and Michel Poirier's edition of *Astrophel et Stella*.

only once in all his verse directly repeated the words of another poet, and he was so disturbed at doing this that he later revised the lines in order to insert an acknowledgement of his indebtedness (see note to OA **9**. 53). Since assimilation rather than imitation was his habitual procedure, it is usually impossible to trace his ideas and images to particular works of others. He, of course, used the poetic vocabulary of his time with its repetitious array of conventional conceits, but these can no more certainly be traced to specific sources than can common proverbs. However, with the Latin poets Ovid, Virgil, and Horace, the Italians Petrarch and Sannazaro, and the Spanish poet Montemayor and his continuators, we are on firm ground. The works of these authors alone, with a few hints from Tottel's *Songes and Sonettes*, would have provided all the models that Sidney needed for all but a handful of his original poems.

The Poems

The *Arcadia* probably grew out of the romances that Sidney read with his sister, and may have started as a game to while away his hours of idleness when visiting her at Wilton. According to Molyneux he began its composition shortly after he returned from his embassy in the spring of 1577, and he completed his first version, or *Old Arcadia*, during a long visit with his sister in the summer of 1580. With his usual gentlemanly self-depreciation he called his work 'a trifle, and that triflingly handled'; but the trifle was a volume of some 180,000 words, and the intricacy of its design and finish of its parts show that it was planned and executed with the greatest of care. The manuscripts reveal that even after it was finished he made minor revisions on at least five different occasions before 1584, when he began the complete recasting and rewriting of the narrative that remains as the unfinished *New Arcadia*.

The *Arcadia*, in both its old and new forms, is the most important original work of English prose fiction produced before the eighteenth century. It has an ingenious plot, a series of strong situations, a varied cast of characters, and a surprising denouement. There is a deal of high-flown language and much dallying with the gentle passion of love, which is treated sometimes sentimentally, sometimes voluptuously, and at other times wittily. But it is much more than a mere love story, for it deals also with kingship and its duties, the proper conduct of public affairs, and vexed problems of personal ethics. Basilius, the Duke of Arcadia, is a ruler who shirks his duties; Euarchus of Macedon is the perfect pattern of the just judge and righteous king. The heroes, Pyrocles and Musidorus, and the heroines, Philoclea and Pamela, struggle with the demands of personal desire and rational conduct, the avoidance of consequences and the maintenance of personal integrity. It is a fundamentally serious romance, concerned with problems of conduct in both public and private life, but fraught with emotion and humour—full of 'delightful teaching'.

In composing it Sidney did not follow the loose structural patterns of the romances of his own and earlier times, but produced an entirely new and original literary form. His strictures on the English plays of his day, which he said were 'neither right Tragedies, nor right Comedies, mingling Kinges and Clownes, not because the matter so carrieth it, but thrust in the Clowne by head and shoulders to play a part in majesticall matters, with neither decencie nor discretion' (iii. 39), have led some critics to assume that he was a neo-classicist who upheld the separation and preservation of the conventional genres in all their theoretical purity. But those critics have not noticed the qualifying phrase 'with neither decencie nor discretion', and have not examined the *Arcadia*. In point of fact Sidney approved the mingling of genres, for he said that 'some Poesies have coupled togither two or three kindes, as the Tragicall and Comicall, where-upon is risen the Tragicomicall, some in [like] maner have mingled prose and verse, as Sanazara and Boetius; some have mingled matters Heroicall and Pastorall, but that commeth all to one in this question, for if severed they be good, the conjunction cannot be hurtfull' (iii. 22). This precisely describes his own *Arcadia*, a mixed kind combining tragic and comic, prose and verse, heroic and pastoral.

Sidney's artistic ideal was to achieve a maximum of variety and complexity within a clearly articulated structure. He achieved this, and overcame the formless meandering of late Greek, medieval, and renaissance long prose tales, by embodying the diverse materials of romance in dramatic form. The *Old Arcadia* is a tragi-comedy in five acts, with a serious double plot (the two pairs of noble lovers with Basilius, Gynecia, and Euarchus) combined with a comic under-plot (Dametas and his wife and daughter). The action is carried on by a small group of characters (there are only eighteen major actors) and is unified in both place and time—most of the events take place in the area around the two country lodges in Arcadia (the travels and other adventures of the princes are reported) and the plot unrolls within the limits of a single year. The renaissance Terentian five-act structure is followed with its movement of protasis, epitasis, and catastrophe. The various strands of action are cleverly intertwined; there is a climax in the third act, a counter-movement in the fourth, and a denouement in the fifth with a totally unexpected anagnorisis and peripeteia. Sidney produced in prose a pastoral tragi-comedy before the earliest examples of the genre, the *Aminta* and *Pastor Fido* of Tasso and Guarini, were available in print.

In addition to giving his prose narrative a dramatic structure, Sidney accentuated the division into acts by placing after each of the first four a set of pastoral pastimes or 'eglogues', in the manner of the *intermezzi* of the learned comedies of Italy. But his eclogues are much more than mere inter-act entertainments, for though they for the most part have a separate cast of characters and do not them-selves advance the plot, they nevertheless set the tone and establish the themes that control the action of the main narrative. Here in the remote and abstract world of the pastoral the actions of the princely characters of the courtly world are mirrored and given perspective in the rural songs of the shepherds.

The eclogues, though they contribute to the design of the main action, also form an isolable unit with a structure of its own that can perfectly well stand by itself. But because they are embedded in the prose of the *Arcadia* as an integral element of a larger whole, they have never been considered by themselves and Sidney has never received his due as a pastoral poet. Discussions of English verse pastoral have always been focused upon Spenser's *Shepheardes Calender*, with never more than a brief reference to an isolated poem or two in the *Arcadia*. But Sidney's four sets of eclogues, containing twenty-seven poems totalling more than 2,500 lines, form a more extensive and varied pastoral work than Spenser's and one that equally deserves attention for its artistic merit. One of the most striking things about Sidney's eclogues is their carefully integrated structure. Each of the four groups develops a situation and explores a theme: the first presents the pangs of unrequited love, the second the struggle between reason and passion, the third the ideals of married love, the fourth the sorrows of lovers and the sorrows of death; and through them all moves the figure of Philisides (Sidney himself), whose identity and full story are not revealed until the very end.

The first two sets of eclogues each contain eight poems arranged in precisely parallel order. In each of the two sets the first poem announces the theme with which all the following poems are concerned, the second begins the development of the theme, the third is a comic interlude satirizing the theme, the fourth returns to the theme, the fifth deals with Philisides and his love, and the last three, recited by the disguised princes Pyrocles and Musidorus, exemplify the application of the theme.

The third set, containing only five poems celebrating the marriage of the shepherds Lalus and Kala, has a different structural pattern. It begins with a formal epithalamium wishing joy to the newly married pair, continues with a humorous fabliau illustrating the effects of unfounded jealousy, follows with a sonnet describing the ideal husband, proceeds with a beast fable about the origins of monarchy narrated by Philisides, and ends with an exhortation to marriage and the proper bearing of the double yoke of wedded life with mutual consent. The beast fable might on a superficial view appear to break the unity of this group; but a little reflection shows that it is entirely appropriate, for it is concerned with discovering the proper form of sovereignty in the state, just as the other marriage poems are concerned with indicating the proper form of sovereignty in the home, which is the point made in the last poem:

> But let us pick our good from out much bad,
> That still our little world may know his king.   (**67.** 62–63)

The fourth eclogues, coming after the supposed death of Basilius and the imprisonment of the princes, exploit the double nature of the renaissance elegy as a song of the sufferings of lovers or a lament for the dead (iii. 22). The set consists of six paired poems. In the first two Strephon and Klaius lament the absence of their beloved Urania, in the second two Philisides tells how he first saw his Mira in a dream and how he bade her farewell after she rejected him, and in the last two Dicus and Agelastus bewail the death of Basilius in a formal pastoral elegy and a rhyming sestina.

Though each of the four sets of eclogues is concerned with a single theme, the individual poems are considerably more varied, both in form and in metrics, than are Spenser's. The conventional pastoral kinds appear—the singing match, the debate, the love lament, the funeral elegy; and also a number of other kinds that are not found in the classical pastoral—the beast fable, the epithalamium, the fabliau, the impresa. The metrics also are amazingly varied, from tetrameter, pentameter, and Alexandrine couplets, terza rima, sixain stanzas, rhyme royal, a nine-line stanza of varied line lengths with refrain, a sonnet, and an echo poem, to a corona of dizains and a double sestina, with polymetric poems containing three or more forms in intricate progression. Each participant is assigned a rhythm appropriate to his character; the native Arcadians recite in the common (that is common for English readers) accentual iambics, the noble strangers use artificial quantitative measures.

In addition to the eclogues there are fifty-one other poems interspersed in the prose narrative of the *Old Arcadia*, for most of the characters, from the members of the Court to the lowliest shepherds, break into song at moments of tension or when they wish to be emphatic. These poems too are varied in form, kind, and mood. There are answer poems, madrigals, blasons, a mock encomium, a hymn, nine varieties of sonnet, &c., some tender, some mocking, some merely ingenious. They have been called experiments, and they were, for Sidney was exploring many of the ways by which language can be patterned. Several were quite successful experiments, and a measure of the esteem with which contemporaries at least regarded his productions can be gained from the first anthology of pastoral lyrics in English, *Englands Helicon* published in 1600, which contains three selections from Spenser, fourteen from Sidney.

Most of these poems gain their full effect only when viewed in the prose contexts in which they occur, which is the reason why I have included in the Commentary a brief account of the situation out of which each arises. The one Arcadian poem that has a place in all the anthologies is the song of the shepherdess Charita (OA 45):

> My true love hath my hart, and I have his.

The late Theodore Spencer, who in 1945 published the best essay that had been written on Sidney's poetry, praised this sonnet for 'the monosyllabic simplicity of the diction . . . and the flawless movement of the rhetoric. The poem is a perfectly drawn circle, ending most contentedly where it began.' It is a pretty poem, not a great one; though it is superior in technique to most of the verse that had been produced in England during the preceding thirty years because of the finish of its form. But people reading it only in anthologies have taken it much too seriously, because the context in which it appears is entirely humorous and it is actually an elaborate *tour de force*.

The narrative episode of which the poem is a part is as follows. The young prince Musidorus has disguised himself as a shepherd in order to gain access to the princess Pamela, who is continually watched by the ugly hag Miso, wife of the lecherous old herdsman Dametas. In order to elope with Pamela Musidorus must somehow get Miso out of the way, so he plays upon her jealous disposition by telling her a completely made-up story of overhearing her husband make an assignation with a young shepherdess.

> So ys yt, Mistris (sayde hee) that, yesterday dryving my Sheepe up to the stately Hill, whiche liftes his heade over the fayre Citty of Mantinea, I hapned uppon the syde of yt . . . to perceyve a younge Mayde, truely of the fynest stamp of Beuty. . . . In her Lapp there lay a Shepeheard so wrapped up in that well liked place, that I coulde discerne no peece of his face . . . [and] her Angelike voyce, strake myne eares with this Songe:

> My true love hath my hart, and I have his . . .

Whereupon the shepherd 'recorded to her Musick this Rurall Poesy' (OA 46):

> O words which fall like sommer deaw on me . . .

'O sweete Charita saide hee . . . when shall youre Blisfull promyse now Due be verifyed with Just performance.' And then, Musidorus continued, he recognized the shepherd as Miso's decrepit husband Dametas, and heard the young shepherdess agree to meet him that night at her house in the Oudemian street. Miso, completely taken in by this story, rushes off to prevent the supposed assignation, and Musidorus is left free to pursue his own courtship.

But the reader is not taken in, and enjoys the comedy of the situation in which the witty prince gulls the stupid countrywoman and deceives her while telling her plainly that she is being deceived—for the Oudemian street means a street without inhabitants, and the songs by their juxtaposition and their stylistic devices mock one another and themselves. Dametas's 'Rurall Poesy' is just as sophisticated a composition as Charita's song, and gains its effect through the clash of its form and content. The images are those that an ignorant country fellow might be expected to use in courtship—'breath more sweete, then is the growing beane', 'haire more gaie then straw', 'flesh . . . as hard, as brawne'; but the ingenious rhetorical structure is completely at variance with the homely imagery. It is built upon the formula of correlative verse, by which a series of terms are distributed and then at the end recapitulated, and the device is carried almost to the ultimate limits of complexity by combining three different sets of distributed terms and their recapitulations. The conclusion makes a complete mockery of Charita's song, because while the young shepherdess sings prettily of the courtly dream of two hearts in one, the old shepherd cares nothing for such idealistic imaginings—for him it is 'skinne' and 'flesh' that 'must pay, the gage of promist weale'.

Sidney did not devote his entire time to the composition of the *Old Arcadia*, for during the years that he was engaged upon it he also wrote a variety of other pieces. Probably in the spring of 1578 he composed *The Lady of May*, a pastoral entertainment devised for Queen Elizabeth when she visited his uncle the Earl of Leicester at Wanstead. He also continued to play the game of Philisides and Mira, and wrote other poems about their courtship for which he did not find a place in the *Arcadia*. One of these he later inserted in a different work (AS v), and another (OP 5) was rescued from his loose papers by his sister and inserted in the composite version of the *New* and *Old Arcadia* that she published in 1593. In addition he wrote a number of other poems, totally unconnected with the *Arcadia*, that he later collected under the title *Certain Sonnets*, all but two of which were composed before the end of 1581.

The *Certain Sonnets* is a gathering of thirty-two poems of various kinds. Five are translations from Latin and Spanish, the rest are original; most are love poems, and though the collection is miscellaneous in nature Sidney gave it some semblance of structure by beginning with two sonnets yielding to love and ending with two others bidding farewell to love. Only thirteen of the poems are properly sonnets; the others are in a variety of metrical forms which show the range and variety of Sidney's poetical experiments even beyond the multiplicity of kinds he had essayed in the eclogues and songs of the *Old Arcadia*. Several of his best poems are here— especially the song on the nightingale with the refrain, 'Thy thorne without, my thorne my heart invadeth'; and the song beginning 'Ring out your bells' with its carefully equipoised passion, the recoil of rage upon itself at the end accentuated by the shift in the refrain, and the whole held together by a stanzaic form whose lines of varying length give just the right pace, pause, and surge to the angry epithets.

Five of the *Certain Sonnets* show his continued preoccupation with quantitative metres. Eight others derive their stanzaic structure and rhythms from contemporary tunes—one Dutch, one English, five Italian, and one Spanish. The only one of these whose music can now be identified (CS 23) shows that Sidney, though changing the sense, patterned his stanza syllable by syllable upon the words of the original, and that the syllables of the original are directly proportioned to the notes of the music. An especially tantalizing problem is raised by CS 7, 26, and 27, the first to a Spanish and the last two to Neapolitan tunes, for they bring a new rhythm into Elizabethan verse:

> This you heare is not my tongue,
> Which once said what I conceavëd,
> For it was of use bereavëd,
> With a cruell answer stong.

These, with one exception, are the first regularly sustained accentual trochaics in English.[1]

After his *Arcadia* and *Certain Sonnets* were completed, Sidney during most of 1581 again became active in courtly affairs, as a Member of Parliament, as a participant in tournaments, and as host to the political exiles the Earl of Angus and Don Antonio. In the latter part of January his aunt, the Countess of Huntingdon, journeyed from the north to present her ward Penelope Devereux at Court, and within two months had affianced her to the young Lord Rich. The wedding was celebrated on 1 November, and some six weeks later Sidney retired from Court and did not return until the following March, when he remained only a short time and again left to spend the summer with his father on the borders of Wales.

---

[1] Schipper and other historians of English versification record no true trochaics before the 1590's. The only examples before Sidney that I have come upon are some metrical translations of Latin hymns in Henry VIII's 1545 Primer—i.e. this translation of *Iam lucis orto sidere*:

> Now the cherefull day doth spryng.
> Unto God, praye we and syng.
> That in all workes of the day
> He preserve and kepe us ay.   (STC 16037, A2)

But these appear to be isolated sports. However, after Sidney accentual trochaic rhythms became exceedingly popular and were used by many poets of the 1590's. One of his earliest followers was Breton, whose trochaics frequently betray the Sidneyan influence in their phrasing as well as in their rhythm.

It was there during the summer of 1582 that he probably composed his *Astrophil and Stella*.[1]

This is a collection of 108 sonnets and eleven songs that tells of the love of a young courtier for a married woman. Sidney went out of his way to identify himself as Astrophil and Stella as Lady Rich, and even wrote three sonnets to reveal her married name. But though the poems are ostensibly autobiographical they do not form a versified diary, for the details are highly selected and most of Sidney's known public and private activities are passed over in silence (see pp. 440–7). Nor are they, like many other collections of sonnets, a series of verse epistles designed to gain the favour of the lady. There is no evidence that the sonnets were ever sent to Stella herself; indeed, many of them were inappropriate for her eyes— there would have been no point to having her guess her own name (37), and no lover attempting to gain favour would tell his mistress of his cynical resolve to break her covenants (69). Stella herself is not directly addressed until sonnet 30, and she is only occasionally addressed thereafter. Astrophil is the central figure, everything is presented from his point of view, and he addresses a variety of persons (a friend, other poets, lordings, envious wits), or things (the moon, a sparrow, his bed), or personifications (Virtue, Reason, Cupid), or he communes with himself. The poems then are a series of conversations or monologues which the reader overhears. The reader and not the lady is the audience, while Astrophil and those he addresses are the actors. As the principal actor Astrophil is also able to observe himself with wry self awareness (31, 53), or even to play a patently sophistical part (75). The mode of presentation is essentially dramatic.

The dramatic development of Sidney's individual poems can be illustrated from the great majority of them—song iv for example, or even from sonnet 54, 'Because I breathe not love to everie one', which is narrated. In this latter piece we are given a little tableau with Astrophil on one side and the young ladies of the Court on the

---

[1] The important recent studies of *Astrophil and Stella* are by Hallett Smith, *Elizabethan Poetry*, 1952, pp. 142–57; J. W. Lever, *The Elizabethan Love Sonnet*, 1956, pp. 53–91; R. L. Montgomery, Jr., 'Reason, Passion, and Introspection in *Astrophel and Stella*', *Texas Studies in English* xxxvi (1957), 127–40; and R. B. Young, 'English Petrarke', *Yale Studies in English* cxxxviii (1958), 1–88. All of these provide valuable insights, though I believe Smith gives the best over-all interpretation. Lever's account suffers from his assumption that CS 31 and 32 form the conclusion of the work, and Young, I think, over-emphasizes Astrophil's awareness of the operation of Petrarchan convention.

other. Astrophil is dressed and acts in a perfectly normal fashion, he wears no lovelocks for a token and heaves no melancholy sighs. The ladies, accustomed to the protestations of conventional courtly lovers, chatter among themselves in charmingly colloquial fashion:

> What, he? say they of me, now I dare sweare,
> He cannot love; no, no, let him alone.

The chatter of the ladies causes Astrophil to recoil, to withdraw within himself and soliloquize:

> And thinke so still. So Stella know my mind,
> Professe in deed I do not Cupid's art.

The word 'art' suggests to him its opposite, the unaffected simplicity of true affection; and he addresses the ladies, telling them what he has learned in the instant, and what they may never feel: the silent swan, not the noisy magpie, is the type of the true lover, who is afraid to express his affection. Astrophil's discovery is scarcely new, is no more than the rephrasing of a proverb; so it is not the thought but the process by which it is arrived at, the way it results from and is developed by a situation, that strikes our attention.

Sidney grouped his poems to mark definite stages in the progress of Astrophil's courtship and gave his work a greater over-all unity than most renaissance collections of sonnets possess. The songs, however, present something of a problem. The six songs in trochaic metres narrate the more important events of the sequence—the stealing of the kiss (ii), the night-time courtship at Stella's window (iv and xi), the climactic episode in which Stella admits her love for Astrophil but at the same time refuses his advances (viii), his lament at her refusal (ix), and his thoughts of her while absent (x). The other five songs, in conventional iambic metres, are little more than fillers, and the grouping, between the trochaic songs iv and viii, of sonnet 86 and the iambic songs v, vi, and vii, shows clumsy joinery. Sidney obviously saw the necessity of separating the two important lovers' meetings described in iv and viii; but in order to provide the needed interval he contented himself with selecting one sonnet he had written to Stella and adding to it three songs, at least one of which (see note to AS v) he had written earlier for quite a different purpose. The results are not very happy, for though the 'change of lookes' of sonnet 86 provides an adequate occasion for the reproaches of song v, it follows strangely upon Stella's inadvertent revelation of her affection in song iv, and though songs vi and vii on the lady's voice and face are related in subject to one another, they again follow strangely after the reproaches of v and do not in any way prepare for the May-time meeting in viii. Neither are all the trochaic songs entirely consistent with the sonnets and with one another, for all the poems are in the first person, except song viii which is narrated in the third person, and Astrophil is consistently portrayed as a courtier, except in song ix where he surprisingly appears as a shepherd. A possible explanation of these inconsistencies is that Sidney first began to write about Astrophil's love for Stella in a set of detached songs in the new trochaic metres he had recently been experimenting with in the *Certain Sonnets*, and that not until after he had written the songs did he think of writing the sonnets and of combining them with the songs in a single sequence.[1] Aside from these slight inconsistencies, Sidney's work is more carefully structured than that of any other Elizabethan sonnet collection.

Though there is some physical action in *Astrophil and Stella*—accounts of tournaments, a stolen kiss, clandestine meetings—the essential action is internal and concerns the play of thought and the workings of emotion. The poem appears to be divided into three parts, which are marked by shifts in the attitude of Astrophil himself. The first part presents the first reactions to being in love of a sensitive, intelligent, and highly principled young man. He does not find it in the least pleasant because for the first time in his life he is experiencing an emotion he cannot control, and like most young men who value their independence he rebels at being under its sway and calls it slavery, hell, and poison (2, 16, 29, 49). He debates the conflicting claims of will and wit, passion and reason; but though he can rationally believe that reason should prevail over the senses, that

[1] Some corroboration of this assumption is furnished by the textual evidence (see p. 453) which indicates that, while Sidney did not allow the sonnets to circulate during his lifetime, at least one of the iambic and four of the trochaic songs were given early and separate manuscript circulation (none of these reveals the identity of Stella). R. B. Young, on the other hand, believes that the shift to the third person and the pastoral disguise in the trochaic songs were deliberately calculated. In song viii he says, 'The lovers are seen from a completely objective point of view, as if at a distance, and from this objective point of view they appear in a new intimacy; the distinction Astrophel is constantly forced to make between "I" and "she" is eliminated in the "they" of the song' (p. 77). In song ix he says, 'Astrophel reappears and sees himself in the role of pastoral lover. . . . He overstresses the pastoral symbols, and makes the pastoral role, as he made his other roles, a kind of deliberate attitudinizing, a vehicle for irony, . . . it is a means of expressing his awareness that the role is not one he has chosen to create but one that is forced upon him' (pp. 79–80).

worship of the loved one is an idolatry that destroys the worshipper, that physical beauty is no more than a dim shadow of the Platonic Good, that our duty is not to regard this life but to prepare for the next, though all this is true, it is 'yet true that I must Stella love' (5). Unlike many other sonneteers who had attempted to transform their emotions by processes of Platonic or religious sublimation, or to escape from their mistresses with cries of 'the Devil take her', Astrophil remains a realist and accepts the power of emotion as an empirical fact that cannot be denied.

He is aware that his love is 'vaine' (4) and brings 'shame' upon him (21), but he cannot free himself from it; so he at first attempts to maintain a measure of self-respect by inventing sophistical arguments to justify his thraldom, to prove by 'reason good, good reason her to love' (10), and to equate passion with virtue (25). He insists that it was the lady's 'knowne worth' that first caused him to love her (2), and that in her 'Vertue is made strong by Beautie's might' (48), while to the charge that love plunges him 'in the mire Of sinfull thoughts' he replies instead that it ennobles and breeds 'A loathing of all loose unchastitie' (14). All this, the reader soon realizes, is an elaborate game of self-deception.

The mask is dropped in the 52nd sonnet, which marks the beginning of the second part of the sequence, where Virtue and Love argue for the possession of Stella, Love claiming her body and Virtue her soul, whereupon Astrophil gives judgement:

> Let Vertue have that Stella's selfe; yet thus,
> That Vertue but that body graunt to us.

The consequences of his change in attitude are shown in the immediately following second tournament sonnet (53). In the first tournament sonnet (41) he had gained the prize, he said, because he was inspired by Stella's eyes; but in this second tournament he is so bemused at her sight that he forgets to fight and makes a complete fool of himself. His change of attitude is made even more emphatic by contrast with the earlier sonnets. Formerly he had at least given intellectual assent to his friend's arguments:

> Your words my friend (right healthfull caustiks) blame
> My young mind marde, whom Love doth windlas so,
>   . . . that to my birth I owe
> Nobler desires, least else that friendly foe,
> Great expectation, weare a traine of shame. (21)

But in the second part he gives over all protestation and goes in active pursuit of Stella:

> No more, my deare, no more these counsels trie,
> O give my passions leave to run their race:
> Let Fortune lay on me her worst disgrace,
>
> . . . .
>
> Let all the earth with scorne recount my case,
> But do not will me from my Love to flie. (64)

A change also occurs in Stella. Previously she had been presented as distant and unresponsive; but one day she blushes when he looks at her (66), and finally she gives him the monarchy of her heart, though only on condition that he maintain a virtuous course. Her admission of affection, instead of ennobling as he had earlier pretended it would, causes him to throw aside all principle and to remark cynically:

> And though she give but thus conditionly
> This realme of blisse, while vertuous course I take,
> No kings be crown'd, but they some covenants make. (69)

Thereafter, until the eighth song, he gives his sensual race the rein. He steals a kiss from her while she sleeps, and thinks what a fool he has been for not taking more than a kiss (ii); he sophistically praises the lecherous Edward IV as the greatest of English kings (75); he hopes Stella will go to bed in a more receptive mood (76); he composes a blason of her visible charms, suggestively concluding with the remark that his 'Mayd'n Muse doth blush to tell the best' (77); and he writes a denunciation of her husband suggesting that it would be no more than justice to cuckold him (78).

The climax of the drama occurs in the eighth song, in which Astrophil urges his suit, and Stella, though admitting her affection, says they must part:

> Trust me while I thee deny,
> In my selfe the smart I try,
> Tyran honour doth thus use thee,
> Stella's selfe might not refuse thee.
>
> Therefore, Deere, this no more move,
> Least, though I leave not thy love,
> Which too deep in me is framed,
> I should blush when thou art named.

She leaves him 'passion rent', and the final section of the poem deals with Astrophil's despair, his sorrow at her absence, and his attempts to see her again. He finally by an act of will gives over the active pursuit of Stella (107); but he does not and cannot cease to love her, for he never frees himself from or sublimates his emotion. It is a fact that must be lived with.

Thomas Nashe, in the preface he wrote for Newman's unauthorized edition of *Astrophil and Stella* in 1591, characterized it as 'the tragicommody of love . . . performed by starlight. . . . The argument cruell chastitie, the Prologue hope, the Epilogue dispaire' (ii. 370). In calling it a tragicomedy Nashe meant that it was comic only in the technical sense 'in respect it wants deaths', for otherwise the action is tragic. Astrophil attains no serenity, and is left alone with 'most rude dispaire' as his 'daily unbidden guest' (108). There is no solution. The interest of the poem lies in its presentation of the emotional states and the psychology of Astrophil himself. Its artistic merit, beyond the excellence of the individual sonnets and songs, resides in its over-all structure. This structure is not rigidly planned, for the *Astrophil and Stella* poems do not have the intricate complication of incident of the plot of the *Arcadia*, nor are the individual poems arranged with the same regard for parallelism and unity of theme that we find in the first two sets of Arcadian eclogues. Instead they present us with a succession of scenes that illustrate emotional attitudes. There are some inconsistencies in the songs, and some of the sonnets could with more appropriateness occupy different positions; but in general there is an orderly progression of mood, the focus of attention remains fixed upon Astrophil as the lover of Stella, no irrelevancies are allowed to intrude, and the courtship is presented as having a beginning, a middle, and an end.

Probably either shortly before or after composing *Astrophil and Stella* Sidney wrote his *Defence of Poesy*.[1] In this, especially in the digression on the contemporary state of English poetry, he describes the principles he had followed and many of the technical innovations he had introduced in his own verses. Thereafter he appears to have written no more than a handful of original poems.

---

[1] Sidney's reference to 'King James of Scotland' as a poet (iii. 35) is probably to the youthful James VI, who according to Calderwood did not begin to write verse until the summer of 1581. Many of the illustrations and critical ideas of the *Defence* are also repeated in the sonnets of *Astrophil and Stella* (see notes to AS 1, 3, 4, 5, 8, 15, &c.), which suggests proximity in time of composition.

At the end of the *Old Arcadia* he had said that some other pen might wish to tell 'the strange continuance of Klaius and Strephons desire' (iv. 389), and he opened the *New Arcadia* with an episode in which the two friends lament the absence of their mistress. Sometime between he began a narrative in ottava rima telling how Strephon and Klaius first fell in love with Urania, and of their pursuit of her during a country game of barley-break (OP 4). This is Sidney's longest poem, over 500 lines, but it breaks off abruptly when the narrative could not have been more than half finished.

In 1584 he began an extensive revision and recasting of his *Old Arcadia*, which he also gave over before it was half finished, though even then the revision was some 50,000 words longer than the completed original version. But he composed only two, or at most three, new poems for his revised narrative, totalling no more than 15 lines (OP 1–3). Between 1582 and 1584 he probably also composed his 'Two Pastoralls' (OP 6 and 7) hymning his friendship with Fulke Greville and Edward Dyer, who made with him 'one Minde in Bodies three'. The second of these two poems is a 'Disprayse of Courtly life':

> Well was I, while under shade
> Oten Reedes me musicke made,
> Striving with my Mates in Song,
> Mixing mirth our Songs among,
> Greater was that shepheard's treasure,
> Then this false, fine, Courtly pleasure.

But the pastoral dream no longer sustained him, and in his later but still young years he turned his attention increasingly to religious subjects. We do not know when he translated the *First Week* of du Bartas (though known to contemporaries the translation no longer survives), but his other works show no evidence of his being acquainted with du Bartas before 1582. Before embarking for the Netherlands he had also begun to translate the prose treatise *De la vérité de la religion chrétienne*, which his friend Phillippe du Plessis Mornay had published in 1581; but he appears to have only begun the translation, and the version that was printed in 1587 as 'finished by Arthur Golding' is probably all the work of the latter.

Perhaps in 1585 also he began the metaphrase of the Psalms, of which he completed only the first forty-three. This, probably his last poetical undertaking, shows him still experimenting with the forms of verse. In part inspired by the model of the French version by Marot and Beza, he set himself the task of rendering each Psalm in a different stanzaic form. In the forty-three Psalms he completed he never once exactly repeated a stanzaic pattern, and forty-one of his stanzas were entirely new creations that he had never used before. But his metaphrase of the Psalms shows no essentially new technical advances, for he continues to use the patterning of masculine and feminine rhymes, the iambic and trochaic rhythms, and the rhetorical structures that he had already mastered.

Then in November 1585 the opportunity for which he had waited all his life arrived, and he sailed for the Netherlands as governor of Flushing and captain of a cornet of horse. He spent the following months in frustrating military campaigns against the Spaniards, and in maintaining the morale of his poorly paid troops and the disheartened Dutch. Though he never had an opportunity to take part in a major engagement, his wisdom as a diplomat and his courage as a soldier aroused the admiration of all he met. After eleven months of indecisive campaigning, he was wounded in a skirmish before the town of Zutphen. He took part in this as a volunteer, signalized his courage by charging three times through the enemies' lines, and though his thigh was shattered by a bullet he rode his horse from the field. Infection set in, and he died on 17 October, having not yet attained his 32nd year. In the following February he was buried with full military honours in St. Paul's, universally lamented, and hymned as 'England's Mars and Muse'.

Characteristics and Innovations

Sidney did not write any poems about his campaigns in the Netherlands, or if he did no record of them survives. His poetry is remarkable for what he did not write about. He was a courtier, but except for some passages in *The Lady of May* he never wrote in praise of the Queen. He was sincerely religious, but he never wrote a poem of personal devotion. He placed a high value upon friendship, but except for his 'Two Pastoralls' and a single mention of Languet he never wrote a commendatory or memorial poem for a real person. The major interest of his life was politics, but only once did he deal with problems of government, and then under the veil of a beast fable. Except for *Astrophil and Stella* his verse was neither official nor personal and dealt almost entirely with imagined situations.

Most of it was concerned with love; but even in his love poetry when he spoke as 'I' he usually did so through a created character, Philisides—and even Astrophil. He remained aloof, and so could view both his productions and himself with a sometimes quizzical detachment.

Until he attained complete mastery of his medium in *Astrophil and Stella*, he devoted his attention more to manner than to matter.[1] When in his idlest times he looked upon the poetry of his own country he did not find it good, and he determined to make it better. He believed that 'the highest flying wit' must have 'a Dedalus to guide him'; and he felt that the greatest defect of his fellow English poets was that with 'neither Artificiall Rules, nor imitative paternes, we much comber our selves withall' (iii. 37). So he set out to be a Daedalus to his countrymen, to teach them rules of right writing, and to provide them with models to follow. His contemporary Spenser, who was also a reformer and proclaimed as 'this our new Poete', sought to revitalize English poetry by amalgamating the native and continental traditions; but Sidney turned his back almost completely upon the English past. Though he admitted the appeal of the old song of Percy and Douglas, he never wrote a ballad; and though he was acquainted with stories of King Arthur, he modelled his own romance upon works from Greece, Italy, and Spain (Heliodorus, Sannazaro, and Montemayor). He had spent his formative years studying the classics at Shrewsbury and Oxford and travelling upon the Continent; so when he commenced poet he followed classical and continental styles and forms more than he did those of his own country.

The Tudor poets had been faced with three major technical problems—forging a poetical language, discovering effective rhythms, and creating new poetical forms—for which they had found various but not always entirely satisfactory solutions. In language Sidney took a middle way, for he avoided both the inkhornisms of the neologizers and the archaisms of the patriotic purists. 'I have found in divers smally learned courtiers', he said, 'a more sound stile, then in some professors of learning' (iii. 43). He therefore did not attempt to create a special poetic diction, but was content to use the language of everyday polite conversation. His verse

---

[1] The first important analysis of the qualities of Sidney's poetry was made by Theodore Spencer, *ELH* xii (1945), 251–78. The first book-length study, *Symmetry and Sense, the Poetry of Sir Philip Sidney*, by R. L. Montgomery, Jr., 1961, appeared after the present edition was in proof.

contains no unusual words, no strange forms; only once did he indulge in Chaucerisms, and that was a single experiment in the manner of Spenser that he never repeated.[1] So restrained was his vocabularly that, again except for isolated experiments (as in OA 34), he avoided the excessive use of polysyllables, and preferred the commonest and shortest words. And yet he made a virtue of the prevailing monosyllabic quality of English. AS 31, for example, opens with ten words in a ten-syllable line—

With how sad steps, ô Moone, thou climb'st the skies—

but the words are not low, nor is the line dull.

Almost the only departures from ordinary prose usage that he permitted himself, aside from tight logical and rhetorical structure, were the occasional use of compound epithets and the frequent use of inversion. Some years after Sidney's death Joseph Hall called the compound epithet

. . . that new elegance,
Which sweet Philisides fetch't of late from France.

(Virgidimiae, 1598, VI. i. 255–6)

But Sidney himself had noted in his *Defence* that English 'is perticularly happy in compositions of two or three wordes togither, neare the Greeke, farre beyond the Latine' (iii. 44), so he probably cultivated the device more in emulation of ancient classical than of contemporary continental writers. His compounds are usually made up of two elements only, as 'thanke worthie frends' (OA 53. 14), but on occasion they are extended to considerable length, as 'long with Love acquainted eyes' (AS 31. 5).

Sidney also used inversion, occasionally in his earlier and with increasing frequency in his later poems. Sometimes the device is a mere ornamental mannerism, and sometimes it produces puzzling ambiguities, as 'Not though thereof the cause her selfe she know' (AS 45. 4); but usually it provides subtle modulations of rhythm and sense, as 'Indeed O you, you that be such of mind' (PS 22. 63), or gives needed emphasis to the most important words: 'And to old age since you your selfe aspire' (OA 15. 13), 'For even the hearbes our hatefull musique stroyes' (OA 72. 103), 'But him her host that unkind guest had slaine' (AS 38. 14).

---

[1] Veré L. Rubel, *Poetic Diction in the English Renaissance*, 1941, pp. 152–5.

Though Sidney was conservative in his choice of words, he was an innovator in his handling of rhythm. In the earlier years of the sixteenth century English prosody had been in a state of anarchy with no generally accepted principles of structure. Followers of the degenerate Lydgate tradition, like Stephen Hawes and William Nevill, wrote verse whose lines had no equivalence in length and no established pattern of stresses, only a tinckle of rhyme at the end. But by the middle decades of the century the earlier anarchy had been reduced to mechanical regularity. As a result George Gascoigne, whose *Certain Notes of Instruction* published in 1575 is the earliest formal treatise on English metrics, recognized only one rhythm, the iambic, and knew of only one way to write English verse: count syllables, have a regular alternation of stresses, and place a caesura in the same position in every line. Absolute regularity had thus become the primary virtue, and Gascoigne and most of his contemporaries maintained in their verses a fixed and never-varying pattern:

> A cloud of care   hath covred all my coste,
> And stormes of strife   doo threaten to appeare:
> The waves of woo,   which I mistrusted moste,
> Have broke the bankes wherein my life lay cleere.
>
> (*Works*, ed. Cunliffe, i. 400)

Sidney set about to combat the monotony of the English verse of his time; but he allowed himself only moderate and not excessive freedom, for he maintained a strict syllable count and an equal number of stresses as the basic pattern of all equivalent lines.[1] To maintain an equal syllable count he made full use of the orthographic schemes that permitted each syllable of a word to receive full pronunciation or to be suppressed at will by elision, apheresis, syncopation, or apocopation, 'as thadvantaige of the verse best serves' (see p. 391); but his scribes were not at all consistent in indicating the suppression of syllables by spelling or apostrophes, and Sidney himself may not have been consistent in using graphical devices for this purpose in his holographs. Since the pronunciation of the lines is made the responsibility of the reader, there is room for a certain amount of individual variation. Whether the last three feet

---

[1] In his *Defence* he noted that modern European poets observe 'onely number, with some regard of the accent', but that English poets 'observe the Accent verie precisely' (iii. 44).

of a line such as OA **70**. 2, 'Since sorow is the follower of evill fortune', should be read as 'the fóll'wer 'f évil fórtune' or as 'the fóll'wer óf 'ill fórtune' is something of an open question; but since Sidney had a more formal conception of metre and was not as disturbed as we are today at a stress falling on an unemphatic word, he may have preferred the second reading. On the other hand, he scarcely ever wrenched pronunciation by diastole to fit his metre. A couplet such as OA **66**. 62–63,

> With neighing, blaying, braying, and barking,
> Roring, and howling for to have a King,

in which the rhyme demands that the last word of the first line be pronounced 'barkíng', is extremely rare.

Some of Sidney's earliest verse is as mechanical as that of Gascoigne (see LM 1); but he almost at once began to vary the tempo of his lines by inversion of feet and shifting of caesuras:

> And keep it joynde, fearing your seate's consumption.   (OA **7**. 42)

> Thus Painters *Cupid* paint, thus Poets do,
> A naked god, young, blind, with arrowes two.   (OA **8**. 5–6)

He introduced variations of this sort sparingly at first, but more frequently as he went on; until in *Astrophil and Stella* he resolved mechanical regularity to a controlled freedom by allowing the rhythms of speech to have an increasing part in introducing variations in the fixed pattern[1]—

'Foole,' said my Muse to me, 'Looke in thy heart and write.'   (AS **1**. 14)

Sidney never achieved the elaborate harmonies of Spenser, but he helped to free English metre from the strait jacket to which poets of the mid century had confined it, and he also sought other rhythms besides the ubiquitous iambic. Following the lead of Ascham and Drant, he for awhile experimented with adapting classical quantitative metres to English (see note to OA 11). But his greatest triumph was naturalizing an entirely new rhythm, the accentual trochaic (see above, p. xliii). He made his first tentative experiments in this new form in three of the *Certain Sonnets*, and brought it to perfection in the songs of *Astrophil and Stella*.

---

[1] See Lever, pp. 86–87; and John Thompson, 'Sir Philip Sidney and the Forsaken Iamb', *Kenyon Review* xx (1958), 90–115, who, however, is overly anxious to have Sidney write like Donne—one of his examples of Sidney's new sense of rhythm (AS **2**. 1) is not Sidney's at all but a unique error in the 1598 folio.

In his handling of rhyme also he was both a meticulous craftsman and an innovator. He almost always rhymed with complete phonetic accuracy. Apparent variations, such as 'bear-were' and 'far-stir', were actually perfect rhymes in Elizabethan pronunciation (in Sidney's holographs they would have been spelled 'bear-wear' and 'fur-stur', but the scribes seldom preserved his phonetic spelling). He sometimes took advantage of variant current pronunciations, but he hardly ever allowed himself the common licence of creating entirely new rhymes by the figure antisthecon, such as 'seech' for 'seek'.

His great innovation was to bring feminine rhyme back into English verse and to make it a formal structural element in the shaping of his stanzas.[1] After the early years of the sixteenth century the Tudor poets had confined themselves almost exclusively to masculine rhyme. Surrey has at most five, and probably only two, pairs of genuine feminine rhymes in all his verse, and an analysis of the selections in a standard anthology such as that of Hebel and Hudson reveals only three pairs of feminine rhymes between Wyatt and Sidney. But Sidney used feminine rhyme in one out of every five of his poems, and even used trisyllabic (*sdrucciola*) rhyme in four poems.[2] He only occasionally introduced it haphazardly as an ornamental variation; most of the time he made it a regularly recurring structural element of his stanzaic patterns. Thus each quatrain of OA 57 has feminine rhyme in its second and fourth lines, and each stanza of CS 23 maintains a pattern of regularly alternating feminine and masculine rhymes. He used feminine rhyme in all of his trochaic poems and in all of his sestinas; but he avoided it in all but three of his early sonnets—none of the *Astrophil and Stella* sonnets contains feminine rhyme, though it regularly appears in the songs. This distinction in its use may be the result of some privately formulated and as yet unexplained principle of decorum. Though feminine rhyme almost never appears in the poetry of the mid century, by the 1590's, probably in part as a result of Sidney's example, it had become an accepted feature of English verse.

---

[1] He had a companion in Spenser who introduced a number of feminine rhymes into his *Shepheardes Calender*; but Spenser used them only as occasional ornaments and never as recurring elements of stanzaic structure. Later in the first three books of his *Faerie Queene* Spenser avoided feminine rhymes almost entirely.

[2] See p. 572. Sidney discussed masculine, feminine, and *sdrucciola* rhyme in his *Defence*, iii. 44–45.

But though Sidney introduced important innovations in rhythm and rhyme, he was even more interested in larger structural patterns which he created by a compact and complex combination of the devices of logic and rhetoric within established or newly invented fixed forms. He prided himself on being 'a peece of a Logician' (iii. 3), and his poems are notable for the orderly progression of their ideas. Some of them are concatenations of arguments (OA 77), others are debates (AS 34), and in all the images are controlled by their logical function and the feeling is guided by thought.[1]

His handling of rhetorical devices also shows a great advance over his predecessors. Though the earlier Tudor poets had been conscious of rhetoric, their range of figures was limited, and they usually contented themselves with the repetitive use of a few simple schemes such as anaphora or alliteration. Sidney structured his verse with an intricate interlacing of the whole panoply of both schemes and tropes. As a result, Abraham Fraunce in his *Arcadian Rhetorike* could illustrate the entire range of figures in the Talaean manual from Sidney's poems. Sometimes he used only a few devices, as in OA 35—

> Sweete glove, the sweete despoyles of sweetest hand,
> Fayre hand, the fayrest pledge of fayrer harte,
> Trew harte, whose trewthe dothe yeeld to trewest bande—

where the controlling scheme gradation is emphasized by polyptoton and some subsidiary devices of repetition. At other times he used tropes as well as schemes in greater variety and related in a more complex manner. In OA 21 the 'brookes', 'aier', and 'sande' on which Cleophila looks, with which he speaks, and in which he writes are the elements water, air, and earth which combine with the fire of his passion; the enumeration is recapitulated in the next to the last line, and the phrases are further related and elaborated by synecdoche, anadiplosis, prosopopoeia, antithesis, and a variety of other figures.[2] In the *Old Arcadia* the rhetoric is sometimes obtrusive, in the best of the *Astrophil and Stella* sonnets it is less obvious because more completely functional. His special contribution was the use, not of one or two figures in isolation, but of a wide variety of figures in intricate combination.

[1] See Rosemond Tuve, 'Imagery and Logic: Ramus and Metaphysical Poetics', *JHI* iii (1942), 365–400, especially pp. 386–8, and *Elizabethan and Metaphysical Imagery*, 1947, pp. 319–29 and passim.

[2] See Rubel, pp. 123–6, 156–8, and passim.

Sidney also enhanced the structure of his poems by following the patterns of the established genres, and by imitating or devising an astonishing number of stanzaic forms. His critical preoccupation is shown by his being the first to introduce into English many of the terms which today are part of our basic vocabulary when talking about poetry—'couplet', 'lyric', 'madrigal', 'masculine rhyme', 'octave', 'stanza', &c. He was also the first Englishman to give a formal list of the traditional classical kinds—pastoral, elegiac, iambic, satiric, comic, tragic, lyric, and heroic (iii. 22–25). He himself, if we include the mixed forms appearing in his prose fiction, produced examples of all of these except the personal invective of the iambic; and in addition he wrote poems modelled on a number of the sub-sidiary kinds, such as the blason, epithalamium, fabliau, and hymn.

But his greatest innovations were in the variety and number of verse forms that he used and introduced. His 286 poems contain 143 different line and stanza patterns (see pp. 569–72), 109 of which he used only once. Most of these were entirely new to English—fewer than 20 appear in Tottel's *Songes and Sonettes*. His lines vary in length from 3 to 14 syllables, his stanzas from 3 to 15 lines; for rhythms he used iambics, trochaics, and 7 varieties of quantitative metre. His *Old Arcadia* contains half a dozen polymetric poems (OA 1, 7, 9, 28, 29, and 50); but in all his later poems, except for introductory quatrains or concluding couplets and partial stanzas, he strictly maintained the same stanza form with which he began, even to the exact patterning of masculine and feminine rhymes. Among the more technically difficult forms that he first introduced were the sestina, the crown, and the canzone. No previous English poet, from Old English to Tudor times, even approached Sidney in the variety and complexity of metrical forms that he used.

The form that he cultivated most assiduously was the sonnet, which after its introduction by Wyatt and Surrey had been strangely neglected by later English poets except Gascoigne. Approximately half of Sidney's poems are sonnets, of which he produced thirty-three different varieties. His handling of the form shows a definite direction of experimentation. He began with the Surreyan form of three quatrains and a couplet—20 of his 34 early sonnets are pat-terned on that model, though he never used it later. The canard that English poets avoided the Italian form because of the difficulty of finding rhymes is effectively refuted by his practice, for sixteen of his earliest sonnets have five rhymes or less—indeed three have only three rhymes, two have two, and one repeats the same rhyme sound in all 14 lines. But he soon began to prefer an octave with only two rhymes, though only once in the *Old Arcadia* did he imitate the strict Italian form (the Petrarchan rhyme scheme and hendecasyllabic lines of OA 69 make the Italian source of his inspiration obvious). The form he eventually found most satisfactory combined an Italian octave with a *cdcdee* sestet, a combination he used in his later composed CS 1 and 2 and in 60 of his *Astrophil and Stella* sonnets. Since Wyatt had written two sonnets of this type (Tottel No. 44 and 102), his model in this case, as Lever observed, may have been English rather than continental. Sidney's earlier sonnets are excellently constructed rhetorical forms exemplifying the Erasmian doctrines of copiousness. His later and better sonnets, instead of being static rhetorical statements, frequently contain a dynamic interaction of feeling and thought by which something is made to happen and through which a discovery is made by both the speaker and the reader.

The poet, Sidney said, is a 'maker' (iii. 7), and from his own practise we can see that he considered him not only as a creator of an ideally ordered world, but also as a creator of artistic forms. His own central preoccupation was with structure, and in his search for form he not only produced single excellently fashioned poems, but also sought to relate them to one another to produce larger and more complex unities. He closely related the verses in the narrative portion of his *Arcadia* to the contexts in which they occur by making them appropriate to the situation and the speaker, and he even so grouped his miscellaneous *Certain Sonnets* that they have a clearly defined beginning and end. But his greatest triumphs in creating larger architectonic patterns are in the between-the-act eclogues of the *Old Arcadia* and in *Astrophil and Stella*. He unified each group of eclogues by making the individual poems illustrate a single theme in different ways, and he related the four groups to one another so that they form an artistic whole that is fully capable of standing by itself. In *Astrophil and Stella*, instead of collecting a mere aggregate of sonnets and songs, he arranged them to provide a narrative and psychological progression, and so produced a sequence that is more dramatic and highly ordered than any other in the renaissance.

Sidney taught his countrymen that a poet should be neither an artisan mechanically performing a task nor an undisciplined enthusiast, but an accomplished craftsman, and in his own poetry he provided both technical models to be followed and examples of excellence. He introduced new techniques of rhythm and rhyme, new stanzaic patterns, and new examples of poetic kinds. What he taught his countrymen in the 1580's, many of them were practising in the 1590's.

Transcription and Publication

Sidney affected an air of nonchalance toward his writings, called them 'trifles', pretended surprise at finding himself numbered 'among the paper blurrers', and said,

> ... I wish not there should be
> Graved in mine Epitaph a Poet's name.   (AS 90)

But this was a pose, the *sprezzatura* of an Elizabethan gentleman. There is abundant evidence that he approached his writing with great seriousness, and was more painstaking than most of the professional artists of his day. His continued and extensive revisions of the *Arcadia*, and his repeated reworkings of a poem like OA 62, indicate the care he took to bring his works as near as he could to perfection. But like other Elizabethan gentlemen, he scorned the commercialism of the stationers' shops, and never himself supervised the printing of any of his works. Except for two anonymous sonnets possibly of his making (PP 4 and 5), which were published by Goldingham in 1581, none of his writings appeared in print until after his death.

This, however, does not mean that he did not publish them, for until well into the seventeenth century manuscript dissemination was an important and just as accepted a means of publication as printing. In sending his *Old Arcadia* to his sister he told her to 'keepe it to yourselfe, *or* to such friendes, who will weigh errors in the ballaunce of good will'. The nine surviving transcripts, all deriving at different times from his own working copy, show that he circulated a number of copies among his friends. There were once more manuscripts than are at present known, for the surviving copies indicate the existence at one time of at least five others (O, P, T, X, Y), and there may also have been other transcripts that have left no trace. His *Certain Sonnets* too were collected and copied in extenso at least twice, and copies of individual poems were given to friends or acquaintances. He also appears to have allowed the songs of *Astrophil and Stella* to circulate; but the sonnets he kept close, because they were too personally revealing, and they do not appear to have come abroad until three or four years after his death. The large number of his poems in the courtly manuscript anthologies that drew their material from works composed in the 1570's and 1580's (especially Ra, which appears to have been compiled in the late 1580's and contained twenty-five of his poems) shows that most of his poems were given early circulation, at least in certain restricted courtly circles.

But manuscript copies were laborious to make and were available only to the few, so that during his own lifetime Sidney was mainly known as a poet by his own particular friends and their associates. He kept his own counsel, avoided recognition for his authorship, and made only one passing reference to his literary work in his surviving correspondence (iii. 132). When Geoffrey Whitney wrote a poem hailing him as the successor of Surrey, he said the verses were more appropriate to his friend Dyer.[1] He was much sought as a patron; but of the 38 dedications addressed to him (a greater number than were addressed to any other contemporary of similar position), in which he was praised for every virtue that the dedicators could think of, only one mentions that he was himself a writer.[2]

The earliest printed reference to Sidney's literary activities is in the *Familiar Letters* of Spenser and Harvey which appeared in the summer of 1580.[3] The following year Thomas Howell, a dependant of Sidney's sister, included a veiled reference to the *Arcadia* in his *Devises* (E4v–F1), and in 1582 Thomas Watson expressed the hope that his *Ekatompathia* might find a place in the book-chests of Sidney or Dyer, though he did not say that they themselves were poets. In 1584 the Huguenot poet du Bartas, who had probably heard of Sidney through their mutual friend du Plessis Mornay, in the second book of the second day of his *Seconde Sepmaine* (lines 623–6) named him as one of the four pillars of the English language, along with Sir Thomas More, Sir Nicholas Bacon, and, of course, Queen Elizabeth. And in the summer of 1586 Edmund Molyneux, in an obituary notice of his master Sir Henry Sidney, mentioned his

---

[1] *A Choice of Emblemes*, 1586, b2.

[2] Scipio Gentile, *In XXV Davidis Psalmos Epicae Paraphrasis*, 1584, *4, said that he was 'poetae ipse longe optimo'.

[3] Paulus Melissus, whom Sidney first met in 1577, addressed him as 'Musarum inclite cultibus' (Buxton, p. 91), but this tribute was not printed until 1586. In 1578 Harvey in his *Gratulationum Valdinensium Libri Quatuor* had hailed Sidney as one 'In quibus ipsae habitent Musae, dominetur Apollo' (K3v), but since he also gave him the attributes of all the other deities of the pantheon, it is doubtful whether his statement has any specific meaning.

heir Sir Philip and 'his booke which he named *Arcadia*', noting that
'a speciall deere freend he should be that could have a sight, but
much more deere that could once obteine a copie of it'.[1]

These few references are the only extant mentions of Sidney as a
man of letters made in his lifetime. They all come from, or can be
traced to, persons close to the Sidney circle. William Webbe, who
in his *Discourse of English Poetrie* published in 1586 showed acquain-
tance only with printed sources, did not mention Sidney in his roster
of contemporary English poets. In the hundreds of poems lamenting
his death that were written at the universities and by men of letters
elsewhere, he was frequently referred to in general terms as a poet,
but few of the writers showed direct acquaintance with his specific
works. Roydon's 'Elegie . . . for his Astrophill', for example, shows
that its author probably knew no more than the titles of Sidney's
works, for he has him taking pleasure 'on the mountaine Parthenie'
in Arcadia, which is a detail found in Sannazaro's story but not in
Sidney's.

Nevertheless, there are several times as many manuscript copies
of Sidney's poems extant as there are those of any other Tudor poet
of his generation or before. After his death his work circulated
even more widely than it had before in manuscript, and it soon was
given still wider dissemination in print. Occasional poems were first
printed by Byrd, Fraunce, and Puttenham between 1587 and 1589.
In 1590 Greville published an excellent edition of the incomplete
New Arcadia, in 1591 Newman brought out two editions of *Astrophil
and Stella* in corrupt texts, and in 1593 the Countess of Pembroke
provided a conclusion to the Arcadian narrative by adding the last
three books of the *Old Arcadia* to the incomplete revised text that
had been published by Greville. In 1598 the Countess brought out a
collected edition of her brother's writings, which reprinted her 1593
version of the *Arcadia* and the previously published *Defence of Poesy*,
and added from manuscripts in her own possession texts of the
Certain Sonnets, *Astrophil and Stella*, and *The Lady of May*. This
had been thirteen times reprinted by 1739 and, except for the collec-
tion of *Miscellaneous Works* edited by William Gray in 1829, re-
mained the standard edition of Sidney's writings until Feuillerat's
edition of 1912–26.

No manuscript of Sidney's verse in his own hand survives; but

---

[1] Holinshed's *Chronicles*, 1587 uncensored edition, p. 1554.

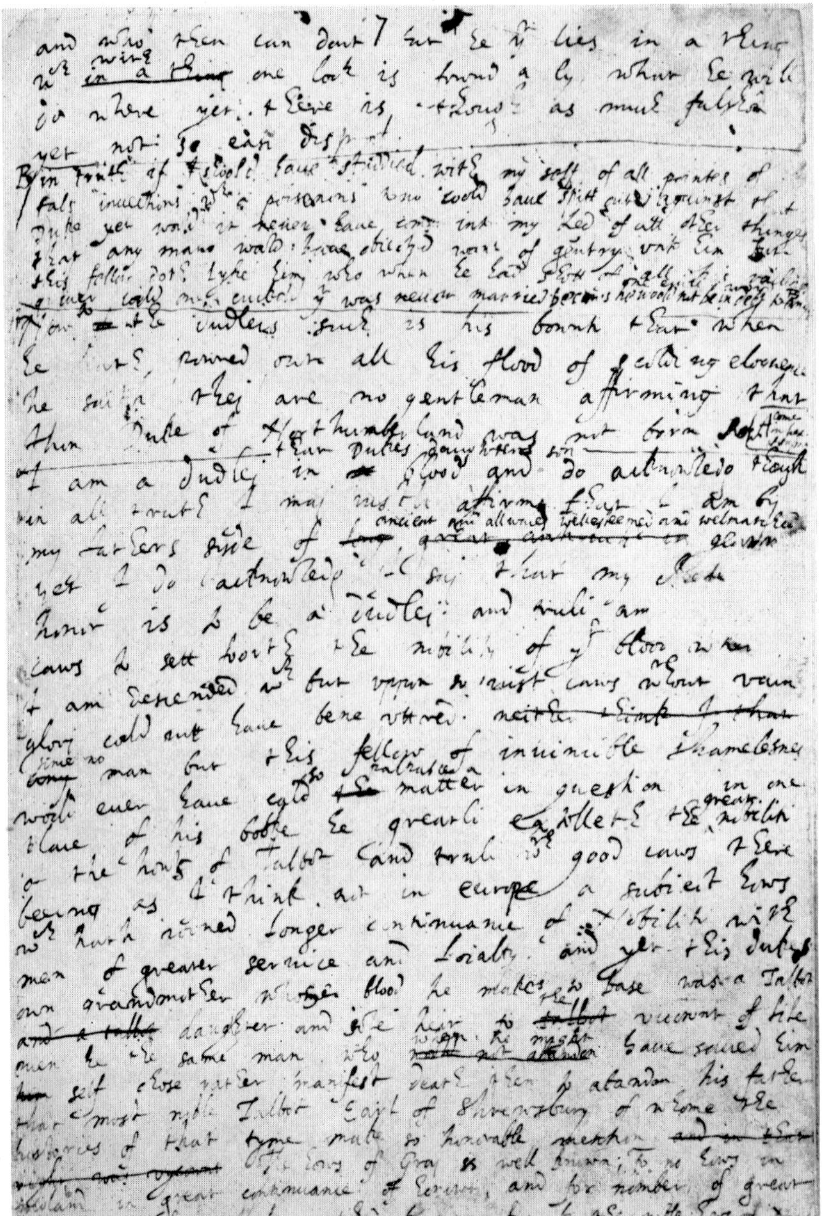
and who then can deny but he that lies in a thing
which wire one loke is found a ly, what he will
do where yet there is though as much falsehood
yet not so easy despr.
For in truth if I shold have studied with my self of all pointes of
fals invections which a poisonous tong cold have spitt out against that
Duke yet wold it never have come into my hed of all other things
that any man wold have obiected want of gentry unto him but
this fellow doth lyke him who when he had shott of all his railing
quiver called one cuckold that was never married
so doth the Libeller such is his bounty that when
he hath powred owt all his flood of scolding eloquence
he saith they are no gentleman affirming that
the Duke of Northumberland was not born so
I am a Dudley in blood, that Dukes daughters son and do acknowledge though
in all truth I may justly affirme that I am by
my fathers side of ancient and allwaies well esteemed and welmatched gentry
yet I do acknowledge I say that my chefest
honor is to be a Dudley and truly am
glad to have cause to sett forth the nobility of that blood wherof
I am descended which but upon so iust cause without vain
glory cold not have bene uttered, since no
man but this fellow of invincible shamelesnes
wold ever have cald so palpable a matter in question. In one
place of his booke he greatly extolleth the great nobility
of the house of Talbot and truly with good cause there
being as I think not in Europe a subiect hows
which hath ioined longer continuance of nobility with
men of greater service and loialty and yet this Dukes
own grandmother whose blood he makes so base was a Talbot
daughter and sole heir to the viscount of Lisle
even he the same man who when he might have saved him
self chose rather manifest death then to abandon his father
that most noble Talbot Earl of Shrewsbury of whome the
histories of that tyme make so honorable mention
The hows of Gray is well known to no hows in
England in great continuance of honor, and for nomber of great
howses sprong of it to be matched by none, but by the noble hows of Stanley

Pierpont Morgan Library MS. 1475, f. 6

from the years during which he was writing poetry there are several
prose holographs—a dozen personal letters, the two-leaf fragment
on Irish Affairs, and his defence of the Earl of Leicester. This last,
now in the Pierpont Morgan Library in New York, is the longest and
most revealing of his holographs. It is the original draft, written with
many deletions, interlineations, and corrections, and shows that Sid-
ney was an extremely rapid writer who composed easily and revised as
his pen travelled. He sometimes would begin a sentence, strike out
a phrase in the middle, and then completely change its direction. A
literatim transcription of a short passage will show something of the
kind of foul papers that his secretary had before him when he made
the first fair copy of his *Arcadia* and his poems. (It is sometimes im-
possible to distinguish *a* from *o* and *u* from *w*. See the eighteenth-
century transcript printed by Feuillerat, iii. 65.)

and who then can dout but he y^t lies in a thing
    with
w^ch ~~in a thing~~ one look is fownd a ly, what he will
do where yet there is though as much falshod
yet not so easi disproof.

B/in truth if I shoold haue studdied with my self of all pointes of
fals inuections wch a poisenous tong coold haue spitt out against that
Duke yet woold it neuer haue come into my hed of all other thinges
that any man woold: haue obiected want of gentry vnto him but
this fellow doth lyke him who when he had shott of all his railing
quiuer cald one a cuckold y^t was neuer married becaws he woold not be
                    one euill word B
                    in debt to any

---

    to
A Now ~~of~~ the dudleis such is his bownti that when
he hath powred out all his flood of scolding eloquence
he saith thei are no gentleman affirming that   come
Ihon Duke of Northumberland was not born so   A in her
                               vt supra
a———————that Dukes daughters son—————
I am a dudlei in—blood and do acknowledg though
in all truth I mai iustli affirme that I am by
            ancient and allwaies wellesteemed and welmatched
my fathers syde of ~~long great antiquiti in~~ gentry

This, however, is an exceptionally disordered passage. Most of

Sidney's holographs are quite clean, with very few deletions or emendations.

Sidney wrote a mixed hand with predominantly Italian characteristics. It is generally clear and legible, with few of the ambiguities that occur in the common secretary hands of his time—his *i* and *e*, and *e* and *d*, for example, could never be confused by a reader, though the same letters can scarcely be distinguished from one another in some secretary hands.

It has sometimes been thought that Elizabethan spelling was completely chaotic; but though it varied from individual to individual, most persons developed fairly regular patterns of their own which are just as significant as the shaping of their letters for identifying their hands. Though Sidney used certain equivalences interchangeably, such as *i*, *ie*, and *y* (he usually signed his name 'Sidnei', but sometimes wrote 'Sidney'), and though he would write 'been' and 'bene' in the same sentence, for the most part his spelling is perfectly consistent and conforms to a regular phonetic pattern. Following are some of his typical spellings, from which he never varied.

able	hable	meant	ment
called	cald	read (*present*)	reed
carrying	cariing	read (*past*)	redd
case	cace	should	shoold
cause	caws(e)	spoken	spokne
could	coold	stir	stur
exceeding	ecceeding	than	then
far	fur(r)	too	to
friend	frend(e)	trouble	troble
further	furdre	weighed	waied
get	gett	were	wear(e)
grant	grawnt	wholly	holy
hear	heer(e)	would	woold
here	he(e)r(e)	you	yow

Sidney did not regularly begin sentences with capitals, and was generally sparing in their use. His punctuation was light, and when composing rapidly he used practically none at all. He used the comma and period (though it is frequently difficult to distinguish the one from the other), and occasionally the colon and parentheses; but he never used the semicolon, question mark, exclamation mark, or dash, and, of course, quotation marks and apostrophes for possessives were not introduced until after his time. Since we do not have any holographs of his verse, it is impossible to tell whether he indicated elision and apocopation by apostrophes. Probably when he indicated them at all he did so by spelling, but he also probably did not consistently provide graphical indications of the suppression of syllables and normally left the perception of the rhythm of his lines to the reader.

None of the surviving manuscripts of his poems preserves more than the slightest trace of Sidney's characteristic pattern of spelling. It is clear that the scribes paid practically no attention to the accidents of their originals, and followed their own individual patterns of spelling when they copied. They may have paid somewhat more attention to punctuation, but since Sidney apparently used very little, they did not have much to go upon. A few of the manuscripts containing his poetry (notably the Clifford manuscript) are heavily punctuated; but most of them (like the St. John's manuscript) are punctuated only lightly, and sometimes not at all—they usually contain no punctuation at the end of a line, and only an occasional comma or set of parentheses within the line. Compositors appear to have been somewhat more conscientious than scribes in following the accidents of their originals (changes in the nature of the printer's copy for the 1593 folio, for example, can sometimes be detected by slight shifts in the pattern of spelling); but most compositors followed their own individual usages and the usages of their printing houses more than they did the accidents of their copy.

None of the surviving manuscripts or early prints appear to have been copied directly from Sidney's own holographs. Indeed, it does not seem to have been the practice in the sixteenth century for gentlemen to keep their 'foul papers'. When they wrote a poem, they usually had a fair copy made by a secretary, and then probably threw the original rough draft away. The three most important authorial manuscripts of gentlemen poets that survive from that period are British Museum MS. Egerton 2711, containing the poems of Wyatt, and MS. Egerton 3165, containing the poems of Sir Arthur Gorges, and the manuscripts of Fulke Greville's poems at Warwick Castle. All of these are scribal copies, with only corrections and additions in the authors' own hands, and in the case of Greville's manuscripts even the corrections were entered by the scribes. This, of course, is what authors who can afford to pay a secretary still do today—they have their original rough drafts typewritten, and make corrections and later changes on the fair copy.

Sidney's own secretaries apparently made fair copies from his holograph foul papers with a high degree of verbal accuracy, though it is unlikely that he enforced any set prescriptions for spelling and punctuation. The scribal originals T and P of the surviving *Old Arcadia* manuscripts, and O* of the *Astrophil and Stella* manuscripts, do not appear to have contained more than a few dozen verbal errors. But none of these fair copies survive. The scribes of the existing manuscripts sometimes worked carefully, but at other times with extreme carelessness. The St. John's manuscript of the *Old Arcadia* (St) contains very few detectable verbal errors; the Phillipps manuscript (Ph) has errors in almost every other line—the scribe, or the scribe of the original from which he copied, was not only extremely careless, but occasionally took the liberty of relieving the boredom of transcription by free embroidery upon the text and made changes and even added phrases of his own composition.

But even Sidney's own secretaries could be distressingly careless if they were not checked. The only surviving manuscript that we know was executed at his personal order (Ba) is a scribal copy on a single sheet of paper of CS 30, which the recipient, Edward Bannister, said had been given him by Sidney himself 'Att pvttenye In svrrye Decembris x° Ann° 1584'. The text contains only 167 words, eight of which are demonstrably wrong—a transcriptional error of 5 per cent. It is therefore not in the least surprising that texts which stand at several removes from Sidney's original—such as the poems appearing in the manuscript anthologies, or Q1 of *Astrophil and Stella*—are to a high degree unreliable.

However, for most of Sidney's poems we are fortunate in having manuscript or printed copies that were carefully made either directly or at no more than one remove from accurate scribal copies of his own holographs. For most of the poems we also have a considerable number of substantive texts, so that it is possible to detect the individual errors of one transcript by comparison with the others. The words of the critical texts that follow I believe represent with a high degree of certainty what Sidney himself wrote. The spelling and punctuation, however, are those of sixteenth-century copyists; they are not Sidney's and do not mirror the usages found in his prose holographs. The reader therefore should attend primarily to the words, and should not allow his interpretation of the poems to be influenced to more than a slight degree by the accidentals.

EDITORIAL PROCEDURE

SINCE no holographs of any of Sidney's poems survive and since none of the extant manuscripts or prints preserves his spelling and punctuation, for each poem the most readable sixteenth-century version has been chosen as copy text, and this has been reproduced literatim except for the correction of demonstrable verbal and punctuation errors. Quotation marks and apostrophes for possessives have been added silently (none exist in any of the originals), and *i*, *j*, *u*, and *v* have been normalized; otherwise all departures from the copy text are recorded in the apparatus. Where punctuation has been emended editorially, the word preceding with the punctuation mark or lack of punctuation in the original is listed in the apparatus without a lemma. Where the spelling of a word in the copy text is ambiguous or misleading, the word is glossed in the Commentary. Since most of the verbal variants in the substantive texts are errors made independently by the scribes or compositors, the apparatus is highly selective. The general principle followed is to list all departures from the copy text, but otherwise only variants occurring in two or more substantive texts. Whenever a variant is listed, the readings of *all* substantive texts in that passage are indicated in the apparatus (except in the *Psalms*, where ordinarily variants are cited only from K and A).

SIGLA

13 *Arcadia . . . with some new Additions*, 1613.

90 *Arcadia*, 1590 (3 books).

93 *Arcadia*, 1593 (5 books). '90–93' indicates that 93 in the passage cited takes its text from 90, '90, 93' indicates that 93 in the passage cited takes its text from manuscript (P or Cm).

98 *Arcadia . . . with sundry new additions*, 1598.

A Viscount De L'Isle and Dudley MS. *Psalms.*

B Bodleian MS. Rawl. poet. 25. *Psalms.*

C Bodleian MS. Rawl. poet. 24. *Psalms.*

D Wadham College MS. 25. *Psalms.*

E The Queen's College MS. 341. *Psalms.*

F Trinity College MS. O. 1. 51. *Psalms.*

G Trinity College MS. R. 3. 16. *Psalms.*

H British Museum MS. Additional 12048. *Psalms.*

I British Museum MS. Additional 12047. *Psalms.*

J Dr. B. E. Juel-Jensen MS. *Psalms.*

K British Museum MS. Additional 46372. *Psalms.*

L Huntington Library MS. HM 100. *Psalms.*

M Huntington Library MS. HM 117. *Psalms.*

N Bibliothèque de l'Université de France MS. 1110. *Psalms.*

As Huntington Library MS. HM 162. Ashburnham MS. of *Old Arcadia.*

Ba British Museum MS. Additional 28253 (Bannister MS. of CS 30).

Bd William Byrd, *Psalmes, Sonets, & songs*, 1588. (AS vi.)

Bd William Byrd, *Songs of sundrie natures*, 1589. (AS x.)

Bn Nicholas Breton, *The Arbor of amorous Deuises*, 1597. (CS 3.)

Bo Bodleian MS. e Museo 37. *Old Arcadia.*

Bt British Museum MS. Additional 15232. Bright MS. of *Astrophil and Stella.*

Cl Folger Library MS. 4009.03. Clifford MS. of *Old Arcadia.*

Cm Cambridge University MS. Kk. 1. 5 (2). *New Arcadia.*

Da British Museum MS. Additional 41204. Davies MS. of *Old Arcadia.*

Dd Cambridge University MS. Dd. 5. 75. (OA 2, 3, 35, 41, 42, 48, 51, 62; CS 3, 30; AS ix.)

Di Henry Constable, *Diana* [1594–7]. (CS 1, 2, 8–11, 18, 20.)

Dn National Library of Scotland MS. 2059. (PP 3.)

Dr University of Edinburgh MS. De. 5. 96. Dymoke-Drummond MS. of *Astrophil and Stella.*

Dv Francis Davison, *A Poetical Rapsody*, 1602. (OP 6, 7.)

Eg British Museum MS. Egerton 2421. (OA 62.)

Fl Folger Library MS. 2071. 7. (OA 17.)

Fo Folger Library MS. 1. 112. The Cornwallis-Lysons MS. (CS 16.)

Fr Abraham Fraunce, *The Arcadian Rhetorike* [1588]. (AS vii, CS 3.)

Go Henry Goldwel, *A briefe declaration* [1581]. (PP 4, 5.)

Ha British Museum MS. Harley 6910. (AS viii; CS 23; OA 3, 15, 64.)

Hn Duke of Norfolk, Arundel-Harington MS. (AS i, x; CS 1, 3, 27, 30; OA 51, 75.)

Hn John Harington, *Orlando Furioso*, 1591. (AS 18; OA 65.)

Ho Arthur A. Houghton, Jr., MS. Briton-Houghton MS. of *Astrophil and Stella.*

Hy British Museum MS. Harley 7392. (CS 3, 16, 19, 23, 30; OA 3, 45, 51, 60; PP 2.)

Je Jesus College MS. 150. *Old Arcadia.*

Le British Museum MS. Additional 41498. Lee MS. of *Old Arcadia.*

Ma Marsh's Library MS. Z 3. 5. 21. (CS 15, 19, 22, 23; OA 17.)

Ph British Museum MS. Additional 38892. Phillipps MS. of *Old Arcadia.*

Pu [George Puttenham], *The Arte of English Poesie*, 1589. (OA 45.)

Q1 *Syr P. S. His Astrophel and Stella*, 1591.

Q2 *Sir P. S. His Astrophel And Stella*, 1591.

Q3 *Syr P. S. His Astrophel and Stella* [1597–1600].

Qu The Queen's College MS. 301. *Old Arcadia.*

Ra Bodleian MS. Rawl. poet. 85. (AS iv, viii, x; CS 3, 8–11, 16, 19, 21, 22, 23, 25; OA 21, 22, 33, 38, 41, 51, 71; PP 2.)

St St. John's College MS. I. 7. *Old Arcadia.*

LOST MANUSCRIPTS

B⁰ The original of *Psalms* MS. B before revision. B¹⁻³ indicate successive revisions of B⁰.

G   The *New Arcadia* MS. that Sidney left with Greville, used as copy for 90.

O   Sidney's holograph originals.

O* Scribal transcript of *Astrophil and Stella* MS. O, the original of X, Y, and Z.

P   *Old Arcadia* MS. given by Sidney to his sister the Countess of Pembroke, used as copy for part of 93.

T   Scribal transcript of *Old Arcadia* MS. O, used by Sidney as his working copy. T¹⁻⁵ indicate successive revisions of T.

X   *Old Arcadia* MS. copied from T¹, the original of Je and Qu.

X   *Astrophil and Stella* MS., the original of 98, Bt, and Fr.

X   *Psalms* MS., from which C D E G H L M N derive.

Y   *Old Arcadia* MS. copied from T², the original of Ph.

Y   *Astrophil and Stella* MS., the original of Dr and the corrections in Q2.

Z   *Astrophil and Stella* MS., the original of Z¹ and ancestor of Q1.

Z¹ *Astrophil and Stella* MS., the original of Hn and Ho.

ABBREVIATIONS FOR SIDNEY'S POEMS

AS   *Astrophil and Stella*, sonnets 1–108 and songs i–xi.

AT   Wrongly Attributed Poems, 1–30.

CS   *Certain Sonnets*, 1–32.

LM   *Lady of May*, poems 1–3.

OA   *Old Arcadia*, poems 1–77.

OP   Other Poems, 1–7.

PP   Poems Possibly by Sidney, 1–5.

PS   *Psalms*, 1–43.

WORKS FREQUENTLY CITED

Sidney's prose writings are cited by volume and page from his *Complete Works*, ed. Albert Feuillerat, 4 vols., Cambridge, 1912–26.

W. Blount. Contemporary manuscript annotations by, in the Folger Library copy of the 1593 *Arcadia*.

Brie. Friedrich Brie, *Sidney's Arcadia*, Strassburg, 1918.

Gray. William Gray, ed., *The Miscellaneous Works of Sir Philip Sidney*, Oxford, 1829.

Grosart. Rev. Alexander B. Grosart, ed., *The Complete Poems of Sir Philip Sidney*, 3 vols., London, 1877.

John. Lisle C. John, *The Elizabethan Sonnet Sequences*, New York, 1938.

Koeppel. Emil Koeppel, 'Studien zur Geschichte des englischen Petrarchismus', *Romanische Forschungen*, v (1890), 90–97.

Poirier. Michel Poirier, ed. and trans., *Astrophel et Stella*, Paris, 1957.

Poirier, *Sidney*. Michel Poirier, *Sir Philip Sidney*, Lille, 1948.

Pollard. Alfred W. Pollard, ed., *Astrophel and Stella*, London, 1888.

Scott. Janet G. Scott [Espiner], *Les Sonnets Élisabéthains*, Paris, 1929.

Brian Twyne. Notes on *Astrophil and Stella*, *c.* 1599, in Corpus Christi College Oxford, MS. 263, f.120.

Wallace. Malcolm W. Wallace, *The Life of Sir Philip Sidney*, Cambridge, 1915.

Wilson. Mona Wilson, ed., *Astrophel and Stella*, London, 1931.

Wilson, *Sidney*. Mona Wilson, *Sir Philip Sidney*, London, 1931.

POEMS FROM
THE LADY OF MAY

THE LADY OF MAY

1

[*The Countrywoman's Supplication to Queen Elizabeth*]

To one whose state is raised over all,
Whose face doth oft the bravest sort enchaunt,
Whose mind is such, as wisest minds appall,
Who in one selfe these diverse gifts can plant;
   How dare I, wretch, seeke there my woes to rest,   [5]
   Where eares be burnt, eyes dazled, harts opprest?

Your state is great, your greatnesse is our shield,
Your face hurts oft, but still it doth delight,
Your mind is wise, your wisedome makes you mild,
Such planted gifts enrich even beggers' sight: [10]
   So dare I, wretch, my bashfull feare subdue,
   And feede mine eares, mine eyes, my hart in you.

2

[*The Singing Match Between Therion and Espilus*]

Therion

Come *Espilus*, come now declare thy skill,
Shew how thou canst deserve so brave desire,
Warme well thy wits, if thou wilt win her will,
For water cold did never promise fire:
   Great sure is she, on whom our hopes do live,   [5]
   Greater is she who must the judgement give.

Espilus   [Shepherds play recorders]

Tune up my voice, a higher note I yeeld,
To high conceipts the song must needes be high,
More high then stars, more firme then flintie field
Are all my thoughts, in which I live or die: [10]
   Sweete soule, to whom I vowed am a slave,
   Let not wild woods so great a treasure have.

1. 98.   5 I wretch 98.   11 I 98.   **2.** 98.

Therion   [Foresters play cornets]

The highest note comes oft from basest mind,
As shallow brookes do yeeld the greatest sound,
Seeke other thoughts thy life or death to find;   [15]
Thy stars be fal'n, plowed is thy flintie ground:
  Sweete soule let not a wretch that serveth sheepe,
  Among his flocke so sweete a treasure keepe.

Espilus   [Shepherds play recorders]

Two thousand sheepe I have as white as milke,
Though not so white as is thy lovely face,   [20]
The pasture rich, the wooll as soft as silke,
All this I give, let me possesse thy grace,
  But still take heede least thou thy selfe submit
  To one that hath no wealth, and wants his wit.

Therion   [Foresters play cornets]

Two thousand deere in wildest woods I have,   [25]
Them can I take, but you I cannot hold:
He is not poore who can his freedome save,
Bound but to you, no wealth but you I would:
  But take this beast, if beasts you feare to misse,
  For of his beasts the greatest beast he is.   [30]

Espilus kneeling to the Queene

Judge you to whom all beautie's force is lent.

Therion

Judge you of Love, to whom all Love is bent.

3

[*Espilus and Therion*]

[*Espilus*] *Silvanus* long in love, and long in vaine,
  At length obtaind the point of his desire,
When being askt, now that he did obtaine
His wished weale, what more he could require:
  'Nothing', sayd he, 'for most I joy in this,   [5]
  That Goddesse mine, my blessed being sees'.

3. 98.   5 Nothing 98.

[*Therion*] When wanton *Pan*, deceiv'd with Lion's skin,
　　Came to the bed, where wound for kisse he got,
　　To wo and shame the wretch did enter in,
　　Till this he tooke for comfort of his lot:　　　　　　[10]
　　　'Poore *Pan*' (he sayd) 'although thou beaten be,
　　　It is no shame, since *Hercules* was he'.

[*Espilus*] Thus joyfully in chosen tunes rejoyce,
　　That such a one is witnesse of my hart,
　　Whose cleerest eyes I blisse, and sweetest voyce,　　[15]
　　That see my good, and judgeth my desert:
[*Therion*] Thus wofully I in wo this salve do find,
　　My foule mishap came yet from fairest mind.

---

7 *Pan* 98.　　　10 lot, 98.

The version of the *Lady of May* at the end of Sir Lionel Tollemache's manuscript
of the *Old Arcadia* now owned by Mr. Arthur A. Houghton, Jr., which is described
above in the Preface, contains the following verbal variants in the songs.

　1. 6 harts] harte.　　7 our shield] you^r shilde.　　12 mine eares, mine eyes, my
hart in] myne eyes, m$\tilde{y}$e eares, myne harte on.

　2. 13 comes oft] come of.　　15 lyfe] self.　　16 Thy stars . . . thy flintie] Thie
starre . . . the flyntie.　　20 lovely] Lowely.　　29 if] of.

　3. 3 askt] axte.　　9 wo] woa.　　10 comfort] comefor.　　13 Thus joyfully
in chosen] This Ioyfull I in ioyfull.　　15 sweetest] sweete of.　　17 Thus wofully
I] This wofull I.

POEMS FROM
THE COUNTESS OF PEMBROKE'S
ARCADIA
(THE OLD ARCADIA)

APPARATUS

The relationships of the extant texts are discussed in the notes (pp. 366–80) and a diagram of the stemma is given on p. 380. The order in which collations from the substantive texts are given is: 90 93 Cm OA (St Bo Cl Le As Da Ph Je Qu) Hn Dd Ra Ha Hy. '90–93' indicates that 93 merely reprints 90, '90, 93' indicates that 93 takes some readings from manuscript (P or Cm). For poems that have been revised, the latest revision is printed in the critical text and the earlier version is given at the bottom of the page within rules.

TO MY DEARE LADIE AND SISTER,
THE COUNTESSE OF PEMBROKE

HERE now have you (most deare, and most worthy to be most deare Lady) this idle worke of mine: which I fear (like the Spider's webbe) will be thought fitter to be swept away, then worn to any other purpose. For my part, in very trueth (as the cruell fathers among the Greekes, were woont to doo to the babes they would not [5] foster) I could well find in my harte, to cast out in some desert of forgetfulnes this child, which I am loath to father. But you desired me to doo it, and your desire, to my hart is an absolute commandement. Now, it is done onelie for you, onely to you: if you keepe it to your selfe, or to such friendes, who will weigh errors in the ballaunce [10] of good will, I hope, for the father's sake, it will be pardoned, perchance made much of, though in it selfe it have deformities. For indeede, for severer eyes it is not, being but a trifle, and that triflinglie handled. Your deare selfe can best witnes the maner, being done in loose sheetes of paper, most of it in your presence, the rest, [15] by sheetes, sent unto you, as fast as they were done. In summe, a young head, not so well stayed as I would it were, (and shall be when God will) having many many fancies begotten in it, if it had not ben in some way delivered, would have growen a monster, and more sorie might I be that they came in, then that they gat out. But his chiefe [20] safetie, shalbe the not walking abroad; and his chiefe protection, the bearing the liverye of your name; which (if much much good will do not deceave me) is worthy to be a sanctuary for a greater offender. This say I, because I knowe the vertue so; and this say I, because it may be ever so; or to say better, because it will be ever so. Read it [25] then at your idle tymes, and the follyes your good judgement wil finde in it, blame not, but laugh at. And so, looking for no better stuffe, then, as in an Haberdasher's shoppe, glasses, or feathers, you will continue to love the writer, who doth excedinglie love you; and most most hartelie praies you may long live, to be a principall [30] ornament to the familie of the *Sidneis*.

Your loving Brother
Philip Sidnei.

THE FIRST BOOK OR ACT

I

[*The Delphic Oracle*]

THY elder care shall from thy carefull face
By princely meane be stolne, and yet not lost.
Thy yonger shall with Nature's blisse embrace
An uncouth love, which Nature hateth most.
Both they themselves unto such two shall wed, [5]
Who at thy beer, as at a barre, shall plead
Why thee (a living man) they had made dead.
In thy owne seate a forraine state shall sit.
And ere that all these blowes thy head doo hit,
Thou, with thy wife, adultry shalt commit. [10]

5-10. OA:

> Thowe with thy wieff adulterie shalt committ
> And in thy throne, a forayne state shall sitte
> All this one the this fatall yere shall hitte.

2

[*Cleophila*]

TRANSFORMD in shew, but more transformd in minde,
I cease to strive, with double conquest foild:
For (woe is me) my powers all I finde
With outward force and inward treason spoild.

For from without came to mine eyes the blowe, [5]
Whereto mine inward thoughts did faintly yeeld;
Both these conspird poore Reason's overthrowe;
False in my selfe, thus have I lost the field.

1. 90-93, Cm (*blank space only*), OA (*wanting in* As Je). 6 plead; 90.
10 shalt] shall 90-93.
2. 90-93, Cm, OA, Dd. 2 striue 90. 4 force, 90. 5 mine] my Bo Le
Da Ph. blowe] blowes Bo Qu. 6 mine] my Bo Le Da Ph Je. 7 Both]
But Qu Dd.

>Thus are my eyes still Captive to one sight:
>Thus all my thoughts are slaves to one thought still: [10]
>Thus Reason to his servants yeelds his right;
>Thus is my power transformed to your will.
>What marvaile then I take a woman's hew,
>Since what I see, thinke, know is all but you?

9-11. OA:

>And thus myne eyes, are plaste still in one sight
>and thus my thoughtes, can thinke but one thing still
>thus reason to his Servantes gyves his right

9 myne] my Bo Le Da.

3

[*Alethes*]

WHAT length of verse can serve brave *Mopsa's* good to show,
Whose vertues strange, and beuties such, as no man them may know?
Thus shrewdly burdned then, how can my Muse escape?
The gods must help, and pretious things must serve to shew her
    shape.
Like great god *Saturn* faire, and like faire *Venus* chaste: [5]
As smooth as *Pan*, as *Juno* milde, like goddesse *Isis* faste.
With *Cupid* she fore-sees, and goes god *Vulcan's* pace:
And for a tast of all these gifts, she borowes *Momus'* grace.
Her forhead jacinth like, her cheekes of opall hue,
Her twinkling eies bedeckt with pearle, her lips of Saphir blew: [10]
Her haire pure Crapal-stone; her mouth O heavenly wyde;
Her skin like burnisht gold, her hands like silver ure untryde.
As for those parts unknowne, which hidden sure are best:
Happie be they which well beleeve, and never seeke the rest.

13-14 *om.* Ph.   14 what] that As Da.
3. 90-93, Cm, OA, Dd, Ha, Hy.   90 *does not indent line* 1.   1 show? 90.
2 beuties] beuty Bo Je.   them may] may them Le Dd, may As.   know 90.
5-14 *om.* Je.   6 as *Juno*] a Iuno St Dd.   *Isis*] Iris 90-93 Cm OA Dd Ha Hy.
faste] faast Cm, fast As Dd.   8 borowes] steales god 90-93 Cm.   9 cheekes]
cheek Le Ph.   10 of] as 90-93 Cm.   11 pure] like 90-93 Cm, of Qu.
13 those] her 90-93 Cm, theis As Da, the Le.   14 be] are Le Ph Dd.   well]
will St Bo As Dd.

4

[*Dorus*]

COME shepheard's weedes, become your master's minde:
Yeld outward shew, what inward change he tryes:
Nor be abasht, since such a guest you finde,
Whose strongest hope in your weake comfort lyes.

Come shepheard's weedes, attend my woefull cryes: [5]
Disuse your selves from sweete *Menalcas*' voice:
For other be those tunes which sorrow tyes,
From those cleere notes which freely may rejoyce.
   Then power out plaint, and in one word say this:
   Helples his plaint, who spoyles himselfe of blisse.   [10]

5

[*Dametas*]

NOW thanked be the great God *Pan*,
That thus preserves my loved life:
Thanked be I that keepe a man,
Who ended hath this fearefull strife:
   So if my man must praises have,   [5]
   What then must I that keepe the knave?

For as the Moone the eie doth please,
With gentle beames not hurting sight:
Yet hath sir Sunne the greatest praise,
Because from him doth come her light: [10]
   So if my man must praises have,
   What then must I that keepe the knave?

4. 90, 93, Cm, OA (*wanting in* Je).   1 shepheard's] shepehearde St Cl As.
2 change] chance 90 Qu.   5 shepheard's] sheepherd St Bo Cl As.   6 your selves]
your selfe Cm As.   10 his] is St Qu.

5. 90, 93, Cm, OA (*wanting in* Le).   90 *indents even numbered lines and begins*
them without a capital.   2 That] which 90-93 Cm.   4 fearefull] bloodie 93 Cm.
5 So] For 90-93 Cm.   7 eie] eies 90 Cm.

6

[The dance of the Arcadian shepherds]

[A.] We love, and have our loves rewarded.
[B.] We love, and are no whit regarded.
[A.] We finde most sweete affection's snare,
[B.] That sweete, but sower despairefull care.
[A.] Who can despaire, whom hope doth beare?   [5]
[B.] And who can hope, who feeles despaire?
[AB.] As without breath, no pipe doth move,
    No musike kindly without love.

7

Lalus and Dorus

Lalus.   Come *Dorus*, come, let songs thy sorowes signifie:
    And if for want of use thy minde ashamed is,
    That verie shame with Love's high title dignifie.
      No stile is held for base, where Love well named is:
    Ech eare suckes up the words a true love scattereth,   [5]
    And plaine speach oft then quaint phrase better framed is.

Dorus.   Nightingales seldome sing, the Pie still chattereth:
    The wood cries most, before it throughly kindled be,
    Deadly wounds inward bleed, ech sleight sore mattereth.
      Hardly they heard, which by good hunters singled be.   [10]
    Shallow brookes murmure most, deep silent slide away;
    Nor true love loves those loves with others mingled be.

6. 90–93, OA (*wanting in* Le).   6 *om.* As.   who feeles] that feeles 90–93 Ph Je.
7. 90, 93, OA (*wanting in* As), Ra (*lines* 152–6 *only*).   1 *Lalus*] *Thyrsis* 93
(*and throughout in lines* 13–174).   5 words, 90.   6 oft, . . . phrase, 90.
8 throughly] thoroughe Le, *om.* Ph Je.   12 those] his 93 St Cl.   others] other
Le Je.

Lalus.   If thou wilt not be seene, thy face goe hide away,
Be none of us, or els maintaine our fashion:
Who frownes at others' feastes, dooth better bide away.   [15]
    But if thou hast a Love, in that Love's passion,
I challenge thee by shew of her perfection,
Which of us two deserveth most compassion.

Dorus.   Thy challenge great, but greater my protection:
Sing then, and see (for now thou hast inflamed me)   [20]
Thy health too meane a match for my infection.
    No, though the heav'ns for high attempts have blamed me,
Yet high is my attempt. O *Muse* historifie
Her praise, whose praise to learne your skill hath framed me.

Lalus.   *Muse* hold your peace: but thou, my God *Pan*, glorifie [25]
My *Kala's* giftes: who with all good gifts filled is.
Thy pipe, ô *Pan*, shall helpe, though I sing sorilie.
    A heape of sweetes she is, where nothing spilled is;
Who though she be no *Bee*, yet full of honie is:
A *Lillie* field, with plowe of *Rose* which tilled is.   [30]
    Milde as a Lambe, more daintie then a Conie is:
Her eyes my eyesight is, her conversation
More gladde to me, then to a miser monie is.
    What coye account she makes of estimation?
How nice to touch? how all her speeches peized be?   [35]
A Nimph thus turnde, but mended in translation.

Dorus.   Such *Kala* is: but ah, my fancies raysed be
In one, whose name to name were high presumption,
Since vertues all, to make her title, pleased be.
    O happie Gods, which by inward assumption   [40]
Enjoy her soule, in bodie's faire possession,
And keep it joynde, fearing your seate's consumption.
    How oft with raine of teares skies make confession,
Their dwellers rapt with sight of her perfection
From heav'nly throne to her heav'n use digression?   [45]
    Of best things then what world can yeeld confection
To liken her? Decke yours with your comparison:
She is her selfe, of best things the collection.

23 my] myne Cl Le Je Qu.   24 whose] who Da Qu.   25 God] good St Da Qu.
26 is] *om.* 93.   30 *Lillie*] Litle Cl Le, seelye Qu.   45 heav'n] heauens Je Qu.

Lalus.   How oft my dolefull Sire cried to me, 'tarrie sonne'
When first he spied my love? how oft he said to me,   [50]
'Thou art no souldier fitte for *Cupid's* garrison.
    My sonne, keepe this, that my long toyle hath laide to me:
Love well thine owne: me thinkes, woolle's whitenes passeth all:
I never found long love such wealth hath paide to me'.
    This winde he spent: but when my *Kala* glasseth all   [55]
My sight in her faire limmes, I then assure my selfe,
Not rotten sheepe, but high crownes she surpasseth all.
    Can I be poore, that her golde haire procure my selfe?
Want I white wooll, whose eyes her white skinne garnished?
Till I get her, shall I to sheep enure my selfe?   [60]

Dorus.   How oft, when reason saw love of her harnished
With armour of my hart, he cried, ' O vanitie,
To set a pearle in steele so meanely varnished?
    Looke to thy selfe; reach not beyond humanitie:
Her minde, beames, state farre from thy weake wings banished:
And Love, which lover hurts is inhumanitie'.   [66]
    Thus Reason said: but she came, Reason vanished;
Her eyes so maistering me, that such objection
Seemde but to spoyle the foode of thoughts long famished.
    Her peereles height my minde to high erection   [70]
Drawes up; and if, hope fayling, ende live's pleasure,
Of fayrer death how can I make election?

Lalus.   Once my well-waiting eyes espied my treasure,
With sleeves turnde up, loose haire, and brestes enlarged,
Her father's corne (moving her faire limmes) measure.   [75]
    'O' cried I, 'of so meane worke be discharged:
Measure my case, how by thy beautie's filling
With seede of woes my hart brimme-full is charged.
    Thy father bids thee save, and chides for spilling.
Save then my soule, spill not my thoughts well heaped,   [80]
No lovely praise was ever got with killing'.

51 garrison? 90.   59 garnished] garnisheth Le Je Qu.   60 sheep] keepe
90–93 OA.   61 saw, 90.   harnished] harnised 90–93.   69 thoughts] thought
Cl Je.   71 if hope-fayling 90.   72 fayrer] fayre Le Qu.   74 brestes] brest
90–93 Je Qu.   75 moving] mowinge Le Ph.   faire] fayres Cl Da.   77 thy]
yᵉ Je Qu.   81 with] by 90–93 Cl.

These bolde words she did heare, this fruite I reaped,
That she, whose looke alone might make me blessed,
Did smile on me, and then away she leaped.

Dorus.   Once, ô sweete once, I saw with dread oppressed   [85]
Her whom I dread; so that with prostrate lying
Her length the earth in Love's chiefe clothing dressed.
    I saw that riches fall, and fell a crying;
'Let not dead earth enjoy so deare a cover,
But deck therewith my soule for your sake dying.   [90]
    Lay all your feare upon your fearefull lover:
Shine eyes on me, that both our lives be guarded;
So I your sight, you shall your selves recover'.
    I cried, and was with open rayes rewarded:
But straight they fledde, summond by cruell honor,   [95]
Honor, the cause, desart is not regarded.

Lalus.   This mayde, thus made for joyes, ô *Pan* bemone her,
That without love she spends her yeares of love:
So faire a fielde would well become an owner.
    And if enchantment can a harde hart move,   [100]
Teach me what circle may acquaint her sprite,
Affection's charmes in my behalfe to prove.
    The circle is my (round about her) sight:
The power I will invoke dwelles in her eyes:
My charme should be, she haunt me day and night.   [105]

Dorus.   Farre other care, ô *Muse*, my sorrow tries,
Bent to such one, in whom, my selfe must say,
Nothing can mend one point that in her lies.
    What circle then in so rare force beares swaye?
Whose sprite all sprites can spoile, raise, damne, or save: [110]
No charme holdes her, but well possesse she may;
    Possesse she doth, and makes my soule her slave:
My eyes the bandes, my thoughts the fatall knot.
No thralles like them that inward bondage have.

---

82 heare] beare 93.   88 riches] richest Bo Je Qu.   89 deare] riche Le, faire
Ph Je Qu.   93 your selves] yor selfe Je Qu.   94 open] opend St Bo Da
Qu.   106 care] case 93 Cl Le.   108 one] that 90-93.   110 spoile] foile
93.   damne] downe Le Da.   114 thralles] thrall 93 Je Qu.

Lalus.   *Kala* at length conclude my lingring lotte: [115]
    Disdaine me not, although I be not faire.
    Who is an heire of many hundred sheepe
    Doth beauties keep, which never Sunne can burne,
    Nor stormes doo turne: fairenes serves oft to wealth.
    Yet all my health I place in your good-will.   [120]
    Which if you will (ô doo) bestow on me,
    Such as you see, such still you shall me finde.
    Constant and kind: my sheep your foode shall breed,
    Their wooll your weede, I will you Musique yeeld
    In flowrie fielde; and as the day begins   [125]
    With twenty ginnes we will the small birds take,
    And pastimes make, as Nature things hath made.
    But when in shade we meet of mirtle bowes,
    Then Love allowes, our pleasures to enrich,
    The thought of which doth passe all worldly pelfe.   [130]

Dorus.   Lady your selfe, whom nether name I dare,
    And titles are but spots to such a worthe,
    Heare plaints come forth from dungeon of my minde.
    The noblest kinde rejects not others' woes.
    I have no shewes of wealth: my wealth is you,   [135]
    My beautie's hewe your beames, my health your deeds;
    My minde for weeds your vertue's liverie weares.
    My foode is teares; my tunes waymenting yeeld:
    Despaire my fielde; the flowers spirits' warrs:
    My day newe cares; my ginnes my daily sight,   [140]
    In which do light small birds of thoughts orethrowne:
    My pastimes none: time passeth on my fall:
    Nature made all, but me of dolours made:
    I finde no shade, but where my Sunne doth burne:
    No place to turne; without, within it fryes: [145]
    Nor helpe by life or death who living dyes.

Lalus.   But if my *Kala* this my suite denies,
    Which so much reason beares,

---

117 hundred] hundreth 93.   118 never] neither Bo Le Da Ph Qu.   119 Nor]
no Je Qu.   130 doth] do Da Qu.   133 Heare] Her Cl Ph Da.   134 "The
90.   137 for] yor Je Qu.   vertue's] vertuous Cl Ph Je.   140 day] days
Da Je Qu.   141 do light] I do delight Ph, delight Je, delightes Qu.   147 this]
thus 93.

Let crowes picke out mine eyes, which saw too much:
If still her minde be such,   [150]
My earthy moulde doth melte in watrie teares.

Dorus.   My earthy moulde doth melte in watrie teares,
And they againe resolve
To aire of sighes, sighes to the harte's fire turne,
Which doth to ashes burne: [155]
So doth my life within it selfe dissolve.

Lalus.   So doth my life within it selfe dissolve,
That I am like a flower
New plucked from the place where it did breed,
Life showing, dead indeed: [160]
Such force hath Love above poore Nature's power.

Dorus.   Such force hath Love above poore Nature's power,
That I growe like a shade,
Which being nought seems somewhat to the eyen,
While that one body shine.   [165]
Oh he is mard that is for others made.

Lalus.   Oh he is mard that is for others made.
Which thought doth marre my piping declaration,
Thinking how it hath mard my shepheard's trade.
    Now my hoarse voice doth faile this occupation,   [170]
And others long to tell their loves' condition:
Of singing take to thee the reputation.

Dorus.   Of singing take to thee the reputation
New friend of mine; I yeeld to thy habilitie:
My hart doth seeke another estimation.   [175]
    But ah my *Muse* I would thou hadst facilitie,
To worke my Goddesse so by thy invention,
On me to cast those eyes, where shine nobilitie.
    Seen, and unknowne; heard, but without attention.

149–50. 93 OA:
              Let crowes picke out mine eyes which too much sawe.
              If shee still hate love's lawe,
149 mine] my Bo Le Qu.

---

151 earthy] earthly St Bo Da Ph Je Ra.   doth] will 90.   152 *90 does not indent.*
earthy] earthly St Bo Ph Je.   doth] do Cl Le Ph Qu.   154 harte's] harte Le Ph.
156 dissolue, 90.   175 hart] soule 90.   176 facilitie] agilitie 90.

156-74. 93 OA:
> Thus doth my life within it selfe dissolve.

Lalus. Thus doth my life within it selfe dissolve
That I growe like the beaste,
Whiche beares the bytt a weaker force doth guide,
Yet patient must abide.   [160]
Such weight it hath which once is full possest.

Dorus. Such weight it hath which once is full possest
That I become a vision,
Which hath in others' head his only being
And lives in fancye's seing.   [165]
O wretched state of man in selfe division!

Lalus. O wretched state of man in selfe division
O well thou saiest! a feeling declaration
Thy toong hath made of *Cupid's* deepe incision.
But now hoarse voyce, doth faile this occupation,   [170]
And others long to tell their loves' condicion.
Of singing thou hast got the reputation.

Dorus. Of singing thou hast got the reputation
Good *Lalus* mine, I yeld to thy abilitie;

156 *om.* St Bo.   157 *Lalus*] *Thyrsis* 93.   160 patient] pacyence Cl Da Ph Qu.
165 fancye's] fancie 93 Da.   166 *om.* Ph.   167 *Lalus*] *Thyrsis* 93.   174 *Lalus*]
Thyrsis 93, lady Qu.

8

[*Dicus*]

POORE Painters oft with silly Poets joyne,
To fill the world with strange but vaine conceits:
One brings the stuffe, the other stamps the coine,
Which breeds nought else but gloses of deceits.
    Thus Painters *Cupid* paint, thus Poets do,   [5]
    A naked god, young, blind, with arrowes two.

8. 90, 93, OA (*wanting in* As). *Stanzas not separated in* 90.   5 do 90.   6 young,
blind] young blind 90, blinde young 93 OA.

Is he a God, that ever flies the light?
Or naked he, disguis'd in all untruth?
If he be blind, how hitteth he so right?
How is he young, that tam'de old *Phœbus'* youth?   [10]
    But arrowes two, and tipt with gold or leade:
    Some hurt accuse a third with horny head.

No, nothing so; an old false knave he is,
By *Argus* got on *Io*, then a cow:
What time for her *Juno* her *Jove* did misse,   [15]
And charge of her to *Argus* did allow.
    Mercury kill'd his false sire for this act,
    His damme a beast was pardon'd beastly fact.

With father's death, and mother's guiltie shame,
With *Jove's* disdaine at such a rival's seed,   [20]
The wretch compell'd a runnagate became,
And learn'd what ill a miser state doth breed,
    To lye, faine, gloze, to steale, pry, and accuse,
    Naught in himselfe ech other to abuse.

Yet beares he still his parents' stately gifts,   [25]
A horned head, cloven foote, and thousand eyes,
Some gazing still, some winking wilye shiftes,
With long large eares where never rumour dyes.
    His horned head doth seeme the heaven to spight:
    His cloven foote doth never treade aright.   [30]

Thus halfe a man, with man he easly haunts,
Cloth'd in the shape which soonest may deceave:
Thus halfe a beast, ech beastly vice he plants,
In those weake harts that his advice receave.
    He proules ech place stil in new colours deckt,   [35]
    Sucking one's ill, another to infect.

To narrow brests he comes all wrapt in gaine:
To swelling harts he shines in honour's fire:

13 is 90.   22 miser] wreched Bo, misers Le Da Je Qu.   23 faine, gloze, to steale,
pry, and] to steale, to pry, and to 93 OA.   26 foote] feete 93 Cl.   29 horned]
hornie Bo Da.   30 foote] feete Cl Le Ph.   31 easly] dayly 90-93.

To open eyes all beauties he doth raine;
Creeping to ech with flattering of desire.   [40]
 But for that Love's desire most rules the eyes,
 Therein his name, there his chiefe triumph lyes.

Millions of yeares this old drivell *Cupid* lives;
While still more wretch, more wicked he doth prove:
Till now at length that *Jove* him office gives,   [45]
(At *Juno's* suite who much did *Argus* love)
 In this our world a hang-man for to be,
 Of all those fooles that will have all they see.

9

Geron Philisides

Geron. Up, up *Philisides*, let sorrowes goe,
 Who yelds to woe, doth but encrease his smart.
 Do not thy hart, to plaintfull custome bring,
 But let us sing, sweet tunes do passions ease,
 An olde man heare, who would thy fancies raise.   [5]

Philisides. Who minds to please the minde drownd in annoyes
 With outward joyes, which inly cannot sincke,
 As well may thincke with oyle to coole the fire:
 Or with desire to make such foe a frend,
 Who doth his soule to endlesse malice bend.   [10]

Geron. Yet sure an end, to each thing time doth give,
 Though woes now live, at length thy woes must dye.
 Then vertue try, if she can worke in thee
 That which we see in many time hath wrought,
 And weakest harts to constant temper brought.   [15]

Philisides. Who ever taught a skillesse man to teach,
 Or stop a breach, that never Cannon sawe?
 Sweet vertue's lawe barres not a causefull mone.

41 Love's desire most] Loue is worst [worse Le, most Ph], which 93 OA. 42 There-
in] Thereon 93 OA.
 9. 93, OA (*wanting in* Le).   3 plaintfull] painefull As Ph Qu.
5 fancies] fancie Je Qu. 7 inly] inward Ph Je. 18 causefull]
cawseles Bo Qu.

Time shall in one my life and sorrowes end,
And me perchaunce your constant temper lend.   [20]

Geron. What can amend where physick is refusde?
   The witts abusde with will no counsayle take.
   Yet for my sake discover us thy griefe.
   Oft comes reliefe when most we seeme in trappe.
   The starres thy state, fortune may change thy happe. [25]

Philisides. If fortune's lappe became my dwelling place,
   And all the starres conspired to my good,
   Still were I one, this still should be my case,
   Ruine's relique, care's web, and sorrowe's foode:
   Since she faire fierce to such a state me calls,   [30]
   Whose wit the starres, whose fortune fortune thralls.

Geron. Alas what falls are falne unto thy minde?
   That there where thou confest thy mischiefe lyes
   Thy wit dost use still still more harmes to finde.
   Whome wit makes vaine, or blinded with his eyes,   [35]
   What counsell can prevaile, or light give light?
   Since all his force against himselfe he tries.
   Then each conceit that enters in by sight,
   Is made, forsooth, a Jurate of his woes,
   Earth, sea, ayre, fire, heav'n, hell, and gastly sprite. [40]
   Then cries to sencelesse things, which neither knowes
   What ayleth thee, and if they knew thy minde
   Would scorne in man (their king) such feeble shows.
   Rebell, Rebell, in golden fetters binde
   This tyran Love; or rather do suppresse   [45]
   Those rebell thoughts which are thy slaves by kinde.
   Let not a glittring name thy fancie dresse
   In painted clothes, because they call it love.
   There is no hate that can thee more oppresse.
   Begin (and halfe the worke is done) to prove   [50]
   By raysing up, upon thy selfe to stand.
   And thinck she is a she, that doth thee move.

22 no] to Je Qu.   26 became] become Bo Qu, became became Ph.   30 a
state] estate Cl As Je.   38 by] his 93, my Ph.   40 sprite] spirites Bo Da Je.
41 neither] never As Ph, ~~neu~~ʳ neyther Da.   43 show's 93.   47 fancie] fancies St
Bo Ph Je.   51 raysing] rising 93 Da.

He water plowes, and soweth in the sand,
And hopes the flickring winde with net to holde,
Who hath his hopes laid up in woman's hand.　　　　　[55]
What man is he that hath his freedome solde?
Is he a manlike man, that doth not know man
Hath power that Sex with bridle to withhold?
A fickle Sex, and trew in trust to no man,
A servant Sex, soone prowde if they be coi'de,　　　　[60]
And to conclude thy mistresse is a woman.

Histor.　Those woordes dyd once the Loveliest shepard use
　　That erst I knewe, and with most plainefull muse;
　　Yet not of wemen Judging as he said,
　　But forste with raige, his raige on theym upbrayde.　[65]

Philisides.　O gods, how long this old foole hath annoi'd
　　My wearied eares! O gods yet graunt me this,
　　That soone the world of his false tong be void.
　　O noble age who place their only blisse
　　In being heard untill the hearer dye　　　　　　　　[70]
　　Uttring a serpent's minde with serpent's hisse.
　　Then who will heare a well autoris'd lye,
　　(And pacience hath) let him goe learne of him
　　What swarmes of vertues did in his youth flye
　　Such hartes of brasse, wise heads, and garments trim　[75]
　　Were in his dayes: which heard, one nothing heares,
　　If from his words the falshood he do skim.
　　And herein most their folly vaine appeares
　　That since they still alledge, *When they were yong*:
　　It shews they fetch their wit from youthfull yeares　[80]
　　Like beast for sacrifice, where save the tong
　　And belly nought is left, such sure is he,
　　This life-deadman in this old dungeon flong.
　　Olde houses are throwne downe for new we see:
　　The oldest Rammes are culled from the flocke:　　　[85]
　　No man doth wish his horse should aged bee.

---

57 know] knowe a Cl Qu.　　58 Sex] seekes Da Qu, sext Je.　　60 coi'de 93.
62–65 *om.* 93.　　62 Those] These Da Ph Je Qu.　　Loveliest] lowliest Da Je.
63 plainefull] paynfull As Je Qu.　　70 the hearer] they heare her Je Qu.　　74 ver-
tues] vertue Ph Qu.　　77 falshood] falsehodes St Cl As.　　do] doth Bo Da Je.
81 beast] beastes Da Ph.　　85 culled] called Cl As Da Qu.

The ancient oke well makes a fired blocke:
Old men themselves, doe love young wives to choose:
Only fond youth admires a rotten stocke.
Who once a white long beard, well handle does, [90]
(As his beard him, not he his beard did beare)
Though cradle witted, must not honnor loose.
Oh when will men leave off to judge by haire,
And thinke them olde, that have the oldest minde,
With vertue fraught and full of holy feare! [95]

Geron. If that thy face were hid, or I were blinde,
I yet should know a young man speaketh now,
Such wandring reasons in thy speech I finde.
He is a beast, that beaste's use will allowe
For proofe of man, who sprong of heav'nly fire [100]
Hath strongest soule, when most his raynes do bowe.
But fondlings fonde, know not your owne desire
Loth to dye young, and then you must be olde,
Fondly blame that to which your selves aspire.
But this light choller that doth make you bolde, [105]
Rather to wrong then unto just defence,
Is past with me, my bloud is waxen colde.
Thy words, though full of malapert offence,
I way them not, but still will thee advize
How thou from foolish love maist purge thy sense. [110]
First thinke they erre, that thinke them gayly wise,
Who well can set a passion out to show:
Such sight have they that see with goggling eyes.
Passion beares high when puffing wit doth blowe,
But is indeed a toy, if not a toy, [115]
True cause of evils, and cause of causelesse woe.
If once thou maist that fancie glosse destroy
Within thy selfe, thou soone wilt be ashamed
To be a player of thine owne annoy.
Then let thy minde with better bookes be tamed, [120]
Seeke to espie her faultes as well as praise,
And let thine eyes to other sports be framed.
In hunting fearefull beastes, do spend some dayes,

90 once] want*es* Je Qu.   94 oldest] eldest As Je.   96 or] and Ph Qu.
110 maist] maye Da Je.   111 erre] are Da Je Qu.   113 that] wch Ph Je.
117 fancie] fancies Bo Cl, fancyed Ph.   122 thine] thy Bo Cl Ph.

Or catch the birds with pitfalls, or with lyme,
Or trayne the fox that traines so crafty laies.   [125]
Ly but to sleepe, and in the earely prime
Seeke skill of hearbes in hills, haunt brookes neere night,
And try with bayt how fish will bite sometime.
Goe graft againe, and seeke to graft them right,
Those pleasant plants, those sweete and frutefull trees,   [130]
Which both the pallate, and the eyes delight.
Cherish the hives of wisely painfull Bees:
Let speciall care upon thy flock be staid,
Such active minde but seldome passion sees.

Philisides. Hath any man heard what this old man said?   [135]
Truly not I, who did my thoughts engage,
Where all my paines one looke of hers hath paid.

Histor. Thus may you see, howe youthe estemeth aige
And never hathe therof arightelye deemde
Whyle hote desyres do Raigne in fancie's rage   [140]
Till aige it self do make it self esteemde.

10

Geron   Mastix

Geron. Downe, downe *Melampus*; what? your fellow bite?
I set you ore the flock I dearly love,
Them to defend, not with your selves to fight.
Do you not thincke this will the wolves remove
From former feare, they had of your good mindes,   [5]
When they shall such devided weakenesse prove?
What if *Lælaps* a better morsell fyndes
Then thow earst knew? rather take part with him
Then jarle: lo, lo, even these how envie blindes.
And thowe *Lælaps* let not pride make thee brim   [10]

124 pitfalls] pitfoldes St Bo Da, pitfold As, pitfall Je Qu.   126 earely] earthly Cl
Da.   128 sometime] sometimes Bo Je.   130 and frutefull] vnfrutfull Je Qu.
135 any] my Bo Da.   137 hers] her 93.   138–41 *om*. 93.   139 arightelye]
rightlye Je Qu.
    10. 93, OA.   2 ore] ou*er* Bo Ph Da, on Qu.   7 *Lælaps*] Lelanx OA.
fyndes] finde? 93.   8 thow] you 93 Da.   10 thowe] then 93 Da.   *Lælaps*]
Lelanx St Bo Cl Le As Ph Je Qu, Lenanx Da.

Because thou hast thy fellow overgone,
But thanke the cause, thou seest, when he is dim.
Here *Lælaps*, here, in deed against the foen
Of my good sheepe, thou never trews time tooke:
Be as thou art, but be with mine at one.   [15]
For though *Melampus* like a wolfe doo looke,
(For age doth make him of a wolvish hew)
Yet have I seene when well a wolfe he shooke.
Foole that I am that with my dogges speake grewe.
Come narr good *Mastix*, tis now full tway score   [20]
Of yeeres (alas) since I good *Mastix* knewe.
Thou heardst even now a yong man snebb me sore,
Because I red him, as I would my son.
Youth will have will: Age must to age therefore.

Mastix. What marvaile if in youth such faults be done,   [25]
Since that we see our saddest Shepheards out
Who have their lesson so long time begonne?
Quickly secure, and easilie in doubt,
Either a sleepe be all if nought assaile,
Or all abroade if but a Cubb start out.   [30]
We shepeheards are like them that under saile
Doe speake high wordes, when all the coaste is cleare,
Yet to a passenger will bonnet vaile.
'I con thee thanke' to whom thy dogges be deare,
But commonly like currs we them entreate,   [35]
Save when great need of them perforce apeare.
Then him we kisse, whom late before we beatt
With such intemperance, that each way grows
Hate of the firste, contempt of later feate:
And such discord twixt greatest shepheards flowes,   [40]
That sport it is to see with howe greate art
By justice' worke they their owne faultes disclose:
Like busie boyes, to winne their tutor's harte,
One saith, He mockes; the other saith, he playes;
The third his lesson mist, till all do smarte.   [45]

12 when] where 93.   13 *Lælaps*] Lelanx St Bo Cl Le As Ph Qu, Lenanx Da,
Lilanx Je.   the] thy Cl Da Ph Je Qu.   14 trew's 93.   16 doo] dothe
Bo Ph Qu.   20 narr] neere 93 Da.   27 lesson] lessons Je Qu.   32 high]
by Ph Qu.   35 we] wee do Cl Qu.   39 feate] feates St Da.

As for the rest, howe shepeheardes spend their daies,
At blowe point, hotcocles, or els at keeles
While, 'Let us passe our time' each shepeheard saies.
So small accompt of time the shepeheard feeles
And doth not feele, that life is nought but time   [50]
And when that time is paste, death holdes his heeles.
To age thus doe they draw there youthfull pryme,
Knowing no more, then what poore tryall showes,
As fishe sure tryall hath of muddy slyme.
This paterne good, unto our children goes,   [55]
For what they see their parents love or hate
Their first caught sence prefers to teacher's blowes.
These cocklinges cockred we bewaile to late,
When that we see our ofspring gaily bent,
Women man-wood, and men effeminate.   [60]

Geron. Fy man, fy man, what wordes hath thy tonge lent?
Yet thou art mickle warse then ere was I,
Thy too much zeale, I feare thy braine hath spent.
We oft are angrier, with the feeble flie
For busines, where it pertaines him not,   [65]
Then with the poisnous todes that quiet lie.
I pray thee what hath ere the *Parret* gott,
And yet they say he talkes in greate men's bowers?
A Cage (guilded perchaunce) is all his lott.
Who of his tongue the lickowr gladly powrs,   [70]
A good foole call'd with paine, perhapps may be,
But even for that shall suffer mightie Lowers.
Let swanne's example siker serve for thee,
Who once all birdes, in sweetly-singing past,
But now to silence turn'd his minstralsie.   [75]
For he woulde sing, but others were defaste;
The peacocke's pride, the pye's pild flatterye,
Cormoraunt's glutt, Kite's spoile, king fisher's waste,
The Falcon's fercenes, Sparrow's letchery,
The Cockow's shame, the Goose's good intent,   [80]
Even turtle toutcht he with hypocrisie.

47 els at] *om.* OA.   56 see, 93.   57 caught] taught Cl Qu.   60 Wemen 93.
62 warse] worsse St Cl Le Ph Qu.   66 poisno'us 93.   77 flatterye] stattery
93.   78 king fisher's] king*es* fishers Bo Cl As Je, Kinges fisher Ph.   waste. 93.
79 letchery 93.

And worse of other more, till by assent
Of all the birdes, but namely those were grieved,
Of fowles there called was a parliament.
There was the swan of dignitie deprived,   [85]
And statute made he never shoulde have voice,
Since when I thinke he hath in silence lived.
I warne thee therefore (since thou maist have choice)
Let not thy tonge become a firy matche,
No sword soe bytes as that evill toole annoyes.   [90]
Lett our unpartiall eyes a litle watche
Our owne demeane, and soone we wondre shall
That huntinge faultes, our selves we did not catch.
Into our mindes let us a little fall,
And we shall find more spottes then Leopard's skinne.   [95]
Then who makes us such judges over all?
But farewell nowe, thy fault is no great sinne,
Come, come my currs, tis late I will goe in.

I I

Dorus

‒ ‒ ‒ ‒ ‒ ᴗᴗ ‒ ᴗᴗ ‒ ᴗᴗ ‒ ‒
‒ ‒ ‒ ᴗᴗ ‒ ‒ ᴗᴗ ‒ ᴗᴗ ‒

FORTUNE, Nature, Love, long have contended about me,
   Which should most miseries, cast on a worme that I am.
Fortune thus gan say; 'misery and misfortune is all one,
   And of misfortune, fortune hath only the gift.
With strong foes on land, on seas with contrary tempests   [5]
   Still doo I crosse this wretch, what so he taketh in hand'.
'Tush, tush', said nature, 'this is all but a trifle, a man's selfe
   Gives happs or mishapps, ev'n as he ordreth his hearte.
But so his humor I frame, in a mould of choller adusted,
   That the delights of life shall be to him dolorouse'.   [10]

86 statute] statutes St Cl As Da Ph.   93 That] at Je Qu.   96 makes] make
Ph Je.
  II. 93, OA. *Scansion only in St Cl As; St strikes through the hexameter scansion and
gives a second version with a spondee in the fourth foot.* 93 *indicates the distichs by a pre-
liminary dash instead of by indentation.* 1 Fortnne 93.   2 miseries] misery Cl Le As.
3 gan] can Bo Cl Le Da.   7 selfe] lyfe Cl Ph, ~~life~~ selffe Je.

Love smiled, and thus said; 'Want joynd to desire is unhappy.
  But if he nought do desire, what can *Heraclitus* aile?
None but I, workes by desire: by desire have I kindled in his soule
  Infernall agonies unto a bewtye divine,
Where thou poore nature left'st all thy due glory, to fortune   [15]
  Her vertue is soveraine, fortune a vassal of hers'.
Nature abasht went back: fortune blusht: yet she replide thus:
  'And ev'n in that love, shall I reserve him a spite'.
Thus, thus, alas! wofull in nature, unhappy by fortune,
  But most wretched I am, now love awakes my desire.   [20]

12

Cleophila

```
 −∪−−∪∪−∪−−
 −∪−−∪∪−∪−−
 −∪−−∪∪−∪−−
       −∪∪−−
```

IF mine eyes can speake to doo harty errande,
Or mine eyes' language she doo hap to judge of,
So that eyes' message be of her receaved,
     Hope we do live yet.

But if eyes faile then, when I most doo need them,   [5]
Or if eyes' language be not unto her knowne,
So that eyes' message doo returne rejected,
     Hope we doo both dye.

Yet dying, and dead, doo we sing her honour;
So become our tombes monuments of her praise;   [10]
So becomes our losse the triumph of her gayne;
     Hers be the glory.

If the sencelesse spheares doo yet hold a musique,
If the Swanne's sweet voice be not heard, but at death,
If the mute timber when it hath the life lost,   [15]
     Yeldeth a lute's tune,

13 workes] worke Bo As Ph.   15 left'st] lefte St Bo Cl Le As Ph Je Qu, leftes Da.
17–19 *om.* Ph.
  12. 90–93, OA. *Scansion only in* St Cl As Qu; St *gives a second scansion with the final
syllable of the first and third line short.*   11 gayne] game Bo Cl Je, mynd Ph.
13 sencelesse spheares] spheares senselesse 90–93.   14 at] a As Ph.   15 the
mute] muett St, mute Bo Cl Le As Je Qu.   16 tune. 90.

Are then humane mindes priviledg'd so meanly,
As that hatefull death can abridge them of powre,
With the voyce of truth to recorde to all worldes,
    That we be her spoiles?   [20]

Thus not ending, endes the due praise of her praise;
Fleshly vaile consumes; but a soule hath his life,
Which is helde in love, love it is, that hath joynde
    Life to this our soule.

But if eyes can speake to doo harty errande,   [25]
Or mine eyes' language she doo hap to judge of,
So that eyes' message be of her receaved,
    Hope we doo live yet.

13

Dorus   Cleofila

−◡◡−◡◡−◡◡−−◡◡−−

Dorus. Lady, reservd by the heav'ns to do pastors' company honnor,
   Joyning your sweete voice to the rurall muse of a deserte,
   Here you fully do finde this strange operation of love,
   How to the woods love runnes as well as rydes to the Pallace,
   Neither he beares reverence to a Prince nor pittie to begger, [5]
   But (like a point in midst of a circle) is still of a neernesse,
   All to a lesson he draws, norr hills nor caves can avoide him.

Cleofila. Worthy shepeheard, by my song to my selfe all favor is
     happned,
   That to the sacred Muse my anoyes somewhat be revealed,
   Sacred Muse, who in one contaynes what nine do in all them. [10]
   But ô happy be you, which safe from fyry reflection
   Of *Phœbus'* violence in shade of stately Ciprus tree,
   Or pleasant mirtell, may teach th'unfortunate *Echo*
   In these woods to resounde the renowmed name of a goddesse.

19 voyce] vowe 90–93 St.   23 hath joynde] ioynde Je, toyned Qu, buckles Ph.
   13. 93, OA, Ra (*lines* 113–39, 141–4, 146–54 *only*). *Scansion only in* St Qu; Qu *lists only a single long syllable for both the third and fourth foot.* 93 *reads* Zelmane *for* Cleofila *throughout.*   1 Lady 93.   4 rydes] ryde St Bo Cl Le As Ph Qu.   5 to begger] to a Begger Cl Je Qu.   7 draw's, 93.   norr] nether 93.   8 shepeheard 93.   9–10 *om.* As *and space left.*   9 anoyes] greiues Bo Ph, ⟨ ⟩ Le.
12 stately Ciprus tree] sweet *Cyparissus* 93, Cyprus tree Je Qu.   13 mirtell] mirthe St Je Qu.   th'] the St Cl Le As Ph Je Qu, *om.* Da.   14 woods] wordes Da Qu.

Happy be you that may to the saint, your onely *Idea*,   [15]
(Although simply atyrde) your manly affection utter.
Happy be those mishapps which, justly proportion holding,
Give right sound to the eares, and enter aright to the judgement;
But wretched be the soules which, vaild in a contrary subject,
How much more we do love, so the lesse our loves be beleeved.
What skill servethe a soare of a wrong infirmity judged?   [21]
What can justice availe, to a man that tells not his owne case?
You, though feares do abash, in you still possible hopes be:
Nature against we do seeme to rebell, seeme fooles in a vaine sute.
But so unheard, condemn'd, kept thence we do seeke to abide in,
Selfe-lost and wandring, banished that place we doe come from,
What meane is there, alas, we can hope our losse to recover?
What place is there left, we may hope our woes to recomfort?
Unto the heav'ns? our wings be too short; th' earth thinks us a
     burden;   [29]
Aire, we do still with sighes encrease; to the fire? we do want none.
And yet his outward heate our teares would quench, but an inward
Fire no liquor can coole: *Neptune's* seate would be dryd up there.
Happy shepheard, with thanks to the Gods, still thinke to be
     thankfull,
That to thy advauncement their wisdomes have thee abased.

Dorus.   Unto the Gods with a thanckfull heart all thankes I do
     render,   [35]
That to my advauncement their wisdomes have me abased.
But yet, alas! O but yet alas! our happs be but hard happs,
Which must frame contempt to the fittest purchase of honnour.
Well may a Pastor plaine, but alas his plaints be not esteem'de.
Silly shepheard's poore pype, when his harsh sound testifis our
     woes,   [40]
Into the faire looker on, pastime, not passion, enters.

16 simply] simple St Qu.   affection] affections Cl Da.   17 which . . . holding
93.   18 iudgement, 93.   19 soules, which . . . subiect: 93.   21 servethe]
salueth 93.   23 You 93.   in you] in youre Bo Cl Ph.   24 a] *om.* Je Qu.
26 and] in 93.   29 short: 93.   th'] *om.* 93, the St Bo Cl Le Ph Je Qu, y^t Da.
burden. 93.   30 Aire . . . encrease, 93.   32 can coole] can coole *changed
by another hand to* cooles St, all wayes Cl As, allaies Le.   *Neptune's* seate] *Neptunes*
realme 93, the great seas Ph.   would be dryd up there] would not auaile vs 93, quyte
would be dryd vp there St.   39 esteem'de] 93.   40 testifis] testifi's 93, testifie
St Bo Je.   our woes] anguish 93, *our* woe Bo, woes Qu.   41 passion] passyons
Le Da.

And to the woods or brookes, who do make such dreery recitall
What be the pangs they beare, and whence those pangs be derived,
Pleasd to receave that name by rebounding answere of *Echo*,
And hope therby to ease their inward horrible anguish,   [45]
Then shall those thinges ease their inward horrible angwish
When trees daunce to the pype, and swift streames stay by the
　　musicke,
Or when an *Echo* begins unmov'd to sing them a love song.
Say then what vantage do we get, by the trade of a Pastor?
(Since no estates be so base, but love vouchsafeth his arrow, [50]
Since no refuge doth serve from woundes we do carry about us,
Since outward pleasures be but halting helpes to decayd soules)
Save that dayly we may discerne what fire we do burne in.
Farre more happy be you, whose greatnes gets a free accesse,
Whose faire bodily gifts are fram'd most lovely to each ey.   [55]
Vertue you have, of vertue you have left proufes to the whole
　　world,
And vertue is gratefull with bewty and richnes adorned,
Neither doubt you a whit, time will your passion utter.
Hardly remains fyer hid, where skill is bent to the hiding,
But in a minde that would his flames should not be repressed,
Nature worketh enough with a small help for the revealing. [61]
Give therefore to the Muse great praise in whose very likenes
You doo approch to the fruite your onely desirs be to gather.

Cleofila. First shall fertill grounds not yeeld increase of a good seed:
First the rivers shall ceasse to repay their fludds to the *Occean*:
First may a trusty Greyhounde transforme himselfe to a Tigre:
First shall vertue be vice, and bewty be counted a blemishe,
Ere that I leave with song of praise her praise to solemnize,
Her praise, whence to the world all praise had his only beginning:
But yet well I doo finde each man most wise in his owne case.   [70]
None can speake of a wound with skill, if he have not a wound felt.
Great to thee my estate seemes, thy estate is blest by my judgement:
And yet neither of us great or blest deemeth his owne selfe.

45 And] May 93.　　　46 *om.* 93 Qu.　　　47 stay] stayd St Bo Da Ph, staies Qu.
48 begins unmov'd] vnmooved begins Cl Qu.　　　53 Save] Synce Cl Le.　　　55 are]
om. Bo Je Qu.　　　56 proufes] proofe 93 Cl.　　　world. 93.　　　57 richnes] riches
Bo Le Da Je Qu.　　　58 awhit 93.　　　60 repressed] expressed Cl Le.　　　63 fruite]
fruytes St Bo Je Qu.　　　desir's 93.　　　69 had] hath 93.　　　only] *om.* Cl As Da.　　　72 my
estate] my state 93, in state Da Ph.　　　thy estate] thy state 93 Da, this state Ph.

For yet (weigh this alas!) great is not great to a greater.
What judge you doth a hillocke shew, by the lofty *Olympus*? [75]
Such this smale greatnes, doth seeme compar'd to the greatest.
When Cedars to the ground be opprest by the weight of an
    emmott,
Or when a rich rubie's just price be the worth of a walnut,
Or to the *Sun* for wonders seeme small sparks of a candle:
Then by my high Cedar, rich *Ruby*, and only shining *Sunne*, [80]
Vertue, richesse, beawties of mine shall great be reputed.
Oh no, no, hardye shepeheard, worth can never enter a title,
Where proofes justly do teach, thus matcht, such worth to be
    nought worth.
Let not a puppet abuse thy sprite, Kings' Crownes do not helpe
    them
From the cruell headache, nor shooes of golde doo the gowt heale,
And preciouse couches full oft are shak't with a feaver. [86]
If then a boddily evill in a boddily gloze be not hidden,
Shall such morning deaws be an ease to the heate of a love's fire?

Dorus. O glittring miseries of man, if this be the fortune
Of those fortune lulls, so small rest rests in a kingdome. [90]
What marvaile tho a Prince transforme himselfe to a Pastor?
Come from marble bowers, many times the gay harbor of anguish,
Unto a silly caban, though weake, yet stronger against woes.
Now by thy words I begin, most famous Lady, to gather
Comfort into my soule. I do finde, I do find what a blessing [95]
Is chaunced to my life, that from such muddy abundance
Of carking agonies (to estates which still be adherent)
Desteny keepes me aloofe. For if all thy estate to thy vertue
Joyn'd, by thy beauty adorn'd, be no meanes these greefes to
    abolish:
If neither by that helpe, thou canst clime up to thy fancie, [100]

74 a] the 93 Cl Da.   76 this smale] my minute 93 Da Je Qu, ~~this smalle~~ my
minute Cl, my smalle Ph.   77 be opprest] fall downe 93, bee prest Ph.
78 just] dew Ph, *om.* Le As.   79 wonders] wonder Je Qu.   80 rich *Ruby*]
right rubie St Bo As Ph Je Qu, ruby right Da.   82 hardye] worthy 93, hardly Ph.
83 worth, 93.   84 puppet] poppet St Bo Ph Je Qu, puppe Da.   85 shooes]
showes St Le Ph.   89 the] thie Da Ph Je.   90 lulls?... kingdome? 93.
92 bowers,] bowres 93 Bo, bowers St Ph Je Qu, bower, As.   95 soule 93.
97 estates] states 93, highe states Ph.   98 aloofe, for 93.   thy estate] this
state 93 Da, this estate Cl, thie state Ph, thie estates Qu.   99 adorn'd 93.   these]
thus St, thy Bo Ph, this Cl.   greefes] greef Cl Ph.

Nor yet, fancy so drest, do receive more plausible hearing:
Then do I thinke in deed, that better it is to be private
In sorrows torments, then, tyed to the pompes of a pallace,
Nurse inwarde maladyes, which have not scope to be breath'd out,
But perforce disgest, all bitter juices of horror   [105]
In silence, from a man's owne selfe with company robbed.
Better yet do I live, that though by my thoughts I be plunged
Into my live's bondage, yet may disburden a passion
(Opprest with ruinouse conceites) by the helpe of an outcrye:
Not limited to a whispringe note, the Lament of a Courtier, [110]
But sometimes to the woods, somtimes to the heavens do de-
    cyphire,
With bolde clamor unheard, unmarckt, what I seeke what I suffer:
And when I meete these trees, in the earth's faire lyvery clothed,
Ease I do feele (such ease as falls to one wholy diseased)
For that I finde in them parte of my estate represented.   [115]

Lawrell shews what I seeke, by the Mirre is show'd how I   A victori
    seeke it,   B Lamentacion
Olive paintes me the peace that I must aspire to by conquest: C Quietnes
Mirtle makes my request, my request is crown'd with a   D Love
    willowe.   E Refusall
Cyprus promiseth helpe, but a helpe where comes no re-   F Death
    comforte.
Sweete *Juniper* saith this, thoh I burne, yet I burne in a sweete
    fire.   [120]
Ewe doth make me be thinke what kind of bow the boy holdeth
Which shootes strongly with out any noyse and deadly without
    smarte.
Firr trees great and greene, fixt on a hye hill but a barrein,
Lyke to my noble thoughtes, still new, well plac'd, to me fruteles.
Figge that yeeldes most pleasante frute, his shaddow is hurtefull,

101 yet . . . drest 93.   more] a Cl Da Qu.   104 out. 93.   105 juices] ioyces
93 Cl, ioyes Qu.   110 Courtier. 93.   111 woods . . . decyphire 93.
heavens] heau'n 93 Da.   do] to As Da.   113 lyvery] liuory 93 Bo As.
115 estate] state 93 Da Ph Ra.   116–19 *Marginal notes only in* St Je Qu Ra.
116 shew's 93.   117 by] by the 93, the Cl, my Le.   118 willowe? 93.
119 recomforte.] recomforte 93 Da Ph, recomfort: Bo, recomfort, Cl As, compforte
St Je Qu Ra.   120 Iuniper, 93.   121 be thinke] thinke 93 Bo Ph Qu Ra.
125 fru'te, . . . hurtefull 93.

Thus be her giftes most sweet, thus more danger to be neere her,
But in a palme when I marke, how he doth rise under a burden,
And may I not (say I then) gett up though griefs be so weightie?
Pine is a maste to a shippe, to my shippe shall hope for a maste
    serve?
Pine is hye, hope is as hie, sharpe leav'd, sharpe yet be my hope's
    budds.   [130]
Elme embraste by a vine, embracing fancy reviveth.
Popler changeth his hew from a rising sunne to a setting:
Thus to my sonne do I yeeld, such lookes her beames do aforde
    me.
Olde aged oke cutt downe, of newe works serves to the building:
So my desires by my feare, cutt downe, be the frames of her
    honour.   [135]
Ashe makes speares which shieldes do resist, her force no repulse
    takes:
Palmes do rejoyce to be joynd by the match of a male to a female,
And shall sensive things be so sencelesse as to resist sence?
Thus be my thoughts disperst, thus thinking nurseth a thinking,
Thus both trees and each thing ells, be the bookes of a fancy. [140]
But to the Cedar, Queene of woods, when I lifte my beteard eyes,
Then do I shape to my selfe that forme which raigns so with in
    me,
And thinke ther she do dwell and heare what plaintes I do utter:
When that noble toppe doth nodd, I beleeve she salutes me;
When by the winde it maketh a noyse, I do thinke she doth
    answer.   [145]
Then kneling to the ground, oft thus do I speake to that Image:
'Onely Juell, O only Juell, which only deservest
That men's harts be thy seate and endlesse fame be thy servant,
O descende for a while, from this greate height to behold me,
But nought els do behold (else is nought worth the beholding) [150]
Save what a worke, by thy selfe is wrought: and since I am altred
Thus by thy worke, disdaine not that which is by thy selfe done.
In meane caves oft treasure abides, to an hostry a king comes.
And so behinde foule clowdes full oft faire starres do ly hidden'.

127 But] Now 93.   128 I not] not I Cl Ra.   129 serue, 93.   131 reuiueth
93.   133 me 93.   134 aged] Age Bo Da.   works] worcke Cl Da, okes Ph.
136 makes] make Le Da.   141 Cedar . . . woods 93.   142 raign's 93.
143 plaintes] plants 93.   146 do I] I do Ph Ra.   150 do, 93.

Cleofila. Hardy shephearde, such as thy meritts, such may be her
  insight [155]
  Justely to graunt thy rewarde, such envie I beare to thy fortune.
  But to my selfe what wish can I make for a salve to my sorrowes,
  Whom both nature seemes to debarr from meanes to be helped,
  And if a meane were found, fortune th' whole course of it hinders.
  Thus plag'de how can I frame to my soare any hope of amende-
  mente? [160]
  Whence may I show to my minde any light of a possible escape?
  Bownd and bownd by so noble bandes, as loth to be unbownd,
  Jaylor I am to my selfe, prison and prisoner to myne owne selfe.
  Yet be my hopes thus plast, here fixed lives my recomforte, [164]
  That that deare *Dyamond*, where wisdome holdeth a sure seate,
  Whose force had such force so to transforme, nay to reforme me,
  Will at length perceave these flames by her beames to be kindled,
  And will pitty the wound festred so strangely within me.
  O be it so, graunte such an event, O Gods, that event give.
  And for a sure sacrifice I do dayly oblation offer [170]
  Of my owne harte, where thoughts be the temple, sighte is an
  aultar.
  But ceasse worthy shepheard, nowe ceasse we to weery the hearers
  With monefull melodies, for enough our greefes be revealed,
  If by the parties ment our meanings rightly be marked,
  And sorrows do require some respitt unto the sences. [175]

156 thy] thee 93.   160 Thus] This 93.   161 a] *om.* 93 Da.   163 myne]
my Bo Cl Le Da Je.   164 fixed] fix'd 93.   lives] liues all 93 Cl Da.   171 my]
mine 93 Da Ph Je Qu.   an] a 93, yᵉ Ph.   175 sorrow's 93.

THE SECOND BOOK OR ACT

14

[*Cleophila*]

IN vaine, mine Eyes, you labour to amende
  With flowing teares your fault of hasty sight:
Since to my hart her shape you so did sende;
  That her I see, though you did lose your light.

In vaine, my Hart, now you with sight are burnd,   [5]
  With sighes you seeke to coole your hotte desire:
Since sighes (into mine inward fornace turnd)
  For bellowes serve to kindle more the fire.

Reason, in vaine (now you have lost my hart)
  My head you seeke, as to your strongest forte: [10]
Since there mine eyes have played so false a parte,
  That to your strength your foes have sure resorte.
    And since in vaine I find were all my strife,
    To this strange death I vainely yeeld my life.

15

[*Basilius*]

LET not old age disgrace my high desire,
  O heavenly soule, in humaine shape conteind:
Old wood inflam'de, doth yeeld the bravest fire,
  When yonger dooth in smoke his vertue spend.

Ne let white haires, which on my face doo grow,   [5]
  Seeme to your eyes of a disgracefull hewe:
Since whitenesse doth present the sweetest show,
  Which makes all eyes doo honour unto you.

14. 90-93, Cm, OA.   2 fault] fainte Cl, fate Je Qu.   7 mine] my Bo Da
Je.   13 And] Then 90-93 Cm, All Qu.
  15. 90, 93, Cm, OA, Ha.   5 doo] dothe Cl Le Da Qu.   8 honour] homage
93 Cm.

Old age is wise and full of constant truth;
   Old age well stayed from raunging humor lives: [10]
Old age hath knowne what ever was in youth:
   Old age orecome, the greater honour gives.
      And to old age since you your selfe aspire,
      Let not old age disgrace my high desire.

16

[*Dorus*]

SINCE so mine eyes are subject to your sight,
That in your sight they fixed have my braine;
Since so my harte is filled with that light,
That onely light doth all my life maintaine;

Since in sweete you all goods so richly raigne,   [5]
That where you are no wished good can want;
Since so your living image lives in me,
That in my selfe your selfe true love doth plant;
    How can you him unworthy then decree,
    In whose chiefe parte your worthes implanted be?   [10]

17

[*Dorus*]

MY sheepe are thoughts, which I both guide and serve:
Their pasture is faire hilles of fruitlesse Love:
On barren sweetes they feede, and feeding sterve:
I waile their lotte, but will not other prove.
My sheepehooke is wanne hope, which all upholdes: [5]
My weedes, Desire, cut out in endlesse foldes.
    What wooll my sheepe shall beare, whyle thus they live,
    In you it is, you must the judgement give.

9–12 *om*. Ha.   10 humor] Honor Cl Le, humors Ph.

  16. 90–93, Cm, OA.   10 parte] plant Bo, partes As Ph Qu.   worthes]
worthies Le Da Je.

  17. 90–93, Cm, OA, Ma, Fl.   3 On] O Da, in St Cl Le As Ph Je Qu Ma Fl.
7 whyle] whiles 90–93 Cm.   they] I Ma Fl.

18

[*Philoclea*]

YEE living powres enclosed in stately shrine
Of growing trees, yee rurall Gods that wield
Your scepters here, if to your eares divine
A voice may come, which troubled soule doth yeld:
    This vowe receave, this vowe ô Gods maintaine;   [5]
    My virgin life no spotted thought shall staine.

Thou purest stone, whose purenesse doth present
My purest minde; whose temper hard doth showe
My tempred hart; by thee my promise sent
Unto my selfe let after-livers know.   [10]
    No fancy mine, nor others' wronge suspect
    Make me, ô vertuous Shame, thy lawes neglect.

O Chastitie, the chiefe of heavenly lightes,
Which makes us most immortall shape to weare,
Holde thou my hart, establish thou my sprights: [15]
To onely thee my constant course I beare.
    Till spotlesse soule unto thy bosome flye,
    Such life to leade, such death I vow to dye.

19

[*Philoclea*]

MY words, in hope to blaze my stedfast minde,
This marble chose, as of like temper knowne:
But loe, my words defaste, my fancies blinde,
Blots to the stone, shame to my selfe I finde:
    And witnesse am, how ill agree in one,   [5]
    A woman's hand with constant marble stone.

18. 90–93, Cm (*blank*), OA.   1 Yee] You 90–93.   2 trees; 90.   yee]
you 90–93 Da Je, the Ph Qu.   3 eares] cares Je Qu.   5 vowe receave] voyce
receyve As Ph.   12 vertuous] vertue Je Qu.   14 makes] makst 90–93 Le.
    19. 90–93, Cm (*blank*), OA.   4 shame] shames 93 St As Le Je, shame is Qu.

My words full weake, the marble full of might;
My words in store, the marble all alone;
My words blacke inke, the marble kindly white;
My words unseene, the marble still in sight,   [10]
    May witnesse beare, how ill agree in one,
    A woman's hand, with constant marble stone.

20

[*Cleophila*]

Loved I am, and yet complaine of Love:
As loving not, accus'd, in Love I die.
When pittie most I crave, I cruell prove:
Still seeking Love, love found as much I flie.
    Burnt in my selfe, I muse at others' fire: [5]
What I call wrong, I doo the same, and more:
Bard of my will, I have beyond desire:
I waile for want, and yet am chokte with store.
    This is thy worke, thou God for ever blinde:
Though thousands old, a Boy entit'led still.   [10]
Thus children doo the silly birds they finde,
With stroking hurt, and too much cramming kill.
    Yet thus much Love, O Love, I crave of thee:
    Let me be lov'd, or els not loved be.

21

[*Cleophila*]

Over these brookes trusting to ease mine eyes,
(Mine eyes even great in labour with their teares)
I layde my face; my face wherein there lyes
Clusters of clowdes, which no Sunne ever cleares.
    In watry glasse my watrie eyes I see: [5]
    Sorrowes ill easde, where sorrowes painted be.

20. 90-93, Cm, OA.
21. 90-93, Cm, OA, Ra.   5 my watrie] my watred Cm Bo Le As Da Ph Je Qu
Ra.

My thoughts imprisonde in my secreat woes,
With flamie breathe doo issue oft in sound:
The sound to this strange aier no sooner goes,
But that it dooth with *Echoe's* force rebound   [10]
   And make me heare the plaints I would refraine:
   Thus outward helps my inward griefes maintaine.

Now in this sande I would discharge my minde,
And cast from me part of my burdnous cares:
But in the sandes my paynes foretolde I finde,   [15]
And see therein how well the writer fares.
   Since streame, aier, sand, mine eyes and eares conspire:
   What hope to quench, where each thing blowes the fire?

22

[*Gynecia*]

WYTH two strange fires of equall heate possest,
The one of Love, the other Jealousie,
Both still do worke, in neither finde I rest:
For both, alas, their strengthes together tie:
The one aloft doth holde the other hie.   [5]
   Love wakes the jealous eye least thence it moves:
   The jealous eye, the more it lookes, it loves.

These fires increase: in these I dayly burne:
They feede on me, and with my wings do flie:
My Lyvelye joyes to dolefull ashes turne: [10]
Their flames mount up, my powers prostrate lie:
They live in force, I quite consumed die.
   One wonder yet farre passeth my conceate:
   The fuell small: how be the fires so great?

8 breathe] breathes 90-93 Cm.   doo] dothe Cl Le.   10 rebound. 90.   rebound]
resound Ph Je Qu Ra.   11 make] makes Cl Da Je.   12 griefes] griefe 93
St Bo Cl.   15 the] thes Je Qu Ra.   sandes] sand 90-93 Cm Le As.   paynes]
tales 90-93, cares Bo.
   22. 90-93, Cm, OA, Ra.   5 holde. 90.   6 wakes] markes Ph Ra, mak*es*
Je Qu.   10 Lyvelye] louely 90-93, lyves Da.   13 farre] fur Bo Je.
14 fires] fyer Le Ph Qu.

23

[*Dorus*]

FEEDE on my sheepe, my chardge my comforte feede,
With sonne's approche your pasture fertill growes,
O only sonne that suche a fruite can breede.

Feede on my sheepe, your fayer sweete feeding flowes,
Eache flower eache herbe dothe to your service yeeld,   [5]
O blessed sonne whence all this blessing goes.

Feede on my sheepe, possesse your fruitefull fyeld,
No woolves dare howle, no murrayne can prevaile,
And from the stormes our sweeteste sonne will shield.

Feede on my sheepe, sorrow hathe stricken sayle,   [10]
Enjoye my joyes, as you dyd taste my payne,
While our sonne shynes no clowdie greeves assaile.
   Feede on my sheepe, your Native joyes mayntayne,
   Your woll is riche: no tonge can tell my gayne.

24

[*Philisides*]

LEAVE of my sheepe: it is no tyme to feede,
My sonne is gon, your pasture barrein growes,
O cruell sonne thy hate this harme dothe breede.

Leave of my sheepe, my shower of teeres oreflowes,
Your sweetest flowers, your herbes, no service yeeld,   [5]
My sonne alas from me for ever goes.

Leave of my sheepe, my sighes burne up your filde,
My plaintes call wolves, my plagues in you prevaile,
My sun is gon, from stormes what shall us sheelde?

23. OA. *Initial capitals and line-end punctuation editorial.*   4 flowes] flowers
Bo, flowers *corrected to* flowes St.   6 blessing] blessinges Ph Qu.   goes]
growes Da Ph, go Qu.   7 sheepe St.   13 Native] nature Le Qu.
24. OA. *Initial capitals and line-end punctuation editorial.*   2 gon St.   3 hate]
heat Ph Je.   5 flowers: yor herbes St.   no] in St.   yeeld] yeelds Le Je Qu.
7 your] my Je Qu.   9 what shall] that shoulde Cl Da, what should Ph.

Leave of my sheepe, sorrowe hathe hoysed sayle,   [10]
Wayle in my woes, taste of your master's payne,
My sun is gon, Nowe clowdie greeves assayle.
    Leave off my sheep my mourninge to maintayne,
    You beare no woll, and losse is all my gayne.

25

[Dametas]

A HATEFULL cure with hate to heale:
A blooddy helpe with blood to save:
A foolish thing with fooles to deale:
Let him be bob'd that bobs will have.
    But who by meanes of wisdome hie   [5]
    Hath sav'd his charge? it is even I.

Let others deck their pride with skarres,
And of their wounds make brave lame showes:
First let them die, then passe the starres,
When rotten Fame will tell their blowes.   [10]
    But eye from blade, and eare from crie:
    Who hath sav'd all? it is even I.

26

[Basilius, Gynecia, Pamela, and Philoclea]

APOLLO great, whose beames the greater world do light,
And in our little world dost cleare our inward sight,
Which ever shines, though hid from earth by earthly shade,
Whose lights do ever live, but in our darkenesse fade;
Thou God, whose youth was deckt with spoyle of *Python*'s skin:
(So humble knowledge can throw downe the snakish sinne)   [6]

12 gon St.   13 off my sheep] Leaving not St Bo Cl Le As Da Je Qu, not to leev
Ph.   14 losse] lost Je Qu.
    25. 90, 93, Cm, OA (*wanting in* Le).   1 cure] care Cm Qu, Cry Cl, Curr Ph.
4 bob'd] bold 90 Bo Cl Da Ph Qu, ~~boulde~~ bobde St.   6 it is] tis St Ph.
7 others] other 90 Cl.   8 brave] *om.* 93.
    26. 90, 93, Cm (*lines* 1–4 *only*), OA (*wanting in* Le).   2 dost] do 90-93 Ph,
does St Bo, dorte Qu.   3 shines] shine 90-93.   4 in our] inward Je Qu.
5 spoyle] spoiles 90-93, *om.* Je.   6 "(So 90.   sinne] kinne 90, skinne Je.

Latona's sonne, whose birth in paine and travaile long
Doth teach, to learne the good what travailes do belong:
In travaile of our life (a short but tedious space)
While brickle houreglas runnes, guide thou our panting race:[10]
Give us foresightfull mindes: give us minds to obaye
What foresight tels; our thoughts upon thy knowledge staye.
Let so our fruites grow up, that nature be maintainde:
But so our hartes keepe downe, with vice they be not stainde.
Let this assured holde our judgements ever take,   [15]
That nothing winnes the heaven, but what doth earth forsake.

7 paine] paynes St Bo Cl As Je Qu.   9 "In 90.   10 race] pace 90–93 Da.
15 judgements] iudgement Da Je.   ever take] ouertake 90–93 Je.   16 "That 90.

27

[*The Arcadian Shepherds*]

Reason. Thou Rebell vile, come, to thy master yelde.
Passion. No, Tyrant; no: mine, mine shall be the fielde.
R. Can *Reason* then a Tyraunt counted be?
P. If *Reason* will, that *Passions* be not free.
R. But *Reason* will, that *Reason* governe most.   [5]
P. And *Passion* will, that *Passion* rule the rost.
R. Your will is will; but *Reason* reason is.
P. Will hath his will, when *Reason's* will doth misse.
R. Whom *Passion* leades unto his death is bent.
P. And let him die, so that he die content.   [10]
R. By nature you to *Reason* faith have sworne.
P. Not so, but fellowlike together borne.
R. Who *Passion* doth ensue, lives in annoy.
P. Who *Passion* doth forsake, lives void of joy.
R. *Passion* is blinde, and treades an unknowne trace.   [15]
P. *Reason* hath eyes to see his owne ill case.
R. Dare *Passions* then abide in *Reason's* light?
P. And is not *Reason* dimde with *Passion's* might?
R. O foolish thing, which glory doeste destroye.
P. O glorious title of a foolish toye.   [20]
R. Weakenes you are, dare you with our strength fight?
P. Because our weaknes weakeneth all your might.
R. O sacred *Reason*, helpe our vertuous toiles.
P. O *Passion*, passe on feeble *Reason's* spoiles.
R. We with ourselves abide a daily strife.   [25]
P. We gladly use the sweetnes of our life.
R. But yet our strife sure peace in end doth breede.
P. We now have peace, your peace we doo not neede.

27. 90–93, OA. *Speech prefixes of 90–93 spell out* Reason *and* Passion *in lines* 3 *and* 4 *only.*   11 have] hathe Cl Ph Qu.   12 *P*, 90.   15 trace 90.   16 hath] hath his Je Qu.   18 dimde] dimme 93 Je.   19 doeste] doth 90–93 Je. 24 spoiles] spoylle Da Je.   25 a] at Je Qu.

R. We are too strong: but *Reason* seekes not blood.
P. Who be too weake, do feigne they be too good. [30]
R. Though we cannot orecome, our cause is just.
P. Let us orecome, and let us be unjust.
R. Yet *Passion*, yeeld at length to *Reason's* stroke.
P. What shall we winne by taking *Reason's* yoke?
R. The joyes you have shall be made permanent. [35]
P. But so we shall with griefe learne to repent.
R. Repent indeed, but that shall be your blisse.
P. How know we that, since present joyes we misse?
R. You know it not: of *Reason* therefore know it.
P. No *Reason* yet had ever skill to show it. [40]
R. P. Then let us both to heavenly rules give place,
　　Which *Passions* kill, and *Reason* do deface.

28

Dicus   Dorus

Dicus.　　*Dorus*, tell me, where is thy wonted motion
　　To make these woods resounde thy lamentation?
　　Thy sainte is dead, or dead is thy devotion.
　　　For who doth holde his love in estimation,
　　To witnes, that he thinkes his thoughts delicious, [5]
　　Seekes to make ech thing badge of his sweet passion.

Dorus.　　But what doth make thee *Dicus* so suspicious
　　Of my due faith, which needs must be immutable?
　　Who others' vertue doubt, themselves are vicious.
　　　Not so; although my mettall were most mutable, [10]
　　Her beames have wrought therin most suer impression:
　　To such a force soone chaunge were nothing sutable.

Dicus.　　The harte well set doth never shunne confession:
　　If noble be thy bandes, make them notorious:
　　Silence doth seeme the maske of base oppression. [15]
　　　Who glories in his love, doth make Love glorious:

29 not] no 90-93.　　36 But] And Cl Le As.　　42 kill] skill 90 St Cl Le Je, bill
Qu.　*Reason*] Passyons Cl, Reasons Le As Da.　do] to Ph Qu, doth Je.
　28. 90-93, OA (*wanting in* Le).　　6 Seekes] Thinks 90-93.　　9 vertue]
vertues As Da Ph Qu.　doubt] dowtes OA.　11 suer] faire 90-93.　12 soone]
some 90-93, sone *changed to* som Je.　15 maske] marke Ph Qu.　oppression]
impression Ph Qu.

But who doth feare, or bideth muet wilfully,
Showes, guilty harte doth deeme his state opprobrious.
   Thou then, that framste both words and voice most skilfully,
Yeeld to our eares a sweet and sound relation,   [20]
If Love tooke thee by force, or caught thee guilefully.

Dorus.   If Sunnie beames shame heav'nly habitation;
If three-leav'd grasse seeme to the sheepe unsavorie,
Then base and sower is Love's most high vocation.
   Or if sheepe's cries can helpe the Sunne's owne braverie, [25]
Then may I hope, my pipe may have abilitie,
To helpe her praise, who decks me in her slaverie.
   No, no: no wordes ennoble selfe-nobilitie.
As for your doubts; her voice was it deceaved me,
Her eyes the force beyond my possibilitie.   [30]

Dicus.   Thy words well voic'd, well gra'ste had almost heaved me
Quite from my selfe to love Love's contemplation;
Till of these thoughts thy sodaine ende bereaved me.
   Goe on therefore, and tell us, by what fashion
In thy owne proofe he gets so straunge possession,   [35]
And how possest he strengthens his invasion?

Dorus.   Sight is his roote, in thought is his progression,
His childhood woonder, prenticeship attention,
His youth delight, his age the soule's oppression:
   Doubte is his sleepe, he waketh in invention;   [40]
Fancie his foode, his clothing is of carefulnes;
Beautie his Booke, his play lovers' dissention:
   His eyes are curious search, but vailde with warefulnesse:
His wings desire oft clipt with desperation:
Largesse his hands could never skill of sparefulnesse.   [45]

Da Ph Je Qu:

       [39] his meanes great shewes, of worth and intercession
       [41] fancy his foode, his cradle Rockt with carefullnes
       [42] to men most lyke, in him breades most discention
       [45] freend to swolne hartes, and enemy of sparefulnes

    41 Rockt] wrackt Da.   42 lyke] lyked Da.

---

30 eyes] eye 90–93 St.   my] all 90–93.   41 is] as St, out Bo, all Cl As.
42 Booke] boote 90 St.

But how he doth by might, or by persuasion
To conquere, and his conquest how to ratifie,
Experience doubts, and schooles holde disputation.

Dicus.　　But so thy sheepe may thy good wishes satisfie
With large encrease, and wooll of fine perfection,　　　　[50]
So she thy love, her eyes thy eyes may gratifie,
　　As thou wilt give our soules a deare refection,
By telling how she was, how now she framed is
To helpe, or hurt in thee her owne infection.

Dorus.　　Blest be the name, wherewith my mistres named is: [55]
Whose wounds are salves, whose yokes please more then pleasure
　　doth:
Her staines are beames; vertue the fault she blamed is.
　　The hart, eye, eare here onely find his treasure doth:
All numbring artes her endlesse graces number not:
Time, place, life, wit scarcely her rare gifts measure doth.　　[60]
　　Is she in rage? so is the Sunne in sommer hot,
Yet harvest brings. Doth she alas absent herselfe?
The Sunne is hid; his kindly shadowe combers not.
　　But when to give some grace she doth content herselfe,
O then it shines; then are the heav'ns distributed,　　　　[65]
And *Venus* seemes, to make up her, she spent herselfe.
　　Thus then (I say) my mischiefes have contributed
A greater good by her divine reflection;
My harmes to me, my blisse to her attributed.
　　Thus she is framde: her eyes are my direction;　　　　[70]
Her love my life; her anger my Instruction;
Lastly what so she be, that's my protection.

Dicus.　　Thy safetie sure is wrapped in destruction:
For that construction thy owne wordes do beare.
A man to feare a woman's moodie eye,　　　　　　　　[75]
Or Reason lie a slave to servile Sense,
Theere seeke defence where weakenesse is the force:
Is Late remorse in follie dearely bought.

47 conquest] conqnest 90.　　　　48 disputation, 90.　　　　54 or] oure Cl Qu.
63 shadowe combers] shadows cumber 90-93.　　　　　　69 attributed, 90.
71 Instruction] destruction 90-93 St (*followed by a period in* 90, *by a comma in* 93).
72 be] is 90-93.　　　that's] that is St Bo Da Ph, ys Cl Je.　　74 thy] thine 90-93.
75 moodie] muddy Cl Da Ph.　　76 Or] Makes 90-93.　　Sense. 90.　　77 Theere
seeke] A weake 90-93.　　the] thy 90-93 Ph.　　78 Is Late] So is 90-93.

Dorus.   If I had thought to heare blasphemous wordes,
  My brest to swords, my soule to hell have solde   [80]
  I sooner would, then thus my eares defile
  With words so vile, which viler breath doth breed.
  O heards take heed; for I a woolfe have found;
  Who hunting round the strongest for to kill,
  His breast doth fill with earth of others' woe,   [85]
  And loden so puls downe, puld downe destroyes.
  O sheepheards' boyes, eschue these tongues of venome,
  Which do envenome both the soule and senses.
  Our best defenses are to flie these adders.
  O tongues right ladders made to clime dishonour,   [90]
  Who judge that honour, which hath scope to slander.

Dicus.   *Dorus* you wander farre in great reproches;
  So love encroches on your charmed reason,
  But it is season for to end our singing,
  Such anger bringing: as for me, my fancie   [95]
     In sicke-man's franzie rather takes compassion,
  Then rage for rage: rather my wish I send to thee,
  Thou soone may have some helpe, or change of passion.

81–90 Da Ph Je Qu:

    I soner would, then have my eares defylde
    with wordes so vyld, from vilder mouth proceeding
    but rotten bleeding argues evill complection
    a foul infection kills or bredeth botches
    men tongd like lotches sucking others sorrowe
      talking time borrowe for to spitt their vennim
    which doeth invennim both the soule and senses
    our best defences are to flie these adders
    whose cries are ladders made to climb dishonor

81 my] mine Je Qu.   85 lotches] leches Da, loches Je, lolhes Qu.   sorrowe] sorrowes Ph Je.   90 dishonor] dishonors Da.

---

81 sooner] rather 90–93.   my] mine 90–93 St As.   85 breast] Chest Cl As. woe] ioyes 90 St, *om.* Bo.   87 sheepheards'] sheepheard St As.   89 flie] flee St Cl.   90 right] like 90–93, even Cl As.   93 on] in Cl Da Qu.   94 our] yor Da Je Qu.   singing. 90.   95 me] *om.* Cl As.   96 franzie] frenzie 90–93, fransey As, fancy Ph.

She oft her lookes, the starres her favour bend to thee:
Fortune store, Nature health, Love grant perswasion.   [100]
    A quiet mind none but thy selfe can lend to thee,
Thus I commend to thee all our former love.

Dorus.   Well do I prove, errour lies oft in zeale,
    Yet is it seale, though errour, of true hart.
Nought could impart such heates to friendly mind.   [105]
But for to find thy words did her disgrace,
Whose onely face the little heaven is,
    Which who doth misse his eyes are but delusions,
Barr'd from their chiefest object of delightfulnesse,
Throwne on this earth the Chaos of confusions.   [110]
    As for thy wish to my enraged spitefulnesse,
The lovely blowe with rare reward, my prayer is
Thou mayest love her that I may see thy sightfulnesse.
    The quiet mind (whereof my selfe empairer is,
As thou doest thinke) should most of all disquiet me   [115]
Without her love, then any mind who fairer is.
    Her onely cure from surfet-woes can diet me:
She holdes the ballance of my contentation:
Her cleared lookes, nought els, in stormes can quiet me.
    Nay rather then my ease discontentation   [120]
Should breed to her, let me for aye dejected be
From any joy, which might her griefe occasion.
    With so sweete plagues my happie harmes infected be:
Paine willes me die, yet will of death I mortifie:
For though life irkes, in life my loves protected be.   [125]
    Thus for ech change my changelesse hart I fortifie.

29

Nico   Pas   Dicus

Nico.   And are you there old *Pas*? in troth I ever thought,
    Among us all we should find out some thing of nought.

100-1 *om*. Ph.   102 loue, 90.   104 is it] it is 90-93 Je.   109 their] his
theyre Cl, his As Da Je Qu, hir Ph.   110 confusions] Confusyon Da Je.
112 blowe] blowne 90, blowen *changed to* blowme St.   113 sightfulnesse]
spytefullnes Cl Qu.   117 cure] Care Cl Ph.   119 lookes] eyes 90-93.
120 my] myne Je Qu.   122 any] my Ph Qu.   124 will] payne Cl Da Ph.
    29. 90, OA (*wanting in* Le). *Heading*] Nico. Dorus. 90, Nico. Pas. Ph.

Pas.   And I am here the same, so mote I thrive and thee,
   Despairde in all this flocke to find a knave, but thee.

Nico.   Ah now I see, why thou art in thy selfe so blind: [5]
   Thy gray-hood hides the thing, that thou despairst to find.

Pas.   My gray-hood is mine owne, all be it be but gray,
   Not as the scrippe thou stalest, while *Dorcas* sleeping lay.

Nico.   Mine was the scrippe: but thou, that seeming raged with love,
   Didst snatch from *Cosma's* hand her greene ywroughten glove.

Pas.   Ah foole; so Courtiers do. But who did lively skippe,   [11]
   When for a treene-dish stolne, thy father did thee whippe?

Nico.   In deed the witch thy dam her crouch from shoulder spred,
   For pilfring *Lalus'* lambe, with crouch to blesse thy head.

Pas.   My voice the lambe did winne, *Menalcas* was our judge: [15]
   Of singing match we made, whence he with shame did trudge.

Nico.   Couldst thou make *Lalus* flie? so nightingales avoide,
   When with the kawing crowes their musicke is annoide.

Pas.   Nay like to nightingales the other birds give eare:
   My pipe and song made him both songe and pipe forsweare. [20]

Nico.   I thinke it well: such voice would make one musicke hate:
   But if I had bene there, th'adst met another mate.

Pas.   Another sure as is a gander from a goose:
   But still when thou dost sing, me thinkes a colt is loose.

Nico.   Well aimed by my hat: for as thou sangst last day;   [25]
   The neighbours all did crie, 'alas what asse doth bray?'

Pas.   But here is *Dicus* old; let him then speake the woord,
   To whether with best cause the Nymphes faire flowers affoord.

3 thrive and thee] thryving bee Cl As, yet surely I Ph.   7 mine] my Bo Da.   8 as]
like 90.   stalest] stol'ste 90 Cl Qu.   *Dorcas*] ~~Dicus~~ Dorcas St, Dorus Bo Cl Da Ph Je Qu.
9 raged] raid 90 Bo Je, rayde St Da, rayed Cl Ph Qu, ray*n*d As.   10 *Cosma's*]
Hyppas Cl As Da Ph Je Qu (*and throughout in lines* 38–134).   greene ywroughten]
greeny wroughtẽ 90 Cl, grene Iwroughten As Da.   12 treene-dish] trindishe
St Bo As Da.   13 shoulder] shoulders Je Qu.   15 our] the Cl Ph.   16 we]
was 90.   whence] when Cl Da Je Qu.   17 flie] flee Cl Da Qu, fly in As.
19 to] ye Je Qu.   20 *indented in* 90.   songe and pipe] pipe and song 90 Bo Da,
songes & pype Qu.   25 hat] hart Je Qu.   28 whether] whither Cl Ph.

Nico. Content: but I will lay a wager hereunto,
    That profit may ensue to him that best can do.   [30]
    I have (and long shall have) a white great nimble cat,
    A king upon a mouse, a strong foe to a rat,
    Fine eares, long taile he hath, with Lion's curbed clawe,
    Which oft he lifteth up, and stayes his lifted pawe,
    Deepe musing to himselfe, which after-mewing showes,   [35]
    Till with lickt beard, his eye of fire espie his foes.
    If thou (alas poore if) do winne, then winne thou this,
    And if I better sing, let me thy *Cosma* kisse.

Pas. Kisse her? now mayst thou kisse. I have a fitter match;
    A prettie curre it is; his name iwis is Catch,   [40]
    No eare nor taile he hath, least they should him disgrace,
    A ruddie haire his cote, with fine long specled face:
    He never musing standes, but with himselfe will play
    Leaping at every flie, and angrie with a flea:
    He eft would kill a mouse, but he disdaines the fight,   [45]
    And makes our home good sport with dauncing bolt upright.
    This is my pawne; the price let *Dicus*' judgement show:
    Such oddes I willing lay; for him and you I know.

Dicus. Sing then my lads, but sing with better vaine then yet,
    Or else who singeth worse, my skill will hardly hit.   [50]

Nico. Who doubts but *Pas*' fine pipe againe will bring
    The auncient prayse to *Arcad* shepheards' skill?
    Pan is not dead, since *Pas* beginnes to sing.

Pas. Who evermore will love *Apollo's* quill,
    Since *Nico* doth to sing so widely gape?   [55]
    Nico his place farre better furnish will.

Nico. Was this not he, who for Siringa's scape
    Raging in woes first pastors tought to plaine?
    Do you not heare his voice, and see his shape?

---

32 a rat] the rat 90 St As.   35 musing] musicke Je Qu.   after-mewing] after
meaning Je Qu.   36 espie] espyes Cl Je Qu.   37 thou . . . thou] yo^u . . . yo^u St
As, yow . . . yow Bo Cl Da Ph Je Qu.   39 fitter] better 90.   40 iwis] I wus
Bo Cl, I wouse Ph.   42 specled] spectled 90.   45 eft] oft As Ph Je.   the]
to 90.   49 but] and St Bo Cl As Je Qu.   50 worse] worst 90 As Ph Je.
will] may Cl As.   52 *Arcad*] Arcades Bo, *Arcadia* Cl, Arcadias Ph, Arcady for Je.
57 this not he, who for Siringa's] not this he, who did for *Syrinx* 90.   58 first
pastors tought] teach pastors first 90.

Pas.   This is not he that failed her to gaine,   [60]
        Which made a Bay, made Bay a holy tree:
        But this is one that doth his musicke staine.

Nico.   O *Faunes*, O *Fairies* all, and do you see,
        And suffer such a wrong? a wrong I trowe,
        That *Nico* must with *Pas* compared be?   [65]

Pas.   O Nymphes, I tell you newes, for *Pas* you knowe:
        While I was warbling out your woonted praise,
        Nico would needes with *Pas* his bagpipe blowe.

Nico.   If never I did faile your holy-dayes,
        With daunces, carols, or with barlybreake: [70]
        Let *Pas* now know, how *Nico* maketh layes.

Pas.   If each day hath bene holy for your sake,
        Unto my pipe, O Nimphes, nowe helpe my pipe,
        For *Pas* well knowes what layes can *Nico* make.

Nico.   Alas how oft I looke on cherries ripe,   [75]
        Me thinkes I see the lippes my *Leuca* hath,
        And wanting her, my weeping eyes I wipe.

Pas.   Alas, when I in spring meete roses rathe,
        And thinke from *Cosma's* sweet red lips I live,
        I leave mine eyes unwipte my cheekes to bathe.   [80]

Nico.   As I of late, neer bushes usde my sive,
        I spied a thrush where she did make her nest,
        That will I take, and to my *Leuca* give.

Pas.   But long have I a sparrow gailie drest,
        As white as milke, and comming to the call,   [85]
        To put it with my hand in *Cosma's* brest.

Nico.   I oft doo sue, and *Leuca* saith, I shall,
        But when I did come neere with heate and hope,
        She ranne away, and threw at me a ball.

61 holy] holly Cl As Je Qu, hollowe Ph.   65 *Pas* 90 (*and so printed throughout in
lines* 66–145).   71 maketh] makes the 90.   73 nowe helpe] helpe now 90.
76 Me thinkes] my think*es* Je Qu.   80 mine] my Bo Cl.   82 a] my Cl Ph.

Pas.   *Cosma* once said, she left the wicket ope,   [90]
   For me to come, and so she did: I came,
   But in the place found nothing but a rope.

Nico.   When *Leuca* dooth appeare, the Sunne for shame
   Dooth hide himselfe: for to himselfe he sayes,
   If *Leuca* live, she darken will my fame.   [95]

Pas.   When *Cosma* doth come forth, the Sun displaies
   His utmost light: for well his witte doth know,
   Cosma's faire beames emblemish much his raies.

Nico.   *Leuca* to me did yester-morning showe
   In perfect light, which could not me deceave,   [100]
   Her naked legge, more white then whitest snowe.

Pas.   But yesternight by light I did receave
   From *Cosma's* eyes, which full in darkenes shine,
   I sawe her arme, where purest Lillies cleave.

Nico.   She once starke nak'd did bathe a little tine;   [105]
   But still (me thought) with beauties from her fell,
   She did the water wash, and make more fine.

Pas.   She once, to coole her selfe, stood in a well,
   But ever since that well is well besought,
   And for Rose-water sould of rarest smell.   [110]

Nico.   To river's banke, being a walking brought,
   She byd me spie her babie in the brooke,
   Alas (said I) this babe dooth nurce my thought.

Pas.   As in a glasse I held she once did looke,
   I said, my hands well paide her for mine eyes,   [115]
   Since in my hands selfe goodly sight she tooke.

Nico.   O if I had a ladder for the skies,
   I would climbe up, and bring a prettie starre,
   To weare upon her neck, that open lies.

93 dooth] did Da Qu.   97 utmost] out most Je Qu.   98 emblemish] embellish
St Bo Da.   100 not me] mee not Cl As.   105 tine] time Bo Da Ph Je Qu.
106 (me thought)] my thought As Da Qu.   107 water] waters 90.   111 To]
The Je Qu.   a walking] on walking 90, to wallking Ph, a washinge Qu.   112 byd]
bad 90, bed As, did Ph, ~~did~~ bidd Je.   119 upon] about Je Qu.

Pas.   O if I had *Apollo's* golden carre,   [120]
   I would come downe, and yeeld to her my place,
   That (shining now) she then might shine more farre.

Nico.   Nothing (O *Leuca*) shall thy fame deface,
   While shepheards' tunes be heard, or rimes be read,
   Or while that shepheards love a lovely face.   [125]

Pas.   Thy name (O *Cosma*) shall with praise be spread,
   As farre as any shepheards piping be:
   As farre as Love possesseth any head.

Nico.   Thy monument is layd in many a tree,
   With name engrav'd: so though thy bodie die,   [130]
   The after-folkes shall wonder still at thee.

Pas.   So oft these woods have heard me 'Cosma' crie,
   That after death, to heav'n in woods' resound,
   With *Echoe's* help, shall 'Cosma, Cosma' flie.

Nico.   Peace, peace good *Pas*, thou weeriest even the ground [135]
   With sluttish song: I pray thee learne to blea,
   For good thou mayst yet proove in sheepish sound.

Pas.   My father hath at home a prettie Jay,
   Goe winne of him (for chattering) praise or shame:
   For so yet of a conquest speake thou may.   [140]

Nico.   Tell me (and be my *Pan*) the monster's name,
   That hath foure legs, and with two onely goes,
   That hath foure eyes, and onely two can frame.

Pas.   Tell this (and *Phœbus* be) what monster growes
   With so strong lives, that bodie cannot rest   [145]
   In ease, untill that bodie life forgoes.

Dicus.   Enough, enough: so ill hath done the best,
   That since the having them to neither's due,
   Let cat and dog fight which shall have both you.

122 farre] fayre Je Qu.   132 me] my Cl Ph.   *Cosma*] *Hyppa* Cl As Da Ph,
happy Je Qu.   134 *Cosma, Cosma*] *Hyppa*, hippa Cl As Da, Hyppa Ph, happy
happy Je Qu.   144 this] me 90.   148 having] having of Cl Ph Je Qu.
neither's] nether is OA.

30

Histor

As I behynde a Busshe dyd sitt
I silent herd more wordes of witt
Then earste I knewe: But first dyd playne
The one, which tother would refrayne.

Plangus   Bowlon

Plangus. Alas how long this pilgrimage doth last?   [5]
    What greater ills have now the heavens in store,
    To couple comming harmes with sorrowes past?
Long since my voice is hoarce, and throte is sore,
    With cries to skies, and curses to the ground,
    But more I plaine, I feele my woes the more.   [10]
Ah where was first that cruell cunning found,
    To frame of Earth a vessell of the minde,
    Where it should be to selfe-destruction bound?
What needed so high sprites such mansions blind?
    Or wrapt in flesh what do they here obtaine,   [15]
    But glorious name of wretched humaine-kind?
Balles to the starres, and thralles to Fortune's raigne;
    Turnd from themselves, infected with their cage,
    Where death is feard, and life is held with paine.
Like players plast to fill a filthy stage,   [20]
    Where chaunge of thoughts one foole to other shewes,
    And all but jests, save onely sorrowe's rage.
The child feeles that; the man that feeling knowes,
    With cries first borne, the presage of his life,
    Where wit but serves, to have true tast of woes.   [25]
A Shop of shame, a Booke where blots be rife
    This bodie is: this bodie so composed,
    As in it selfe to nourish mortall strife.
So divers be the Elements disposed
    In this weake worke, that it can never be   [30]
    Made uniforme to any state reposed.

30. 90, 93, Cm (*lines 5–37 only*), OA.   1–4 *om.* 90–93 Cm Le.   4 re-
frayne St.   *Bowlon*] *Basilius* 90–93 (*and throughout*).   6 ills] euill Je Qu.
14 so] such Je Qu.   mansions] Mansion Bo Je.   18 cage] aige St Bo Ph, rage As.
20 pla'st 90.   31 state] estate Cl Je.

Griefe onely makes his wretched state to see
   (Even like a toppe which nought but whipping moves)
   This man, this talking beast, this walking tree.
Griefe is the stone which finest judgement proves: [35]
   For who grieves not hath but a blockish braine,
   Since cause of griefe no cause from life removes.

Boulon. How long wilt thou with monefull musicke staine
   The cheerefull notes these pleasant places yeeld,
   Where all good haps a perfect state maintaine?   [40]

Plangus. Curst be good haps, and curst be they that build
   Their hopes on haps, and do not make despaire
   For all these certaine blowes the surest shield.
Shall I that saw *Eronae's* shining haire
   Torne with her hands, and those same hands of snow   [45]
   With losse of purest blood themselves to teare,
Shall I that saw those brests, where beauties flow,
   Swelling with sighes, made pale with minde's disease,
   And saw those eyes (those Sonnes) such shoures to shew,
Shall I, whose eares her mournefull words did seaze,   [50]
   Her words in syrup laid of sweetest breath,
   Relent those thoughts, which then did so displease?
No, no: Despaire my dayly lesson saith,
   And saith, although I seeke my life to flie,
   Plangus must live to see *Eronae's* death.   [55]
Plangus must live some helpe for her to trie
   Though in despaire, for love so forcethe me;
   Plangus doth live, and shall *Erona* dye?
Erona dye? O heaven (if heaven there be)
   Hath all thy whirling course so small effect?   [60]
   Serve all thy starrie eyes this shame to see?
Let doltes in haste some altars faire erect
   To those high powers, which idly sit above,
   And vertue do in greatest need neglect.

35 judgement] iudgement*es* Je Qu.   37 from] of Bo Ph.   38 monefull] mourne-
full Da Qu.   40 all] as Cl Le.   43 these] those Bo As, ye Je Qu.   shield]
yeald Je Qu.   46 teare? 90.   49 shoures] showes Le Da, shrowd Ph, shewers
As Je.   50 did] do Cl Le.   57 for love so forcethe] so Loue enforceth 90,
so Loue so forceth 93.   58 shall] must 90.   59 if heaven] of heauens Je Qu.
60 thy] the Cl Le.   62 altars] alter Je Qu.

Boulon. O man, take heed, how thou the Gods do move   [65]
　　　To causefull wrath, which thou canst not resist.
　　　Blasphemous words the speaker vaine do prove.
　　Alas while we are wrapt in foggie mist
　　　Of our selfe-love (so passions do deceave)
　　　We thinke they hurt, when most they do assist.   [70]
　　To harme us wormes should that high Justice leave
　　　His nature? nay, himselfe? for so it is.
　　　What glorie from our losse can he receave?
　　But still our dazeled eyes their way do misse,
　　　While that we do at his sweete scourge repine,   [75]
　　　The kindly way to beate us on to blisse.
　　If she must dye, then hath she past the line
　　　Of lothsome dayes, whose losse how canst thou mone,
　　　That doost so well their miseries define?
　　But such we are with inward tempest blowne   [80]
　　　Of windes quite contrarie in waves of will:
　　　We mone that lost, which had we did bemone.

Plangus. And shall shee dye? shall cruell fier spill
　　　Those beames that set so many harts on fire?
　　　Hath she not force even death with love to kill?   [85]
　　Nay even cold Death enflamde with hot desire
　　　Her to enjoy, where joy it selfe is thrall,
　　　Will spoile the earth of his most rich attire.
　　Thus Death becomes a rivall to us all,
　　　And hopes with foule embracements her to get,   [90]
　　　In whose decay Vertue's faire shrine must fall.
　　O Vertue weake, shall death his triumph set
　　　Upon thy spoiles, which never should lye waste?
　　　Let Death first dye; be thou his worthy let.
　　By what eclipse shall that Sonne be defaste?   [95]
　　　What myne hath erst throwne downe so faire a tower?
　　　What sacriledge hath such a saint disgrast?
　　The world the garden is, she is the flower
　　　That sweetens all the place; she is the guest
　　　Of rarest price, both heav'n and earth her bower.   [100]

66 causefull] irefull 90, carefull St Qu, cawseles Bo.   67 do] dothe Cl Le.
76 on to] to our 90.   79 doost] doth Je Qu.   81 windes] mindes 90.
quite] cleane Cl Le.   82 lost] Losse Cl Ph.   97 disgra'st 90.

And shall (ô me) all this in ashes rest?
　　Alas, if you a *Phœnix* new will have
　　Burnt by the Sunne, she first must build her nest.
But well you know, the gentle Sunne would save
　　Such beames so like his owne, which might have might　[105]
　　In him, the thoughts of *Phaëton's* damme to grave.
Therefore, alas, you use vile *Vulcan's* spight,
　　Which nothing spares, to melt that Virgin-waxe
　　Which while it is, it is all *Asia's* light.
O *Mars*, for what doth serve thy armed axe?　　　　　[110]
　　To let that witolde beast consume in flames
　　Thy *Venus'* child, whose beautie *Venus* lackes?
O *Venus* (if her praise no envy frames,
　　In thy high minde) get her thy husband's grace.
　　Sweete speaking oft a currish hart reclaimes.　　　　[115]
O eyes of mine, where once she saw her face,
　　Her face which was more lively in my hart;
　　O braine, where thought of her hath onely place;
O hand, which toucht her hand when we did part;
　　O lippes, that kist that hand with my teares sprent;　[120]
　　O toonge, then dumbe, not daring tell my smart;
O soule, whose love in her is onely spent,
　　What ere you see, thinke, touch, kisse, speake, or love,
　　Let all for her, and unto her be bent.

Boulon.　Thy wailing words do much my spirits move,　[125]
　　They uttred are in such a feeling fashion,
　　That sorrowe's worke against my will I prove.
Me-thinkes I am partaker of thy passion,
　　And in thy case do glasse mine owne debilitie:
　　Selfe-guiltie folke must prove to feele compassion.　[130]
Yet Reason saith, Reason should have abilitie,
　　To hold these worldly things in such proportion,
　　As let them come or go with even facilitie.
But our Desire's tyrannicall extortion

<hr>

102 new] now Cl Le Da.　　have] saue Je Qu.　　　　108 Virgin-waxe] virgins waxe
St Da Ph Je Qu.　　　111 witolde] wit-old 90-93 Da, withold Bo, wittalde Je, witt
holde Qu.　　112 child] sheld Je, sheilde Qu.　　115 "Sweete 90.　　119 we]
she 90.　　120 that hand] her hand 90 Je.　　129 mine] my St Bo As.　　130 must
prove] most prone 90-93 St, must proue (*or* prone, *can't distinguish* u *and* n) Bo.
132 worldly] wordly St Ph.

Doth force us there to set our chiefe delightfulnes,   [135]
    Where but a baiting place is all our portion.
But still, although we faile of perfect rightfulnes,
    Seeke we to tame these childish superfluities:
    Let us not winke though void of purest sightfulnes.
For what can breed more peevish incongruities,   [140]
    Then man to yeeld to female lamentations?
    Let us some grammar learne of more congruities.

Plangus. If through mine eares pearce any consolacyons
    By wise discourse, sweete tunes, or Poet's fiction;
    If ought I cease these hideous exclamations,   [145]
While that my soule, she, she lives in affliction;
    Then let my life long time on earth maintained be,
    To wretched me, the last worst malediction.
Can I, that know her sacred parts, restrained be
    From any joy, know fortune's vile displacing her,   [150]
    In morall rules let raging woes contained be?
Can I forget, when they in prison placing her,
    With swelling hart in spite and due disdainfulnes
    She lay for dead, till I helpt with unlasing her?
Can I forget, from how much mourning plainfulnes   [155]
    With Diamond in window-glasse she graved,
    '*Erona* dye, and end this ougly painefulnes'?
Can I forget in how straunge phrase she craved
    That quickly they would her burne, drowne, or smother,
    As if by death she onely might be saved?   [160]
Then let me eke forget one hand from other:
    Let me forget that *Plangus* I am called:
    Let me forget I am sonne to my mother,
But if my memory thus must be thralled
    To that strange stroke which conquer'd all my senses,   [165]
    Can thoughts still thinking so rest unappalled?

138 these] the 90, those Je.   140 breed] yelde Da Je Qu.   142 more] oure Cl Le.
143 mine] my Le Da Qu.   consolacyons] consolation 90-93 St Bo Je, consultacions
Qu.   145 these] this Ph Qu.   hideous] Odyous Cl Da.   146 she lives]
lyveth Da Ph Je.   147 long time on earth] on earthe longe tyme Cl Le Ph Je.
149 know] knewe Cl Le Da.   sacred] secret Ph Je Qu.   parts . . . be, 90.
150 From] For 90 Da.   151 morall] mortall Da Ph Je.   155 mourning]
murnefull Bo, mourfull Je.   plainfulnes] painefulnes Le Ph Je.   157 this] thy 90.
159 drowne] downe Cl Qu.   164-6 *om.* Je.   164 thus must] must thus 90-93.
166 thoughts] thoughte Cl Le.

Boulon. Who still doth seeke against himselfe offences,
    What pardon can availe? or who employes him
    To hurt himselfe, what shields can be defenses?
Woe to poore man: ech outward thing annoyes him   [170]
    In divers kinds; yet as he were not filled,
    He heapes in inward griefe, that most destroyes him.
Thus is our thought with paine for thistles tilled:
    Thus be our noblest parts dryed up with sorrow:
    Thus is our mind with too much minding spilled.   [175]
One day layes up stuffe of griefe for the morrow:
    And whose good happ, doth leave him unprovided,
    Condoling cause of friendship he will borrow.
Betwixt the good and shade of good divided,
    We pittie deeme that which but weakenes is: [180]
    So are we from our high creation slided.
But *Plangus*, lest I may your sicknesse misse
    Or rubbing hurt the sore, I here doo end.
    The asse did hurt when he did thinke to kisse.

Histor. Thus dyd they saye and then awaye dyd wende;   [185]
    Hye tyme for me, for scattered were my sheepe
    While I there speache in my rude ryminge pende.
Yet for that night, my Caban dyd them kepe
    While Plangus dyd a storie strainge declare.
    But hoarse and drye, my pipes I nowe must spare.   [190]

31

Philisides   *Echo*

‒ ‒ ‒ ∪∪ ‒ ‒ ‒ ∪∪ ‒ ∪∪ ‒ ‒

FAIRE Rocks, goodly rivers, sweet woods, when
    shall I see peace?   Peace.
Peace? what barrs me my tongue? who is it that
    comes me so ny?   I.

169 shields] sheild As Ph.   172 inward] outward 93 Da.   that] which 90.
173 Thus] This Bo Le Je.   177 happ, doth] haps do 90-93.   182 *Plangus* 90.
185-90 *om.* 90-93 Le.   185 *Histor*] *om.* Cl Qu.   wende St.   187 pende St.
189 declare St.   190 pipes] pipe Je Qu.   spare St.
    31. 93, 90, OA. (*All verbal variants in* 90 *listed*). *The scansion appears twice in* St, *before the first and after the fourth line, and elsewhere only in* Cl *and* As *after the fourth line*; Je *and* Qu *leave a space after the fourth line.*   1 Peace, 93.   2 what barrs me] who debars me 90, who is yt that barres Bo, who barres me Da, what answerethe me Ph, what bar*res* Je Qu.

Oh! I do know what guest I have mett; it is Echo.   'T is Echo.

Well mett Echo, aproche: then tell me thy will too.   I will too.

  Echo, what do I gett yelding my sprite to my
    grieves?   [5]
    Grieves.

What medecin may I finde for a paine that draw's
  me to death?   Death.

O poisonous medecin! what worse to me can be
  then it?   It.

In what state was I then, when I tooke this deadly
  disease?   Ease.

And what manner a mind which had to that humor
  a vaine?   Vaine.

Hath not Reason enough vehemence the desire to   [10]
  reprove?   Prove.

Oft prove I: but what salve, when Reason seeks to
  be gone?   One.

Oh! what is it? what is it that may be a salve to my
  Love?   Love.

What do lovers seeke for, long seeking for to enjoy?   Joy.

What be the joyes for which to enjoy they went to
  the paines?   Paines.

Then to an earnest Love what doth best victorie   [15
  lend?   Ende.

End? but I can never end, love will not give me the
  leave.   Leave.

How be the minds dispos'd that can not tast thy
  physick?   Sick.

Yet say againe thy advise for th' ev'lls that I told thee.   I told thee.

Doth th'infected wretch, of his ev'll th'extremity
  know?   No.

But if he know not his harms what guides hath he   [20]
  whil'st he be blind?   Blind.

What blinde guides can he have that leanes to a
  fancy?   A fancy.

3 have mett] doo meete 90.   'T is] 't is 93, T' is 90, it is OA.   4 then] and 90.
5 sprite] spirits Le Ph Qu.   6 paine] griefe 93.   7 to me can be] can bee to
mee Ph Qu.   9 And what manner a] And what maner of Bo Qu, What maner of
a Cl Le Ph.   humor] Honor Cl Je.   10 vehemence] vehemency Cl Da Ph Je Qu.
11 One 93.   14 for which] which for 93.   went] want Cl Le.   16 the leaue? 93.
17 thy] the 90 Da.   18 thy] th' 90.   that I told thee? 93.   19 ev'll] harme
93, ill 90, evill OA.   20 whil'st he be] while hee ys Cl Le Je.   21 leanes] leades 90.

Can fancies want eies, or he fall that steppeth aloft?   Oft.

What causes first made these torments on me to
light?   Light.

Can then a cause be so light that forceth a man to
go die?   Aye.

Yet tell what light thinge I had in me to draw me   [25]
to die?   Eye.

Eysight made me to yeelde, but what first pierst to
myne eies?   Eies.

Eies' hurters, eies hurt, but what from them to me
fall's?   Fall's.

But when I first did fal, what brought most fall to
my hart?   Arte.

Arte? what can be that art which thou dost meane
by thy speche?   Speche.

What be the fruites of speaking arte? what growes   [30]
by the words?   Words.

O much more then words: those words serv'd more
to me blesse.   Lesse.

Oh when shall I be knowne, wher most to be
knowne I do longe?   Long.

Long be thy woes for such newes, but how recks she
my thoughts?   Oughts.

Then then what do I gaine, since unto hir will I do
winde?   Winde.

Winde, tempests, and stormes, yet in ende what   [35]
gives she desire?   Ire.

Silly rewarde! yet among women hath she of vertu
the most.   Most.

What great name may I give to so heav'nly a woman?   A woe-man.

Woe, but seems to me joy, that agrees to my thought
so.   I thought so.

Think so, for of my desired blisse it is only the course.   Curse.

24 Aye] Yea 93, I 90 St Bo Cl Le Da Ph, dye As, eye Je Qu.   25 *om.* Je Qu.
tell] tell mee Cl Da Ph.   26 myne] my 93 90 Bo.   27 hurt. 93.   29 which]
that 93, whearof Ph.   30 the words] thy wordes Da Ph Je Qu.   31 serv'd]
seemd Cl Le As, sind Da, sved Qu.   to me] me to 93 90, to my Je Qu.   32 do] *om.*
Da Qu.   33 newes, but] bad newes: 90.   recks] reck's 93, rockes St Bo Ph Qu,
wreckes Je.   35 Ire, 93.   36 among] aboue 90.   of vertu the most. Most] a
title. A tittle 90.   the most, 93.   37 woe-man, 93.   38 my thought] my
thoughtes Bo Cl Le Da Ph.   39 of] *om.* Je Qu.   Curse] Course 90 As Qu.

Curs'd be thy selfe for cursing that which leades me   [40]
    to joies.   Toies.

What be the sweet creatures wher lowly demaunds
    be not heard?   Hard.

Harde to be gott, but got constant, to be helde like
    steeles.   Eeles.

Howe can they be unkind? speake for th'hast
    narroly pri'de.   Pride.

Whence can pride come there, since springs of
    beawty be thence?   Thence.

Horrible is this blasphemy unto the most holy.   O lie.   [45]

Thou li'st false Echo, their minds as vertu be just.   Just.

Mock'st thou those Diamonds which only be matcht
    by the gods?   Ods.

Ods? what an ods is there since them to the heav'ns
    I prefer?   Erre.

Tell yet againe me the names of these faire form'd
    to do ev'lls.   Dev'lls.

Dev'lls? if in hell such dev'lls do abide, to the hells   [50]
    I do go.   Go.

32

[*Cleophila*]

◡–◡–◡––

MY muse what ails this ardour
To blase my onely secretts?
Alas it is no glory
To sing my owne decaid state.
Alas it is no comfort,   [5]
To speake without an answere.
Alas it is no wisdome
To shew the wound without cure.

41 lowly] louely Cl Le Je Qu.   42 *om.* 93.   like] uery 90.   43 Howe can
they be] What makes them be 93, How be they helde 90.   narroly] neerly St Bo Cl
Le As Da Je Qu, newlie Ph.   44 Whence] How 90 Je.   since] suche Ph Qu.
Thence, 93.   45 this] thy Cl Le As Da, the Qu.   46 be iust, 93.   47 those]
thes Je Qu.   48 there] their 93.   erre. 93.   49 Tell yet againe, how name
ye the goodly made euill? A deuill. 90.   50 Deuill? in hell where such Deuill is,
to that hell I doo goe. Goe. 90.   a bide, 93.
    32. 93, OA. *Scansion in* St Bo Cl As *only.*   1 ail's 93.   4 my] myne St As.
8 wound] woundes Cl Le.   cure, 93.

My muse what ails this ardour?
My eys be dym, my lyms shake,   [10]
My voice is hoarse, my throte scorcht,
My tong to this my roofe cleaves,
My fancy amazde, my thoughtes dull'd,
My harte doth ake, my life faints,
My sowle beginnes to take leave.   [15]
So greate a passion all feele,
To think a soare so deadly
I should so rashly ripp up.

My muse what ails this ardour?
If that to sing thou arte bent   [20]
Go sing the fall of old *Thebes*,
The warres of ougly Centaurs,
The life, the death of *Hector*,
So may thy songe be famous;
Or if to love thou art bent,   [25]
Recount the rape of *Europe*,
Adonis' end, *Venus*' nett,
The sleepy kisse the moone stale:
So may thy song be pleasant.

My muse what ails this ardour   [30]
To blase my onely secretts?
Wherein do only flowrish
The sorry fruites of anguish,
The song thereof a last will,
The tunes be cryes, the words plaints,   [35]
The singer is the song's theame
Wherin no eare can have joy,
Nor ey receaves due object,
Ne pleasure here, ne fame gott.

9 ail's 93.   10 My eys] Mine eys 93 Da.   11 scorcht] scerchte 93, scortche
Cl, is scortche Da.   13 thoughtes] thought 93.   19 ail's 93.   20 that
to sing] vnto singe St Bo Le As Je, vnto Songe Cl Da Ph Qu.   21 fall] songe Le
Qu.   old, *Thebes* 93.   23 *Hector* 93.   *Hector*] Hestor Le Qu.   24 thy]
the 93.   famous, 93.   26 Recounte] Rocount 93.   27–28 *om.* Je.   27 nett
93.   28 stale] stall St Bo Le As Qu, full Ph.   30 ail's 93.   33 anguish. 93.
34 a last] alas Cl Da Ph, elect Je.   37 Wherin] When 93.   38 receaves] receaue
93 Je Qu, revives Ph.   due] an Bo Cl.   obiect 93.   39 ne fame] ne fancie Bo,
in fame Cl, in fancie Le, no fame As, me fame Ph.   gott] gett 93 Da Qu, get*es* Je.

My muse what ails this ardour? [40]
'Alas' she saith 'I am thine,
So are thy pains my pains too.
Thy heated harte my seat is
Wherein I burne, thy breath is
My voice, too hott to keepe in. [45]
Besides, lo here the auther
Of all thy harmes: Lo here she,
That only can redresse thee,
Of her I will demaund helpe'.

My muse I yeeld, my muse singe, [50]
But all thy songe herein knitt:
The life we leade is all love,
The love we holde is all death,
Nor ought I crave to feede life,
Nor ought I seeke to shun death, [55]
But onely that my goddesse
My life my death do counte hers.

33

[Cleophila]

−−−◡◡−◡−◡−◡

REASON, tell me thy mind, if here be reason
In this strange violence, to make resistance.
Where sweet graces erect the stately banner
Of vertue's regiment, shining in harnesse
Of fortune's Diademes, by beauty mustred. [5]
Say then Reason, I say what is thy counsell?

Her loose haire be the shott, the brestes the pykes be,
Skowts each motion is, the hands the horsmen,
Her lipps are the riches the warres to maintaine,
Where well couched abides a coffer of pearle, [10]
Her legges carriage is of all the sweet campe:
Say then Reason I say what is thy counsell?

40 ail's 93.   44 burne 93.   45 in, 93.   46 Besides 93.   lo here] to
heere St, to heare Bo Le Ph, ~~to~~ Lo heare Cl.   47 thy] my Cl Le As Je.
51 knitt, 93.   52 loue: 93.   57 do] dothe Cl Le, om. Qu.
    33. 93, OA, Ra. Scansion in St Bo Cl As only.   1 here] this Da Ra.   7 brestes]
breaste 93 Le Qu.   8 the horsmen] be horsmen 93 Da Je.

Her cannons be her eys, myne eys the walls be,
Which at firste voly gave too open entry,
Nor ramper did abide; my braine was up blowne,   [15]
Undermin'd with a speech the pearcer of thoughts.
Thus weakned by my selfe, no helpe remaineth.
Say then Reason; I say, what is thy counsell?

And now fame the herald of her true honour,
Doth proclaime with a sound made all by men's mouths [20]
That nature, soverayne of earthly dwellers,
Commands all creatures, to yeeld obeysance
Under this, this her owne, her only dearling.
Say then Reason I say what is thy counsell?

Reason sighes but in end he thus doth answere.   [25]
'Nought can reason availe in heav'nly matters'.
Thus nature's Diamond, receave thy conquest,
Thus pure pearle, I do yeeld, my senses and soule.
Thus sweete paine, I do yeeld, what ere I can yeelde.
Reason looke to thy selfe, I serve a goddesse.   [30]

34

[Dorus]

```
---UU--UU-UU
```

O SWEET woods the delight of solitarines!
O how much I do like your solitarines!
Where man's mind hath a freed consideration
Of goodnes to receive lovely direction.
Where senses do behold th'order of heav'nly hoste,   [5]
And wise thoughts do behold what the creator is:
Contemplation here holdeth his only seate:
Bownded with no limitts, borne with a wing of hope
Clymes even unto the starres, Nature is under it.

13–20 om. Je.   15 braine] trayne St Ph.   17 remaineth 93.   21 nature 93.
23 this, this] this Cl Je Ra.   27 Diamond 93.   receave] receaues 93.
29 yeelde, 93.
  34. 93, OA (wanting in Je). Scansion in St Bo Cl As only.   3 where 93.
5 th'] the Bo Cl Le Da Ph Qu.

Nought disturbs thy quiet, all to thy service yeeld, [10]
Each sight draws on a thought, thought mother of science,
Sweet birds kindly do graunt harmony unto thee,
Faire trees' shade is enough fortification,
Nor danger to thy selfe if be not in thy selfe.

O sweete woods the delight of solitarines! [15]
O how much I do like your solitarines!
Here no treason is hidd, vailed in innocence,
Nor envie's snaky ey, finds any harbor here,
Nor flatterers' venomous insinuations,
Nor conning humorists' puddled opinions, [20]
Nor courteous ruin of proffered usury,
Nor time pratled away, cradle of ignorance,
Nor causelesse duty, nor comber of arrogance,
Nor trifling title of vanity dazleth us,
Nor golden manacles, stand for a paradise, [25]
Here wrong's name is unheard: slander a monster is.
Keepe thy sprite from abuse, here no abuse doth haunte.
What man grafts in a tree dissimulation?

O sweete woods the delight of solitarines!
O how well I do like your solitarines! [30]
Yet deare soile, if a soule closed in a mansion
As sweete as violetts, faire as a lilly is,
Streight as Cedar, a voice staines the Cannary birds,
Whose shade safety doth hold, danger avoideth her:
Such wisedome, that in her lives speculation: [35]
Such goodnes that in her simplicitie triumphs:
Where envie's snaky ey, winketh or els dyeth,
Slander wants a pretext, flattery gone beyond:
Oh! if such a one have bent to a lonely life
Her stepps, gladd we receave, gladd we receave her eys. [40]
    And thinke not she doth hurt our solitarines,
    For such company decks such solitarines.

10 yeeld] yeelds 93 Da Qu.   14 if be] yf Cl, if it be Le Da Ph Qu.   16 I do]
do I Cl Le Da Ph Qu.   17 no] nor 93, not Bo.   innocence] Innocency Cl Le Da
Ph Qu.   20 conning] comming 93, Common Ph.   21 ruin] Ruyning Cl Le.
23 *om.* Cl Le.   arrogance] arrogancie Da Qu.   26 is 93.   30 I do] do I Cl
Le Da Qu.   31 if] of Ph Qu.   32 a] *om.* 93 Qu.   33 as] as a Cl Le Da
Qu.   34 safety] safely 93 St Da.   35 *om.* Le.   38 wants] wanteth Cl Le,
watches Ph.   pretext] prelext 93.   39 bent, . . . life, 93.   40 stepps 93.

35

[Dorus]

SWEETE glove the wittnes of my secrett blisse
(Whiche hyding didest preserve that beawtie's light,
That opened furthe my seale of compforte is)
Be thow my starre in this my darkest night,
Nowe that myne eyes their cheerefull sunn dothe misse   [5]
Whiche dazeling still, dothe still maynteine my sight;
   Be thow, sweete glove, the Anker of my mynde,
   Till my frayle barke his haven agayn do fynde.

Sweete glove, the sweete despoyles of sweetest hand,
Fayre hand, the fayrest pledge of fayrer harte,   [10]
Trew harte, whose trewthe dothe yeeld to trewest bande,
Chief band I saye, which tyes my chiefest parte,
My cheefest parte, wherin do chieflye stand
Those secrett joyes, which heaven to me emparte,
   Unite in one, my state thus still to save;   [15]
   You have my thankes, Let me your comforte have.

36

[Dorus]

THE marchante man, whome gayne dothe teache the Sea
Where rockes do wayte, for theym the wyndes do chase,
Beaten with waves, no sooner kennes the baye
Wheare he was bounde, to make his marting place,
   But feare forgott, and paynes all overpaste,   [5]
   Make present ease receave the better taste.

---

35. OA (*wanting in* Je), Dd. *Initial capitals and line-end punctuation (except at lines 2 and* 10) *editorial.*   1 Sweete] O sweete Cl Le Ph.   2 didest] did Cl Ph. 3 furthe] St.   5 their] his St Bo Da Dd, this Qu.   6 dothe] doste Cl Qu. my] *om.* Ph Qu.   7 thow St.   10 fayrer] farest Bo Da.   11 to] the As Qu Dd.   trewest] trusty Cl Ph.

   36. OA. *Initial capitals and line-end punctuation editorial.*   1-6 *om.* Je. 6 better] bitter Da Qu.

The laborer, which cursed earthe up teares
With sweatie browes, sometyme with watrie eyes,
Ofte scorching sonne, ofte clowdie darkenes feares,
Whyle upon chaunce, his fruite of labour lyes;   [10]
    But harveste come, and corne in fertill store,
    More in his owne he toyld he gladdes the more.

Thus in my pilgrimaige of mated mynde,
Seeking the Sainct in whome all graces dwell,
What stormes founde me, what tormentes I dyd fynde,   [15]
Who seekes to knowe, acquaintes hym self with hell;
    But nowe successe hathe gott above annoyes,
    That sorrowe's weight dothe balance up thies joyes.

37

[*Cleophila*]

THE marchante man, whome many seas have toughte
What horrors breede, wheare wynd dominion beares,
Yet never rock, nor race, suche terror brought,
As neere his home, when storme or shelf he feares;
    For nature hathe that never fayling scoope,   [5]
    Moste lothe to loose, the moste approching hope.

The labourer, whome tyred boddie makes
Hold deere his work, with sighes eache change attendes,
But at no change, so pinching care he takes,
As happie shewes of corne when harvest sendes;   [10]
    For reason will, great sight of hoped blisse,
    Make great the losse, so grete the feare to misse.

Thus tossed in my shipp of huge desyre,
Thus toyled in my work of raging love,

8 sometyme] some tymes Cl Le Ph Qu.   watrie] watered St As Da Ph Je.
    37. OA. *Initial capitals and line-end punctuation editorial.* 1 have] hath Le As Ph Qu.
2 breede] breedes Cl Le Ph Je.   wynd] mynde Le Qu.   4 As neere his home]
om. Je Qu.   5 hathe, St.   7 whome] whose Je Qu.   8 sighes] sighe
Cl Le As.   9 at] as Le Je Qu.   10 shewes] shew Je Qu.   11 will . . .
sight] would . . . light Je Qu.   14 toyled] toyling Da Je Qu.   work] mind Je Qu.

Nowe that I spye the haven my thoughtes requyre,   [15]
Nowe that some flower of fruict, my paynes do prove,
  My dreeades augment the more in passion's mighte,
  Synce love with care, and hope with feare do fight.

38

[*Basilius*]

PHÆBUS farewell, a sweeter Saint I serve,
The high conceits thy heav'nly wisedomes breed
My thoughts forget: my thoughts, which never swerve
From her, in whome is sowne their freedome's seede,
And in whose eyes my dayly doome I reede.   [5]

Phœbus farewell, a sweeter Saint I serve.
Thou art farre off, thy kingdome is above:
She heav'n on earth with beauties doth preserve.
Thy beames I like, but her cleare rayes I love:
Thy force I feare, her force I still do prove.   [10]

Phœbus yeelde up thy title in my minde.
She doth possesse, thy Image is defaste,
But if thy rage some brave revenge will finde,
On her, who hath in me thy temple raste,
Employ thy might, that she my fires may taste.   [15]
  And how much more her worth surmounteth thee,
  Make her as much more base by loving me.

39

[*Cleophila*]

SINCE that the stormy rage of passions darcke
(Of passions darke, made darke by beautie's light)

16 fruict] ffruites Cl Qu.
  38. 93, OA, Ra. (Je *transcribes the lines in the order* 6–10, 1–5, 11–17).   2 wise-
domes] wisdome Cl Le Da Ph Je Ra.   3 which] will Da Ra.   4 freedome's]
freedom Bo Je Qu.   5 eyes] eye Je Qu.   8 with] wch Cl Qu.   14 On]
or St (*might be* on) As.
  39. 93, OA.   2 by] of 93, my Ph.

With rebell force, hath closde in dungeon darke
My minde ere now led foorth by reason's light:

Since all the thinges which give mine eyes their light [5]
Do foster still, the fruite of fancies darke:
So that the windowes of my inward light
Do serve, to make my inward powers darke:

Since, as I say, both minde and sences darke
Are hurt, not helpt, with piercing of the light: [10]
While that the light may shewe the horrors darke
But cannot make resolved darkenes lighte:
   I like this place, wheare at the least the darke
   May keepe my thoughtes, from thought of wonted light

40

[*Gynecia*]

HARKE plaintfull ghostes, infernall furies harke
Unto my woes the hatefull heavens do sende,
The heavens conspir'd, to make my vitall sparke
A wreched wracke, a glasse of Ruine's ende.

Seeing, Alas, so mightie powers bende [5]
Their ireful shotte against so weake a marke,
Come cave, become my grave, come death, and lende
Receipte to me, within thy bosome darke.

For what is life to dayly dyinge minde,
Where drawing breath, I sucke the aire of woe: [10]
Where too much sight, makes all the bodie blinde,
And highest thoughts, downeward most headlong throw?
   Thus then my forme, and thus my state I finde,
   Death wrapt in flesh, to living grave assign'd.

3 With] Whith 93.   5 give] gives Cl Le Qu.   mine] my Cl As Da Ph.   their]
the Bo Qu.   6 fruite] fruites 93 Le Ph Qu.   8 Do] to Je Qu.   9 sences]
sence is Je Qu.   10 Are] or Je Qu.   11 the horrors] my horrours Je Qu.
13 wheare at] whereat 93.
   40. 93, OA (*wanting in* Ph).   5 Alas; 93.   9 dyinge] dieng 93.
14 to living] to live in Da Qu, liuing, my Je.

41

[*Gynecia*]

LIKE those sicke folkes, in whome strange humors flowe,
Can taste no sweetes, the sower onely please:
So to my minde, while passions daylie growe,
Whose fyrie chaines, uppon his freedome seaze,
  Joie's strangers seeme, I cannot bide their showe,   [5]
Nor brooke oughte els but well acquainted woe.
Bitter griefe tastes me best, paine is my ease,
Sicke to the death, still loving my disease.

42

[*Gynecia*]

HOWE is my Sunn, whose beames are shining bright,
Become the cause of my darke ouglie night?
Or howe do I, captiv'd in this darke plight,
Bewaile the case, and in the cause delight?

My mangled mind huge horrors still doe fright,   [5]
With sense possest, and claim'd by reason's right:
Betwixt which two in me I have this fight,
Wher who so wynns, I put my selfe to flight.

Come clowdie feares, close up my daseled sight,
Sorowe suck up the marowe of my might,   [10]
Due sighes blowe out all sparkes of joyfull light,
Tyre on, despaier, uppon my tyred sprite.
  An ende, an ende, my dulde penn cannot write,
  Nor mas'de head thinke, nor faltring tonge recite.

41. 93, OA (*wanting in* Ph), Dd, Ra.   2 sweetes] sweet Da Je Qu Ra.   sower]
sower doeth Da Dd Ra.   5 strangers seeme] Straunges seeme Le, straunger
seames As, straunges seemes Qu.   7 griefe tastes] greves taste As Ra, greef taste
Da.   7 best 93.
    42. 93, OA (*wanting in* Ph), Dd (*lines* 1–8 *only*).   1 bright 93.   3 I 93.
9 feares 93.   10 Sorowe] Sorrowes 93.   12 on despaier 93.   13 dulde]
dull As Je.   14 faltring] flattering Je Qu.

43

[*Gynecia*]

THIS cave is darke, but it had never light.
  This waxe doth waste it selfe, yet painelesse dyes.
    These wordes are full of woes, yet feele they none.

I darkned am, who once had clearest sight.
  I waste my harte, which still newe torment tryes.   [5]
    I plaine with cause, my woes are all myne owne.

      No cave, no wasting waxe, no wordes of griefe,
        Can holde, shew, tell, my paines without reliefe.

44

[*Aristomenes*]

A BANISHT man, long bard from his desire
By inward letts, of them his state possest,
Hid heere his hopes, by which he might aspire
To have his harmes with wisdome's helpe redrest.

Seeke then and see, what man esteemeth best,   [5]
All is but this, this is our labour's hire,
Of this we live, in this wee finde our rest,
Who hold this fast no greater wealth require.
    Looke further then, so shalt thou finde at least,
    A baite most fit, for hungrie minded guest.   [10]

45

[*Charita*]

MY true love hath my hart, and I have his,
By just exchange, one for the other giv'ne.
I holde his deare, and myne he cannot misse:
There never was a better bargaine driv'ne.

---

43. 93, OA.   2 yet] it As Da.   4 who] wch Le Je.   5 torment] tor-
ments Le As Ph Je Qu.   6 are all] are still Cl Le, all are Ph.   myne] my
Bo Da Ph Qu.   owne, 93.

44. 93, OA.   8 hold] holdes Cl Da Je.   9 least] last Ph Je.   10 baite]
hart Ph Qu.

45. 93, OA, Hy, Pu (*lines 1–8 only with first line repeated after each quatrain*).   2 the
other] thother St, another Qu Hy Pu.   3 his] it Da Ph.

His hart in me, keepes me and him in one,   [5]
My hart in him, his thoughtes and senses guides:
He loves my hart, for once it was his owne:
I cherish his, because in me it bides.

His hart his wound receaved from my sight:
My hart was wounded, with his wounded hart,   [10]
For as from me, on him his hurt did light,
So still me thought in me his hurt did smart:
    Both equall hurt, in this change sought our blisse:
    My true love hath my hart and I have his.

46

[Dametas]

O WORDS which fall like sommer deaw on me,
O breath more sweete, then is the growing beane,
O toong in which, all honyed likoures bee,
O voice that doth, the Thrush in shrilnes staine,
    Do you say still, this is her promise due,   [5]
    That she is myne, as I to her am true.

Gay haire more gaie then straw when harvest lyes,
Lips red and plum, as cherrie's ruddy side,
Eyes faire and great, like faire great oxe's eyes,
O brest in which two white sheepe swell in pride: [10]
    Joyne you with me, to seale this promise due,
    That she be myne, as I to her am true.

But thou white skinne, as white as cruddes well prest,
So smooth as sleekestone-like, it smoothes each parte,
And thou deare flesh, as soft as wooll new drest,   [15]
And yet as hard, as brawne made hard by arte:
    First fower but say, next fowr their saying seale,
    But you must pay, the gage of promist weale.

5 me and him] him & me Hy Pu.   12 me thought] my thought Ph Je.   hurt]
hart Ph Hy.
   46. 93, OA.   6 as] and Le Je, and as As.   8 plum] plaine Da Ph.
13 cruddes] curdes Bo Cl Le Je.

47

[Pamela]

Do not disdaine, ô streight up raised Pine,
That wounding thee, my thoughtes in thee I grave:
Since that my thoughtes, as streight as streightnes thine,
No smaller wound, alas! farr deeper have.

Deeper engrav'd, which salve nor time can save,   [5]
Giv'ne to my harte, by my fore wounded eyne:
Thus cruell to my selfe how canst thou crave
My inward hurte should spare thy outward rine?

Yet still, faire tree, lifte up thy stately line,
Live long, and long witnesse my chosen smarte,   [10]
Which barde desires, (barde by my selfe) imparte.

And in this growing barke growe verses myne.
My harte my worde, my worde hath giv'ne my harte.
The giver giv'n from gifte shall never parte.

48

[Pamela]

Sweete roote say thou, the roote of my desire
Was vertue cladde in constant love's attire.

49

[Musidorus]

You goodly pines, which still with brave assent
In nature's pride your heads to heav'nwarde heave,
Though you besides such graces earth hath lent,
Of some late grace a greater grace receave,

47. 93, OA (wanting in Je).   1 Pine 93.   3 thine 93.   4 deeper] deep
Da Qu.   8 hurte] harte As Ph.   outward] inward Da Qu.   9 still 93.
11 Which] With Cl Le Da Qu.   imparte 93.
48. 93, OA (wanting in Je), Dd.
49. 93, OA (wanting in Je).

By her who was (O blessed you) content,   [5]
With her faire hande, your tender barkes to cleave,
And so by you (O blessed you) hath sent,
Such pearcing wordes as no thoughts els conceave:

Yet yeeld your graunt, a baser hand may leave
His thoughtes in you, where so sweete thoughtes were spent, [10]
For how would you the mistresse' thoughts bereave
Of waiting thoughts all to her service ment?

Nay higher thoughtes (though thralled thoughtes) I call
My thoughtes then hers, who first your ryne did rente,
Then hers, to whom my thoughts alonely thrall   [15]
Rysing from lowe, are to the highest bente;
    Where hers, whom worth makes highest over all,
    Comming from her, cannot but downewarde fall.

50

[*Pamela and Musidorus*]

Pamela. Like divers flowers, whose divers beauties serve
    To decke the earth with his well-colourde weede,
    Though each of them, his private forme preserve,
    Yet joyning formes one sight of beautie breede.
    Right so my thoughts, whereon my hart I feede: [5]

    Right so my inwarde partes, and outward glasse,
    Though each possesse a divers working kinde,
    Yet all well knit to one faire end do passe:
        That he, to whome these sondrie giftes I binde,
        All what I am, still one, his owne, doe finde.   [10]

6 barkes] Barcke Le Ph Qu.   8 thoughts] thought Bo As, thing Cl.   14 rente. 93.
15 alonely] a lonely 93, a Lovely Cl Le Qu.   16 lowe] Love Cl Le As Da Ph Qu.
17 all 93.
    50. 93, OA (*wanting in* Je). *Space after line 4.*   5 whereon] where on 93.
9 he to whome, ... binde 93.   these] this As Qu, the Ph.

Musidorus. All what you are still one, his owne to finde,
   You that are borne to be the worlde's eye,
   What were it els, but to make each thing blinde?
   And to the sunne with waxen winges to flie?

No no, such force with my small force to trye   [15]
   Is not my skill, nor reach of mortall minde.
   Call me but yours, my title is most hye:
   Holde me most yours, then my longe suite is signde.

You none can clayme but you your selfe by right,
   For you do passe your selfe, in vertue's might.   [20]
   So both are yours: I, bound with gaged harte:
   You onely yours, too farr beyond desarte.

51

[*Musidorus*]

LOCKE up, faire liddes, the treasures of my harte:
   Preserve those beames, this age's onely lighte:
   To her sweete sence, sweete sleepe, some ease imparte,
   Her sence too weake to beare her spirit's mighte.

And while ô sleepe thou closest up her sight,   [5]
   (Her sight where love did forge his fayrest darte)
   O harbour all her partes in easefull plighte:
   Let no strange dreme make her fayre body starte.

But yet ô dreame, if thou wilt not departe
   In this rare subject from thy common right: [10]
   But wilt thy selfe in such a seate delighte,

Then take my shape, and play a lover's parte:
   Kisse her from me, and say unto her spirite,
   Till her eyes shine, I live in darkest night.

---

11 what] that Cl Le.   16 nor] or 93.   19 none] nowe St Bo As Da Ph.   by
right] aright 93.
   51. 93, OA (*wanting in* Je), Dd, Hn, Hy, Ra.   1 Locke] Looke Cl As Da.
treasures] treasure 93 Qu Hy Ra.   3 sleepe 93.   7 ô 93.   10 rare] fair
Dd Hn.   thy] the 93.   14 night] lighte Cl Le.

52

[Basilius]

WHY doost thou haste away
O *Titan* faire the giver of the daie?
Is it to carry newes
To Westerne wightes, what starres in East appeare?
Or doost thou thinke that heare   [5]
Is left a Sunne, whose beames thy place may use?
Yet stay and well peruse,
What be her giftes, that make her equall thee,
Bend all thy light to see
In earthly clothes enclosde a heavenly sparke.   [10]
Thy running course cannot such beawties marke:
No, no, thy motions bee
Hastened from us with barre of shadow darke,
Because that thou, the author of our sight,
Disdainst we see thee staind with other's light.   [15]

53

[Philoclea]

O STEALING time the subject of delaie,
(Delay, the racke of unrefrain'd desire)
What strange dessein hast thou my hopes to staie,
My hopes which do but to mine owne aspire?

Mine owne? ô word on whose sweete sound doth pray [5]
My greedy soule, with gripe of inward fire:
Thy title great, I justlie chalenge may,
Since in such phrase his faith he did attire.

O time, become the chariot of my joyes:
As thou drawest on, so let my blisse draw neere.   [10]
Each moment lost, part of my hap destroyes:

---

52. 93, OA.   4 appeare] appeares Le Je Qu.   7 peruse] *perceaue* Je Qu.
8 make] makes Ph Je Qu.   9 to] & Je Qu.   11 *om.* Qu.   13 shadow]
shadowes Ph Je Qu.   14 thou . . . sight 93.   15 Disdainst] disdaines OA.   thee
staind] distaind Je Qu.
53. 93, OA.   2 vnrefram'd 93.   3 dessein] desyer Cl Ph, ⟨ ⟩ Je.   staie 93.

Thou art the father of occasion deare:
Joyne with thy sonne, to ease my long annoys.
In speedie helpe, thanke worthie frends appeare.

54

[*Gynecia*]

MY Lute within thy selfe thy tunes enclose,
Thy mistresse' song is now a sorrow's crie,
Her hand benumde with fortune's daylie blows,
Her minde amaz'de can neither's helpe applie.
Weare these my words as mourning weedes of woes,   [5]
Blacke incke becommes the state wherein I dye.
   And though my mones be not in musicke bound,
   Of written greefes, yet be the silent ground.

The world doth yeeld such ill consorted shows,
With circkled course, which no wise stay can trye,   [10]
That childish stuffe which knowes not frendes from foes,
(Better despisde) bewondre gasing eye.
Thus noble golde, downe to the bottome goes,
When worthlesse corke, aloft doth floting lye.
   Thus in thy selfe, least strings are loudest founde,   [15]
   And lowest stops doo yeeld the hyest sounde.

55

[*Basilius*]

WHEN two Sunnes do appeare
Some say it doth betoken wonders neare
As Prince's losse or change:
Two gleaming Sunnes of splendour like I see,
And seeing feele in me   [5]
Of Prince's harte quite lost the ruine strange.

13 annoy's. 93.   14 frends] frend Je Qu.
54. 93, OA.   1 within] which in 93.   5 weedes] weede 93 St Bo Le As.
6 becommes] become Cl Le Da.   8 the] the they Cl, they Ph Qu, ihe As.
11 frendes] frend Je Qu.   12 bewondre] by wonder Ph Qu, bee wonder Cl Je.
55. 93, OA.

But nowe each where doth range
With ouglie cloke the darke envious night:
Who full of guiltie spite,
Such living beames should her black seate assaile,   [10]
Too weake for them our weaker sighte doth vaile.

'No' saies faire moone, 'my lighte
Shall barr that wrong, and though it not prevaile
Like to my brother's raies, yet those I sende
Hurte not the face, which nothing can amende'.   [15]

56

[*Cleophila*]

AURORA now thou shewst thy blushing light
(Which oft to hope laies out a guilefull baite,
That trusts in time, to finde the way aright
To ease those paines, which on desire do waite)

Blush on for shame: that still with thee do light   [5]
On pensive soules (in steede of restfull baite)
Care upon care (in steede of doing right)
To over pressed brestes, more greevous waight.

As oh! my selfe, whose woes are never lighte
(Tide to the stake of doubt) strange passions baite,   [10]
While thy known course, observing nature's right,
Sturres me to thinke what dangers lye in waite.

For mischeefes greate, daye after day doth showe:
Make me still feare, thy faire appearing showe.

57

[*Cleophila*]

BEAUTIE hath force to catche the humane sight.
Sight doth bewitch, the fancie evill awaked.
Fancie we feele, encludes all passion's mighte,
Passion rebelde, oft reason's strength hath shaked.

14 raies] raise 93 As.
   56. 93, OA.   3 trusts] trust Bo Da Je Qu.   7 Care] Or Cl Da Qu, are Le.
11 known] knowe Da Qu, vnknowne Je.   right 93.   13 doth] do Cl Da Je.
14 still feare] feare still Cl Le As.
   57. 93, OA.   3 encludes] eludes Cl Da, include Je.

No wondre then, though sighte my sighte did tainte,   [5]
And though thereby my fancie was infected,
Though (yoked so) my minde with sicknes fainte,
Had reason's weight for passion's ease rejected.

But now the fitt is past: and time hath giv'ne
Leasure to weigh what due deserte requireth.   [10]
All thoughts so spronge, are from their dwelling driv'n,
And wisdome to his wonted seate aspireth.
  Crying in me: eye hopes deceitefull prove.
  Thinges rightelie prizde, love is the bande of love.

58

[Inscription on Gynecia's Love Potion]

LET him drinke this, whome long in armes to folde
Thou doest desire, and with free power to holde.

59

[Basilius]

GET hence foule Griefe, the canker of the minde:
Farewell Complaint, the miser's only pleasure:
Away vayne Cares, by which fewe men do finde
          Their sought-for treasure.

Ye helplesse Sighes, blowe out your breath to nought,   [5]
Teares, drowne your selves, for woe (your cause) is wasted,
Thought, thinke to ende, too long the frute of thought
          My minde hath tasted.

But thou, sure Hope, tickle my leaping heart.
Comfort, step thou in place of wonted sadnes.   [10]
Fore-felt Desire, begin to savour parte
          Of comming gladnes.

14 *not indented in* 93.
  58. 93, OA.
  59. 93, OA.   3 Cares] care Je Qu.   5 Ye] Yet Je Qu.   Sighes] sightes
As Je.   10 step] sleepe Cl As Qu, slepp Da.   11 parte] parts 93.   12 comming]
my Cunning Cl, cunning Da Ph.

Let voice of Sighes into cleare musike runne,
Eyes, let your Teares with gazing now be mended,
In stede of Thought, true pleasure be begunne,   [15]
　　　　　And never ended.

60

[Philoclea]

VERTUE, beawtie, and speach, did strike, wound, charme,
My harte, eyes, eares, with wonder, love, delight:
First, second, last, did binde, enforce, and arme,
His workes, showes, suites, with wit, grace, and vow's might.

Thus honour, liking, trust, much, farre, and deepe,   [5]
Held, pearst, possest, my judgement, sence, and will,
Till wrong, contempt, deceipt, did growe, steale, creepe,
Bandes, favour, faith, to breake, defile, and kill.

Then greefe, unkindnes, proofe, tooke, kindled, tought,
Well grounded, noble, due, spite, rage, disdaine,   [10]
But ah, alas! (In vayne) my minde, sight, thought,
Doth him, his face, his words, leave, shunne, refraine,
For no thing, time, nor place, can loose, quench, ease,
Mine owne, embraced, sought, knot, fire, desease.

15 Thought] thoughtes Je Qu.
　60　93. OA. Hy. Je Hy *do not number the words.*　　　　3 binde] blinde Je Qu.
4 suites] ffruites Cl Da Qu.

61

[*Philoclea*]

THE love which is imprinted in my soule
With beautie's seale, and vertue faire disguis'de,
With inward cries putts up a bitter role
Of huge complaintes, that now it is despis'de.

Thus thus the more I love, the wronge the more   [5]
Monstrous appeares, long trueth receaved late,
Wrong sturres remorsed greefe, griefe's deadly sore
Unkindnes breedes, unkindnes fostreth hate.

But ah the more I hate, the more I thinke
Whome I doe hate, the more I thinke on him,   [10]
The more his matchlesse giftes do deepely sinck
Into my breste, and loves renewed swimme.
What medicin then, can such desease remove
Where love draws hate, and hate engendreth love?

62

[*Pyrocles repeating Philisides*]

WHAT toong can her perfections tell
In whose each part all pens may dwell?
Her haire fine threeds of finest gould
In curled knots man's thought to hold:
But that her fore-head sayes in me   [5]
A whiter beautie you may see.
Whiter indeed; more white then snow,
Which on cold winter's face doth grow.

Cl Le As Da Ph Je Qu:

    [3] Her hayre fyne Laces made of golde

---

61. 93, OA, Pu (*lines* 13–14 *only*).   2 vertue] vertues Ph Je.   3 up] out
Je Qu.   role] roole St Bo Da Qu, Rowle Cl Le As Ph Je.   8 hate] hath 93.
    62. 90–93, Cm (*lines* 1–8 *only*), OA, Dd, Eg (*lines* 143–6 *only*).   3 threeds of
finest] lockes made of Cm.   4 thought] thoughtes Bo Le Da Qu Dd.   5 sayes]
said Cm, saies *overwritten as* saied Bo, sures Je, layes Qu.   7 white] whiter As Qu.

That doth present those even browes,
Whose equall lynes their angles bowes,   [10]
Like to the Moone when after chaunge
Her horned head abroad doth raunge:
And arches be to heavenly lids,
Whose winke ech bold attempt forbids.
For the blacke starres those Spheares containe,   [15]
The matchlesse paire, even praise doth staine.
No lampe, whose light by Art is got,
No Sunne, which shines, and seeth not,
Can liken them without all peere,
Save one as much as other cleere: [20]
Which onely thus unhappie be,
Because themselves they cannot see.
   Her cheekes with kindly claret spred.
Aurora like new out of bed,
Or like the fresh Queene-apple's side,   [25]
Blushing at sight of *Phœbus'* pride.
   Her nose, her chinne pure ivorie weares:
No purer then the pretie eares.
So that therein appeares some blood,
Like wine and milke that mingled stood.   [30]
In whose Incirclets if you gaze,
Your eyes may tread a Lover's maze.
But with such turnes the voice to stray,
No talke untaught can finde the way.

Cl Le As Da Ph Je Qu:

   [9] That dothe present those prety Browes,
   [12] Her Horned face in Heaven dothe Range,
   [13] And Arches bee to those fayre Lyddes
   [15] As for the Starres, those spheares conteene,
   [24] Like Christall, vnderlayde with Redd,
   [27] Her Nose and Chynn suche Ivory weares,
   [28] No *Elephant* so perfect beares.

9 those] thes Je Qu.   13 those] thes Je Qu.   15 those] whose Cl Qu.

---

9 those] these Bo Je Qu.   even] eben *overwritten as* even St, ebeene Bo.   10 lynes]
line 90-93 Je Qu.   16 paire] praise OA Dd.   24 *om.* Bo.   25-26 *not in*
Cl Le As Da Ph Je Qu.   29-36 *om.* Cl Le As Ph Je Qu.   31 In] on St Bo.
you] ye 90-93.   33 stray] staye Da (Ph *marginal addition*).   34 *om.* Dd.

The tippe no jewell needes to weare: [35]
The tippe is jewell of the eare.
    But who those ruddie lippes can misse?
Which blessed still themselves doo kisse.
Rubies, Cherries, and Roses new,
In worth, in taste, in perfitte hewe: [40]
Which never part but that they showe
Of pretious pearle the double rowe,
The second sweetly-fenced warde,
Her heav'nly-dewed tongue to garde.
Whence never word in vaine did flowe.   [45]
    Faire under these doth stately growe,
The handle of this plesant worke,
The neck, in which strange graces lurke.
Such be I thinke the sumptuous towers
Which skill dooth make in Princes' bowers.   [50]
So good a say invites the eye,
A little downward to espie,
The lovely clusters of her brests,
Of *Venus'* babe the wanton nests:
Like pomels round of Marble cleere: [55]
Where azurde veines well mixt appeere.
With dearest tops of porphyrie.
    Betwixt these two a way doth lie,
A way more worthie beautie's fame,
Then that which beares the mylken name.   [60]
This leades unto the joyous field,
Which onely still doth Lillies yeeld:
But Lillies such whose native smell
The Indian odours doth excell.
Waste it is calde, for it doth waste   [65]
Men's lives, untill it be imbraste.

Cl Le As Da Ph Je Qu:
    [51] So true a Taste invites the Eye,
    [57] With Lycoras stalkes of Porphiry,

---

35 needes] nede Bo Dd.   46 these] this Le Dd.   47 plesant] pretious 90-93.
50 skill] still Le Qu Dd.   53 lovely] liuelie 90-93.   54 babe] Babb Cl, babes
Da, Bayt*es* Je, bayte Qu.   60 mylken] *Milkie* 90-93, milker Je.   61 This]
These Cl Le Qu.   unto] into 90-93 Qu.   64 doth] doo Cl Le Ph Dd.

There may one see, and yet not see
Her ribbes in white well armed be.
More white then *Neptune's* fomie face,
When strugling rocks he would imbrace.   [70]
  In thies delights the wandring thought
Might of each side astray be brought,
But that her navel doth unite,
In curious circle, busie sight:
A daintie seale of virgin-waxe,   [75]
Where nothing but impression lackes.
  The bellie there gladde sight doth fill,
Justly entitled *Cupid's* hill.
A hill most fitte for such a master,
A spotlesse mine of Alablaster.   [80]
Like Alablaster faire and sleeke,
But soft and supple satten like.
In that sweete seate the Boy doth sport:
Loath, I must leave his chiefe resort.
For such an use the world hath gotten,   [85]
The best things still must be forgotten.
  Yet never shall my song omitte
Those thighes, for *Ovid's* song more fitte;
Which flanked with two sugred flankes,
Lift up their stately swelling bankes;   [90]
That *Albion* clives in whitenes passe:
With hanches smooth as looking glasse.

Cl Le As Da Ph Je Qu:

[68] Her tender Ribbes well armed bee,
[69] Like Whitest Snowe, in silver Brooke,
[70] ffayre, thorow fayre strykes of heedefull Looke.

69–70 *om.* Je (*because following leaf is missing, but has catchword* like *to line* 69). Da *has*
Cl-Qu *lines* Like . . . Looke, *but in margin has* alius *and* St-Bo *lines* More . . . imbrace.
70 of] *om.* Le As Da Ph.

---

68 well] all 90–93.   71–86 *om.* As. Je *has these lines in its margin.*   71–92 *om.*
Qu.   71 thies] those 90–93.   77–92 *om.* Ph.   77 The] Her 90–93.
there] then 90–93.   83–84 *om.* Cl.   85 "For 90.   an] a 90–93.   86 "The
90.   87–146 *om.* Je (*leaves wanting*).   88 Those thighes] Thighes 90, Hir
thighes 93.

But bow all knees, now of her knees
My tongue doth tell what fancie sees.
The knottes of joy, the gemmes of love,   [95]
Whose motion makes all graces move.
Whose bought incav'd doth yeeld such sight,
Like cunning Painter shadowing white.
The gartring place with child-like signe,
Shewes easie print in mettall fine.   [100]
But there againe the flesh doth rise
In her brave calves, like christall skies.
Whose *Atlas* is a smallest small,
More white then whitest bone of whall.

 There ofte steales out that round cleane foote   [105]
This noble Cedar's pretious roote:
In shewe and sent pale violets,
Whose steppe on earth all beautie sets.

 But back unto her back, my *Muse*,
Where *Leda's* swanne his feathers mewes,   [110]
Along whose ridge such bones are met,
Like comfits round in marchpane set.

 Her shoulders be like two white Doves,
Pearching within square royall rooves,
Which leaded are with silver skinne,   [115]
Passing the hate-spott Ermelin.
And thence those armes derived are;
The *Phœnix* wings be not so rare

Cl Le As Da Ph [Je ?] Qu:

 [102] In her brave Calves, lyke morning skyes,
 [103] That Limitt*es* have in smallest smalle,
 [104] Whose eeven descent makes equall falle,
 [114] Pearching vppon square Royall Rooves,
 [115] Whose gentle rayes suche Luster fynde,
 [116] Lyke thynnest Lawne with Tynsell lynde,

95 gemmes] Gynnes Cl, iemes Le Dd, Iinnes Ph. 97 incav'd] enchaynde Cl,
engraved As. sight] light As Qu. 98 Painter] paynters Cl Le Qu. 101 there]
then 90-93. 104 whall] all 90-93, whale Dd. 105 There ofte] Thereout
90-93, Therof As Dd. 110 *Leda's*] lo as Da, ⟨ ⟩ Ph. mewes] muse Bo
Le As Da, mewse Dd, *om.* Cl Ph. 116 hate-spott] hate-sport 90 St. 118 be]
are 90-93 As Da, but Qu.

For faultlesse length, and stainelesse hewe,
 Ah woe is me, my woes renewe;   [120]
Now course doth leade me to her hand,
Of my first love the fatall band.
Where whitenes dooth for ever sitte:
Nature her selfe enameld it.
For there with strange compact dooth lie   [125]
Warme snow, moyst pearle, softe ivorie.
There fall those Saphir-coloured brookes,
Which conduit-like with curious crookes,
Sweete Ilands make in that sweete land.
As for the fingers of the hand,   [130]
The bloudy shaftes of *Cupid's* warre,
With amatists they headed are.
 Thus hath each part his beautie's part,
But how the Graces doo impart
To all her limmes a spetiall grace,   [135]
Becomming every time and place,
Which doth even beautie beautifie,
And most bewitch the wretched eye,
How all this is but a faire Inne
Of fairer guest, which dwells within,   [140]
Of whose high praise, and praisefull blisse,
Goodnes the penne, heaven paper is,
The inke immortall fame dooth lende:
As I began, so must I ende.
 No tongue can her perfections tell,   [145]
 In whose each part all pens may dwell.

124 her selfe] it selfe Ph, y^t y^t selfe Qu. 125 dooth] doe Le Ph Qu. 128 with]
om. Bo Dd. 129 make] makes Cl Le As. 130 the hand] that hand As Dd.
135 a spetiall] especiall Cl Ph. 136 place. 90. 138 eye. 90. 140 guest]
guestes 90-93 Bo Qu. dwells] dwell 90-93 Bo Da Ph. within. 90. 142 is. 90.
145 perfections] p*erfecton* As Eg. 146 pens] tongues 90-93.

63

[*Dicus*]

LET mother earth now decke her selfe in flowers,
To see her ofspring seeke a good increase,
Where justest love doth vanquish *Cupid's* powers
And warr of thoughts is swallow'd up in peace
    Which never may decrease   [5]
    But like the turtells faire
    Live one in two, a well united paire,
    Which that no chaunce may staine,
    O *Himen* long their coupled joyes maintaine.

O heav'n awake shewe forth thy stately face,   [10]
Let not these slumbring clowds thy beawties hide,
But with thy cheerefull presence helpe to grace
The honest Bridegroome, and the bashfull Bride,
    Whose loves may ever bide,
    Like to the Elme and Vyne,   [15]
    With mutuall embracements them to twyne:
    In which delightfull paine,
    O *Himen* long their coupled joyes maintaine.

Yee Muses all which chaste affects allow,
And have to Lalus shewd your secret skill,   [20]
To this chaste love your sacred favours bow,
And so to him and her your giftes distill,
    That they all vice may kill:
    And like to lillies pure
    Do please all eyes, and spotlesse do endure.   [25]
    Where that all blisse may raigne,
    O *Himen* long their coupled joyes maintaine.

63. 93, OA.   1–31 *om.* Je.   3 justest] iustice Le As, iustide Da, simple
Ph.   4 warr] ware 93.   19 affects] effectes Ph Qu, affectes do Le.
20 Lalus] *Thyrsis* 93.   24 to] as Cl Je.   25 Do . . . do] May . . . may 93.

Yee Nymphes which in the waters empire have,
Since Lalus' musick oft doth yeeld you praise,
Graunt to the thing which we for Lalus crave.   [30]
Let one time (but long first) close up their daies,
  One grave their bodies seaze:
  And like two rivers sweete,
  When they though divers do together meete:
  One streame both streames containe,   [35]
  O *Himen* long their coupled joyes maintaine.

Pan, father *Pan*, the god of silly sheepe,
Whose care is cause that they in number growe,
Have much more care of them that them do keepe,
Since from these good the others' good doth flowe,   [40]
  And make their issue showe
  In number like the hearde
  Of yonglings, which thy selfe with love hast rearde,
  Or like the drops of raine.
  O *Himen* long their coupled joyes maintaine.   [45]

Vertue (if not a God) yet God's chiefe parte,
Be thou the knot of this their open vowe,
That still he be her head, she be his harte,
He leane to her, she unto him do bow:
  Each other still allow: [50]
  Like Oke and Mistletoe.
  Her strength from him, his praise from her do growe.
  In which most lovely traine,
  O *Himen* long their coupled joyes maintaine.

But thou foule *Cupid*, syre to lawlesse lust,   [55]
Be thou farre hence with thy empoyson'd darte,
Which though of glittring golde, shall heere take rust
Where simple love, which chastnesse doth imparte,
  Avoydes thy hurtfull arte,
  Not needing charming skill,   [60]
  Such mindes with sweet affections for to fill,

28 empire] empyres Cl As Da, *om.* Ph.   29 Lalus] *Thyrsis* 93.   30 Lalus]
Thyrsis 93.   33 two] to Cl Le Ph Je.   34 though] through Bo Cl Le, thought
Da.   40 others'] other As Ph Je Qu.   doth] do Bo As Je Qu.   43 hast]
hath Bo Je.   49 leane] cleave Cl Le Ph, leave Qu.   55 *Cupid* 93.
59 thy] the Cl Le As Je Qu.

Which being pure and plaine,
O *Himen* long their coupled joyes maintaine.

All churlish wordes, shrewd answeres, crabbed lookes,
All privatenes, selfe-seeking, inward spite,   [65]
All waywardnes, which nothing kindly brookes,
All strife for toyes, and clayming master's right:
    Be hence aye put to flight,
    All sturring husband's hate
    Gainst neighbors good for womanish debate   [70]
    Be fled as things most vaine,
O *Himen* long their coupled joyes maintaine.

All peacock pride, and fruites of peacock's pride
Longing to be with losse of substance gay
With recklesness what may thy house betide,   [75]
So that you may on hyer slippers stay
    For ever hence awaye:
    Yet let not sluttery,
    The sinke of filth, be counted huswifery:
    But keeping holesome meane,   [80]
O *Himen* long their coupled joyes maintaine.

But above all away vile jealousie,
The evill of evils, just cause to be unjust,
(How can he love suspecting treacherie?
How can she love where love cannot win trust?)   [85]
    Goe snake hide thee in dust,
    Ne dare once shew thy face,
    Where open hartes do holde so constant place,
    That they thy sting restraine,
    O *Himen* long their coupled joyes maintaine.   [90]

The earth is deckt with flowers, the heav'ns displaid,
Muses graunt guiftes, Nymphes long and joyned life,
Pan store of babes, vertue their thoughts well staid,
Cupid's lust gone, and gone is bitter strife,

67 for . . . master's] or . . . masteryes Je Qu.   69 sturring . . . hate] stirring*es*
. . . hat*es* Je Qu.   70 womanish] womanly Je Qu.   73 peacock] Peacock*es*
Cl Da Je Qu.   75 recklesness] retchlesnes 93, wretchlesnes As Qu, racklesnes Je.
thy] the Ph Je.   83 euils 93.   88 do] doth Da Ph.   89 sting] string Bo,
stinges Le Je.

Happy man, happy wife.   [95]
No pride shall them oppresse,
Nor yet shall yeeld to loathsome sluttishnes,
And jealousie is slaine:
For *Himen* will their coupled joyes maintaine.

64

[*Nico*]

A NEIGHBOR mine not long agoe there was,
(But namelesse he, for blamelesse he shall be)
That married had a trick and bonny lasse
As in a sommer day a man might see:
  But he himselfe a foule unhansome groome,   [5]
  And farre unfit to hold so good a roome.

Now whether mov'd with selfe unworthines,
Or with her beawtie fit to make a pray,
Fell jealousie did so his braine oppresse,
That if he absent were but halfe a daye,   [10]
  He gest the worst (you wot what is the worst)
  And in himselfe new doubting causes nurst.

While thus he fear'd the silly innocent,
Who yet was good, because she knewe none ill,
Unto his house a jollie shepeheard went,   [15]
To whome our prince did beare a great good will,
  Because in wrestling and in pastorall
  He farre did passe the rest of Shepheards all.

And therefore he a courtier was benamed,
And as a courtier was with cheere receaved,   [20]
(For they have toongs to make a poore man blamed
If he to them his dutie misconceaved)
  And for this Courtier should well like his table,
  The goodman bad his wife be serviceable.

99 For] O Le Qu.
64. 93, OA, Ha.   4 sommer] Somers Bo Je Qu Ha.   8 with her] whether
Cl Le Da, her fayr Ph.   9 braine] Braynes Cl Da Ph Je, mynd Ha.   11 wot]
know Je Ha.   12 doubting] doting As Ha.   14 none] no Bo Da Je Qu Ha,
not Ph.   21 blamed. 93.   23 well like] like well Bo Le.   his]
~~this~~ his Cl, this Da Ph.

And so she was, and all with good intent,   [25]
But fewe dayes past while she good maner us'de,
But that her husband thought her service bent
To such an end as he might be abus'de.
    Yet like a coward fearing stranger's pride,
    He made the simple wench his wrath abide.   [30]

With chumpish lookes, hard words, and secret nips,
Grumbling at her when she his kindnes sought,
Asking her how she tasted Courtier's lips,
He forst her thinke that which she never thought.
    In fine he made her gesse, there was some sweet   [35]
    In that which he so fear'd that she should meet.

When once this entred was, in woman's hart,
And that it had enflam'd a new desire,
There rested then, to play a woman's part,
Fuell to seeke and not to quench the fire: [40]
    But (for his jealous eye she well did finde)
    She studied cunning how the same to blinde.

And thus she did. One day to him she came,
And (though against his will) on him she leand,
And out gan cry, 'ah well away for shame,   [45]
If you helpe not our wedlocke will be staind'.
    The goodman starting, askt what did her move?
    She sigh'd and sayd, the bad guest sought her love.

He little looking that she should complaine
Of that, whereto he feard she was enclinde,   [50]
Bussing her oft, and in his hart full faine,
He did demaunde what remedy to finde;
    How they might get that guest, from them to wend,
    And yet the prince (that lov'd him) not offend.

'Husband', quoth she, 'go to him by and by,   [55]
And tell him that you finde I doo him love,
And therefore pray him that of courtesie
He will absent himselfe, least he should move
    A young girle's hart, to that were shame for both,
    Whereto you knowe, his honest harte were loath.   [60]

26 maner] maners Cl Le Da Ph Je Ha.   30 wench] wretch Da Qu.   31 chum-
pish] Clumpish Cl Je, Lumpishe As, crumpish Ph Ha, thumpishe Qu.   35 he] yt
Bo Cl Le As Da Ph.   37 entred] entrye Je Qu, kindled Ha.   44 his] her Je Qu.
46 staind, 93.   55 quoth] qd. Bo As.   56 that you] you do 93 Ha.

'Thus shall you show that him you do not doubt,
And as for me (sweete husband) I must beare'.
Glad was the man when he had heard her out,
And did the same, although with mickle feare.
    For feare he did, least he the young man might   [65]
    In choller put, with whom he would not fight.

The Courtlie shepheard much agast at this,
Not seeing earst such token in the wife,
Though full of scorne, would not his duty misse,
Knowing that evill becommes a houshold strife,   [70]
    Did goe his way, but sojourn'd neere thereby,
    That yet the ground hereof he might espie.

The wife thus having settled husband's braine,
Who would have sworne his spowse *Diana* was,
Watched when she a furder point might gaine,   [75]
Which little time did fitlie bring to passe.
    For to the Courte her man was calld by name,
    Whether he needes must goe for feare of blame.

Three dayes before that he must sure depart,
She written had (but in a hand disguisde)   [80]
A letter such which might from either part
Seeme to proceede, so well it was devisde.
    She seald it first, then she the sealing brake,
    And to her jealous husband did it take.

With weeping eyes (her eyes she taught to weepe)   [85]
She told him that the Courtier had it sent:
'Alas', quoth she, 'thus women's shame doth creepe'.
The goodman read on both sides the content,
    It title had, *Unto my only love*,
    Subscription was, *Yours most, if you will prove*.   [90]

The pistle selfe, such kinde of wordes it had,
'My sweetest joy, the comfort of my sprite,
So may thy flockes encrease, thy deere hart glad,
So may each thing, even as thou wishest lighte,
    As thou wilt deigne to reade, and gentlie reede,   [95]
    This mourning inck, in which my hart doth bleede.

68 token] tokens As Ha.   72 hereof] thereof Bo Cl Je Ha.   78 Whether]
Whither 93 Qu.   81 which] as Le Ha.   89 title] little 93 Da.   93 en-
crease 93.   95 reade . . . reede 93.

'Long have I lov'd, (alas thou worthy arte)
Long have I lov'd, (alas love craveth love)
Long have I lov'd thy selfe, alas my harte
Doth breake, now toong unto thy name doth move,   [100]
   And thinke not that thy answere answere is,
   But that it is my doome of bale or blisse.

'The jealous wretch must now to Courte be gone:
Ne can he faile, for prince hath for him sent:
Now is the time we may be here alone,   [105]
And geve a long desire a sweet content.
   Thus shall you both reward a lover true,
   And eke revenge his wrong suspecting you'.

And this was all, and this the husband read
With chafe enough, till she him pacified: [110]
Desiring, that no griefe in him he bread
Now that he had her words so truely tried:
   But that he would, to him the letter show
   That with his fault he might her goodnes know.

That streight was done with many a boistrous threat,   [115]
That to the Duke, he would his sinne declare,
But now the Courtier gan to smell the feate,
And with some words which shewed little care,
   He stayd untill the goodman was departed,
   Then gave he him the blow which never smarted.   [120]

Thus may you see, the jealous wretch was made
The Pandare of the thing, he most did feare,
Take heed therefore, how you ensue that trade,
Least that some markes of jealousie you beare.
   For sure, no jealousie can that prevent,   [125]
   Whereto two parties once be full content.

111 he] bee Cl Le As Ph Je.   113 he] shee Cl Da Je.   114 fault] shame Ph Ha.
116 Duke] King 93 Ha, ~~Duke~~ prince Ph.   120 which] that Bo Qu Ha.   124
that some] the same 93, that same As, you like Ha.

65

[*Pas*]

WHO doth desire that chaste his wife should be,
First be he true, for truth doth truth deserve:
Then such be he, as she his worth may see,
And one man still, credit with her preserve.

Not toying kinde, nor causlesly unkinde,   [5]
Not sturring thoughts, nor yet denying right,
Not spying faults, nor in plaine errors blinde,
Never hard hand, nor ever raines too light.

As farre from want, as farre from vaine expence,
(The one doth force, the latter doth entise)   [10]
Allow good company, but kepe from thence
Al filthy mouths that glory in their vice.
   This done, thou hast no more, but leave the rest
   To vertue, fortune, time and woman's brest.

66

[*Philisides*]

As I my little flocke on *Ister* banke
(A little flocke; but well my pipe they couthe)
Did piping leade, the Sunne already sanke
Beyond our worlde, and ere I gatt my boothe
Each thing with mantle black the night doth soothe;   [5]
   Saving the glowe worme, which would curteous be
   Of that small light oft watching shepheards see.

The welkin had full niggardly enclosed
In cofer of dimme clowdes his silver groates,
Icleped starres; each thing to rest disposed: [10]
The caves were full, the mountaines voide of goates:
The birds' eyes closde, closed their chirping notes.

65. 93, OA, Hn.   4 still 93.   5 causlesly] yet causeles As Da.   6 right
93.   8 ever] never Cl Le.   10 latter] later 93 St Cl Le Da, tother Hn.
12 mouth's 93.   13 This] Thus Cl Da Ph.
   66. 90-93, OA.   2 they] the 93 Ph.   4 gatt] got 90-93 St As Da Ph Je Qu.
5 soothe] scothe 90-93 St.   9 dimme] deuine Je Qu.   10 Icleped] yeeldeped
As, eclipsed Je Qu.   12 closde 90.   closed] closde St Le Qu, closde vp Cl, did
close As Da, *om.* Ph Je.

As for the Nightingale, woodmusique's King,
It *August* was, he daynde not then to sing.

Amid my sheepe, though I sawe nought to feare, [15]
Yet (for I nothing sawe) I feared sore;
Then founde I which thing is a charge to beare
For for my sheepe I dreaded mickle more
Then ever for my selfe since I was bore:
   I sate me downe: for see to goe ne could, [20]
   And sange unto my sheepe lest stray they should.

The songe I sange old Languet had me taught,
Languet, the shepheard best swift *Ister* knewe,
For clerkly reed, and hating what is naught,
For faithfull hart, cleane hands, and mouth as true: [25]
With his sweet skill my skillesse youth he drewe,
   To have a feeling tast of him that sitts
   Beyond the heaven, far more beyond your witts.

He said, the Musique best thilke powers pleasd
Was jumpe concorde betweene our wit and will: [30]
Where highest notes to godlines are raisd,
And lowest sinke not downe to jote of ill:
With old true tales he woont mine eares to fill,
   How sheepheards did of yore, how now they thrive,
   Spoiling their flock, or while twixt them they strive. [35]

He liked me, but pitied lustfull youth:
His good strong staffe my slippry yeares upbore:
He still hop'd well, because I loved truth;
Till forste to parte, with harte and eyes even sore,
To worthy Coredens he gave me ore. [40]
   But thus in oke's true shade recounted he
   Which now in night's deepe shade sheep heard of me.

14 Nightingale 90.   woodmusique's] wood Musak Cl Le.   15 feare 90.
17 founde] fonde 90 St.   18 For] As 90-93.   dreaded] dradded 90-93 St Le,
~~feared~~ dreaded Cl.   20 sate] satt Cl Le As Da Ph.   see] so Cl Le Da.   22
Languet] *Lanquet* 90-93.   23 Languet] *Lanquet* 90-93.   28 heaven] heauens
Je Qu.   33 mine] my Bo Cl.   38 I] he 90-93.   39 harte] hartes St
Bo Ph.   40 Coredens] *Coriden* 90-93, Coridens Ph, Corydens Je, Corydus Qu.
41 thus] this As Da Ph Je.   he] be St Ph Qu.

Such maner time there was (what time I n'ot)
When all this Earth, this damme or mould of ours,
Was onely won'd with such as beastes begot: [45]
Unknowne as then were they that buylden towers:
The cattell wild, or tame, in nature's bowers
    Might freely rome, or rest, as seemed them:
    Man was not man their dwellings in to hem.

The beastes had sure some beastly pollicie: [50]
For nothing can endure where order n'is.
For once the Lion by the Lambe did lie;
The fearefull Hinde the Leopard did kisse:
Hurtles was Tyger's pawe and Serpent's hisse.
    This thinke I well, the beasts with courage clad [55]
    Like Senators a harmeles empire had.

At which, whether the others did repine,
(For envie harbreth most in feeblest hartes)
Or that they all to chaunging did encline,
(As even in beasts their dammes leave chaunging parts) [60]
The multitude to *Jove* a suite empartes,
    With neighing, blaying, braying, and barking,
    Roring, and howling for to have a King.

A King, in language theirs they said they would:
(For then their language was a perfect speech) [65]
The birdes likewise with chirpes, and puing could,
Cackling, and chattring, that of *Jove* beseech.
Onely the owle still warnde them not to seech
    So hastily that which they would repent:
    But sawe they would, and he to deserts went. [70]

Jove wisely said (for wisedome wisely sayes)
'O beasts, take heed what you of me desire.
Rulers will thinke all things made them to please,
And soone forget the swincke due to their hire.
But since you will, part of my heav'nly fire [75]

44 ours 90.   ours] cures Je Qu.   45 won'd] wened Je Qu.   46 as then were
they] were they as then Bo Le.   buylden] builded 90-93 Bo Le Ph Je Qu.   48 rome]
Ronne Cl Qu, run*n*e As.   49 in to] into 93 St Qu, even to As, had not Ph.
51 n'is] misse As Da Ph Je Qu.   57 which 90.   66 puing] pyinge Cl Ph Qu,
pyninge Le, p̄ving Da.   could 90.   68 still] *om.* Cl Le Ph.   70 deserts]
desert Je Qu.   72 you] ye As Ph.

I will you lende; the rest your selves must give,
That it both seene and felte may with you live'.

Full glad they were and tooke the naked sprite,
Which streight the Earth yclothed in his claye:
The Lion, harte; the Ounce gave active might; [80]
The Horse, good shape; the Sparrow, lust to playe;
Nightingale, voice, entising songes to saye.
    Elephant gave a perfect memorie:
    And Parot, ready tongue, that to applie.

The Foxe gave crafte; the Dog gave flatterie; [85]
Asse, pacience; the Mole, a working thought;
Eagle, high looke; Wolfe secrete crueltie:
Monkie, sweet breath; the Cow, her faire eyes brought;
The Ermion, whitest skinne, spotted with nought;
    The sheep, mild-seeming face; climing, the Beare; [90]
    The Stagge did give the harme eschewing feare.

The Hare, her sleights; the Cat, his melancholie;
Ante, industrie; and Connie, skill to builde;
Cranes, order; Storkes, to be appearing holie;
Camæleon, ease to chaunge; Ducke, ease to yelde; [95]
Crocodile, teares, which might be falsely spilde:
    Ape great thing gave, though he did mowing stand,
    The instrument of instruments, the hand.

Ech other beast likewise his present brings:
And (but they drad their Prince they ofte should want) [100]
They all consented were to give him wings:
And aye more awe towards him for to plant,
To their owne worke this priviledge they graunt,
    That from thenceforth to all eternitie,
    No beast should freely speake, but onely he. [105]

Thus Man was made; thus Man their Lord became:
Who at the first, wanting, or hiding pride,
He did to beastes' best use his cunning frame;
With water drinke, herbes meate, and naked hide,
And fellow-like let his dominion slide; [110]

83 a] *om.* Je Qu.   89 *om.* Le.   92 Hare] Beare Cl Le, harte Je.   his] her Le Je Qu.   95 ease . . . ease] easie . . . easy Je Qu.   97 mowing] mooving Cl Da Je Qu.   100 drad] dread Bo Ph Je Qu, dreed As.   ofte] ought 90-93, *om.* Je.

Not in his sayings saying I, but we:
As if he meant his lordship common be.

But when his seate so rooted he had found,
That they now skilld not, how from him to wend;
Then gan in guiltlesse earth full many a wound,   [115]
Iron to seeke, which gainst it selfe should bend,
To teare the bowels, that good corne should send.
    But yet the common Damme none did bemone;
    Because (though hurt) they never heard her grone.

Then gan he factions in the beastes to breed;   [120]
Where helping weaker sort, the nobler beastes,
(As Tygers, leopards, beares, and Lions' seed)
Disdaind with this, in deserts sought their restes;
Where famine ravine taught their hungrie chestes,
    That craftily he forst them to do ill,   [125]
    Which being done he afterwards would kill.

For murdre done, which never erst was seene,
By those great beastes, as for the weaker's good,
He chose themselves his guarders for to bene,
Gainst those of might, of whom in feare they stood,   [130]
As horse and dogge, not great, but gentle blood:
    Blith were the commons, cattell of the fielde,
    Tho when they saw their foen of greatnes kilde.

But they or spent, or made of slender might,
Then quickly did the meaner cattell finde,   [135]
The great beames gone, the house on shoulders light:
For by and by the horse faire bitts did binde:
The dogge was in a coller taught his kinde.
    As for the gentle birds, like case might rewe
    When falcon they, and gossehauke saw in mewe.   [140]

Worst fell to smallest birds, and meanest heard,
Who now his owne, full like his owne he used.
Yet first but wooll, or fethers off he teard:
And when they were well us'de to be abused,
For hungrie throte their flesh with teeth he brused: [145]

111 sayings] sayinge Cl Le As Ph.   116 gainst] ageanst Cl Da.   120 he] the
90-93.   126 afterwards] after ward As Da Qu.   127 murdre] murthers 90-93 St.
128 weaker's] weaker Je Qu.   132 commons 90.   135 the] theyre Cl Da.
136 great] greaters Bo, greter Je Qu.   138 coller] choller St As Je.   139 birds
90.   142 Who] Whom 90-93.   145 throte] teeth 90-93.

At length for glutton taste he did them kill:
At last for sport their sillie lives did spill.

But yet ô man, rage not beyond thy neede:
Deeme it no gloire to swell in tyrannie.
Thou art of blood; joy not to make things bleede: [150]
Thou fearest death; thinke they are loth to die.
A plaint of guiltlesse hurt doth pierce the skie.
    And you poore beastes, in patience bide your hell,
    Or know your strengths, and then you shall do well.

Thus did I sing, and pipe eight sullen houres   [155]
To sheepe, whom love, not knowledge, made to heare,
Now fancie's fits, now fortune's balefull stowers:
But then I homeward call'd my lambkins deare:
For to my dimmed eyes beganne t'appeare
    The night growne old, her blacke head waxen gray,   [160]
    Sure shepherd's signe, that morne would soone fetch day.

67

Geron   Histor

Geron.   In faith, good *Histor*, long is your delay,
    From holy marriage, sweete and surest meane
    Our foolish lustes in honest rules to stay.
        I pray thee doo to *Lalus*' sample leane:
    Thou seest, how friske, and jolly now he is,   [5]
    That last day seem'd, he could not chew a beane.
        Beleeve me man, there is no greater blisse,
    Then is the quiet joy of loving wife;
    Which who so wants, halfe of himselfe doth misse.
        Friend without change, playfellow without strife,   [10]
    Foode without fulnes, counsaile without pride,
    Is this sweet doubling of our single life.

147 their] the St Bo Ph Qu.   149 gloire] glorie 93 Bo Ph Je Qu, glore St Da, prayse
Cl Le As.   150 make] see 90-93, mak St.   155 sullen] solempne Cl Le Da Ph.
158 homeward] homewards 90-93.   159 t'] to Bo Cl As Da Ph Qu.   161 would]
should 90-93.
    67. 90-93, OA.   2 marriage . . . meane: 90.   3 lustes] lust 90-93.
4 *Lalus*'] kalas Da.   6 chew] chawe St Da Qu, chowe Bo, shewe Ph.

Histor.   No doubt to whom so good chance did betide,
As for to finde a pasture strowed with golde,
He were a foole, if there he did not bide.   [15]

Who would not have a *Phœnix* if he could?
The humming Waspe, if it had not a stinge,
Before all flies the Waspe accept I would.

But this bad world, few golden fieldes doth bring,
Phœnix but one, of Crowes we milllions have: [20]
The Waspe seemes gay, but is a combrous thing.

If many *Kalaes* our *Arcadia* gave,
Lalus' example I would soone ensue,
And thinke, I did my selfe from sorrow save.

But of such wives we finde a slender crew;   [25]
Shrewdnes so stirres, pride so puffes up their hart,
They seldome ponder what to them is due.

With meager lookes, as if they still did smart;
Puiling, and whimpring, or else scolding flat,
Make home more paine then following of the cart.   [30]

Either dull silence, or eternall chat;
Still contrarie to what her husband sayes;
If he do praise the dog, she likes the cat.

Austere she is, when he would honest playes;
And gamesome then, when he thinkes on his sheepe;   [35]
She bids him goe, and yet from jorney stayes.

She warre doth ever with his kinsfolke keepe,
And makes them fremb'd, who frendes by nature are,
Envying shallow toyes with malice deepe.

And if forsooth there come some new found ware,   [40]
The little coine his sweating browes have got,
Must goe for that, if for her lowres he care:

Or els; 'Nay faith, mine is the lucklest lot,
That ever fell to honest woman yet:
No wife but I hath such a man, God wot'.   [45]

Such is their speech, who be of sober wit;

14 strowed] strawed 90–93, strewde Cl Qu, araide Je.   18 flies] flees St Cl, theis Qu.
19 doth] do Da Ph Je.   26 their] the 90–93.   31–33 *om.* Da Ph Je Qu.
31 Either] Ether 90.   37 kinsfolke] kinsfolk*es* Bo As.   38 fremb'd] fremd foe
Cl, frend Da, freme Ph, frend*es* Je, fiende Qu.   frendes] frinds 90–93.   41 have]
hathe Cl Le As Je.   42 lowres] Love Cl Le As Da.   43 lucklest] looklest St,
lucliest Bo Je, Luckless Cl Le Da Ph.   45 hath] haue Bo Cl As Je.

But who doo let their tongues shew well their rage,
Lord, what bywords they speake, what spite they spit?
   The house is made a very lothsome cage,
Wherein the birde doth never sing but cry;   [50]
With such a will that nothing can asswage.
   Dearely the servants doo their wages buy,
Revil'd for ech small fault, sometimes for none:
They better live that in a gaile doo lie.
   Let other fowler spots away be blowne;   [55]
For I seeke not their shame, but still me thinkes,
A better life it is to lye alone.

Geron.   Who for ech fickle feare from vertue shrinkes,
Shall in this life embrace no worthy thing:
No mortall man the cuppe of suretie drinkes.   [60]
   The heav'ns doo not good haps in handfuls bring,
But let us pick our good from out much bad:
That still our little world may know his king.
   But certainly so long we may be glad,
While that we doo what nature doth require,   [65]
And for th'event we never ought be sad.
   Man oft is plag'de with aire, is burnt with fire,
In water dround, in earth his buriall is;
And shall we not therefore their use desire?
   Nature above all things requireth this,   [70]
That we our kind doo labour to maintaine;
Which drawne-out line doth hold all humane blisse.
   Thy father justly may of thee complaine,
If thou doo not repay his deeds for thee,
In granting unto him a grandsire's gaine.   [75]
   Thy common-wealth may rightly grieved be,
Which must by this immortall be preserved,
If thus thou murther thy posteritie.
   His very being he hath not deserved,
Who for a selfe-conceipt will that forbeare,   [80]

47 doo] dothe Cl Le As Da.   51 that] as 90–93.   53 sometimes] some tyme
Cl Le Qu, soneetynee As.   54 gaile] gayole St, geile Bo, Gayle Cl Ph, Gaole Le
As Qu, gaoyle Da, goyall Je.   57 lye] live Cl Je Qu.   59 this] his 90–93.
62 let] lett*es* St Le As.   pick our] pike our 90–93, pick or Bo, pick oute Cl As, o*r* Qu.
65 what] that Le As.   73 justly may of thee] may of thee iustly Le Je.   74 deeds]
debt*es* Je Qu.   78 posteritie] prosperitie Da Je.

Whereby that being aye must be conserved.
    And God forbid, women such cattell were,
As you paint them: but well in you I finde,
No man doth speake aright, who speakes in feare.
    Who onely sees the ill is worse then blind.   [85]
These fiftie winters maried have I beene;
And yet finde no such faults in womankind.
    I have a wife worthie to be a Queene,
So well she can command, and yet obay;
In ruling of a house so well shee's seene.   [90]
    And yet in all this time, betwixt us tway,
We beare our double yoke with such consent,
There never past foule word, I dare well say.
    But these be your love-toyes, which still are spent
In lawlesse games, and love not as you should,   [95]
But with much studie learne late to repent.
    How well last day before our Prince you could
Blinde *Cupid's* workes with wonder testifie?
Yet now the roote of him abase you would.
    Goe to, goe to, and *Cupid* now applie   [100]
To that where thou thy *Cupid* maist avowe,
And thou shalt finde, in women vertues lie.
    Sweete supple mindes which soone to wisdome bowe
Where they by wisdome's Rules directed are,
And are not forst fonde thraldome to allow.   [105]
    As we to get are fram'd, so they to spare:
We made for paine, our paines they made to cherish:
We care abroad, and they of home have care.
    O *Histor*, seeke within thy selfe to flourish:
Thy house by thee must live, or els be gone: [110]
And then who shall the name of *Histor* nourish?
    Riches of children passe a Prince's throne;
Which touch the father's hart with secret joy,
When without shame he saith, 'these be mine owne'.

84 who] y^t As Da, which Je Qu.   86 winters] yeares Le Je Qu.   90 shee's]
shee ys Cl, ys Ph Je.   91 tway] twaine Da Je Qu.   93 There] That 90-93,
their As.   94 be] are Cl Le As.   97 our] yor Cl Je Qu.   103 supple]
simple Je Qu.   104 Where they by] wherby all Je, whereby Qu.   Rules] rule
90-93 Le.   105 are] yet Cl Le As.   107 our paines they made] they made
oure paynes Cl Le As.   108 home] whome Da Ph.   112 Prince's] Princesse
St Le, princely Da.   114 mine] my Da Qu.

Marrie therefore; for marriage will destroy   [115]
Those passions which to youthfull head doo clime,
Mothers and Nurses of all vaine annoy.

Histor.   Perchaunce I will, but nowe me thinkes it tyme
We go unto the Bryde, and use this daye
To speak with her, while freely speak we maye.   [120]

116 passions] poysons Je Qu.   head] head*es* Je Qu.   clime 90.   118–20 *om.*
90–05 (*restored from MS. by* 13).   118 Perchaunce] P*er*happes Je Qu.   me
thinkes] I think Bo Da Ph.   119 We] To 13.

68

[*Aristomenes*]

WHO hath his hire, hath well his labour plast:
Earth thou didst seeke, and store of earth thou hast.

69

[*Basilius*]

O NIGHT, the ease of care, the pledge of pleasure,
Desire's best meane, harvest of hartes affected,
The seate of peace, the throne which is erected
Of humane life to be the quiet measure,

Be victor still of *Phœbus'* golden treasure: [5]
Who hath our sight with too much sight infected,
Whose light is cause we have our lives neglected
Turning all nature's course to selfe displeasure.

These stately starrs in their now shining faces,
With sinlesse sleepe, and silence, wisdome's mother,   [10]
Witnesse his wrong which by thy helpe is eased:

Thou arte therefore of these our desart places
The sure refuge, by thee and by no other
My soule is bliste, sence joyde, and fortune raysed.

70

[*Agelastus*]

SINCE wayling is a bud of causefull sorowe,
Since sorow is the follower of evill fortune,
Since no evill fortune equalls publique damage:

68. 93, OA (*wanting in* Le).   2 didst] dost Bo Cl As Je.
69. 93, OA.   1 Night . . . care 93.   2 harvest] harnest 93.   9 now]
new Ph Je.   10 silence 93.
70. 93, OA.

Now Prince's losse hath made our damage publique,
Sorow pay we unto the rights of Nature, [5]
And inward griefe seale up with outward wailing.

Why should we spare our voice from endlesse wailing,
Who justly make our hearts the seates of sorow?
In such a case where it appeares that nature
Doth add her force unto the sting of fortune: [10]
Choosing alas! this our theatre publique,
Where they would leave trophees of cruell damage,

Then since such pow'rs conspire unto our damage
(Which may be know'n, but never help't with wailing)
Yet let us leave a monument in publique [15]
Of willing teares, torne heare, and cries of sorrow.
For lost, lost is by blowe of cruell fortune
Arcadia's gemme the noblest childe of nature.

O nature doting olde, ô blinded nature,
How hast thou torne thy selfe! sought thine owne damage! [20]
In graunting such a scope to filthy fortune,
By thy impe's losse to fill the world with wailing.
Cast thy stepmother eyes upon our sorowe,
Publique our losse: so, see, thy shame is publique.

O that we had, to make our woes more publique, [25]
Seas in our eyes, and brasen tongues by nature,
A yelling voice, and heartes compos'd of sorow,
Breath made of flames, wits knowing nought but damage,
Our sports murdering our selves, our musiques wailing,
Our studies fixt upon the falles of fortune. [30]

No, no, our mischiefe growes in this vile fortune,
That private panges can not breath out in publique
The furious inward griefes with hellish wailing:

4 Prince's] Princesse St Cl Le Ph.   5 Sorow, 93.   unto the] to thee 93.
6 wailing] waylinges Ph Qu.   8 make] makes Le Ph Qu.   seates] seate 93 Je.
13 conspire] conspir'd 93 Ph Je Qu.   16 heare] haires 93 As Da, cheare Je, hartes
Qu.   18 nature, 93.   20 thine] thy St Bo Ph Je Qu.   22 wai'ling. 93.
24 so] to Cl Da Ph.   27 yelling] yeilding As Qu.   28 wits] with Cl Qu.
29 musiques] Musicke Ph Da Je Qu.   32 panges] paines 93.

But forced are to burthen feeble nature
With secret sense of our eternall damage,
And sorow feede, feeding our soules with sorow.

[35]

Since sorow then concludeth all our fortune,
With all our deathes shew we this damage publique.
His nature feares to die who lives still wailing.

37 fortune 93.

71

Strephon   Klaius

Strephon. Yee Gote-heard Gods, that love the grassie mountaines,
  Yee Nimphes which haunt the springs in pleasant vallies,
  Ye Satyrs joyde with free and quiet forrests,
  Vouchsafe your silent eares to playning musique,
  Which to my woes gives still an early morning: [5]
  And drawes the dolor on till wery evening.

Klaius. O *Mercurie*, foregoer to the evening,
  O heavenlie huntresse of the savage mountaines,
  O lovelie starre, entitled of the morning,
  While that my voice doth fill these wofull vallies,   [10]
  Vouchsafe your silent eares to plaining musique,
  Which oft hath *Echo* tir'd in secrete forrests.

Strephon. I that was once free-burges of the forrests,
  Where shade from Sunne, and sporte I sought in evening,
  I that was once esteem'd for pleasant musique,   [15]
  Am banisht now among the monstrous mountaines
  Of huge despaire, and foule affliction's vallies,
  Am growne a shrich-owle to my selfe each morning.

Klaius. I that was once delighted every morning,
  Hunting the wilde inhabiters of forrests,   [20]
  I that was once the musique of these vallies,
  So darkened am, that all my day is evening,
  Hart-broken so, that molehilles seeme high mountaines,
  And fill the vales with cries in steed of musique.

71. 90, 93, OA, Ra.   1 Yee] You 90 Ra.   2 Yee] You 90 Ra.   which]
that 90 Da Qu Ra.   3 Ye] You 90 Ra.   4 playning] playing Cl Da Ph.
5 gives] giue 93 Ra.   11 plaining] playing Cl Da, pleasaunte Qu Ra.   12 tir'd]
tryed St Je Qu, cryde Ra.   14 sporte] sports 90-93 St.   in] at 90-93.
16 Am] And Cl Le.   among] amongst Cl Le Je Qu Ra.   20 of] of the Cl As
Qu Ra.   21 these] the Cl, those As Da.   24 vales] valleyes Cl As Ph Qu Ra.

Strephon. Long since alas, my deadly Swannish musique   [25]
    Hath made it selfe a crier of the morning,
    And hath with wailing strength clim'd highest mountaines:
    Long since my thoughts more desert be then forrests:
    Long since I see my joyes come to their evening,
    And state throwen downe to over-troden vallies.   [30]

Klaius. Long since the happie dwellers of these vallies,
    Have praide me leave my strange exclaiming musique,
    Which troubles their daye's worke, and joyes of evening:
    Long since I hate the night, more hate the morning:
    Long since my thoughts chase me like beasts in forrests, [35]
    And make me wish my selfe layd under mountaines.

Strephon. Me seemes I see the high and stately mountaines,
    Transforme themselves to lowe dejected vallies:
    Me seemes I heare in these ill-changed forrests,
    The Nightingales doo learne of Owles their musique: [40]
    Me seemes I feele the comfort of the morning
    Turnde to the mortall serene of an evening.

Klaius. Me seemes I see a filthie clowdie evening,
    As soon as Sunne begins to clime the mountaines:
    Me seemes I feele a noysome sent, the morning   [45]
    When I doo smell the flowers of these vallies:
    Me seemes I heare, when I doo heare sweete musique,
    The dreadfull cries of murdred men in forrests.

Strephon. I wish to fire the trees of all these forrests;
    I give the Sunne a last farewell each evening;   [50]
    I curse the fidling finders out of Musicke:
    With envie I doo hate the loftie mountaines;
    And with despite despise the humble vallies:
    I doo detest night, evening, day, and morning.

Klaius. Curse to my selfe my prayer is, the morning: [55]
    My fire is more, then can be made with forrests;
    My state more base, then are the basest vallies:
    I wish no evenings more to see, each evening;
    Shamed I hate my selfe in sight of mountaines,
    And stoppe mine eares, lest I growe mad with Musicke. [60]

35 beasts] beast St Bo Je.   42 Turnde] Turne Cl Qu Ra.   serene] *Siren* Cl Da
Qu Ra, Sereme Le Ph, Syryen Je.   53 despise] do spyte Cl Da.   57 state]
estate Cl Da.   are] ys Cl Da Qu Ra.   58 evenings] Eevening Cl Le Da Ph Qu
Ra.   59 hate] haue 90-93.

Strephon. For she, whose parts maintainde a perfect musique,
    Whose beawties shin'de more then the blushing morning,
    Who much did passe in state the stately mountaines,
    In straightnes past the Cedars of the forrests,
    Hath cast me, wretch, into eternall evening,   [65]
    By taking her two Sunnes from these darke vallies.

Klaius. For she, with whom compar'd, the Alpes are vallies,
    She, whose lest word brings from the spheares their musique,
    At whose approach the Sunne rase in the evening,
    Who, where she went, bare in her forhead morning,   [70]
    Is gone, is gone from these our spoyled forrests,
    Turning to desarts our best pastur'de mountaines.

Strephon. These mountaines witnesse shall, so shall these vallies,
Klaius. These forrests eke, made wretched by our musique,
    Our morning hymne this is, and song at evening.   [75]

72

Strephon   Klaius

Strephon. I Joye in griefe, and doo detest all joyes:
    Despise delight, am tyrde with thought of ease;
    I turne my minde to all formes of annoyes,
    And with the chaunge of them my fancie please.
    I studie that which moste may me displease,   [5]
    And in despite of that displeasure's might,
    Embrace that most, that most my soule destroyes.
    Blinded with beames, fell darkenes is my sight:
    Dwell in my ruines, feede with sucking smarte,
    I thinke from me, not from my woes to parte.   [10]

Klaius. I thinke from me, not from my woes to parte,
    And loth this time, calld life, nay thinke, that life
    Nature to me for torment did emparte;
    Thinke, my harde haps have blunted death's sharpe knife,

---

62 beawties] beautie 90-93 Ra.   65 me wretch 90.   67 with] to 90-93 Ra,
that Qu.   68 word] woordes As Ra.   69 rase] rose 90-93 Qu Ra.   75 this
is] is this 90-93.
    72. 90, 93, OA.   2 am tyrde] and tyrde 90 Ph, ame tryed St, and tyer Cl.
thought] thoughtes Cl Da.   ease 90.   5 moste maye me] may me most 90-93.
9 Dwell in my ruines, feede] Dole on my ruine feedes, 90, Dwell in my ruyns, fedd
Cl Ph, Dwell in my ruyns fled Da, Dull in my ruyns, feede Qu.   12 nay] may Cl Da.

Not sparing me, in whom his workes be rife: [15]
And thinking this, thinke Nature, Life, and Death
Place Sorrowe's triumph on my conquered harte:
Whereto I yeeld, and seeke no other breath,
But from the sent of some infectious grave:
Nor of my fortune ought, but mischieve crave.   [20]

Strephon. Nor of my fortune ought but mischiefe crave,
And seeke to nourish that, which now contaynes
All what I am: if I my selfe will save,
Then must I save, what in my chiefly raignes,
Which is the hatefull web of Sorowe's paines.   [25]
Sorow then cherish me, for I am sorowe:
No being now, but sorowe I can have:
Then decke me as thine owne; thy helpe I borowe,
Since thou my riches arte, and that thou haste
Enough to make a fertill minde lie waste.   [30]

Klaius. Enough to make a fertill minde lie waste
Is that huge storme, which powres it selfe on me:
Hailestones of teares, of sighes a monstrous blast,
Thunders of cries; lightnings my wilde lookes be,
The darkened heav'n my soule which nought can see;   [35]
The flying sprites which trees by rootes up teare
Be those despaires, which have my hopes quite wast.
The diffrence is; all folkes those stormes forbeare:
But I cannot; who then my selfe should flie,
So close unto my selfe my wrackes doo lie.   [40]

Strephon. So close unto my selfe my wrackes doo lie;
Both cause, effect, beginning, and the ende
Are all in me: what helpe then can I trie?
My ship, my selfe, whose course to love doth bende,
Sore beaten doth her mast of Comforte spende: [45]
Her cable, *Reason*, breakes from anchor, *Hope*:
Fancie, her tackling, torne away doth flie:
Ruine, the winde, hath blowne her from her scope:
Brused with waves of Care, but broken is
On rocke, *Despaire*, the buriall of my blisse.   [50]

17 harte] brest 90.   18 no] none 90–93 St.   36 teare] teares Cl Ph.   37 wast]
raste Cl Le As.   39 flie 90.   44 my selfe; 90.   49 Care] *Cares* 90–93.

Klaius. On rocke, *Despaire*, the buriall of my blisse
    I long doo plowe with plough of deepe *Desire*:
    The seed *Fast-meaning* is, no truth to misse:
    I harowe it with *Thoughts*, which all conspire
    Favour to make my chiefe and onely hire.   [55]
    But, woe is me, the yeare is gone about,
    And now I faine would reape, I reape but this,
    Hate fully growne, *Absence* new sprongen out.
    So that I see, although my sight empaire,
    Vaine is their paine, who labour in *Despaire*.   [60]

Strephon. Vaine is their paine, who labour in *Despaire*.
    For so did I, when with my angle, *Will*,
    I sought to catch the fish *Torpedo* faire.
    Ev'n then *Despaire* did *Hope* already kill:
    Yet *Fancie* would perforce employ his skill,   [65]
    And this hath got; the catcher now is caught,
    Lamde with the angle, which it selfe did beare,
    And unto death, quite drownde in *Dolours*, brought
    To death, as then disguisde in her faire face.
    Thus, thus alas, I had my losse in chase.   [70]

Klaius. Thus, thus alas, I had my losse in chase,
    When first that crowned *Basiliske* I knewe,
    Whose footesteps I with kisses oft did trace,
    Till by such hap, as I must ever rewe,
    Mine eyes did light upon her shining hewe,   [75]
    And hers on me, astonisht with that sight.
    Since then my harte did loose his wonted place,
    Infected so with her sweet poyson's might,
    That, leaving me for dead, to her it went:
    But ah her flight hath my dead reliques spent.   [80]

Strephon. But ah her flight hath my dead reliques spent,
    Her flight from me, from me, though dead to me,
    Yet living still in her, while her beames lent
    Such vitall sparke, that her mine eyes might see.

52 doo] to Da Qu.   58 new] nowe Le Da.   sprongen] springe Bo, spronge Cl
Le As.   62 my] myne Cl As.   70 alas, I had] I had, alas, 90.   71 alas.
I had] I had, alas, 90.

But now those living lights absented be,   [85]
Full dead before, I now to dust should fall,
But that eternall paines my soule have hent,
And keepe it still within this body thrall:
That thus I must, while in this death I dwell,
In earthly fetters feele a lasting hell.   [90]

Klaius. In earthly fetters feele a lasting hell
        Alas I doo; from which to finde release,
        I would the earth, I would the heavens sell.
        But vaine it is to thinke those paines should cease,
        Where life is death, and death cannot breed peace. [95]
        O faire, ô onely faire, from thee, alas,
        These foule, most foule, disastres to me fell;
        Since thou from me (ô me) ô Sunne didst passe.
        Therefore esteeming all good blessings toyes,
        I joy in griefe, and doo detest all joyes.   [100]

Strephon. I joye in griefe, and doo detest all joyes.
        But now an ende, (ô *Klaius*) now an ende,
        For even the hearbes our hatefull musique stroyes,
        And from our burning breath the trees doo bende.

73

[*Philisides*]

Now was our heav'nly vaulte deprived of the light
With Sunne's depart: and now the darkenes of the night
Did light those beamye stars which greater light did darke:
Now each thing which enjoy'd that firie quickning sparke
(Which life is cald) were mov'd their spirits to repose,   [5]
And wanting use of eyes their eyes began to close:

87 have] should 90, hath Je Qu.   89 That] Thus Da Je Qu.   93 sell] fell
90-93 Da Ph Qu.   94 those] these 90-93 Ph Je Qu.   97 disastres] distresses
90 Ph.   fell] fall Cl, tell Qu.   99 toyes 90.   102 But] And 90-93.   *Klaius*]
Claius 90-93.   ende 90.   103 hatefull] mournefull 90.
    73. 90-93, OA.   4 which] that 90-93 Je.

A silence sweet each where with one consent embraste
(A musique sweet to one in carefull musing plaste)
And mother Earth, now clad in mourning weeds, did breath
A dull desire to kisse the image of our death: [10]
When I, disgraced wretch, not wretched then, did give
My senses such release, as they which quiet live,
Whose braines boile not in woes, nor brests with beatings ake,
With nature's praise are wont in safest home to take.
Far from my thoughts was ought, whereto their minds aspire, [15]
Who under courtly pompes doo hatch a base desire.
Free all my powers were from those captiving snares,
Which heav'nly purest gifts defile in muddy cares.
Ne could my soule it selfe accuse of such a faulte,
As tender conscience might with furious panges assaulte.   [20]
But like the feeble flower (whose stalke cannot sustaine
His weighty top) his top doth downeward drooping leane:
Or as the silly birde in well acquainted nest
Doth hide his head with cares but onely how to rest:
So I in simple course, and unentangled minde   [25]
Did suffer drousie lids mine eyes then cleare to blinde;
And laying downe my head, did nature's rule observe,
Which senses up doth shut the senses to preserve.
They first their use forgot, then fancies lost their force;
Till deadly sleepe at length possest my living coarse.   [30]
A living coarse I lay: but ah, my wakefull minde
(Which made of heav'nly stuffe no mortal chaunge doth bynde)
Flew up with freer wings of fleshly bondage free;
And having plaste my thoughts, my thoughts thus placed me.
Me thought, nay sure I was, I was in fairest wood   [35]
Of *Samothea* lande; a lande, which whilom stood
An honour to the world, while Honour was their ende,
And while their line of yeares they did in vertue spende.
But there I was, and there my calmie thoughts I fedd
On Nature's sweet repast, as healthfull senses ledd.   [40]
Her giftes my study was, her beauties were my sporte:
My worke her workes to know, her dwelling my resorte.

7 A] And Cl As Qu.   8 musing] Musick Cl Ph Qu.   12 release] reliefe 90–93.
13 boile] broile 90–93, boyles Le Qu.   14 safest] safty Cl Le, saftest Je.
22 drooping] dropping Bo Cl Da Ph.   26 mine] my Bo As.   31 lay] say As
Ph Qu.   32 bynde] blind 90–93 St Da.

Those lampes of heav'nly fire to fixed motion bound,
The ever-turning spheares, the never-moving ground;
What essence dest'nie hath; if fortune be or no;　　　　　　[45]
Whence our immortall soules to mortall earth doo flowe:
What life it is, and how that all these lives doo gather,
With outward maker's force, or like an inward father.
Such thoughts, me thought, I thought, and straind my single mind
Then void of neerer cares, the depth of things to find.　　　[50]
When lo with hugest noise (such noise a tower makes
When it blowne up with myne a fall of ruine takes)
(Or such a noise it was, as highest thunders sende,
Or canons thunder-like, all shot togither, lende)
The moone a sunder rent (O godes, o pardon me,　　　　　[55]
That forced with grief reveales what greeved eyes dyd see)
The Moone a sunder rent; whereat with sodaine fall
(More swift then falcon's stoope to feeding Falconer's call)
There came a chariot faire by doves and sparrowes guided:
Whose stormelike course staid not till hard by me it bided.　[60]
I, wretch, astonisht was, and thought the deathfull doome
Of heaven, of earth, of hell, of time and place was come.
But streight there issued forth two Ladies (Ladies sure
They seemd to me) on whom did waite a Virgin pure:
Straunge were the Ladies' weeds; yet more unfit then strange. [65]
The first with cloth's tuckt up as Nymphes in woods do range;
Tuckt up even with the knees, with bowe and arrowes prest:
Her right arme naked was, discovered was her breast.
But heavy was her pace, and such a meagre cheere,
As little hunting minde (God knowes) did there appeere.　　[70]
The other had with arte (more then our women knowe,
As stuffe meant for the sale set out to glaring showe)
A wanton woman's face, and with curld knots had twinde
Her haire, which by the helpe of painter's cunning, shinde.
When I such guests did see come out of such a house,　　　[75]
The mountaines great with childe I thought brought foorth a mouse.
But walking forth, the first thus to the second saide,

47 doo gather] dothe gather St Bo, together As.　　　　50 depth] Depthes Cl Da.
51 When] Who Cl Ph Qu.　　a] as Cl, no Ph Da Je Qu.　　　52 up with myne]
downe with winde 90-93.　　　53 Or] But Da Ph Je Qu.　　thunders] thunder Bo As.
55-56 om. 90-93.　　　55 rent O godes o pardon me St.　　　56 with] muche St.
see St.　　　57 whereat] whereout 90-93.　　　61 I wretch 90.　　　67 with] to Cl
Le.　　70 did there] there did Da Qu.

'*Venus* come on': said she, '*Diane* you are obaide'.
Those names abasht me much, when those great names I hard:
Although their fame (me seemd) from truth had greatly jard.   [80]
As I thus musing stood, *Diana* cald to her
Her waiting Nymphe, a Nymphe that did excell as farr
All things that earst I sawe, as orient pearles exceed,
That which their mother hight, or els their silly seed.
Indeed a perfect hewe, indeed a sweet consent   [85]
Of all those Graces' giftes the heavens have ever lent.
And so she was attirde, as one that did not prize
Too much her peerles parts, nor yet could them despise.
But cald, she came apace; a pace wherein did move
The bande of beauties all, the little world of Love.   [90]
And bending humbled eyes (ô eyes the Sunne of sight)
She waited mistresse' will: who thus disclosd her spright.
'Sweet *Mira* mine' (quoth she) 'the pleasure of my minde,
In whom of all my rules the perfect proofe I finde,
To onely thee thou seest we graunt this speciall grace   [95]
Us to attend, in this most private time and place.
Be silent therefore now, and so be silent still
Of what thou seest: close up in secrete knot thy will'.
She answer'd was with looke, and well perform'd behest:
And *Mira* I admirde: her shape sank in my brest.   [100]
But thus with irefull eyes, and face that shooke with spite
Diana did begin. 'What mov'd me to invite
Your presence (sister deare) first to my Moony spheare,
And hither now, vouchsafe to take with willing eare.
I know full well you know, what discord long hath raign'd   [105]
Betwixt us two; how much that discord foule hath stain'd
Both our estates, while each the other did deprave,
Proofe speakes too much to us that feeling triall have.
Our names are quite forgot, our temples are defac'd:
Our offrings spoil'd, our priests from priesthood are displac'd. [110]
Is this thy fruite O strife? those thousand churches hie,
Those thousand altars faire now in the dust to lie?

78 *Diane*] *Diana* Cl Le Da Ph Qu.   82 Her] The 90–93.   88 Too] So **Cl Le Da.**
91 Sunne] soñe St, summ Bo Le As Je.   sight] Lighte Cl Da Ph.   92 thus] this
As Qu.   98 what] that 90–93.   100 sank] sonke 90–93, canke Bo.   101 **face
that shooke**] face trembling Ph Je, tremblinge face Qu.   103 Moony] moovy Cl Da,
moonishe As, Mony Ph Qu.   110 *om.* Qu.   priests] priest 90.   displac'd 90.
111 thy] the 90–93 Da Ph Je.   O] of 90–93 Cl Je, or As.

In mortall mindes our mindes but planets' names preserve:
No knee once bowed, forsooth, for them they say we serve.
Are we their servants growne? no doubt a noble staye: [115]
Celestiall powers to wormes, *Jove's* children serve to claye.
But such they say we be: this praise our discord bred,
While we for mutuall spight a striving passion fed.
But let us wiser be; and what foule discorde brake,
So much more strong againe let fastest concorde make.   [120]
Our yeares doo it require: you see we both doo feele
The weakning worke of Time's for ever-whirling wheele.
Although we be divine, our grandsire *Saturne* is
With age's force decay'd, yet once the heaven was his.
And now before we seeke by wise *Apollo's* skill   [125]
Our young yeares to renew (for so he saith he will)
Let us a perfect peace betwixt us two resolve:
Which lest the ruinous want of government dissolve;
Let one the Princesse be, to her the other yeeld:
For vaine equalitie is but contention's field.   [130]
And let her have the giftes that should in both remaine:
In her let beautie both, and chastnesse fully raigne.
So as if I prevaile, you give your giftes to me:
If you, on you I lay what in my office be.
Now resteth only this, which of us two is she,   [135]
To whom precedence shall of both accorded be.
For that (so that you like) hereby doth lie a youth
(She beckned unto me) as yet of spotlesse truth,
Who may this doubt discerne: for better, witt, then lot
Becommeth us: in us fortune determines not.   [140]
This crowne of amber faire (an amber crowne she held)
To worthiest let him give, when both he hath beheld:
And be it as he saith'. *Venus* was glad to heare
Such proffer made, which she well showd with smiling cheere.
As though she were the same, as when by *Paris'* doome   [145]
She had chiefe Goddesses in beautie overcome.
And smirkly thus gan say. 'I never sought debate
Diana deare; my minde to love and not to hate

114 knee] knees 90-93.   121 it] yet Cl Le Da Ph Qu.   126 he saith] saithe
hee Le Ph.   127 betwixt] betweene 90-93.   129 to her the other] the other
to her As Qu.   130 contention's] a Contentious Ph Qu.   field 90.   135-6 *om.*
Je.   136 precedence] precedentes St Cl Le Qu, president As.

Was ever apt: but you my pastimes did despise.
I never spited you, but thought you overwise.   [150]
Now kindnesse profred is, none kinder is then I:
And so most ready am this meane of peace to trie.
And let him be our judge: the lad doth please me well'.
Thus both did come to me, and both began to tell
(For both togither spake, each loth to be behinde)   [155]
That they by solemne oth their Deities would binde
To stand unto my will: their will they made me know.
I that was first agast, when first I saw their showe:
Now bolder waxt, waxt prowde, that I such sway might beare:
For neere acquaintance dooth diminish reverent feare.   [160]
And having bound them fast by *Styx*, they should obaye
To all what I decreed, did thus my verdict saye.
'How ill both you can rule, well hath your discord taught:
Ne yet for what I see, your beauties merite ought.
To yonder Nymphe therefore (to *Mira* I did point)   [165]
The crowne above you both for ever I appoint'.
I would have spoken out: but out they both did crie;
'Fie, fie, what have we done? ungodly rebell fie.
But now we muste needs yeelde, to what our othes require'.
'Yet thou shalt not go free (quoth *Venus*) such a fire   [170]
Her beautie kindle shall within thy foolish minde,
That thou full oft shalt wish thy judging eyes were blinde'.
'Nay then (*Diana* said) the chastnesse I will give
In ashes of despaire (though burnt) shall make thee live'.
'Nay thou (said both) shalt see such beames shine in her face   [175]
That thou shalt never dare seeke helpe of wretched case'.
And with that cursed curse away to heaven they fled,
First having all their giftes upon faire *Mira* spred.
The rest I cannot tell, for therewithall I wak'd
And found with deadly feare that all my sinewes shak'd.   [180]
Was it a dreame? O dreame, how hast thou wrought in me,
That I things erst unseene should first in dreaming see?
And thou ô traytour Sleepe, made for to be our rest,
How hast thou framde the paine wherewith I am opprest?

---

150 overwise] eu*er* wise Ph Qu.   159 might] must 90-93, should Ph.   164 what]
ought 90-93 Cl, *om.* Le.   165-86 *om.* Je (*blank leaf*).   169 muste needes . . .
what] needs must . . . that 90-93.   173 the] thee Cl Le Ph.   177 heaven]
heavens Cl Le As.   180 sinewes] sences Le Qu.   183 thou] then Bo Cl Da Ph.

O cowarde *Cupid* thus doost thou thy honour keepe,   [185]
Unarmde (alas) unwarn'd to take a man asleepe?

74

[Philisides]

˗◡◡˗˗˗˗˗˗˗˗◡◡˗˗
˗˗˗◡◡˗˗◡◡˗◡◡˗

UNTO the caitife wretch, whom long affliction holdeth,
  and now fully beleeves helpe to be quite perished;
Grant yet, grant yet a looke, to the last monument of his anguish,
  O you (alas so I find) cause of his onely ruine.
Dread not a whit (O goodly cruell) that pittie may enter   [5]
  into thy hart by the sight of this Epistle I send:
And so refuse to behold of these strange wounds the recitall,
  least it might thee allure home to thy selfe to returne,
(Unto thy selfe I do meane those graces dwell so within thee,
  gratefulnes, sweetnes, holy love, hartie regard)   [10]
Such thing cannot I seeke (Despaire hath giv'n me my answer
  despaire most tragicall clause to a deadly request)
Such thing cannot he hope, that knowes thy determinat hardnes;
  hard like a rich marbell: hard, but a faire Diamond.
Can those eyes, that of eyes drownd in most harty flowing teares, [15]
  (teares and teares of a man) had no returne to remorse;
Can those eyes now yeeld to the kind conceit of a sorow,
  which inke onely relates, but ne laments, ne replies?
Ah, that, that do I not conceive, though that to me leefe were
  more then *Nestor's* yeares, more then a King's diademe.   [20]
Ah, that, that do I not conceive; to the heaven when a mouse climes
  then may I hope t'atchieve grace of a heavenly tiger.
But, but alas, like a man condemn'd doth crave to be heard speake,
  not that he hopes for amends of the desaster he feeles,

186 unwarn'd] vnwares 90, vnarmde Cl As Da Ph Qu.
 74. 90, 93, Cm (*lines 1–16 only*), OA, Hn. *Scansion in* St Bo Cl As Qu *only*;
St Bo *show extra final syllable.*   1–28 *om.* Je.   1 the] a 90–93 Cm, ~~the~~ a St.
3 monument] moment As Ph, momt Qu.   8 thee] th' 90–93, the Cm Bo As, the'
Hn.   15 those] these Da Qu.   eyes that 90.   19–20 *om.* Da.   19–21
though . . . conceive] *om.* As.   19 that do I] that I do I 90–93 Bo, I do Cl.   con-
ceiue (though . . . were) 90.   me leefe] my blisse 90–93, me life Bo Le, mee sure Ph.
21 that do I] that I do 90 Hn, I do Cl Da.   23 speake 90.

But finding th'approch of death with an inly relenting,   [25]
  gives an adieu to the world, as to his onely delight:
Right so my boiling hart, enflam'de with fire of a faire eye,
  bubling out doth breathe signes of his hugie dolours:
Now that he finds to what end his life and love be reserved,
  and that he thence must part where to live onely I lyved.   [30]
O faire, O fairest, are such the triumphs to thy fairnesse?
  can death beautie become? must I be such a monument?
Must I be onely the marke, shall prove that Vertue is angrie?
  shall prove that fiercenes can with a white dove abide?
Shall to the world appeare that faith and love be rewarded   [35]
  with mortall disdaine, bent to unendly revenge?
Unto revenge? O sweete, on a wretch wilt thou be revenged?
  shall such high Plannets tend to the losse of a worme?
And to revenge who doo bend, would in that kind be revenged,
  as th'offence was done, and goe beyond if he can.   [40]
All my'offence was Love: with Love then must I be chastned,
  and with more, by the lawes that to Revenge doo belong.
If that love be a fault, more fault in you to be lovely:
  Love never had me opprest, but that I saw to be lov'd.
You be the cause that I love: what Reason blameth a shadowe, [45]
  that with a body't goes? since by a body it is.
If the Love hate you dyd, you should your beautie have hidden:
  you should those faire eyes have with a veile covered.
But foole, foole that I am, those eyes would shine from a dark
  cave.
  what veiles then doo prevaile, but to a more miracle?   [50]
Or those golden lockes, those lockes which lock me to bondage,
  torne you should disperse unto the blasts of a winde.
But foole, foole that I am, tho I had but a hair of her head found,
  ev'n as I am, so I should unto that haire be a thrall.
Or with a fair hand's nailes (ô hand which nailes me to this death)
  you should have your face (since Love is ill) blemished.   [56]

25 inly] ougly 90.   28 breathe] breath 90-93 Bo As Hn.   30 thence] hence
90 Cl.   live onely I lyved] liue onely he lou'd 90, liue onely he liu'd 93.   31 the]
thy 93 Da, to the Bo, om. As.   32 I be such a] be such a 90, I be such 93 Bo
Cl Je Qu Hn.   34 that] the that Cl, the Ph.   38-39 om. Cl.   38 tend]
ende 90, tread Da.   40 was] ys Cl Ph.   45 love] lou'd 90-93.   47 the] that
90-93 Ph Hn. Hate St. hate you dyd] you did hate 90-93, you hate Ph.   51 lock]
locks Le Ph, lookt Da, lockt Je.   54 I should] shoulde I Da Qu.   55 with
a] with 90-93 Da Je. hands-nailes 90. this] om. Cl As.

O wretch, what do I say? should that faire face be defaced?
  should my too-much sight cause so true a Sunne to be lost?
First let *Cimmerian* darknes be my onel'habitaco'n:
  first be mine eyes pulde out, first be my braine perished;   [60]
Ere that I should consent to doo such excessive a dammage
  unto the earth, by the hurt of this her heavenly jewell.
O not but such love you say you could have afoorded,
  as might learne Temp'rance voyde of a rage's events.
O sweet simplicitie: from whence should Love be so learned? [65]
  unto *Cupid* that boy shall a Pedante be found?
Well: but faultie I was: Reason to my Passion yeelded,
  Passion unto my rage, Rage to a hastie revenge.
But what's this for a fault, for which such faieth be abolisht,
  such faith, so staineles, inviolate, violent?   [70]
Shall I not? ô may I not thus yet refresh the remembrance,
  what sweete joyes I had once, and what a place I did hold?
Shall I not once object, that you, you graunted a favour
  unto the man, whom now such miseries you awarde?
Bend your thoghts to the dear sweet words which then to me giv'n
    were: [75]
  think what a world is now, think who hath altred her hart.
What? was I then worthie such good, now worthie so muche evill?
  now fled, then cherished? then so nie, now so remote?
Did not a rosed breath, from lips more rosie proceeding,
  say, that I well shuld finde in what a care I was had?   [80]
With much more: now what doo I finde, but Care to abhor me,
  Care that I sinke in griefe, Care that I live banished?
And banished doo I live, nor now will seeke a recov'rie,
  since so she will, whose will is to me more then a lawe.
If then a man in most ill case may give you a farewell;   [85]
  farewell, long farewell, all my woe, all my delight.

57 do] did Cl As Hn.   61 a] *om.* Le Qu.   62 jewell] Ivill Bo, evell Cl,
Iswell Qu.   63 not] no: 90.   64 a rage's] outragius Cl, rages Le Ph Je.
65 be so] so be 90.   66 shall] shoulde Cl Le As.   Pedante] Padante St,
pechante Bo, pendaunt Cl Le, picture Ph, pelante Je, pendan*tes* Qu, pedantee Hn.
69 faieth be] fault is 90, faithe is Le.   77 such] of suche Cl As Hn.   so muche]
such 90-93, to muche Ph.   80 well shuld] should well 90-93, will should As.

75

[*Dicus*]

SINCE that to death is gone the shepheard hie,
  Who most the silly shepheard's pipe did pryse,
  Your dolefull tunes sweete *Muses* now applie.

And you ô trees (if any life there lies
  In trees) now through your porous barkes receave   [5]
  The straunge resounde of these my causefull cries:
And let my breath upon your braunches cleave,
  My breath distinguish'd into wordes of woe,
  That so I may signes of my sorrowe leave.
But if among yourselves some one tree growe,   [10]
  That aptest is to figure miserie,
  Let it embassage beare your grieves to showe.
The weeping Myrrhe I thinke will not denie
  Her helpe to this, this justest cause of plaint.
  Your dolefull tunes sweet *Muses* now applie.   [15]

And thou poore Earth, whom fortune doth attaint
  In Nature's name to suffer such a harme,
  As for to lose thy gemme, our earthly Sainct,
Upon thy face let coaly Ravens swarme:
  Let all the Sea thy teares accounted be: [20]
  Thy bowels with all killing mettals arme.
Let golde now rust, let Diamonds waste in thee:
  Let pearls be wan with woe their damme doth beare:
  Thy selfe henceforth the light doo never see.
And you, ô flowers, which sometimes Princes were,   [25]
  Till these straunge altrings you did hap to trie,
  Of Prince's losse your selves for tokens reare.
Lilly in mourning blacke thy whitenes die:
  O *Hiacinthe* let *Ai* be on thee still.
  Your dolefull tunes sweet *Muses* now applie.   [30]

---

75. 90, 93, OA.   2 Who] Whom 90.   7 cleave] leaue 90.   12 em-
bassage] Embasshade St, embassade Bo As, (embraced) Cl, imbassage Le, ambassage
Da Je, imbusshed Ph, embashed Qu.   18 lose] loose 90-93 Cl Le Ph Je Qu.
our earthly] and such a 90-93, or earthly Cl, thy earthly Je.   28 mourning]
Morning Cl Le, morne in Da Ph Je Qu.

O *Echo*, all these woods with roaring fill,
    And doo not onely marke the accents last,
    But all, for all reach not my wailefull will:
One *Echo* to another *Echo* cast
    Sounde of my griefes, and let it never ende,   [35]
    Till that it hath all woods and waters past.
Nay to the heav'ns your just complayninges sende,
    And stay the starrs' inconstant constant race,
    Till that they doo unto our dolours bende:
And aske the reason of that speciall grace,   [40]
    That they, which have no lives, should live so long,
    And vertuous soules so soone should lose their place?
Aske, if in great men good men so do thronge,
    That he for want of elbowe roome must die?
    Or if that they be skante, if this be wronge?   [45]
Did Wisedome this our wretched time espie
    In one true chest to rob all Vertue's treasure?
    Your dolefull tunes sweete *Muses* now applie.

And if that any counsell you to measure
    Your dolefull tunes, to them still playning say,   [50]
    To well felte griefe, plainte is the onely pleasure.
O light of Sunne, which is entit'led day,
    O well thou doost that thou no longer bidest;
    For mourning night her blacke weedes may display.
O *Phœbus* with good cause thy face thou hidest,   [55]
    Rather then have thy all-beholding eye
    Fould with this sight, while thou thy chariot guidest.
And well (me thinks) becomes this vaultie skie
    A stately tombe to cover him deceased.
    Your dolefull tunes sweet *Muses* now applie.   [60]

O *Philomela* with thy brest oppressed
    By shame and griefe, helpe, helpe me to lament
    Such cursed harmes as cannot be redressed.

31 roaring] roaringes St Bo Je, scritching Ph.   32–34 *om*. As.   33 not] out
90–93.   37 complayninges] complaining 90–93 Da Qu.   38 inconstant] in
constant St Da Ph, vnconstant Cl Le, Inconst As, Constants Qu.   39 our] your
As Ph.   42 lose] loose 90–93 Bo Ph Je Qu, leave Cl.   43 so do] doo so 90–93
Da Ph.   47 Vertue's] vertuous Cl Qu.   50 playning] playinge Bo Cl Da.
54 night] light 90–93.   57 thy] the Cl Ph.

Or if thy mourning notes be fully spent,
   Then give a quiet eare unto my playning: [65]
   For I to teach the world complainte am bent.
Yee dimmy clowdes, which well employ your stayning
   This cheerefull aire with your obscured cheere,
   Witnesse your wofull teares with daily rayning.
And if, ô Sunne, thou ever didst appeare,   [70]
   In shape, which by man's eye might be perceived;
   Vertue is dead, now set thy triumph here.
Now set thy triumph in this world, bereaved
   Of what was good, where now no good doth lie;
   And by thy pompe our losse will be conceaved.   [75]
O notes of mine your selves together tie:
   With too much griefe me thinkes you are dissolved.
   Your dolefull tunes sweete *Muses* now applie.

Time ever old, and yonge is still revolved
   Within it selfe, and never taketh ende: [80]
   But mankind is for aye to nought resolved.
The filthy snake her aged coate can mende,
   And getting youth againe, in youth doth flourish:
   But unto Man, age ever death doth sende.
The very trees with grafting we can cherish,   [85]
   So that we can long time produce their time:
   But Man which helpeth them, helplesse must perish.
Thus, thus the mindes, which over all doo clime,
   When they by yeares' experience get best graces,
   Must finish then by death's detested crime.   [90]
We last short while, and build long lasting places:
   Ah let us all against foule Nature crie:
   We Nature's workes doo helpe, she us defaces.
For how can Nature unto this reply?
   That she her child, I say, her best child killeth?   [95]
   Your dolefull tunes sweete Muses now apply.

Alas, me thinkes, my weakned voice but spilleth,
   The vehement course of this just lamentation:
   Me thinkes, my sound no place with sorrow filleth.

67 Yee] You 90–93.   75 thy] the Cl Da Ph.   80 taketh] tasteth 90–93, takeste
St.   81 resolved] dissolved Le As Da Ph Je Qu.   83 againe, in youth doth]
in yowth ageane can Cl Qu.   90 then] them Le Qu.   94 reply] apply Cl Le.

I know not I, but once in detestation   [100]
   I have my selfe, and all what life containeth,
   Since Death on Vertue's fort hath made invasion.
One word of woe another after traineth:
   Ne doo I care how rude be my invention,
   So it be seene what sorrow in me raigneth.   [105]
O Elements, by whose (they say) contention,
   Our bodies be in living power maintained,
   Was this man's death the fruite of your dissention?
O Phisicke's power, which (some say) hath refrayned
   Approch of death, alas thou helpest meagerly,   [110]
   When once one is for *Atropos* distrained.
Great be Physitions' brags, but aid is beggerly,
   When rooted moisture failes, or groweth drie,
   They leave off al, and say, death comes too eagerlie.
They are but words therefore which men do buy,   [115]
   Of any since God *AEsculapius* ceased.
   Your dolefull tunes sweete Muses now applie.

Justice, justice is now (alas) oppressed:
   Bountifulnes hath made his last conclusion:
   Goodnes for best attire in dust is dressed.   [120]
Shepheards bewaile your uttermost confusion;
   And see by this picture to you presented,
   Death is our home, life is but a delusion.
For see alas, who is from you absented.
   Absented? nay I say for ever banished   [125]
   From such as were to dye for him contented.
Out of our sight in turne of hand is vanished
   Shepherd of shepherds, whose well setled order
   Private with welth, publike with quiet garnished.
While he did live, farre, farre was all disorder;   [130]
   Example more prevailing then direction,
   Far was homestrife, and far was foe from border.
His life a law, his looke a full correction:
   As in his health we healthfull were preserved,
   So in his sicknesse grew our sure infection.   [135]

106 they] men 90-93.   107 power] powers Le Qu.   109 refrayned] restrained
90-93 Cl.   115 which] that 90-93.   116 God] good Bo Ph Je Qu, *om.* Cl.
124 absented? 90.   126 contented? 90.

His death our death. But ah; my Muse hath swarved,
 From such deepe plaint as should such woes descrie,
 Which he of us for ever hath deserved.
The stile of heavie hart can never flie
 So high, as should make such a paine notorious: [140]
 Cease Muse therfore: thy dart ô Death applie;
And farewell Prince, whom goodnesse hath made glorious.

76

[*Agelastus*]

FAREWELL ô Sunn, *Arcadia's* clearest light:
Farewell ô pearl, the poore man's plenteous treasure:
Farewell ô golden staffe, the weake man's might:
Farewell ô Joy, the wofull's onely pleasure.
Wisdome farewell, the skillesse man's direction: [5]
Farewell with thee, farewell all our affection.

For what place now is lefte for our affection,
Now that of purest lampe is queint the light,
Which to our darkned mindes was best direction;
Now that the mine is lost of all our treasure,   [10]
Now death hath swallow'd up our worldly pleasure,
We Orphans lefte, void of all publique might?

Orphans in deede, depriv'd of father's might:
For he our father was in all affection,
In our well-doing placing all his pleasure,   [15]
Still studying how to us to be a light.
As well he was in peace a safest treasure:
In warr his wit and word was our direction.

Whence, whence alas, shall we seeke our direction!
When that we feare our hatefull neighbours' might,   [20]
Who long have gap't to get *Arcadians'* treasure.
Shall we now finde a guide of such affection,
Who for our sakes will thinke all travaile light,
And make his paine to keepe us safe his pleasure?

137 plaint] playntes Le Qu.
76. 93, OA. 1 clearest] cheifest Bo Je, cearest Ph. 4 wofull's] ioyfulls 93.
5 skillesse] skill of Da, skillest Ph Je. 8 queint] quench'd 93 Ph, quynt Le, quienct
As, quenchest Je, quentch Qu. 9 direction? 93. 10 treasure? 93. 12 lefte]
made 93, *om.* Ph.

No, no, for ever gone is all our pleasure;   [25]
For ever wandring from all good direction;
For ever blinded of our clearest light;
For ever lamed of our suerest might;
For ever banish'd from well plac'd affection;
For ever robbed of our royall treasure.   [30]

Let teares for him therefore be all our treasure,
And in our wailfull naming him our pleasure:
Let hating of our selves be our affection,
And unto death bend still our thoughts' direction.
Let us against our selves employ our might,   [35]
And putting out our eyes seeke we our light.

Farewell our light, farewell our spoiled treasure:
Farewell our might, farewell our daunted pleasure:
Farewell direction, farewell all affection.

28 suerest] sured 93, fairest Ph.   30 robbed of] robd of all 93.   31 for him
therefore] therefore for hym Le Da.   36 our eyes] of eyes Cl Le.   38 daunted]
dainted Bo Cl, dampned Qu.

77

[*Musidorus*]

SINCE nature's workes be good, and death doth serve
As nature's worke: why should we feare to dye?
Since feare is vaine, but when it may preserve,
Why should we feare that which we cannot flye?

Feare is more paine, then is the paine it feares, [5]
Disarming humane mindes of native might:
While each conceate an ouglie figure beares,
Which were not evill, well vew'd in reason's light.

Our owly eyes, which dimm'd with passions bee,
And scarce discerne the dawne of comming day, [10]
Let them be clearde, and now begin to see,
Our life is but a step in dustie way.
  Then let us holde the blisse of peacefull minde,
  Since this we feele, great losse we cannot finde.

77. 93, OA.   2 worke] worckes Cl Le.   4 feare, 93.   6 mindes, 93.
7 conceate, 93.   8 well vew'd] well wayed Cl Le, *om*. Ph.   9 owly] onely
As Ph.   12 step, 93.   13–14 *om*. Ph.   13 holde, 93.   14 this] that
Da Je.

CERTAIN SONNETS

CERTAIN SONNETS

I

SINCE shunning paine, I ease can never find:
Since bashfull dread seekes where he knowes me harmed:
Since will is won, and stopped eares are charmed:
Since force doth faint, and sight doth make me blind:

Since loosing long, the faster still I bind: [5]
Since naked sence can conquer reason armed:
Since heart in chilling feare with yce is warmed:
In fine, since strife of thought but marres the mind,

I yeeld, ô Love, unto thy loathed yoke,
Yet craving law of armes, whose rule doth teach,   [10]
That hardly usde, who ever prison broke,
In justice quit, of honour made no breach:
    Whereas if I a gratefull gardien have,
    Thou art my Lord, and I thy vowed slave.

2

WHEN Love puft up with rage of hy disdaine,
Resolv'd to make me patterne of his might,
Like foe, whose wits inclin'd to deadly spite,
Would often kill to breed more feeling paine,

He would not arm'd with beautie, only raigne   [5]
On those affectes which easily yeeld to sight,
But vertue sets so high, that reason's light,
For all his strife can onlie bondage gaine.

Title in 98 Cl Bo *only*: Certaine Sonets Written By Sir Philip Sidney: Neuer before
printed 98, Dyuers and sondry Sonett*es* Cl, Certein lowse Sonnett*es* and songes Bo.
1. 98, Bo, Hn, Di.   4 blind. 98.
2. 98, Bo, Di.   4 paine. 98.

So that I live to pay a mortall fee,
Dead palsie sicke of all my chiefest parts: [10]
Like those whom dreames make uglie monsters see,
And can crie helpe with nought but grones and starts:
  Longing to have, having no wit to wish,
  To starving minds such is God *Cupid's* dish.

3

To the tune of *Non credo gia che piu infelice amante*

THE fire to see my wrongs for anger burneth:
The aire in raine for my affliction weepeth:
The sea to ebbe for griefe his flowing turneth:
The earth with pitie dull the center keepeth:
  Fame is with wonder blazed: [5]
  Time runnes away for sorow:
  Place standeth still amazed
To see my night of evils, which hath no morow.
  Alas, all onely she no pitie taketh,
  To know my miseries, but chaste and cruell: [10]
  My fall her glorie maketh,
  Yet still her eyes give to my flames their fuell.

Fire burne me quite, till sense of burning leave me:
Aire let me draw no more thy breath in anguish:
Sea drownd in thee, of tedious life bereave me: [15]
Earth take this earth, wherein my spirits languish.
  Fame say I was not borne:
  Time haste my dying hower:
  Place see my grave uptorne:
  Fire, aire, sea, earth, fame, time, place, shew your power. [20]

3. 98, Fr, 93; Cl, Bo, St; Cm (*incipit only*), 90; Hn; Dd; Ra, Bn, Hy.   *Heading in* 98 Cl Bo St *only*: To the tune of] *om.* St.   *gia*] giu St.   *amante*] avante Cl, anute St. *Headed* A Louers complaint Bn.   1 wrongs] woes Cm 90 Hn, wrong Dd.   2 my] myne Ra Bn.   4 the] his Cl Bo St 90-93.   center] Centure Cl St.   keepeth] turneth 90, kepes Dd.   8 night] nyghtes Ra Bn.   evils] ill Fr, ils 90, woes Hn, greife Ra, euill Bn Hy.   which] that Fr Hn Ra.   hath] haue Bo Bn Hy.   9 all onely] a louely 98, alonely Bo Hn, onely Bn Hy.   10 know] see Hn Ra Bn.   miseries] mystryes Hn, misery Ra Hy.   12 their] the Fr Cl, onely Hn.   13 quite] quick Bn Hy.   me] *om.* Ra Bn.   14 no more thy breath] no more my breathe Cl Hy, thy breath no more 90-93, no more this breath Hn, my breathe no more Ra Bn.   15 drownd] drowne me Ra Bn, drownde me Hy.   16 my] these Ra Bn Hy.   18 haste my dying] draw my dismall Bn Hy.

Alas, from all their helps I am exiled,
For hers am I, and death feares her displeasure.
Fie death, thou are beguiled,
Though I be hers, she makes of me no treasure.

4

To the same tune

THE Nightingale, as soone as Aprill bringeth
Unto her rested sense a perfect waking,
While late bare earth, proud of new clothing springeth,
Sings out her woes, a thorne her song-booke making:
   And mournfully bewailing,   [5]
   Her throate in tunes expresseth
   What griefe her breast oppresseth,
For *Thereus'* force on her chaste will prevailing.
    O *Philomela* faire, ô take some gladnesse,
    That here is juster cause of plaintfull sadnesse: [10]
    Thine earth now springs, mine fadeth,
    Thy thorne without, my thorne my heart invadeth.

Alas she hath no other cause of anguish
But *Thereus'* love, on her by strong hand wrokne,
Wherein she suffring all her spirits' languish,   [15]
Full womanlike complaines her will was brokne.
   But I who dayly craving,
   Cannot have to content me,
   Have more cause to lament me,
Since wanting is more woe then too much having.   [20]
    O *Philomela* faire, ô take some gladnesse,
    That here is juster cause of plaintfull sadnesse:
    Thine earth now springs, mine fadeth:
    Thy thorne without, my thorne my heart invadeth.

21 their] yor Cl Ra.   helps] helpe 98 Cl St 90.   22 hers am I] I am hers Hn,
hers I am Ra Hy.   23 Fie] O Ra Bn Hy.   24 she makes of me] of me she
makes Fr, shee set*tes* by mee Cl St 90.

4. 98, Cl, Bo.   *Heading in* 98 *only.*   1 Nightingale 98.   21–24 O
Philomela fayre, O take &c vt antea. Cl, O Philomela fare o take &c vt supra. Bo.

5

O MY thoughtes' sweete foode, my my onely owner,
   O my heavens for taste by thie heavenly pleasure,
O the fayre *Nymphe* borne to doo woemen honor,
               Lady my Treasure.

Where bee now those Joyes, that I lately tasted?   [5]
   Where bee nowe those eyes ever Inly persers?
Where bee now those wordes never Idelly wasted,
           Woundes to Rehersers?

Where ys Ah that face, that a Sunne defaces?
   Where bee those wellcomes by no worthe deserved?   [10]
Where bee those movinges, the Delights, the graces?
          Howe bee wee swerved?

O hideous absence, by thee am I thralled.
   O my vayne worde gon, Ruyn of my glory.
O deue allegiance, by thee am I called   [15]
          Still to be sory.

But no more wordes, thoughe [? such] a worde bee spoken,
   Nor no more wording with a worde to spill mee.
Peace Due alledgeance, Duty must bee broken,
         Yf Duety kill mee.   [20]

Then come, O come, then do I come, receyve [mee],
   Slay mee not, for stay doo not hyde thy blisses,
But betweene those armes, never else do leave mee;
         Give mee my kisses.

O my Thoughtes' sweete foode, my [my] onely Owner, [25]
   O my heavens for Taste, by thy heavenly pleasure,
O the fayre *Nymphe* borne to doo woemen honor,
              Lady my Treasure.

---

5. Cl, St.   1 thoughtes, . . . foode Cl.   my my] my Cl.   2 thie] the Cl.
4 Treasure, Cl.   7 wasted? Cl.   8 Rehersers, Cl.   9 Ah] ay Cl.
defaces] defaceth Cl St.   11 movinges,] mooving Cl, movinges St.   13 am I]
I am Cl.   thralled? Cl.   14 glory? Cl.   15 O deue] Ah dew St.
allegiance] Aleageaunce St.   17 more] moe St.   such] *om.* Cl St.   18 mee?
Cl.   19 alledgeance] Aleageaunce St.   21 do I] I do Cl St.   mee] *om.* Cl
St.   22 blisses] bleses St.   23 mee Cl.   25–28 *om.* St.   25 Thoughtes,
Cl.   my my] my Cl.   Owner? Cl.   26 thy] the Cl.   pleasure? Cl.
27 hono^r? Cl.

6

To the tune of *Basciami vita mia*

Sleepe Babie mine, Desire, nurse Beautie singeth:
Thy cries, ô Babie, set mine head on aking:
The Babe cries 'way, thy love doth keepe me waking'.

Lully, lully, my babe, hope cradle bringeth
Unto my children alway good rest taking: [5]
The babe cries 'way, thy love doth keepe me waking'.

Since babie mine, from me thy watching springeth,
Sleepe then a litle, pap content is making:
The babe cries 'nay, for that abide I waking'.

7

To the tune of the Spanish song,
Se tu señora no dueles de mi

O Faire, ô sweet, when I do looke on thee,
In whom all joyes so well agree,
Heart and soule do sing in me.
  This you heare is not my tongue,
  Which once said what I conceaved,   [5]
  For it was of use bereaved,
With a cruell answer stong.
    No, though tongue to roofe be cleaved,
    Fearing least he chastisde be,
    Heart and soule do sing in me.   [10]

O faire, O sweete, when I do looke on thee,
In whom all joyes so well agree,
Heart and soule do sing in me.

---

6. 98, Cl, Bo, St.   *Heading*: *Basciami*] Basitam Cl, Basciamy Bo, Basciam St.
1 Desire 98.

7. 98, Cl, Bo.   *Heading*: *no dueles*] no dules Cl, ne dueles Bo.   11–13 O
faire, O sweete, &c. 98 Bo, O fayre O sweete &c vt antea Cl.

Just accord all musike makes;
In thee just accord excelleth,   [15]
Where each part in such peace dwelleth,
One of other beautie takes.
    Since then truth to all minds telleth,
    That in thee lives harmonie,
    Heart and soule do sing in me.   [20]

O faire, O sweet, when I do looke on thee,
In whom all joyes so well agree,
Heart and soule do sing in me.
    They that heav'n have knowne, do say
    That who so that grace obtaineth,   [25]
    To see what faire sight there raigneth,
    Forced are to sing alway;
        So then since that heaven remaineth,
        In thy face I plainly see,
        Heart and soule do sing in me.   [30]

O faire, O sweete, when I do looke on thee,
In whom all joyes so well agree,
Heart and soule do sing in me.
    Sweete thinke not I am at ease,
    For because my cheefe part singeth,   [35]
    This song from deathe's sorrow springeth:
    As to Swanne in last disease:
        For no dumbnesse nor death bringeth
        Stay to true love's melody:
        Heart and soule do sing in me.   [40]

8

*These foure following Sonnets were made when his Ladie had
paine in her face*

THE scourge of life, and death's extreame disgrace,
    The smoke of hell, the monster called paine,

15 thee] the Cl Bo.   19 thee] the Cl Bo.   21–23 O faire, O sweet, &c. 98 Cl
Bo.   31–33 O faire, O sweete, &c. 98 Cl Bo.
    8. 98, Cl, Bo, Di, Ra.   *Heading in* 98 Cl Ra *only.* These 4 Sonnets followinge|
wer made by Sʳ P: Sidney|when his Ladye hadd|[*added between the lines in a different
hand and ink* the small poxe]|a payne in her|face. Ra. 98 *also indents lines* 3, 7, *and* 11.

Long sham'd to be accurst in every place,
  By them who of his rude resort complaine,
Lyke crafty wretch by time and travell tought,   [5]
  His ugly evill in other's good to hide,
Late harbers in her face whom nature wrought,
  As treasure house where her best gifts abyde.
And so by priviledge of sacred seate,
  A seate where beauty shines and vertue raignes,   [10]
He hopes for some small praise since she hath great,
  Within her beames wrapping his cruell staines.
    Ah saucy paine let not thy errour last,
    More loving eyes she draws, more hate thou hast.

9

Wo, wo to me, on me returne the smart:
  My burning tongue hath bred my mistresse paine,
For oft in paine to paine my painefull heart
  With her due praise did of my state complaine.
I praisde her eyes whom never chance doth move,   [5]
  Her breath which makes a sower answer sweete,
Her milken breasts the nurse of child-like love,
  Her legges (O legges) her ay well stepping feete.
Paine heard her praise, and full of inward fire,
  (First sealing up my heart as pray of his)   [10]
He flies to her, and boldned with desire,
  Her face (this age's praise) the thiefe doth kisse.
    O paine I now recant the praise I gave,
    And sweare she is not worthy thee to have.

10

Thou paine the onely guest of loath'd constraint,
  The child of curse, man's weaknesse foster-child,
Brother to woe, and father of complaint:
  Thou paine, thou hated paine, from heav'n exilde,

4 complaine. 98.   8 abyde] do bide 98 Ra.
  9. 98, Cl, Bo, Di, Ra. 98 *also indents lines* 3, 7, *and* 11.   1 Wo, wo, 98.
11 flies] flees Cl Ra.
  10. 98, Cl, Bo, Di, Ra. 98 *also indents lines* 3, 7, *and* 11.

How holdst thou her, whose eyes constraint doth feare,   [5]
    Whom curst do blesse, whose weakenesse vertues arme,
Who others' woes and plaints can chastly beare:
    In whose sweete heav'n Angels of high thoughts swarme?
What courage strange hath caught thy caitife hart,
    Fear'st not a face that oft whole harts devowres,   [10]
Or art thou from above bid play this part,
        And so no helpe gainst envy of those powers?
        If thus, alas: yet while those partes have wo,
        So stay her toung, that she no more say no.

II

AND have I heard her say, 'ô cruell paine!'
    And doth she know what mould her beautie beares?
Mournes she in truth, and thinks that others faine?
    Feares she to feele, and feeles not others' feares?
Or doth she thinke all paine the minde forbeares?   [5]
    That heavie earth, not fierie sprites may plaine?
That eyes weepe worse then hart in bloodie teares?
    That sense feeles more then what doth sense containe?
No, no, she is too wise, she knowes her face
    Hath not such paine as it makes others have: [10]
She knows the sicknesse of that perfect place
    Hath yet such health, as it my life can save.
        But this she thinks, our paine hye cause excuseth,
        Where her who should rule paine, false paine abuseth.

12

Translated out of Horace, *which beginnes* Rectiùs viues

YOU better sure shall live, not evermore
    Trying high seas, nor while Sea rage you flee,
    Pressing too much upon ill harbourd shore.

8 swarme. 98.   13 thus 98.
    11. 98, Cl, Bo, Di, Ra. 98 *also indents lines* 3, 7, *and* 11.   1 say? 98.   6 not]
no Di Ra.   13 paine] paines Di Ra.
    12. 98, Cl, Bo.   *Heading*: Horace] Homer Cl; *beginnes*] beginneth Bo.   2 Sea]
seas 98.

The golden meane who loves, lives safely free
   From filth of foreworne house, and quiet lives, [5]
   Releast from Court, where envie needes must be.

The wynde most oft the hugest Pine-tree greeves:
   The stately towers come downe with greater fall:
   The highest hills the bolt of thunder cleeves:

Evill happes do fill with hope, good happes appall [10]
   With feare of change, the courage well preparde:
   Fowle Winters as they come, away they shall.

Though present times and past with evils be snarde,
   They shall not last: with Citherne silent muse
   Apollo wakes, and bow hath sometime sparde. [15]

In hard estate with stowt shew valor use,
   The same man still in whom wysdome prevailes,
   In too full winde draw in thy swelling sailes.

13
Out of Catullus

Nulli se dicit mulier mea nubere malle,
   Quam mihi non si se Iupiter ipse petat,
Dicit sed mulier Cupido quæ dicit amanti,
   In vento aut rapida scribere oportet aqua.

UNTO no body my woman saith she had rather a wife be,
   Then to my selfe, not though *Jove* grew a suter of hers.
These be her words, but a woman's words to a love that is eager,
   In wind or water streame do require to be writ.

14

Qui sceptra sævus duro imperio regit,
   Timet timentes, metus in Authorem redit.

FAIRE seeke not to be feard, most lovely beloved by thy servants,
   For true it is, that they feare many whom many feare.

7 wynde] windes 98.   14 muse, 98.   15 bow hath sometime] Boz sometyme
hathe Cl, he that sometime Bo.   17 wysdome] wise doome 98.   18 In too]
Into Cl, In to Bo.
   13. 98, Cl, Bo.   *Heading*: Catullus] Latullus Bo; *quæ dicit*] *dicit* Cl, que dicit
Bo; *oportet*] *optet* 98, *oported* Bo.   4 water] waters 98.
   14. 98, Cl, Bo.

15

Uppon the Devyse of a Seeled Dove, with this worde of
Petrarch: Non mi vuol e non mi trahe d'Impaccio

LIKE as the Dove which seeled up doth flie,
   Is neither freed, nor yet to service bound,
But hopes to gaine some helpe by mounting hie,
   Till want of force do force her fall to ground;

Right so my minde, caught by his guiding eye   [5]
   And thence cast off, where his sweete hurt he found,
Hath neither leave to live, nor doome to dye,
   Nor held in evill, nor suffered to be sound,

But with his wings of fancies up he goes,
   To hie conceits whose fruits are oft but small,   [10]
Till wounded, blind, and wearied Spirites, lose
   Both force to flie and knowledge where to fall.
     O happie Dove if she no bondage tried:
     More happie I, might I in bondage bide.

16a

Edward Dyer

PROMETHEUS *when first from heaven hie,*
   He brought downe fire, ere then on earth not seene,
Fond of Delight, a Satyre standing by,
   Gave it a kisse, as it like sweete had beene.

Feeling forthwith the other burning power,   [5]
   Wood with the smart, with showts and shryking shrill,
He sought his ease in river, field, and bower,
   But for the time his griefe went with him still.

---

15. 98, Cl, Bo, Ma.   *Heading:* om. 98 Bo; *this worde*] these Ma; e] & Cl, et
Ma. 98 *also indents lines* 3, 7, *and* 11.   4 ground. 98.   5 minde caught . . .
eye, 98.   6 off] of Cl Bo Ma.   7 neither] neuer 98 Cl Bo Ma.   8 sound.
98.   9 fancies] fancy Cl Ma.   11 Spirites] spirite 98.   lose] loose
Cl Ma.
  16a. 98, Cl, Bo, Ha, Ra, Hy, Fo.   *Heading:* E. D. 98, Edw: D. Cl, *om.* Bo Ha
Ra Hy Fo.   98 *also indents lines* 3, 7, *and* 11.   3 *Delight*] the Lighte Cl Ha.
5 *other*] others Ha, outwarde Ra Hy Fo.   6 smart 98.

So silly I, with that unwonted sight
In humane shape, an Angell from above, [10]
Feeding mine eyes, the impression there did light,
That since I runne and rest as pleaseth love.
The difference is, the Satire's lippes, my hart,
He for a while, I evermore have smart.

16

A SATYRE once did runne away for dread,
With sound of horne, which he him selfe did blow,
Fearing and feared thus from himselfe he fled,
Deeming strange evill in that he did not know.

Such causelesse feares when coward minds do take, [5]
It makes them flie that which they faine would have:
As this poore beast who did his rest forsake,
Thinking not why, but how himselfe to save.

Even thus might I, for doubts which I conceave
Of mine owne wordes, my owne good hap betray, [10]
And thus might I for feare of may be, leave
The sweete pursute of my desired pray.
Better like I thy Satyre deerest Dyer,
Who burnt his lips to kisse faire shining fire.

17

MY mistresse lowers and saith I do not love:
I do protest and seeke with service due,
In humble mind a constant faith to prove,
But for all this I can not her remove
From deepe vaine thought that I may not be true. [5]

9 I 98.   10 shape 98.   11 *the impression*] thimpression Ha Ra Hy.
12 *runne and rest*] reste and runn Ra Hy Fo.   loue, 98.   13 *is*] *om.* Hy Fo.
14 *while*] tyme Ra Hy Fo.   *Subscribed:* Mᵣ Dier Ra, DY. Hy, Dier Fo.
16. 98, Cl, Bo, Ra, Hy, Fo. 98 *also indents lines* 3, 7, *and* 11.   **2** With] Of
Ra Hy Fo.   which] that Ra, wᶜʰ *corrected to* yᵗ Hy.   **5** coward] cowardes
Ra Hy Fo.   **7** who] that Ra, wᶜʰ Hy Fo.   **9** thus] so Ra Hy Fo.   I 98.
doubts] doubte Ra Fo.   **10** wordes] harte Ra Hy Fo.   my] myne Cl Ra Hy.
betray] bewray Hy Fo.   **11** thus] so Ra Hy Fo.   **13** like I] be lyke Ra, I lyke
Hy Fo.   thy] the Cl Fo.   **14** Who] That Ra Hy Fo.   *Subscribed:* S. P. S.
Ra, SY. Hy, S p. Sydney Fo.
17. 98, Cl, Bo.   **4** for all] all for Cl Bo.

If othes might serve, even by the Stygian lake,
    Which Poets say, the gods them selves do feare,
    I never did my vowed word forsake:
    For why should I, whom free choise slave doth make,
    Else what in face, then in my fancie beare?   [10]

My Muse therefore, for onely thou canst tell,
    Tell me the cause of this my causelesse woe,
    Tell how ill thought disgrac'd my doing well:
    Tell how my joyes and hopes thus fowly fell
    To so lowe ebbe that wonted were to flowe.   [15]

O this it is, the knotted straw is found
    In tender harts, small things engender hate:
    A horse's worth laid wast the Troyan ground:
    A three foote stoole in *Greece*, made Trumpets sound,
    An Asse's shade ere now hath bred debate.   [20]

If *Greekes* themselves were mov'd with so small cause
    To twist those broyles, which hardly would untwine:
    Should Ladies faire be tyed to such hard lawes,
    As in their moodes to take a lingring pawse?
    I would it not, their mettall is too fine.   [25]

My hand doth not beare witnesse with my hart,
    She saith, because I make no wofull laies,
    To paint my living death, and endlesse smart:
    And so for one that felt god *Cupid's* dart,
    She thinks I leade and live too merrie daies.   [30]

Are *Poets* then the onely lovers true,
    Whose hearts are set on measuring a verse:
    Who thinke themselves well blest, if they renew
    Some good old dumpe, that *Chaucer's* mistresse knew,
    And use but you for matters to rehearse?   [35]

Then good *Apollo* do away thy bowe:
    Take harp and sing in this our versing time:
    And in my braine some sacred humour flowe:
    That all the earth my woes, sighes, teares may know,
    And see you not that I fall now to ryme?   [40]

9 make? 98.   10 beare. 98.   11 therefore 98.   21 cause, 98.
31 true? 98.   35 rehearse. 98.   36 good] god Bo.   40 ryme. 98.

As for my mirth, how could I but be glad,
  Whilst that methought I justly made my bost
  That onely I the onely Mistresse had:
  But now, if ere my face with joy be clad:
  Thinke *Hanniball* did laugh when Carthage lost. [45]

Sweet Ladie, as for those whose sullen cheare,
  Compar'd to me, made me in lightnesse found:
  Who Stoick-like in clowdie hew appeare:
  Who silence force to make their words more deare:
  Whose eyes seeme chaste, because they looke on ground: [50]
    Beleeve them not, for Phisicke true doth finde,
    Choler adust is joyed in woman-kinde.

18

IN wonted walkes, since wonted fancies change,
  Some cause there is, which of strange cause doth rise:
For in each thing wherto mine eye doth range,
  Part of my paine me seemes engraved lyes.

The Rockes which were of constant mind the marke [5]
  In clyming steepe, now hard refusall show:
The shading woods seeme now my Sunne to darke,
  And stately hilles disdaine to looke so low.

The restfull Caves now restlesse visions give,
  In Dales I see each way a hard assent: [10]
Like late mowne meades, late cut from joy I live.
  Alas sweete Brookes do in my teares augment:
    Rockes, woods, hilles, caves, dales, meads, brookes, answere me,
    Infected mindes infect each thing they see.

19

IF I could thinke how these my thoughts to leave,
  Or thinking still my thoughts might have good end:
  If rebell sence would reason's law receave;
  Or reason foyld would not in vaine contend:

51 not 98.
18. 98, Cl, Bo, Di. 98 *also indents lines* 3, 7, *and* 11.   5 mind, 98.   mind]
myndes Cl Di.
  19. 98, Cl, Bo, St, Ma, Ra, Hy.   2 good] an Ra Hy.

Then might I thinke what thoughts were best to thinke: [5]
Then might I wisely swimme or gladly sinke.

If either you would change your cruell hart,
  Or cruell (still) time did your beautie staine:
If from my soule this love would once depart,
  Or for my love some love I might obtaine, [10]
    Then might I hope a change or ease of minde,
    By your good helpe, or in my selfe to finde.

But since my thoughts in thinking still are spent,
  With reason's strife, by senses overthrowne,
You fairer still, and still more cruell bent, [15]
I loving still a love that loveth none,
    I yeeld and strive, I kisse and curse the paine:
    Thought, reason, sense, time, you, and I, maintaine.

20

A Farewell

Oft have I musde, but now at length I finde,
  Why those that die, men say they do depart:
Depart, a word so gentle to my minde,
  Weakely did seeme to paint death's ougly dart.

But now the starres with their strange course do binde [5]
  Me one to leave, with whome I leave my hart.
I heare a crye of spirits faint and blinde,
  That parting thus my chiefest part I part.

Part of my life, the loathed part to me,
  Lives to impart my wearie clay some breath. [10]
But that good part, wherein all comforts be,
  Now dead, doth shew departure is a death.
    Yea worse then death, death parts both woe and joy,
    From joy I part still living in annoy.

8 did] would Ra Hy.   10 some love I might] I mighte some Love Cl St Ma
16 none. 98.   18 Thought] Though Ra Hy.
  20. 98, Cl, Bo, Di.   *Heading*: *om.* Bo Di. 98 *also indents lines* 3, 7, *and* 11.
9 me 98.   12 death, 98.

21

FINDING those beames, which I must ever love,
  To marre my minde, and with my hurt to please,
I deemd it best some absence for to prove,
  If further place might further me to ease.

Myne eyes thence drawne, where lived all their light,   [5]
  Blinded forthwith in darke dispaire did lye,
Like to the Mowlle with want of guiding sight,
  Deepe plunged in earth, deprived of the skie.

In absence blind, and wearied with that woe,
  To greater woes by presence I returne,   [10
Even as the flye, which to the flame doth goe,
  Pleased with the light, that his small corse doth burne:
    Faire choice I have, either to live or dye
    A blinded Mowlle, or else a burned flye.

22

The 7. Wonders of England

NEERE *Wilton* sweete, huge heapes of stones are found,
  But so confusde, that neither any eye
  Can count them just, nor reason reason trye,
What force brought them to so unlikely ground.

To stranger weights my minde's waste soile is bound,   [5]
  Of passyon's hilles reaching to reason's skie,
From fancie's earth passing all numbers' bound,
  Passing all ghesse, whence into me should fly
    So mazde a masse, or if in me it growes,
    A simple soule should breed so mixed woes.   [10]

21. 98, Cl, Bo, Ra. 98 *also indents lines* 3, 7, *and* 11.   5 Myne] My 98.
7 Mowlle] Molde 98, mould Bo.   14 Mowlle] Molde 98 Bo.
  22. 98, Cl, Bo, Ma, Ra.   *Heading*: *The*] loue fashyoned to the Ra; 7] *om.* Bo;
of] in Cl.   6 passyon's] passion 98.   8 fly] flee Cl Ra.

The *Bruertons* have a Lake, which when the Sunne
  Approching warmes (not else) dead logges up sends,
  From hidnest depth, which tribute when it ends,
  Sore signe it is, the Lord's last thred is spun.

My lake is sense, whose still streames never runne,   [15]
  But when my Sunne her shining twinnes there bends,
  Then from his depth with force in her begunne,
  Long drowned hopes to watrie eyes it lends:
    But when that failes, my dead hopes up to take,
    Their master is faire warn'd his will to make.   [20]

We have a fish, by strangers much admirde,
  Which caught, to cruell search yeelds his chiefe part:
  (With gall cut out) closde up againe by art,
  Yet lives untill his life be new requirde.

A stranger fish, my selfe not yet expirde,   [25]
  Though rapt with beautie's hooke, I did impart
  My selfe unto th' Anatomy desirde,
  In steade of gall, leaving to her my hart:
    Yet live with thoughts closde up, till that she will
    By conquest's right in steade of searching kill.   [30]

Peake hath a Cave, whose narrow entries finde
  Large roomes within, where droppes distill amaine:
  Till knit with cold, though there unknowne remaine,
  Decke that poore place with Alablaster linde.

Mine eyes the streight, the roomie cave, my minde,   [35]
  Whose clowdie thoughts let fall an inward raine
  Of sorrowe's droppes, till colder reason binde
  Their running fall into a constant vaine
    Of trueth, farre more then Alablaster pure,
    Which though despisde, yet still doth truth endure.   [40]

A field there is where, if a stake be prest
  Deepe in the earth, what hath in earth receipt
  Is chang'd to stone, in hardnesse, cold, and weight,
  The wood, above doth soone consuming rest.

11 *Bruertons*] bruretons Bo, Bruertone Ra.   Sunne, 98.   13 hidnest] hideous
98, hydnoust Cl, hindest Ma, hyndemost Ra.   14 Sore] ffor Ma Ra, So Cl.
27 th'] the Cl Ma Ra.   28 In steade] In steed 98.   30 in steade] in steed 98.
31 finde, 98.   36 thoughts, 98.   37 droppes 98.   41 is, where . . .
prest, 98.   42 receipt, 98.

The earth, her eares: the stake is my request: [45]
  Of which, how much may pierce to that sweet seate,
  To honor turnd, doth dwell in honor's nest,
  Keeping that forme, though void of wonted heate:
    But all the rest, which feare durst not applie,
    Failing themselves, with withered conscience dye.   [50]

Of ships, by shipwrack cast on *Albion* coast,
  Which rotting on the rockes, their death do dye:
  From wooden bones, and bloud of pitch doth flie
  A bird which gets more life then ship had lost.

My ship, desire, with winde of lust long tost,   [55]
  Brake on faire cleeves of constant chastitie:
  Where plagu'd for rash attempt, gives up his ghost,
  So deepe in seas of vertue beauties ly.
    But of his death flies up a purest love,
    Which seeming lesse, yet nobler life doth move.   [60]

These wonders England breedes, the last remaines,
  A Ladie in despite of nature chaste,
  On whome all love, in whom no love is plaste,
  Where fairenesse yeelds to wisdome's shortest raines.

An humble pride, a skorne that favour staines: [65]
  A woman's mould, but like an Angell graste,
  An Angell's mind, but in a woman caste:
  A heaven on earth, or earth that heaven containes:
    Now thus this wonder to my selfe I frame,
    She is the cause that all the rest I am.   [70]

23

To the tune of Wilhelmus *van* Nassaw, &c.

  WHO hath his fancie pleased,
    With fruits of happie sight,
  Let here his eyes be raised
    On nature's sweetest light.

51 *Albion*] *Albions* Cl Ra.   53 wooden] wodden 98, wood ye Ma, wodye Ra.
59 his] this 98 Bo.   62 chaste. 98.
  23. 98, Cl, Bo, Ma, Ha, Ra, Hy.   *Heading: om.* Ha Ra Hy; Wilhelmus]
Wilhemus 98, Willelmus Cl, Williclmus Bo, Wyllielmus Ma.

A light which doth dissever,   [5]
   And yet unite the eyes,
A light which dying never,
   Is cause the looker dyes.

She never dies but lasteth
   In life of lover's hart,   [10]
He ever dies that wasteth
   In love, his chiefest part.
Thus is her life still guarded,
   In never dying faith:
Thus is his death rewarded,   [15]
   Since she lives in his death.

Looke then and dye, the pleasure
   Doth answere well the paine:
Small losse of mortall treasure,
   Who may immortall gaine.   [20]
Immortall be her graces,
   Immortall is her minde:
They fit for heavenly places,
   This heaven in it doth binde.

But eyes these beauties see not,   [25]
   Nor sence that grace descryes:
Yet eyes deprived be not,
   From sight of her faire eyes:
Which as of inward glorie
   They are the outward seale: [30]
So may they live still sorie
   Which die not in that weale.

But who hath fancies pleased,
   With fruits of happie sight,
Let here his eyes be raysed   [35]
   On nature's sweetest light.

---

11 ever] never Ha Ra.   14 In] with Ha Ra Hy.   23 fit for] tell of Ra Hy.
24 This . . . doth binde] That . . . do fynde Ra Hy.   25 these beauties] this
Bewtye Ma Ha Ra Hy.   26 that] this Ra Hy.   31 live still] lyue full Ma
Ha, still be Hy.   32 Which] That Ra Hy.   33–36 *om.* Ha.   33 fancies]
fancye Ra Hy.

24

To the tune of *The smokes of Melancholy*

WHO hath ever felt the change of love,
And knowne those pangs that the losers prove,
  May paint my face without seeing mee,
  And write the state how my fancies bee,
  The lothsome buds growne on sorrowe's tree.   [5]
But who by hearesay speakes, and hath not fully felt
What kind of fires they be in which those spirits melt,
  Shall gesse, and faile, what doth displease,
  Feeling my pulse, misse my disease.

O no, O no, tryall onely shewse   [10]
The bitter juice of forsaken woes,
  Where former blisse present evils do staine,
  Nay former blisse addes to present paine,
  While remembrance doth both states containe.
Come learners then to me, the modell of mishappe,   [15]
Engulfed in despaire, slid downe from fortune's lappe:
  And as you like my double lot,
  Tread in my steppes, or follow not.

For me alas I am full resolv'd,
Those bands alas shall not be dissolv'd,   [20]
  Nor breake my word though reward come late,
  Nor faile my faith in my failing fate,
  Nor change in change, though change change my state.
But alwayes one my selfe with eagle eyde trueth to flie,
Up to the sunne, although the sunne my wings do frie: [25]
  For if those flames burne my desire,
  Yet shall I die in *Phænix* fire.

24. 98, Cl, Bo.   *Heading*: To the tune of] *om*. 98 Cl.   *Stanza division and*
indentation from Cl.   2 losers] loosers 98 Cl Bo.   25 vp 98.

25

−◡◡−◡−−

WHEN to my deadlie pleasure,
When to my livelie torment,
Ladie mine eyes remained,
Joyned alas to your beames,

With violence of heav'nly   [5]
Beautie tied to vertue,
Reason abasht retyred,
Gladly my senses yeelded.

Gladly my senses yeelding,
Thus to betray my hart's fort,   [10]
Left me devoid of all life;

They to the beamie Sunnes went,
Where by the death of all deaths,
Finde to what harme they hastned,

Like to the silly *Sylvan*,   [15]
Burn'd by the light he best liked,
When with a fire he first met.

Yet, yet, a life to their death,
Lady you have reserved,
Lady the life of all love;   [20]

For though my sense be from me,
And I be dead who want sense,
Yet do we both live in you.

Turned anew by your meanes,
Unto the flowre that ay turnes,   [25]
As you, alas, my Sunne bends;

Thus do I fall to rise thus,
Thus do I dye to live thus,
Changed to a change, I change not.

25. 98, Cl, Ra (*lines* 27–34 *only*). *Scansion in* Cl *only*.   4 beames. 98.   6 tied,
98.   11 life. 98.   14 hastned. 98.   15 *Sylvan*] Sillman Cl.   20 loue.
98.   26 bends. 98.   *After* 28 Ra *adds*: Turnde with yll turnes I turne not.

Thus may I not be from you: [30]
Thus be my senses on you:
Thus what I thinke is of you:
Thus what I seeke is in you:
    All what I am, it is you.

26

To the tune of a Neapolitan *song, which
    beginneth*: No, no, no, no

No, no, no, no, I cannot hate my foe,
    Although with cruell fire,
    First throwne on my desire,
    She sackes my rendred sprite.
        For so faire a flame embraces   [5]
            All the places,
        Where that heat of all heates springeth,
            That it bringeth
        To my dying heart some pleasure,
            Since his treasure   [10
        Burneth bright in fairest light. No, no, no, no.

No, no, no, no, I cannot hate my foe,
    Although with cruell fire,
    First throwne on my desire,
    She sackes my rendred sprite.   [15]
        Since our lives be not immortall,
            But to mortall
        Fetters tyed, do waite the hower
            Of deathe's power,
        They have no cause to be sorie,   [20]
            Who with glorie
        End the way, where all men stay. No, no, no, no.

After 34 Ra *adds*: Thus what I feel is for you.
   26. 98, Cl, Bo (*lines 7–33 only*).   *Heading: beginneth*] Beginns Cl. *Indentation
from* Cl.   5 so] so a 98.   faire, 98.   flame] face Cl.   13–15 Al-
though, &c. 98 Cl, &c. Bo.   19 of . . . power. 98.

No, no, no, no, I cannot hate my foe,
  Although with cruell fire,
  First throwne on my desire,   [25]
She sackes my rendred sprite.
  No man doubts, whom beautie killeth,
    Faire death feeleth,
  And in whome faire death proceedeth,
    Glorie breedeth: [30]
  So that I in her beames dying,
    Glorie trying,
  Though in paine, cannot complaine. No, no, no, no.

27

To the tune of a Neapolitan Villanell

AL my sense thy sweetnesse gained,
Thy faire haire my heart enchained,
My poore reason thy words moved,
So that thee like heaven I loved.
  Fa la la leridan, dan dan dan deridan: [5]
  Dan dan dan deridan deridan dei:
    While to my minde the out side stood,
    For messenger of inward good.

Now thy sweetnesse sowre is deemed,
Thy haire not worth a haire esteemed: [10]
Reason hath thy words removed,
Finding that but words they proved.
  Fa la la leridan dan dan dan deridan,
  Dan dan dan deridan deridan dei,
    For no faire signe can credit winne,   [15]
    If that the substance faile within.

No more in thy sweetnesse glorie,
For thy knitting haire be sorie:
Use thy words but to bewaile thee,
That no more thy beames availe thee.   [20]

24–26 Although, &c. 98 Cl, &c., Bo.
  27. 98, Cl, Bo, Hn, Pu (*lines* 39–40 *only*).   *Heading*: *om.* Hn Pu. *Indentation and stanza division editorially regularized.*   5–6 *om.* Hn.   10 not] *om.* Cl Hn.
13–14 *om.* Hn.   16 substance] Inne do Cl Bo.

Fa la la leridan dan dan dan deridan,
Dan dan dan deridan deridan dei:
    Lay not thy colours more to view,
    Without the picture be found true.

Wo to me, alas she weepeth!   [25]
Foole in me, what follie creepeth,
Was I to blaspheme enraged,
Where my soule I have engaged?
    Fa la la leridan, dan dan dan deridan:
    Dan dan dan deridan deridan dei: [30]
        And wretched I must yeeld to this,
        The fault I blame her chastnesse is.

Sweetnesse sweetly pardon folly,
Ty me haire your captive wholly,
Words, ô words of heavenlie knowledge,   [35]
Know my words their faults acknowledge.
    Fa la la leridan, dan dan dan deridan:
    Dan dan dan deridan deridan dei:
        And all my life I will confesse,
        The lesse I love, I live the lesse.   [40]

28

Translated out of the Diana *of Montemaior in Spanish. Where* Sireno *a shepheard pulling out a litle of his Mistresse* Diana's *haire, wrapt about with greene silke, who now had utterlie forsaken him: to the haire he thus bewaild himselfe*

WHAT changes here, ô haire,
    I see since I saw you:
How ill fits you this greene to weare,
    For hope the colour due.

21–22 Dan, dan, Dan, dan, 98 Cl Bo, *om.* Hn.   28 engaged. 98.   29–30 Dan, dan, Dan, dan, 98 Cl Bo, *om.* Hn.   34 haire] here Cl Bo Hn.   wholly] holly 98 Cl Bo, holy Hn.   36 faults] fault Cl Bo.   37–38 Dan, dan, Dan, dan. 98 Cl Bo, *om.* Hn.   40 lesse, 98.
    28. 98, Cl, Bo (*lines 1–24 only*).

Indeed I well did hope,   [5]
    Though hope were mixt with feare,
    No other shepheard should have scope,
    Once to approch this hayer.

Ah haire, how many dayes,
    My *Diane* made me shew,   [10]
    With thousand pretty childish plaies,
    If I ware you or no,
    Alas how oft with teares,
    O teares of guilefull breast,
    She seemed full of jealous feares,   [15]
    Whereat I did but jeast.

Tell me ô haire of gold,
    If I then faultie be,
    That trust those killing eyes, I would,
    Since they did warrant me.   [20]
    Have you not seene her mood,
    What streames of teares she spent,
    Till that I sware my faith so stood,
    As her words had it bent?

Who hath such beautie seene   [25]
    In one that changeth so,
    Or where one's love so constant bene,
    Who ever saw such woe?
    Ah haire are you not griev'd,
    To come from whence you be,   [30]
    Seeing how once you saw I liv'd,
    To see me as you see?

On sandie banke of late,
    I saw this woman sit,
    Where, 'sooner die then change my state',   [35]
    She with her finger writ:
    Thus my beleefe was staid,
    Behold Love's mightie hand
    On things, were by a woman said,
    And written in the sand.   [40]

8 hayer] heare 98 Bo.   12 ware] were Cl Bo.   14 *om*. Bo.   26 so? 98.
27 one's] one Cl.   bene? 98.   35 Where 98.   state] fate Cl.

29

The same Sireno *in Montemaior holding his mistresse' glasse before her, looking upon her while she viewed her selfe, thus sang:*

OF this high grace with blisse conjoyn'd
  No further debt on me is laid,
Since that in selfe same mettall coin'd,
  Sweet Ladie you remaine well paid.
    For if my place give me great pleasure,   [5]
    Having before me Nature's treasure,
    In face and eyes unmatched being,
    You have the same in my hands, seeing
    What in your face mine eyes do measure.

Nor thinke the match unev'nly made,   [10]
  That of those beames in you do tarie:
The glasse to you but gives a shade,
  To me mine eyes the true shape carie.
    For such a thought most highlie prized,
    Which ever hath Love's yoke despised: [15]
    Better then one captiv'd perceiveth,
    Though he the lively forme receiveth:
    The other sees it but disguised.

30

RING out your belles, let mourning shewes be spread,
  For love is dead:
    All Love is dead, infected
    With plague of deepe disdaine:
    Worth as nought worth rejected,   [5]
    And Faith faire scorne doth gaine.

29. 98, Cl. *Indentation from* Cl; 98 *also indents lines* 3 *and* 12.   8 hands seeing, 98.

30. 98, Cl, St, Ba, Dd, Hn, Hy. *All verbal variants in* Ba *are listed.*   5–6 *om.* Hn.   6 faire] fowle Ba.

From so ungratefull fancie,
From such a femall franzie,
From them that use men thus,
Good Lord deliver us.　　　　　　　　　　　　　[10]

Weepe neighbours, weepe, do you not heare it said,
　That Love is dead?
　　His death-bed peacock's follie,
　　His winding sheete is shame,
　　His will false-seeming holie,　　　　　　　　[15]
　　His sole exec'tour blame.
　　From so ungratefull fancie,
　　From such a femall franzie,
　　From them that use men thus,
　　Good Lord deliver us.　　　　　　　　　　　[20]

Let Dirge be sung, and Trentals rightly read,
　For Love is dead:
　　Sir wrong his tombe ordaineth,
　　My mistresse' Marble hart,
　　Which Epitaph containeth,　　　　　　　　　[25]
　　'Her eyes were once his dart'.
　　From so ungratefull fancie,
　　From such a femall franzie,
　　From them that use men thus,
　　Good Lord deliver us.　　　　　　　　　　　[30]

Alas, I lie: rage hath this errour bred,
　Love is not dead.
　　Love is not dead, but sleepeth
　　In her unmatched mind:
　　Where she his counsell keepeth,　　　　　　[35]
　　Till due desert she find.

8 franzie] frenseye Ba Hy.　　　11 do . . . heare] have . . . hard Ba Hn.　　　12 dead:
98.　　　15 His will, false, seeming holly Cl, Whose witt false seming holly Hy, his
will false seeminge hollie St Ba Dd Hn.　　　16 sole] soules *corrected to* sole St,
sowle Ba, soules Hn.　　exec'tour] exectour 98 Hn, dxecutor St, Executors Ba.
17–20 From so vngratefull, &c. 98 St Dd, ffrom so vngratefull &c vt antea Cl, From &c
Ba, from so Hn.　　　21 sung] songe Cl St Ba Dd Hn, songs Hy.　　　23 ordaineth: 98.
ordaineth] ordeinth Ba.　　　24 Marble hart] Marble-heart 98 Dd.　　　25 Which]
whose Ba, his Dd Hn.　　　27–30 From so vngratefull, &c. 98 St Dd, ffrom so
vngratefull &c vt antea Cl, From &c Ba, from so Hn.

Therefore from so vile fancie,
To call such wit a franzie,
Who love can temper thus,
Good Lord deliver us. [40]

31

THOU blind man's marke, thou foole's selfe chosen snare,
Fond fancie's scum, and dregs of scattred thought,
Band of all evils, cradle of causelesse care,
Thou web of will, whose end is never wrought;

Desire, desire I have too dearely bought, [5]
With price of mangled mind thy worthlesse ware,
Too long, too long asleepe thou hast me brought,
Who should my mind to higher things prepare.

But yet in vaine thou hast my ruine sought,
In vaine thou madest me to vaine things aspire, [10]
In vaine thou kindlest all thy smokie fire;

For vertue hath this better lesson taught,
Within my selfe to seeke my onelie hire:
Desiring nought but how to kill desire.

32

LEAVE me ô Love, which reachest but to dust,
And thou my mind aspire to higher things:
Grow rich in that which never taketh rust:
What ever fades, but fading pleasure brings.

Draw in thy beames, and humble all thy might, [5]
To that sweet yoke, where lasting freedomes be:
Which breakes the clowdes and opens forth the light,
That doth both shine and give us sight to see.

37 Therefore] Wherfore Ba Hy, then Hn.   38 franzie] frensey Ba Hy.   39 Who]
that Ba Hy, whom Hn.

31. 98, Cl, Bo.   4 wrought. 98.   6 price] prise 98, pryse Cl.   11 fire.
98.

32. 98, Cl.   4 What] Whiche Cl.   7 opens] peanes Cl.   light. 98.
8 sight] light Cl.

O take fast hold, let that light be thy guide,
In this small course which birth drawes out to death,   [10]
And thinke how evill becommeth him to slide,
Who seeketh heav'n, and comes of heav'nly breath.
    Then farewell world, thy uttermost I see,
    Eternall Love maintaine thy life in me.

Splendidis longum valedico nugis.

13 thy] the Cl.

ASTROPHIL AND STELLA

Title: Astrophel and Stella, Written by the Noble Knight Sir Philip Sidney 98, *om.* Bt, Songs and Sonets Fr; *om.* Dr; Sonnetts of Sr Phillip Sydneys vppon to ye Lady Ritch Hn, Sonnetts wrytten by Sr Philipp Sydney Knight Ho, Syr P. S. His Astrophel and Stella Q1–2.

APPARATUS

The relationships of the extant texts are discussed in the notes (pp. 447–57) and a diagram of the stemma is given on p. 455. Variants from the three branches of the stemma (X Y Z) are separated by semicolons (i.e. **2.** 3 X mind Bt; Y my mynde Dr; Z myne [? *or* mynd] Ho, tract Q1).

I

LOVING in truth, and faine in verse my love to show,
That the deare She might take some pleasure of my paine:
Pleasure might cause her reade, reading might make her know,
Knowledge might pitie winne, and pitie grace obtaine,
   I sought fit words to paint the blackest face of woe,   [5]
Studying inventions fine, her wits to entertaine:
Oft turning others' leaves, to see if thence would flow
Some fresh and fruitfull showers upon my sunne-burn'd braine.
   But words came halting forth, wanting Invention's stay,
Invention, Nature's child, fled step-dame Studie's blowes,   [10]
And others' feete still seem'd but strangers in my way.
Thus great with child to speake, and helplesse in my throwes,
   Biting my trewand pen, beating my selfe for spite,
   'Foole,' said my Muse to me, 'looke in thy heart and write.'

2

   NOT at first sight, nor with a dribbed shot
      Love gave the wound, which while I breathe will bleed:
      But knowne worth did in mine of time proceed,
   Till by degrees it had full conquest got.
   I saw and liked, I liked but loved not,   [5]
      I loved, but straight did not what *Love* decreed:
      At length to *Love's* decrees, I forc'd, agreed,
   Yet with repining at so partiall lot.

1. 98, Bt, Fr (*lines 1–5 only*); Dr, Q2; Hn, Ho, Q1.   1 in verse my love] in verse Dr; my love in verse Hn Ho Q1–2.   2 the deare She] she (deare she) 98, thee (deer ⟨ ⟩he Bt [*damaged*].   8 showers] showre Hn Q1–2, shewr Ho.   9 forth] out Hn Ho Q1–2.   10 Inuention 98.   11 feete] sute Hn Ho.   13 trewand] tongue and Hn Ho Q1.

2. 98, Bt; Dr, Q2; Ho, Q1.   1 at] at the 98.   dribbed] dribbing Ho Q1–2. 3 mine] mind Bt; my mynde Dr; myne [? *or* mynd] Ho, tract Q1.   6 straight did not] strayte had not Dr; did not straight Ho Q1–2.   7 forc'd] first Ho Q1.

Now even that footstep of lost libertie
Is gone, and now like slave-borne *Muscovite*,   [10]
I call it praise to suffer Tyrannie;
And now employ the remnant of my wit,
    To make my selfe beleeve, that all is well,
    While with a feeling skill I paint my hell.

3

LET daintie wits crie on the Sisters nine,
That bravely maskt, their fancies may be told:
Or *Pindare's* Apes, flaunt they in phrases fine,
Enam'ling with pied flowers their thoughts of gold:
    Or else let them in statelier glorie shine,   [5]
Ennobling new found Tropes with problemes old:
Or with strange similies enrich each line,
Of herbes or beastes, which *Inde* or *Afrike* hold.
    For me in sooth, no Muse but one I know:
    Phrases and Problemes from my reach do grow,   [10]
And strange things cost too deare for my poore sprites.
    How then? even thus: in *Stella's* face I reed,
    What Love and Beautie be, then all my deed
But Copying is, what in her Nature writes.

4

VERTUE alas, now let me take some rest,
Thou setst a bate betweene my will and wit,
If vaine love have my simple soule opprest,
Leave what thou likest not, deale not thou with it.
    Thy scepter use in some old *Catoe's* brest;   [5]
Churches or schooles are for thy seate more fit:
I do confesse, pardon a fault confest,
    My mouth too tender is for thy hard bit.

13 my selfe] me selfe 98 Bt.
  3. 98, Bt; Dr, Q2; Ho, Q1.   4 with pied flowers their thoughts of] their pyde
flowrs their thoughts wth Ho, their pride with flowers of Q1.   5 statelier] state-
lyee Q2; stately Q1.
  4. 98, Bt; Dr, Q2; Ho, Q1.   2 will and wit] loue and me Q1.   3 opprest:
98.   4 not, deale not thou] nor deale thow not Ho, and deale thou not Q1.
6 more] most Ho Q1.   7 confest: 98.

But if that needs thou wilt usurping be,
The litle reason that is left in me, [10]
And still th'effect of thy perswasions prove:
I sweare, my heart such one shall shew to thee,
That shrines in flesh so true a Deitie,
That *Vertue*, thou thy selfe shalt be in love.

5

IT is most true, that eyes are form'd to serve
The inward light: and that the heavenly part
Ought to be king, from whose rules who do swerve,
Rebels to Nature, strive for their owne smart.
It is most true, what we call *Cupid's* dart, [5]
An image is, which for our selves we carve;
And, fooles, adore in temple of our hart,
Till that good God make Church and Churchman starve.
True, that true Beautie Vertue is indeed,
Whereof this Beautie can be but a shade, [10]
Which elements with mortall mixture breed:
True, that on earth we are but pilgrims made,
And should in soule up to our countrey move:
True, and yet true that I must *Stella* love.

6

SOME Lovers speake when they their Muses entertaine,
Of hopes begot by feare, of wot not what desires:
Of force of heav'nly beames, infusing hellish paine:
Of living deaths, deare wounds, faire stormes and freesing fires:
Some one his song in *Jove*, and *Jove's* strange tales attires, [5]
Broadred with buls and swans, powdred with golden raine:
Another humbler wit to shepheard's pipe retires,
Yet hiding royall bloud full oft in rurall vaine.

10 The] that Ho Q1.   left] Least Dr.
  5. 98, Bt; Dr, Q2; Ho, Q1.   1–8 *In the order* 5–8, 1–4 *in* Ho Q1.   1 form'd]
found Q2; Ho, bound Q1.   3 do] doth Q1–2.   4 Nature 98.   8 Church-
man] Church-men Q2; Churh-men Q1.   10 be but] but he Q1–2.   14 yet]
most Ho Q1–2.
  6. 98, Bt; Dr, Q2; Ho, Q1.   5 song] songes Q1–2.   6 Broadred] Bordred
98 Bt; Bordered Ho Q1–2.

To some a sweetest plaint, a sweetest stile affords,
  While teares powre out his inke, and sighs breathe out his words:
His paper, pale dispaire, and paine his pen doth move.   [11]
  I can speake what I feele, and feele as much as they,
  But thinke that all the Map of my state I display,
When trembling voice brings forth that I do *Stella* love.

7

WHEN Nature made her chiefe worke, *Stella's* eyes,
  In colour blacke, why wrapt she beames so bright?
  Would she in beamie blacke, like painter wise,
  Frame daintiest lustre, mixt of shades and light?
    Or did she else that sober hue devise,   [5]
  In object best to knit and strength our sight,
  Least if no vaile those brave gleames did disguise,
  They sun-like should more dazle then delight?
    Or would she her miraculous power show,
  That whereas blacke seemes Beautie's contrary,   [10]
  She even in blacke doth make all beauties flow?
Both so and thus, she minding *Love* should be
    Placed ever there, gave him this mourning weed,
    To honor all their deaths, who for her bleed.

8

LOVE borne in *Greece*, of late fled from his native place,
  Forc'd by a tedious proofe, that Turkish hardned hart,
  Is no fit marke to pierce with his fine pointed dart:
And pleasd with our soft peace, staid here his flying race.
But finding these North clymes do coldly him embrace,   [5]
  Not usde to frozen clips, he strave to find some part,
  Where with most ease and warmth he might employ his art:
At length he perch'd himself in *Stella's* joyfull face,

10 While] Whiles Q1–2.   11 paper 98.
  7. 98, Bt; Dr, Q2; Ho, Q1.   6 knit and strength] streingth and knyt Ho Q1–2.
7 those] these 98; Q1–2.   gleames] beams Ho Q1.   14 who] which Q2; that Ho.
  8. 98, Bt; Dr, Q2; Ho, Q1.   2 Forc'd] first Bt; Ho.   hart] harts Ho Q1.
3 Is] was Ho, Were Q1–2.   dart] dartes Ho Q1.   4 flying] flinging Ho, fleeting
Q1–2.   5 North] colde Ho Q1.   do] to Ho, too Q1–2.   8 he perch't him-
self] he preach'd himselfe Q2; himself he peartcht Ho Q1.

Whose faire skin, beamy eyes, like morning sun on snow,
Deceiv'd the quaking boy, who thought from so pure light, [10]
Effects of lively heat, must needs in nature grow.
But she most faire, most cold, made him thence take his flight
    To my close heart, where while some firebrands he did lay,
    He burnt unwares his wings, and cannot fly away.

9

QUEENE *Vertue's* court, which some call *Stella's* face,
    Prepar'd by Nature's chiefest furniture,
    Hath his front built of Alablaster pure;
Gold is the covering of that stately place.
The doore by which sometimes comes forth her Grace, [5]
    Red Porphir is, which locke of pearle makes sure:
    Whose porches rich (which name of cheekes endure)
Marble mixt red and white do enterlace.
    The windowes now through which this heav'nly guest
Looks over the world, and can find nothing such, [10]
Which dare claime from those lights the name of best,
Of touch they are that without touch doth touch,
    Which *Cupid's* selfe from Beautie's myne did draw:
    Of touch they are, and poore I am their straw.

10

REASON, in faith thou art well serv'd, that still
Wouldst brabling be with sence and love in me:
I rather wisht thee clime the Muses' hill,
Or reach the fruite of Nature's choisest tree,
    Or seeke heavn's course, or heavn's inside to see: [5]
Why shouldst thou toyle our thornie soile to till?
Leave sense, and those which sense's objects be:
Deale thou with powers of thoughts, leave love to will.

9 eyes 98.   on] in Dr; Q1.
    9. 98, Bt; Dr, Q2; Ho, Q1.   [2 chiefest] choisest 98 Bt.   5 comes] romes Q2;
runnes Q1.   7 which] with Q1–2.   10 over] ore Q2; on Q1.   11 lights]
sights Ho Q1.   best. 98.   12 doth] do Dr; Ho Q1.   13 myne] mind 98.
    10. 98, Bt; Dr, Q2; Ho, Q1.   2 brabling] arguing Bt; Dr.   3 wisht]
wyshe Ho Q1–2.   4 choisest] chiefest Q1–2.   5 heau'ns . . . heau'ns 98.
7 which] that Ho Q1–2.   8 love] thow Ho Q1.

But thou wouldst needs fight both with love and sence,
With sword of wit, giving wounds of dispraise,   [10]
Till downe-right blowes did foyle thy cunning fence:
For soone as they strake thee with *Stella's* rayes,
    Reason thou kneel'dst, and offeredst straight to prove
    By reason good, good reason her to love.

I I

IN truth, ô Love, with what a boyish kind
    Thou doest proceed in thy most serious wayes:
    That when the heav'n to thee his best displayes,
Yet of that best thou leav'st the best behind.
For like a child that some faire booke doth find,   [5]
    With guilded leaves or colourd Velume playes,
    Or at the most on some fine picture stayes,
But never heeds the fruit of writer's mind:
    So when thou saw'st in Nature's cabinet
Stella, thou straight lookst babies in her eyes,   [10]
In her cheeke's pit thou didst thy pitfould set,
And in her breast bopeepe or couching lyes,
    Playing and shining in each outward part:
    But, foole, seekst not to get into her hart.

12

CUPID, because thou shin'st in *Stella's* eyes,
    That from her lockes, thy day-nets, none scapes free,
    That those lips swell, so full of thee they bee,
That her sweete breath makes oft thy flames to rise,
That in her breast thy pap well sugred lies,   [5]
    That her Grace gracious makes thy wrongs, that she

12 For] So Q1–2.   13 kneel'dst, and offeredst] knewest and offered Ho Q1–2.
    11. 98, Bt; Dr, Q2; Ho, Q1.   5 For] that Ho Q1–2.   6 guilded] gilden
Q1–2.   or] of Ho Q1–2.   Velume] volume Dr; Ho.   7 fine] fayr Ho Q1–2.
11 pitfould] pittfall Ho Q1–2.   set: 98.   12 or couching] or touching Q2; or
lowting Ho, a lowting Q1.
    12. 98, Bt; Dr, Q2; Ho, Q1.   2 lockes] look*es* Dr; Ho Q1–2.   day-nets,]
daunces 98, daynties Bt; Dr; dint*es* Ho, dimnesse Q1.   none] nowe Q1–2.   3 swell]
sweld 98 Bt; Dr; Q1–2.   4 her sweete breath makes] sweeet breth maketh Ho Q1.
6 her Grace gracious makes thy] grac evn gracious make thy Ho, grace euen makes thy
gracious Q1.

What words so ere she speakes perswades for thee,
That her cleare voyce lifts thy fame to the skies.
　　Thou countest *Stella* thine, like those whose powers
Having got up a breach by fighting well,　　　　　　　[10]
Crie, 'Victorie, this faire day all is ours.'
O no, her heart is such a Cittadell,
　　So fortified with wit, stor'd with disdaine,
　　That to win it, is all the skill and paine.

13

PHŒBUS was Judge betweene *Jove*, *Mars*, and *Love*,
　　Of those three gods, whose armes the fairest were:
　　Jove's golden shield did Eagle sables beare,
Whose talents held young *Ganimed* above:
But in Vert field *Mars* bare a golden speare,　　　　　[5]
　　Which through a bleeding heart his point did shove:
　　Each had his creast, *Mars* caried *Venus'* glove,
Jove on his helme the thunderbolt did reare.
Cupid then smiles, for on his crest there lies
　　Stella's faire haire, her face he makes his shield,　[10]
　　Where roses gueuls are borne in silver field.
Phœbus drew wide the curtaines of the skies
　　To blaze these last, and sware devoutly then,
　　The first, thus matcht, were scarcely Gentlemen.

14

ALAS have I not paine enough my friend,
　　Upon whose breast a fiercer Gripe doth tire
　　Then did on him who first stale downe the fire,
While *Love* on me doth all his quiver spend,
But with your Rubarb words yow must contend　　　　　[5]
　　To grieve me worse, in saying that Desire

7 speakes] speake 98.　　　　8 lifts thy fame to the] lifteth thy fame to Ho, lifteth the
Sunne to Q1.　　　11 faire day all] happy day Ho Q1.
　13. 98, Bt; Dr, Q2; Ho, Q1.　　　　　1 betweene *Jove*] twixt Iove & Ho Q1.
5 bare] beare Ho, beares Q1.　　10 haire] hear Bt; Ho.　　12 curtaines] Cur-
taine Ho Q1–2.　　skies, 98.　　13 these] the Bt; Ho Q1–2.　　sware] swere Ho,
swore Q1–2.　　14 scarcely] scantly 98 Bt.
　14. 98, Bt; Dr, Q2; Ho, Q1.　　2 tire, 98.　　　　3 stale] stole Ho Q1–2.
5 yow] ye 98 Bt.　　contend, 98.

Doth plunge my wel-form'd soule even in the mire
Of sinfull thoughts, which do in ruine end?
If that be sinne which doth the maners frame,
Well staid with truth in word and faith of deed,   [10]
Readie of wit and fearing nought but shame:
If that be sinne which in fixt hearts doth breed
    A loathing of all loose unchastitie,
    Then Love is sinne, and let me sinfull be.

15

YOU that do search for everie purling spring,
    Which from the ribs of old *Parnassus* flowes,
    And everie floure, not sweet perhaps, which growes
Neare therabout, into your Poesie wring;
You that do Dictionarie's methode bring   [5]
    Into your rimes, running in ratling rowes:
    You that poore *Petrarch's* long deceased woes,
With new-borne sighes and denisend wit do sing;
    You take wrong waies, those far-fet helpes be such,
    As do bewray a want of inward tuch: [10]
And sure at length stolne goods do come to light.
    But if (both for your love and skill) your name
    You seeke to nurse at fullest breasts of Fame,
Stella behold, and then begin to endite.

16

IN nature apt to like when I did see
    Beauties, which were of manie Carrets fine,
    My boiling sprites did thither soone incline,
And, Love, I thought that I was full of thee:

12 that] yt Ho Q1–2.   hearts] hart Q1–2.
    15. 98, Bt; Dr, Q2; Ho, Q1.   3 floure 98.   4 therabout] thereabouts 98.
Poesie] posy Dr; Ho, Poems Q1.   wring. 98.   7 poore *Petrarch's*] petrarkas
Ho, old *Petrarchs* Q1.   8 denisend wit do] ⟨ ⟩ witt to Dr, deuised wit do Q2;
wytt devysing Ho, wit disguised Q1.   sing. 98.   9 waies 98.   12 your
name] you name Q1–2.   13 breasts] brest Ho Q1–2.   14 to endite] t' indyte
Dr Q2; to wryte Ho Q1.
    16. 98, Bt; Dr, Q2; Ho, Q1.   3 sprites] Spirittis Dr; spirits Q1–2.   soone]
then Ho Q1.

But finding not those restlesse flames in me,   [5]
   Which others said did make their soules to pine:
   I thought those babes of some pinne's hurt did whine,
By my love judging what Love's paine might be.
   But while I thus with this yong Lyon plaid;
Mine eyes (shall I say curst or blest) beheld   [10]
Stella; now she is nam'd, need more be said?
In her sight I a lesson new have speld,
   I now have learn'd Love right, and learn'd even so,
   As who by being poisond doth poison know.

17

His mother deare *Cupid* offended late,
   Because that *Mars*, growne slacker in her love,
   With pricking shot he did not throughly move,
To keepe the pace of their first loving state.
The boy refusde for feare of *Marse's* hate,   [5]
   Who threatned stripes, if he his wrath did prove:
   But she in chafe him from her lap did shove,
Brake bow, brake shafts, while *Cupid* weeping sate:
   Till that his grandame *Nature* pittying it,
Of *Stella's* browes made him two better bowes,   [10]
And in her eyes of arrowes infinit.
   O how for joy he leapes, ô how he crowes,
   And straight therewith, like wags new got to play,
   Fals to shrewd turnes, and I was in his way.

18

With what sharpe checkes I in my selfe am shent,
   When into Reason's audite I do go:
   And by just counts my selfe a banckrout know
Of all those goods, which heav'n to me hath lent:

8 love] soule 98.   paine] paines Ho Q1–2.   9 yong] *om.* 98.   14 who by
being poisond doth] who be being poyson'd doth Dr; they that being poysoned Ho Q1.
17. 98, Bt; Dr, Q2; Ho, Q1.   2 *Mars* 98.   growne] grew Ho Q1–2.
4 pace] place Ho Q1.   8 while] wher Ho Q1–2.   13 therewith 98.
18. 98, Bt; Dr, Q2; Hn, Ho, Q1. *All verbal variants listed for this sonnet.*
1 sharpe] strange Q1–2.   2 audite] recknings Hn Ho.   3 just] such Hn Ho
Q1.   4 hath] haue 98; Ho.

Unable quite to pay even Nature's rent,   [5]
   Which unto it by birthright I do ow:
And which is worse, no good excuse can show,
But that my wealth I have most idly spent.
   My youth doth waste, my knowledge brings forth toyes,
My wit doth strive those passions to defend,   [10]
Which for reward spoile it with vaine annoyes.
I see my course to lose my selfe doth bend:
   I see and yet no greater sorow take,
   Then that I lose no more for *Stella's* sake.

19

ON *Cupid's* bow how are my heart-strings bent,
   That see my wracke, and yet embrace the same?
When most I glorie, then I feele most shame:
I willing run, yet while I run, repent.
My best wits still their owne disgrace invent: [5]
   My verie inke turnes straight to *Stella's* name;
   And yet my words, as them my pen doth frame,
Avise themselves that they are vainely spent.
   For though she passe all things, yet what is all
That unto me, who fare like him that both   [10]
Lookes to the skies, and in a ditch doth fall?
O let me prop my mind, yet in his growth
   And not in Nature for best fruits unfit:
   'Scholler,' saith *Love*, 'bend hitherward your wit.'

20

FLIE, fly, my friends, I have my death wound; fly,
   See there that boy, that murthring boy I say,

6 do] did Hn.   9 youth] wit Q1.   11 Which for reward spoile it with]
With my reward (spoyled with Hn Ho, With my rewarde, the spoile of Q1.   12 see]
find Hn.   lose] loose 98 Bt; Dr; Hn Q1, leese Ho.   my selfe] it selfe Hn.   13 and
yet] yet do Hn.   14 lose] loose 98 Bt; Dr; Ho Q1–2, leese Hn.
   19. 98, Bt; Dr, Q2; Ho, Q1.   7 them] then Dr; Ho.   8 *Line omitted by* Q1
which on preceding page has catchword Accuse.   Avise] Against Q2; Ho.   10 who]
that Ho Q1.   fare] fars Bt; fares Dr; fair Ho.   12 prop] prove Ho Q1.   mind
98.   growth, 98.   13 Nature, 98.   14 your] thy Bt; Ho Q1.
   20. 98, Bt; Dr, Q2; Ho, Q1.   1 death wound] deathes woonde Ho Q1–2.

Who like a theefe, hid in darke bush doth ly,
Till bloudie bullet get him wrongfull pray.

   So Tyran he no fitter place could spie,   [5]
Nor so faire levell in so secret stay,
As that sweete blacke which vailes the heav'nly eye:
There himselfe with his shot he close doth lay.

   Poore passenger, passe now thereby I did,
And staid pleasd with the prospect of the place,   [10]
While that blacke hue from me the bad guest hid:
But straight I saw motions of lightning' grace,
    And then descried the glistring of his dart:
    But ere I could flie thence, it pierc'd my heart.

21

YOUR words my friend (right healthfull caustiks) blame
   My young mind marde, whom *Love* doth windlas so,
   That mine owne writings like bad servants show
My wits, quicke in vaine thoughts, in vertue lame:
That *Plato* I read for nought, but if he tame   [5]
   Such coltish gyres, that to my birth I owe
   Nobler desires, least else that friendly foe,
Great expectation, weare a traine of shame.
   For since mad March great promise made of me,
If now the May of my yeares much decline,   [10]
What can be hoped my harvest time will be?
Sure you say well, your wisdome's golden mine
   Dig deepe with learning's spade, now tell me this,
   Hath this world ought so faire as *Stella* is?

22

IN highest way of heav'n the Sunne did ride,
   Progressing then from faire twinnes' gold'n place:

3 darke] a Q1–2.   6 faire] farre Q1–2.   secret] ⟨ ⟩ Dr.   7 vailes the] veiles thy Q2; wales the Ho, walles thy Q1.   10 with the] with Q2; Ho.   12 lightning] lightnings Ho Q1–2.   13 then] there Ho Q1–2.   glistring] glisterings Ho Q1–2.
   21. 98; Dr, Q2; Ho, Q1.   1 friend (right healthfull caustiks)] frend right helthfull ⟨ ⟩ Dr; frinds doth cawslesly me Ho, freends me causelesly doe Q1.
2 windlas] wenlasse Ho, menace Q1.   3 mine] my Q1–2.   6 gyres] yeeres 98; Ho Q1; geers Dr, giers Q2.   8 weare] were Ho Q1–2.   9 of] to Q1–2.
12 mine, 98.   13 Dig] Diggs Ho Q1–2.
   22. 98; Dr, Q2; Ho, Q1.

Having no scarfe of clowds before his face,
But shining forth of heate in his chiefe pride;
When some faire Ladies, by hard promise tied,   [5]
    On horsebacke met him in his furious race,
    Yet each prepar'd, with fanne's wel-shading grace,
From that foe's wounds their tender skinnes to hide.
Stella alone with face unarmed marcht,
    Either to do like him, which open shone,   [10]
    Or carelesse of the wealth because her owne:
Yet were the hid and meaner beauties parcht,
    Her daintiest bare went free; the cause was this,
    The Sunne which others burn'd, did her but kisse.

23

THE curious wits, seeing dull pensivenesse
    Bewray it selfe in my long setled eyes,
    Whence those same fumes of melancholy rise,
With idle paines, and missing ayme, do guesse.
Some that know how my spring I did addresse,   [5]
    Deeme that my Muse some fruit of knowledge plies:
    Others, because the Prince my service tries,
Thinke that I thinke state errours to redresse.
    But harder Judges judge ambition's rage,
Scourge of it selfe, still climing slipprie place,   [10]
Holds my young braine captiv'd in golden cage.
O fooles, or over-wise, alas the race
    Of all my thoughts hath neither stop nor start,
    But only *Stella*'s eyes and *Stella*'s hart.

24

RICH fooles there be, whose base and filthy hart
Lies hatching still the goods wherein they flow:

3 scarfe] maske Q1–2.   5 Ladies 98.   7 prepar'd 98.   10 him 98.
12 the] thy Dr; their Ho Q1.   13 daintiest] daytiest Ho; dainties Q2.   14 which]
that Ho Q1.
    23. 98, Fr (*lines 12–14 only*); Dr, Q2; Ho, Q1.   1 wits 98.   4 do] doth
Ho Q1.   9 ambition's] Ambitiowse Dr; Q1–2, ambitious [? *or* ambitions] Ho.
12 or over-wise] or other wyse Dr; far otherwyse Ho Q1.   race] case Q1–2.
13 hath] have Dr; Ho Q1–2.
    24. 98; Dr, Q2; Q1.

And damning their owne selves to *Tantal's* smart,
Wealth breeding want, more blist, more wretched grow.
    Yet to those fooles heav'n such wit doth impart, [5]
As what their hands do hold, their heads do know,
And knowing, love, and loving, lay apart
As sacred things, far from all daunger's show.
    But that rich foole, who by blind Fortune's lot
The richest gemme of Love and life enjoyes, [10]
And can with foule abuse such beauties blot;
Let him, deprived of sweet but unfelt joyes,
    (Exil'd for ay from those high treasures, which
    He knowes not) grow in only follie rich.

25

THE wisest scholler of the wight most wise
By *Phœbus'* doome, with sugred sentence sayes,
That Vertue, if it once met with our eyes,
Strange flames of *Love* it in our soules would raise;
    But for that man with paine this truth descries, [5]
While he each thing in sense's ballance wayes,
And so nor will, nor can, behold those skies
Which inward sunne to *Heroicke* minde displaies,
    Vertue of late, with vertuous care to ster
Love of her selfe, takes *Stella's* shape, that she [10]
To mortall eyes might sweetly shine in her.
    It is most true, for since I her did see,
    Vertue's great beautie in that face I prove,
    And find th'effect, for I do burne in love.

26

THOUGH dustie wits dare scorne Astrologie,
And fooles can thinke those Lampes of purest light,

4 blist] blest Dr; rich Q1–2.   5 such wit doth] doth such wit Q1–2.   7 knowing *Loue*, and louing lay apart, 98.   8 sacred] scattered Q1–2.   9 foole who
. . . lot, 98.   12 him 98.   14 rich] Riche Dr.
  25. 98; Dr, Q2; Q1.   1 wise, 98.   3 Vertue 98.   met] meete Q1–2.
4 raise. 98.   6 While] Whiles 98; Whilst Dr.   7 can behold . . . skies, 98.
8 sunne] Sonn Dr; Summe Q1–2.   minde] mindes Q1–2.   displaies. 98.   9 late
98.   10 *Loue* 98.   her selfe . . . she] himselfe . . . hee Q1–2.   take s
tooke 98; take Q1.   13 that] her Q1–2.
  26. 98; Dr, Q2; Ho, Q1.   1 dustie] dusky Ho Q1–2.

Whose numbers, wayes, greatnesse, eternitie,
Promising wonders, wonder to invite,
   To have for no cause birthright in the skie,   [5]
But for to spangle the blacke weeds of night:
Or for some brawle, which in that chamber hie,
They should still daunce to please a gazer's sight.
   For me, I do Nature unidle know,
And know great causes, great effects procure: [10]
And know those Bodies high raigne on the low.
And if these rules did faile, proofe makes me sure,
   Who oft fore-judge my after-following race,
   By only those two starres in *Stella's* face.

27

BECAUSE I oft in darke abstracted guise,
   Seeme most alone in greatest companie,
   With dearth of words, or answers quite awrie,
To them that would make speech of speech arise,
They deeme, and of their doome the rumour flies,   [5]
   That poison foule of bubling pride doth lie
   So in my swelling breast that only I
Fawne on my self, and others to despise:
   Yet pride I thinke doth not my soule possesse,
Which lookes too oft in his unflattring glasse: [10]
But one worse fault, *Ambition*, I confesse,
That makes me oft my best friends overpasse,
   Unseene, unheard, while thought to highest place
   Bends all his powers, even unto *Stella's* grace.

28

YOU that with allegorie's curious frame,
   Of other's children changelings use to make,

3 numbers weighs greatnesse 98.   numbers] number Ho Q1–2.   wayes] weighs
98; Dr.   4 wonders, wonder] wondrous wonders Q1–2.   to] do 98.   inuite:
98.   5 skie] skyes Q1–2.   7 brawle, which in] brave wthin Ho Q1.   13 fore-
judge] foresee Q2; forceye Ho, bewraies Q1.
    27. 98; Dr, Q2; Ho, Q1.   2 companie: 98.   3 or] & Ho Q1–2.   4 make
speech of] of speache make Dr; make naked Ho Q1.   arise. 98.   6 lie: 98.
8 my self] me selfe 98.   others] all Ho Q1–2.   10 his] this Q1–2.   11 fault
Ambition 98.
    28. 98; Dr, Q2; Q1.

With me those paines for God's sake do not take:
I list not dig so deepe for brasen fame.
When I say '*Stella*', I do meane the same   [5]
   Princesse of Beautie, for whose only sake
   The raines of *Love* I love, though never slake,
And joy therein, though Nations count it shame.
   I beg no subject to use eloquence,
Nor in hid wayes to guide Philosophie: [10]
Looke at my hands for no such quintessence;
But know that I in pure simplicitie,
   Breathe out the flames which burne within my heart,
   Love onely reading unto me this art.

29

LIKE some weake Lords, neighbord by mighty kings,
   To keepe themselves and their chiefe cities free,
   Do easly yeeld, that all their coasts may be
Ready to store their campes of needfull things:
So *Stella's* heart, finding what power *Love* brings,   [5]
   To keepe it selfe in life and liberty,
   Doth willing graunt, that in the frontiers he
Use all to helpe his other conquerings:
   And thus her heart escapes, but thus her eyes
   Serve him with shot, her lips his heralds arre: [10]
Her breasts his tents, legs his triumphall carre:
Her flesh his food, her skin his armour brave,
   And I, but for because my prospect lies
   Upon that coast, am giv'n up for a slave.

30

WHETHER the Turkish new-moone minded be
   To fill his hornes this yeare on Christian coast;

3 God's sake] god*es* Love Dr, good now Q2; God-sake Q1.   5 say, 98.   say] see
Q1–2.   6 sake, 98.   10 to] do 98.   14 reading unto me] leading me into Q1–2.
   29. 98; Dr, Q2; Ho, Q1.   3 coasts] cost Ho, coast Q1–2.   4 store their
campes] serv their camp Ho Q1–2.   5 heart 98.   7 frontiers] Frontire Q1–2.
11 carre] Chair Ho Q1–2.   12 Her flesh] her self Ho Q1–2.   14 that] the
Ho Q1.
   30. 98; Dr, Q2; Ho, Q1.   2 his hornes this yeare on] her hornes this yeere
on Q2; their hono^rs here on Ho, her hornes vppon the Q1.   coast: 98.

How *Poles'* right king meanes, without leave of hoast,
To warme with ill-made fire cold *Moscovy*;
If French can yet three parts in one agree;   [5]
    What now the Dutch in their full diets boast;
    How *Holland* hearts, now so good townes be lost,
Trust in the shade of pleasing *Orange* tree;
    How *Ulster* likes of that same golden bit,
Wherewith my father once made it halfe tame;   [10]
If in the Scottishe Court be weltring yet;
These questions busie wits to me do frame;
    I, cumbred with good maners, answer do,
    But know not how, for still I thinke of you.

31

WITH how sad steps, ô Moone, thou climb'st the skies,
How silently, and with how wanne a face,
What, may it be that even in heav'nly place
That busie archer his sharpe arrowes tries?
Sure, if that long with *Love* acquainted eyes   [5]
    Can judge of *Love*, thou feel'st a Lover's case;
    I reade it in thy lookes, thy languisht grace,
To me that feele the like, thy state descries.
    Then ev'n of fellowship, ô Moone, tell me
Is constant *Love* deem'd there but want of wit?   [10]
Are Beauties there as proud as here they be?
Do they above love to be lov'd, and yet
    Those Lovers scorne whom that *Love* doth possesse?
    Do they call *Vertue* there ungratefulnesse?

32

MORPHEUS, the lively sonne of deadly sleepe,
    Witnesse of life to them that living die:

3 *Poles'*] Polands Q1–2.   meanes 98.   meanes] myndes Ho Q1–2.   4 *Moscouy.* 98.
5 agree, 98.   6 boast, 98.   7 be] have Ho, are Q1–2.   8–9 *om.* Q1.   8 tree.
98.   10 once made it] made it once Q1–2.   tame, 98.   11 Scottishe
Court be] *Scotch* Court be no 98; Scottishe Court be as Dr.   yet. 98.   13 I 98.
14 of] on Ho Q1–2.
    31. 98; Dr; Ho, Q1–2.   2 wanne] meane Q1–2.   3 What may it be, 98.
5 Sure 98.   6 a] of Q1–2.   7 it in] within Q1–2.   grace 98.   8 thy]
my Q1–2.   11 they] there Q1–2.   14 ungratefulnesse. 98.
    32. 98; Dr, Q2; Ho, Q1.   1 *Morpheus* 98.

A Prophet oft, and oft an historie,
A Poet eke, as humours fly or creepe,
Since thou in me so sure a power doest keepe, [5]
   That never I with clos'd-up sense do lie,
   But by thy worke my *Stella* I descrie,
Teaching blind eyes both how to smile and weepe,
   Vouchsafe of all acquaintance this to tell,
Whence hast thou Ivorie, Rubies, pearle and gold, [10]
To shew her skin, lips, teeth and head so well?
'Foole,' answers he, 'no *Indes* such treasures hold,
   But from thy heart, while my sire charmeth thee,
   Sweet *Stella's* image I do steale to mee.'

33

I MIGHT, unhappie word, ô me, I might,
And then would not, or could not see my blisse:
Till now, wrapt in a most infernall night,
I find how heav'nly day wretch I did misse.
   Hart rent thy selfe, thou doest thy selfe but right, [5]
No lovely *Paris* made thy *Hellen* his:
No force, no fraud, robd thee of thy delight,
Nor Fortune of thy fortune author is:
   But to my selfe my selfe did give the blow,
While too much wit (forsooth) so troubled me, [10]
That I respects for both our sakes must show:
And yet could not by rising Morne foresee
   How faire a day was neare, ô punisht eyes,
   That I had bene more foolish or more wise.

34

COME let me write, 'And to what end?' To ease
   A burthned hart. 'How can words ease, which are
   The glasses of thy dayly vexing care?'
Oft cruell fights well pictured forth do please.

3 and oft an historie] of hidden mysterie Q1.   4 or] and Q1–2.   6 clos'd-up]
close vp 98.   7 (my *Stella*) 98.   8 weepe. 98.
   33. 98; Dr, Q2; Ho, Q1.   1 ô me] (woe me) Q1–2.   2 or] nor Q1–2.
3 now 98.   4 I did] did I Q1–2.   12 yet could] could I Ho Q1.   13 punisht]
pnnisht Q2; pinisht Ho.
   34. 98; Dr, Q2; Ho, Q1.   1 write, and to . . . to 98.   2 hart, how 98.

'Art not asham'd to publish thy disease?'
   Nay, that may breed my fame, it is so rare:
   'But will not wise men thinke thy words fond ware?'
Then be they close, and so none shall displease.
   'What idler thing, then speake and not be hard?'
What harder thing then smart, and not to speake?   [10]
Peace, foolish wit, with wit my wit is mard.
Thus write I while I doubt to write, and wreake
   My harmes on Ink's poore losse, perhaps some find
   Stella's great powrs, that so confuse my mind.

35

WHAT may words say, or what may words not say,
Where truth it selfe must speake like flatterie?
Within what bounds can one his liking stay,
Where Nature doth with infinite agree?
   What *Nestor's* counsell can my flames alay,   [5]
Since Reason's selfe doth blow the cole in me?
And ah what hope, that hope should once see day,
Where *Cupid* is sworne page to Chastity?
Honour is honour'd, that thou doest possesse
   Him as thy slave, and now long needy Fame   [10]
   Doth even grow rich, naming my *Stella's* name.
Wit learnes in thee perfection to expresse,
   Not thou by praise, but praise in thee is raisde:
   It is a praise to praise, when thou art praisde.

36

STELLA, whence doth this new assault arise,
A conquerd, yelden, ransackt heart to winne?
Whereto long since, through my long battred eyes,
Whole armies of thy beauties entred in.

8 so none shall] they shall none Ho Q1-2.   11 Peace 98.   13 on] in Q1-2.
14 powrs, that so confuse] powr that confusd Ho, power, that so confus'd Q1-2.
   35. 98; Dr, Q2; Q1.   6 Reason's] Reason 98.   cole in] coles to Q1-2.
11 naming] meaning Q1-2.   14 when] where Q1-2.
   36. 98; Dr, Q2; Ho, Q1.   1 this new assault] this new assaults Ho, these newe
assautts Q1-2.   2 conquerd golden 98.   yelden] golden 98; yelding Dr;
yeelding Q1-2.   3 since 98.

And there long since, *Love* thy Lieutenant lies,   [5]
My forces razde, thy banners raisd within:
Of conquest, do not these effects suffice,
But wilt new warre upon thine owne begin?
With so sweete voice, and by sweete Nature so,
In sweetest strength, so sweetly skild withall,   [10]
In all sweete stratagems sweete Arte can show,
That not my soule, which at thy foot did fall,
　　Long since forc'd by thy beames, but stone nor tree
　　By Sence's priviledge, can scape from thee.

37

MY mouth doth water, and my breast doth swell,
　　My tongue doth itch, my thoughts in labour be:
　　Listen then Lordings with good eare to me,
For of my life I must a riddle tell.
Towardes *Aurora's* Court a Nymph doth dwell,   [5]
　　Rich in all beauties which man's eye can see:
　　Beauties so farre from reach of words, that we
Abase her praise, saying she doth excell:
　　Rich in the treasure of deserv'd renowne,
Rich in the riches of a royall hart,   [10]
Rich in those gifts which give th'eternall crowne;
Who though most rich in these and everie part,
　　Which make the patents of true worldly blisse,
　　Hath no misfortune, but that Rich she is.

38

THIS night while sleepe begins with heavy wings
　　To hatch mine eyes, and that unbitted thought
　　Doth fall to stray, and my chiefe powres are brought
To leave the scepter of all subject things,
The first that straight my fancie's error brings   [5]
　　Unto my mind, is *Stella's* image, wrought

7 do not] what doe Q1–2.   8 new] now 98.   9 Nature so 98.   11 strata-
gems, 98.
　37. 98; Dr.   5 Towardes] Toward 98.
　38. 98; Dr, Q2; Ho, Q1.   2 hatch] close Ho Q1–2.   that unbitted] the vnbitted
Q2; that my troubled Q1.   4 things. 98.

By *Love*'s owne selfe, but with so curious drought,
That she, me thinks, not onely shines but sings.
I start, looke, hearke, but what in closde up sence
Was held, in opend sense it flies away,   [10]
Leaving me nought but wailing eloquence:
I, seeing better sights in sight's decay,
   Cald it anew, and wooed sleepe againe:
   But him her host that unkind guest had slaine.

39

COME sleepe, ô sleepe, the certaine knot of peace,
The baiting place of wit, the balme of woe,
The poore man's wealth, the prisoner's release,
Th'indifferent Judge betweene the high and low;
   With shield of proofe shield me from out the prease   [5]
Of those fierce darts, dispaire at me doth throw:
O make in me those civill warres to cease;
I will good tribute pay if thou do so.
   Take thou of me smooth pillowes, sweetest bed,
A chamber deafe to noise, and blind to light: [10]
A rosie garland, and a wearie hed:
And if these things, as being thine by right,
   Move not thy heavy grace, thou shalt in me,
   Livelier then else-where, *Stella*'s image see.

40

AS good to write as for to lie and grone.
   O *Stella* deare, how much thy power hath wrought,
   That hast my mind, none of the basest, brought
My still kept course, while others sleepe, to mone.
Alas, if from the height of Vertue's throne,   [5]
   Thou canst vouchsafe the influence of a thought

9 in closde up] enclosd vp Ho Q1-2.   10 opend] open Ho Q1-2.   12 I 98.
sight's] sighes Q1-2.   13 Cald it] ⟨ ⟩ yt Dr; Conclude Q2.
   39. 98; Dr, Q2; Ho, Q1.   2 baiting place of wit] bathing place of witts Ho
Q1-2.   4 Th'] the Ho Q1-2.   6 those] these Ho Q1-2.   10 to ... to]
of ... of Ho Q1-2.   12 by] in Ho Q1-2.   13 me 98.   14 else-where 98.
   40. 98; Dr, Q2; Q1.   1 grone, 98.   3 none] now Q1-2.   4 others]
other 98; Dr.   sleepe 98.   5 from] ~~thau~~ from Dr; thou Q1.

Upon a wretch, that long thy grace hath sought;
Weigh then how I by thee am overthrowne:
  And then, thinke thus, although thy beautie be
  Made manifest by such a victorie,   [10]
Yet noblest Conquerours do wreckes avoid.
  Since then thou hast so farre subdued me,
  That in my heart I offer still to thee,
O do not let thy Temple be destroyd.

41

HAVING this day my horse, my hand, my launce
  Guided so well, that I obtain'd the prize,
  Both by the judgement of the English eyes,
And of some sent from that sweet enemie *Fraunce*;
Horsemen my skill in horsmanship advaunce;   [5]
  Towne-folkes my strength; a daintier judge applies
  His praise to sleight, which from good use doth rise;
Some luckie wits impute it but to chaunce;
  Others, because of both sides I do take
My bloud from them, who did excell in this,   [10]
Thinke Nature me a man of armes did make.
How farre they shoote awrie! the true cause is,
  Stella lookt on, and from her heavenly face
  Sent forth the beames, which made so faire my race.

42

O EYES, which do the Spheares of beautie move,
Whose beames be joyes, whose joyes all vertues be,
Who while they make *Love* conquer, conquer *Love*,
The schooles where *Venus* hath learn'd Chastitie.
  O eyes, where humble lookes most glorious prove,   [5]
  Only lov'd Tyrants, just in cruelty,

7 that] which Q1–2.   8 Weigh] Way Q1–2.
  41. 98; Dr, Q2; Ho, Q1.   4 from] by Ho Q1.   *Fraunce.* 98.   5 aduaunce:
98.   6 Towne-folkes] townffolke Ho Q1–2.   strength, 98.   7 rise: 98.
8 chaunce: 98.   9 of] from Ho Q1–2.   10 who did] that do Ho Q1–2.
11 of] at Q1–2.   12 shoote] shot 98; Dr; sute Ho.   awrie? 98.   13 heavenly]
hau'nly 98.   14 the] her Ho Q1.   my] a Ho Q1–2.
  42. 98; Dr, Q2; Ho, Q1.   2 be joyes] all ioys Ho Q1–2.

Do not, ô do not from poore me remove,
Keepe still my Zenith, ever shine on me.
    For though I never see them, but straight wayes
My life forgets to nourish languisht sprites;   [10]
Yet still on me, ô eyes, dart downe your rayes:
And if from Majestie of sacred lights,
    Oppressing mortall sense, my death proceed,
    Wrackes Triumphs be, which *Love* (high set) doth breed.

43

FAIRE eyes, sweet lips, deare heart, that foolish I
Could hope by *Cupid's* helpe on you to pray;
Since to himselfe he doth your gifts apply,
As his maine force, choise sport, and easefull stay.
    For when he will see who dare him gainesay,   [5]
Then with those eyes he lookes, lo by and by
Each soule doth at *Love's* feet his weapons lay,
Glad if for her he give them leave to die.
    When he will play, then in her lips he is,
Where blushing red, that *Love's* selfe them doth love,   [10]
With either lip he doth the other kisse:
But when he will for quiet's sake remove
    From all the world, her heart is then his rome,
    Where well he knowes, no man to him can come.

44

MY words I know do well set forth my mind,
    My mind bemones his sense of inward smart;
    Such smart may pitie claime of any hart,
Her heart, sweete heart, is of no Tygre's kind:
And yet she heares, yet I no pitty find;   [5]
    But more I crie, lesse grace she doth impart,
    Alas, what cause is there so overthwart,
That Noblenesse it selfe makes thus unkind?

7 ô] *om.* Ho Q1–2.   poore me] poore me, once Q2; me pore me Ho Q1.   14 be]
best Q1–2.
    43. 98; Dr, Q2; Ho, Q1.   4 choise] chiefe Q1–2.   10 doth] doe Q1–2.
    44. 98, Fr (*lines* 1–4 *only*); Dr, Q2; Ho, Q1.   5 yet I no pitty] and yet no
pitie I 98; & I no pitty Ho Q1–2.

I much do guesse, yet find no truth save this,
That when the breath of my complaints doth tuch   [10]
Those daintie dores unto the Court of blisse,
The heav'nly nature of that place is such,
   That once come there, the sobs of mine annoyes
   Are metamorphosd straight to tunes of joyes.

45

STELLA oft sees the verie face of wo
   Painted in my beclowded stormie face:
   But cannot skill to pitie my disgrace,
Not though thereof the cause her selfe she know:
Yet hearing late a fable, which did show   [5]
   Of Lovers never knowne, a grievous case,
   Pitie thereof gate in her breast such place
That, from that sea deriv'd, teares' spring did flow.
   Alas, if Fancy drawne by imag'd things,
Though false, yet with free scope more grace doth breed   [10]
Then servant's wracke, where new doubts honor brings;
   Then thinke my deare, that you in me do reed
   Of Lover's ruine some sad Tragedie:
   I am not I, pitie the tale of me.

46

I CURST thee oft, I pitie now thy case,
   Blind-hitting boy, since she that thee and me
   Rules with a becke, so tyrannizeth thee,
That thou must want or food, or dwelling place.
For she protests to banish thee her face,   [5]
   Her face? O *Love*, a Rogue thou then shouldst be,
   If *Love* learne not alone to love and see,
Without desire to feed of further grace.

9 save] but Ho Q1.   10 doth] do Ho Q1-2.   12 *om*. Ho Q1.   13 mine]
my Q1-2.
   45. 98; Dr, Q2; Q1.   1 wo] woes Q1-2.   4 No Not thoughe she the
Cause her self do knowe Dr, No though thereof the cause her selfe she knowes Q2; No
though the cause heereof herselfe she knowes Q1.   7 gate] gat Dr; got Q1-2.
place, 98.   8 That from ... deriu'd 98.   As from *her* eyes, a Spring of teares
did flow Q1-2.   12 Then ... you in me] Than ... in me you Q1-2.
   46. 98; Dr, Q2; Q1.   6 be! 98.   8 of] on Dr Q2.

Alas poore wag, that now a scholler art
To such a schoole-mistresse, whose lessons new   [10]
Thou needs must misse, and so thou needs must smart.
Yet Deare, let me this pardon get of you,
    So long (though he from booke myche to desire)
    Till without fewell you can make hot fire.

47

WHAT, have I thus betrayed my libertie?
    Can those blacke beames such burning markes engrave
    In my free side? or am I borne a slave,
Whose necke becomes such yoke of tyranny?
Or want I sense to feele my miserie?   [5]
    Or sprite, disdaine of such disdaine to have?
    Who for long faith, tho dayly helpe I crave,
May get no almes but scorne of beggerie.
    Vertue awake, Beautie but beautie is,
I may, I must, I can, I will, I do   [10]
Leave following that, which it is gaine to misse.
    Let her go. Soft, but here she comes. Go to,
    Unkind, I love you not: O me, that eye
Doth make my heart give to my tongue the lie.

48

SOULE'S joy, bend not those morning starres from me,
    Where Vertue is made strong by Beautie's might,
    Where *Love* is chastnesse, Paine doth learne delight,
And Humblenesse growes one with Majestie.
What ever may ensue, ô let me be   [5]
    Copartner of the riches of that sight:
    Let not mine eyes be hel-driv'n from that light:
O looke, ô shine, ô let me die and see.

12 this] his 98.   14 you] *thou* Q1–2.

    47. 98, Fr (*lines* 9–14 *only*); Dr, Q2; Ho, Q1.   1 What 98.   7 tho] the
Q2; Ho, some Q1.   12 her do: soft, . . . comes, go 98.   go] do 98 Fr.   here]
hear Dr; there Q1–2.   13 O me, that eye] (woe me) that I Ho Q1.   14 Doth
. . . give to] must . . . thus give Ho Q1.

    48. 98; Dr, Q2; Ho, Q1.   4 growes one] grows on Dr Q2; Ho, is linckt Q1.
7 hel-driv'n] held even Dr, driuen Q2; blyndfold Ho, blinded Q1.

For though I oft my selfe of them bemone,
That through my heart their beamie darts be gone,   [10]
Whose curelesse wounds even now most freshly bleed:
  Yet since my death-wound is already got,
  Deare Killer, spare not thy sweet cruell shot:
A kind of grace it is to slay with speed.

49

I ON my horse, and *Love* on me doth trie
  Our horsmanships, while by strange worke I prove
  A horsman to my horse, a horse to *Love*;
And now man's wrongs in me, poore beast, descrie.
The raines wherewith my Rider doth me tie,   [5]
  Are humbled thoughts, which bit of Reverence move,
  Curb'd in with feare, but with guilt bosse above
Of Hope, which makes it seeme faire to the eye.
  The Wand is Will, thou Fancie Saddle art,
Girt fast by memorie, and while I spurre   [10]
My horse, he spurres with sharpe desire my hart:
  He sits me fast, how ever I do sturre:
  And now hath made me to his hand so right,
That in the Manage myselfe takes delight.

50

STELLA, the fulnesse of my thoughts of thee
Cannot be staid within my panting breast,
But they do swell and struggle forth of me,
Till that in words thy figure be exprest.
  And yet as soone as they so formed be,   [5]
According to my Lord *Love's* owne behest:
With sad eyes I their weake proportion see,
To portrait that which in this world is best.

10 gone: 98.   12 death-wound] deaths woonde Ho Q1–2.   14 slay] kill Ho Q1.
  49. 98; Dr, Q2; Ho, Q1.   2 horsmanships] horsemanship Q1–2.   by strange
worke] to straing work*es* Ho, two strong works Q1.   4 me poore beast 98.   5 raines]
raine 98; Ho; Reyne Dr.   my] the Ho Q1.   6 Reverence] reuerent Q1–2.
11 desire] desires Ho Q1–2.   14 myselfe takes] my selfe do take Q2; I my self Ho Q1.
  50. 98; Dr, Q2; Ho, Q1.   1–2 of my thoughts of thee | Cannot be staid] cannot
stayed be | of hidden thowghts Ho Q1.   5 so] thus Ho Q1.   8 that which in]
what within Q1–2.   best] ~~blest~~ best Ho, blest Q1.

So that I cannot chuse but write my mind,
And cannot chuse but put out what I write,   [10]
While those poore babes their death in birth do find:
And now my pen these lines had dashed quite,
But that they stopt his furie from the same,
Because their forefront bare sweet *Stella's* name.

51

PARDON mine eares, both I and they do pray,
So may your tongue still fluently proceed,
To them that do such entertainment need,
So may you still have somewhat new to say.
On silly me do not the burthen lay,   [5]
Of all the grave conceits your braine doth breed;
But find some *Hercules* to beare, in steed
Of *Atlas* tyr'd, your wisedome's heav'nly sway.
For me, while you discourse of courtly tides,
Of cunningst fishers in most troubled streames,   [10]
Of straying wayes, when valiant errour guides:
Meane while my heart confers with *Stella's* beames,
And is even irkt that so sweet Comedie,
By such unsuted speech should hindred be.

52

A STRIFE is growne betweene *Vertue* and *Love*,
While each pretends that *Stella* must be his:
Her eyes, her lips, her all, saith *Love* do this,
Since they do weare his badge, most firmely prove.
But *Vertue* thus that title doth disprove,   [5]
That *Stella* (ô deare name) that *Stella* is
That vertuous soule, sure heire of heav'nly blisse:
Not this faire outside, which our hearts doth move.

11 those] these 98.   13 stopt] stop Q1–2.   14 bare] beares Q1–2.
51. 98; Dr, Q2; Ho, Q1.   2 fluently] flauntingly Ho Q1–2.   3 entertain-
ment] entertainments Q1–2.   4 somewhat] something Ho Q1.   5 the] your
Ho Q1–2.   10 cunningst] cunning 98.   11 wayes] wawes Ho, waues Q1–2.
13 And ys even reck't that sweet Comedie Dr, And is euen woe that so sweet Comedie
Q2; as pitty twas so sweet a commody Ho, As pittie tis so sweete a Comedie Q1.
14 unsuted] vnfuted Q2; vnfitted Q1.
52. 98; Dr, Q2; Ho, Q1.   2 must] may Ho Q1.   3 her all, saith *Love* do]
loue says that he knows Ho, Loue saith that he owes Q1.   8 hearts] hart Ho Q1–2.

And therefore, though her beautie and her grace
Be *Love's* indeed, in *Stella's* selfe he may   [10]
By no pretence claime any maner place.
Well *Love*, since this demurre our sute doth stay,
  Let *Vertue* have that *Stella's* selfe; yet thus,
  That *Vertue* but that body graunt to us.

53

In Martiall sports I had my cunning tride,
  And yet to breake more staves did me addresse:
  While with the people's shouts I must confesse,
Youth, lucke, and praise, even fild my veines with pride.
When *Cupid*, having me his slave describe   [5]
  In *Marse's* liverie, prauncing in the presse:
  'What now sir foole,' said he, 'I would no lesse,
Looke here, I say.' I look'd, and *Stella* spide,
  Who hard by made a window send forth light.
My heart then quak'd, then dazled were mine eyes,   [10]
One hand forgott to rule, th'other to fight.
  Nor trumpets' sound I heard, nor friendly cries;
    My Foe came on, and beat the aire for me,
    Till that her blush taught me my shame to see.

54

Because I breathe not love to everie one,
  Nor do not use set colours for to weare,
  Nor nourish speciall lockes of vowed haire,
Nor give each speech a full point of a grone,
The courtly Nymphs, acquainted with the mone   [5]
  Of them, who in their lips *Love's* standerd beare;
  'What he?' say they of me, 'now I dare sweare,
He cannot love: no, no, let him alone.'

53. 98; Dr, Q2; Ho, Q1.   **2** did] I did Ho Q1–2.   **3** with the people's shouts] that the peopl's showtes Q2; people show*tes* indeed Ho Q1.   **4** praise] *om.* Ho Q1.   **5** *Cupid* hauing . . . describe, 98.   **6** *Marse's*] Mars his Ho Q1–2.   **7** What now] Now what Ho Q1.   **8** say, I look'd and . . . spide: 98.   **9** made a window send forth] through a window sent forth Q2; throwgh a wyndow sent her Ho Q1.   **9** light, 98.   **10** mine] my Q1–2.   **11** forgott] forgat 98.   **12** Nor trumpets'] no trompett*es* Ho, No trumpet Q1–2.

54. 98, Fr (*line* 14 *only*); Dr, Q2; Ho, Q1.   **3** of] wth Ho Q1–2.   **4** grone. 98.   **7** now] no Ho Q1.

And thinke so still, so *Stella* know my mind,
Professe in deed I do not *Cupid's* art;   [10]
But you faire maides, at length this true shall find,
That his right badge is but worne in the hart:
    Dumbe Swannes, not chatring Pies, do Lovers prove,
    They love indeed, who quake to say they love.

55

MUSES, I oft invoked your holy ayde,
    With choisest flowers my speech to engarland so;
    That it, despisde in true but naked shew,
Might winne some grace in your sweet skill arraid.
And oft whole troupes of saddest words I staid,   [5]
    Striving abroad a foraging to go,
    Untill by your inspiring I might know,
How their blacke banner might be best displaid.
    But now I meane no more your helpe to trie,
Nor other sugring of my speech to prove,   [10]
But on her name incessantly to crie:
For let me but name her whom I do love,
    So sweete sounds straight mine eare and heart do hit,
    That I well find no eloquence like it.

56

FY, schoole of Patience, Fy, your lesson is
    Far far too long to learne it without booke:
    What, a whole weeke without one peece of looke,
And thinke I should not your large precepts misse?

10 Professe . . . do . . . art] protest . . . know . . . darte Ho Q1.   12 but worne]
learned Ho Q1.   14 quake to] dare not Ho Q1.
  55. 98; Dr, Q2; Ho, Q1. *Sonnet 55 follows 56 in* Ho Q1-2.   1 invoked] have
cravd Ho Q1.   holy] holly Dr; Ho, whole Q2.   2 to] t' Dr; Q1-2.   3 it
98.   despisde] disguisde Q1-2.   4 skill] grace 98.   6 go; 98.   8 banner]
banners Ho Q1-2.   9 now I meane . . . trie] I meane now . . . prove Ho Q1.
10 Nor other sugering of speech to proue Q2; no other sugaring of speech to try Ho Q1.
11 incessantly] vncessantly Q1-2.   13 sounds straight mine eare] sownd straight
my eares Ho Q1-2.   14 like] but Dr; to Ho Q1.
  56. 98; Dr, Q2; Ho, Q1. *Sonnet 56 precedes 55 in* Ho Q1-2.   1 Fy 98.   3 with-
out one peece of] without a peece of Ho, and yet not halfe a Q1.

When I might reade those letters faire of blisse,   [5]
   Which in her face teach vertue, I could brooke
   Somewhat thy lead'n counsels, which I tooke
As of a friend that meant not much amisse:
   But now that I, alas, do want her sight,
What, dost thou thinke that I can ever take   [10]
In thy cold stuffe a flegmatike delight?
No Patience, if thou wilt my good, then make
   Her come, and heare with patience my desire,
   And then with patience bid me beare my fire.

57

Wo, having made with many fights his owne
   Each sence of mine, each gift, each power of mind,
   Growne now his slaves, he forst them out to find
The thorowest words, fit for woe's selfe to grone,
Hoping that when they might find *Stella* alone,   [5]
   Before she could prepare to be unkind,
   Her soule, arm'd but with such a dainty rind,
Should soone be pierc'd with sharpnesse of the mone.
   She heard my plaints, and did not only heare,
But them (so sweete is she) most sweetly sing,   [10]
With that faire breast making woe's darknesse cleare:
   A prety case! I hoped her to bring
   To feele my griefes, and she with face and voice
So sweets my paines, that my paines me rejoyce.

58

Doubt there hath bene, when with his golden chaine
   The Oratour so farre men's harts doth bind,

5 those] these Ho Q1.   6 Which in her face teach] w^thin her face ech Ho Q1.
7 Somewhat thy . . . which] from what the . . . that Ho Q1.   tooke, 98.   8 that]
wch Ho Q1.   9 that I, alas] alas that I Ho Q1-2.   I alas 98.

57. 98; Dr, Q2; Ho, Q1.   1 fights] sighes Ho Q1-2.   7 soule 98.   but]
om. Ho Q1-2.   8 pierc'd] prest Dr; hurt Ho Q1-2.   10 is she] she did Ho
Q1.   12 A prety case! I hoped her] my privy cares to her I hope Ho, My priuie
cares I holpe to her Q1.   case 98.   13 feele] tell Ho Q1.   griefes] griefe Ho
Q1-2.   voice, 98.

58. 98; Dr, Q2; Ho, Q1.   1 bene when . . . chaine, 98.

That no pace else their guided steps can find,
But as he them more short or slacke doth raine,
Whether with words this soveraignty he gaine,   [5]
    Cloth'd with fine tropes, with strongest reasons lin'd,
    Or else pronouncing grace, wherewith his mind
Prints his owne lively forme in rudest braine.
    Now judge by this: in piercing phrases late,
    Th' anatomy of all my woes I wrate,   [10]
Stella's sweete breath the same to me did reed.
    O voice, ô face, maugre my speeche's might,
    Which wooed wo, most ravishing delight
Even those sad words even in sad me did breed.

59

DEARE, why make you more of a dog then me?
    If he do love, I burne, I burne in love:
    If he waite well, I never thence would move:
If he be faire, yet but a dog can be.
    Litle he is, so litle worth is he;   [5]
    He barks, my songs thine owne voyce oft doth prove:
    Bid'n, perhaps he fetcheth thee a glove,
But I unbid, fetch even my soule to thee.
    Yet while I languish, him that bosome clips,
    That lap doth lap, nay lets, in spite of spite,   [10]
This sowre-breath'd mate tast of those sugred lips.
    Alas, if you graunt only such delight
    To witlesse things, then Love I hope (since wit
    Becomes a clog) will soone ease me of it.

60

WHEN my good Angell guides me to the place,
    Where all my good I do in Stella see,

3 pace . . . guided . . . can] place . . . giddy . . . could Ho Q1.   4 short or slacke
doth] slack or sharpe did Ho, slacker short did Q1.   raine. 98.   5 this] his Ho
Q1.   6 with strongest reasons] with strongest reason Q2; as his strongest Q1.
8 lively forme] forme lyvely Ho Q1.   braine: 98.   9 this, 98.   10 Th'] The
98; Q1.   13 Which wooed wo] With wooed woe Q2; wth woed wordes Ho Q1.
delight, 98.   14 words, 98.   even in sad] a ioy in Ho, a ioy to Q1-2.
    59. 98; Dr, Q2; Ho, Q1.   2 love, I burne] love alas Ho Q1-2.   7 Bid'n
98.   10 lets 98.   11 sowre-breath'd] fawning Ho Q1.   13 Loue, 98.
    60. 98; Dr, Q2; Ho, Q1.

That heav'n of joyes throwes onely downe on me
Thundred disdaines and lightnings of disgrace:
But when the ruggedst step of Fortune's race   [5]
  Makes me fall from her sight, then sweetly she
  With words, wherein the Muses' treasures be,
Shewes love and pitie to my absent case.
  Now I, wit-beaten long by hardest Fate,
So dull am, that I cannot looke into   [10]
The ground of this fierce *Love* and lovely hate:
  Then some good body tell me how I do,
  Whose presence, absence, absence presence is;
Blist in my curse, and cursed in my blisse.

61

OFT with true sighes, oft with uncalled teares,
Now with slow words, now with dumbe eloquence
I *Stella's* eyes assayll, invade her eares;
But this at last is her sweet breath'd defence:
  That who indeed infelt affection beares,   [5]
So captives to his Saint both soule and sence,
That wholly hers, all selfnesse he forbeares,
Thence his desires he learnes, his live's course thence.
  Now since her chast mind hates this love in me,
  With chastned mind, I straight must shew that she   [10]
Shall quickly me from what she hates remove.
  O Doctor *Cupid*, thou for me reply,
  Driv'n else to graunt by Angel's sophistrie,
That I love not, without I leave to love.

62

LATE tyr'd with wo, even ready for to pine
With rage of *Love*, I cald my Love unkind;

3 heav'n of] hevenly Ho Q1.   4 lightnings] lightning Q1–2.   9 I 98.   wit-
beaten] wth beating Ho Q1.   11 lovely] loving Ho Q1–2.   12 I] to Q1–2.
14 Blist] Blest Dr; Ho Q1–2.

  61. 98; Dr, Q2; Ho, Q1.   3 assayll] assaid 98; assaild Ho Q1–2.   invade]
I cloyd Ho, I closde Q1.   4 sweet breath'd] sweetest Ho Q1.   6 sence]
mynd Ho Q1.   8 Thence] Then 98.   desires] desyre Ho Q1–2.   learnes 98,
9 her...mind] this...love Ho Q1–2.   10 straight] needs Ho Q1–2.   13 Angel's]
Angell Q1–2.

  62. 98; Dr, Q2; Ho, Q1.   2 cald] call Q1–2.

She in whose eyes *Love*, though unfelt, doth shine,
Sweet said that I true love in her should find.
    I joyed, but straight thus watred was my wine,   [5]
That love she did, but loved a Love not blind,
Which would not let me, whom she loved, decline
From nobler course, fit for my birth and mind:
    And therefore by her Love's authority,
    Willd me these tempests of vaine love to flie,   [10]
And anchor fast my selfe on *Vertue's* shore.
    Alas, if this the only mettall be
    Of *Love*, new-coind to helpe my beggery,
Deare, love me not, that you may love me more.

63

O GRAMMER rules, ô now your vertues show;
So children still reade you with awfull eyes,
    As my young Dove may in your precepts wise
Her graunt to me, by her owne vertue know.
For late with heart most high, with eyes most low,   [5]
    I crav'd the thing which ever she denies:
    She lightning *Love*, displaying *Venus'* skies,
Least once should not be heard, twise said, No, No.
    Sing then my Muse, now *Io Pean* sing,
    Heav'ns envy not at my high triumphing: [10]
But Grammer's force with sweet successe confirme,
    For Grammer sayes (ô this deare *Stella* weighe,)
    For Grammer sayes (to Grammer who sayes nay)
That in one speech two Negatives affirme.

First song

DOUBT you to whom my Muse these notes entendeth,
Which now my breast orecharg'd to Musicke lendeth?
To you, to you, all song of praise is due,
Only in you my song begins and endeth.

3 *Loue* though vnfelt 98.   4 Sweet said that] sweetly sayd Ho Q1–2.   find, 98.
6 loved] wth Ho Q1–2.   10 Willd] Wild 98; Q2; Wilde Q1.   flie] flee Q1–2.
14 you] ye 98.
    63. 98; Dr, Q2; Ho, Q1.   8 once] one Q1–2.   9 *om.* Q1.   11 con-
firme: 98.   12 ô] ah Ho Q1–2.   weighe] nay 98; waye Ho Q1–2.
    i. 98; Dr; Q1.   *Heading*: The .1. Song Dr; First Sonnet Q1.   2 lendeth: 98.

Who hath the eyes which marrie state with pleasure,   [5]
Who keepes the key of Nature's chiefest treasure?
To you, to you, all song of praise is due,
Only for you the heav'n forgate all measure.

Who hath the lips, where wit in fairenesse raigneth,
Who womankind at once both deckes and stayneth?   [10]
To you, to you, all song of praise is due,
Onely by you *Cupid* his crowne maintaineth.

Who hath the feet, whose step all sweetnesse planteth,
Who else for whom *Fame* worthy trumpets wanteth?
To you, to you, all song of praise is due,   [15]
Onely to you her Scepter *Venus* granteth.

Who hath the breast, whose milke doth passions nourish,
Whose grace is such, that when it chides doth cherish?
To you, to you, all song of praise is due,
Onelie through you the tree of life doth flourish.   [20]

Who hath the hand which without stroke subdueth,
Who long dead beautie with increase reneweth?
To you, to you, all song of praise is due,
Onely at you all envie hopelesse rueth.

Who hath the haire which, loosest, fastest tieth,   [25]
Who makes a man live then glad when he dieth?
To you, to you, all song of praise is due:
Only of you the flatterer never lieth.

Who hath the voyce, which soule from sences sunders,
Whose force but yours the bolts of beautie thunders?   [30]
To you, to you, all song of praise is due:
Only with you not miracles are wonders.

Doubt you to whom my Muse these notes intendeth,
Which now my breast orecharg'd to Musicke lendeth?
To you, to you, all song of praise is due: [35]
Only in you my song begins and endeth.

6 treasure: 98.   10 stayneth: 98.   13 step all] step of 98; steps al Q1.
14 wanteth: 98.   18 cherish, 98.   19 you all 98.   22 reneweth: 98.
25 which loosest 98.   loosest, fastest] loosing faster Dr; most loose most fast Q1.
26 dieth: 98.   30 thunders: 98.   32 not] all Dr; no Q1.   34 lendeth: 98.

64

No more, my deare, no more these counsels trie,
  O give my passions leave to run their race:
  Let Fortune lay on me her worst disgrace,
Let folke orecharg'd with braine against me crie,
Let clouds bedimme my face, breake in mine eye,   [5]
  Let me no steps but of lost labour trace,
  Let all the earth with scorne recount my case,
But do not will me from my *Love* to flie.
  I do not envie *Aristotle's* wit,
Nor do aspire to *Cæsar's* bleeding fame,   [10]
Nor ought do care, though some above me sit,
Nor hope, nor wishe another course to frame,
  But that which once may win thy cruell hart:
  Thou art my Wit, and thou my Vertue art.

65

Love by sure proofe I may call thee unkind,
That giv'st no better eare to my just cries:
Thou whom to me such my good turnes should bind,
As I may well recount, but none can prize:
  For when, nak'd boy, thou couldst no harbour find   [5]
In this old world, growne now so too too wise:
I lodg'd thee in my heart, and being blind
By Nature borne, I gave to thee mine eyes.
  Mine eyes, my light, my heart, my life, alas,
If so great services may scorned be: [10]
Yet let this thought thy Tygrish courage passe:
That I perhaps am somewhat kinne to thee;
  Since in thine armes, if learnd fame truth hath spread,
  Thou bear'st the arrow, I the arrow head.

64. 98; Dr, Q2; Ho, Q1.   4 crie. 98.   5 bedimme my face, breake in
mine eye] be dimme, my face breake in my eye Q2; be dymme my face bereav myne
eyes Ho, be dimme, my fate bereaues myne eyes Q1.   6 trace: 98.   trace] try
Ho Q1–2.   7 with] in Q1–2.   case] race Ho Q1–2.   10 fame; 98.
11 do] to Q1–2.   sit: 98.   12 wishe] with 98.   13 hart 98.

65. 98; Dr, Q2; Ho, Q1.   2 giv'st . . . eare] gevs . . . eares Ho Q1–2.
3 should] shouldst Q1–2.   4 recount, but none can] accowmpt but cannot Ho
Q1.   5 when nak'd boy 98.   8 mine] my Ho Q1–2.   9 heart, my life]
heart Ho, life, my hart Q1–2.   13 if learnd fame truth hath] if fame the truth
hav Ho, of Fame most truely Q1.

66

AND do I see some cause a hope to feede,
Or doth the tedious burd'n of long wo
In weakened minds, quicke apprehending breed,
Of everie image, which may comfort show?
    I cannot brag of word, much lesse of deed, [5]
Fortune wheeles still with me in one sort slow,
My wealth no more, and no whit lesse my need,
Desire still on the stilts of feare doth go.
    And yet amid all feares a hope there is
Stolne to my heart, since last faire night, nay day, [10]
Stella's eyes sent to me the beames of blisse,
Looking on me, while I lookt other way:
    But when mine eyes backe to their heav'n did move,
    They fled with blush, which guiltie seem'd of love.

67

HOPE, art thou true, or doest thou flatter me?
    Doth *Stella* now begin with piteous eye,
    The ruines of her conquest to espie:
Will she take time, before all wracked be?
Her eye's-speech is translated thus by thee: [5]
    But failst thou not in phrase so heav'nly hie?
    Looke on againe, the faire text better trie:
What blushing notes doest thou in margine see?
    What sighes stolne out, or kild before full borne?
Hast thou found such and such like arguments? [10]
Or art thou else to comfort me forsworne?
Well, how so thou interpret the contents,
    I am resolv'd thy errour to maintaine,
    Rather then by more truth to get more paine.

66. 98; Dr, Q2; Ho, Q1.   3 apprehending] apprehension Q1-2.   6 Fortune wheeles] Fortunes wheeles 98; Dr; Ho, Fortunes windes Q1.   slow] blow Ho Q1.   8 the] *om.* Q1-2.   9 amid] amids Q1-2.   is, 98.   10 heart 98.   12 while I lookt other] while I looke other Q2; I looke an other Q1.

    67. 98; Q2; Ho, Q1.   3 ruines of her] raigne of this Ho Q1-2.   5 eye's-speech] eye speech Ho Q1-2.   7 on] ons Ho, ore Q1.   trie] prye Q1-2.   12 the] my Ho Q1.

68

STELLA, the onely Planet of my light,
 Light of my life, and life of my desire,
 Chiefe good, whereto my hope doth only aspire,
World of my wealth, and heav'n of my delight.
Why doest thou spend the treasures of thy sprite,   [5]
 With voice more fit to wed *Amphion's* lyre,
 Seeking to quench in me the noble fire,
Fed by thy worth, and kindled by thy sight?
 And all in vaine, for while thy breath most sweet,
With choisest words, thy words with reasons rare,   [10]
Thy reasons firmly set on *Vertue's* feet,
Labour to kill in me this killing care:
 O thinke I then, what paradise of joy
 It is, so faire a Vertue to enjoy.

69

O JOY, too high for my low stile to show:
 O blisse, fit for a nobler state then me:
 Envie, put out thine eyes, least thou do see
What Oceans of delight in me do flow.
My friend, that oft saw through all maskes my wo,   [5]
 Come, come, and let me powre my selfe on thee;
 Gone is the winter of my miserie,
My spring appeares, ô see what here doth grow.
 For *Stella* hath with words where faith doth shine,
Of her high heart giv'n me the monarchie: [10]
I, I, ô I may say, that she is mine.
And though she give but thus conditionly
 This realme of blisse, while vertuous course I take,
 No kings be crown'd but they some covenants make.

68. 98; Q2; Ho, Q1.   3 only aspire] onely' spire Q2; sole aspire Q1.
5 treasures] Treasure Q1–2. 8 Fed] set Ho Q1.   kindled] blinded 98.
9 most] so Ho Q1. 11 on] are Q1–2. *feet*, 98.
 69. 98; Q2; Ho, Q1. 1 low stile] Loue still Q1–2.   2 state] seat Ho
Q1–2. 4 Oceans] *Ouans* Q1. do] doth Q1–2. 5 saw] sawst Ho Q1–2.
8 ô] lo Ho Q1. 11 I, I, ô] And I o Ho, And *Io* Q1. 12 thus] this [? or
thus] Ho, this Q1. 13 vertuous] vertues Q1–2. 14 covenants] couenant
Q1–2. make, 98.

70

MY Muse may well grudge at my heav'nly joy,
If still I force her in sad rimes to creepe:
She oft hath drunke my teares, now hopes to enjoy
Nectar of Mirth, since I *Jove's* cup do keepe.
    Sonets be not bound prentise to annoy: [5]
Trebles sing high, as well as bases deepe:
Griefe but *Love's* winter liverie is, the Boy
Hath cheekes to smile, as well as eyes to weepe.
    Come then my Muse, shew thou height of delight
In well raisde notes, my pen the best it may   [10]
Shall paint out joy, though but in blacke and white.
Cease eager Muse, peace pen, for my sake stay,
    I give you here my hand for truth of this,
    Wise silence is best musicke unto blisse.

71

WHO will in fairest booke of Nature know,
    How Vertue may best lodg'd in beautie be,
    Let him but learne of *Love* to reade in thee,
Stella, those faire lines, which true goodnesse show.
There shall he find all vices' overthrow,   [5]
    Not by rude force, but sweetest soveraigntie
    Of reason, from whose light those night-birds flie;
That inward sunne in thine eyes shineth so.
    And not content to be Perfection's heire
Thy selfe, doest strive all minds that way to move,   [10]
Who marke in thee what is in thee most faire.
So while thy beautie drawes the heart to love,
    As fast thy Vertue bends that love to good:
    'But ah,' Desire still cries, 'give me some food.'

70. 98; Q2; Ho, Q1.   2 in sad rimes to creepe] thus in woe to weepe Ho Q1.
3 to] t' Q1–2.   4 cup do] Cupid Ho Q1.   6 as] so Ho Q1–2.   8 as well]
so well Q1–2.   to weepe] weepe Q2.   9 thou height] the height Q2; Ho, the
force Q1.

71. 98; Q2; Ho, Q1.   3 thee 98.   4 goodnesse show] vertue know Ho,
Beautie showe Q1.   7 light those] *om.* Ho, light, the Q1–2.   10 doest] doth
Q2.   moue: 98.   11 marke in thee what is in thee] marke in thee what is in
deede Q2; marking thee wch art indeed Ho Q1.   12 drawes the] dryvs thy Ho,
driues my Q1–2.

72

DESIRE, though thou my old companion art,
   And oft so clings to my pure Love, that I
   One from the other scarcely can descrie,
While each doth blow the fier of my hart;
Now from thy fellowship I needs must part,   [5]
   Venus is taught with *Dian's* wings to flie:
   I must no more in thy sweet passions lie;
Vertue's gold now must head my *Cupid's* dart.
   Service and Honor, wonder with delight,
Feare to offend, will worthie to appeare,   [10]
Care shining in mine eyes, faith in my sprite,
These things are left me by my only Deare;
   But thou Desire, because thou wouldst have all,
   Now banisht art, but yet alas how shall?

Second song

HAVE I caught my heav'nly jewell,
Teaching sleepe most faire to be?
Now will I teach her that she,
When she wakes, is too too cruell.

Since sweet sleep her eyes hath charmed,   [5]
The two only darts of *Love*:
Now will I with that boy prove
Some play, while he is disarmed.

Her tongue waking still refuseth,
Giving frankly niggard No: [10]
Now will I attempt to know,
What No her tongue sleeping useth.

See the hand which waking gardeth,
Sleeping, grants a free resort:
Now will I invade the fort;   [15]
Cowards *Love* with losse rewardeth.

72. 98; Q2; Ho, Q1.   1 my] mine Q2.   4 doth] do Ho Q1.   10 will]
well Ho Q1-2.   11 sprite. 98.   14 but] *om.* Q2.   alas how shall] alas who shall
Ho, within my call Q1.
   ii. 98; Q1.   13 which] that Q1.   15 will I] I wil Q1.

But ô foole, thinke of the danger,
Of her just and high disdaine:
Now will I alas refraine,
Love feares nothing else but anger.   [20]

Yet those lips so sweetly swelling,
Do invite a stealing kisse:
Now will I but venture this,
Who will read must first learne spelling.

Oh sweet kisse, but ah she is waking,   [25]
Lowring beautie chastens me:
Now will I away hence flee:
Foole, more foole, for no more taking.

73

LOVE still a boy, and oft a wanton is,
School'd onely by his mother's tender eye:
What wonder then if he his lesson misse,
When for so soft a rod deare play he trie?
   And yet my Starre, because a sugred kisse   [5]
In sport I suckt, while she asleepe did lie,
Doth lowre, nay, chide; nay, threat for only this:
Sweet, it was saucie *Love*, not humble I.
   But no scuse serves, she makes her wrath appeare
In Beautie's throne, see now who dares come neare   [10]
Those scarlet judges, threatning bloudy paine?
   O heav'nly foole, thy most kisse-worthie face,
   Anger invests with such a lovely grace,
That Anger' selfe I needs must kisse againe.

74

I NEVER dranke of *Aganippe* well,
Nor ever did in shade of *Tempe* sit:
And Muses scorne with vulgar braines to dwell,
Poore Layman I, for sacred rites unfit.

23 will I but venture] but venture will I Qı.   27 away] for feare Qı.
   73. 98; Q2; Ho, Qı.   6 suckt] sucke Qı-2.   14 Anger'] Angers Qı-2.
   74. 98; Q2; Ho, Qı.   2 ever] neuer Qı-2.

Some do I heare of Poets' furie tell, [5]
But (God wot) wot not what they meane by it:
And this I sweare by blackest brooke of hell,
I am no pick-purse of another's wit.
　　How falles it then, that with so smooth an ease
My thoughts I speake, and what I speake doth flow [10]
In verse, and that my verse best wits doth please?
Guesse we the cause: 'What, is it thus?' Fie no:
　　'Or so?' Much lesse: 'How then?' Sure thus it is:
　　My lips are sweet, inspired with *Stella's* kisse.

75

OF all the kings that ever here did raigne,
Edward named fourth, as first in praise I name,
Not for his faire outside, nor well lined braine,
Although lesse gifts impe feathers oft on Fame,
　　Nor that he could young-wise, wise-valiant frame [5]
His Sire's revenge, joyn'd with a kingdome's gaine:
And gain'd by *Mars*, could yet mad *Mars* so tame,
That Ballance weigh'd what sword did late obtaine,
　　Nor that he made the Flouredeluce so fraid,
Though strongly hedg'd of bloudy Lyon's pawes, [10]
That wittie *Lewis* to him a tribute paid.
Nor this, nor that, nor any such small cause,
　　But only for this worthy knight durst prove
　　To lose his Crowne, rather then faile his Love.

76

SHE comes, and streight therewith her shining twins do move
　　Their rayes to me, who in her tedious absence lay
　　Benighted in cold wo, but now appeares my day,
The onely light of joy, the onely warmth of *Love*.

12 cause, what is it thus? fie 98.　　thus] this Ho Q1-2.　　13 much . . . how . . .
sure 98.　　14 sweet] sure Q1-2.
　　75. 98; Q2; Ho, Q1.　　3 braine; 98.　　4 gifts impe] guift, imp Q2; guift,
are Q1.　　oft on] oft no Q2; of ow^r Ho, of high Q1.　　Fame 98.　　8 obtaine.
98.　　9 Flouredeluce] Flower de lys Q2.　　13 knight] King Q1-2.　　14 lose]
loose 98; Q1-2.　　faile] lose Ho, loose Q1.
　　76. 98; Q2; Ho, Q1.　　1 moue, 98.　　3 Benighted] bathed Ho, Bath'de Q1.
my] my shining Q1-2.

She comes with light and warmth, which like *Aurora* prove   [5]
   Of gentle force, so that mine eyes dare gladly play
   With such a rosie morne, whose beames most freshly gay
Scortch not, but onely do darke chilling sprites remove.
   But lo, while I do speake, it groweth noone with me,
Her flamie glistring lights increase with time and place;   [10]
My heart cries 'ah', it burnes, mine eyes now dazled be:
No wind, no shade can coole, what helpe then in my case,
   But with short breath, long lookes, staid feet and walking hed,
   Pray that my sunne go downe with meeker beames to bed.

77

THOSE lookes, whose beames be joy, whose motion is delight,
That face, whose lecture shewes what perfect beautie is:
That presence, which doth give darke hearts a living light:
That grace, which *Venus* weepes that she her selfe doth misse:
   That hand, which without touch holds more then *Atlas* might;
Those lips, which make death's pay a meane price for a kisse: [6]
That skin, whose passe-praise hue scorns this poore terme of white:
Those words, which do sublime the quintessence of blisse:
   That voyce, which makes the soule plant himselfe in the eares:
That conversation sweet, where such high comforts be,   [10]
As consterd in true speech, the name of heav'n it beares,
Makes me in my best thoughts and quietst judgement see,
   That in no more but these I might be fully blest:
   Yet ah, my Mayd'n Muse doth blush to tell the best.

78

   O HOW the pleasant aires of true love be
      Infected by those vapours, which arise
      From out that noysome gulfe, which gaping lies
    Betweene the jawes of hellish Jealousie.

6 force . . . mine] force . . . my Q2; face . . . my Ho Q1.   7 freshly] fresh & Ho
Q1.   10 glistring] glittering Ho Q1–2.   12 can] no Ho Q1.   14 meeker]
me her Q2.
   77. 98; Q2; Ho, Q1.   1 be] my Ho Q1.   6 make] makes Q1–2.
7 passe-praise] past-praise Q2; passing Ho Q1.   white] whit Q2.   8 which]
that Ho Q1.   11 consterd] construed Ho, constru'd Q1–2.   12 quietst
judgement] quyetts iudgm^t Ho, quiet iudgements Q1–2.
   78. 98; Q2; Ho, Q1.

A monster, other's harme, selfe-miserie, [5]
 Beautie's plague, Vertue's scourge, succour of lies:
 Who his owne joy to his owne hurt applies,
And onely cherish doth with injurie.
 Who since he hath, by Nature's speciall grace,
 So piercing pawes, as spoyle when they embrace, [10]
So nimble feet as stirre still, though on thornes:
 So manie eyes ay seeking their owne woe,
 So ample eares as never good newes know:
Is it not evill that such a Devill wants hornes?

79

SWEET kisse, thy sweets I faine would sweetly endite,
 Which even of sweetnesse sweetest sweetner art:
 Pleasingst consort, where each sence holds a part,
Which, coupling Doves, guides *Venus'* chariot right.
Best charge, and bravest retrait in *Cupid's* fight, [5]
 A double key, which opens to the heart,
 Most rich, when most his riches it impart:
Neast of young joyes, schoolmaster of delight,
 Teaching the meane, at once to take and give
The friendly fray, where blowes both wound and heale, [10]
The prettie death, while each in other live.
Poore hope's first wealth, ostage of promist weale,
 Breakefast of *Love*, but lo, lo, where she is,
 Cease we to praise, now pray we for a kisse.

80

SWEET swelling lip, well maist thou swell in pride,
 Since best wits thinke it wit thee to admire;
 Nature's praise, Vertue's stall, *Cupid's* cold fire,
Whence words, not words, but heav'nly graces slide.

5 harme] harmes Q1–2. 7 hurt] hart Ho Q1–2. 8 injurie] iniuries Q1–2.
11 still, though] though still Ho Q1–2. 12 ay] as Ho Q1. 13 as] that Ho Q1–2.
 79. 98; Q2; Ho, Q1. 2 sweetner] sweeter Ho Q1–2. 3 Pleasingst]
pleasing Ho Q1. 4 Which coupling Doues 98. Which] wth Ho Q1–2.
6 opens] openeth Ho Q1–2. 9 meane] meanes Q1–2. 10 both] doth Ho,
do Q1–2. 12 ostage of promist] a stage of promised Q2; A ⟨ ⟩ promyse Ho, a
pledge of promised Q1.
 80. 98; Q2; Ho, Q1. 2 wit] best Ho Q1.

The new *Pernassus*, where the Muses bide,   [5]
   Sweetner of musicke, wisedome's beautifier:
   Breather of life, and fastner of desire,
Where Beautie's blush in Honour's graine is dide.
   Thus much my heart compeld my mouth to say,
   But now spite of my heart my mouth will stay,   [10]
Loathing all lies, doubting this Flatterie is:
   And no spurre can his resty race renew,
   Without how farre this praise is short of you,
Sweet lip, you teach my mouth with one sweet kisse.

81

O KISSE, which doest those ruddie gemmes impart,
Or gemmes, or frutes of new-found *Paradise*,
Breathing all blisse and sweetning to the heart,
Teaching dumbe lips a nobler exercise.
   O kisse, which soules, even soules together ties   [5]
By linkes of *Love*, and only Nature's art:
How faine would I paint thee to all men's eyes,
Or of thy gifts at least shade out some part.
   But she forbids, with blushing words, she sayes,
   She builds her fame on higher seated praise: [10]
But my heart burnes, I cannot silent be.
   Then since (deare life) you faine would have me peace,
   And I, mad with delight, want wit to cease,
Stop you my mouth with still still kissing me.

82

NYMPH of the gard'n, where all beauties be:
   Beauties which do in excellencie passe
   His who till death lookt in a watrie glasse,
Or hers whom naked the *Trojan* boy did see.

6 Sweetner] swetnes Ho Q1–2.   beautifier] *om.* Ho.   7 fastner] fastnes Ho Q1.
9 compeld my mouth] my mouth compeld Ho Q1.   10 mouth] tongue Q1–2.
12 his] this Ho Q1–2.   13–14 *om.* Ho, Wherefore to trie if that I said be true, |
How can I better proue then with a kisse? Q1.
   81. 98; Q2; Ho, Q1.   1 doest] doth Q1–2.   3 sweetning] sweetnes
Q1–2.   8 shade] set Ho Q1.   12 life] kisse Ho Q1.
   82. 98; Q2; Ho, Q1.   2 passe: 98.   3 lookt] lockt Q1–2.   4 hers] her
Ho Q1.

Sweet gard'n Nymph, which keepes the Cherrie tree,   [5]
    Whose fruit doth farre th'*Esperian* tast surpasse:
    Most sweet-faire, most faire-sweet, do not alas,
From comming neare those Cherries banish me:
    For though full of desire, emptie of wit,
Admitted late by your best-graced grace,   [10]
I caught at one of them a hungrie bit;
Pardon that fault, once more graunt me the place,
    And I do sweare even by the same delight,
    I will but kisse, I never more will bite.

83

GOOD brother *Philip*, I have borne you long,
    I was content you should in favour creepe,
    While craftily you seem'd your cut to keepe,
As though that faire soft hand did you great wrong.
I bare (with Envie) yet I bare your song,   [5]
    When in her necke you did *Love* ditties peepe;
    Nay, more foole I, oft suffered you to sleepe
In Lillies' neast, where *Love's* selfe lies along.
    What, doth high place ambitious thoughts augment?
    Is sawcinesse reward of curtesie?   [10]
Cannot such grace your silly selfe content,
But you must needs with those lips billing be?
    And through those lips drinke Nectar from that toong;
    Leave that sir *Phip*, least off your necke be wroong.

Third song

IF *Orpheus'* voyce had force to breathe such musicke's love
Through pores of sencelesse trees, as it could make them move:
If stones good measure daunc'd, the *Theban* walles to build,
To cadence of the tunes, which *Amphyon's* lyre did yeeld,
More cause a like effect at leastwise bringeth: [5]
O stones, ô trees, learne hearing, *Stella* singeth.

6 th' *Esperian*] the hemisperian Ho, the Hesperian Q1–2.   8 those] these Ho Q1–2.
13 I do] so I Ho Q1–2.   even by the same] by the self same Ho Q1.
   83. 98; Q2; Ho, Q1.   1 borne] forborne Ho Q1–2.   5 yet] heare Q1–2.
14 *Phip*, least off] philippe lest Ho Q1.
   iii. 98; Q1.

If Love might sweet'n so a boy of shepheard' brood,
To make a Lyzard dull to taste Love's daintie food:
If Eagle fierce could so in *Grecian* Mayd delight,
As his light was her eyes, her death his endlesse night: [10]
Earth gave that Love, heav'n I trow Love refineth:
O birds, ô beasts, looke Love, lo, *Stella* shineth.

The birds, beasts, stones and trees feele this, and feeling *Love*:
And if the trees, nor stones stirre not the same to prove,
Nor beasts, nor birds do come unto this blessed gaze,   [15]
Know, that small Love is quicke, and great Love doth amaze:
They are amaz'd, but you with reason armed,
O eyes, ô eares of men, how are you charmed!

84

HIGHWAY since you my chiefe *Pernassus* be,
   And that my Muse to some eares not unsweet,
   Tempers her words to trampling horses feet,
More oft then to a chamber melodie;
Now blessed you, beare onward blessed me   [5]
   To her, where I my heart safeliest shall meet.
   My Muse and I must you of dutie greet
With thankes and wishes, wishing thankfully.
   Be you still faire, honourd by publike heed,
By no encrochment wrongd, nor time forgot: [10]
Nor blam'd for bloud, nor sham'd for sinfull deed.
   And that you know, I envy you no lot
      Of highest wish, I wish you so much blisse,
      Hundreds of yeares you *Stella's* feet may kisse.

85

I SEE the house, my heart thy selfe containe,
   Beware full sailes drowne not thy tottring barge:

7 shepheard] Shepheards Q1.   8 daintie] *om.* Q1.   10 his light was her
eyes] her eyes were his light Q1.   12 O birds, ô beasts,] O beasts, ô birds 98; O
beasts, birds Q1.   looke, 98.

   84. 98; Q2; Ho, Q1.   1 High way 98.   2 unsweet] vnmeete Q1-2.   4 oft
then to] often than to Q2; often then Ho Q1.   melodie. 98.   5 onward]
onwards Q1-2.   6 I my heart safeliest] I my heart safelest 98; my heart
safliest Ho Q1   meet, 98.   9 faire, honourd] carefull kept Q1-2.

   85. 98; Q2; Ho, Q1.

Least joy, by Nature apt sprites to enlarge,
Thee to thy wracke beyond thy limits straine.
Nor do like Lords, whose weake confused braine,   [5]
    Not pointing to fit folkes each undercharge,
    While everie office themselves will discharge,
With doing all, leave nothing done but paine.
    But give apt servants their due place, let eyes
See Beautie's totall summe summ'd in her face: [10]
Let eares heare speech, which wit to wonder ties,
Let breath sucke up those sweetes, let armes embrace
    The globe of weale, lips *Love's* indentures make:
    Thou but of all the kingly Tribute take.

Fourth song

ONELY joy, now here you are,
Fit to heare and ease my care:
Let my whispering voyce obtaine,
Sweete reward for sharpest paine:
Take me to thee, and thee to me.   [5]
'No, no, no, no, my Deare, let be.'

Night hath closd all in her cloke,
Twinckling starres Love-thoughts provoke:
Danger hence good care doth keepe,
Jealousie it selfe doth sleepe: [10]
Take me to thee, and thee to me.
'No, no, no, no, my Deare, let be.'

Better place no wit can find,
Cupid's yoke to loose or bind:
These sweet flowers on fine bed too,   [15]
Us in their best language woo:
Take me to thee, and thee to me.
'No, no, no, no, my Deare, let be.'

This small light the Moone bestowes,
Serves thy beames but to disclose,   [20]

3 ioy 98.   10 summ'd] found Ho Q1.   her] their Q1-2.   11 wit] will
Ho Q1-2.   ties. 98.   13-14 *om.* Ho Q1.
  vi. 98; Q1; Ra.   15 on] our Q1; in Ra.

So to raise my hap more hie;
Feare not else, none can us spie:
Take me to thee, and thee to me.
'No, no, no, no, my Deare, let be.'

That you heard was but a Mouse, [25]
Dumbe sleepe holdeth all the house:
Yet a sleepe, me thinkes they say,
Yong folkes, take time while you may:
Take me to thee, and thee to me.
'No, no, no, no, my Deare, let be.' [30]

Niggard Time threats, if we misse
This large offer of our blisse,
Long stay ere he graunt the same:
Sweet then, while each thing doth frame:
Take me to thee, and thee to me. [35]
'No, no, no, no, my Deare, let be.'

Your faire mother is a bed,
Candles out, and curtaines spread:
She thinkes you do letters write:
Write, but first let me endite: [40]
Take me to thee, and thee to me.
'No, no, no, no, my Deare, let be.'

Sweet alas, why strive you thus?
Concord better fitteth us:
Leave to *Mars* the force of hands, [45]
Your power in your beautie stands:
Take me to thee, and thee to me.
'No, no, no, no, my Deare, let be.'

Wo to me, and do you sweare
Me to hate? But I forbeare, [50]
Cursed be my destines all,
That brought me so high to fall:
Soone with my death I will please thee.
'No, no, no, no, my Deare, let be.'

28 folkes] fooles Q1; ~~fols~~ Foole Ra. 32 blisse: 98. 33 Long stay ere he]
Long stay ere she Q1; No longer stay but Ra. 40 first let me] let me first 98.
44 fitteth] fitteh 98. 47 Take thee to me, and me to thee. 98; Ioyne the to me.
&c. Ra. 50 hate, but 98.

86

ALAS, whence came this change of lookes? If I
   Have chang'd desert, let mine owne conscience be
   A still felt plague, to selfe condemning me:
Let wo gripe on my heart, shame loade mine eye.
But if all faith, like spotlesse Ermine ly   [5]
   Safe in my soule, which only doth to thee
   (As his sole object of felicitie)
With wings of *Love* in aire of wonder flie,
   O ease your hand, treate not so hard your slave:
In justice paines come not till faults do call;   [10]
Or if I needs (sweet Judge) must torments have,
Use something else to chast'n me withall,
   Then those blest eyes, where all my hopes do dwell,
   No doome should make one's heav'n become his hell.

Fift song

WHILE favour fed my hope, delight with hope was brought,
Thought waited on delight, and speech did follow thought:
Then grew my tongue and pen records unto thy glory:
I thought all words were lost, that were not spent of thee:
I thought each place was darke but where thy lights would be,   [5]
And all eares worse then deafe, that heard not out thy storie.

I said, thou wert most faire, and so indeed thou art:
I said, thou wert most sweet, sweet poison to my heart:
I said, my soule was thine (ô that I then had lyed)
I said, thine eyes were starres, thy breasts the milk'n way,   [10]
Thy fingers *Cupid's* shafts, thy voyce the Angels' lay:
And all I said so well, as no man it denied.

But now that hope is lost, unkindnesse kils delight,
Yet thought and speech do live, though metamorphosd quite:

86. 98; Q2; Ho, Q1.   1 came] comes Ho Q1–2.   if 98.   4 eye] eyes
Ho Q1.   8 flie. 98.   9 O ease your hand, treate] Cease yow^r hard hand
threat Ho Q1.   10 call, 98.   14 one's] once 98.
    v. 98; Q1.   3 grew] drew Q1.   8 wert] art 98.   9 that] would Q1.
10 thine] thy Q1.   12 I . . . as] is . . . that Q1.   14 metamorphosd] meta-
morphisde Q1 (*the same misprint appears in* Q2).

For rage now rules the reynes, which guided were by Pleasure. [15]
I thinke now of thy faults, who late thought of thy praise,
That speech falles now to blame, which did thy honour raise,
The same key op'n can, which can locke up a treasure.

Thou then whom partiall heavens conspir'd in one to frame,
The proofe of Beautie's worth, th'enheritrix of fame, [20]
The mansion seat of blisse, and just excuse of Lovers;
See now those feathers pluckt, wherewith thou flewst most high:
See what clouds of reproch shall darke thy honour's skie,
Whose owne fault casts him downe, hardly high seat recovers.

And ô my Muse, though oft you luld her in your lap, [25]
And then, a heav'nly child, gave her Ambrosian pap:
And to that braine of hers your hidnest gifts infused,
Since she disdaining me, doth you in me disdaine:
Suffer not her to laugh, while both we suffer paine:
Princes in subjects wrongd, must deeme themselves abused. [30]

Your Client poore my selfe, shall *Stella* handle so?
Revenge, revenge, my Muse, Defiance' trumpet blow:
Threat'n what may be done, yet do more then you threat'n.
Ah, my sute granted is, I feele my breast doth swell:
Now child, a lesson new you shall begin to spell: [35]
Sweet babes must babies have, but shrewd gyrles must be beat'n.

Thinke now no more to heare of warme fine odourd snow,
Nor blushing Lillies, nor pearles' ruby-hidden row,
Nor of that golden sea, whose waves in curles are brok'n:
But of thy soule, so fraught with such ungratefulnesse, [40]
As where thou soone mightst helpe, most faith dost most oppresse,
Ungratefull who is cald, the worst of evils is spok'n.

Yet worse then worst, I say thou art a theefe, a theefe?
Now God forbid. A theefe, and of worst theeves the cheefe:

15 reynes] raines 98.   16 thought] wrote Q1.   19 Thou then] Then thou Q1]
20 worth, th' enheritrix] worke, the inheritance Q1.   21 seat] state Q1.   22 flewst.
flew 98.   24 casts . . . seat] casteth . . . state Q1.   26 then a . . . child 98.
27 hidnest] highest Q1.   29 while] and Q1.   30 wrongd] wrongs Q1.   32 Muse.
98.   33 Threat'n] Threate, threat, Q1.   37 odourd] shining Q1.   40 so]
om. Q1.   41 faith dost most] there thou dost Q1.   42 spok'n: 98.   44 the
cheefe] a thiefe Q1.

Theeves steal for need, and steale but goods, which paine recovers,
But thou rich in all joyes, doest rob my joyes from me,   [46]
Which cannot be restor'd by time nor industrie:
Of foes the spoile is evill, far worse of constant lovers.

Yet gentle English theeves do rob, but will not slay;
Thou English murdring theefe, wilt have harts for thy pray: [50]
The name of murdrer now on thy faire forehead sitteth:
And even while I do speake, my death wounds bleeding be:
Which (I protest) proceed from only Cruell thee,
Who may and will not save, murder in truth committeth.

But murder, private fault, seemes but a toy to thee,   [55]
I lay then to thy charge unjustest Tyrannie,
If Rule by force without all claime a Tyran showeth,
For thou doest lord my heart, who am not borne thy slave,
And which is worse, makes me most guiltlesse torments have,
A rightfull Prince by unright deeds a Tyran groweth.   [60]

Lo you grow proud with this, for tyrans make folke bow:
Of foule rebellion then I do appeach thee now;
Rebell by Nature's law, Rebell by law of reason,
Thou, sweetest subject, wert borne in the realme of Love,
And yet against thy Prince thy force dost dayly prove: [65]
No vertue merits praise, once toucht with blot of Treason.

But valiant Rebels oft in fooles' mouthes purchase fame:
I now then staine thy white with vagabunding shame,
Both Rebell to the Sonne, and Vagrant from the mother;
For wearing *Venus'* badge, in every part of thee,   [70]
Unto *Dianae's* traine thou runaway didst flee:
Who faileth one, is false, though trusty to another.

What, is not this enough? nay farre worse commeth here;
A witch I say thou art, though thou so faire appeare;

45 but] for Q1.   46 joyes] goods Q1.   48 worse] more Q1.   49 but]
and Q1.   55 murder] murthers Q1.   murder priuate fault 98.   56 unjustest]
vniustice Q1.   58 doest lord my heart] art my hearts Lord Q1.   60 unright]
vnrightfull Q1.   61 make] makes Q1.   63 Rebell . . . law . . . law] Rebels
. . . lawes . . . way Q1.   64 Thou sweetest subiect 98.   68 vagabunding]
blackest blot of Q1.   69 Sonne] Sunne 98.   71 flee] flie 98 Q1.   73 What
98.

For I protest, my sight never thy face enjoyeth,   [75]
But I in me am chang'd, I am alive and dead:
My feete are turn'd to rootes, my hart beccommeth lead,
No witchcraft is so evill, as which man's mind destroyeth.

Yet witches may repent, thou art far worse then they,
Alas, that I am forst such evill of thee to say,   [80]
I say thou art a Devill, though clothd in Angel's shining:
For thy face tempts my soule to leave the heav'n for thee,
And thy words of refuse, do powre even hell on mee:
Who tempt, and tempted plague, are Devils in true defining.

You then ungratefull thiefe, you murdring Tyran you,   [85]
You Rebell run away, to Lord and Lady untrue,
You witch, you Divill, (alas) you still of me beloved,
You see what I can say; mend yet your froward mind,
And such skill in my Muse you reconcil'd shall find,
That all these cruell words your praises shall be proved.   [90]

Sixt song

O YOU that heare this voice,
O you that see this face,
Say whether of the choice
Deserves the former place:
Feare not to judge this bate,   [5]
For it is void of hate.

This side doth beauty take,
For that doth Musike speake,
Fit oratours to make
The strongest judgements weake: [10]
The barre to plead their right,
Is only true delight.

Thus doth the voice and face,
These gentle Lawyers wage,
Like loving brothers' case   [15]
For father's heritage,

75 my sight . . . face] mine eyes . . . sight Q1.   81 Deuill 98.   82 heav'n]
heauens Q1.   84 tempt, . . . plague] tempts, . . . plagues Q1.   87 Diuill 98.
90 all] by Q1.
    vi. 98; Q1; Bd.   15 case, 98.   16 heritage: 98.

That each, while each contends,
It selfe to other lends.

For beautie beautifies,
With heavenly hew and grace,   [20]
The heavenly harmonies;
And in this faultlesse face,
The perfect beauties be
A perfect harmony.

Musicke more loftly swels   [25]
In speeches nobly placed:
Beauty as farre excels,
In action aptly graced:
A friend each party drawes,
To countenance his cause: [30]

Love more affected seemes
To beautie's lovely light,
And wonder more esteemes
Of Musick's wondrous might:
But both to both so bent,   [35]
As both in both are spent.

Musike doth witnesse call
The eare, his truth to trie:
Beauty brings to the hall,
The judgement of the eye,   [40]
Both in their objects such,
As no exceptions tutch.

The common sence, which might
Be Arbiter of this,
To be forsooth upright,   [45]
To both sides partiall is:
He layes on this chiefe praise,
Chiefe praise on that he laies.

17 each 98.   25 loftly] lustie Q1; loftie Bd.   34 Musick's] Musike 98 Bd.
40 The judgement] Eye-iudgement 98; eye witnesse Bd.   47 this] this side 98.

Then reason, Princesse hy,
Whose throne is in the mind,   [50]
Which Musicke can in sky
And hidden beauties find,
Say whether thou wilt crowne,
With limitlesse renowne.

Seventh song

WHOSE senses in so evill consort, their stepdame Nature laies,
That ravishing delight in them most sweete tunes do not raise;
Or if they do delight therein, yet are so cloyed with wit,
As with sententious lips to set a title vaine on it: [4]
O let them heare these sacred tunes, and learne in wonder's schooles,
To be (in things past bounds of wit) fooles, if they be not fooles.

Who have so leaden eyes, as not to see sweet beautie's show,
Or seeing, have so wodden wits, as not that worth to know;
Or knowing, have so muddy minds, as not to be in love;
Or loving, have so frothy thoughts, as easly thence to move: [10]
O let them see these heavenly beames, and in faire letters reede
A lesson fit, both sight and skill, love and firme love to breede.

Heare then, but then with wonder heare; see but adoring see,
No mortall gifts, no earthly fruites, now here descended be:
See, do you see this face? a face? nay image of the skies,   [15]
Of which the two life-giving lights are figured in her eyes:
Heare you this soule-invading voice, and count it but a voice?
The very essence of their tunes, when Angels do rejoyce.

Eighth song

IN a grove most rich of shade,
Where birds wanton musicke made,
May then yong his pide weedes showing,
New perfumed with flowers fresh growing,

49 reason 98.
   vii. 98, Fr; Q1.   3 cloyed] closde 98.   6 be in . . . wit 98.
   viii. 98, Bt; Q1 (*lines* 1–16 *and* 101–4 *only*); Ha, Ra.   *Heading*: Eight song
98 Bt; The eighth Q1; *om.* Ha Ra.   3 pide] new Ha Ra.   4 New perfumed
with] New perfumes with Q1; Deckte with pyde Ha Ra.   fresh] sweetly Ha, swetly
a Ra.

Astrophil with *Stella* sweete,   [5]
Did for mutuall comfort meete,
Both within themselves oppressed,
But each in the other blessed.

Him great harmes had taught much care,
Her faire necke a foule yoke bare,   [10]
But her sight his cares did banish,
In his sight her yoke did vanish.

Wept they had, alas the while,
But now teares themselves did smile,
While their eyes by love directed,   [15]
Enterchangeably reflected.

Sigh they did, but now betwixt
Sighs of woes were glad sighs mixt,
With armes crost, yet testifying
Restlesse rest, and living dying.   [20]

Their eares hungry of each word,
Which the deere tongue would afford,
But their tongues restraind from walking,
Till their harts had ended talking.

But when their tongues could not speake,   [25]
Love it selfe did silence breake;
Love did set his lips asunder,
Thus to speake in love and wonder:

'*Stella* soveraigne of my joy,
Faire triumpher of annoy,   [30]
Stella starre of heavenly fier,
Stella loadstar of desier.

'*Stella*, in whose shining eyes,
Are the lights of *Cupid's* skies,
Whose beames, where they once are darted,   [35]
Love therewith is streight imparted.

---

5 *Astrophil*] *Astrophel* 98; Q1; Ha Ra.   8 each in the other] either in each other
Q1; yet ech in either Ha, each of yᵉ other Ra.   11–12 *Lines reversed in* Ra.
17 Sigh they did] Sighd they had Q1; Sighte they did Ha, Syghed they did Ra.
18 Sighs] sightes Ha, sigtes Ra.   28 and] a Ha Ra.   30 triumpher of]
Triumphres in Q1; triumphe on Ha, triumphante in Ra.   35 beames 98.   where]
when Ha, whence Ra.

'*Stella*, whose voice when it speakes,
Senses all asunder breakes;
Stella, whose voice when it singeth,
Angels to acquaintance bringeth. [40]

'*Stella*, in whose body is
Writ each character of blisse,
Whose face all, all beauty passeth,
Save thy mind which yet surpasseth.

'Graunt, ô graunt, but speech alas, [45]
Failes me fearing on to passe,
Graunt, ô me, what am I saying?
But no fault there is in praying.

'Graunt, ô deere, on knees I pray,
(Knees on ground he then did stay) [50]
That not I, but since I love you,
Time and place for me may move you.

'Never season was more fit,
Never roome more apt for it;
Smiling ayre allowes my reason, [55]
These birds sing: "Now use the season."

'This small wind which so sweete is,
See how it the leaves doth kisse,
Ech tree in his best attiring,
Sense of love to love inspiring. [60]

'Love makes earth the water drink,
Love to earth makes water sinke;
And if dumbe things be so witty,
Shall a heavenly grace want pitty?'

There his hands in their speech, faine [65]
Would have made tongue's language plaine;
But her hands his hands repelling,
Gave repulse all grace excelling.

42 Writ each character of] Writ the caracters of Q1; Write each character of Ha, Eche
character of heauenly Ra.   43 Whose face all] Whose sweete face Q1; Whose fayer
face Ha, Stella whose face Ra.   44 thy] the Q1; Ha Ra.   51 I 98.   56 sing;
now 98.   61 drink] drinek 98.   68 excelling] expelling Q1; Ha.

Then she spake; her speech was such,
As not eares but hart did tuch: [70]
While such wise she love denied,
As yet love she signified.

'*Astrophil*' sayd she, 'my love
Cease in these effects to prove:
Now be still, yet still beleeve me,   [75]
Thy griefe more then death would grieve me.

'If that any thought in me,
Can tast comfort but of thee,
Let me, fed with hellish anguish,
Joylesse, hopelesse, endlesse languish.   [80]

'If those eyes you praised, be
Half so deere as you to me,
Let me home returne, starke blinded
Of those eyes, and blinder minded.

'If to secret of my hart,   [85]
I do any wish impart,
Where thou art not formost placed,
Be both wish and I defaced.

'If more may be sayd, I say,
All my blisse in thee I lay;   [90]
If thou love, my love content thee,
For all love, all faith is meant thee.

'Trust me while I thee deny,
In my selfe the smart I try,
Tyran honour doth thus use thee,   [95]
Stella's selfe might not refuse thee.

'Therefore, Deere, this no more move,
Least, though I leave not thy love,
Which too deep in me is framed,
I should blush when thou art named.'   [100]

73 *Astrophil*] *Astrophel* 98 Bt; Ha Ra.   75 yet] bvt Ha Ra.   78 tast . . . of]
take . . . in Ha Ra.   79 me 98.   fed] feele Ha Ra.   90 in] on Ha, one Ra.
94 In my selfe the smart] The torment in my selfe Ha, The smarte within my selfe Ra.
95 Tyran, 98.   doth thus] thus doth Ha Ra.   97 Deare no more this matter
move Ha Ra.   98 Least 98.

Therewithall away she went,
Leaving him so passion rent,
With what she had done and spoken,
That therewith my song is broken.

Ninth song

Go my flocke, go get you hence,
Seeke a better place of feeding,
Where you may have some defence
From the stormes in my breast breeding,
And showers from mine eyes proceeding.   [5]

Leave a wretch, in whom all wo
Can abide to keepe no measure,
Merry flocke, such one forgo,
Unto whom mirth is displeasure,
Only rich in mischiefe's treasure.   [10]

Yet alas before you go,
Heare your wofull maister's story,
Which to stones I els would show:
Sorrow onely then hath glory,
When tis excellently sory.   [15]

Stella fiercest shepherdesse,
Fiercest but yet fairest ever;
Stella whom ô heavens do blesse,
Tho against me shee persever,
Tho I blisse enherit never.   [20]

Stella hath refused me,
Stella who more love hath proved,
In this caitife hart to be,
Then can in good eawes be moved
Toward *Lamkins* best beloved.   [25]

102 so] to 98; with Q1.   103 what] that Ha Ra.   104 is] was Ha Ra.
ix. 98; Dr; Q1; Dd.   4 From] Fro 98; Dr.   16 fiercest] fairest Q1; Dd.
17 Fiercest . . . fairest] Fairest . . . cruelst Q1.   25 Toward] Towards Q1; vnto
Dd.

Stella hath refused me,
Astrophil that so wel served,
In this pleasant spring must see
While in pride flowers be preserved,
Himselfe onely winter-sterved.   [30]

Why alas doth she then sweare,
That she loveth me so dearely,
Seing me so long to beare
Coles of love that burne so clearely;
And yet leave me helplesse meerely?   [35]

Is that love? forsooth I trow,
If I saw my good dog grieved,
And a helpe for him did know,
My love should not be beleeved,
But he were by me releeved.   [40]

No, she hates me, wellaway,
Faining love, somewhat to please me:
For she knowes, if she display
All her hate, death soone would seaze me,
And of hideous torments ease me.   [45]

Then adieu, deere flocke adieu:
But alas, if in your straying
Heavenly *Stella* meete with you,
Tell her in your piteous blaying,
Her poore slave's unjust decaying.   [50]

87

W HEN I was forst from *Stella* ever deere,
Stella food of my thoughts, hart of my hart,
Stella whose eyes make all my tempests cleere,
By iron lawes of duty to depart:

27 *Astrophil*] *Astrophel* 98; Dr; Q1.   31 doth she then] then doth she Q1; Dd.
35 helplesse] hopelesse Q1; haplesse Dd.   43 Knowing, if she should display Q1;
Dd.
  87. 98; Dr, Q2; Ho, Q1.   2 hart of] hurt of Ho Q1–2.   3 tempests]
temples Q1–2.   4 iron] ⟨ ⟩ Ho, *Stellaes* Q1.

Alas I found, that she with me did smart,   [5]
I saw that teares did in her eyes appeare;
I saw that sighes her sweetest lips did part,
And her sad words my sadded sence did heare.
    For me, I wept to see pearles scattered so,
    I sighd her sighes, and wailed for her wo,   [10]
Yet swam in joy, such love in her was seene.
    Thus while th' effect most bitter was to me,
    And nothing then the cause more sweet could be,
I had bene vext, if vext I had not beene.

88

OUT traytour absence, darest thou counsell me,
From my deare Captainnesse to run away?
Because in brave array heere marcheth she,
That to win me, oft shewes a present pay?
    Is faith so weake? Or is such force in thee?   [5]
When Sun is hid, can starres such beames display?
Cannot heavn's food, once felt, keepe stomakes free
From base desire on earthly cates to pray?
    Tush absence, while thy mistes eclipse that light,
    My Orphan sence flies to the inward sight,   [10]
Where memory sets foorth the beames of love.
    That where before hart loved and eyes did see,
    In hart both sight and love now coupled be;
United powers make each the stronger prove.

89

NOW that of absence the most irksome night,
    With darkest shade doth overcome my day;
    Since *Stella's* eyes, wont to give me my day,
Leaving my Hemisphere, leave me in night,

---

8 sadded] saddest 98; sayd ded Ho, sad deare Q1.   9 wept] weepe Q1-2.
12 th' effect] the'ffect 98; the effect Dr; Q1-2.   13 nothing then the cause]
nothing than that cause Q2; then the cawse nothing Ho Q1.
88. 98; Dr, Q2; Ho, Q1.   5 or 98.   7 heau'ns food once . . . free, 98.
8 pray. 98.   9 absence 98.   11 sets] feeds Ho Q1.   13 both] my Q1-2.
89. 98, Fr (*lines 9-14 only*); Dr, Q2; Ho, Q1.   1 night] nigh 98.   2 my] the
Q1-2.   3 eyes 98.   4 leave me in] leaues mee in Q2; o'recast with Q1.

Each day seemes long, and longs for long-staid night, [5]
  The night as tedious, wooes th'approch of day;
  Tired with the dusty toiles of busie day,
Languisht with horrors of the silent night,
Suffering the evils both of the day and night,
  While no night is more darke then is my day, [10]
Nor no day hath lesse quiet then my night:
  With such bad mixture of my night and day,
That living thus in blackest winter night,
  I feele the flames of hottest sommer day.

90

STELLA thinke not that I by verse seeke fame,
  Who seeke, who hope, who love, who live but thee;
  Thine eyes my pride, thy lips my history:
If thou praise not, all other praise is shame.
Nor so ambitious am I, as to frame [5]
  A nest for my yong praise in Lawrell tree:
  In truth I sweare, I wish not there should be
Graved in mine Epitaph a Poet's name:
  Ne if I would, could I just title make,
That any laud to me thereof should grow, [10]
Without my plumes from others' wings I take.
For nothing from my wit or will doth flow,
  Since all my words thy beauty doth endite,
  And love doth hold my hand, and makes me write.

91

STELLA, while now by honour's cruell might,
  I am from you, light of my life, mis-led,
  And that faire you my Sunne, thus overspred
With absence' Vaile, I live in Sorowe's night.

7 Tired . . . busie] toyled . . . busyed Ho Q1. 8 night; 98. 9 the day] day Fr;
Ho Q1-2. 14 flames] steames Ho, gleames Q1. sommer] summers Fr; Q1-2.
 90. 98; Dr, Q2; Ho, Q1. 2 live] like Ho Q1-2. 3 my history] mine
history 98. 4 not] me Ho Q1-2. 8 mine] my Ho Q1-2. 9 Ne] No Ho,
Nor Q1-2. could I] I could 98; Dr; Ho. 10 to me thereof] thereof to me Q1-2.
 91. 98; Dr, Q2; Ho, Q1. 2 life 98. life] light Ho Q1-2. 3 ouerspred,
98.

If this darke place yet shew like candle light,   [5]
 Some beautie's peece, as amber colourd hed,
 Milke hands, rose cheeks, or lips more sweet, more red,
Or seeing jets, blacke, but in blacknesse bright.
 They please I do confesse, they please mine eyes,
But why? because of you they models be,   [10]
Models such be wood-globes of glistring skies.
Deere, therefore be not jealous over me,
 If you heare that they seeme my hart to move,
 Not them, ô no, but you in them I love.

92

BE your words made (good Sir) of Indian ware,
 That you allow me them by so small rate?
 Or do you cutted Spartanes imitate?
Or do you meane my tender eares to spare,
That to my questions you so totall are?   [5]
 When I demaund of *Phenix Stella's* state,
 You say forsooth, you left her well of late.
O God, thinke you that satisfies my care?
 I would know whether she did sit or walke,
How cloth'd, how waited on, sighd she or smilde,   [10]
Whereof, with whom, how often did she talke,
With what pastime, time's journey she beguilde,
 If her lips daignd to sweeten my poore name.
 Say all, and all well sayd, still say the same.

Tenth song

O DEARE life, when shall it be,
 That mine eyes thine eyes may see?
 And in them thy mind discover,
Whether absence have had force
Thy remembrance to divorce,   [5]
 From the image of thy lover?

5 like] by Q1–2. 6 peece 98. 8 seeing jets, blacke] seeing gets blacke 98;
Dr; Ho, seeming iett black Q1–2. 14 ô] no Ho Q1–2.
 92. 98; Dr, Q2; Ho, Q1. 2 me them] them mee Q1–2. 3 cutted Spar-
tanes] cutted Sparta Ho, the *Caconians* Q1. imitate, 98. 4 spare? 98. 5 are,
98. 7 late, 98. 9 did] *om.* 98. 12 pastime . . . journey] pastyms . . .
iorneys Ho Q1–2. 13 daignd] deyne Ho Q1–2. name, 98. 14 all, well 98.
 x. 98; Dr; Q1 (*lines* 1–24 *and* 43–48 *only*); Hn, Ra, Bd (*lines* 1–18 *only*). 3 thy
mind] my mind Dr; Ra Bd, thy thoughts Hn. 6 thy] the 98; Dr.

O if I my self find not,
    After parting ought forgot,
    Nor debard from beautie's treasure,
    Let no tongue aspire to tell, [10]
    In what high joyes I shall dwell,
    Only thought aymes at the pleasure.

Thought therefore I will send thee,
    To take up the place for me;
    Long I will not after tary, [15]
    There unseene thou maist be bold,
    Those faire wonders to behold,
    Which in them my hopes do cary.

Thought see thou no place forbeare,
    Enter bravely every where, [20]
    Seaze on all to her belonging;
    But if thou wouldst garded be,
    Fearing her beames, take with thee
    Strength of liking, rage of longing.

Thinke of that most gratefull time, [25]
    When my leaping hart will clime,
    In my lips to have his biding,
    There those roses for to kisse,
    Which do breath a sugred blisse,
    Opening rubies, pearles deviding. [30]

Thinke of my most Princely power,
    When I blessed shall devower,
    With my greedy licorous sences,
    Beauty, musicke, sweetnesse, love
    While she doth against me prove [35]
    Her strong darts, but weake defences.

Thinke, thinke of those dalyings,
    When with Dovelike murmurings,

With glad moning passed anguish,
We change eyes, and hart for hart,   [40]
Each to other do imparte,
Joying till joy make us languish.

O my thought my thoughts surcease,
Thy delights my woes increase,
My life melts with too much thinking;   [45]
Thinke no more but die in me,
Till thou shalt revived be,
At her lips my Nectar drinking.

93

O FATE, ô fault, ô curse, child of my blisse,
    What sobs can give words grace my griefe to show?
    What inke is blacke inough to paint my wo?
Through me, wretch me, even *Stella* vexed is.
Yet truth (if Caitif's breath mighte call thee) this   [5]
    Witnesse with me, that my foule stumbling so,
    From carelesnesse did in no maner grow,
But wit confus'd with too much care did misse.
    And do I then my selfe this vaine scuse give?
I have (live I and know this) harmed thee,   [10]
Tho worlds quite me, shall I my selfe forgive?
Only with paines my paines thus eased be,
    That all thy hurts in my hart's wracke I reede;
    I cry thy sighs; my deere, thy teares I bleede.

39 With glad] when with Hn, And with Ra.   41 do imparte] do depart 98; then
ymparts Hn.   43 my thought] my Thoughts Q1; Hn, thoughtes now Ra.
thought my 98.   44 *om.* Dr.   Thy] Your Q1; Hn, These Ra.   woes] payns
Hn Ra.   45 My life melts] My life fleetes Q1; ah I dye Hn, And I dy Ra.
46 Whearfore thoughts com sleep w^(th) me Hn, Thoughte! therfore come sleepe w^(th) me
Ra.   47 thou shalt revived] yee may awaked Hn, thou maist awaked Ra.
   93. 98; Dr, Q2; Ho, Q1.   1 curse] cruse Dr; Curst Ho Q1-2.   5 breath]
om. Dr; brath Q1-2.   mighte] may 98.   this] his Ho Q1.   6 my foule] I
foole Ho Q1.   10 I have (live I] I do sweete Loue, Q1-2.   11 Tho worlds]
the wourld Ho Q1-2.   quite] quitt Dr; Q1-2.   my selfe] me selfe 98.   12 my
paines] *om.* Ho, thy paines Q1.

94

GRIEFE find the words, for thou hast made my braine
　　So darke with misty vapors, which arise
　　From out thy heavy mould, that inbent eyes
Can scarce discerne the shape of mine owne paine.
Do thou then (for thou canst) do thou complaine,　　　　[5]
　　For my poore soule, which now that sicknesse tries,
　　Which even to sence, sence of it selfe denies,
Though harbengers of death lodge there his traine.
　　Or if thy love of plaint yet mine forbeares,
As of a caitife worthy so to die,　　　　　　　　　　[10]
Yet waile thy selfe, and waile with causefull teares,
That though in wretchednesse thy life doth lie,
Yet growest more wretched then thy nature beares,
By being placed in such a wretch as I.

95

YET sighs, deere sighs, indeede true friends you are,
　　That do not leave your least friend at the wurst,
　　But as you with my breast I oft have nurst,
So gratefull now you waite upon my care.
Faint coward joy no longer tarry dare,　　　　　　　[5]
　　Seeing hope yeeld when this wo strake him furst:
　　Delight protests he is not for the accurst,
Though oft himselfe my mate-in-armes he sware.

---

94. 98; Dr, Q2; Ho, Q1. *Complete* Ho *and* Q1 *variants given for this sonnet.*
1 braine] vaine Q1.　　　3 inbent] ⟨ ⟩ Ho, euen mine Q1.　　　6 now] not Ho, wit
Q1.　　　8 lodge there] & of Ho Q1.　　　9 Or if thy love of plaint yet mine] Or if
the loue of plaint yet mind Q2; or if the loue of plaint yet mine Ho, The execution of
my fate Q1.　　　10 worthy so] worthy for Dr; not vouchsaft Q1.　　　11 waile thy
selfe, and waile with causefull] waye thy selfe and wayle in causefull Q2; shewe thy
hate of life in liuing Q1.　　　13 Yet growest] yet grown Ho, Thou maist Q1.　　　then
thy] be than Q1.　　　14 By] as Ho Q1.

95. 98; Dr, Q2; Ho, Q1.　　　2 least] left 98; best Q1.　　　6 hope] hope did
Ho Q1.　　　7 protests] exclaims Q1–2.　　　not for the accurst] not for thee accurst
Dr; not for thee curst Ho, for my fault curst Q1–2.　　　8 Though oft himselfe my
mate-in-armes] Though oft himselfe my mate in arme 98; Dr; thought of him self my
make in arme Ho, Although my mate in Armes himselfe Q1–2.

Nay sorrow comes with such maine rage, that he
Kils his owne children, teares, finding that they   [10]
By love were made apt to consort with me.
Only true sighs, you do not go away,
   Thanke may you have for such a thankfull part,
   Thanke-worthiest yet when you shall breake my hart.

96

THOUGHT with good cause thou likest so well the night,
   Since kind or chance gives both one liverie,
   Both sadly blacke, both blackly darkned be,
Night bard from Sun, thou from thy owne sunne's light;
Silence in both displaies his sullen might,   [5]
   Slow heavinesse in both holds one degree,
   That full of doubts, thou of perplexity;
Thy teares expresse night's native moisture right.
   In both a mazefull solitarinesse:
In night of sprites the gastly powers stur,   [10]
In thee or sprites or sprited gastlinesse:
But, but (alas) night's side the ods hath fur,
   For that at length yet doth invite some rest,
   Thou though still tired, yet still doost it detest.

97

DIAN that faine would cheare her friend the Night,
   Shewes her oft at the full her fairest face,
   Bringing with her those starry Nimphs, whose chace
From heavenly standing hits each mortall wight.
But ah poore Night, in love with *Phœbus'* light,   [5]
   And endlesly dispairing of his grace,
   Her selfe (to shew no other joy hath place)
Silent and sad in mourning weedes doth dight:

9 that] as Ho Q1–2.   10 teares 98.
   96. 98; Dr; Ho, Q1.   2 liverie] Lybertye Ho Q1.   3 both] hoth 98.
4 sunne's] Sun 98.   6 heavinesse . . . holds] heavens . . . do hold the Ho Q1.
9 a mazefull] amazefull Dr; a wayfull Ho, a wofull Q1.   10 powers] powers to
98; powr Ho Q1.   12 But but 98.   13 some] to Ho Q1.   14 doost] doth
Dr; Ho.
   97. 98; Dr; Ho, Q1.   4 hits] hates Dr; hurts Ho Q1.   5 Night 98.

Even so (alas) a Lady *Dian*'s peere,
With choise delights and rarest company, [10]
Would faine drive cloudes from out my heavy cheere.
But wo is me, though joy it selfe were she,
 She could not shew my blind braine waies of joy,
 While I dispaire my Sunne's sight to enjoy.

98

Ah bed, the field where joye's peace some do see,
 The field where all my thoughts to warre be traind,
 How is thy grace by my strange fortune staind!
How thy lee shores by my sighes stormed be!
With sweete soft shades thou oft invitest me [5]
 To steale some rest, but wretch I am constraind,
 (Spurd with love's spur, though gald and shortly raind
With care's hard hand) to turne and tosse in thee.
 While the blacke horrors of the silent night,
 Paint woe's blacke face so lively to my sight, [10]
That tedious leasure marks each wrinckled line:
 But when *Aurora* leades out *Phœbus*' daunce,
 Mine eyes then only winke, for spite perchance,
That wormes should have their Sun, and I want mine.

99

When far spent night perswades each mortall eye,
 To whom nor art nor nature graunteth light,
 To lay his then marke wanting shafts of sight,
Clos'd with their quivers in sleep's armory;
With windowes ope then most my mind doth lie, [5]
 Viewing the shape of darknesse and delight,
 Takes in that sad hue, which with th'inward night
Of his mazde powers keepes perfit harmony:

10 delights] delight Ho Q1. 12 it selfe] her selfe Ho Q1. 14 I] *om.* Ho.
 98. 98; Dr; Ho, Q1. 4 lee shores] loe shores Ho, low shrowdes Q1. 7 though gald] though gold 98; Dr; thus held Ho, this held Q1. 10 to] in Ho Q1.
11 marks] makes 98; Dr.
 99. 98; Dr; Ho, Q1. 2 graunteth] graunted Ho Q1. 5 ope] *om.* Dr.
mind] hart Ho Q1. 7 which with] wth wch Ho Q1. night, 98.

But when birds charme, and that sweete aire, which is
Morne's messenger, with rose enameld skies [10]
Cals each wight to salute the floure of blisse;
In tombe of lids then buried are mine eyes,
    Forst by their Lord, who is asham'd to find
    Such light in sense, with such a darkned mind.

100

O TEARES, no teares, but raine from beautie's skies,
    Making those Lillies and those Roses grow,
    Which ay most faire, now more then most faire show,
While gracefull pitty beauty beautifies.
O honied sighs, which from that breast do rise, [5]
    Whose pants do make unspilling creame to flow,
    Wing'd with whose breath, so pleasing *Zephires* blow,
As can refresh the hell where my soule fries.
    O plaints conserv'd in such a sugred phraise,
    That eloquence it selfe envies your praise, [10]
While sobd out words a perfect Musike give.
    Such teares, sighs, plaints, no sorrow is, but joy:
    Or if such heavenly signes must prove annoy,
All mirth farewell, let me in sorrow live.

101

STELLA is sicke, and in that sicke bed lies
Sweetnesse, that breathes and pants as oft as she:
And grace, sicke too, such fine conclusions tries,
That sickenesse brags it selfe best graced to be.
    Beauty is sicke, but sicke in so faire guise, [5]
That in that palenesse beautie's white we see;
And joy, which is inseperate from those eyes,
Stella now learnes (strange case) to weepe in thee.

9 charme, and] Charme ayre Ho, chirpe aire Q1.   11 floure] ⟨ ⟩ Ho, heauen Q1.
   100. 98; Dr; Ho, Q1.   3 more then most faire] fayrer needs must Ho Q1.
4 gracefull] gratefull Dr; Ho Q1.   5 which] that Ho Q1.   9 sugred] surged
98.   10 it selfe envies your] her selfe enuies yor Dr; envyes & yet doth Ho Q1.
13 signes] sighes Ho Q1.
   101. 98; Dr; Ho, Q1.   2 that] which 98.   3 grace 98.   4 brags]
brings Ho Q1.   to] *om.* Ho.   6 paleness] palanesse 98.   see, 98.   7 ioy 98.
inseperate] vnsevered Ho Q1.   eyes: 98.

Love moves thy paine, and like a faithfull page,
As thy lookes sturre, runs up and downe to make   [10]
All folkes prest at thy will thy paine to 'swage,
Nature with care sweates for her darling's sake,
   Knowing worlds passe, ere she enough can find
   Of such heaven stuffe, to cloath so heavenly mynde.

102

WHERE be those Roses gone, which sweetned so our eyes?
   Where those red cheeks, which oft with faire encrease did frame
   The height of honor in the kindly badge of shame?
Who hath the crimson weeds stolne from my morning skies?
How doth the colour vade of those vermillion dies,   [5]
   Which Nature' selfe did make, and selfe engraind the same?
   I would know by what right this palenesse overcame
That hue, whose force my hart still unto thraldome ties?
   Gallein's adoptive sonnes, who by a beaten way
   Their judgements hackney on, the fault on sicknesse lay,   [10]
But feeling proofe makes me say they mistake it furre:
   It is but love, which makes his paper perfit white
   To write therein more fresh the story of delight,
While beautie's reddest inke *Venus* for him doth sturre.

103

O HAPPIE Tems, that didst my *Stella* beare,
I saw thy selfe with many a smiling line
Upon thy cheerefull face, joye's livery weare:
While those faire planets on thy streames did shine.
   The bote for joy could not to daunce forbeare,   [5]
While wanton winds with beauties so devine
Ravisht, staid not, till in her golden haire
They did themselves (ô sweetest prison) twine.

9 page 98.   10 runs] comes 98.   11 'swage] asswage 98; swage Dr; Ho, Q1.
14 mynde] amind 98.
   102. 98; Dr; Ho, Q1.   1 sweetned so] so sweetend erst Ho Q1.   2 Where]
where be Ho Q1.   oft with] wth Ho, *om.* Q1.   3 The] No Ho Q1.   5 vade]
fade Ho Q1.   6 Nature] *om.* Dr.   engraind] engrav Ho Q1.   8 still unto]
in so great Ho Q1.   9 adoptive] adopted Ho Q1.   11 (say they) 98.   12 loue
which ... white, 98.   which makes his] that makes this Ho Q1.
   103. 98; Dr; Ho Q1.   1 Tems] *Thames* Q1.   2 thy selfe with] thee wth
full Ho Q1.

And faine those *Æols'* youthes there would their stay
Have made, but forst by Nature still to flie,   [10]
First did with puffing kisse those lockes display:
She so discheveld, blusht; from window I
 With sight thereof cride out; ô faire disgrace,
 Let honor' selfe to thee graunt highest place.

104

ENVIOUS wits what hath bene mine offence,
 That with such poysonous care my lookes you marke,
 That to each word, nay sigh of mine you harke,
As grudging me my sorrowe's eloquence?
Ah, is it not enough, that I am thence,   [5]
 Thence, so farre thence, that scarcely any sparke
 Of comfort dare come to this dungeon darke,
Where rigrows exile lockes up all my sense?
 But if I by a happy window passe,
If I but stars upon mine armour beare,   [10]
Sicke, thirsty, glad (though but of empty glasse:)
Your morall notes straight my hid meaning teare
 From out my ribs, and puffing prove that I
 Do *Stella* love. Fooles, who doth it deny?

Eleventh song

'WHO is it that this darke night,
Underneath my window playneth?'
It is one who from thy sight,
Being (ah) exild, disdayneth
Every other vulgar light.   [5]

9 And] but Ho Q1. *Æols'* youthes] *Æols* youth 98; friendly windes Q1. 12 dis-
cheveld] discheued Dr; discoverd Ho Q1. 13 ô] ah Ho Q1. 14 honor']
honours Q1.
 104. 98; Dr; Ho, Q1. 2 poysonous] poysoned Ho Q1. 6 thence] *om.* Dr.
scarcely] scantly Ho Q1. 8 rigrows] rigours 98; rigorous Dr; Q1. 12 morall
notes . . . teare] morrals note . . . there Ho Q1. teare, 98. 13 and puffing prove]
and puffing proues 98; a whirlewind proues Q1. 14 loue, fooles 98.
 xi. 98; Bt; Dr. *Heading*: Eeleuenth song 98, Ele ⟨ ⟩ Bt [*damaged*]; xi^th Song Dr.

'Why alas, and are you he?
Be not yet those fancies changed?'
Deere when you find change in me,
Though from me you be estranged,
Let my chaunge to ruine be.   [10]

'Well in absence this will dy,
Leave to see, and leave to wonder.'
Absence sure will helpe, if I
Can learne, how my selfe to sunder
From what in my hart doth ly.   [15]

'But time will these thoughts remove:
Time doth worke what no man knoweth.'
Time doth as the subject prove,
With time still th' affection groweth
In the faithfull Turtle dove.   [20]

'What if you new beauties see,
Will not they stir new affection?'
I will thinke theye pictures be,
(Image like of Saints' perfection)
Poorely counterfeting thee.   [25]

'But your reason's purest light,
Bids you leave such minds to nourish.'
Deere, do reason no such spite,
Never doth thy beauty florish
More then in my reason's sight.   [30]

'But the wrongs love beares, will make
Love at length leave undertaking.'
No, the more fooles it do shake,
In a ground of so firme making,
Deeper still they drive the stake.   [35]

'Peace, I thinke that some give eare:
Come no more, least I get anger.'
Blisse, I will my blisse forbeare,
Fearing (sweete) you to endanger,
But my soule shall harbour there.   [40]

12 wonder: 98.   17 knoweth, 98.   19 th'] the 98.   21 you] thou Dr.
23 theye] thy 98.   27 nourish? 98.   30 More, 98.   32 vndertaking;
98.   33 No 98.   fooles it do] fooldes it doth Dr.   40 there] thee 98.

'Well, be gone, be gone I say,
Lest that *Argus* eyes perceive you.'
O unjustest fortune's sway,
Which can make me thus to leave you,
And from lowts to run away.   [45]

105

UNHAPPIE sight, and hath she vanisht by
  So neere, in so good time, so free a place?
  Dead glasse, doost thou thy object so imbrace,
As what my hart still sees thou canst not spie?
I sweare by her I love and lacke, that I   [5]
  Was not in fault, who bent thy dazling race
  Onely unto the heav'n of *Stella's* face,
Counting but dust what in the way did lie.
  But cease mine eyes, your teares do witnesse well
That you, guiltlesse thereof, your Nectar mist: [10]
Curst be the page from whome the bad torch fell,
Curst be the night which did your strife resist,
  Curst be the Cochman which did drive so fast,
  With no worse curse then absence makes me tast.

106

O ABSENT presence *Stella* is not here;
  False flattering hope, that with so faire a face,
  Bare me in hand, that in this Orphane place,
Stella, I say my *Stella*, should appeare.
What saist thou now, where is that dainty cheere   [5]
  Thou toldst mine eyes should helpe their famisht case?
  But thou art gone, now that selfe felt disgrace
Doth make me most to wish thy comfort neere.

42 that] *om.* Dr.   you, 98.   43 unjustest] vniust 98.
  105. 98, Bt; Dr; Ho, Q1.   2 time 98.   3 glasse 98.   thy] thine Ho Q1.
5 I love and] love & my Ho Q1.   6 who bent thy] that bent my Ho Q1.   8 what
in the] that in her Ho Q1.   9 well, 98.   10 you 98.   thereof, your Nectar]
therfore yow^r necklass Ho Q1.   11 whome] whence 98.   12 strife] will Ho
Q1.   13 which] that Ho Q1.   14 worse] lesse Ho Q1.
  106. 98, Bt; Dr; Ho, Q1.   5 cheere, 98.   6 toldst] woldst Ho Q1.
famisht] famist 98; vanisht Dr.   7 gone now . . . disgrace, 98.

But heere I do store of faire Ladies meete,
Who may with charme of conversation sweete,   [10]
Make in my heavy mould new thoughts to grow:
Sure they prevaile as much with me, as he
That bad his friend, but then new maim'd, to be
Mery with him, and not thinke of his woe.

107

STELLA since thou so right a Princesse art
Of all the powers which life bestowes on me,
That ere by them ought undertaken be,
They first resort unto that soueraigne part;
Sweete, for a while give respite to my hart,   [5]
Which pants as though it still should leape to thee:
And on my thoughts give thy Lieftenancy
To this great cause, which needs both use and art,
And as a Queene, who from her presence sends
Whom she imployes, dismisse from thee my wit,   [10]
Till it have wrought what thy owne will attends.
On servants' shame oft Maister's blame doth sit;
O let not fooles in me thy workes reprove,
And scorning say, 'See what it is to love.'

108

WHEN sorrow (using mine owne fier's might)
Melts downe his lead into my boyling brest,
Through that darke fornace to my hart opprest,
There shines a joy from thee my only light;
But soone as thought of thee breeds my delight,   [5]
And my yong soule flutters to thee his nest,
Most rude dispaire my daily unbidden guest,
Clips streight my wings, streight wraps me in his night,

13 friend 98.
   107. 98, Bt; Dr; Ho, Q1.   5 Sweete 98.   7 thoughts] thought Ho Q1.
8 art. 98.   11 Till it] till they Dr; still to Ho Q1.   14 see 98.
   108. 98, Bt; Dr; Ho, Q1.   1 mine] my Ho Q1.   3 to] of Ho Q1.
6 flutters to thee his] onc flutters to her Ho Q1.

And makes me then bow downe my head, and say,
Ah what doth *Phœbus'* gold that wretch availe,   [10]
Whom iron doores do keepe from use of day?
So strangely (alas) thy works in me prevaile,
   That in my woes for thee thou art my joy,
   And in my joyes for thee my only annoy.

11 doores] darts Ho Q1.   *Following line* 14: The end of Astrophel and Stella. 98; Other Sonnets Of Variable Verse. [*followed by songs* i–x *and at the end* Finis Syr P. S.] Q1–2.

OTHER POEMS

OTHER POEMS

1

[*A shepherd attending Philisides*]

ME thought some staves he mist: if so, not much amisse:
For where he most would hit, he ever yet did misse.
One said he brake acrosse; full well it so might be:
For never was there man more crossely crost then he.
But most cryed, 'O well broke': O foole full gaily blest: [5]
Where failing is a shame, and breaking is his best.

2

[*Dametas*]

MISO mine owne pigsnie, thou shalt heare news o' *Damœtas.*

3

The Epitaph

HIS being was in her alone:
And he not being, she was none.
    They joi'd one joy, one griefe they griev'd,
    One love they lov'd, one life they liv'd.
    The hand was one, one was the sword   [5]
    That did his death, hir death afford.
As all the rest, so now the stone
That tombes the two, is justly one.

Argalus and Parthenia.

1. 90, Cm.
2. 90, Cm.   1 *Miso*] *om.* Cm.   o'] of Cm.   *Damœtas*] *om.* Cm.
3. 93 (Cm *and* 90 *leave a blank space*).
917.26   R

4

[*Lamon*]

A SHEPHEARD'S tale no height of stile desires
To raise in words what in effect is lowe:
A plaining songe plaine-singing voice requires,
For warbling notes from inward chearing flow.
I then, whose burd'ned brest but thus aspires   [5]
Of shepheards two the seely case to show,
   Nede not the stately Muses' helpe invoke
   For creeping rimes, which often sighings choke.
But you, ô you, that thinke not teares too deare
To spend for harms, although they touch you not: [10]
And deigne to deeme your neighbors' mischefe neare,
Although they be of meaner parents gott:
You I invite with easie eares to heare
The poore-clad truth of love's wrong-ordred lot.
   Who may be glad, be glad you be not such: [15]
   Who share in woe, weygh others have as much.
Ther was (ô seldome blessed word of was!)
A paire of frends, or rather one cal'd two,
Train'd in the life which on short-bitten grasse
In shine or storme must sett the clowted shoe: [20]
He, that the other in some yeares did passe,
And in those gifts that years distribute doe,
   Was *Klaius* cald, (ah *Klaius*, wofull wight!)
   The later borne, yet too soone, *Strephon* hight.
Epeirus high, was honest *Klaius*' nest,   [25]
To *Strephon Æole's* land first breathing lent:
But East and West were join'd by frendship's hest.
As *Strephon's* eare and heart to *Klaius* bent:
So *Klaius*' soule did in his *Strephon* rest.
Still both their flocks flocking togither went,   [30]
   As if they would of owners' humour be,
   And eke their pipes did well, as frends, agree.

---

4. 93. (*All verbal and punctuation variants in 98 also listed.*)   6 case] cause 98.
9 too] to 93.   20 clowted] doubted 93.   27 But] Put 98.   32 frends
93-98.

Klaius for skill of herbs and shepheard's art
Among the wisest was accounted wise,
Yet not so wise, as of unstained harte: [35]
Strephon was yonge, yet markt with humble eies
How elder rul'd their flocks, and cur'd their smart,
So that the grave did not his words despise.
 Both free of minde, both did clear-dealing love,
 And both had skill in verse their voice to move. [40]
Their chearfull minds, till pois'ned was their cheare,
The honest sports of earthy lodging prove;
Now for a clod-like hare in fourm they peere,
Now bolt and cudgill squirrels' leape do move.
Now the ambitiouse Larke with mirror cleare [45]
They catch, while he (foole!) to himself makes love:
 And now at keels they trie a harmles chaunce,
 And now their curr they teach to fetch and daunce.
When mery May first early calls the morne,
With mery maids a Maying they do go, [50]
Then do they pull from sharpe and niggard thorne
The plenteous sweets, (can sweets so sharply grow?)
Then some grene gowns are by the lasses worne
In chastest plaies, till home they walke a rowe,
 While daunce about the may-pole is begun, [55]
 When, if nede were, they could at quintain run:
While thus they ran a low, but leaveld race,
While thus they liv'd, (this was indede a life)
With nature pleas'd, content with present case,
Free of proud feares, brave begg'ry, smiling strife [60]
Of clime-fall Court, the envy-hatching place:
While those restles desires in great men rife
 To visite so low folkes did much disdaine,
 This while, though poore, they in themselves did raigne.
One day (ô day, that shin'de to make them darke!) [65]
While they did ward sun-beames with shady bay,
And *Klaius* taking for his yonglings carke,
(Lest greedy eies to them might challenge lay)
Busy with oker did their shoulders marke,
(His marke a Piller was devoid of stay, [70]

33 herbs] hearb's 93. 50 a Maying] a mayeng 93. 59 case. 93. 67 yong-lings] yongling 93-98.

As bragging that free of all passions' mone
Well might he others beare, but leane to none)
Strephon with leavy twiggs of *Laurell* tree
A garland made on temples for to weare,
For he then chosen was the dignitie   [75]
Of village-Lord that whitsontide to beare:
And full, poore foole, of boyish bravery,
With triumph's shews would shew he nought did feare.
　　But fore-accounting oft makes builders misse,
　　They found, they felt, they had no lease of blisse.   [80]
For ere that either had his purpose done,
Behold (beholding well it doth deserve)
They saw a maid who thitherward did runne,
To catch hir sparrow which from hir did swerve,
As she a black-silke cap on him begunne   [85]
To sett, for foile of his milke-white to serve.
　　She chirping ran, he peeping flew away,
　　Till hard by them both he and she did stay.
Well for to see they kept themselves unsene,
And saw this fairest maid of fairer minde,   [90]
By fortune meane, in Nature borne a Queene,
How well apaid she was hir birde to finde:
How tenderly hir tender hands betweene
In ivory cage she did the micher binde:
　　How rosy moist'ned lipps about his beake   [95]
　　Moving, she seem'd at once to kisse, and speake.
Chastned but thus, and thus his lesson tought,
The happy wretch she putt into hir breast,
Which to their eies the bowles of *Venus* brought,
For they seem'd made even of skie-mettall best,   [100]
And that the bias of hir bloud was wrought.
Betwixt them two the peeper tooke his nest,
　　Where snugging well he well appear'd content
　　So to have done amisse, so to be shent.
This done, but done with captive-killing grace,   [105]
Each motion seeming shott from beautie's bow,
With length laid downe she deckt the lonely place.
Proud grew the grasse that under hir did growe,

77 foole 93.　　　　brauery 93-98.　　　91 By, 93.　　　meane] meare 93.
97 tought 93-98.

The trees spred out their armes to shade hir face,
But she on elbow lean'd, with sighs did show [110]
   No grasse, no trees, nor yet hir sparrow might
   To long-perplexed minde breed long delight.
She troubled was (alas that it mought be!)
With tedious brawlings of her parents deare,
Who would have hir in will and worde agree [115]
To wedd *Antaxius* their neighbour neare.
A heardman rich of much account was he,
In whome no evill did raigne, nor good appeare,
   In some such one she lik'd not his desire,
   Faine would be free, but dreadeth parents' ire. [120]
Kindly, sweete soule, she did unkindnes take,
That bagged baggage of a miser's mudd,
Should price of hir, as in a market, make.
But golde can guild a rotten piece of wood,
To yeeld she found hir noble heart did ake: [125]
To strive she fear'd how it with vertue stoode.
   These doubting clouds ore-casting heav'nly braine,
   At length in rowes of Kisse-cheeke teares they raine.
Cupid the wagg, that lately conquer'd had
Wise Counsellors, stout Captaines, puissant Kings, [130]
And ti'de them fast to leade his triumph badd,
Glutted with them now plaies with meanest things.
So oft in feasts with costly chaunges cladd
To crammed mawes a spratt new Stomake brings.
   So Lords with sport of *Stagg and Hearon* full [135]
   Sometimes we see small birds from nests do pull.
So now for pray these shepheards two he tooke,
Whose mettall stiff he knew he could not bende
With hear-say, pictures, or a window looke,
With one good dawnce, or letter finely pend, [140]
That were in Court a well proportion'd hooke,
Where piercing witts do quickly apprehend,
   Their sences rude plaine objects only move,
   And so must see great cause before they love.
Therfore Love arm'd in hir now takes the fielde, [145]

---

110 lean'd 93–98.   sighs] sigh's 93–98.   117 he 93.   121 take 93–98.
127 These] This 93–98.   128 Kisse-cheeke] Kisse-cheeks 98.   130 Captaines
93.   136 see] vse 93.   137 tooke 93–98.

Making hir beames his bravery and might:
Hir hands which pierc'd the soule's seav'n-double shield,
Were now his darts leaving his wonted fight.
Brave crest to him hir scorn-gold haire did yeeld,
His compleat harneis was hir purest white.   [150]
    But fearing lest all white might seeme too good,
    In cheeks and lipps the Tyran threatens bloud.
Besides this force, within hir eies he kept
A fire, to burne the prisoners he gaines,
Whose boiling heat encreased as she wept: [155]
For ev'n in forge colde water fire maintaines.
Thus proud and fierce unto the hearts he stept
Of them, poore soules: and cutting Reason's raines,
    Made them his owne before they had it wist.
    But if they had, could shephookes this resist?   [160]
Klaius streight felt, and groned at the blowe,
And cal'd, now wounded, purpose to his aide:
Strephon, fond boy, delighted did not knowe,
That it was Love that shin'de in shining maid:
But lickrous, Poison'd, faine to her would goe,   [165]
If him new-learned manners had not stai'd.
    For then *Urania* homeward did arise,
    Leaving in paine their wel-fed hungry eies.
She went, they staid; or rightly for to say,
She staid in them, they went in thought with hyr: [170]
Klaius in deede would faine have puld a way
This mote from out his eye, this inward burre,
And now, proud Rebell gan for to gainsay
The lesson which but late he learn'd too furre:
    Meaning with absence to refresh the thought   [175]
    To which hir presence such a feaver brought.
Strephon did leape with joy and jolitie,
Thinking it just more therein to delight
Then in good Dog, faire field, or shading tree.
So have I sene trim bookes in velvet dight   [180]
With golden leaves, and painted babery,
Of seely boies please unacquainted sight:
    But when the rod began to play his part,
    Faine would, but could not fly from golden smart.

153 force 93.   155 heat] hart 98.   158 them 93-98.   181 babery 93-98.

He quickly learn'd *Urania* was her name,   [185]
And streight for failing, grav'd it in his heart:
He knew hir haunt, and haunted in the same,
And taught his shepe hir shepe in food to thwart.
Which soone as it did batefull question frame,
He might on knees confesse his faulty part,   [190]
 And yeeld himselfe unto hir punishment,
 While nought but game, the selfe-hurt wanton ment.
Nay ev'n unto hir home he oft would go,
Where bold and hurtles many plays he tries,
Her parents liking well it should be so,   [195]
For simple goodnes shined in his eyes.
There did he make hir laugh in spite of woe,
So as good thoughts of him in all arise,
 While into none doubt of his love did sinke,
 For not himselfe to be in love did thinke.   [200]
But glad Desire, his late embosom'd guest,
Yet but a babe, with milke of Sight he nurst:
Desire the more he suckt, more sought the brest,
Like dropsy folke still drinke to be a thyrst.
Till one faire eav'n an howr ere Sun did rest,   [205]
Who then in Lion's cave did enter fyrst,
 By neighbors prai'd she went abroad therby,
 At Barly brake hir swete swift foot to trie.
Never the earth on his round shoulders bare
A maid train'd up from high or low degree,   [210]
That in her doings better could compare
Mirth with respect, few words with curtesy,
A careles comelines with comely care,
Self-gard with mildnes, Sport with Majesty:
 Which made hir yeeld to deck this shepheards' band,   [215]
 And still, beleve me, *Strephon* was at hand.
A-field they goe, where many lookers be,
And thou, seke-sorow *Klaius*, them among:
In dede thou said'st it was thy frend to see,
Strephon, whose absence seem'd unto thee long,   [220]
While most with hir he lesse did kepe with thee.
No, no, it was in spite of wisdome's song,

194 plays] play 93-98. 207 therby. 93-98.   217 A field 93-98.
218 thou 93-98. *Klaius* 93-98. 219 see 93-98. 222 song 93-98.

Which absence wisht: love plai'd a victor's part:
The heav'n-love lodestone drew thy iron hart.
Then couples three be streight allotted there,   [225]
They of both ends the middle two doe flie,
The two that in mid place, Hell called were,
Must strive with waiting foot, and watching eye
To catch of them, and them to hell to beare,
That they, aswell as they, Hell may supplie: [230]
    Like some which seeke to salve their blotted name
    With others' blott, till all do tast of shame.
There may you see, soone as the middle two
Do coupled towards either couple make,
They false and fearfull do their hands undoe,   [235]
Brother his brother, frend doth frend forsake,
Heeding himselfe, cares not how fellow doe,
But of a straunger mutuall help doth take:
    As perjur'd cowards in adversity
    With sight of feare from frends to fremb'd do flie.   [240]
These sports shepheards deviz'd such faults to show.
Geron, though olde yet gamesome, kept one ende
With *Cosma*, for whose love *Pas* past in woe.
Faire *Nous* with *Pas* the lott to hell did sende:
Pas thought it hell, while he was *Cosma* fro.   [245]
At other end *Uran* did *Strephon* lend
    Her happy-making hand, of whome one looke
    From *Nous* and *Cosma* all their beauty tooke.
The play began: *Pas* durst not *Cosma* chace,
But did entend next bout with her to meete,   [250]
So he with *Nous* to *Geron* turn'd their race,
With whome to joyne fast ran *Urania* sweet:
But light-legd *Pas* had gott the middle space.
Geron strave hard, but aged were his feet,
    And therfore finding force now faint to be,   [255]
    He thought gray haires afforded subtletie.
And so when *Pas* hand-reached him to take,
The fox on knees and elbowes tombled downe:
Pas could not stay, but over him did rake,
And crown'd the earth with his first touching crowne: [260]
His heels grow'n proud did seme at heav'n to shake.
But *Nous* that slipt from *Pas*, did catch the clowne.

So laughing all, yet *Pas* to ease some dell,
Geron with *Uran* were condemn'd to hell.
Cosma this while to *Strephon* safely came,   [265]
And all to second barly-brake are bent:
The two in hell did toward *Cosma* frame,
Who should to *Pas*, but they would her prevent.
Pas mad with fall, and madder with the shame,
Most mad with beames which he thought *Cosma* sent, [270]
    With such mad haste he did to *Cosma* goe,
    That to hir breast he gave a noysome blowe.
She quick, and proud, and who did *Pas* despise,
Up with hir fist, and tooke him on the face,
'Another time', quoth she, 'become more wise'.   [275]
Thus *Pas* did kisse hir hand with little grace,
And each way luckles, yet in humble guise
Did hold hir fast for feare of more disgrace,
    While *Strephon* might with preatie *Nous* have met,
    But all this while another course he fet.   [280]
For as *Urania* after *Cosma* ran,
He ravished with sight how gracefully
She mov'd hir lims, and drew the aged man,
Left *Nous* to coast the loved beauty ny.
Nous cri'de, and chafd, but he no other can.   [285]
Till *Uran* seing *Pas* to *Cosma* fly,
    And *Strephon* single, turned after him.
    Strephon so chas'd did seme in milke to swimme.
He ran, but ran with eye ore shoulder cast,
More marking hir, then how himselfe did goe,   [290]
Like *Numid* Lions by the hunters chas'd,
Though they do fly, yet backwardly do glowe
With proud aspect, disdaining greater hast.
What rage in them, that love in him did show.
    But God gives them instinct the man to shun,   [295]
    And he by law of Barly-brake must run.
But as his heate with running did augment,
Much more his sight encreast his hote desire:
So is in her the best of Nature spent,
The aire hir swete race mov'd doth blow the fire.   [300]
Hir feet be Pursevants from *Cupid* sent,

263 dell 93-98.

With whose fine stepps all loves and joyes conspire.
   The hidden beauties seem'd in waite to lye,
   To downe proud hearts that would not willing dye.
Thus, fast he fled from her he follow'd sore,   [305]
Still shunning *Nous* to lengthen pleasing race,
Till that he spied old *Geron* could no more,
Then did he slack his love-enstructed pace.
So that *Uran*, whose arme old *Geron* bore,
Laid hold on him with most lay-holding grace.   [310]
   So caught, him seem'd he caught of joyes the bell,
   And thought it heav'n so to be drawn to hell.
To hell he goes, and *Nous* with him must dwell.
Nous sware it was no right; for his default
Who would be caught, that she should go to hell: [315]
But so she must. And now the third assault
Of Barly-brake among the six befell.
Pas Cosma matcht, yet angry with his fault,
   The other end *Geron* with *Uran* garde.
   I thinke you thinke *Strephon* bent thitherward.   [320]
Nous counseld *Strephon Geron* to pursue,
For he was olde, and easly would be cought:
But he drew hir as love his fancy drew,
And so to take the gemme *Urania* sought.
While *Geron* olde came safe to *Cosma* true,   [325]
Though him to meete at all she sturred nought.
   For *Pas*, whether it were for feare, or love,
   Mov'd not himselfe, nor suffred hir to move.
So they three did togither idly stay,
While deare *Uran*, whose course was *Pas* to meet,   [330]
(He staying thus) was faine abroad to stray
With larger round, to shun the folowing feet.
Strephon, whose eies on hir back-parts did play,
With love drawne on, so fast with pace unmeet
   Drew dainty *Nous*, that she not able so   [335]
   To runne, brake from his hands, and let him goe.
He single thus, hop'd soone with hir to be,
Who nothing earthly, but of fire and aire,
Though with soft leggs, did run as fast as he.
He thrise reacht, thrise deceiv'd, when hir to beare   [340]

       327 whether] whither 93.

He hopes, with dainty turns she doth him flee.
So on the downs we see, neere *Wilton* faire,
   A hast'ned Hare from greedy Grayhound goe,
   And past all hope his chapps to frustrate so.
But this straunge race more straunge conceits did yeeld: [345]
Who victor seem'd, was to his ruine brought:
Who seem'd orethrown was mistresse of the field:
She fled, and tooke: he folow'd, and was cought.
So have I heard to pierce pursuing shield
By Parents train'd the *Tartars* wilde are tought,   [350]
   With shafts shott out from their back-turned bow.
   But, ah! hir darts did farre more depely goe.
As *Venus'* bird the white, swift, lovely Dove
(O happy Dove that art compar'd to hir!)
Doth on hir wings hir utmost swiftnes prove,   [355]
Finding the gripe of Falcon fierce not furr:
So did *Uran*, the narr the swifter move,
(Yet beauty still as fast as she did sturre)
   Till with long race deare she was breathles brought,
   And then the *Phœnix* feared to be cought.   [360]
Among the rest that there did take delight
To see the sportes of double-shining day,
And did the tribute of their wondring sight
To Nature's heir, the faire *Urania*, pay,
I tolde you *Klaius* was the haples wight   [365]
Who earnest found what they accounted play.
   He did not there doe homage of his eies,
   But on his eies his heart did sacrifise.
With gazing looks, short sighs, unsettled feet,
He stood, but turn'd, as *Girosol*, to Sun: [370]
His fancies still did hir in half-way meet,
His soule did fly as she was seen to run.
In sum, proud *Boreas* never ruled fleet
(Who *Neptune's* webb on daunger's distaff spun)
   With greater powr, then she did make them wend [375]
   Each way, as she, that age's praise, did bend.
Till spying well she welnigh weary was,
And surely taught by his love-open eye,
His eye, that ev'n did marke hir troden grasse,

342 down's 93–98.   *Wilton*] Helis 13.   373 sum 93–98.   377 spying] spieng 93.

That she would faine the catch of *Strephon* flie,   [380]
Giving his reason pasport for to passe,
Whither it would, so it would let him dy,
   He that before shund hir to shun such harmes,
   Now runnes, and takes hir in his clipping armes.
For with pretence from *Strephon* hir to garde,   [385]
He met hir full, but full of warefulnes,
With inbow'd bosome well for hir prepar'd,
When *Strephon*, cursing his owne backwardnes,
Came to hir back, and so with double warde
Emprison hir, who both them did possesse   [390]
   As heart-bound slaves: and happy then embrace
   Vertue's proofe, fortune's victor, beautie's place.
Hir race did not hir beautie's beames augment,
For they were ever in the best degree,
But yet a setting foorth it some way lent: [395]
As rubies lustre, when they rubbed be.
The dainty dew on face and body went
As on sweet flowrs when morning's drops we see.
   Her breath, then short, seem'd loth from home to pas,
   Which more it mov'd, the more it sweeter was.   [400]
Happy, ô happy! if they so might bide,
To see hir eies, with how true humblenes
They looked down to triumph over pride:
With how sweet sawes she blam'd their sawcines:
To feele the panting heart, which through hir syde   [405]
Did beate their hands, which durst so neere to presse.
   To see, to feele, to heare, to tast, to know
   More then, besides hir, all the earth could show.
But never did *Medea's* golden weed
On *Creon's* child his poison sooner throw,   [410]
Then those delights through all their sinews breed
A creeping serpentlike of mortall woe.
Till she brake from their armes (although in deed
Going from them, from them she could not go)
   And fare-welling the flocke did homeward wend,   [415]
   And so that even the barly-brake did end.
It ended, but the others' woe began,
Began at least to be conceiv'd as woe,

388 *Strephon* 93-98.   backwardnes 93.   399 breath 93-98.   short 93.

For then wise *Klaius* found no absence can
Help him, who can no more hir sight foregoe.　　　　[420]
He found man's vertue is but part of man,
And part must folowe where whole man doth goe.
　　He found that Reason's self now reasons found
　　To fasten knotts, which fancy first had bound.
So doth he yeeld, so takes he on his yoke,　　　　[425]
Not knowing who did draw with him therin;
Strephon, poore youth, because he saw no smoke,
Did not conceive what fire he had within.
But after this to greater rage it broke,
Till of his life it did full conquest win,　　　　[430]
　　First killing mirth, then banishing all rest,
　　Filling his eies with teares, with sighs his brest.
Then sports grew paines, all talking tediouse,
On thoughts he feeds, his lookes their figure chaunge,
The day seemes long, but night is odious,　　　　[435]
No sleeps, but dreams, no dreams, but visions straunge,
Till finding still his evill encreasing thus,
One day he with his flock abroad did raunge:
　　And comming where he hop'd to be alone,
　　Thus on a hillock set, he made his mone.　　　　[440]
'Alas! what weights are these that lode my heart!
I am as dull as winter-sterved sheep,
Tir'de as a jade in overloden carte,
Yet thoughts do flie, though I can scarcely creep.
All visions seeme, at every bush I start:　　　　[445]
Drowsy am I, and yet can rarely slepe.
　　Sure I bewitched am, it is even that:
　　Late neere a crosse I met an ougly Cat.
'For, but by charms, how fall these things on me,
That from those eies where heav'nly apples bene,　　　　[450]
Those eies, which nothing like themselves can see,
Of faire *Urania*, fairer then a greene,
Proudly bedeckt in Aprill's livory,
A shot unheard gave me a wound unseene?
　　He was invisible that hurt me so,　　　　[455]
　　And none invisible, but Spirites, can goe.
'When I see her, my sinewes shake for feare,

And yet, deare soule, I know she hurteth none:
Amid my flock with woe my voice I teare,
And, but bewitch'd, who to his flock would mone?   [460]
Her chery lipps, milke hands, and golden haire
I still do see, though I be still alone.
    Now make me thinke that there is not a fende,
    Who hid in Angel's shape my life would ende.
'The sportes wherin I wonted to do well,   [465]
Come she, and sweet the aire with open brest,
Then so I faile, when most I would do well,
That at me so amaz'd my fellowes jest:
Sometimes to her newes of my selfe to tell
I go about, but then is all my best   [470]
    Wry words, and stam'ring, or els doltish dombe,
    Say then, can this but of enchantment come?
'Nay each thing is bewitcht to know my case:
The Nightingales for woe their songs refraine:
In river as I look'd my pining face,   [475]
As pin'd a face as mine I saw againe.
The courteous mountaines, griev'd at my disgrace,
Their snowy haire teare off in melting paine.
    And now the dropping trees do wepe for me,
    And now faire evenings blush my shame to see.   [480]
'But you my pipe, whilome my chief delight,
Till straunge delight, delight to nothing ware;
And you my flock, care of my carefull sight,
While I was I, and so had cause to care;
And thou my dogg, whose truth and valiant might   [485]
Made wolves (not inward wolves) my ewes to spare;
    Go you not from your master in his woe:
    Let it suffise that he himselfe forgoe.
'For though like waxe, this magique makes me waste,
Or like a lambe whose dam away is fet,   [490]
(Stolne from her yoong by theeves' unchoosing hast)
He treble beas for helpe, but none can get:
Though thus, and worse, though now I am at last,
Of all the games that here ere now I met:
    Do you remember still you once were mine,   [495]
    Till my eies had their curse from blessed eine.

477 mountaines 93-98.   disgrace 93-98.   478 off] of 93.

'Be you with me while I unheard do cry,
While I do score my losses on the winde,
While I in heart my will write ere I die.
In which by will, my will and wits I binde: [500]
Still to be hers, about her aye to flie,
As this same sprite about my fancies blinde,
   Doth daily haunt: but so, that mine become
   As much more loving, as lesse combersome.
'Alas! a cloud hath overcast mine eies: [505]
And yet I see her shine amid the cloud.
Alas! of ghostes I heare the gastly cries:
Yet there, me seemes, I heare her singing loud.
This song she singes in most commaunding wise:
Come shepheard's boy, let now thy heart be bowd   [510]
   To make it selfe to my least looke a slave:
   Leave sheepe, leave all, I will no piecing have.
'I will, I will, alas! alas! I will:
Wilt thou have more? more have, if more I be.
Away ragg'd rams, care I what murraine kill?   [515]
Out shreaking pipe made of some witched tree.
Go bawling curre, thy hungry maw go fill,
On yond foule flocke belonging not to me.'
   With that his dogge he henc'd, his flocke he curst:
   With that (yet kissed first) his pipe he burst.   [520]
This said, this done, he rase even tir'd with rest,
With heart as carefull, as with carelesse grace,
With shrinking legges, but with a swelling brest,
With eyes which threatned they would drowne his face,
Fearing the worst, not knowing what were best,   [525]
And giving to his sight a wandring race,
   He saw behind a bush where _Klaius_ sate:
   His well knowne friend, but yet his unknowne mate,
Klaius the wretch, who lately yelden was
To beare the bondes which Time nor wit could breake, [530]
(With blushing soule at sight of judgement's glasse,
While guilty thoughts accus'd his Reason weake)
This morne alone to lonely walke did passe,
With in himselfe of hir deare selfe to speake,

512 sheepe] sleepe 98.   519 henc'd,] henst 93.   528 know'ne 93.

Till *Strephon's* plaining voice him nearer drew,   [535]
Where by his words his self-like cause he knew.
For hearing him so oft with wordes of woe
Urania name, whose force he knew so well,
He quickly knew what witchcraft gave the blow
Which made his *Strephon* think himselfe in hell.   [540]
Which when he did in perfect image show,
To his owne witt, thought upon thought did swell,
 Breeding huge stormes with in his inward parte,
 Which thus breath'd out with earthquake of his hart.

5

[*Philisides*]

THE ladd *Philisides*
Lay by a river's side,
In flowry fielde a gladder eye to please:
His pipe was at his foote,
His lambs were him beside,   [5]
A widow turtle neere on bared root
Sate wailing without boot.
Each thing both sweet and sadd
Did draw his boyling braine
To thinke, and thinke with paine   [10]
Of *Mira's* beames eclipst by absence bad.
And thus, with eyes made dimme
With teares, he saide, or sorrow said for him.

'O earth, once answere give,
So may thy stately grace   [15]
By north or south still rich adorned live:
So *Mira* long may be
On thy then blessed face,
Whose foote doth set a heav'n on cursed thee,
I aske, now answere me.   [20]

---

535 plaining] planing 93. 536 cause] case 98. 538 Vrania 93. 544 *Not indented in* 93.
 5. 93. (*All verbal and punctuation variants in* 98 *and* 13 *also listed.*) 93–13 *do not separate stanzas.* 2 river's] riuer 13. 4 foote 93. 5 beside] besides 93–98. 6 root] rootes 93. 7 boot] bootes 93. 13 him: 98–13.
16 north, 93–13. liue, 98–13. 17 *Long* 93.

If th' author of thy blisse,
Phœbus, that shepheard high,
Do turne from thee his eye,
Doth not thy selfe, when he long absent is,
Like Rogue, all ragged goe,   [25]
And pine away with daily wasting woe?

'Tell me you wanton brooke,
So may your sliding race
Shunn lothed-loving bankes with conning crooke:
So in you ever new   [30]
Mira may looke her face,
And make you faire with shadow of her hue:
So when to pay your due
To mother sea you come,
She chide you not for stay,   [35]
Nor beat you for your play,
Tell me, if your diverted springs become
Absented quite from you,
Are you not dried? Can you your self renew?

'Tell me you flowers faire,   [40]
Cowslipp and Columbine,
So may your Make, this wholsome springtime aire,
With you embraced lie,
And lately thence untwine:
But with dew dropps engendre children hy: [45]
So may you never dy,
But pulld by *Mira's* hande,
Dresse bosome hers or hedd,
Or scatter on her bedd,
Tell me, if husband springtime leave your lande,   [50]
When he from you is sent,
Wither not you, languisht with discontent?

'Tell me my seely pipe,
So may thee still betide
A clenly cloth thy moistnes for to wipe: [55]

21 blisse 93-13   22 high 93-13.   29 crooke? 98.   37 me 93-13.
39 self] selues 93-13.   40 faire 93-13.   41 Cowslipp] Cowslop 98-13.
42 Make 93-13.   aire 93-13.   47 hande 93   48 hers, 98-13.   49 bed.
98-13.   52 Wither] Whither 93.   53 me, 98-13.

917.26   S

So may the cheries redd
Of *Mira's* lipps divide
Their sugred selves to kisse thy happy hedd:
So may her eares be ledd,
Her eares where Musique lives,   [60]
To heare, and not despise
Thy liribliring cries,
Tell, if that breath, which thee thy sounding gives,
Be absent farre from thee,
Absent alone canst thou then piping be?   [65]

'Tell me my lamb of gold,
So maist thou long abide
The day well fed, the night in faithfull folde:
So grow thy wooll of note,
In time that, richly di'de,   [70]
It may be part of *Mira's* peticoate,
Tell me, if wolves the throte
Have cought of thy deare damme,
Or she from thee be staide,
Or thou from her be straide,   [75]
Canst thou, poore lamme, become another's lamme?
Or rather, till thou die,
Still for thy Dam with bea-waymenting crie?

'Tell me ô Turtle true,
So may no fortune breed   [80]
To make thee nor thy better-loved rue:
So may thy blessings swarme
That *Mira* may thee feede
With hand and mouth, with lapp and brest keepe warme,
Tell me if greedy arme,   [85]
Do fondly take away
With traitor lime the one,
The other left alone,
Tell me poore wretch, parted from wretched prey,
Disdaine not you the greene,   [90]
Wayling till death, shun you not to be seene?

58 head; 98-13.   61 heare 13.   62 Thy] The 93.   cries: 13.   68 fed; 93.
70 that 93-13.   di'de 93-13.   77 rather 93-13.   die 93-13.
84 mouth; 98-13.   88 alone: 98-13.   89 prey,] pray 93-13.   91 death 93-13.

'Earth, brooke, flowrs, pipe, lambe, Dove
Say all, and I with them,
"Absence is death, or worse, to them that love."
So I unlucky lad   [95]
Whome hills from her do hemme,
What fitts me now but teares, and sighings sadd?
O fortune too too badd,
I rather would my sheepe
Thad'st killed with a stroke,   [100]
Burnt *Caban*, lost my cloke,
Then want one hower those eyes which my joyes keepe.
Oh! what doth wailing winne?
Speeche without ende were better not begin.

'My song clime thou the winde   [105]
Which *Holland* sweet now gently sendeth in,
That on his wings the leavell thou maist finde
To hit, but Kissing hit,
Her ears the weights of wit.
If thou know not for whome thy Master dies,   [110]
These markes shall make thee wise:
She is the heardesse faire that shines in darke
And gives her kidds no food, but willow's barke.'

This said, at length he ended
His oft sigh-broken dittie,   [115]
Then rase, but rase on leggs with faintnes bended,
With skinne in sorrow died,
With face the plot of pittie,
With thoughts which thoughts their owne tormentors tried,
He rase, and streight espied   [120]
His Ramme, who to recover
The Ewe another loved,
With him proud battell proved.
He envied such a death in sight of lover,
And alwaies westward eying,   [125]
More envied *Phœbus* for his westerne flyinge.

92 flowr's 93-13.   93 all 13.   101 *Caban* 93-13.   102 Then] When 93.
105 wind, 98-13.   106 *Holland*] holland 93-98, Ciprus 13.   108 Kiss-
ing hit 93-13.   109 ear's 93-13.   112 darke, 98-13.   114 ended, 93.
116 raise, but raise 93-13.   on] no 98.   leggs: 93-98.   with] which 93-98.
119 tried. 98-13.   125 eying 93.

6

Two Pastoralls, made by Sir *Philip Sidney*, never yet published

Upon his meeting with his two worthy Friends
and fellow-Poets, Sir Edward Dier,
and Maister Fulke Grevill.

JOYNE Mates in mirth to me,
Graunt pleasure to our meeting:
Let *Pan* our good God see,
How gratefull is our greeting.
   Joyne hearts and hands, so let it be,   [5]
   Make but one Minde in Bodies three.

Ye Hymnes, and singing skill
Of God *Apolloe's* giving,
Be prest our reedes to fill,
With sound of musicke living.   [10]
   Joyne hearts and hands, so let it be,
   Make but one Minde in Bodies three.

Sweete *Orpheus'* Harpe, whose sound
The stedfast mountaynes moved,
Let heere thy skill abound,   [15]
To joyne sweete friends beloved.
   Joyne hearts and hands, so let it be,
   Make but one Minde in Bodies three.

My two and I be met,
A happy blessed Trinitie;   [20]
As three most joyntly set,
In firmest band of Unitie.
   Joyne hearts and hands, so let it be,
   Make but one Minde in Bodies three.

6. *A Poetical Rapsody,* 1602, which repeats only the incipit of the refrain in all except the first and last stanzas.

Welcome my two to me,   E.D. F.G. P.*S.*   [25]
The number best beloved,
Within my heart you be
In friendship unremoved.
 Joyne hearts and hands, so let it be,
 Make but one Minde in Bodies three.   [30]

Give leave your flockes to range,
Let us the while be playing,
Within the Elmy grange,
Your flockes will not be straying.
 Joyne hearts and hands, so let it be,   [35]
 Make but one Minde in Bodies three.

Cause all the mirth you can,
Since I am now come hether,
Who never joy, but when
I am with you together.   [40]
 Joyne hearts and hands, so let it be,
 Make but one Minde in Bodies three.

Like Lovers do their Love,
So joy I, in you seeing;
Let nothing mee remove   [45]
From alwayes with you beeing.
 Joyne hearts and hands, so let it be,
 Make but one Minde in Bodies three.

And as the Turtle-Dove
To mate with whom he liveth,   [50]
Such comfort, fervent love
Of you, to my hart giveth.
 Joyne hearts and hands, so let it be,
 Make but one Minde in Bodies three.

Now joyned be our hands,   [55]
Let them be ne'r a sunder,
But linkt in binding bands
By metamorphoz'd wonder.
 So should our sever'd bodies three
 As one for ever joyned bee.   [60]

7

Disprayse of a Courtly life

WALKING in bright *Phœbus*' blaze
Where with heate oppreste I was,
I got to a shady wood,
Where greene leaves did newly bud.
And of grasse was plenty dwelling,   [5]
Deckt with pyde flowers sweetely smelling.

In this wood a man I met,
On lamenting wholy set:
Rewing change of wonted state,
Whence he was transformed late,   [10]
Once to Shepheard's God retayning,
Now in servile Court remayning.

There he wandring malecontent,
Up and downe perplexed went,
Daring not to tell to mee,   [15]
Spake unto a sencelesse tree,
One among the rest electing
These same words, or this effecting:

'My old mates I grieve to see,
Voyde of me in field to bee,   [20]
Where we once our lovely sheepe,
Lovingly like friends did keepe,
Oft each other's friendship proving,
Never striving, but in loving.

'But may Love abiding bee   [25]
In poore shepheard's base degree?
It belongs to such alone
To whom arte of Love is knowne:
Seely shepheards are not witting
What in art of Love is fitting.   [30]

7. *A Poetical Rapsody*, 1602.

'Nay, what neede the Arte to those,
To whom we our love disclose?
It is to be used then,
When we doe but flatter men:
Friendship true in hart assured,   [35]
Is by nature's giftes procured.

'Therefore shepheardes wanting skill,
Can Love's duties best fulfill:
Since they know not how to faine,
Nor with Love to cloake Disdaine,   [40]
Like the wiser sorte, whose learning,
Hides their inward will of harming.

'Well was I, while under shade
Oten Reedes me musicke made,
Striving with my Mates in Song,   [45]
Mixing mirth our Songs among,
Greater was that shepheard's treasure,
Then this false, fine, Courtly pleasure.

'Where, how many Creatures be,
So many pufft in minde I see,   [50]
Like to *Junoe's* birdes of pride,
Scarce each other can abide,
Friends like to blacke Swannes appearing,
Sooner these than those in hearing.

'Therefore *Pan*, if thou mayst be   [55]
Made to listen unto me,
Grant, I say (if seely man
May make treaty to god *Pan*)
That I, without thy denying,
May be still to thee relying.   [60]

'Only for my two loves' sake,   *Sir Ed. D. and M. F. G.*
In whose love I pleasure take,
Only two do me delight
With their ever-pleasing sight,
Of all men to thee retaining,   [65]
Grant me with those two remaining.

'So shall I to thee alwayes,
With my reedes, sound mighty praise;
And first Lambe that shall befall,
Yearely decke thine Altar shall: [70]
If it please thee be reflected,
And I from thee not rejected.'

So I left him in that place,
Taking pitty on his case,
Learning this among the rest,   [75]
That the meane estate is best,
Better filled with contenting,
Voyde of wishing and repenting.

THE PSALMS OF DAVID
TRANSLATED INTO ENGLISH VERSE
BY THAT NOBLE AND
VIRTUOUS GENTLEMAN
SIR PHILIP SYDNEY

To the Angell spirit of the most excellent
Sir Phillip Sidney

To thee pure sprite, to thee alone's addres't
  this coupled worke, by double int'rest thine:
  First rais'de by thy blest hand, and what is mine
inspird by thee, thy secrett power imprest.
    So dar'd my Muse with thine it selfe combine,   [5]
    as mortall stuffe with that which is divine,
Thy lightning beames give lustre to the rest,

That heaven's King may daigne his owne transform'd
  in substance no, but superficiall tire
  by thee put on; to praise, not to aspire   [10]
To, those high Tons, so in themselves adorn'd,
  which Angells sing in their cælestiall Quire,
  and all of tongues with soule and voice admire
Theise sacred Hymnes thy Kinglie Prophet form'd.

Oh, had that soule which honor brought to rest   [15]
  too soone not left and reft the world of all
  what man could showe, which wee perfection call
This halfe maim'd peece had sorted with the best.
  Deepe wounds enlarg'd, long festred in their gall
  fresh bleeding smart; not eie but hart teares fall.   [20]
Ah memorie what needs this new arrest?

Yet here behold, (oh wert thou to behold!)
  this finish't now, thy matchlesse Muse begunne,
  the rest but peec't, as left by thee undone.
Pardon (oh blest soule) presumption too too bold: [25]
  if love and zeale such error ill-become
  'tis zealous love, Love which hath never done,
Nor can enough in world of words unfold.

And sithe it hath no further scope to goe,
  nor other purpose but to honor thee,   [30]
  Thee in thy workes where all the Graces bee,

J. 9 'no.   27 ti's.

As little streames with all their all doe flowe
  to their great sea, due tribute's gratefull fee:
  so press my thoughts my burthened thoughtes in mee,
To pay the debt of Infinits I owe   [35]

To thy great worth; exceeding Nature's store,
  wonder of men, sole borne perfection's kinde,
  Phœnix thou wert, so rare thy fairest minde
Heav'nly adorn'd, Earth justlye might adore,
  where truthfull praise in highest glorie shin'de: [40]
  For there alone was praise to truth confin'de;
And where but there, to live for evermore?

Oh! when to this Accompt, this cast upp Summe,
  this Reckoning made, this Audit of my woe,
  I call my thoughts, whence so strange passions flowe;   [45]
Howe workes my hart, my sences striken dumbe?
  that would thee more, then ever hart could showe,
  and all too short who knewe thee best doth knowe
There lives no witt that may thy praise become.

Truth I invoke (who scorne else where to move   [50]
  or here in ought my blood should partialize)
  Truth, sacred Truth, Thee sole to solemnize
Those precious rights well knowne best mindes approve:
  and who but doth, hath wisdome's open eies,
  not owly blinde the fairest light still flies   [55]
Confirme no lesse? At least 'tis seal'd above.

Where thou art fixt among thy fellow lights:
  my day put out, my life in darkenes cast,
  Thy Angell's soule with highest Angells plac't
There blessed sings enjoying heav'n-delights   [60]
  thy Maker's praise: as farr from earthy tast
  as here thy workes so worthilie embrac't
By all of worth, where never Envie bites.

As goodly buildings to some glorious ende
  cut of by fate, before the Graces hadde   [65]
  each wondrous part in all their beauties cladde,

34 mee.   35 owe.   56 ti's.

Yet so much done, as Art could not amende;
  So thy rare workes to which no witt can adde,
  in all men's eies, which are not blindely madde,
Beyonde compare above all praise, extende.   [70]

Immortall Monuments of thy faire fame,
  though not compleat, nor in the reach of thought,
  howe on that passing peece time would have wrought
Had Heav'n so spar'd the life of life to frame
  the rest? But ah! such losse hath this world ought   [75]
  can equall it? or which like greevance brought?
Yet there will live thy ever praised name.

To which theise dearest offrings of my hart
  dissolv'd to Inke, while penn's impressions move
  the bleeding veines of never dying love: [80]
I render here: these wounding lynes of smart
  sadd Characters indeed of simple love
  not Art nor skill which abler wits doe prove,
Of my full soule receive the meanest part.

Receive theise Hymnes, theise obsequies receive;   [85]
  if any marke of thy sweet sprite appeare,
  well are they borne, no title else shall beare.
I can no more: Deare Soule I take my leave;
  Sorrowe still strives, would mount thy highest sphere
  presuming so just cause might meet thee there,   [90]
Oh happie chaunge! could I so take my leave.

          By the Sister of that
          Incomparable Sidney

          93 Incomporable.

THE PSALMS OF DAVID

Psalm I

Beatus vir, qui non

1 HE blessed is, who neither loosely treads
    The straying stepps as wicked Counsel leades;
Ne for bad mates in way of sinning waiteth,
    Nor yet himself with idle scorners seateth:
2 But on God's law his heart's delight doth bind,   [5]
    Which night and day he calls to marking mind.

3 He shall be lyke a freshly planted tree,
    To which sweet springs of waters neighbours be,
Whose braunches faile not timely fruite to nourish,
    Nor withered leafe shall make yt faile to flourish.   [10]
So all the things whereto that man doth bend,
    Shall prosper still, with well succeeding end.

4 Such blessings shall not wycked wretches see:
    But lyke vyle chaffe with wind shal scattred be.
5 For neither shall the men in sin delighted   [15]
    Consist, when they to highest doome are cited,
Ne yet shall suffred be a place to take,
    Wher godly men do their assembly make.

The copy text is B, *with Woodford's marginal notes of the earliest readings transferred to the body of the text. Variants, except for special cases, are cited only from* K *and* A. *See note in Commentary (pp. 508–9) on end-of-line punctuation. The title, from* F, *is wanting in* A B I J K; *for titles of the other manuscripts see* C, D, E H L N, G, *and* M *in the Bibliography.*   **1.** *Wanting in* A.   3 waiteth] wayeth B.   8 be. B. 10 withered] with red B, with'red J.   13–22 *Woodford notes:* 'In the margin is written. *these altered.* Q[*uœre*]. & both this staffe & yᵗ wᶜʰ followes is crossed.' *The Countess of Pembroke's revision is preserved only in* J:

> Not soe the wicked; Butt like chaff with wind
>   scatt'red, shall neither stay in Iudgment find
> nor with the iust, bee in their meetings placed:
>   for good mens waies by God are knowne & graced.
> Butt who from Iustice sinnfully doe stray,
>   the way they goe, shall be their ruins way.

13 blessings] blessing K.   16 cited. B.

[6] For God doth know, and knowing doth approve
    The trade of them, that just proceeding love;   [20]
But they that sinne, in sinfull breast do cherish;
    The way they go shal be their way to perish.

Psalm II

Quare fremuerunt gentes

1. WHAT ayles this heathenish rage? What do theis people meane
    To mutter murmures vaine?
2. Why do these earthly kings and lords such meetings make,
    And counsel jointly take,
    Against the lord of lords, the lord of every thing,   [5]
    And his anoynted King?
3. Come let us break their bonds, say they, and fondly say:
    And cast their yoakes away.
4. But He shall them deride, who by the heavns is borne,
    He shall laugh them to scorn,   [10]
5. And bravely speake to them, with breath of wrathful fire,
    And vex them in his ire.
6. And say (O kings) yet have I set my King upon
    My Holy Hill Syon.
7. And I will (sayeth His King) the lord's decree display,   [15]
    And say that he did say:
8. Thou art my son in deed, this day begott by me:
    Ask I will give yt Thee,
    The Heathen for thy Child's right, and will thy realme extend
    Farr as World's farthest end.   [20]
9. With Iron scepter bruse thou shalt, and peece meale breake
    These men like potshards weake.
10. Therfore (O Kings), be wise, O Rulers rule your mind,
    That knowledg you may find.
11. Serve God, serve him with feare: Rejoyce in him but so,   [25]
    That joy with trembling go.

---

2. *Wanting in* A.   1 theis] this J.   3 meetings] meeting B K.   9 heaun's
B.   11 bravely] *after* B K J. *Woodford notes:* 'twas *brauely* but y^t is blotted out.'
18 yt] to B K J. *Woodford notes:* '*yt* blotted out.'   19 realme] realme B K J.
Woodford notes: 'another word bl[otted].'

12. With loving homage kisse that only son he hath,
    Least you enflame his wrath.
Wherof if but a sparke once kindled be, you all
    From your way perish shall   [30]
And then they that in him their only trust do rest,
    O they be rightly blest.

Psalm III

Domine quid multiplic[ati sunt]

1. LORD how do they encrease
    That hatefull never cease
    To breed my grievous trouble,
How many Ones there be
    That all against poore me   [5]
    Their numbrous strength redouble.

2. Even multitudes be they
    That to my soul do say,
    No help for you remaineth
3. In God on whom you build,   [10]
    Yet lord thou art my shield,
    In thee my glory raigneth.

4. The lord lifts up my head,
    To him my voyce I spread,
    From Holy hill he heard me.   [15]
5. I layd me down and slept,
    For he me safely kept
    And safe again He rear'd mee.

6. I will not be afraid
    Though legions round be layd,   [20]
    Which all against me gather:
7. I say no more but this:
    Up lord now time it is:
    Help me my God and Father.

---

3. *Wanting in* A.   6 strength] strengthes K.   17 For] While B K J.
Woodford notes: '*For.* bl[otted].'   18 again He] from sleep I B J, from sleepe hee
K. *Woodford notes*: '*again He.* bl[otted].'

For thou with cruel blowes, [25]
  On jaw-bones of my foes,
    My causeless wrongs hast wroken.
Thou those men's teeth which byte,
  Venom'd with godless spight,
    Hast in their malice broken. [30]

8. Salvation doth belong
  Unto the lord most strong:
    He is he that defendeth;
And on those blessed same,
  Which beare his people's name, [35]
    His blessing he extendeth.

Psalm IV

Cum invocarem

1. HEARE me, O heare me when I call
  O God, God of my Equity,
  Thou sett'st me free, when I was thrall,
  Have mercy therfore still on me,
  And hearken how I pray to Thee. [5]

2. O men, whose Fathers were but men,
  Till when will ye my honour high
  Staine with your blasphemys? till when
  Such pleasure take in Vanity,
  And only hunt, where lyes do ly? [10]

3. Yet know this too, that God did take
  When He chose me, a godly One:
  Such one I say, that when I make
  My crying plaints to him alone,
  He will give good eare to my moane. [15]

4. O tremble then with awfull will:
  Sinne from all rule in you depose,
  Talk with your hearts, and yet be still:
  And when your chamber you do close,
  Yourselves yet to yourselves disclose. [20]

27 hast] hath J.
4. 3 sett'st] setdst B, settest K.

6 [i.e. 5]   The sacrifices sacrify
    Of just desires, on justice stayd,
    Trust in that lord, that cannot ly,
    Indeed full many folkes have said,
    From whence shall come to us such ayd ?   [25]

6. But, lord, lift Thou upon our sight
    The shining clearness of thy face:
    Where I have found more heart's delight
    Than they whose stoare in harvest space
    Of grain and wine fills stoaring place.   [30]

7. So I in peace, and peacefull blisse
    Will lay me down, and take my rest:
    For it is thou lord, Thou it is,
    By power of whose only brest,
    I dwell, layd up in safest neast.   [35]

Psalm V

Verba mea auribus

[1] PONDER the words, O lord, that I do say,
    Consider what I meditate in me:
2 O, hearken to my voice, which calls on Thee,
    My King, my God for I to thee will pray.
3 So shall my voice clime to thyne eares betime: [5]
    For unto Thee I will my prayer send,
    With earlyest entry of the Morning prime,
4:   And will my waiting eyes to thee ward bend.

For Thou art that same God, far from delight
    In that, which of fowle wickedness doth smel: [10]
5 No, nor with Thee the naughty Ones shall dwel,
    Nor glorious Fooles stand in Thy awfull sight.

---

23 that lord] the lord B.   24 folkes] folk B.   29 harvest] haruests A.
34 whose] whose Owne B K A. *Woodford notes*: 'own is added aboue the line by an-
cther hand.'
   5. 8 waiting] wayling B K A. *Woodford notes*: 'wayling. bl[otted].'

6 Thou hatest all whose works in evill are plac't
  And shalt root out the tongues to lying bent:
  For Thou the lord in endless hatred hast   [15]
  The murdrous man, and so the fraudulent.

7. But I my self will to Thy house addresse
   With passe-port of thy graces manifold:
   And in thy feare knees of my heart will fold
   Towards the Temple of Thy Holyness.   [20]
8 Thou lord, Thou lord, the saver of Thyne Owne
  Guide me, O in thy justice be my guide:
  And make Thy wayes to me more plainly known,
  For all I neede, that with such foes do byde.

9 For in their mouth not One cleere word is spent, [25]
  Their soules fowl sinns for inmost lyning have:
  Their throat, it is an Open swallowing grave,
  Wherto their tongue is flattring Instrument.
10. Give them their due unto their guiltiness,
    Let their vile thoughts the thinkers' ruin be   [30]
    With heaped weights of their own sins oppresse
    These most ungratefull rebels unto Thee.

11. So shall all they that trust in thee do bend,
    And love the sweet sound of thy name, rejoyce.
    They ever shall send thee their praysing voyce, [35]
    Since ever thou to them wilt succour send.
12 Thy work it is to blesse, thou blessest them;
   The just in Thee, on thee and justice build:
   Thy work it is such men safe in to hemm
   With kindest care, as with a certein shield.   [40]

14 shalt] shall K.   18 manifold] many fold B.   26 Their soules fowl sinns]
Mischeif ther soules B A, mischiefes theire Soules K. *Woodford notes*: '*Their soules
fowl sinns* but alterd as here.'   33 in] on B K A. *Woodford notes*: '*in* bl[otted].'
34 name B.   37 blesse B.   thou blessest] they blessed B K, thou blessedst ['st'
in different ink] A.

Psalm VI

Domine ne in furore

j. LORD, let not me a worme by thee be shent,
    While Thou art in the heat of thy displeasure:
    Ne let thy rage, of my due punishment
        Become the measure.

2 But mercy, lord, let Mercy thyne descend   [5]
    For I am weake, and in my weakness languish;
    Lord help, for ev'en my bones their marrow spend
        With cruel anguish.

3 Nay ev'n my soul fell troubles do appall;
    Alas, how long, my God, wilt Thou delay me?   [10]
4   Turne Thee, sweet lord, and from this Ougly fall
        My Deare God stay me.

5 Mercy, O Mercy lord, for Mercy's sake,
    For death doth kill the Witness of thy glory;
    Can of thy prayse the tongues entombed make   [15]
        A heavnly story?

6. Lo, I am tir'd, while still I sigh and groane:
    My moystned bed proofes of my sorrow showeth:
    My bed, while I with black night mourn alone,
        With my tears floweth.   [20]

7. Woe, lyke a moth, my face's beauty eates
    And age pull'd on with paines all freshness fretteth:
    The while a swarm of foes with vexing feates
        My life besetteth.

8 Get hence you ev'ill, who in my ev'ill rejoyce,   [25]
    In all whose workes vainess is ever raigning:
    For God hath heard the weeping sobbing voice
        Of my complaining.

9. The lord my suite did heare, and gently heare,
    They shall be sham'd and vext, that breed my crying,
10.   And turn their backs, and strait on backs appeare   [31]
        Their shamefull flying.

6. 7 for ev'en] mee for ~~even~~ K.   11 Thee] thou K.   14 doth] dos B.
24 besetteth] be setteth B.   29–32 *Wanting in* K (*torn*).

Psalm VII

Domine Deus meus

j. O LORD my God, Thou art my trustfull stay
   O save me from this Persecution's showre:
   Deliver me in my endangerd way

2 Least lion like He do my soule devoure,
   And cruely in many peices teare   [5]
   While I am voyd of any helping pow'r.

3 O lord, my God, if I did not forbeare
   Ever from deed of any such desart:
   If ought my hands of wyckednes do bear:

4 If I have been unkynd for friendly part: [10]
   Nay if I wrought not for his Freedome's sake
   Who causeless now, yeelds me a hatefull heart,

5 Then let my Foe chase me, and chasing take:
   Then let his foot uppon my neck be set:
   Then in the Dust let him my honour rake.   [15]

6 Arise, O lord, in wrath thy self upsett
   Against such rage of foes: Awake for me
   To that high doome, which I by Thee must get.

7. So shall all men with laudes inviron thee.
   Therfore, O lord, lift up Thy throne on high   [20]
   That evry folk Thy wondrous Acts may see.

8 Thou, lord, the people shalt in judgment try:
   Then lord, my lord, give sentence on my side
   After my clearness, and my Equity.

9 O let their wickedness no longer bide   [25]
   From coming to the well deserved end,
   But still be Thou to just men justest guide.

10 Thou righteous proofes to hearts, and reines dost send,
   And all my help from none but Thee is sent,
   Who dost Thy saving health to true men bend.   [30]

11 Thou righteous art, Thou strong, thou patient,
12   Yet each day art provoakt, thyne Ire to show,

---

7. *Wanting in* K (*torn*).   1 trustfull] trust full B.   6 pow'r] power B.   12 a]
an B.   20 Thy throne] Thy self B.   29 And] All B.   32 Yet] And B A.
Woodford notes: '*yet*. bl[otted].'

For this same man will not learn to repent,

13 Therfore thou whetst Thy sword, and bend'st Thy bow,
 And hast Thy deadly armes in order brought [35]
 And ready art to let Thyne arrowes go.

14. Lo he that first conceiv'd a wretched thought,
 And great with child of mischeif travaild long,
 Now brought abed, hath brought nought foorth, but nought.

15. A pitt was digg'd, by this man vainly strong, [40]
 But in the pitt he ruind first did fall,
 Which fall he made to do his neighbor wrong.

16 He against me doth throw, but down it shall
 Upon his pate, his pain employed thus
 And his own evill his own head shall appall. [45]

17 I will give thanks unto the lord of Us
 According to his heavnly equity
 And will to highest Name yeild prayses high.

Psalm VIII

Domine Dominus

[1] O Lord that rul'st Our mortall lyne
 How through the World thy Name doth shine:
 That hast of thine unmatched glory
 Upon the heavns engrav'n the story.

2. From sucklings hath Thy honour sproong, [5]
 Thy force hath flow'd from Babie's tongue
 Wherby Thou stop'st Thyne Enemy's prating
 Bent to revenge and ever hating.

[3] When I upon the Heav'ns do look
 Which all from Thee their Essence took [10]
 When Moone and starrs my thoughtes beholdeth
 Whose life no life but of Thee holdeth,

[4] Then think I, Ah, what is this Man,
 Whom that Great God remember can?

33 For this same] And if this B A. *Woodford notes*: '*For this same.* bl[otted].'
34 Therfore thou] For him thou B A. *Woodford notes*: '*Therfore* thou bl[otted]. & a second amendment *Then dost thou.* bl[otted].'   39 foorth] out B.   41 fall. B.
 8. 1–16 *Damaged in* K.   3 thine] Thy B.   4 engrav'n the] engrav'd Thy B.
7 Thyne] thy K.   8 ever hating] ouer-hating A.   11 thoughtes] thought B.
12 life no life] life no life B K A. *Woodford notes*: 'Qu[ære]: if not *light* bis.'

And what the race of him descended   [15]
　　It should be ought of God attended.
[5] For though in lesse than Angel's state
　　Thou planted hast this earthly mate
　　Yet hast Thou made even him an owner
　　Of glorious Croune, and crouning honour.   [20]
[6] Thou placest him upon all lands
　　To rule the Works of Thyne own hands
　　And so thou hast all things ordained
　　That even his feet have on them raigned.
[7] Thou under his Dominion plac't   [25]
　　Both sheep and Oxen wholy hast,
　　And all the beasts for ever breeding
　　Which in the fertile fields be feeding,
[8] The Bird free Burgess of the ayre,
　　The Fish of Sea the Native heire,   [30]
　　And what thinges els of waters traceth
　　The unworn paths, his rule embraceth.
[9]　　　　O lord that rulest Our mortall lyne,
　　　　How through the World Thy name doth shine.

Psalm IX

Confitebor tibi

1 WITH all my heart O lord I will prayse Thee,
　　My speeches all Thy marvailes shall descry:
2 　In Thee my joyes and comforts ever be,
　　Yea even my songs thy name shall magnify,
　　　　　O Lord most high.   [5]
3 Because my Foes to fly are now constraind
　　And they are faln, nay perisht at Thy sight:
4. 　For Thou my cause, my right Thou hast maintaind,
　　Setting Thy self in Throne, which shined bright
　　　　　Of judging right.   [10]
5 The Gentiles Thou rebuked sorely hast,
　　And wyked folkes from thee to wrack do wend.

---

30 Sea] seas B.　　　31 thinges els of waters] thing else of water B.
9. 12 folkes] folk B.

And their Renoune, which seemd so lyke to last,
Thou dost put out, and quite consuming send
   To endless end.   [15]

6 O bragging Foe, where is the endless wast
 Of Conquerd states, wherby such fame you gott?
 What? Doth their Memory no longer last?
 Both ruines, ruiners, and ruin'd plott
   Be quite forgott.   [20]

7. But God shall sit in his Eternal chaire
 Which He prepar'd, to give his judgments high:
8 Thither the World for justice shall repaire,
 Thence he to all his judgments shall apply
   Perpetualy.   [25]

9 Thou lord also th' Oppressed wilt defend
 That they to Thee in troublous tyme may flee:
10. They that know Thee, on Thee their trust will bend,
 For Thou lord found by them wilt ever be
   That seek to Thee.   [30]

11. O prayse the lord, this Syon dweller good,
 Shew forth his Acts, and this as Act most high,
12 That He enquiringe, doth require just blood,
 Which he forgetteth not, nor letteth dy
   Th' afflicted cry.   [35]

13. Have mercie, mercie lord I once did say,
 Ponder the paines, which on me loaden be
 By them whose minds on hatefull thoughts do stay:
 Thou lord that from Death' gates hast lifted me,
   I call to Thee.   [40]

14. That I within the ports most beautyfull
 Of syon's Daughter may sing forth Thy prayse:
 That I, even I of heavnly comfort full,
 May only joy in all Thy saving wayes
   Throughout my days.   [45]

15. No sooner said, but (lo) myne Enemyes sink
 Down in the pitt, which they themselves had wrought:
 And in that nett, which they well hidden think,
 Is their own foot, ledd by their own ill thought,
   Most surely caught.   [50]

27 tyme] times B. 33 enquiringe] in quiring B. 36 mercie, mercie lord]
mercy lord mercy B. 38 stay] straie K A. 42 sing] sound A.

16 For then the lord in judgment shewes to raigne
    When Godless men be snar'd in their own snares:
    When Wycked soules be turn'd to hellish paine,
    And that forgetfull sort, which never cares
            What God prepares.   [55]
17 But of the Other side, the poore in sprite
    Shall not be scrap'd from out of heavnly scoar:
    Nor meek abiding of the patient wight
    Yet perish shall (although his paine be sore)
            For ever more.   [60]
18 Up lord, and judg the Gentyls in Thy right
    And let not man have upper hand of Thee,
    With terrors great, O Lord, do thou them fright:
    That by sharp proofes, the heathen themselves may see
            But men to be.   [65]

Psalm X

Vt quid Domine

1.   WHY standest Thou so farr,
        O God our only starr,
        In time most fitt for Thee
        To help who vexed be!

2. For lo with pride the wicked man   [5]
    Still plagues the poore the most he can:
    O let proud him be throughly caught
    In craft of his own crafty thought!

3   For he himself doth prayse,
        When he his lust doth ease,   [10]
        Extolling ravenous gain:
        But doth God' self disdain.

4 Nay so proud is his puffed thought
    That after God he never sought,
    But rather much he fancys this   [15]
    That Name of God a fable is.

---

56 of] on A.   57 of] the B.   59 paine] paines K.
  10. *Lines 18–24 and 61–64 wanting in K (torn).*   10 ease] rayse K (*blotted*).
12 God' self] gods self A.   13 is his] is his B K A. *Woodford notes:* 'hee is. but
blotted out & put as in the text being a fault of the scribe.'   16 That] the A.

5   For while his wayes do prove,
          On them he sets his love:
          Thy judgments are too high
          He cannot them espy,   [20]

6 Therfore he doth defy all those
          That dare themselves to him oppose,
          And sayeth in his bragging heart,
          This gotten blisse shall never part,

7.   Nor he removed be   [25]
          Nor danger ever see:
          Yet from his mouth doth spring
          Cursing and cosening,

8. Under his tongue do harbour'd ly
          Both mischeif and iniquity.   [30]
          For proof, oft lain in wait he is
          In secret by-way villages.

          In such a place Unknown
          To slay the hurtless One,
          With winking eyes aye bent   [35]
          Against the Innocent,

9. Like lurking lion in his denn
          He waites to spoyle the simple men:
          Whom to their losse he still doth get
          When hee once drau'th his wily nett.   [40]

10.   O with how simple look
          He oft layeth out his hook,
          And with how humble showes
          To trap poore soules he goes!

11 Thus freely saith he in his sprite: [45]
          God sleeps, or hath forgotten quite,
          His farr off sight now hoodwinkt is,
          He leasure wants to mark all this.

12   Then rise and come abroad,
          O lord Our only God,   [50]
          Lift up Thy heavnly hand
          And by the syly stand.

20 cannot them] can them not A.   22 dare themselves to him]
dare to him themselues B.   29 do] doth K.   39 doth] dos B.   40 hee
once] once he B A.   47 hoodwinkt] hud-winck A.

13 Why should the evill, so evill despise
    The power of Thy through-seing eyes?
    And why should he in heart so hard   [55]
    Say, Thou dost not Thyn Own regard?

14.   But nake'd before thine eyes
    All wrong and mischeife lyes,
    For of them in Thy hands
    The ballance evnly stands;   [60]
But who aright poore-minded be
    Commit their Cause, themselves, to Thee,
    The succour of the succourless
    And Father of the Fatherlesse.

15   Breake Thou the wyked arm   [65]
    Whose fury bends to harme:
    Search them, and wyked he
    Will streight-way nothing be.
16 So lord we shall Thy Title sing
    Ever and ever to be King,   [70]
    Who hast the heath'ny folk destroyd
    From out Thy land by them anoy'd.

17   Thou openest heavnly Doore
    To prayers of the poore:
    Thou first prepare'dst their mind   [75]
    Then eare to them enclin'd.
18 O be thou still the Orphan's aide
    That poore from ruine may be stayd:
    Least we should ever feare the lust
    Of earthly man, a lord of dust.   [80]

Psalm XI

In Domino Confido

[1] SINCE I do trust Jehova still,
    Your fearfull words why do you spill
    That like a byrd to some strong hill
    I now should Fall aflying?

62 Cause themselues B.   69 So] o A.   71 heath'ny] heathney B.
75 prepare'dst] prepar'd A.

[2] Behold the evill have bent their bow   [5]
   And set their arrows in a rowe
   To give unwares a Mortall blow
     To hearts that hate all lying.

3. But that in building they begunne
   With ground plot's fall shall be undone: [10]
   For what, alas, have just men done?
    In them no cause is growing.
4. God in his Holy Temple is,
   The throne of Heav'n is only His:
   Naught his allseing sight can miss,   [15]
    His eyelidds peyse our going.

5 The lord doth search the just man's reines,
   But hates, abhorrs the wycked braines,
[6]   On them storms, brimstone, coales he raines,
    That is their share assigned.   [20]
[7] But so of happy other side
   His lovely face on them doth bide
   In race of life their Feet to guide
    Who be to God enclined.

Psalm XII

Salvum me fac

1. LORD help, it is high time for me to call,
   No men are left, that charity do love,
   Nay even the race of good men are decay'd.
2 Of things vain, with vaine mates they bable all,
   Their abject lips no breath but flattery move   [5]
   Sent from false heart, on double meaning stay'd.
3. But Thou (O lord) give them a thorough fall,
   Those lying lipps from Cousening head remove,
   In falsehood wrapt, but in their pride display'd.

11. 5 Behold] Behold B K A. *Woodford notes*: '*Perhaps* bl[otted].'   9 begunne]
began B.   21 so of] of so B.   other side] otherside B.   24 enclined: B.
12. 2 do] doth A.

4. Our tongues, say they, beyond them all shall go,   [10]
    Wee both have power, and will our tales to tell,
    For what lord rules our bold emboldned breast.

5 Ah, now even for their sakes, that taste of Woe,
    Whom troubles tosse, whose natures need doth quell,
    Even for the sighs, true sighs of man distrest,   [15]

6 I will get up saith God, and my help show
    Against all them, that against him do swell,
    Maugre their force I will set him at rest.

7 These are God's words, God's words are ever pure,
    Pure, Purer than the silver throughly try'd   [20]
    When fire seven times hath spent his earthly parts.

8 Then Thou (O lord) shalt keep the Good stil sure.
    By Thee preserv'd, in Thee they shall abide,
    Yea in no age thy blisse from them departs.

9 Thou seest each side the walking doth endure   [25]
    Of these bad folkes, more lifted up with pride
    Which if it last, Woe to all simple Hearts.

Psalm XIII

Vsque quo Domine

1. How long, O Lord, shall I forgotten be?
        What? ever?
  How long wilt Thou Thy hidden face from me
        Dissever?

2. How long shall I consult with carefull sprite   [5]
        In anguish?
  How long shall I with foes' triumphant might
        Thus languish?

3. Behold me, lord, let to Thy hearing creep
        My crying: [10]
  Nay give me eyes, and light, least that I sleep
        In dying.

11 to] too B.   12 bold] braue B K A. *Woodford notes*: '*bold* blotted out.'
14 quell] quell B K A. *Woodford notes*: '*quayl* expungd.'   15 the] their B.
18 their force] his foes B K A. *Woodford notes*: '*their force*, exp[unged].'   18 set
him] him sett A.   21 earthly] earthy A.   26 folkes] folk B.

4. Least my Foe bragg, that in my ruin hee
        Prevailed,
   And at my fall they joy that, troublous, me   [15]
        Assailed.

5. No, No I trust on thee, and joy in Thy
        Great Pity.
   Still therfore of Thy Graces shall be my
        Song's Ditty.   [20]

Psalm XIV

Dixit Insipiens

1. THE foolish man by flesh and fancy led
   His guiltie heart with this fond thought hath fed,
      There is no God that raigneth.
And so thereafter He, and all his Mates
   Do works which earth corrupt and Heaven hates,   [5]
      Not One that good remaineth.

2 Even God himself sent down his peircing ey
   If of this Clayey race he could espy
      One that his Wisdom learneth.
3. And, lo, he finds that all astraying went,   [10]
   All plung'd in stinking filth, not One well bent,
      Not One, that God discerneth.

4. O madness of these folks, thus loosely led,
   These Canibals, who as if they were bread
      God's people do devower,   [15]
5 Nor ever call on God, but they shall quake
   More than they now do bragg, when He shall take
      The just into his power.

13. 15 that, troublous,] that trouble B, that troublouse K.
   14. *Woodford notes*: 'This Psalm has a Crosse (mark of expunction) set over against its Title Quære'; *and* K *notes in the margin opposite the fourth stanza*: 'Varying, and wanting 4: stanses' [*i.e. verses* 5–7 *of the Psalter*].   2 guiltie] *om.* B.   fond] one K.   5 corrupt] corrupts B.   15 devower] devoure B K.

6. Indeed the poore opprest by you, you mock,
　　Their Counsills are your Common jesting stock,　　[20]
　　　　But God is Their recomfort.
7 Ah, when from syon shall the saver come,
　　That Jacob freed by Thee may glad become
　　　　And Israel full of Comfort?

Psalm XV

Domine quis habitabit

1. In Tabernacle Thyne, O lord, who shall remayne?
　　Lord, of Thy Holy Hill who shall the rest obtayne?
2 Even he, that leads of life an uncorrupted traine,
　　Whose deeds of Righteous heart, whose hearty words be plain,
3. Who with deceitfull tongue hath never usd to faine,　　[5]
　　Nor neighbour hurts by deed, nor doth with slaunder stain.
4. Whose eyes a person vile do hold in vile disdain,
　　But doth with honour great the Godly entertaine;
　Who word to neighbour given doth faithfully maintain
　　Although some Worldly losse therby he may sustaine,　　[10]
5. Frome bitinge Usury who ever doth refrain,
　　Who sells not guiltlesse cause, for filthy love of gain:
　　　Who thus proceeds, for aye, in sacred Mount shall raign.

Psalm XVI

Conserva me

1. Save me lord, for why Thou art
　　All the hope of all my heart,
2.　　Witness Thou my soule with me
　　That to God my God I say
　　Thou my lord, Thou art my stay,　　[5]
　　Though my Works reach not to Thee.

---

15. 2 Lord B.　　　　3 of life an] a life of K A.　　　6 neighbour] neighbo[rs] K.
7 do] doth A.　　in vile] in high K.　　　　9 word to neighbour] oath & promise
B K A. *Woodford notes:* '*word to neighbour* exp[unged].'　　　10 losse] *om.* B.

3. This is all the best I prove,
    Good and godly men I love
    And forsee their wretched paine
4.   Who to other Gods do run,   [10]
    Their blood offrings I do shun,
    Nay to name their names disdain.

5. God my only portion is
    And of my Child's part the blisse,
    He then shall maintayn my lott.   [15]
6   Say then, Is not my lot found
    In a goodly pleasant ground?
    Have not I fair partage gott?

7. Ever, lord, I will blesse Thee,
    Who dost ever counsell mee,   [20]
    Ev'n when night with his black wing
    Sleepy darkness doth o're cast,
    In my inward reynes I taste
    Of my faults and chastening.

8. My eyes still my God regard   [25]
    And he my right hand doth guard,
    So can I not be opprest,
9.   So my heart is fully glad,
    So in joy my glory clad,
    Yea my flesh in hope shall rest.   [30]

10. For I know the deadly grave
    On my soul no power shall have:
    For I know thou wilt defend
    Ev'en the body of Thyne Own,
    Deare beloved Holy One,   [35]
    From a foule corrupting end.

[11] Thou the path wilt make me tread
    Which to life true life doth lead:

16. 8 Good] God B.   22 doth] dos B.   31-32 *Opposite these lines in
different ink* K *adds:*

                    ffor I know y^t thow in hell
                    wilt not leave my sowl to dwell.

37-44 *om.* K F I. K *notes:* '.12. Wants' [i.e. *verse 12 of the Psalter*]. *Woodford notes:*
'The last staff of this Psalm is put by the Author, & as I judg under his own hand as in

Where who may contemplate Thee
Shall feel in Thy face's sight   [40]
All the fulness of delight,
And whose bodys placed be
On thy blessed making hand
Shall in endlesse pleasures stand !

Psalm XVII

Exaudi Domine [iustitiam]

1 MY suite is just, just lord to my suite hark;
  I plain sweet Lord, my plaint for pitty mark;
    And since my lipps feign not with Thee,
    Thyne Ears voutchsafe to bend to me.

2 O let my sentence passe from Thyne own face;   [5]
  Show that Thy eyes respect a faithfull case;
3   Thou that by proofe acquainted art
    With Inward secrets of my heart.
  When silent night might seeme all faults to hide,
  Then was I by thy searching insight try'd,   [10]
    And then by Thee was guiltless found
    From Ill word, and ill meaning sound.

4 Not weighing ought how fleshly fancys run,
  Led by Thy Word the Rav'ner's stepps I shun,
    And pray that still Thou guide my way   [15]
5   Least yet I slip or go astray.
6 I say again that I have calld on Thee
  And boldly say Thou wilt give eare to me,

yᵉ text, instead of the following wch is expung'd, & whence in the margin. *Leaue roome
for this staff*. viz yᵗ in yᵉ text sett [Quotes 37–44]. Expungd possibly it was because two
verses longer than the rest.' *The Countess of Pembroke's revision appears in B, set in the
text by Woodford, and in* X A J:

    Thou lifes Path wilt make me know
    In whose vieue with [X A J doth] plenty grow
    All delights that soules can craue:
    And whose bodys placed stand
    On Thy blessed Making Hand
    They all joyes like endless haue.

17. 3 with] to A.   6 Thy] thine A.   9 When] Where B K A. *Woodford*
notes: 'fortè pro *when*.'   might] did K.

    Then let my Words, my Crys ascend,
    Which to Thy self my soul will send.   [20]

7 Shew then O Lord Thy wondrous kindness show,
   Make us in mervailes of Thy mercy know
     That Thou by Faithfull Men wilt stand
     And save them from rebellious hand.

8 Then keep me as the Apple of an Eye,   [25]
  In Thy wings' shade then let me hidden ly

9   From my destroying Wicked Foes
     Who for my Death still me enclose.

10 Their eyes do swim, their face doth shine in fatt,
    And cruel Words their swelling tongues do chatt,   [30]

11   And yet their high hearts look so low
     As how to watch our overthrow,

12 Now like a lion gaping to make preyes,
   Now like his Whelp in den that lurking stayes.

13   Up lord prevent those gaping jawes   [35]
     And bring to naught those watching pawes.

14 Save me from them Thou usest as thy blade,
   From men I say, and from men's worldly trade,
     Whose life doth seeme most greatly blest
     And count this life their Portion best,   [40]
   Whose bellyes so with daintys Thou dost fill
 And so with hidden treasures grant their Will,
     That they in riches flourish do
     And children have to leave it to.

15 What would they more? And I would not their case.   [45]
  My joy shall be pure to enjoy thy face,
     When waking of this sleep of mine
     I shall see Thee in likeness Thine.

Psalm XVIII

Diligam te

1 THEE will I love, O Lord, with all my heart's delight,
   My strength my strongest rock, which my defence hast borne,
[2] My God, and helping God, my might and trustfull might,
   My never peirced shield, my ever saving horn,

21 then] me B.   28 still] do A.   29 doth] doe K.   40 best. B.
42 treasures] treasure B.
  18. 2 borne] been B.

3   My refuge, refuge then, when moste I am forlorn;   [5]
Whom then shall I invoke but Thee most worthy prayse,
On whom against my Foes my only safty stayes?

4 On me the paines of death already gan to prey,
The floods of wickedness on me did horrors throw,

5 Like in a winding sheet, wretch I already lay,   [10]
All ready, ready to my snaring grave to go.

6   This my Distresse to God with wailfull cryes I show,
My cryes clim'd up and he bent down from sacred throne,
His eyes unto my Case, his eares unto my moane.

7 And so the Earth did fall to tremble, and to quake   [15]
The Mountains proudly high, and their ffoundations bent
With motion of his rage did to the bottom shake.

8   He came, but came with smoake from out his nostrills sent,
Flames issued from his mouth, and burning coales out went;

9 He bow'd the heav'ns, and from the bow'd heav'ns did discend
With hugy darknes, which about his feet did wend.   [21]

10 The Cherubins their backs, the winds did yeild their wings,
To beare his sacred flight, in secret place then clos'd,

11 About which hee dimme clouds like a Pavilion brings,
Cloudes even of Waters dark, and thickest ayre compos'd; [25]

12   But streight his shining eyes this misty masse disclos'd.

13 Then hayle, then firie coales, then thundred heavnly sire,
Then spake he his lowd voyce, then hailestones coales and fire.

14 Then out his arrowes fly, and streight they scatterd been,
Lightning on lightning he did for their wrack augment;   [30]

15 The gulfs of waters then were through their Chanels seen,
The World's foundations then lay bare because he shent
With blasting breath O Lord, that in thy chiding went.

16 Then sent he from above, and took me from below,
Ev'n from the Waters' depth my God preserved me so.   [35]

17 So did he save me from my mighty furious foe,
So did he save me from their then prevailing hate,

18 For they had caught me up, when I was weake in Woe;
But He, staffe of my age, He staid my stumbling state

5 refuge, refuge . . . moste I am] refuge . . . I am most B.   22 Cherubins]
Cherubyms B.   24 hee] hee B K A. *Woodford notes*: '*high* exp[unged]: & error
librarij.'   26 this] his K.   27 coales B.   31 waters] water B.
39 He staffe B.

  This much, yet more, when I by him this freedom gate, [40]
[19] By him because I did find in his eyes' sight grace,
  He lifted me unto a largly noble place.

20 My justice, my just hands thus did the lord reward,
21 Because I walk'd his wayes, nor gainst him ev'ly went,
22 Still to his judgments lookt, still for his statutes car'd, [45]
23 Sound and upright with him, to wickednes not bent.
24 Therfore I say again this goodness he me sent,
  As he before his eyes did see my justice stand,
  According as he saw the pureness of my hand.

25 Meeke to the Meek Thou art, The good thy goodness taste; [50]
26 Pure to the pure, Thou dealst with crooked crookedly;
27 Up then thou liftst the poore, and down the proud wilt cast;
28 Up Thou dost light my light, and cleare my darkned eye.
29 I hosts by thee orecome, by Thee ore walls I fly;
30 Thy way is soundly sure, Thy word is purely tryd; [55]
  To them that trust in Thee a shield thou dost abide.

31 For who is God, besides this Great Jehova Ours?
  And so besides our God, who is indue'd with might?
32 This God then girded me in his Almighty pow'rs,
  He made my cumbrous way to me most plainly right. [60]
33 To match with light foot staggs he made my foot so light
34 That I Climb'd highest hill, he me warr points did show,
  Strengthning mine arms that they could break an Iron bow.

35 Thou gavest me saving shield, Thy right hand was my stay;
  Me in encreasing still, Thy kindness did maintaine; [65]
36 Unto my strengthned stepps Thou didst enlarge the way,
  My heeles and plants thou didst from stumbling slip sustaine;
37 What Foes I did persue my force did them attaine,
38 That I e're I return'd destroyd them utterly
  With such brave wounds, that they under my feet did ly. [70]

39 For why, my fighting strength by Thy strength strengthned was.
  Not I but thou throw'st down those, who 'gainst me do rise;
40 Thou gavest me their necks, on them Thou mad'est me passe.
41 Behold they cry, but who to them his help applys?

41 eyes' sight] ey-sight A. 46 wickednes] wycked ness B. . . . 52 liftst] lift*es*
K A. wilt] will B. 54 by thee orecome] orecome by Thee B A. 56 a shield
thou dost] Thou dost a sheild B. 57 besides] beside B. 58 besides] beside B.
59 pow'rs] powers B. 70 that] as A.

Nay unto Thee they cry'd, but thou heardst not their cryes.
I bett those folks as small as dust, which wind doth rayse;   [76]
42 I bett them as the clay is bett in beaten wayes.

43 Thus freed from mutin men, thou makest me to raign,
Yea Thou dost make me serv'd by folks I never knew;
44 My name their eares, their eares their hearts to me enchaine;
Ev'en Feare makes strangers shew much love though much
untrue.   [81]
45   But they do faile, and in their mazed corners rew.
Then live Jehova still, my rock still blessed be;
46 Let him be lifted up, that hath preserved me!

47 He that is my revenge, in whom I realmes subdue,   [85]
48   Who freed me from my foes, from rebells guarded me,
And rid me from the wrongs which cruel Witts did brew;
49   Among the Gentiles then I, Lord, yeild thanks to Thee,
I to Thy Name will sing, and this my song shall bee:
50 He nobly saves his King, and kindness keeps in store,   [90]
For David his Anoynt, and his seed ever more.

Psalm XIX

Cæli enarrant

1 THE heavnly Frame sets forth the Fame
    Of him that only thunders;
  The firmament, so strangely bent,
    Shewes his handworking wonders.

2 Day unto day doth it display,   [5]
    Their Course doth it acknowledg,
  And night to night succeding right
    In darkness teach cleere knowledg.

3 There is no speech, no language which
    Is so of skill bereaved,   [10]
  But of the skyes the teaching cryes
    They have heard and conceived.

76 those] these B.   doth] dos B.   77 the] they B.   79 yea B.
80 enchaine] enchain'd A.   85 realmes] Realm's B.   88 I B.
  19. 4 handworking] hand working B.   5 doth it] hee doth K, it doth A.
9 no language] nor language A.

4 There be no eyn but reade the line
From so fair book proceeding,
Their Words be set in letters great   [15]
For evry body's reading.

Is not he blind that doth not find
The tabernacle builded,
There by his Grace for sun's fair face
In beams of beauty guilded.   [20]

5 Who forth doth come like a bridegrome
From out his veiling places,
As glad is he, as Giants be
To runne their mighty races.

6 His race is even from ends of heaven   [25]
About that Vault he goeth,
There be no Rea'ms hidd from his beames,
His heat to all he throweth.

7 O law of his How perfect 'tis
The very soul amending,   [30]
God's witness sure for aye doth dure
To simplest Wisdom lending.

8 God's doomes be right, and cheer the sprite,
All his commandments being
So purely wise it gives the eyes   [35]
Both light and force of seing.

9 Of him the Feare doth cleaness beare
And so endures for ever,
His judgments be self verity,
They are unrighteous never.   [40]

10 Then what man would so soon seek gold
Or glittering golden mony?
By them is past in sweetest taste
Hony or Comb of hony.

30 amending] a mending B.   35 it gives] as giue B A. *Woodford notes: 'it gives.*
exp[unged].'

11 By them is made Thy servants' trade   [45]
    Most circumspectly guarded,
    And who doth frame to keep the same
      shall fully be rewarded.

12 Who is the man that ever can
     His faults know and acknowledg?   [50]
    O lord cleanse me from faults that be
     Most secret from all knowledg.

13 Thy servant keep, least in him creep
    Præsumptuous sins' offences,
    Let them not have me for their slave   [55]
     Nor reign upon my senses.

    So shall my spryte be still upright
     In thought and conversation,
    So shall I bide well purify'd
     From much abomination.   [60]

14 So let words sprung from my weake tongue,
    And my heart's meditation,
    My saving might, lord in Thy sight,
    Receive good acceptation!

Psalm XX

Exaudiat te Deus

1   LET God the lord heare Thee,
Ev'n in the day when most Thy troubles be;
   Let name of Jacob's God,
   When Thou on it dost cry,
Defend Thee still from all Thy foes abroad.   [5]

2   From sanctuary high
Let him come down, and help to Thee apply
   From Syon's holy top;
   Thence let him undertake
With heavnly strength Thy earthly strength to prop. [10]

            20. 7 down B.

3   Let him notorious make
That in good part he did Thy Offrings take;
    Let fyre for tryall burn,
    Yea fire from himself sent,
Thy offrings so that they to ashes turn.   [15]

4   And so let him consent
To grant Thy Will and perfect Thy entent,
5   That in thy saving We
    May joy and banners raise
Up to Our God, when Thy suites granted be.   [20]

6   Now in mee knowledg sayes
That God from fall his own Anoynted stayes.
    From heavnly holy land
    I know that He heares Thee,
Yea heares with powers and helps of helpfull hand.   [25]

7   Let trust of some men be
In chariots arm'd, Others in chivalry;
    But let all our conceit
    Upon God's holy name,
Who is our Lord, with due remembrance wayte.   [30]

8   Behold their broken shame!
Wee stand upright, while they their fall did frame.
[9]   Assist us Saviour deare;
    Let that King deign to heare,
When as to him Our Prayers do appeare.   [35]

Psalm XXI

Domine in Virtute

1 NEW joy, new joy unto Our King,
    Lord from Thy strength is growing;
Lord what delight to him doth bring
    His safety from Thee flowing!

21 mee] my B.   30 lord B.

2 Thou hast given what his heart would have, [5]
　　Nay soon as he but moved
　His lips to crave, what he would crave
　　He had as him behoved.

3 Yea thou prevent'st e're ask he could,
　　With many liberall blessing; [10]
　Croune of his head with croune of Gold
　　Of purest Metal dressing.
4 He did but ask a life of Thee,
　　Thou him a long life gavest;
　Lo! ev'en unto Eternity [15]
　　The life of him Thou savest.

5 Wee may well call his glory great
　　That springs from Thy salvation;
　Thou, Thou it is that hast him set
　　In so high estimation. [20]
6 Like storehouse Thou of blessings mad'st,
　　This man for everlasting;
　Unspeakably his heart Thou glad'st,
　　On him Thy Count'nance casting.

7 And why all this? Because Our King [25]
　　In heaven his trust hath layed;
　He only leanes on highest Thing,
　　So from base slip is stayed.
8 Thy hand thy foes shall overtake,
　　That Thee so ev'ill have hated; [30]
9 Thou as in fiery Ov'en shalt make
　　These mates to be amated.

The Lord on them with causfull Ire
　　Shall use destroying power,
　And flames of never quenched fire [35]
　　Shall these bad wights devouer.
10 Their fruit shalt Thou from earthly face
　　Send unto desolation,
　And from among the humane race
　　Root out their generation. [40]

21. *Lines* 17–52 *wanting in* K (*torn*).　　7 would crave] would have K.　　22 for]
of A.　　30 have] *om.* A.　　33 causfull] cause full B.　　35 And] All B.

11 For they to overthrow Thy Will
　　Full Wylily intended;
　　But all their bad mischeivous skill
　　Shall fruitlesly be ended.

12 For like a marke Thou shalt arow   [45]
　　Set them in pointed places,
　　And ready make Thy vengefull bowe
　　Against their guilty faces.

13　Lord in Thy strength, lord in Thy might,
　　　Thy Honour high be raised,   [50]
　　And so shall in Our songs' delight,
　　　Thy power still be praised.

Psalm XXII

Deus Deus meus

1 My God my God why hast Thou me forsaken?
　　Woe me, from me why is Thy presence taken?
　　So farr from seing myne unhealthfull eyes,
　　So farr from hearing to my roaring cryes.

2 O God my God I cry while day appeareth;   [5]
　　But God Thy eare my crying never heareth.
　　O God the night is privy to my plaint,
　　Yet to my plaint Thou hast not audience lent.

3 But Thou art Holy and dost hold Thy dwelling
　　Where Israel Thy lawdes is ever telling;   [10]
4　Our Fathers still in thee their trust did beare,
　　They trusted and by Thee deliverd were.

5 They were set free when they upon Thee called,
　　They hop'd on Thee, and they were not appalled.

---

45 arow] a row B A.
　22. *Lines* 1–36 *wanting in* K (*torn*).   2 me from B.   7–8 C *and* M *contain*
unique revisions:
　　　　The night (O God) my Plainte haue wholie spent
　　　　yet to my Plainte thow hast no Audience lent   C.

　　　　O God the night in moane to thee I spend
　　　　Yet to my moane thou dost no audience lend.   M.

8 not] no A.   10 lawdes is] lawes are B.   11 in] to B A. *Woodford notes*:
'*in* exp[unged].'

6   But I a worm, not I of mankind am,   [15]
      Nay shame of men, the people's scorning game.
7 The lookers now at me poore wretch be mocking,
      With mowes and nodds they stand about me flocking.
8   Let God help him (say they) whom he did trust;
      Let God save him, in whom was all his lust.   [20]
9 And yet ev'en from the womb thy self did'st take me;
      At mother's breastes, thou didst good hope betake me.
10   No sooner my child eyes could look abroad,
      Than I was giv'en to Thee, Thou wert my God.
11 O be not farr, since pain so nearly presseth,   [25]
      And since there is not One, who it redresseth.
12   I am enclosed with young Bulls' madded route,
      Nay Basan mighty Bulls close me about.
13 With gaping mouthes, these folks on me have charged,
      Like lions fierce, with roaring jawes enlarged.   [30]
14   On me all this, who do like water slide;
      Whose loosed bones quite out of joint be wryde;
    Whose heart with these huge flames, like wax o're heated,
      Doth melt away though it be inmost seated.
15   My moystning strength is like a potsherd dride,   [35]
      My cleaving tongue close to my roofe doth bide.
    And now am brought, alas, brought by Thy power
      Unto the dust of my death's running hower;
16   For bawling doggs have compast me about,
      Yea worse than doggs, a naughty wicked rout.   [40]
    My humble hands, my fainting feet they peirced;
17   They look, they gaze, my boanes might be rehearsed;
      Of my poore weedes they do partition make
18   And do cast lots, who should my vesture take.
19 But be not farr O Lord, my strength, my comfort;   [45]
      Hasten to help me, in this deep discomfort.
20   Ah! from the sword yet save my vital sprite,
      My desolated life from dogged might.
21 From lion's mouth O help, and shew to heare me
      By aiding when fierce unicorns come neare me.   [50]
22   To Brethren then I will declare Thy Fame,

19 (say they)] they say, B.   21 did'st] did B.   22 breastes] breast B.
29 mouthes, these] mouth those B.   33 flames B.   37 alas B.
40 doggs B.   42 look B.   gaze] gazed K.   49 mouth] mouths B.

And with these Words, when they meet, prayse Thy Name.

23 Who feare the lord all prayse and glory beare him;
    You Isra'el's seed, you come of Jacob, feare him.

24   For he hath not abhorrd nor yet disdain'd   [55]
    The seely wretch with foule affliction staind,

25 Nor hidd from him his face's faire appearing;
    But when he calld this lord did give him hearing.
    In congregation great I will prayse Thee,
    Who feare Thee shall my vowes performed see.   [60]

26 The' afflicted then shall eat, and be well pleased,
    And God shall be by those his seekers praysed.
    Indeed O you, you that be such of mind,
    You shall the life that ever liveth find.

27 But what? I say from earth's remotest border   [65]
    Unto due thoughts mankind his thoughts shall order,
    And turn to God, and all the Nations be
    Made worshipers before Almighty Thee.

28 And reason, since the Croune to God pertaineth,
    And that by right upon all Realmes he raigneth.   [70]

29   They that be made even fatt, with earth's fatt good,
    shall feed and laud the giver of their food.
To him shall kneel who to the dust be stricken,
    Even he whose life no help of man can quicken.

[30] As they so theirs, Him shall their ofspring serve,   [75]
    And God shall them in his own court reserve.

[31]   They shall to children's children make notorious
    His righteousness, and this his doing glorious.

---

54 Iacob B.   56 staind. B.   65 remotest] remoted'st K A.   73–78 *om.*
K F I X. K *notes*: '3 verses wanting' [i.e. *verses 29–31 of the Psalter*]. *Woodford notes*:
'Instead of the four last Verses it stood thus [Quotes 73–78]. But these six verses are
scratched out as being two supernumerary, & in the margin is writen as I conceiue
under Sr Philips oun hand. *leaue space for this* staff. viz ye staffe wch I haue set in y^e
text.' *The Countess of Pembroke's revision appears in B, set in the text by Woodford,
and in A J:*
                To him shall kneel even who to dust be stricken
                Even he whose life no help of man can quicken
                His service shall from child to child descend
                His Doomes one age shall to another send.

Psalm XXIII

Dominus regit me

1 THE lord the lord my shepheard is,
  And so can never I
  Tast misery.

2 He rests me in green pasture his.
  By waters still and sweet   [5]
  He guides my feet.

3 He me revives, leads me the way
  Which righteousness doth take,
  For his name's sake.

4 Yea tho I should thro vallys stray   [10]
  Of death's dark shade I will
  No whit feare ill.

  For thou Deare lord Thou me besetst,
  Thy rodd and Thy staffe be
  To comfort me.   [15]

5. Before me Thou a table setst,
  Ev'en when foe's envious ey
  Doth it espy.

  With oyle Thou dost anoynt my head,
  And so my cup dost fill   [20]
  That it doth spill.

6. Thus thus shall all my days be fede,
  This mercy is so sure
  It shall endure,
  And long yea long abide I shall,   [25]
  There where the Lord of all
  Doth hold his hall.

23. G M *rephrase to make the third and sixth line of each stanza a trimeter.*   4 pas-
ture] pastures B.   19–27 *These lines appear in* B K F I X. *Woodford notes:* 'The
last staff before the Authors Correction stood thus. [Quotes 19–27]. But these nine
verses are expung'd, & in ye margin under the Authors hand *leaue space for six lines.*
viz those in yᵉ text.' *The Countess of Pembroke's revision appears in* B, *set in the text by*
Woodford, and in A J:

       Thou oylst my head thou filst my cup
       Nay more Thou endlesse good
             shalt geue me food
       To Thee I say ascended up
       Where Thou the lord of all
             Dost hold Thy Hall.

Psalm XXIV

Domini est terra

1 THE earth is God's, and what the Globe of earth containeth,
    And all who in that Globe do dwell;
2 For by his power the land upon the Ocean raigneth,
    Through him the floods to their beds fell.
3   Who shall climb to the hill which God's own hill is named,
      Who shall stand in his Holy place?   [6]
4   He that hath hurtless hands, whose inward heart is framed
      All pureness ever to embrace;
  Who shunning vanity and works of vaineness leaving,
    Vainly doth not puff up his mind;   [10]
  Who never doth deceive, and much lesse his deceaving
    With perjury doth falsly bind.

5 A blessing from the lord, from God of his salvation
    Sweet Righteousness shall he receive,
6 Jacob this is Thy seed, God seeking generation,   [15]
    Who search of God's face never leave.
7   Lift up your heads you Gates, and you doores ever biding,
      In comes the King of glory bright.
8   Who is this glorious King in might and power riding?
      The lord whose strength makes battails fight.   [20]
9   Lift up your heads you Gates, and you doores ever biding,
      In comes the King of glory bright.
10   Who is This Glorious King? The lord of armyes guiding,
      Even He the King of glory hight.

Psalm XXV

Ad te Domine

1   To thee, O Lord most just,
      I lift my in ward sight;
2   My God in Thee I trust,
      Let me not ruin quite;

24. 6 Who] And who B.   7 hands B.   inward] in ward B.   12 falsly] falsly
B K A. *Woodford notes*: 'safely exp[unged].'   13 lord B.   15 God] good K.

Let not those foes that me annoy   [5]
On my complaint build up their joy.

3   Sure, sure who hope in Thee
        shall never suffer shame;
4   Let them confounded be
        That causeless wrongs do frame.   [10]
Yea Lord to me Thy wayes do show;
Teach me, thus vext, what path to go.

5   Guide me as Thy Truth guides;
        Teach me for why Thou art
    The God in whom abides   [15]
        The saving me from smart,
For never day such changing wrought
That I from trust in Thee was brought.

6   Remember, only King,
        Thy Mercy's tenderness;   [20]
    To Thy remembrance bring
        Thy kindnes, lovingnes;
Let those things Thy remembrance grave,
Since they Eternal Essence have.

7   But Lord remember not   [25]
        Sins brew'd in youthfull glass,
    Nor my Rebellious blott,
        Since youth and they do passe;
But in Thy kindness me record,
Ev'n for Thy mercy's sake, O Lord.   [30]

8   Of grace and righteousness
        The lord such plenty hath,
    That he deigns to express
        To sinning men his path.
9 The meek he doth in judgment lead,   [35]
And teach the humble how to tread.

25. C *revises* 15–16, 47–48, 71–72, *and* 77–78; G *and* M *each have different versions of* 77–78; G M *revise* 71–72; C G M *revise* 66; *and* M *also rephrases* 11 *and* 23.   6 build] lift K.   12 me B.   22 kindnes B.   27 Rebellious] rebellions A.   blott] spot B.

10   And what think you may be
       The Paths of my great God?
    Ev'en spotless verity
       And mercy spredd abroad   [40]
To such as keep his Covenant
And on his Testimonys plant.

11   O Lord for Thy name's sake
       Let my iniquity
    Of thee some mercy take,   [45]
       Though it be great in me.
12 Oh, is there one with his Feare fraught?
He shall be by best teacher taught.

13   Lo, how his blessing budds
       Inward, an inward rest,   [50]
14   Outward, all outward goods
       By his seed eke possest.
For such he makes his secret know,
To such he doth his Cov'nant show.

15   Where then should my eyes be   [55]
       But still on this Lord set?
16   Who doth, and will set free
       My feet from tangling net.
O look, O help, let mercy fall,
For I am poore, and left of all.   [60]

17   My woes are still encreast;
       Shield me from these assaults;
18   See how I am opprest
       And pardon all my faults.
19 Behold my Foes, what store they be,   [65]
Who hate, yea hate me cruely.

20   My soul, which Thou didst make,
       Now made, O Lord maintain,
    And me from these ills take
       Least I rebuke sustain;   [70]
For Thou the Lord, Thou only art,
Of whom the trust lives in my heart.

---

43 name's] name A.   54 doth] dos B.   show: B.   60 left] least K A.
62 these] those K.   72 lives] lyes B.

[21]   Let my uprightness gaine
       Some safty unto me;
    I say, and say again,   [75]
       My hope is all in thee.
[22] In fine deliver Israel,
       O Lord from all his troubles fell.

Psalm XXVI

Iudica me Deus

1   LORD judg me, and my case,
     For I have made my race
Within the bounds of Innocence to byde,
     And setting Thee for scope
     Of all my trustfull hope,   [5]
I held for sure that I should never slyde.

2   Prove me O Lord most high,
     Me with Thy touch-stone try,
3 Yea sound my reines, and inmost of my heart;
     For so Thy loving hand   [10]
     Before my eyes did stand
That from Thy truth will not depart.

4   I did not them frequent
     Who be to vaineness bent,
Nor kept with base dissemblers company;   [15]
5   Nay I did even detest
     Of wicked wights the nest,
And from the haunts of such bad folks did fly.

6   In th' Innocence of Me
     My hands shall washed be,   [20]
7 And with those hands about Thy Altar waite,
     That I may still expresse
     With voyce of thankfulness
The works perform'd by Thee most wondrous great.

26. 9 inmost] in most B.   12 will not depart] ~~will not depart~~ I would not
once depart K.   18 haunts] haunt K.

8   Lord I have loved well   [25]
     The House where Thou dost dwell,
   Ev'n where Thou makest Thy honour's biding place.
9   Sweet lord, write not my soul
     Within the sinners' roll,
   Nor my life's cause match with bloodseeker's case,   [30]
10   Whose hands do handle nought,
     But led by wicked thought
   That hand whose strength should help of bribes is full.
11   But in integrity
     My stepps shall guided be,   [35]
   Then me redeem Lord then be mercifull.
[12]   Even truth that for me sayes
       My foot on justice stayes,
   And tongue is prest to publish out thy prayse.

Psalm XXVII

Dominus Illuminatio

1   THE shining Lord he is my light,
    The strong God my salvation is.
    Who shall be able me to fright?
    This lord with strength my life doth blisse;

---

30 bloodseekers] blood suckers B.   case. B.   31–39 *These lines appear in* B K
F I. *Woodford notes:* 'The last staff e're alterd by the Author ran thus. [Quotes 31–39]
but these verses are expungd & in ye margin under his hand *Leaue space,* (viz for it
as it is putt).' *The Countess of Pembroke's revision appears in* B, *set in the text by Wood-*
ford, and in A J:

                With hands of wicked chifts [A J shifts]
                With right hands staind with gifts
            But while I walk in my unspotted ways
                Redeem & shew me Grace
                So I in Public place
            Set on plain ground will Thee Iehova prayse.

X *retains* 31–36 *and for* 37–39 *substitutes*:

                Now firme my foote doth stand
                    supported by thy hand
                        in course of iustice, truth, and righteousnes.
                My tongue shall daie by daie
                    thy wondrous workes displaie
                        where Congregacions meete wth thankfullnes.

37 that] thus K.

And shall I then [5]
Feare might of men?

2 When wicked folk, even they that be
My foes, to utmost of their pow'r
With rageing jaws environ me
My very flesh for to devoure, [10]
They stumble so
That down they go.

3 Then though against me armys were,
My Courage should not be dismaid.
Though battaile's brunt I needs must beare, [15]
While battaile's brunt on me were laid
In this I would
My trust still hold.

4 One thing in deed I did and will
For ever crave, that dwell I may [20]
In house of High Jehova still,
On beauty His my eyes to stay
And look into
His Temple too.

5 For when great griefes to me be ment, [25]
In Tabernacle His hee will
Hide me, ev'n closely in his Tent;
Yea noble hight of Rocky Hill
He makes to be
A seat for me. [30]

6 Now, Now shall He lift up my head
On my beseiging Enemyes;
So shall I sacrifices spred,
Offrings of joy in Temple His,
And song accord [35]
To prayse the lord.

7 Heare lord when I my voice display,
Heare to have mercy eke of me.

8 Seek ye my Face, when Thou didst say,
In Truth of heart I answerd Thee, [40]

27. 8 foes B. 22 my] mine A. 23 in to B. 26 hee] I B. 33–34
X *rephrases*:

Soe I in temple his shall spread
Offrings of ioye; and Sacrifice.

O Lord I will
Seek Thy face still.

9 Hide not therfore from me that face,
Since all my ayd in Thee I got.
In rage Thy servant do not chase.   [45]
Forsake not me, O leave me not,
O God of my
Salvation high.

10 Though Father's Care, and Mother's love
Abandond me, yet my decay   [50]

11 Should be restor'd by him above.
Teach lord, lord lead me Thy right way,
Because of those
That be my Foes,

12 Unto whose ever hating lust   [55]
Oh, give me not, for there are sproong
Against me witnesses unjust,
Ev'n such I say, whose lying tongue
Fiercly affords
Most cruel words.   [60]

13 What had I been, except I had
Beleiv'd God's goodness for to see,
In land with living creatures clad?

14 Hope, Trust in God, bee strong, and he
Unto Thy heart   [65]
Shall joy impart.

Psalm XXVIII

Ad te Domine clamabo

1 To thee Lord my cry I send.
O my strength stop not Thine eare,
Least, if answer Thou forbeare,
I be like them that descend
To the pitt where flesh doth end.   [5]

---

53 Because] Be cause B.   54 Foes. B.   64 strong B.
  28. 1 thee Lord] Thee O lord B.   3 Least B.

2 Therfore while that I may cry,
  While I that way hold my hands
  Where Thy sanctuary stands,
  To thy self those words apply
  Which from suing voice do fly. [10]

3 Link not me in self same chain
  With the wicked working folk
  Who, their spotted thoughts to cloak,
  Neighbors friendly entertain
  When in hearts they malice meane. [15]

4 Spare not them, give them reward
  As their deeds have purchas'd it,
  As deserves their wicked witt;
  Fare they as their hands have far'd,
  Ev'en so be their guerdon shar'd. [20]

5 To Thy Works they give no ey.
  Let them be thrown down by Thee;
6   Let them not restored be;
  But let me give prayses high
  To the Lord that heares my cry. [25]

7 That God is my strength my shield;
  All my trust on him was sett;
  And, so I did safety gett,
  So shall I with joy be filld,
  So my songs his lauds shall yeeld. [30]

8 God on them his strength doth lay
  Who his Anoynted helped have.
9   Lord then still Thy people save,
  Blesse Thyne heritage I say,
  Feed and lift them up for aye. [35]

Psalm XXIX

Afferte Domino

1 ASCRIBE unto the lord of light,
  ye men of Pow'er even by birth-right,
  Ascribe all glory and all might.

13 Who B.   to] do B.   26 my shield] & shield B.   28 And B.   safety]
safely A.

2 Ascribe due glory to his Name,
   And in his ever glorious frame   [5]
   Of sanctuary do the same.

3 His voice is on the Waters found,
   His voyce doth threatning thunders sound,
   Yea through the Waters doth resound.

4 The Voice of that lord ruling us   [10]
   Is strong though he be gracious,
   And ever, ever glorious.

5 By voice of high Jehova we
   The highest Cedars broken see,
   Ev'en Cedars, which on liban be,   [15]

6 Nay like young Calves in leapes are born,
   And Liban' self with Nature's skorn,
   And shirion like young Unicorn.

7 His voice doth flashing flames divide,

8   His voice have trembling deserts try'd,   [20]
   Ev'en Deserts where the Arabs byde.

9 His voice makes hindes their calves to cast,
   His voice makes bald the forest wast;
   But in his church his Fame is plac't.

10 His justice seat the World sustains,   [25]
   Of furious floods he holds the reines,
   And this his rule for aye remains.
     God to his people strength shall give,
     That they in peace shall blessed live.

Psalm XXX

Exaltabo te Domine

1 O LORD Thou hast exalted me
   And sav'd me from foes' laughing scorn;
   I owe Thee prayse, I will prayse Thee.

29. 17 Liban'] libans B.   25–29 *These lines appear in* B K X. *Woodford notes*:
'The 10 V[erse] before Correction stood thus. [Quotes 25–29]. But hauing two super-
numerary verses is expunged & yᵉ other putt in its place.' *The Countess of Pembroke's
revision appears in* B, *set in the text by Woodford, and in* A F J:

     He sits on seas, he endlesse raigns
      His strength his peoples strength maintains
      Wᶜʰ blest by him in peace remains.

26 floods] floude K.
  30. 3 prayse B.

2 For when my heart with woes was torn,
   In Cryes to Thee I shewd my Cause   [5]
   And was from evill by Thee upborn,
3 Yea from the grave's most hungry jawes;
   Thou wouldst not set me on their score
   Whom Death to his cold bosom drawes.
4 Prayse, Prayse this lord then evermore   [10]
   Ye saints of his, remembring still
   With thanks his Holyness therfore;
5 For quickly ends his wrathfull Will,
   But his deare favour where it lyes
   From age to age life joyes doth fill.   [15]
Well may the Evening cloath the eyes
   In clouds of teares, but soon as sun
   Doth rise again, new joyes shall rise.
6 For proof, while I my race did run
   Full of successe, fond I did say   [20]
   That I should never be undone,
7 For then my Hill Good God did stay;
   But, ah he strait his face did hide,
   And what was I but wretched clay?
8 Then thus to Thee I praying cry'd: [25]
   What serves alas the blood of me
   When I within the pitt do bide;
9 Shall ever dust give thanks to Thee,
   Or shall Thy Truth on mankind layd
   In deadly dust declared be?   [30]
10 Lord heare, let mercy thine be stay'd
   On me, from me help this annoy.
   Thus much I said, this being said
11 Lo I that waild, now daunce for joy.
   Thou didst ungird my dolefull sack   [35]
   And madest me gladsom weeds enjoy,
12 Therfore my tongue shall never lack
   Thy endless prayse: O God my King
   I will thee thanks for ever sing.

11 his B.   19 proof B.   20 successe B.   I did] did I B.   23 ah]
O B.   28 dust] earth B K A. *Woodford notes: 'dust* exp[unged].'

Psalm XXXI

In te Domine

1 ALL, all my trust lord I have put in Thee,
  Never therfore let me confounded be,
    But save me, save me in Thy righteousness,
2 Bow down thine eare to heare how much I need,
  Deliver me, Deliver me in speed,   [5]
    Be my strong rock, be Thou my forteress.

3 Indeed Thou art my rock, my Forteress;
  Then since my tongue delights that name to blesse,
    Direct me how to go, and guide me right,
4 Preserve me from the wyly wrappinge nett   [10]
  Which they for me with privy craft have set,
    For still I say Thou art my only might.

5 Into Thy hands I do commend my sprite,
  For it is Thou, that hast restord my light,
    O lord that art the God of verity.   [15]
6 I hated have those men whose thoughts do cleave
  To Vanitys, which most trust most deceave,
    For all my hope fixt upon God doth ly.

7 Thy mercy shall fill me with jollity,
  For my annoyes have come before thyne eye,   [20]
    Thou well hast known what plung my soul was in
8 And thou hast not for aye enclosed me
  Within the hand of hatefull enmitie,
    But hast enlargd my feet from mortall ginn.

9 O Lord, of Thee let me still mercy winn,   [25]
  For troubles of all sides have me within.
    My eye, my Gutts, yea my soul grief doth wast,
10 My life with heavyness, my yeares with moane
  Do pine, my strength with pain is wholy gon,
    And ev'en my bones consume where they be plac't. [30]

31. 1 I have] haue I B.   4 thine] Thy B.   10 wrappinge] trapping B.
23 enmitie] emnity B.   25 Lord of Thee, B.   27 eye B.

11 All my fierce Foes reproach on mee did cast;
   Yea neighbors, more, my mates were so agast
     That in the streets from sight of me they fled.

12 Now I, now I my self forgotten find,
   Ev'n like a dead man dreamed out of mind,   [35]
     Or like a broken pott in myer tredd.

13 I understand what rayling great men spred;
   Feare was each where, while they their counsells led
     All to this point, how my poore life to take.

14 But I did trust in Thee, lord, I did say   [40]
   Thou art my God, my time on thee doth stay;
15   Save me from foes who seek my bane to bake.

16 Thy Face to shine upon Thy servant make,
   And save me in, and for Thy mercie's sake.
     Let me not tast of shame, O lord most high,   [45]
17 For I have call'd on Thee, let wicked folk
   Confounded be, and passe away like smoake,
     Let them in bedd of endless silence dy.

18 Let those lips be made dumbe which love to ly,
   Which full of spight, of Pride and cruelty,   [50]
     Do throw their words against the most upright.
19 Oh! of thy grace what endlesse pleasure flowes
   To whom feare Thee? what thou hast done for those
     That trust in Thee, ev'n in most open sight!

20. And when neede were, from pride in privy plight   [55]
   Thou hast hid them: yet leaving them thy light,
     From strife of tongues in Thy Pavilions plac't.
21. Then prayse, then prayse I do the lord of us,
   Who was to me more than most gracious,
     Farr farr more sure, than walls most firmly fast.   [60]

22 Yet I confess in that tempestuous haste
   I said that I from out Thy sight was cast;
     But Thou didst heare, when I to Thee did moane.

31 reproach on mee] on me reproach B.   32 neighbors B.   39 point B.
41 my time on thee] on Thee my time B.   44 mercie's] mercy B.   49 dumbe]
drunck B.   54 That] Who B.   58–59 M *rephrases*:

        Then let me ever praise the Lord who thus
        Was vnto me more than most gracious.

61 haste] time B.   63 did moane] did cry B (*in text, but* did moane *in margin*).

23 Then love him ye all ye that feel his grace,
   For this Our lord preserves the faith full race   [65]
      And to the proud in deeds pays home their own.
[24] Bee strong I say his strength confirm in you,
   You that do trust in him who still is true,
      And he shall your establishment renew.

Psalm XXXII

Beati quorum remissa sunt

1 Bless'ed is the man whose filthy stain
   The lord with pardon doth make cleane,
      Whose fault well hidden lyeth.
2 Blessed in deed to whom the lord
   Imputes not sins to be abhord,   [5]
      Whose spirit falshood flyeth.

64–69 *These lines appear in* B K *and* C D E H L N. *Woodford notes*: 'The three last
verses of the Psalm (before correction under the Authors hand), stood thus—[Quotes
last two words of 63, 'did moane', and 64–69].' *The Countess of Pembroke's revision
appears in* B, *set in the text by Woodford, and in* A F J:

> Then loue the lord all ye that feel his grace
> Who pares the proud, preserues the faith full race
>   Be strong in hope his strength shall you supply.

G *and* M *contain independent revisions of these lines*:

> Then loue him ye all ye that feele his grace:
> For this our Lord preserves the faithful race,
>   And to the proud in deede payes home their owne.
> All you therefore, that in the Lord alone
> Your trust repose, doe, & in others none
>   Confirme with strength this confidence in you:
> And this our God, on whome you so depend
> Shall you in all your waies still so defend
>   That he your hearts establisht shall renewe.   G.

> Then loue him ye, all ye that feele his grace
> For this our Lord preserues the faithfull race
>   And to the prowde in deede paies home theire owne.

> You there fore that on God doe trust alone,
> And on his blessed name, & others none
>   With constant zeale, O still therein remaine
> And he your hear*tes* (wch so him feare & loue
> That no distresse, can yo^u from him remoue)
>   Shall still establish, & in grace sustaine.   M.

67 his] this K.
   32. 1 Bless'ed is the man] Blessed is He B K A. *Woodford notes*: '*Bless'ed is the man*
exp[unged].'   2 doth] dos B.

3. Thus I prest down with weight of pain,
  Whether I silent did remain,
    Or roar'd, my bones still wasted;
4 For so both day and night did stand   [10]
  On wretched mee thy heavy hand,
    My life hott torments tasted.

5 Till my self did my faults confess
  And open'd mine own wickedness,
    Wherto my heart did give me;   [15]
  So I my self accus'd to God,
  And his sweet grace streight easd the rod
    And did due pain forgive me.

6 Therfore shall evry godly One
  In fitt time make to Thee his moane,
    When Thou wilt deign to heare him.   [20]
  Sure, sure the Floods of straying streames
  However they putt in their claimes,
    Shall never dare come neare him.

7 Thou art my safe and secret place   [25]
  Who savest me from troblous case,
    To songs and joyfull byding.
8 But who so will instructed be
  Come, Come, the way I will teach Thee,
    Guide Thee by my eyes' guiding.   [30]

9 Oh be not like a horse or mule,
  Wholy devoy'd of Reason's rule,
    Whose mouths Thy self dost bridle,
  Knowing full well that beasts they be
  And therfore soon would mischeife Thee   [35]
    If Thou remainedst Idle.

10 Woes, woes shall come to wicked folks;
  But who on God his trust invokes,
    All mercys shall be swarmed.

---

9 roar'd B.   10–11 E G H L M *reverse and rephrase*:
      On wretched me thy heauie hand
      Both day and night did sorely stand.
11 mee] my B.   22 Floods] floud K A.   36 remainedst] remainest B.

11 Be glad you good, in God have joy,　　　　　[40]
　　Joy be to you, who do enjoy
　　Your hearts with clearness armed.

Psalm XXXIII

Exultate justi

1 REJOICE in God, O ye
　　That righteous be;
　　For cherfull thankfulness,
　　It is a comely part
　　　In them whose heart　　　　　[5]
　　Doth cherish rightfulness.

2 　O prayse with harp the lord,
　　　O now accord
　　Viols with singing Voice,
　　Let ten-stringd instrument　　　　　[10]
　　　O now be bent
　　To witness you rejoice.

3 A new, sing a new song
　　To him most strong,
4 Sing lowd and merrily,　　　　　[15]
　　Because that word of his
　　　Most righteous is
　　And his deeds faithfull bee.

5 　He righteousness approves
　　　And judgment loves,　　　　　[20]
　　God's goodness fills all lands,
6 　His Word made heavnly Coast,
　　　And all that Host
　　By breath of his mouth stands.

7 The waters of the seas　　　　　[25]
　　　In heapes he layes,
　　And depths in treasure his.

8 Let all the earth feare God,
  And who abroad
  Of world a dweller is.   [30]

9   For he spake not more soone
  Than it was done;
  He badd and it did stand.

10   He doth heath'n counsell breake,
  And maketh weak   [35]
  The might of people's hand.

11 But ever, ever shall
  His Counsells all
  Throughout all ages last.
  The thinckinges of that mind   [40]
  No end shall find
  When time's times shall be past.

12   That Realm in deed hath blisse
  Whose God he is,
  Who him for their lord take;   [45]
  Ev'en people that, ev'en those
  Whom this lord chose,
  His heritage to make.

13 The lord looks from the sky,
  Full well his ey   [50]
  Beholds our mortall race;

14 Ev'en where he dwelleth hee
  Throughout doth see
  Who dwell in dusty place.

15   Since he their hearts doth frame,   [55]
  He knowes the same,
  Their works he understands.

16   Hosts do the King not save,
  Nor strong men have
  Their help from mighty hands.   [60]

17   Of quick strength is an horse,
  And yet his force

40 thinckinges] thinking B.   42 time's times] Times time B.   58 the] ye B.
61 strength] help B.   an] a K.

Is but a succour vaine,
Who trusts him sooner shall
   Catch harmfull fall   [65]
Than true deliverance gain.

18 But lo Jehova's sight
   On them doth light
Who him do truly feare,
And them who do the scope   [70]
   Of all their hope
Upon his mercy beare.

19   His sight is them to save
     Ev'en from the grave
   And keep from Famin's paine.   [75]
20   Then on that lord most kind
     Fix We our mind,
   Whose shield shall us maintaine.

21 Our hearts sure shall enjoy
     In him much joy,   [80]
   Who hope on his Name just.
22 O let thy mercy great
     On us be set,
   We have no plea but trust.

Psalm XXXIV

Benedicam Domino

1   I EV'EN I will always
  Give hearty thanks to him on high,
  And in my mouth continualy
2 Inhabit shall his prayse.
    My soul shall glory still   [5]
  In that deare lord with true delight,
  That hearing it the hearts contrite,
  May learn their joyes to fill.

81 Who] Whose B.

3   Come then and join with me,
Somewhat to speake of his due praise,   [10]
Strive we that in some worthy phrase
His Name may honourd be.

4   Thus I begin. I sought
This lord and he did heare my cry,
Yea and from dreadfull misery   [15]
He me, he only brought.

5   This shall men's fancys frame
To looke and run to him for aid,
Whose faces on his comfort staid
Shall never blush for shame.   [20]

6   For lo, this Wretch did call,
And lo, his Call the skyes did clime;
And God freed him, in his worst time
From out his troubles all.

7   His Angels Armys round   [25]
About them pitch who him do feare,
And watch and ward for such do beare
To keep them safe and sound.

8   I say but tast and see
How sweet how gracious is his grace.   [30]
Lord he is in thrice blessed case
Whose trust is all on thee.

9   Feare God ye saints of his,
For nothing they can ever want
Who faithfull feares in him do plant;   [35]
They have and shall have blisse.

10   The lions oft lack food,
Those raveners' whelps oft starved be,
But who seek God with constancy
Shall need nought that is good.   [40]

11   Come children, lend your eare
To me and mark what I do say,

34. 33–48 *Woodford notes:* 'In the Originall Copy the 11ᵗʰ & 12ᵗʰ Verses [of the Geneva version], were set before the 9ᵗʰ & 10ᵗʰ, so yᵗ against the staffe is written as I judg by Sʳ Philip Sydney himself *These verses must be transplaced* (as here I haue put them) *according to* yʳ *Ciphars* (viz. 9. & 10. when they stood before 11. 12.) *namely the fower following.'*   41 children B.

For I will teach to you the way
How this Our lord to feare.

12　Among you, who is here　　　　　　　　　[45]
That life and length of life requires,
And blessing such with length desires,
As life may good appeare?

13　Keep well thy lipps and tongue
Least inward evills do them defile,　　　　　[50]
Or that by words enwrapt in guile
Another man be stonge.

14　Do good, from faults decline,
Seek peace and follow after it,

15　For God's own eyes on good men sit　　　[55]
And eares to them encline.

16　So his high heavnly face
Is bent, but bent against those same
That wicked be, their very name
From earth quite to displace.　　　　　　　[60]

[17]　The just when harms approach
Do cry, their cry of him is heard,
And by his care from them is barr'd
All trouble, all reproche.

18　To humble broken minds　　　　　　　　[65]
This lord is ever ever neare,
And will save whom his sight cleere
In sprite afflicted finds.

19　Indeed the very best
Most great and grievous paines doth beare,　[70]
But God shall him to safety reare
When most he seemes opprest.

20　His bones he keepeth all
So that not one of them is broke;

21　But malice shall the wicked choake,　　　[75]
Who hate the good shall fall.

45 you B.　　　48 appeare. B.　　　52 stonge] strong B.　　　53 good B.
64 trouble B.　　all reproche.] & reproach B.　　66 ever ever] ever B.

22 God doth all soules redeeme
 Who weare his blessed livery;
 None, I say still, shall ruind be
 Who him their trust esteeme. [80]

Psalm XXXV

Iudica Domine

1 SPEAKE thou for me against wrong speaking foes,
 Thy force O Lord against their force oppose,
2 Take up Thy shield and for my succour stand,
 Yea take Thy lance and stop the way of those
3 That seek my bane, O make me understand [5]
 In sprite that I shall have Thy helping hand.

4 Confound those folks, thrust them in shamefull hole
 That hunt so poore a prey as is my soule.
 Rebuke and wracke on those wrong doers throw,
 Who for my hurt each way their thoughts did roll. [10]
5 And as vile chaff away the wind doth blow,
 Let Angel thine a scattring make them go.

6 Let Angel thine persue them as they fly,
 But let their flight be dark and slippery;
7 For causeless they both pitt and net did sett, [15]
 For causeles they did seek to make me dy.
8 Let their sly witts unwares destruction get,
 Fall in self pitt, be caught in their own nett.

9 Then shall I joy in thee, then sav'd by Thee
 I both in mind, and bones shall gladded be. [20]
10 Ev'en bones shall say O God, who is Thy peere,
 Who poore and weake from rich and strong dost free,
 Who helpest those, whose ruin was so neere,
 From him whose force did in their spoiles appeare.

79 None I say still B.
 35. *Line* 10 *indented and* 1 *and* 9 *not indented in* B. 5 bane B. **9 wracke]**
wreck B. 16 me] my B. 17 unwares] unware B.

11   Who did me wrong, against me witness beare   [25]
      Laying such things, as never in mee weare;

12   So my good deeds they pay with this ev'ill share,
      With cruel minds my very soul to teare.

13   And whose? Ev'n his who when they sickness bare
      With inward wo, an outward sack cloth ware.   [30]

      I did pull down my self, fasting for such;
      I prayd with prayers which my breast did touch;

14   In summe, I shew'd, that I to them was bent
      As Brothers, or as Friends beloved much;

      Still still for them I humbly mourning went   [35]
      Like one that should his Mother's death lament.

15   But lo, soon as they did me staggering see,
      Who joy but they, when they assembled bee?

      Then abjects, while I was unwitting quite,
      Against me swarm, ceaseless to raile at me.   [40]

16   With scoffers false I was their feast's delight,
      Ev'en gnashing teeth, to witness more their spight.

17   Lord wilt thou see, and wilt Thou suffer it?
      Oh! on my soul let not these tumults hitt.

      Save me distrest from lion's cruel kind.   [45]

18   I will thank Thee, where congregations sitt,
      Even where I do most store of people find;
      Most to Thy lawdes will I my speeches bind.

19   Then, then let not my foes unjustly joy;
      Let them not fleere, who me would causeless stroy,   [50]

20   Who never word of peace yet utter would,
      But hunt with craft the quiet man's annoy;

21   And said to me wide mowing as they could,
      Aha! Sir, now we see you where we should.

22   This thou hast seen, and wilt thou silent be?   [55]
      O lord, do not absent Thy self from me!

23   But rise, but wake that I may judgment gett.

24 My lord my God ev'en to my equity
      Judg lord, judg God, ev'en in Thy justice great,
      Let not their joy upon my woes be sett.   [60]

25 wrong B.   26 never in mee] in me never B.   weare] were B K.   27 this]
om. A.   30 ware] weare B.   39 while] when B.   48 lawdes] laues B.

25   Let them not, Lord, within their hearts thus say:
    O Soul, rejoyce, we made this wretch our prey.
26   But throw them down, put them to endlesse blame,
    Who make a Cause to joy of my decay;
        Let them be cloathd in most confounding shame,   [65]
    That lift themselves my ruin for to frame.

27   But make such glad, and full of joyfulness,
    That yet beare love unto my righteousness;
        Yet let them say, laud be to God always
    Who loves with good his servants good to blesse.   [70]
28   As for my tongue, while I have any dayes,
    Thy justice witness shall and speake Thy prayse.

Psalm XXXVI

Dixit injustus

1 ME thinks amid my heart I heare
    What guilty wickedness doth say,
    Which wicked folks do hold so deare;
    Ev'n thus it self it doth display,
    Noe feare of God doth once appeare   [5]
    Before his eyes that so doth stray.

2 For those same eyes his flatterers be
    Till his known ev'ill do hatred get.
3 His words deceit, iniquity
    His deeds, yea thoughtes all good forgett;   [10]
4 Abed on mischief museth he,
    Abroad his stepps be wrongly sett.

5 Lord, how the heav'ns thy mercy fills,
    Thy truth above the Clouds, most high,
6 Thy Righteousness like hugest hills,   [15]
    Thy judgments like the depths do ly,
    Thy grace with safety man fulfills,
    Yea beasts made safe thy goodness try.

61 not Lord B.   65 in] with A.   69 Yet] Yea B.
  36. 5 *om.* B.   6 so doth stray] doth so sway B.   10 thoughtes] thought B.
11 Abed] A bed B A.   16 depths] depth K, deepes A.

7 O Lord how excellent a thing
   Thy Mercy is! which makes mankind   [20]
8 Trust in the shadow of thy wing.
   Who shall in Thy house fatness find
And drink from out Thy pleasures' spring,
   Of pleasurs past the reach of mind?

9 For why the Well of life Thou art   [25]
   And in thy light shall We see light.
10 O then extend Thy loving heart
   To them that know Thee and Thy might,
O then Thy righteousness impart
   To them that be in soules upright.   [30]

11 Let not proud feet make me their thrall,
   Let not ev'ill hands discomfit me;
12 Lo there I now foresee their fall
   Who do ev'ill works: lo I doe see
They are cast down, and never shal   [35]
   Have power again to raised be.

Psalm XXXVII

Noli æmulari

1 FRETT not Thy self, if thou do see
   That wicked men do seeme to flourish,
   Nor envy in thy bosome nourish
Though ill deeds well succeeding be.
2   They soone shall be cutt down like grasse   [5]
   And wither like green herb or flower;
   Do well and trust on heavnly power,
3   Thou shalt have both good food and place.

4 Delight in God and he shall breed
   The fulness of thy own heart's lusting;   [10]
5   Guide Thee by him, lay all thy trusting
On him and he will make it speed.

26 shall We] we shall A.   34 I doe] there I B.   36 to raised] raysed to B.
37. 11 him B.

6   For like the light he shall display
      Thy justice in most shining luster,
      And of Thy Judgement make a muster   [15]
    Like to the glory of noone day.

7 Wait on the lord with patient hope,
      Chafe not at some man's great good fortune
      Though all his plotts without misfortune
  Attain unto their wished scope.   [20]
8   Fume not, rage not, frett not I say,
      Least such things sin in Thy self cherish,
      For those badd folks at last shall perish,
9   Who stay for God, in blisse shall stay.

10 Watch but a while, and Thou shalt see   [25]
      The wicked by his own pride bannisht;
      Look after him, he shall be vannisht
  And never found again shal be.
11   But meek men shall the earth possesse,
      In quiet home they shall be planted,   [30]
      And this delight to them is granted,
    They shall have peace in plenteousness.

12 Ev'ill men work ill to utmost right,
      Gnashing their teeth full of disdeigning;
      But God shall scorn their moody meaning,   [35]
13 For their short time is in his sight.
      The ev'ill bent bowes, and swords they drew,
14   To have their hate on good soules wroken;
      But lo their bowes, they shall be broken,
15   Their swords shall their own hearts embrew.   [40]

16 Small goodes in good men better is
    Than of bad folks the wealthy wonder,
17   For wycked arms shall breake asunder,
  But God upholds the just in blisse.
18   God keeps account of good men's dayes,   [45]
      Their heritage shall last for ever,
19   In perill they shall perish never,
    Nor want in dearth their want to ease.

15 Judgement] judgments B.   41 goodes] good B.

20 Badd folks shall fall, and fall for aye,
Who to make warr with God præsumed;   [50]
Like fatt of lambs shall be consumed,
21 Ev'en with the smoake shall wast away.
The Naughty borrowes paying not,
22   The good is kind and freely giveth;
Lo whom God blest he blessed liveth,   [55]
Whom he doth curse to naught shall rott.

23 The man whom God directs doth stand
Firm on his way, his way God loveth,
24   Though he do fall no wracke he proveth,
He is upheld by heavnly hand.   [60]
25   I have been younge now old I am,
Yet I the man that was betaken
To justice never saw forsaken,
Nor that his seed to begging came.

26 He lends, he gives, more he doth spend   [65]
The more his seed in blessing flourish;
27   Then fly all ev'ill and goodness nourish,
And Thy good state shall never end.
28   God, loving right, doth not forsake
His Holy ones; they are preserved   [70]
From time to time, but who be swerved
To ev'ill, both they and theirs shall wrack.

29 I say, I say the Righteous minds
Shall have the land in their possessing,
Shall dwell thereon, and this their blessing   [75]
No time within his limites binds.
30   The good mouth will in Wisdom bide,
His tongue of heavnly judgments telleth,
31   For God's high law in his heart dwelleth.
What comes therof? He shall not slide.   [80]

32 The Wicked watch the righteous much
And seek of life for to bereave him;

55 Lo] To B.   blest] blesse B.   59 do] doth A.   wracke] wreck B.
61 younge now] young & now B.   64 to] a A.   65 doth] dos B.   69 God
loving right B.   70 ones B.   71 be] are B.   72 ev'ill B.   73 I say I B.
75 thereon] therin B.

33   But in their hand God will not leave him,
Nor let him be condemn'd by such.

34   Wait thou on God and keep his way,   [85]
       He will exalt thee unto honour
       And of the earth make Thee an owner,
Yea thou shalt see the ev'ill decay.

35 I have the Wicked seen full sound,
       Like laurell fresh himself out spreading.   [90]

36   Lo, he was gon, print of his treading,
Though I did seek, I never found.

37   Mark the upright, the just attend,
       His end shall be in peace enjoyed;

38   But strayers vile shall be destroyed   [95]
       And quite cutt off, with helpless end.

39 Still, still the godly shall be stay'd
       By God's most sure, and sweet salvation;
       In time of greatest tribulation
He shall be their true strength and aid.   [100]

40   He shall be their true strength and aid,
       He shall save them from all the fetches
       Against them usd by wicked wretches,
Because on him their trust is laid.

Psalm XXXVIII

Domine ne in furore

1 LORD while that thy rage doth bide,
       Do not chide
    Nor in anger chastise me;

2 For thy shafts have pierc't me sore,
       And yet more,   [5]
    Still Thy hands upon me be.

3 No sound part (causd by Thy wrath)
       My flesh hath,
    Nor my sins let my bones rest;

4 For my faults are highly spred   [10]
       On my head,
    Whose foule weights have me opprest.

85 thou] then B.   97 Still still B.
38. 7 part causd by Thy wrath B.

5 My wounds putrify and stink,
   In the sinck
6 Of my filthy folly lai'd;   [15]
Earthly I do bow and crooke,
   With a look
Still in mourning chear arayd.

7 In my reines hot torment raignes,
   There remains   [20]
8 Nothing in my body sound;
I am weake and broken sore,
   Yea I roare,
In my heart such grief is found.

9 Lord before Thee I do lay   [25]
   What I pray;
My sighs are not hid from thee;
10 My heart pants, gon is my might;
   Ev'en the light
Of mine eyes abandons me.   [30]

11 From my plague, kynn, neighbour, Friend,
   Farr off wend;
12 But who for my life do waite,
They lay snares they nimble be.
   Who hunt me,   [35]
Speaking ev'ill, thinking deceit.

13 But I like a man become,
   Deaf and dumb,
Little hearing, speaking lesse;
14 I ev'en as such kind of wight,   [40]
   Senseles quite,
Word with word do not represse.

15 For on Thee, lord, without end
   I attend,
My God Thou wilt heare my voice;   [45]
16 For I sayd, heare, least they be
   Glad on me,
Whom my fall doth make rejoyce.

---

19 torment] torments A.   31 neighbour B.   43 Thee] the A.   lord B.

17 Sure I do but halting go,
    And my woe   [50]
    Still my orethwart neighbour is.
18 Lo I now to mourn begin
    For my sin,
    Telling mine iniquityes.

19 But the while they live and grow   [55]
    In great show,
20 Many mighty wrongfull foes,
    Who do ev'ill for good, to me
        Enemys be—
    Why? because I virtue chose.   [60]

21 Do not, Lord, then me forsake,
    Do not take
22 Thy deare presence farr from me;
    Hast O Lord, that I be stayd
        By thy aid;   [65]
    My salvation is in thee.

Psalm XXXIX

Dixi custodiam

1 THUS did I think: I well will mark my way,
    Least by my tongue I hap to stray;
    I mussle will my mouth while in the sight
    I do abide of wicked wight.
2 And so I nothing said, I muët stood,   [5]
    I silence kept ev'n in the good.
    But still the more that I did hold my peace,
    The more my sorrow did encrease,
3 The more me thought my heart was hott in me;
    And as I mus'd such World to see,   [10]
    The fire took fire and forcibly out brake,
    My tongue would needs and thus I spake:
4 Lord unto me my time's just measure give,
    Shew me how long I have to live.

58 good B.   64 Lord B.
39. 1 think B.   5 said B.

5 Lo Thou a span's length madest my living line;   [15]
    A span? nay nothing in Thyn eyne.
  What do we seeke? the greatest state I see
    At best is merely vanity.

6 They are but shades not true things where we live,
    Vain shades and vain, in vain to grieve.   [20]
  Look but on this: man still doth riches heape
    And knowes not who the fruit shall reap.

7 This being thus, For what O Lord wait I?
    I wait on Thee with hopefull ey.

8 O helpe o help me, this farr yet I crave,   [25]
    From my transgressions me to save.
  Let me not be thrown down to so base shame
    That fooles of me may make their game.

9 But I do hush, Why do I say thus much,
    Since it is Thou that makest one such?   [30]

10 Ah! yet from me let Thy plagues be displac't,
    For with thy handy stroakes I wast.

11 I know that man's foule sin doth cause Thy wrath.
    For when his sin Thy scourging hath,
  Thou moth like mak'st his beauty fading be;   [35]
    So what is man but vanity?

12 Heare lord my suits and cryes, stop not thyn eares
    At these my words all cloath'd in teares;
  For I with Thee on earth a stranger am
    But baiting, as my Fathers came;   [40]

13 Stay then Thy wrath, that I may strength receive
    E're I my earthly being leave.

Psalm XL

Expectans expectavi

1 WHILE long I did with patient constancy
    The pleasure of my God attend,
    He did himself to me ward bend,

16 span B.   17 state] that B.   21 on, this man B.   22 fruit] fruits B.
23 thus? . . . I B.   25 helpe o] help me, B.   30 one] me B.   such. B.
35 mak'st] makes A.

2 And hearkned how, and why that I did cry,
    And me from pitt bemyred, [5]
    From dungeon he retired,
    Where I in horrors lay,
    Setting my feet upon
    A steadfast rocky stone,
    And my weake steps did stay. [10]

3 So in my mouth he did a song afford,
    New song unto our God of prayse,
    Which many seeing hearts shall rayse
To feare with trust, and trust with feare the Lord.
4   O he indeed is blessed, [15]
    Whose trust is so addressed,
    Who bends not wandring eyes
    To great men's peacock pride,
    Nor ever turns aside
    To follow after lyes. [20]

5 My God Thy wondrous works how manifold,
    What man Thy thoughts can count to Thee.
    I fain of them would speaking be;
But they are more than can by me be told.
6   Thou sacrifice nor offring, [25]
    Burnt offring nor sin offring,
    Didst like, much lesse didst crave;
    But thou didst peirce my eare,
    Which should Thy lessons beare
    And witness me Thy slave. [30]

7 Thus bound I said, lo, lord I am at hand,
    For in Thy book's roll I am writt,
8   And sought with deeds Thy will to hitt;
Yea lord Thy law within my heart doth stand;
9   I to great congregation, [35]
    Thou knowst made declaration,
    Of This sweet righteousness.
    My lipps shall still reveale,
10   My heart shall not conceale
    Thy Truth, health, gratiousness. [40]

40. 5 bemyred] bemir'd B.   6 retired] retir'd B.   27 like B.

11 Then lord from me draw not Thy tender grace,
   Me still in truth and mercy save,
   For endless woes me compast have,
12 So prest with sins I cannot see my case.
     But tryall well doth teach me,   [45]
     Foul faults sore pains do reach me,
     More than my head hath haires;
     So that my surest part,
     My life-maintaining heart,
     Failes me, with ugly feares.   [50]

13 Vouchsafe me help O Lord, and help with hast;
14   Let them have shame, yea blush for shame,
   Who jointly sought my bale to frame;
Let them be curst away that would me wast;
     Let them with shame be cloyed;   [55]
15   Yea let them be destroyed
     For guerdon of their shame,
     Who so unpitteous be
     As now to say to me,
     Aha! This is good game.   [60]

16 But fill their hearts with joy, who bend their wayes
   To seek Thy beauty past conceit;
   Let them that love Thy saving seat
Still gladly say, Unto our God bee prayse.
17   Tho I in want be shrinking,   [65]
     Yet God on me is thinking,
     Thou art my help for aye;
     Thou only, Thou, art hee
     That dost deliver me,
     My God, O make no stay.   [70]

Psalm XLI

Beatus qui intelligit

1 HE blessed is, who with wise temper can
   Judg of th' afflicted man;
For God shall him deliver in the time
   When most his troubles clime.

51-70 *om*. K.   52 for] with B.   54 me] my B.   68 only Thou B.

2 The Lord will keep his life yet safe and sound   [5]
     With blessings of the ground,
And will not him unto the will expose
     Of them that be his foes.

3 When bedd from rest becomes his seat of woe,
     In God his strength shall grow,   [10]
And turn his couch, where sick he couched late,
     To well recoverd state.
4 Therfore I said in most infirmity,
     Have mercy lord on me,
O heale my soul, let there Thy cure begin   [15]
     Where 'gainst Thee lay my sin.

5 My Foes' ev'ill words their hate of me display
     While thus, alas, they say:
When, when will death o'retake this wretched wight
     And his name perish quite?   [20]
6 Their courteous visitings are courting lyes,
     They inward ev'ills disguise,
Ev'en heapes of wicked thoughts which streight they show
     As soon as out they go.

7 For then their hatefull heads close whispring be   [25]
     With hurtfull thoughts to me.
8 Now is hee wrackt say they, lo, there he lyes
     Who never more must rise.
9 O yea, my Friend to whom I did impart
     The secrets of my heart,   [30]
My Friend I say, who at my table sate,
     Did kick against my state.

10 Therfore, O Lord, abandond thus of all,
     On me let mercy fall,
And rayse me up that I may once have might   [35]
     Their merits to requite.
11 But what? This doth already well appeare
     That I to Thee am deare,
Since foes nor have, nor shall have cause to be
     Triumphing over me.   [40]

41. *Stanzas not spaced in* B.   15 cure] care B.   18 thus alas B.
27 is hee] he is A.   say they] they say B.   33 Therfore O Lord B.

12 But triumph well may I, whom Thou dost stay
   In my sound rightfull way,
  Whome Thou, O place of places all, dost place
   For aye before Thy face.
[13] So then be blest now, then, at home, abroad,   [45]
   Of Israel the God.
  World without end, let still his blessing flow;
   Oh so! O be it so!

Psalm XLII

[*Quemadmodum*]

1. As the chafed hart which brayeth
   Seeking some refreshing brook,
   So my soul in panting playeth,
   Thirsting on my God to look.

2.   My soul thirsts indeed in me   [5]
    After ever living thee;
    Ah, when comes my blessed being,
    Of Thy face to have a seing?

3. Day and night my teares out flowing
   Have been my ill feeding food,   [10]
   With their dayly questions throwing:
   Where is now Thy God so good?

4.   My heart melts remembring so,
    How in troops I wont to go,
    Leading them his prayses singing,   [15]
    Holy daunce to God's house bringing.

5 Why art Thou my soul so sorry
   And in me so much dismaid?
   Wait on God, for yet his glory
   In my song shall be display'd.   [20]

6   When but with one look of his
    He shall me restore to blisse,
    Ah my soul it self appaleth,
    In such longing thoughts it falleth.

41 I B.   43 Whome] Whence B.   all B.   45 home B.   47 still] this A.
42. 19 God B.

For my mind on my God bideth,   [25]
Ev'n from Hermon's dwelling led,
From the grounds where Jordan slideth
And from Mizzar's hilly head.

7.   One deep with noyse of his fall
      Other deeps of Woes doth call,   [30]
      While my God with wasting wonders
      On me wretch his tempest thunders.

All Thy floods on me abounded,
Over me all thy waves went;
Yet thus still my hope is grounded,   [35]
8 That Thy anger being spent,
      I by day thy love shall tast,
      I by night shall singing last,
      Praying, prayers still bequeathing
      To my God that gave me breathing.   [40]

9. I will say: O lord my tower,
Why am I forgott by Thee?
Why should grief my heart devower,
While the Foe oppresseth me?
10.   Those vile scoffes of naughty ones   [45]
       Wound and rent me to the bones,
       When foes ask with foule deriding,
       Where hath now your God his biding?

11 Why art Thou my soul so sorry
And in me so much dismaid?   [50]
Wait on God, for yet his glory
In my song shall be displayed.
      To him my thanks shall be said
      Who is still my present aid;
      And in fine my soul be raysed,   [55]
      God is my God, by me praysed.

27 jordan B.   39 Praying B.   41 say B.   48 hath . . . his biding] is . . .
abiding A.   51 God B.   53–56 *These lines appear in* B K D A F J; *four
different revisions appear in* X:
            Trust in him, on him relie
            Yeeld him praise contynuallie
            Whoe hath beene (thee failing never)
            Thy true God, & wilbe ever. C.   [*cont. overleaf*]

Psalm XLIII

Iudica me Deus

1. JUDG of all, judg me
   And Protector bee
      Of my Cause oppressed
   By most cruel sprites,
   Save me from bad wights   [5]
      In false colours dressed.

2. For my God Thy sight
   Giveth me my might,
      Why then hast thou left me?
   Why walk I in woes   [10]
   While prevayling foes
      Have of joyes bereft me?

3. Send Thy truth and light,
   Let them guide me right
      From the paths of folly,   [15]
   Bringing me to thy
   Tabernaclee high
      In thy hill most holy.

4. To God's Altars tho
   Will I boldly go   [20]
      shaking off all sadnes,
   To that God that is
   God of all my blisse,
      God of all my gladness.

To him my thanckfull hart singe
Who is still my god my kinge
& with ayde me neare attendeth
When my foes my thrall entendeth.   E H L N.

Unto him a songe of praise
Still my thankfull heart shall raise
He who helpes my case distressed
Even my God for ever blessed.   G.

He it is who hath and will
Beene my comfort reddy still
   He it is who faild me neuer
   God my blessed God for euer.   M.

43. 1 all B.   3 B *does not indent.*   5 wights. B.   17 Tabernacle]
Tabernacles B K.

Then lo, then I will [25]
With sweet musick's skill
   Gratefull meaning show thee,
Then God, yea my God,
I will sing abroad
   What great thanks I ow thee. [30]

5 Why art Thou my soul
Cast down in such dole,
   What ayles Thy discomfort?
Wait on God, for still
Thank my God I will, [35]
   Sure aid present comfort.

25 I will] will I B K.   34 God B.   *After* 36 Hitherto S^r Ph. Sidney B J, Hactenus
Sr Phillip Sydneye E H N.

LOST POEM

Translation of du Bartas, *La Semaine ou Creation du Monde*

DU BARTAS'S *La Semaine*, a versified account of the creation in seven books or days, was first published in 1578; Sidney had become acquainted with it by 1582, for he made use of it in *Astrophil and Stella*. Fulke Greville, in his letter to Walsingham of November 1586, said that Sidney had translated 'bartas his semeyne'; in 1587 Matthew Gwinne mentioned the translation in the Oxford *Exequiae*; and on 23 August 1588 William Ponsonby entered it for publication, but apparently never printed it. In 1593 Thomas Moffet mentioned it as Sidney's in *Nobilis* (ed. Heltzel and Hudson, p. 74); in 1595 the anonymous rhyme-royal translator of du Bartas's *First Day* said that he had withheld publication of his translation for some time in expectation of the appearance of Sidney's; in 1603 John Florio said he had 'seene' Sidney's version of the 'first septmaine' (*Essayes of Montaigne*, R3); and in 1605 Josuah Sylvester, in a sonnet prefacing his own translation of *Bartas His Devine Weekes & Workes*, wrote that Sidney 'This Lovely Venus first to Limne beganne', but 'that Holy-Relique' is now 'shrin'd | In som High Place, close lockt from common light'. Thereafter we hear no more of Sidney's translation, and no trace remains of the manuscript. Sylvester's translation runs to 7,696 lines; so if Sidney translated the whole of the first *Semaine*, as Greville and Florio say he did, we have lost a body of his verse equal in bulk to more than half of that which survives.

POEMS POSSIBLY BY SIDNEY

I

A Dialogue betweene two shepherds, utterd in a pastorall
shew, at Wilton.

Will. *Dick*, since we cannot dance, come let a chearefull voyce
Shew that we do not grudge at all when others do rejoyce.
Dick. Ah *Will*, though I grudge not, I count it feeble glee
With sight made dymme with dayly teares another's sport to see.
Who ever Lambkins saw (yet lambkins love to play)   [5]
To play when that their loved dammes, are stoln or gone astray?
If this in them be true, as true in men think I
A lustles song for sooth thinks hee that hath more lust to cry.
Will. A tyme there is for all, my Mother often sayes,   [9]
When she with skirts tuckt very hy, with girles at stoolball playes.
When thou hast mynd to weepe, seeke out som smoky room:
Now let those lightsomme sights we see thy darknes overcome.
Dick. What joy the joyfull sunne gives unto bleared eyes:
That comfort in these sports you like, my mynde his comfort tryes.
Will. What? is thy Bagpipe broke, or are thy lambs miswent; [15]
Thy wallet or thy Tarbox lost, or thy new rayment rent?
Dick. I would it were but thus, for thus it were too well.
Will. Thou seest my eares do itch at it: good *Dick* thy sorow tell.
Dick. Here then and learne to sigh: a mistress I doo serve,
Whose wages makes me beg the more, who feeds me till I sterve,
Whose lyverie is such, as most I freeze apparelled most,   [21]
And lookes so neere unto my cure that I must needes be lost.
Will. What? these are riddles sure, art thou then bound to her?
Dick. Bound as I neither power have, nor would have power to stir.
W[ill]. Who bound thee? *D[ick].* Love my Lord. *W[ill].* What
witnesses therto?   [25]
Dick. Faith in my self and worth in her, which no proofe can undoo.
W[ill]. What seale? *D[ick].* My hart deepe graven. *W[ill].* Who
made the band so fast?
D[ick]. Wonder that by two so black eyes the glittring stars be past.

Will. What keepeth safe thy band? *D[ick].* Remembrance is the
   Chest
  Lockt fast with knowing that she is, of worldly things the best. [30]
Will. Thou late of wages playn'dst: what wages mayst thou have?
D[ick]. Her heavenly looks, which more and more do give me cause
   to crave.
W[ill]. If wages make you want, what food is that she gives?
D[ick]. Teares drink, sorowes meat, wherewith, not I, but in me
   my death lives.
Will. What living get you then? *D[ick].* Disdayne; but just dis-
   dayne.   [35]
  So have I cause my selfe to plaine, but no cause to complayne.
Will. What care takes shee for thee? *D[ick].* Hir care is to prevent
  My freedom, with show of hir beames, with virtue my content.
Will. God shield us from such Dames. If so our Downes be sped,
  The shepheards will grow leane I trow, their sheep will ill be fed.
  But *Dick* my counsell marke: run from the place of wo: [41]
  The Arrow being shot from far, doth give the smaller blowe.
Dick. Good *Will*, I cannot take thy good advice, before
  That Foxes leave to steale, because they finde they dy therefore.
Will. Then *Dick* let us go hence lest wee great folkes annoy. [45]
  For nothing can more tedious bee, then plaint, in time of joy.
Dick. Oh hence! o cruell word! which even doggs do hate:
  But hence, even hence, I must needes goe; such is my dogged fate.

2

THE darte, the beames, the stringe so stronge I prove;
Whiche my chefe partte, dothe passe throughe, parche, and tye,
That of the stroke, the heat, and knott of love,
Wounded, inflam'de, knitt to the deathe I dye.

Hardned, and coulde, farr from affectione's snare   [5]
Was once my mynde, my temper, and my lyfe,
Whille I that syghte, desyre, and vowe forbare,
Whiche to avoyde, quenche, loose noughte booted stryfe.

2. Ra, Hy. Hy *indents even numbered lines.*   2 tye Ra.   3 loue Ra.
5 farrr Ra.   6 my mynde] mynde Ra.   lyfe Ra.   7 forbare Ra.
8 loose] lose Ra.   booted] booteth Hy.   stryfe Ra.

Yet will not I greife, ashes, thralldom change
For other's ease, their frutte, or free estate,   [10]
So brave a shott, deere fyre and bewtye strange
Did me pearce, burne, and bynde, longe since and late,
   And in my woundes, my flames and bondes I fynde
   A salve, freshe ayre, and hyghe contented mynde.

3

[Inscription on Sidney's portrait at Longleat, 1577]

WHO gives him selfe, may well his picture give
   els weare it vayne since both short tyme doe lyve.

4

[The Challenge of the Four Foster Children of Desire]

YEELDE yeelde, O yeelde, you that this FORTE do holde,
   which seated is, in spotlesse honor's fielde,
Desire's great force, no forces can withhold:
   then to DESIER's desire, O yeelde O yeelde.

Yeelde yeelde O yeelde, trust not on beautie's pride,   [5]
   fayrenesse though fayer, is but a feeble shielde,
When strong Desire, which vertue's love doth guide,
   claymes but to gaine his due, O yeelde O yeelde.

Yeelde yeelde O yeelde, who first this Fort did make,
   did it for just Desire's true children builde,   [10]
Such was his minde, if you another take:
   defence herein doth wrong, O yeelde O yeelde,

Yeelde yeelde O yeelde, now is it time to yeelde,
   Before thassault beginne, O yeelde O yeelde.

---

10 their] theirs Ra.   or] of Hy.   estate Ra.   12 late Ra.   14 *[subscription]*
Finis S P S Ra, FINIS Hy.
   4. Henry Goldwel, *A briefe declaration*, 1581 (Go).   10 Desires, Go.

5

[*The Defiance of the Fortress of Perfect Beauty*]

ALLARME allarme, here will no yeelding be,
  such marble eares, no cunning wordes can charme,
Courage therefore, and let the stately see
  that naught withstandes DESIRE, Allarme allarme.

Allarme allarme, let not their beauties move   [5]
  remorse in you to doe this FORTRESSE harme,
For since warre is the ground of vertue's love,
  no force, though force be used, Allarme allarme.

Allarme allarme, companions nowe beginne,
  about these never conquered walles to swarme,   [10]
More prayse to us we never looke to winne,
  much may that was not yet, Allarme allarme.

Allarme allarme, when once the fight is warme,
then shall you see them yelde, Allarme allarme.

5. Henry Goldwel, *A briefe declaration*, 1581 (Go).   3 see. Go.   8 vsed
Go.   10 these] this Go.   13 allarme when Go.   14 Go *indents*.

WRONGLY ATTRIBUTED POEMS

WRONGLY ATTRIBUTED POEMS

THIRTY-FIVE poems have at one time or another been improperly attributed to Sidney. I presented detailed evidence for rejecting most of these from the canon in an article in *Studies in Philology*, xlvii (1950), 126–51. I list these below, alphabetically by first lines and numbered as in the article for ease in cross-reference, with only a summary statement of the reasons for rejecting them. A few items that have come to my attention since the publication of the article I insert in the alphabetical sequence and number 10a, 12a, &c. Poems numbered 8, 16, 24, and 28 in the article I accept as genuine or as possibly by Sidney, and have printed them above as PP 1, OP 6, PP 2, and OP 7. At the end of this list I print the texts of AT 5, 14, 19, and 21, poems which cannot positively be rejected from the canon, but which I am personally convinced are not by Sidney.

Ah poore love whi dost thou live, lines 9–36 of AT 5.

1. All my sences stand amazed, 32 lines.

This and Nos. 17 and 22 attributed on merely impressionistic grounds by Mary Bowen, *MLN* x (1895), 239–44.

2. All things that are, or ever were, or shall hereafter bee, 204 lines.

The first line of 54 passages of verse in *The trewnesse of the Christian Religion*, 1587, a translation begun by Sidney and finished by Golding. All the verse is Golding's.

3. Allusion of words is no sure ground, 2 lines.

This and Nos. 23 and 27 wrongly attributed in *Englands Parnassus*, 1600. No. 3 is by W. Lisle, 23 by Spenser, and 27 by John Dolman.

4. Are women faire? yea wondrous faire to see too, 26 lines.

Attributed only in Rosenbach MS. 186 of the second quarter of the seventeenth century. Ten earlier seventeenth-century transcripts are anonymous.

5. At my harte there is a payne—printed below.

6. Cloathed in state and girt with might, 16 lines.

Attributed in the second edition of Zouch's *Memoirs of*

Sidney (1809), p. 398. Metaphrase of Psalm 93 by the Countess of Pembroke.

7. Come live with me and be my love, 28 lines.

Attributed in Morgan Library MS. 'Rulers of England'. By Christopher Marlowe.

9. Faint amorist; what, do'st thou think, 28 lines.

Attributed in J. H[owell's] *Cottoni Posthuma*, 1651. Composed in the seventeenth century.

10. Harke all youe Ladies that doe sleepe, 35 lines.

Attributed in British Museum MS. Additional 28253. By Thomas Campion.

10a. Heare ye how faintlie now and timidlie, 14 lines.

Professor Earl R. Wasserman pointed out to me that this is attributed in an anonymous communication, 'Unpublished Sidney MSS', *The European Magazine*, lxxxvi (1824), 315–18, with Nos. 12a, 18a, and 29b. The unknown author said that another person had allowed him to make copies of 'a number of old manuscripts, which he averred were autographs of Sir Philip Sidney'. He printed the four poems noted, the last of which he said appeared in 'a projected classic pastoral' partly in prose, the scene of which is laid in the vale of Tempe. The poems are obvious nineteenth-century fabrications.

11. Her inward worth all outward Show transcends, 6 lines.

Attributed in a manuscript now at Wilton House. A nineteenth-century fabrication.

12. How can the feeble forts but fall and yeild at last, 30 lines.

Attributed only in Rosenbach MS. 186 of the second quarter of the seventeenth century. Subscribed 'M^{rs} M: R:' in the earlier Bodleian MS. Rawl. poet. 85.

12a. I slept, and lo! methoughte, beneathe a tree, 14 lines, *see* No. 10a.

13. Iffe that [p]ynes and dyes, 68 lines.

Suggested by Grosart (1. xxxiii) on the basis of handwriting; but the hand is not Sidney's.

14. In a field full fayer of flowers—printed below.

15. It is not I that die, I do but leave an Inn, 6 lines.

Attributed, as Mr. John Crow pointed out to me, in *Wits Recreations* (1645), R1^{v}; also in Winstanley's *Lives of the . . . English Poets*

(1687), and in five manuscripts of the second quarter of the seven-teenth century or later. By William Crashaw.

La cuisse rompue [title only].

Fulke Greville in his *Life of Sidney*, chap. 13, reported that shortly before his death Sidney 'cals for Musick; especially that song which himself had intitled, *La cuisse rompue*. Partly (as I conceive by the name) to shew that the glory of mortal flesh was shaken in him: and by that Musick it self, to fashion and enfranchise his heavenly soul into that everlasting harmony of Angels, whereof these Concords were a kinde of terrestriall *Echo*.' Thomas Zouch (*Sidney*, 1809, p. 258) and others have assumed that this is a song which Sidney himself composed; but Greville said only that Sidney so designated a song he knew which he considered to apply to his own case. Thomas Moffet (*Nobilis*, ed. Heltzel and Hudson, p. 92) said that on his deathbed Sidney 'made known the thankfulness of his soul in hymns'.

17. Leave me O life, the prison of my minde, 10 lines, *see* No. 1.

18. Nigh seated where the river flows, 40 lines.

Attributed in Steele's *Guardian*, No. 18, and by Zouch, p. 399. Metaphrase of Psalm 137 by the Countess of Pembroke.

18a. Now lette us shede the brinie teare, 44 lines, *see* No. 10a.

18b. O Lord, how vain are all our frail delights, 18 lines.

This and 29a attributed by E. H. Fellowes, *Collected Vocal Works of William Byrd*, xv (1948), 40–43 and xvi. 59–67. The attributions must have been made in error, for none of the manuscripts from which Fellowes drew these texts contain an ascription to Sidney.

19. Philisides, the Shepherd good and true—printed below.

20. Philoclea and Pamela sweet, 86 lines.

Attributed in the 1655 and later editions of the *Arcadia*, and in four late seventeenth-century manuscripts. Composed in the mid-seventeenth century, probably by Sir John Mennes or James Smith.

21. Singe neighbours singe, here yow not Say—printed below.

22. Some men will saie, there is a kinde of muse, 66 lines, *see* No. 1.

23. Such is the crueltie of women-kind, 9 lines, *see* No. 3.

25. The gentle season of the yeere, 42 lines. By Sir Arthur Gorges.

The Life and Death of Mary Magdalene: or, Her Life in Sin and Death to Sin [title only].

According to *N & Q*, 5th ser., vii (1877), 48, a poem with this title which its editor suggested was 'probably written by Sir Philip Sidney' was printed in the February 1869 number of *Westminster Abbey; or, Reminiscences of Past Literature*. The only recorded file of that periodical, in the British Museum, was destroyed in World War II, so there is no way of testing the suggestion.

26. The Tyme hath beene that a Taudry lace, 12 lines.

Attributed by William Percy, *The Faery Pastorall*, early seventeenth century. By Percy himself.

26a. The worldes faire rose and Henries frostye fire, 14 lines.

An anonymous sonnet in Bodleian MS. Douce 280, f. 124ᵛ, enumerating the works of Michael Drayton. Listed in error as by Sidney in the *Catalogue of the Printed Books and Manuscripts bequeathed by Francis Douce Esq.* (1840), p. 47.

27. Unpunisht scapes, from hainous crime some one, 2 lines, *see* No. 3.

29. Wert thou a Kinge, yet not commaunde content, 6 lines.

Headed 'Answered thus by Sʳ P. S.' in Chetham College Manchester MS. 8012, p. 84, and subscribed 'Vere' in Folger MS. 1. 112, f. 6, the only other text. In my earlier study of the canon I thought these verses might possibly be by Sidney, but I now definitely reject them. They are an 'answer' to a six-line poem beginning 'Weare I a Kinge I coulde commande content' which appears alone near the end of British Museum MS. Additional 22583 (a collection of his own writings made by William Gager in the late 1580's and 1590's), and which was printed with a musical setting in John Mundy's *Songs and Psalms*, 1594. Gager and Mundy's texts of 'Weare I a Kinge' vary from one another in only a single word; but the Folger text changes eight of Gager's words, and the Chetham text changes nine. The corruptions in the text of the first poem in the Chetham MS., which was transcribed some fifty years after Sidney's death and contains several erroneous attributions, indicates that it stands at several removes from the author's original and suggests that the 'answer' stands similarly removed. The unique and late ascription to Sidney in the unreliable Chetham MS. cannot be accepted.

29a. What vaileth it to rule the cities great, 10 lines, *see* 18b.

29b. Whoe hath not hearde of Tempe's beauteous vale,
16 lines, *see* 10a.

30. Woe to mine eyes, the organs of my ill, 14 lines.
Erroneously attributed by Grosart (i. 229) on the basis of style.

I print below AT 5, 14, 19, and 21, which are attributed to Sidney
in late sixteenth-century manuscripts, though I believe the attribu-
tions are mistaken.

AT 5 is subscribed 'S. P. S.' in Ra, whose attributions are usually,
though not invariably, accurate; but it also appears without attribu-
tion in British Museum MS. Additional 34064 as one of a group of
poems that are probably all the work of Breton. Ra is an inferior
text, manifestly wrong in lines 27, 28, and 32; both texts are prob-
ably wrong in line 30, 'snake', which Grosart emended to 'make'
(meaning 'mate'). Lines 9–36 of Ra were first printed, attributed to
Sidney, by Philip Bliss in his edition of Anthony à Wood's *Athenae
Oxonienses*, i (1813), 525; and the first two stanzas by Mary Bowen,
MLN x (1895), 239. I believe the poem is by Breton.

AT 14 was first printed from Ha, the only text, by Grosart
(ii. 78–79), who attributed it to Sidney. The letter 'S' of the sub-
scription has been crossed out in the manuscript and is not clearly
decipherable, and Ha is not a dependable authority for about a
quarter of its other attributions are doubtful or wrong. Sidney
never used the name Phillis, but Phillis and Coridon were Breton's
stock characters in the 1590's. The poem is probably by Breton or
some other imitator of Sidney.

AT 19 and 21 appear only in Hy and were first printed by
B. M. Wagner, *PMLA* liii (1938), 118–24, who considered them to
be Sidney's; but Hy is not a dependable authority, for more than
a third of its attributions of authorship are wrong. Professor Wagner
himself observed of AT 19 that the description of the characters
and the occasion of their meeting 'usurp the function of Sidney's
prose, which invariably supplies just these details', and that Menalcas
in the *Old Arcadia* is a shepherd and not a husbandman; and of
AT 21 that it adapts the stanza form of CS 30 and was probably
designed as a laudation of Queen Elizabeth on one of the anni-
versaries of her Accession Day. Sidney was not in the habit of
writing poems in praise of the Queen. I believe both are by imitators
of Sidney.

AT 5

AT my harte there is a payne.
   Never payne so pinchte my harte.
More than haulfe with sorrow slayne.
   And the payne yet will not parte.

Ah my harte how it doth bleede.   [5]
   Into dropps of bitter teares
Whyle my faythefull love doth feede.
   But one fancyes onlye feares.

Ah poore love whi dost thou live.
   Thus to se thy service loste   [10]
Ife she will no comforte geve
   Make an end yeald up the goaste

That she may at lenghte aprove.
   That she hardlye long beleived
That the harte will dy for love   [15]
   That is not in tyme releived

Ohe that ever I was borne.
   Service so to be refused
Faythfull love to be forborne.
   Never love was so abused.   [20]

But swet love be still a whylle
   She that hurte the sone maye healle the
Sweet I see within her smylle
   More than reason can reveall the

For thoughe she be riche and fayre   [25]
   Yet she is both wise and kynde.
And therfore do thou not despayre.
   But thy faythe may fancy fynde.

Yet allthoughe she be a quene
   That maye suche a snake despyse   [30]
Yet withe sylence all unseene
   Runn and and hid the in her eyes.

AT 5. Ra, British Museum MS. Additional 34064 (*here designated* Co).   4 yet will] will yitt Co.   5 Ah] Oh Co.   12 yeald] giue Co.   13 lenghte] last Co.   19 forborne] forlorne Co.   26 she is] is she Co.   27 thou] *om.* Co.   28 fancy] favor Co.   29 Yet] And Co.   32 and and] and Co.

Where if she will let the dye
   Yet at latest gaspe of breathe.
Say that in a ladyes eye   [35]
   Love both tooke his lyfe and deathe.

finis S: P. S.

AT 14

In a field full fayer of flowers
Where the *Muses* made their bowers
And more sweeter Hony grew
Then the sence of Nature knew
Preevie sweete with hartsease springing   [5]
While sweet *Philomel* was singing
Coridon and *Phillis* fayer
Went abroad to take the ayer
Each in absence long diseased
But in presence either pleased   [10]
Where begun their pritle pratle
Ther was prety title tatle.
Coridon quoth shee a tryall
Must in truth have no denyall
True quoth he and then he proved   [15]
Well I hope shalbe beloved.
Yea *Quoth shee* but where is true love
Where *quoth hee* both you and I love
Yea *quoth shee* but truly tell me
And in these fewe letters spell me.   [20]
C O R I D O N
Where was I when these were gon
Sweet *quoth hee* how to devise the
And by letters to suffice the
P H I L L I S   [25]
All my joye both was and is
In my hart thou art inclosed
Where thy love cannot be losed
Trust me *Phillis* in good sadnes
Is it not a very maddnes.   [30]

After 36 finis S: P. S.] Finis Co.
AT 14. Ha.

To refuse a good thing offered
When it was of good will proffered
And what better thing to proove
Then how good a thing is love
Many a wench and if shee knew it   [35]
What it were and how to use it
In her hart full soone would rue it
When shee thought shee did refuse it
It is a humor that doth tickle
And like Thistle downe doth prickle   [40]
Veines and sinnewes, witts and senses
With the sweete of such deffences
Which dame Nature gave to me
Onely to bestowe on thee
Take it duly even and morrowe   [45]
It will drive out care and sorrowe
Use it kindly sweetly trie it
Then unto thine hart applye it

finis P. [S.?]

AT 19

PHILISIDES, the Shepherd good and true,
   Came by Menalchas house, the husbandman,
With Tonges of Love, and praise of Mirrhaes hue,
   Whose faire sweet lokes, make him loke pale and wan.
Yt erly was; Menalcha forth was bound,   [5]
   With Horse and man, to sow and till the ground.

Menalcha softe; this Shepeherd to him saies,
   Wilt thou with worke, this holy time defile?
This is the chief of Cupides Sabaothe daies,
   The Wake of those that honour Samos Ile.   [10]
Where great, and small, rich, poore, and eche degree.
   Yeld, fayth, Love, Joy, and prove what in them bee,

AT **19.** Hy. *The subscription first contained the initials* H. C. *which were crossed out and* P. Sidney *added.*

Menalcha who of longe his thoughtes had tild,
  With ffancies plow, that they might plesure beare,
And with his Love the Empty ffurrowes fild,   [15]
  Which alwais sprange to him againe in feare,
Was well content the plow and all to yeeld,
  Unto this Sabothe day, and sacred feeld.

And on is past by course amonge the reste,
  Wyth Layes of Joy, and Lyrickes all of Praise,   [20]
His Hart as theirs, in service of the beste,
  ffor other Saintes, he knoweth not their daies.
Yf any Juste, his whip must be his Speare,
  And of his teeme the *till horse, must him beare. *mill

When he runnes well, then well to her betide,   [25]
  When yll, then ill. a plaine faith is exprest,
Yf neither well nor ill light on his side,
  His course is yet rewarded with the best:
ffor of all Runners, this the ffortune is.
  That who runnes best, is fortunde on[e] to misse.   [30]

        FINIS.   P. Sidney.

AT 21

Nec habent occulta sepulchrum.

SINGE neighbours singe, here yow not Say,
    This Sabaothe day:
  A Sabaoth is reputed,
    Of such a roiall Saincte,
  As all Sayntes els confuted,   [5]
    Is Love without constrainte.

  Let such a Sainte be praised,
    Which so her worth hath raised,
ffrom him that wold not thus,
    Good Lord delyver us.   [10]

      AT 21. Hy.

Sound up your pypes, do yow not see,
    That yond is Shee,
yeaven She that most respecteth,
    The faithfull loving myndes,
And no on thought rejecteth,   [15]
    That upon Honor byndes.

Let such a Sainte be praysed,
    Which so her worth hath raysed,
ffrom him that wold not thus
    Good Lorde deliver us.   [20]

Shew forth yowr Joy, let moorninge stay,
    This is Her day:
Her day on which shee entred,
    And with her entry Peace,
Whiche shee hath not adventred,   [25]
    But kepte for our encrease.

Let such a Saynte be praysed,
    Which so her worth hath raysed
ffrom him that wold not thus
    Good Lord delyver us.   [30]

All Joy is full, like for no moe,
    Let Sorrow goe;
Let Sorrow goe despised,
    And mirth be made a Queene,
The Heavens highly praised,   [35]
    That we this day have seene.

Let suche a Saynte be praised,
    Which so her worthe hath raysed,
ffrom him that wold not thus,
    Good Lorde delyver us.   [40]

FINIS.   Sr P. Sy.

COMMENTARY

COMMENTARY

POEMS FROM THE LADY OF MAY

THIS pastoral entertainment was first printed as the last item in the 1598 *Arcadia . . . with sundry new additions*, Bbb3ᵛ–6ᵛ, the only substantive text, from which it was reprinted in the later folios and collected editions of Sidney's works. There is no evidence that it circulated in manuscript, for the extracts in Corpus Christi College Oxford MS. 263, f. 120, National Library of Scotland MS. 2059, ff. 294ᵛ–9ᵛ, and British Museum MS. Sloane 161, ff. 29–30, all derive from the 1599 folio or later prints. Since the 98 text does not reflect Sidney's characteristic pattern of spelling (for example, in the prose 'far excell' [ii. 337] would have been written 'fur eccel' by Sidney), the printer's copy was probably a scribal transcript rather than the holograph original. The folios set the opening words in capitals—'HER MOST EXCELLENT MAIESTIE WALKING IN WANSTEED GARDEN'—but give the piece no title. In 1600 the editor of *Englands Helicon* called it 'The May Lady', and the editor of the 1725–24 *Works* called it 'The Lady of May, A Masque', a designation which was adopted by all subsequent editors. It is, of course, not technically a masque, and though when first mentioned in the text the heroine is called 'the Lady of May', in the speech headings she is always called 'the May Lady'.

Queen Elizabeth, walking in Wanstead garden, receives a 'Supplication' (LM 1) from a countrywoman whose daughter, the Lady of May, has two suitors. Six shepherds and six foresters then enter, each trying to pull the Lady of May to their side. The old shepherd Lalus and the pedantical schoolmaster Rombus try to explain the cause of the contest, and the Lady of May herself asks the Queen to help her decide which suitor to choose: the forester Therion (θηρίον, wild beast), who has 'many deserts and many faults', or the shepherd Espilus (εἰς πῖλος, felt presser), who has 'verie small deserts and no faults'. Therion and Espilus engage in a singing match (LM 2). The old shepherd Dorcas and the young forester Rixus debate which sang the better, and Rombus tries to 'endoctrinate' their 'plumbeous cerebrosities' in schoolboy techniques of argumentation. The Queen decides in favour of Espilus, who brings the playlet to a close with a song of joy (LM 3).

It is a slight piece, entertaining mainly because of the laughable pedantry of Rombus, whose speeches recall the burlesque 'inkhorn' epistle in the *Arte of Rhetorique* by Sidney's friend Thomas Wilson. Its operatic combination of song and spectacle resembles earlier royal entertainments, such as that at Woodstock in 1575, and its shepherds and foresters are the stock figures of continental pastoral romances and dramas; but it draws upon no specific sources. It is historically interesting as the earliest example in English of conventionalized pastoral drama.

The most likely dates for the presentation are either 6–16 May 1578, or 1–2 May 1579. It concerns 'the lady of the whole moneth of May', and the opening lines say it was acted before Queen Elizabeth at Wanstead. The Earl of Leicester acquired the house and manor of Wanstead, near the royal palace at Greenwich, in 1577. The Queen visited there eight times, but only in 1578 and 1579 did her visits occur in the month of May. The old shepherd Lalus appears in the First Eclogues of the *Old Arcadia* as a young shepherd, Dorcas is mentioned in OA **29.** 8, and the anecdote of Pan and Hercules in LM **3** is also used in Book III of the *Old Arcadia*. These resemblances and variations, and also the jog-trot versification and commonplace sixain stanzas, suggest that the *Lady of May* is early work, composed before the *Old Arcadia* had completely taken form. I therefore favour the spring of 1578 as the date of composition and presentation, though 1579 is also possible. The actors may have been members of the Earl of Leicester's company of professional players; if they were, it is possible that Rombus was played by Richard Tarlton, to whose son Sidney was godfather in 1582.

Royal entertainments of this sort were expected to contain topical allusions and hidden significances, and the Lady of May tells the Queen, 'in judging me, you judge more then me in it'. Perhaps it concerns the chief point of national policy at issue in 1578–9, whether England should actively support the cause of continental Protestantism by giving military aid to the Netherlands. To do so would mean an open conflict with Spain, and the Queen wanted to maintain the peace by any means; Leicester and his followers favoured a warlike policy, which the Queen, if she considered this the implication of the piece, rejected by giving judgement in favour of the peaceful Espilus. Though Sidney's playlet concerns a choice of suitors, I doubt that he intended it to reflect (as William Gray suggested) the marriage proposal of the Duke of Anjou to the Queen, which after being in abeyance for two years she again began to consider in the spring of 1578, for he here allows Therion both deserts and faults, but in the letter against the marriage proposal which he addressed to the Queen in the summer or autumn of 1579, he allowed Anjou only faults and no merits at all.

1

Sidney differed from the majority of his fellow courtiers who made flattery of the Queen the main business of their pens, for this is his only poem in praise of Elizabeth. It is mechanically fashioned of two triads: state, face, mind—ears, eyes, heart. Cf. CS 3, 17, 18.

2

The singing match is a recurring device in Greek and Latin pastoral (Theocritus v, Virgil iii) which was revived by the neo-Latin and vernacular poets of the renaissance. This I believe is the earliest example in English; others close in time are OA 7 and 29, and Spenser's August eclogue.

14. Proverbial since classical times. Cf. OA **7.** 11 and Ralegh's

> Our Passions are most like to Floods and streames;
> The shallow Murmure; but the Deep are Dumb.

19. Virgil's Corydon similarly seeks the favour of Alexis by enumerating his wealth:

Mille meae Siculis errant in montibus agnae;
lac mihi non aestate novum, non frigore defit.
                                        (*Ecl.* ii. 21–22.)

Cf. OA **7.** 115–17.

28 *would*. Sidney's own spelling 'woold' gives a satisfactory eye-rhyme.

3

The prose introducing these lines says: 'Then did Espilus sing this song, tending to the greatnesse of his owne joy, and yet to the comfort of the other side, since they [Therion and his followers] were overthrowne by a most worthy adversarie [the Queen]'; but it is obvious from the song itself that lines 7–12 and 17–18 are sung by Therion. The poem was ingeniously devised to be appropriate to whichever suitor was adjudged victor by the Queen.

7 *Lion's skin*, the identifying garment of Hercules. Ovid, *Fasti*, ii. 303–58, tells how Faunus (whom he equates with Pan), seeking Omphale's bed, gets into that of Hercules. Sidney refers to the anecdote again in the *Old Arcadia* (iv. 213), making the mistress of Hercules Iole rather than Omphale.

POEMS FROM THE OLD ARCADIA

(i) *The* Old *and the* New Arcadia. *The Countesse of Pembrokes Arcadia* was first printed in 1590 in a version divided into three books, with eclogues after the first and second books, and the narrative of the third book ending abruptly in the middle of a sentence. Three years later a second edition in five books appeared, the first part of which was a reprint of the 1590 edition except for a few verbal variants and some rearrangements and additions in the eclogues. After the incomplete third book a note was added: 'How this combate ended . . . is altogether unknowne. What afterward chaunced, out of the Author's owne writings and conceits hath bene supplied, as followeth.' There then followed a lengthy addition to the third book, plus a fourth and fifth book, with eclogues after the third and fourth. These additions dealt with the same characters and completed the story of the 1590 edition, but were not entirely consistent with the earlier part of the narrative. The 1593 edition, with the narrative hiatus in the middle, was reprinted many times, and for over 300 years was the only form in which Sidney's major prose work was known to the general public.

However, Temple's mention of the 'Arcadiae . . . fabrica texta nouae' in the Cambridge *Lachrymae* (1587), Fraunce's quotations in the *Arcadian Rhetorike* (1588), and references by Greville in his letter to Walsingham, by Harington in his *Orlando Furioso*, and by the editor of the 1613 edition to Sidney's 'old' or 'first Arcadia', indicate that at least some of his contemporaries were acquainted with an earlier form of his work that differed from the printed editions. But later generations did not know that this earlier version existed until in 1907 and 1909 Bertram Dobell told of finding three manuscripts of the *Old Arcadia*.[1] From his analysis of these manuscripts, Dobell was able to show that the continuation of Book III, and Books IV and V in the 1593 edition were, except for a few minor changes, actually the last three books of the *Old Arcadia*, the first two books of which differed radically from the revised version, or *New Arcadia*, printed in 1590. In 1926 Professor Feuillerat printed the *Old Arcadia* from Cl (the Clifford MS.), and for the first time made Sidney's original version generally available. However, St (the St. John's MS.) is more accurate and contains later revisions. Miss Jean Robertson is preparing a critical edition based upon a collation of all the substantive texts.

[1] The *Athenaeum*, 7 Sept. 1907, and *Quarterly Review*, cxi. 74–100. Later researches of Feuillerat, Mona Wilson, and Margaret Beese raised the known number of *Old Arcadia* manuscripts to nine. R. W. Zandvoort, *Sidney's Arcadia, A Comparison Between the Two Versions* (1929), provided a valuable analysis of the processes by which Sidney transformed the *Old Arcadia* into the *New*. Unfortunately he was unable to determine the precise relationships of the *Old Arcadia* manuscripts, and some of his remarks on the editing of the printed editions need revision because he was unaware of the existence of Cm (the Cambridge MS.). His suggestion (p. 67) that Sidney transferred actual pages of his *Old Arcadia* manuscript to the *New* with scissors and paste is not borne out by the textual evidence, for all transference of material appears to have been done by the making of transcripts.

(ii) *Dates of Composition.* The first version of the *Old Arcadia* appears to have been composed at intervals over a period of three years, from the latter part of 1577 to the latter part of 1580. Edmund Molyneux, the Sidney family's confidential secretary, reported that Sir Philip, 'Not long after his returne from that jorneie [to the Emperor in June 1577], and before his further imploiment by hir majestie [as governor of Flushing in 1585], at his vacant and spare times of leisure . . . made his booke which he named *Arcadia*';[1] and Ph (the Phillipps MS.) is headed, 'A treatis . . . of certeyn accidents in Arcadia, made in the year 1580'. The work was certainly completed by the end of 1580, for Sidney read parts of it to his friend the Earl of Angus in the summer of 1581, and in the same year Thomas Howell, after describing the finished narrative, complained that it had been kept from circulation 'all to[o] long'.[2] On 18 October 1580 Sidney promised his brother Robert, who was travelling on the Continent, 'My toyfull booke I will send with God's helpe by February',[3] which probably means that by this date he had sent the completed manuscript to a scribe for copying.

Sidney said in his dedication that he had written most of his book in the presence of the Countess of Pembroke. His first visits to his sister after her marriage were in August, September, and December 1577, when according to Molyneux the work was begun. But it probably took shape slowly, for the Arcadian characters in the *Lady of May*, which could not have been composed earlier than the spring of 1578, are described in a way which indicates that the *Old Arcadia* itself had not yet assumed definite form. Some of the poems in classical metres were probably written before Drant's death in the spring of 1578; Spenser's one early sonnet and one sestina, probably inspired by Sidney's example, indicate that poems in those forms had been composed by 1579; while OA 66 may have been written as a result of Sidney's association with Spenser in the autumn of 1579. The book was probably completed during his long visit with his sister at Wilton from March to August 1580.

The incomplete *New Arcadia*, which is a recasting and expansion of the narrative in the first two books of the *Old Arcadia*, must have been composed in 1584, the date written on the first page of Cm, the only extant manuscript. Greville, in his letter of November 1586, wrote of 'a correction of that old one don 4 or 5 years since which he left in trust with me'. I take '4 or 5 years since' as a reference to the revision, which would put its composition in the latter part of 1581 or 1582; but Greville is often inaccurate when dealing with matters of fact, and there is strong evidence to show that the revision was begun after 1582. First, the textual tradition of the *Old Arcadia* shows that Sidney continued to authorize transcriptions of the first version of his work with no more than minor changes in the text until about 1582. Second, several images in both earlier and later prose passages of the *New Arcadia* derive from *Astrophil and Stella*, which was composed in 1582. Third, many of the geographical references in the *New Arcadia* result from Sidney's study of Mercator's maps, probably those in Ptolemy's *Geographia*, 1584, though they appeared separately in 1578. Fourth, the

---

[1] Holinshed, *Chronicles* (1587 uncensored version), p. 1554.
[2] David Hume of Godscroft (a member of the Earl of Angus's train), *The History of . . . Douglas and Angus* (1648), p. 362; Thomas Howell, *Devises* (1581), E4ᵛ–F1.
[3] iii. 132. A passage in an earlier letter to Robert (iii. 125), probably written in Feb. 1579, is similar in idea and phrasing to a passage in Book IV of the *Old Arcadia* (iv. 313).

trick at the end of the *New Arcadia*, by which Cecropia apparently beheaded
Philoclea without harming her, was probably suggested by Reginald Scot's
Discoverie of Witchcraft, which was printed in 1584.[1]

(iii) *The Text of the* Old Arcadia. In dedicating the *Old Arcadia* to his sister,
Sidney said that the work had been written 'in loose sheetes of paper, most of it
in your presence, the rest, by sheetes, sent unto you, as fast as they were done'.
There is no reason to question the accuracy of his statement; but we should not
infer from it, as the 1613 editor erroneously did, that what he had written was
'never after reviewed, nor somuch as seene al together by himself' (ii. 350), for
variants in the texts of the surviving manuscripts show that Sidney retained in
his own possession a transcript of his work which he afterwards revised on at
least five different occasions.

The eight manuscripts of the *Old Arcadia* and a ninth containing the poems
only are described in the bibliography and designated by the abbreviations As,
Bo, Cl, Da, Je, Le, Ph, Qu, and St.[2] These are scribal transcripts in different
hands, with various omissions and peculiarities of reading which show that none
could have been copied from another, so all are substantive witnesses to the text.
The title of Ph indicates that it was transcribed after Sidney's death; Bo is on

---

[1] Sara R. Watson, 'Sidney at Bartholomew Fair', *PMLA* liii (1938), 125–30. Scot
notes in the margin of his account, 'This was donne by one Kingsfield of London, at
a Bartholomewtide, An. 1582'. Miss Watson suggests that Sidney may have seen this
performance; but in Aug. 1582 he was probably with his father on the borders of Wales.
It is more likely that Sidney got the suggestion for his Arcadian episode from a reading
of Scot's book, for he not only describes the apparent beheading but also gives Scot's
explanation of how the trick was done. See also D. E. Baughan, *JEGP* li (1952), 35–41.

[2] In addition to these and Cm (the manuscript of the *New Arcadia*), substantive
manuscript texts of the poems are preserved in Dd (2, 3, 35, 41, 42, 48, 51, 62), Eg (62),
Fl (17), Ha (3, 15, 64), Hn (51, 74), Hy (3, 45, 51, 60), Ma (17), and Ra (7, 13, 21, 22,
33, 38, 41, 51, 70). Aside from the 90 and 93 editions of the *Arcadia*, substantive printed
texts of the poems are also in Hn (65) and Pu (45, 61). The Hn manuscript and printed
texts probably derive from an *Old Arcadia* manuscript owned by Sir John Harington
that has since been lost; the other texts probably derive independently from copies of
individual poems circulated on separate sheets of paper or from other now lost manu-
script anthologies. Fl and Ma have agreements in error that indicate they descend from
a common ancestor; but none of the other miscellaneous texts give evidence of being
related to one another or to any other known text.

Early texts deriving from other known manuscripts or printed editions, and therefore
not substantive, are found in British Museum MS. Additional 12515 (77), Additional
15117 (45), Additional 27406 (62), Additional 34064 (2, 14, 15, 16, 21, 27, 47, 62),
Egerton 2877 (77), Harley 3511 (21), Loan 35 (34, 54), and Sloane 1925 (17, 20, 62);
Bodleian MS. Douce 280 (34), Rawlinson poet. 142 (3), Rawlinson poet. 148 (21, 68),
and Rawlinson poet. 172 (15); Corpus Christi College Oxford MS. 328 (62); National
Library of Scotland MS. 2059 (3, 8, 19, 21, 25, 27, 40, 41, 43, 46, 52, 54, 59, 60, 65, 69,
and parts of others); Viscount De L'Isle and Dudley MS. 'Arcadia' (1, 2, 4, 5, 15, 22,
25, 52, 58, and part of 62); Folger MS. 452. 4 (62); Rosenbach MS. 197 (15); and The
Melvill Book of Roundels (5). Early printed derivative texts are in Fraunce's *Arcadian
Rhetorike*, 1588 (199 lines from 31 *Old Arcadia* poems); Dowland's *Second Book*, 1600
(34); *Englands Helicon*, 1600 (4, 6, 17, 60); *Englands Parnassus*, 1600 (413 lines from
36 *Old Arcadia* poems); Jones's *Second Booke*, 1601 (21); Ravenscroft's *Pammelia*,
1609 (5); Ward's *First Set*, 1613 (30, 45); Vautor's *First Set*, 1619 (51); Peerson's *Private
Musicke*, 1620 (51); Pilkington's *Second Set*, 1624 (4); and Dousa's *Echo*, 1638 (31).

paper with the same watermark as one of Sidney's letters dated 28 December 1581; Je and Cl are on paper with a garter watermark of Elizabethan manufacture; As has written in it the name of a family agent who can be traced no later than 1583; and all are in late sixteenth-century hands. With the exception of Ph, and possibly Je and Qu, they were probably transcribed during the years 1580-2, for the watermark of Bo, which has the same state of text as St, indicates that it was probably transcribed late in 1581 or early in 1582, and all the other manuscripts derive from earlier versions of the text. After the printing of the *New Arcadia* in 1590, no incentive would have remained to justify the enormous labour of copying by hand some 180,000 words.

None of the nine manuscripts shows any appreciable trace of Sidney's characteristic pattern of spelling, and several manifest errors occurring in all of them (at **3**. 6, **7**. 60, **10**. 7, **10**. 10, **10**. 13, **10**. 47, **11**. 15, **12**. 15, **13**. 4, **13**. 80, **17**. 3, **21**. 5, **24**. 13, **26**. 7, **28**. 9, **28**. 109, **29**. 9, **29**. 49, **31**. 43, **32**. 20, **49**. 16, **50**. 19, **52**.15, and **62**. 16) indicate that they do not derive directly from the holograph original, but instead descend from it through a scribal transcript (T) which must have been Sidney's own working copy. St and As appear to be the most accurately transcribed manuscripts, closely followed by Bo, Cl, Le, and Da; but Ph, Je, and Qu are extremely corrupt with between 5 and 7 per cent. of their words wrong. The extreme inaccuracy of Ph, Je, and Qu suggests that they descend from T through intermediaries rather than directly, and other evidence corroborates this assumption. Though Ph was transcribed after Sidney's death in 1586, it contains the original version of OA 28 which was revised in T about 1581 (before St, Bo, Cl, Le, and As were transcribed); therefore it must descend from T through an intermediary (Y). Je-Qu agree in error against all the other texts in several hundred passages, which is clear evidence that they descend from T through a common intermediary (X). Since no clear patterns of agreements in error relate the other more accurate texts, they are probably direct transcripts of T.[1]

A few omissions in one or more of the extant manuscripts evidently occurred because some of the scribes overlooked items written in the margin of their original (a common failing) or because the material itself was inserted after some transcripts had been made. Only St, Je, and Qu contain the side-note to OA 13, and only St indicates the scansions of all eight quantitative poems (Cl contains seven, Bo and As four, Qu three, and the others omit the scansions entirely). These omissions appear to have been accidental or deliberate oversights. Only St contains in its margin opposite OA 11 the 'Nota' for the rules of syllabic quantities, though a blank space was left for it in As. This may have been a later addition. Cl, Le, As, Da, Ph, Qu, and probably Je (which has lost a leaf and

---

[1] In the first ten poems the nine manuscripts contain 91 errors which occur in two or more texts, in addition to almost an equal number of unique errors. In these ten poems Je-Qu agree in error in 16 passages, Da-Qu in five, and Ph-Je in four; five other combinations of texts (Bo-Qu, Cl-Da, Le-Ph, Ph-Je-Qu, Ph-Qu) have three agreements in error each, six (Bo-Je, Bo-Da, Bo-Da-Je, Cl-Le, Cl-As-Da-Qu, Da-Je) have two, and 39 combinations have one. Since most of these agreements in error indicate contradictory and therefore impossible patterns of relationship, they cannot derive from errors in the originals that were being copied but must result from mere chance. Human minds and hands are prone to similar lapses, and two or more scribes copying the same original will from time to time make identical mistakes.

consequently wants all after line 86) contain a version of OA 62 varying in length from 114 to 144 lines, a variation resulting from the presence or absence of lines 29–36, 71–76, 77–86, and 87–92. OA 62 is a catalogue poem in which the parts of a woman's anatomy are praised in orderly fashion from head to foot—lines 29–36 describe her ears, 71–76 her navel, 77–86 her belly, and 87–92 her thighs. The lines in question were evidently additions to the original draft of the poem which were inserted in the margin and which some of the scribes noticed and copied and others did not—lines 77–86 actually appear in the margin of Je.[1]

Aside from these omissions, the only variations of consequence among the manuscripts occur in the prose at the end of the First Eclogues[2] and in a few other scattered passages, and in the texts of OA 28, 29, and 62, which give every indication of being authorial revisions. Je-Qu contain, in the prose at the end of the First Eclogues, a discussion of quantitative versifying that appears in none of the other manuscripts; Je-Qu-Da-Ph contain a version of OA 28 in

[1] The appearance or absence of one or more of these four sets of lines in OA 62 is the one puzzling phenomenon that makes establishment of the order of transcription of the nine manuscripts difficult. Da, which on other evidence appears to have been transcribed relatively early, contains all four passages in its text and an alternative version of lines 69–70 in the margin; Cl-Le-As, which on other evidence appear to have been transcribed later than Da, all omit lines 29–36 and the alternative version of lines 69–70. The explanation I offer, that the lines in question were added by Sidney in the margin of his working copy—or possibly on appended slips of paper—and that some transcribers copied them and others overlooked them, makes it possible to arrange the manuscripts in order in accordance with the other evidence. Some readers may consider this more a device for the editor's convenience than an explanation. But I can think of no other theory that will explain the facts, and must reiterate that Elizabethan scribes frequently *did* omit material in the margins of their copy.

[2] After OA 13 all texts have the sentence, 'What exclaiming praises . . . through it', and then continue as follows (italics indicate material peculiar to a particular revision):

Je-Qu

. . . and then yt is neaver longe tyed (where fitt condmendacones is so likewise) ofered vnto yt. *But amongst . . . commendable* rose remembring Cleofilas hurt, and therfore though vnwillingly perswaded her to take that farre spent nightes rest and so of all sides they went to recommend them selues to the elder brother of death.

and then . . . vnto yt] *om.* Je.   rose] rare Je.   so of all] so all Qu.

Da

. . . But ye wastinge of the torches, made them finde ye nightes waste: and therefore remembring Cleofilas hurte, Basilius rose from his seate: and soe the pastoralls ended.

Ph

. . . And then is it never tong tyed from the ffitt Commendacon.

St Bo Cl [*om.* Le] As

. . . and then is it never tonge tyed where fitt commendacon (wherof woman kynde is so licorus) is offered vnto it, But the wasting of the torches served as a watch vnto theym, to make theym see the tyme waste, And therefore the Duke though vnwilling rase from his seate wch he thought excellently setled of thone syde, and considering Cleophilas late hurtes persuaded her to tak that farr spent nightes reste, And so of all sydes they went to recommende theym selves to thelder brother of Death.

hurtes] hurt Bo Cl As.

which lines 39–45 and 81–90 are different from the text in the other manuscripts; and St-Bo have the name 'Cosma' for 'Hyppa' in OA 29, and contain a 146-line version of OA 62 in which lines 25–26 are additions and 17 other scattered lines are rephrased. These variations are evidence of 'continuous copy'; that is, they indicate that all nine manuscripts were transcribed, either directly or through intermediaries, at different times from a single original which itself underwent successive revisions at the hands of the author. The manuscripts fall into four groups (Je-Qu, Da-Ph, Cl-Le-As, and St-Bo), indicating four successive stages of revision by Sidney himself. The processes of composition, revision, and transcription appear to have taken place as follows.

(1) Sidney, as he composed, presented a copy of what he had written to his sister (P), and had a scribal fair copy made for his own use (T^1). Though T^1 was executed with considerable care, it contained a few verbal errors and inadvertently omitted OA **67**. 31–33. Its First Eclogues ended with a prose debate concerning the merits of quantitative verse; in its Second Eclogues OA 28 contained several lines in a form that was later changed; and at the end of Book III, OA 62 appeared in a short version of 130 lines (probably only 114 of the 130 lines were written consecutively and lines 71–76 and 77–86 were added in the margin). After he completed his work in the latter part of 1580, Sidney allowed a transcript (X) to be made from T^1. X was carelessly executed, for it omitted OA **31**. 25 and introduced a large number of additional verbal errors; and it probably mechanically followed its original in placing OA **62**. 71–76 and 77–86 in the margin (these lines were omitted by Qu, and Je which retained them placed 77–86 in the margin). Je and Qu are carelessly made direct transcripts of X.

(2) After X had been transcribed from T^1, Sidney revised his working copy (and so transformed it into T^2) by crossing out the discussion of versification at the end of the First Eclogues and substituting a two-sentence conclusion in the margin, and by inserting in the margin of OA 62 lines 29–36 and 87–92 and an alternative version of 69–70. Da is a moderately careful transcript of T^2 which reproduces all the additions to OA 62, but only the first of the two sentences in the new conclusion to the First Eclogues. Shortly before or after Da was copied, a second transcript (Y) was made from T^2. Y was carelessly executed, for it introduced a large number of verbal errors, and though it omitted the deleted discussion of versification at the end of the First Eclogues it failed to include the new two-sentence conclusion, and it omitted all the marginal additions to OA 62 except lines 71–76. Several years later, after Sidney's death, Ph was copied from Y.

(3) After Da and Y had been transcribed from T^2, Sidney revised his working copy (and so transformed it into T^3) by probably abstracting the leaf containing the crossed-out discussion of versification at the end of the First Eclogues and making a fair copy of the substituted two-sentence conclusion on an insert sheet, and by rewriting part of OA 28 and restoring the hiatus in OA 67; but he allowed OA 62 to remain with only part of its lines written consecutively and part written in the margin. These changes were probably made sometime in 1581. Perhaps at this time he also gathered together his miscellaneous poems under the title 'Divers and Sundry [or Certain] Sonnets' and filed them with his *Arcadia* manuscript. Cl, Le, and As are fairly careful transcripts of T^3. Cl and

Le are moderately accurate and omit lines 29–36 in OA 62; As, though it generally maintains a higher level of accuracy, omits lines 29–36 and 71–86 in OA 62. At the end of Cl and written in the same hand is a collection of 31 'Dyuers and sondry Sonnettes'; these do not appear in As, nor in Le, which is a collection of Arcadian poems only.

(4) After Cl, Le, and As had been transcribed from T³, Sidney again revised his working copy (and so transformed it into T⁴) by further revising OA 62 by adding lines 25–26 and rephrasing 17 other scattered lines, and by substituting the name 'Cosma' for 'Hyppa' in OA 29. These changes were probably made about the latter part of 1581 or early part of 1582, since Bo is on paper with the same watermark as a letter of Sidney's dated December 1581. St and Bo are transcripts of T⁴, Bo being executed with fair accuracy and St being an almost perfect reproduction of its original. Bo has at its end, on the same paper and in the same hand, a collection of 27 'Certein lowse Sonnettes and songes'; St has at its end, on different paper and in a different hand, five scattered and untitled *Certain Sonnets.*

(iv) *The Text of the* New Arcadia *and the 1590 Edition.* In 1584 Sidney began a complete and radical recasting of his *Old Arcadia*; but he had only carried his revision through the first two books of the original version, by which time he had produced more than a quarter of a million words, when he broke off abruptly in the middle of a sentence. Fulke Greville reported that Sidney (probably when he went to the Netherlands in 1585) had left the unique manuscript (G) of this 'New Arcadia' in trust with him along with 'a direction sett doun vndre his own hand how and why' it was to be further amended. This manuscript has disappeared, but there are two witnesses to its text: Cambridge University MS. Kk. 1. 5 (Cm), and *The Countesse of Pembrokes Arcadia* published in 1590 by William Ponsonby (90).

Cm is a transcript of G, the manuscript Sidney left with Greville, made by an unimaginative scribe who worked hastily and therefore made many verbal errors and frequently omitted words or phrases, but otherwise mechanically copied what was before him. It consists of the narrative portion of the text only, written continuously without division into books and with no trace of the eclogues, though the narrative promises 'pastorall pastymes' at ff. 65 and 149. In the earlier part of the manuscript, where characters assume a new name, the old name is written and scored through and the new name written above; in the latter part of the manuscript blank spaces are left for many of the names. It contains or provides blank spaces for 26 poems, though only the complete text of 14 shorter poems and the opening lines of four others are preserved.

90, which was edited by Fulke Greville and Matthew Gwinne, appears to have been printed from G with some material added from an *Old Arcadia* manuscript. The narrative, which is the same as that in Cm, is divided into three books which contain the complete text of 25 poems with a blank space for a 26th (OP 3, also blank in Cm) in the same order as in Cm; eclogues with prose introductions are inserted at the end of Books I and II, the first set containing six and the second five poems. The editors appear to have followed their original conscientiously, and to have made only such changes and additions as they thought had been intended by Sidney himself. Their changes (except in OA 31) went no further than the occasional correction of manifest transcriptional errors affecting single words or phrases; their additions consisted only of dividing the work into books and chapters 'for the more ease of the Readers', of supplying the proper names and the complete texts of poems for which blank spaces had been left in the manuscript, and of adding eclogues from the *Old Arcadia* at the two places where the revised narrative itself promised 'pastorall pastymes'. The text of 90 is much more accurate than that of Cm, for in many places it preserves the correct reading where Cm is obviously in error—as i. 6. 12 'the' for Cm 'her', 6. 17 '(me thought)' for Cm 'in thought', 6. 29 'here' for Cm 'where', &c. Some of these may be conjectural emendations by the editors, but most of the superior readings in 90 must result from its following the original (G) more accurately than did the careless scribe of Cm.

Comparison of Cm and 90 shows that their common original G was a scribal copy and not a holograph, for neither of them retains more than a trace of Sidney's characteristic pattern of spelling, and in several passages both agree in manifest errors (as Cm f. 2^v and 90 i. 8. 36 'cast destruction and'; Cm f. 61^v and 90 118. 22 'shewed'; Cm f. 62 and 90 121. 21 'courrage'; &c.). In the 222 lines and two incipits of verse which Cm and 90 have in common, they agree together against the *Old Arcadia* manuscripts in 16 lines (CS **3.** 1; OA **2.** 9, **2.** 10, **2.** 11, **3.** 8, **3.** 10, 3. 11, **3.** 13, **5.** 2, **5.** 5, **14.** 13, **17.** 3, **17.** 7, **21.** 8, **21.** 15, and **74.** 1), all but four of which are certainly or probably scribal errors. The scribe of G therefore appears to have been somewhat less accurate than the one who prepared T, Sidney's working copy of his *Old Arcadia*.

Comparison of Cm and 90 also indicates that Sidney, in his own foul papers of the *New Arcadia*, instead of writing out the texts of the poems instructed his scribe to copy them from T, and that the scribe copied only a few of the shorter poems and the beginnings of others, which is what we find in Cm. Proof of this is afforded by **62.** 3, which in the earlier *Old Arcadia* manuscripts reads 'Laces made of', but which in St and Bo was revised to read 'threeds of finest'. Cm has 'lockes made of', an inaccurate transcription of the original reading, which must have appeared in G. Therefore G in copying these lines from T must have overlooked the revised reading in the margin and transcribed the original reading. But 90 has the revised reading 'threeds of finest', which could not come from G. This suggests that G contained only the opening lines of the poem (Cm has only the first eight), and that the editors of 90 went to T for the complete text, and accurately reproduced all the revisions that Sidney had written in the margin.

90's texts of OA 29 and 62 contain Sidney's latest revisions, otherwise preserved only in St and Bo (which were transcribed from T^4). But 90 also contains revisions in other poems that do not appear in any of the *Old Arcadia* manuscripts. Thus lines 9–11 in OA 2, which appears in the text of Book I in 90, contain authorial revisions; and lines 149–76 in OA 7 and several lines in OA 8, which appear in the First Eclogues in 90 and so must derive from T, are also revised. These changes show that, after making his fourth set of revisions (T^4), Sidney again went over his *Old Arcadia* manuscript and began to make a fifth set of revisions (T^5) affecting OA 2, 7, and 8. But it appears that he soon gave over making minor changes in the *Old Arcadia*, and began to rewrite his story entirely anew.

Sidney carried through less than half the recasting of his narrative, which is the incomplete *New Arcadia* preserved in Cm and 90. In this last revision he confined his attention almost entirely to the prose text. He included 23 *Old Arcadia* poems and another previously written poem (CS 3) in the new version of his story, but he composed only two or three new poems (OP 1, 2, and perhaps 3). The Delphic oracle, OA 1, he transferred to Book II of the *New Arcadia*, and when he did so he added three lines that indicate he planned a different denouement for the revised version of his story. Aside from this revision in OA 1, and the previously made revisions in OA 2, 7, and 8, the texts of the poems in the *New Arcadia* do not differ in any significant way from those of the later *Old Arcadia* manuscripts St and Bo.

Cm does not contain any eclogues, and the editors of 90 explained in a prefatory note that Sidney had postponed revision of that material 'till the worke had bene finished'; but he never completed his narrative, and so apparently never himself came to a conclusion on which eclogues 'should have bene taken, and in what maner brought in' to the *New Arcadia*. In the absence of definite instructions from the author, the editors of 90 used their own judgement and took over from the eclogues of T⁵ the poems and prose links they considered appropriate to the revised narrative, 'chosen and disposed as the overseer thought best'.

From the original First Eclogues they retained only OA 6, 7, and 12. They omitted OA 8 because Sidney had used it in the narrative of Book II; they omitted the companion poems OA 9 and 10, because the first concerned Philisides whose characterization had been altered in the revised narrative; and they omitted OA 11 and 13, probably because they did not approve of quantitative verse. To make up for the poems left out, they inserted OA 66, 67, and 71 from the Third and Fourth Eclogues. In the Second Eclogues they omitted OA 30 because Sidney had used it in the narrative of Book II; they omitted the quantitative poems OA 32, 33, and 34; and though they retained the quantitative poem OA 31, they emended it heavily and transferred it from Philisides to an unnamed shepherd. To make up for the poems left out they inserted OA 72 from the Fourth Eclogues. This was an intelligent selection generally consistent with the implications of the revised narrative; but the rearrangement destroyed the thematic unity and parallel structure that was so important a consideration in Sidney's own grouping of the First and Second Eclogues in the *Old Arcadia*.

Greville in his letter to Walsingham had said that the works Sidney left in manuscript required 'the care of his frends, not to amend for I think it fales within the reach of no man living, but only to see to the paper and other common errors of mercenary printing'. 90 appears to have been edited in that spirit, for aside from filling in the blanks left for proper names and supplying the full text of poems that were only partially copied in G, the editors appear to have contented themselves with presenting Sidney's own words as well as they could be deciphered. Because they lacked specific instructions from the author, they were forced to make their own arrangement of the eclogues; otherwise their only departure from conservative editorial practice was in silently emending OA 31. The printer of 90 did his work with moderate accuracy, for verbal errors occur only about once in every eight or ten lines of text, which is not below normal Elizabethan standards. But the narrative was incomplete and ended strangely in the middle of a sentence, and the text did contain some verbal errors.

(v) *The text of the 1593 edition.* Three years after the appearance of the 1590 edition there was published, also by William Ponsonby, a second edition of *The Countesse of Pembrokes Arcadia . . . now since the first edition augmented and ended*. This contained a preface by Hugh Sanford, secretary to the Earl of Pembroke, who said that the Countess, undertaking to wipe away the 'spottes' of the first edition, had 'begonne in correcting the faults' but 'ended in supplying the defectes'; that the improvements in the 1593 edition had been carried through 'most by her doing, all by her directing'; and that in it the reader will find 'the conclusion, not the perfection of *Arcadia*: and that no further then the Authour's own writings, or knowen determinations could direct'.

The first part of 93 reprinted the narrative portion of 90, but rearranged some of the poems in the eclogues, omitting OA 29 and inserting an entirely new poem OP 4. At the point where the *New Arcadia* narrative ended, in the middle of Zelmane's fight with Anaxius, 93 appended the complete narrative text of Books III–V of the *Old Arcadia*, with changes of the proper names and a few other small revisions designed to bring the old story into partial conformity with the new; and also appended the eclogues after Books III and IV, with some changes of the *Old Arcadia* order and the addition of a second new poem OP 5.

90 was used as printer's copy for the first part of 93; but the 'spottes' of 90, its verbal errors—which actually were not very numerous—were corrected partly by conjecture and partly by reference to a manuscript of the *New Arcadia*. This manuscript was not G, the authoritative draft of the *New Arcadia* which Sidney had left with Greville and from which 90 had been printed, but another less accurate transcript which appears to have been the still existing Cm itself. Though the editors of 93 compared the text of 90 with Cm, they did so in only a cursory fashion. Thus though they supplied from Cm words omitted by 90 at i. 11. 15 'nothing *wherewith* to', 125, 20 'mistrusting *greatly* Cecropia', and 145. 29 'to *be* witnesse of'; they also cancelled obviously authentic passages in 90 at i. 83. 4–5, 147. 34–36, 198. 31–32, and 408. 18–21 because they were omitted by Cm. In the poems, though the 93 editors corrected an error in 90 by introducing the Cm reading at OA 4. 2, they also substituted Cm errors for the correct readings of 90 at OA 5. 4, 15. 18, and 25. 4. In addition they made a few conjectural emendations that corrected manifest errors in both Cm and 90, as i. 118. 22 'sued' for 'shewed', and 121. 21 'cowardes' for 'courage'; but at the same time either they or the printer introduced an even greater number of new errors, as i. 10. 11 'of the' for 90–Cm 'of', 10. 30 'such' for 'such a', 10. 36 'corde' for 'rope', &c.

The appended Books III–V and the eclogues, which 93 printed for the first time, probably derive from the manuscript (P) of the *Old Arcadia* that Sidney himself had presented to his sister. The relationship of the Countess's now lost manuscript to the nine extant *Old Arcadia* manuscripts is somewhat difficult to determine, because the passages (in OA 28, 29, 62, and 67) that help us to trace the chronological order of Sidney's later revisions and corrections are either omitted by 93 or reprinted without change from 90. But there is some evidence in the prose that permits us to determine the characteristics of the Countess's manuscript. For example, in the prose of Book IV (iv. 265. 13) St-Bo comment on the sorrowfulness of Agelastus, 'the cares of which as it were to long to tell, so yet the effect was of an athenian senatour to become an Arcadian shepherd'; but 93 (ii. 138. 13) and the earlier *Old Arcadia* manuscripts read instead, 'wherewith hee seemed to despise the workes of nature'. And in the prose at the end of the First Eclogues, in 93 and Je-Qu Basilius calls a halt to the singing 'remembring' Pyrocles's 'hurt'; this detail is omitted in Da, Ph, and Le, but in 90, St, Bo, Cl, and As he does so 'considering' Pyrocles's 'late hurt'. These readings indicate that P is closer to Je-Qu than to the later *Old Arcadia* manuscripts, and that therefore it preserves the earliest version of Sidney's text.

Indeed, the Countess's manuscript appears to preserve a version of the text even earlier than that of any of the nine extant *Old Arcadia* manuscripts that descend from T. For example, 93 omits OA **9**. 62–65, an obvious afterthought that interrupts the linked rhymes of the terza rima, but that appears in all the *Old Arcadia* manuscripts. In OA 13 the text of 93 differs from the consensus of the *Old Arcadia* manuscripts in 38 of its 175 lines. A large proportion of these variants are manifest errors in 93; but two (lines 4 and 80) are corrections of demonstrable errors in T, and at least half a dozen others appear to be original readings of Sidney's foul papers that he later corrected or emended. Thus 93 in line 12 reads 'sweet Cyparissus', the manuscripts 'stately Ciprus tree'; and 93 in line 32 reads 'Neptunes realme would not auaile vs', the manuscripts 'Neptunes seate quyte would be dryd vp there'. Since these readings of 93 and the manuscripts both make equally good sense and both scan perfectly in accordance with Sidney's own rules for determining quantities, they have every appearance of being genuine authorial variants.

These earlier authorial variants in 93 actually lend greater authority to the descendants of T, for they indicate that after T had been transcribed Sidney proof-read it with some care and made a number of small changes in its text. Since 93 does not contain these changes, the majority of its unique variants, when they are not errors by the scribe of P, must be readings that Sidney himself later discarded.

It has already been shown that the nine extant *Old Arcadia* manuscripts agree in a small number of errors because they descend from the scribal transcript T. That 93 does not show any trace of these errors is additional proof that it derives, not from T, but from the 'loose sheetes' which Sidney said he had sent to his sister. Whether these 'loose sheetes' (P) were Sidney's holographs or scribal copies is a debatable question. If we can guess the appearance of the foul papers of the *Old Arcadia* from the holograph Morgan Library manuscript of Sidney's *Defence of the Earl of Leicester*, with its numerous excisions and interlineations, they would have been unsightly and difficult to read, not at all a proper manuscript to present as a gift. Furthermore, 93 does not reproduce Sidney's characteristic pattern of spelling, though the printer (as the text of OP 4 shows) appears to have been influenced by the spelling of his manuscript copy. Thus what little evidence there is favours the assumption that P was a scribal transcript rather than the holograph foul papers themselves.

In addition to printing the last three books of 93 from P, the Countess also used her *Old Arcadia* manuscript as the basis for occasional corrections in the text of the poems she reprinted from 90. But her collations were neither complete nor accurate, for she or her assistants compared with P the texts of only nine of the 33 *Old Arcadia* poems in 90 (OA 7, 8, 26, 30, 31, 71, 72, 74, 75). For example, in 90 the text of OA 71 contained nine errors; the Countess corrected three of these, allowed six to remain, and added one new error. She noticed that the editors of 90 had emended the text of OA 31 and quite properly restored the *Old Arcadia* text, but in the process she introduced five new errors. She also noticed that a 20-line passage in OA 7 was different from that of her own manuscript and restored the earlier readings; but the text of 90 preserved a later revision that had been made by Sidney himself. On the other hand, OA 28 and 62, which had also been revised by Sidney, she allowed to stand in their revised form, and reprinted them from 90 with only six changes, four of which were successful conjectural emendations and two of which were new errors.

Books III–V of the *Old Arcadia*, which 93 printed from P, for the most part contain the wording of the other *Old Arcadia* manuscripts; but a few changes were introduced, mainly for the purpose of bringing the last part of the older narrative into conformity with the revised first part.[1] Proper names and titles that had been altered in the revision are made consistent, and references to past actions are omitted or altered to conform to the revised narrative. These are all minor changes that could have been made independently by any editor.

Of more importance is a second set of revisions that significantly modify the conduct of the heroes. In the *Old Arcadia*, Musidorus while eloping with Pamela breaks his vow of respecting her chastity by making ready to attack her while she sleeps (iv. 190, 285–6); but in 93, by the deletion of 22 lines, all reference to his intended attack is omitted (ii. 27, 118–19). Again, in the *Old Arcadia* Pyrocles visits Philoclea's chamber expressly for the purpose of seducing her (iv. 215–27); but in 93 he does so only to persuade her to flee with him to his own country in order that they may be married (ii. 51–61). These changes in the conduct of the heroes necessitate some revision of the final trial scene, though the revisions are not carried out consistently. In the trial scene of the *Old Arcadia* Pyrocles confesses that he had attempted, though unsuccessfully, to rape Philoclea, and is therefore condemned to be thrown from a high tower, while Musidorus who is accused only of abduction is condemned to be beheaded (iv. 358–89). In 93 Pyrocles maintains that he visited Philoclea only to persuade her to flee with him; but Philanax in his charge still says he had confessed rape, and though Euarchus in his summing up says both princes are 'equallie culpable' of abduction, he assigns each a different punishment as in the *Old Arcadia* (ii. 177–207). A third set of revisions, though they do not affect the characterization or plot, considerably change the accounts of how and why Euarchus and Kalodulus come to Arcadia (iv. 331–3 and 381; ii. 149–53 and 199).

Scholarly opinion has been divided on the question of who was responsible for these changes. Zandvoort and Wiles assume that the Countess of Pembroke introduced all but the third set of changes on her own authority, and accuse her of bowdlerizing her brother's work; Myrick and Rowe[2] argue that the revisions

---

[1] Most of the changes have been tabulated and analysed by Zandvoort, pp. 27–40, and A. G. D. Wiles, *SP* xxxix (1942), 167–206.

[2] See preceding note and K. O. Myrick, *Sir Philip Sidney as a Literary Craftsman*, 1935, pp. 285–9, and K. T. Rowe, *PMLA* liv (1939), 122–38. Rowe suggests that Sidney wrote out the changes in Books III–V in his own *Old Arcadia* manuscript which the Countess of Pembroke later used for 93; but Sidney's own manuscript was T⁵, and the textual evidence proves that the Countess used her own earlier and unrevised manuscript P.

are in accord with the more serious ethical tone of the *New Arcadia* and conclude that the changes appearing in 93 had been authorized by Sidney himself. The latter hypothesis is attractive, especially since Greville in his letter to Walsingham said that Sidney had left 'a direction sett doun undre his own hand how and why' his *New Arcadia* was to be 'amended'. But the direction is not extant, and we are left to wonder whether Sidney did wish to change the conduct of his heroes when we notice that in the earlier part of his revision he sometimes accentuated rather than toned down their amorousness. Thus in the *Old Arcadia* (iv. 116) Pyrocles and Philoclea kissed and 'passed the promys of mariage'; but in retelling the episode in the *New Arcadia* (i. 261), after they kissed Sidney added, 'which faine Pyrocles would have sealed with the chiefe armes of his desire, but Philoclea commaunded the contrary; and yet they passed the promise of mariage'. Evidence of another kind, less subject to personal interpretations, is needed before the question of who was responsible for the changes in 93 can be decided. This evidence can be obtained, I believe, by investigating the apparently unrelated subject of the sources of the geographical references in the *Old* and *New Arcadia*.

The geography of the *Old Arcadia* is vague, sometimes inaccurate, and embodies no specialized knowledge beyond recollection of general reading in the Roman poets and Greek and Latin historians. We are given the names of 23 countries, seven cities, two rivers, and one valley of the eastern Mediterranean regions—all places frequently mentioned in classical writings. Arcadia is improperly described as having a sea-coast and none of its neighbouring states in the Peloponnesus are mentioned; we are told the name of one city within its borders (Mantinea—mentioned by Herodotus, Plutarch, and others), and one town (Phagona, a name invented from φαγών, glutton).

But in the *New Arcadia* more than thirty new place-names are introduced, and the geography becomes clear and precise. The heroes, instead of wandering over all Asia Minor, Palestine, and Egypt—too great an expanse of territory for the adventures of a single year, confine their travels to a small area of Asia Minor. Arcadia is now accurately described as landlocked, and we are given the names of seven cities, two rivers, and a mountain within its boundaries. Evidently before undertaking his revision Sidney must have made a special study of the geography of Greece and Asia Minor in order to give his action a local habitation as well as a name. As Brie (p. 210) noted, he may have consulted Strabo VIII. viii for his revised description of Arcadia; but he could not have derived all his new geographical information from Strabo or from any of the other ancients. He must have studied maps of his own time for some of his place-names and for the boundaries of the various countries.

Of all the sixteenth-century maps of the eastern Mediterranean region, the only ones I have found adequate for explaining the geographical references of the *New Arcadia* are those prepared by Mercator for the edition of Ptolemy's *Geographiae Libri Octo* published at Cologne early in 1584 (and apparently also issued separately in 1578). Mercator's Map X of Europe provides a more detailed delineation of Greece than any other map published in the sixteenth century. The island of Cythera appears off the coast of Laconia. Arcadia is shown as landlocked, and the location of nine cities and two mountain ranges within its borders are indicated. The boundaries of the other countries of the Peloponnesus are outlined, making it possible to trace the itinerary of Musidorus in his search for Pyrocles (i. 74). Mercator's Map I of Asia provides all the information we need to follow the wanderings of the princes in Asia Minor. Paphlagonia is shown as a province of Galatia, which explains why Sidney used both names in his famous episode of the 'unkind king' that provided Shakespeare the germ of *King Lear*.

Most of 93's departures from the *Old Arcadia* text involve no more than the deletion of material, the change of a word, or the replacing of a sentence here and there. Only two passages contain any considerable amount of new writing—the accounts of the visit of Pyrocles to Philoclea's chamber and of the journey of Euarchus to Arcadia—each of which contains about four pages of completely new material. In the first episode, in the *Old Arcadia* (iv. 215–27) Pyrocles goes to Philoclea's chamber 'to satisfy his greedy desyer', he places her on her bed and there comes into his mind a song detailing the beauties of a woman's anatomy (OA 62), and the author leaves him 'feighting ageanst a Weyke resistance whiche did stryve to bee overcome'. The *New Arcadia* transferred OA 62 to an earlier episode where Pyrocles saw Philoclea bathing in the river Ladon. In 93 (ii. 51–61) when he goes to her chamber he does so only for the purpose of eloping with her. He hopes they may reach the frontiers of Arcadia and receive help from the Helots, who were 'newly againe up in armes against the Nobilitie', and he imagines himself 'safelie arrived with his Ladie at the stately pallace of Pella . . . geving order for . . . sumptuous shewes and triumphes against their mariage'. Philoclea agrees to flee with him to Macedon, but is so overcome with emotion that she is unable to travel; so both fall asleep, with only their necks 'subject each to others chaste embracements'.

In the second episode, in the *Old Arcadia* (iv. 331–3) when Euarchus of Macedon hears of the retirement of his 'Neighboure' Basilius of Arcadia, he decides to visit him and accordingly sails to the 'Arcadian shore' and lands at a port not far from Mantinea. In the *New Arcadia* (ii. 149–53) Euarchus, having fortified the western coast of his country to prevent an invasion from Italy, agrees to aid Queen Erona who is imprisoned in Armenia. He accordingly sails from his port of Aulon for Byzantium to raise a force for her release. But on the way southward around the Peloponnesus his ships are scattered by a storm and he is cast upon the 'coast of Laconia', which he finds devastated because a second civil war had broken out between the Helots and the nobles; so he goes inland to the peaceful country of Arcadia to await the reassembly of his fleet.

These two episodes are closely linked by the reference in each to the second uprising of the Helots, which is not mentioned elsewhere in either the *Old* or *New Arcadia*, and by the fact that only a person who had studied Mercator's maps could have corrected the *Old Arcadia* errors and supplied the details of Pyrocles's intended and Euarchus's actual journey. Though Pella (named once in a different context in the *Old Arcadia*, iv. 381) was known as the birth-place of Philip and Alexander; in ancient times Macedonia did not extend westward to the coast, and Aulon (modern Valona in Albania) was of no consequence. But in Mercator's map Macedonia is shown extending from sea to sea in northern Greece, with the capital city of Pella on the east and the principal port of Aulon on the west, just as it is described in 93.

These two episodes could not have been written by any editor, but only by

Sidney himself. And if Sidney revised the account of the visit of Pyrocles to Philoclea's chamber, then it is probable that he at least authorized the deletion of Musidorus's intended attack on Pamela, and the revisions in the trial scene. The 'direction' Greville said that Sidney had left with him must have consisted of several sheets of paper in which the episodes of Cleophila's chamber and Euarchus's journey to Arcadia, and perhaps some other detached paragraphs, were written out substantially as they appear in 93, with a general instruction to bring the rest of the narrative into conformity with these changes.

Thus the narrative portion of the last three books of 93 preserves several additional pages of Sidney's own composition and gives us some imperfect hints of how he intended to continue his revision of the story. But the handling of the eclogues in 93 was considerably less satisfactory. Greville said that Sidney himself had not decided 'which should have bene taken, and in what manner brought in', and there is nothing to indicate that the Countess of Pembroke had any knowledge of her brother's plans for grouping the eclogues beyond what could be learned from the *Old Arcadia*.

Some rearrangement of the *Old Arcadia* eclogues was necessary, because Sidney had himself transferred five of the poems to the narrative text of the *New Arcadia*, and furthermore had revised his fictional self-portrait, Philisides, by making him the lover of a 'Star' (Stella) rather than of Mira, and in the process had transferred three poems dealing with Mira (OA 62, 73, 74) to other characters. The editors of 90 gave full consideration to the changes that had been introduced in the incomplete revision, and in their own careful selection of material for the eclogues excluded all references to Philisides, which was in evident harmony with Sidney's own intentions. But the editors of 93, instead of following the implications of the text before them and the lead of the 90 editors, mechanically rearranged the poems in the eclogues to conform to their original order in the *Old Arcadia*, but with some strange inconsistencies. This was an indefensible procedure, for it involved restoring OA 75 to its original place in the Fourth Eclogues, though it appears that Sidney himself had placed it in the *New Arcadia* narrative, and of telling at length the original story of Philisides, which Sidney's own narrative indicated he intended either to omit or revise. And even so they did not consistently restore the *Old Arcadia* order, but transferred OA 9 and 10, omitted in 90, from the First Eclogues to the second, and OA 71 and 72 from the Fourth Eclogues to the Second. Furthermore, they transferred OA 70 from its original position in the narrative of Book IV to the Fourth Eclogues, and unaccountably omitted the pleasantly humorous OA 29.

The 93 editors also failed to note an indication in the *New Arcadia* of a change Sidney intended to make in the final denouement, which is the most unsatisfactory part of the *Old Arcadia*. At their trial Pyrocles and Musidorus are, first, jointly accused of responsibility for the supposed murder of Basilius, which they both deny; and second, Pyrocles is accused of offering violence to Philoclea and Musidorus of abducting Pamela, which they both admit. Euarchus finds the evidence to support the first charge insufficient, but in accordance with the laws of the country condemns them to death on the second. Even when he learns that the two young men are his son and nephew he insists that the sentence be carried out, saying 'yf Rightly I have judged, then rightly I have judged myne owne Children' (iv. 383). But then the supposedly dead Basilius revives, and pardons the princes by abrogating the laws. This completely undercuts the heroic adherence of Euarchus to 'sacred Rightfullnes', for the princes escape punishment, not by any revelation of a change in the nature of their offence, but by coming before a less impartial and less idealistic judge. Sidney himself apparently became aware of the ethical ambiguity of this scene, and when he transferred OA 62 to the middle of Book II of his *New Arcadia*, he began to prepare for a different handling of the trial by removing all references to the heroes' attempts upon the chastity of the princesses. But he must have realized that this would not solve the essential difficulty, for the princes would still be guilty of the crime of abduction. However, as he was writing the last part of Book II of his *New Arcadia* he saw how to solve the problem—he revised the oracle (OA 1) to indicate that the charge against the heroes would be, not elopement with the princesses, but responsibility for the death of Basilius. By this change, when Basilius revives there has been no crime committed, and even Euarchus with his determination never 'to chaunge the never chaunging Justice' may pardon the princes without inconsistency. But though Sidney indicated his final intention in his revision of the oracle, he did not carry through the changes in the trial scene itself.

John Florio was justified in his criticism of the 1593 edition when he said that 'this end wee see of it . . . now is not answerable to the precedents'; though he was unduly harsh on the editors when he said they did 'more marring that was well, then mending what was amisse' (*Essayes of Montaigne*, 1603, R3). The Countess of Pembroke and her assistants appear to have performed their editorial labours, if not with perfect accuracy and consistency, at least conservatively. They do not appear to have introduced any significant changes in the narrative beyond those warranted by Sidney's written instructions, they preserved three poems and at least two passages of prose that otherwise would have been lost, and they provided the story with a 'conclusion' of sorts from Sidney's own writings. They could not provide the 'perfection' of the *New Arcadia* because Sidney had not finished it and did not fully spell out his intentions in the 'direction' he left behind.

The 1593 text, containing the *New Arcadia* 'ended' by the addition of the last three books of the *Old*, was reprinted without significant change in all subsequent folio editions. It is a tribute to the vitality of Sidney's writing that this strange hermaphrodite, two different versions of the story with a narrative hiatus in the middle, continued to be the most admired and most popular work of English fiction for more than a century. But today I believe we should read the *New Arcadia* in a text based only upon the narrative part of 90 corrected by Cm, the *Old Arcadia* in a text based upon St and corrected by the other manuscripts, with the changes introduced in the last three books of 93 indicated in appended notes, and the Eclogues only in the order in which they appear in the *Old Arcadia*, for their rearrangement in 90 and 93 destroys their artistic unity.

(vi) *Editorial procedure*. The relationships of the extant texts, described in the preceding discussion, is summarized in the diagram on p. 380.

The extant texts all derive from three now lost manuscripts. The most important of these (T) was a scribal transcript that Sidney himself used as his working copy, and in which he later made minor revisions on five different occasions. T can be reconstructed from the nine *Old Arcadia* manuscripts and

from the poems printed in 90 that do not appear in Cm. The second in impor-
tance (P) was the 'loose sheetes' of the first draft of the *Old Arcadia*, probably
also scribal transcripts, that Sidney presented to his sister. P can be partially
reconstructed from the additions to 90 that appear in 93. The third (G) was a
scribal transcript of Sidney's revised version, the incomplete *New Arcadia*.
G can be reconstructed from Cm and 90.

These three lost transcripts were executed by scribes working under Sidney's
own supervision; but being transcripts they inevitably contained a few scribal
errors, even after being proof-read, that were transmitted to their descendants.
Some of these errors can be detected by a comparison of the reconstructed

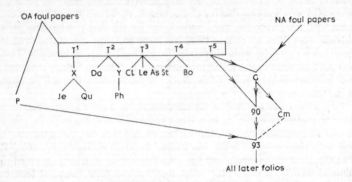

readings of T, P, and G; but more than half of the poems are preserved in texts
that descend only from T, and errors in these must be corrected by conjectural
emendation. I have therefore admitted emendations into the critical text at
3. 6, **7.** 60, **24.** 13, and **29.** 9. Where T and P differ in readings that appear
equally appropriate in their contexts, I accept the reading of T because it con-
tains Sidney's later revisions and corrections. I accept unique readings in 93
only when the consensus of the *Old Arcadia* manuscripts is manifestly in error.

The logical choice of copy text for an edition of the complete *Old Arcadia*
would be St, because it is slightly more accurate in wording than the other
substantive witnesses and contains the latest state of the *Old Arcadia* text; but
it does not contain all of Sidney's revisions in the poems (some of which appear
only in 90), and its spelling, which is no closer to Sidney's own than that of the
other texts, and its lack of punctuation, are likely to confuse the present-day
reader. 90 and 93 are almost as accurate in wording as St, taken together they
contain Sidney's latest revisions, and on the whole they are adequately punctu-
ated in accordance with Elizabethan principles. I therefore use 90 as copy text
for all the poems it contains except OA 31, which was improperly emended by
the editors; 93 for the remaining poems it printed; and St for the five poems
(OA 23, 24, 35, 36, 37) that do not appear in the early printed editions.

In constructing the critical text all substantive variants have been taken into
account, but as a general rule only variants occurring in two or more substantive
texts have been listed in the apparatus. The poems are printed in the order in
which they first appeared in the *Old Arcadia*, for which they were first composed,

and later changes in order or assignment of speakers are indicated in the notes. The order of the eclogues in the *Old Arcadia*, 90, and 93 is shown in the following table.

Old Arcadia	1590	1593
FIRST ECLOGUES		
6 Arcadians	6 Arcadians	6 Arcadians
7 Lalus and Dorus	7 Lalus and Dorus	7 Thyrsis and Dorus
8 Dicus	[8 Miso in Bk. II]	[8 Miso in Bk. II]
9 Geron and Philisides		
10 Geron and Mastix		
	66 young shepherd	
	67 Geron and Histor	
	71 Strephon and Klaius reported by Lamon	
11 Dorus		11 Dorus
12 Cleophila	12 Zelmane	12 Zelmane
13 Dorus and Cleophila		13 Dorus and Zelmane
		OP 4 reported by Lamon
SECOND ECLOGUES		
27 Arcadians	27 Arcadians	27 Arcadians
28 Dicus and Dorus	28 Dicus and Dorus	28 Dicus and Dorus
29 Nico and Pas	29 Nico and Pas	
		71 Strephon and Klaius reported by Histor and Damon
30 Plangus and Boulon reported by Histor	[30 Plangus and Basilius in in Bk. II]	[30 Plangus and Basilius in Bk. II]
	72 Strephon and Klaius reported by Lamon	72 Strephon and Klaius reported by Histor and Damon
		9 Geron and Philisides
		10 Geron and Mastix
31 Philisides	31 young shepherd	31 Philisides
32 Cleophila		32 Zelmane
33 Cleophila		33 Zelmane
34 Dorus		34 Dorus
THIRD ECLOGUES		
63 Dicus		63 Dicus
64 Nico		64 Nico
65 Pas		65 Pas
		OP 5 Philisides
66 Philisides		66 Philisides
67 Geron and Histor		67 Geron and Histor
FOURTH ECLOGUES		
71 Strephon and Klaius		
72 Strephon and Klaius		
73 Philisides	[73 Amphialus in Bk. III]	[73 Amphialus in Bk. III]

Old Arcadia	1590	1593
74 Philisides	[74 Dorus in Bk. III]	[74 Dorus in Bk. III]
		70 Agelastus [from Bk. IV]
75 Dicus	[75 unnamed in Bk. III]	75 unnamed
76 Agelastus		76 unnamed

NAMES OF THE RECITERS OR COMPOSERS OF THE POEMS

Agelastus (ἀγέλαστος, not laughing): 70, 76.

Alethes (ἀληθής, truthful): 3.

Arcadian shepherds: 6, 27.

Aristomenes: 44 and 68 (composed by Musidorus).

Basilius (βασιλεύς, ruler): 15, 26, 38, 52, 55, 59, 69.

Boulon (βουλεύω, counsel): 30 (with Plangus—reported by Histor).

Charita (χάρις, grace): 45 (composed by Musidorus).

Cleophila (an anagram of Philoclea), name assumed by Pyrocles.

Dametas: 5, 25, 46 (composed by Musidorus).

Delphic Oracle: 1.

Dicus (δίκη, right, custom): 8, 28 (with Musidorus), 63, 75.

Dorus, name assumed by Musidorus.

Geron (γέρων, old man): 9 (with Philisides), 10 (with Mastix), 67 (with Histor).

Gynecia (γυναικεῖος, womanly): 22, 40, 41, 42, 43, 54 (58 motto on potion).

Histor (ἱστορία, history): 30 (reporting Plangus and Boulon), 67 (with Geron).

Klaius (κλαίω, weep): 71 and 72 (with Strephon).

Lalus (λάλος, babbler): 7 (with Musidorus).

Mastix (μάστιξ, scourge): 10 (with Geron).

Musidorus (Μοῦσα δῶρον, gift of the Muses): 4, 7 (with Lalus), 11, 13 (with Pyrocles), 16, 17, 23, 28 (with Dicus), 34, 35, 36, 44 (attributed to Aristomenes), 45 (attributed to Charita), 46 (attributed to Dametas), 49, 50 (with Pamela), 51, 68 (attributed to Aristomenes), 77.

Nico (νίκη, victory): 29 (with Pas), 64.

Pamela (παμ-μελι, all sweetness): 47, 48, 50 (with Musidorus).

Pas (πᾶς, the whole): 29 (with Nico), 65.

Philisides (φιλ-sidus, lover of a constellation or star, Philip Sidney): 9 (with Geron), 24, 31, 62 (reported by Pyrocles), 66, 73, 74.

Philoclea (φίλος κλέος, lover of glory): 18, 19, 53, 60, 61.

Plangus (plangor—lamentation): 30 (with Boulon—reported by Histor).

Pyrocles (πῦρ κλέος, fire and glory): 2, 12, 13 (with Musidorus), 14, 20, 21, 32, 33, 37, 39, 56, 57, 62 (reporting Philisides).

Strephon (στρέφω, writhe): 71 and 72 (with Klaius).

DEDICATION

This was printed before the 1590 edition of the incomplete *New Arcadia*, the only substantive text, and reprinted in all later folios. As Dobell noted, it obviously was composed to accompany a completed work ('now, it is done'), and therefore must have been written in 1580 to accompany the finished manuscript copy (P) of the *Old Arcadia* which Sidney presented to his sister. The fact that it was printed in the 1590 edition indicates that the editors, Greville and Gwinne, consulted the Countess of Pembroke, and that she co-operated with them at least to the extent of providing a copy of this dedicatory letter, just as they three years later transmitted to her Sidney's 'direction' for amending the *New Arcadia*. The Countess of Pembroke's dedicatory poem to the metaphrase of the Psalms shows how entirely she reciprocated her brother's affection and admiration.

Even in the intimacy of his own family Sidney assumed a mask and maintained the pose of graceful negligence that was expected of a renaissance gentleman. His 'idle worke' had consumed most of his leisure for some three years; the 'trifle, and that triflinglie handled' ran to some 180,000 words, and was a composition more carefully structured and more artfully executed than anything in English of its time.

THE FIRST BOOK OR ACT

I

Basilius, Duke of Arcadia, consults the Delphic oracle about his future and receives this reply, which summarizes in riddling fashion the plot of the narrative that follows. To avoid the misfortunes that are prophesied, he hands the government over to a regent and retires into the country with his wife and two daughters; but everything foretold comes to pass.

Pyrocles, son of King Euarchus of Macedon, and his cousin Musidorus, Duke of Thessaly, visit Arcadia, hear of the two princesses living in retirement, and to gain access to them disguise themselves as an Amazon named Cleophila and a shepherd named Dorus. Basilius's elder daughter Pamela elopes with Musidorus (the Arcadians think she has been abducted), but is brought back by some shepherds (lines 1–2). His younger daughter Philoclea takes Pyrocles as her lover, who is disguised as a woman (lines 3–4). Basilius and his wife Gynecia fall in love with the disguised Pyrocles, who makes an assignation with both of them for the same night; Basilius meets Gynecia in the dark, and thinking she is Pyrocles commits adultery with his wife (line 10). Basilius drinks what Gynecia had supposed was a harmless love potion and falls into a swoon with the appearance of death (lines 6–7). At this point King Euarchus arrives in Arcadia, accepts the office of protector of the country (line 8), and condemns Gynecia for causing the death of Basilius, and Pyrocles and Musidorus for their violence toward the princesses. But before the sentences can be carried out, Basilius revives and pardons everyone. All this takes place within a single year.

The text of the oracle is reported at the very beginning of the *Old Arcadia*, but in the *New Arcadia* it is not revealed until the end of Book II. Lines 5–7, added in the 1584 revision, show that Sidney planned a different denouement for the *New Arcadia*, for they indicate that Pyrocles and Musidorus marry Philoclea and Pamela before their trial, and that the main point at issue in the trial is that they are accused of responsibility for the supposed death of Basilius rather than of violence toward the princesses. The seven-line *Old Arcadia* text was first printed (from Ph) by Bertram Dobell in the *Quarterly Review*, ccxi (1909), 83.

6 *beer*, bier.

2

Pyrocles, disguised as the Amazon Cleophila, expresses his love for Philoclea in this 'songe'. It is the first of the 18 sonnets, in nine different rhyme schemes, that Sidney wrote for the *Old Arcadia*. The only earlier English poets to write more than an occasional sonnet were Wyatt, Surrey, the anonymous translator in British Museum MS. Additional 36529, and Gascoigne.

6 *faintly*, timidly.

9–11. The revision, preserved in 90–93 and Cm, was made after St and Bo had been transcribed; it regularizes the rhetorical structure, and gives clearer emphasis to the idea of the lover's enforced servitude.

3

The boorish shepherd Dametas, to whose care the Princess Pamela had been entrusted, had an ugly and ill-natured daughter named Mopsa (probably from Mopsus, a shepherd in Virgil's *Eclogues*) whose praises had been set forth in verse by Alethes, 'an honest man of that tyme'. In the *New Arcadia* the verses are reported by Kalander as having been written by 'a pleasant fellow' of his acquaintance. There are many precedents for this kind of ironic praise, a form of 'contreblason' (see notes to OA 62). Skelton, in his *Garland of Laurel* (lines 926–53 and 1038–61) pretended to praise one lady by comparing her to Canace and Phaedra, who were incestuous, and another by comparing her to Pasiphae, who loved a bull. Stowe, in his edition of Chaucer (1561, Ppp 6), printed *A balade pleasaunte* in which a lady is praised whose 'beautie is to none other like', whose 'skin is smothe as any Oxes tong', and who is meek as a hornet. C. W. Lemmi (*MLN* xlii [1927], 78) cited Francesco Berni's sonnet, beginning 'Chiome d'argento fin', in which a lady is described as having 'un bel viso d'oro', 'occhi di perle vaghi', and 'bocca ampia celeste'.

1 *What length of verse*. The verse is the popular long-lined poulter's measure, which Sidney considered awkward and old fashioned, and the burlesque is heightened by indenting the 14 lines like a Surreyan sonnet.

3 *shrewdly*, severely.

5–8. Saturn is ugly, Venus wanton, Pan rough and shaggy, Juno wrathful, Isis faced like a cow, Cupid blind, Vulcan lame, and Momus censorious.

6 *Isis faste*. All the texts read 'Iris', the beautiful messenger of the gods who *is* 'fast', which is not ironical; so 'Iris' must be a slip of the pen in T for 'Isis', and 'faste' must be a variant spelling of 'faced' (see OA **10.** 76 and **68.** 1).

8–13. The variants in 90–93 and Cm are not revisions, but inferior readings resulting from repetitions and substitutions by the scribe of G (thus in 8 'god Momus', who is not a god, repeats 'god Vulcan's' from 7).

9–12. Jacinth is blue or yellow, opal many-coloured, crapal (crapaud) stone the jewel in the head of a toad described in the bestiaries, and untried (unsmelted) silver ore black.

13–14. Opposite these lines W. Blount quotes Ovid's account of Phoebus gazing upon Daphne, 'si qua latent meliora putat' [*Met.* i. 502].

14 *well*. The scribes differ in their reading of T, for 'e' and 'i' are often difficult to distinguish in secretary hand. Sidney may have written St-Bo-As-Dd's 'will'.

4

Musidorus, in order to be near Pamela, changes clothes with the shepherd Menalcas (the name is from Virgil's *Eclogues*), and then sings these 'verses'. Francis Pilkington, *The Second Set of Madrigals and Pastorals* (1624), No. 14, provided a setting for five voices of lines 5–10.

1 *become*, befit.
2 *tryes*, experiences.
3 *guest*, his body in shepherd's clothes.
9 *power*, pour.

5

When Pamela was attacked by a bear her guardian, the cowardly Dametas, hid in a bush; but his servant Dorus (Musidorus) killed the bear and saved the princess. When the danger was past Dametas came from his hiding-place and 'sange this Songe, for Joy of *theyre* success'. Damoetas is a traditional name for a shepherd used by Theocritus and Virgil. The variants in the *New Arcadia* texts derive from scribal errors in G. This was set as a round for six voices by Thomas Ravenscroft, *Pammelia* (1609), No. 95.

THE FIRST ECLOGUES

6

The Arcadian shepherds begin their pastoral sports before Basilius and his entourage by holding hands and dancing in a circle 'singing some shorte Coup-lettes, whereto the one half beginning, the other half answered'. Their song announces the theme of unrequited love which is the subject of the following poems.

7

Lalus, accounted one of the best singers among the shepherds, began 'first with his pype, and then with his voyce' to challenge Dorus (Musidorus). The song contest was a standard fixture of the classical pastoral (see LM 2 and note), but Sidney here plays the game in accordance with far more difficult rules, which he appears to have learned from the second eclogue of Sannazaro's *Arcadia* and perhaps from the third song in the sixth book of Montemayor's *Diana*. Though he in part imitates the general structure and metrical form of Sannazaro and Montemayor's poems, the content and phrasing are his own.

Lalus, believing Dorus to be no more than a simple shepherd, urges him to sing, and Dorus at first refuses. Lalus, not perceiving the ingenuity of his refusal, which consists entirely of proverbs feigning 'plaine speach' but artfully grouped together, issues a direct challenge which Dorus accepts (lines 1–24). In the contest itself (lines 25–166), which consists of seven pairs of answer poems (see note to OA 24), Lalus sets the pattern, and Dorus exhibits his technical virtuosity by replying in stanzas of the same metrical form, and using images similar to those Lalus applies to Kala changes the meaning to apply to his own love for Pamela. Lalus begins in terza rima with three-syllable rhyme, but is not able to keep up the pace and descends to feminine and then to masculine rhyme (lines 26–114). In an effort to outdistance Dorus, who has easily followed him, he shifts to an intricate system of medial rhyme in which the final syllable of one line is made to rhyme with the fourth syllable of the following line (lines 115–46). When Dorus follows him in this device also, in a final desperate effort he changes to an intricate five-line stanza rhyming a⁵b³c⁵c³b⁵ (lines 147–66); but Dorus surpasses him by beginning his reply with the last line of Lalus's stanza and then repeating the same form. The roles are now reversed, for Lalus is forced to reply to Dorus by beginning with his last line. He manages to do so for one stanza, but when Dorus again successfully caps his effort, he returns to the terza rima with which he had begun and acknowledges defeat. Dorus, like Spenser's Calidore later, courteously insists that Lalus is the better singer.

Sannazaro had begun with terza rima in feminine rhyme, shifted to medial rhyme, and ended with five-line linked stanzas; Montemayor had begun with terza rima, first in feminine and then in masculine rhyme, continued with five-line linked stanzas and eight-line stanzas, and ended with terza rima. Sidney's metrical form (he experimented with simpler varieties of it in OA 9 and 28) is even more intricate than that of his models, his images are more ingeniously paralleled, and he handles the turns and changes in the contest with far more dramatic skill. His practice here justifies his argument in the *Defence of Poesie* that English is superior to the other modern languages because it provides a greater variety of rhymes, for the Italians use feminine and three-syllable (*sdrucciola*) rhyme, but not masculine; the French masculine and feminine rhyme, but not three-syllable; 'where the English hath all three' (iii. 44–45). Sir John Harington especially admired Sidney's polysyllabic rhymes and quoted this poem, though he suggested that 'to part them with a one syllable meeter between them would give it best grace. For . . . I would have the eare fed but not cloyed with these pleasing and sweet falling meeters' (*Orlando Furioso*, 1591, ¶ 8ᵛ).

1 *Lalus* is a young shepherd, mentioned again in OA 29 and 67, whose marriage with Kala is celebrated in OA 63; in the *Lady of May* the name had been used for an old shepherd. 93 changes Lalus to Thyrsus throughout except in OA 67.

6. Cf. Sidney's criticism of the professor of learning who 'using art to shew art and not [to] hide art . . . flieth from nature, and indeed abuseth art' (*Defence of Poesie*, iii. 43).

10 *heard*, herd. *singled*, separated.

11. Cf. LM **2.** 14.

24 *Her*, Pamela's. *learne*, show or teach.

35 *peized*, weighed.

46 *confection*, a combination of objects.

60 *sheep*. T's 'keepe' makes no sense in this context and must be a scribal error.

61 *harnished*, an eye rhyme for 'harnised', clad in armour.

63 *varnished*, embellished.

71 *and . . . pleasure*, and if the failing of hope should end the pleasure of life.

85–96. Dorus here refers to the episode at the end of Book I when Pamela, pursued by the bear, had swooned in fear. He killed the bear and took Pamela in his arms; but when she recovered from her swoon, she 'with greate disdayne putt him from her' (iv. 48).

103 *prove*, experience.

117–19. W. Blount quotes Virgil (*Ecl.* ii. 19–21):

> Despectus tibi sum nec, qui sim, quaeris, Alexi,
> Quam dives pecoris, nivei quam lactis abundans:
> Mille meae Siculis errant in montibus agnae;
> Lac mihi non aestate novum, non frigore defit.

138 *waymenting*, lamenting.

151 *moulde*, shape.

163 *growe like a shade*, increase like a shadow.

165. While that sun (Pamela) shines.

175–6 *hart . . . facilitie*. 90's 'soule' and 'agilitie' are probably errors rather than authorial revisions.

8

After Lalus and Dorus had praised their mistresses, the grave shepherd Dicus, who hated love, came with a whip in one hand, a naked Cupid in the other, and wearing on his breast:

A paynted Table, wherein hee had given Cupide a quite newe forme, making him sitt upon a payre of gallows like a Hangman, aboute whiche there was a Rope very handsomely provyded; hee him self paynted all ragged and torne so that his Skinne was bare in moste places, where a man mighte perceyve his body full of eyes, his heade horned with the hornes of a Bull, with longe eares, accordingly, his face ould and wrinckled and his feete Cloven. In his Right hand hee was paynted holdinge a Crowne of Lawrell, in his lefte a purse of money, and oute of his mouthe hange a lase, whiche helde the pictures of a goodly man and an excellent fayre woman.

The 'paynted Table' and verses that follow form an emblem in the manner, but not with the matter, of Alciati, whose No. 107, 'Vis Amoris', pictures Cupid conventionally as a naked, winged boy with a bow and arrow. In the *New Arcadia* this poem is transferred to the old hag Miso who recites it in Book II; this removes an inconsistency in the characterization of Dicus, who praises married love in OA 63.

Sidney appears to have carried the last correction and revision of his *Old Arcadia* manuscript (T⁵) through this poem, for the changes in lines 6, 23, and 41–42 appearing in 90 are definite improvements and seem to be authorial (but in line 31 'dayly' looks like an error made by a compositor mentally substituting a common for an uncommon modifier). 93 returns to the earlier OA readings of P.

1–2 *Poore*, incompetent. *silly*, ignorant. Cf. Horace, *AP* 1.

10. Cupid caused Phoebus to fall in love with Daphne (Ovid, *Met.* i. 452 ff.). That Love was the youngest and oldest of the gods had been a commonplace since the time of Plato (*Symposium*, 178 B and 195 A).

11–12. The arrow of gold kindles love, that of lead causes disdain (*Met.* i. 470–1); the third arrow with the head of horn (for cuckoldry) is Sidney's invention.

13–18. Jove's amour with Io, her transformation into a heifer, and being guarded by Argus who was killed by Mercury, is narrated in *Met.* i. 588 ff. That the hundred-eyed Argus begot Cupid on Io is Sidney's invention.

18 *fact*, deed.

21 *runnagate*, vagabond.

47 *hang-man*, the most debased and shameful of all occupations; so at the end of the *Old Arcadia* Dametas is punished by being made a hangman.

9

Young Histor, shocked at Dicus's irreverence, begins to tell in prose the story of Erona, which illustrates Cupid's revenge on those who are disrespectful to him. Geron interrupts him, and turning to the melancholy Philisides (Sidney—see notes to OA 73), 'thus began his Eglogue unto him'. 90 omitted this and its companion poem OA 10, and 93 transferred both to the Second Eclogues. The poem begins with an attack on women similar to Mantuan's fourth eclogue, and concludes with advice on how to fall out of love reminiscent of Ovid's *Remedia Amoris*; but Sidney's immediate model appears to have been the eighth eclogue of Sannazaro's *Arcadia*, in which Eugenio attempts to relieve the love melancholy of Clonico with good advice. Sannazaro wrote his eclogue in terza rima throughout, but Sidney has a more intricate metrical structure in which the changes in verse form are related to changes in the tone of the discussion. He also improves upon Sannazaro by dramatically developing the clash of character between old Geron and young Philisides.

39 *Jurate*, jurat, sworn witness.

53–55. The idea had been a commonplace since the time of Ovid (*Heroides*, v. 115–16); but Sidney here directly translates lines 10–12 of Sannazaro's eighth eclogue:

> Nel'onde solca e nel'arene semena;
> E'l vago vento spera in rete accogliere
> Chi sue speranze fonda in cor de femina.

He later boasted that he was 'no pick-purse of another's wit' (AS 74) and, so far as I am aware, his translation of these lines is the only verbatim borrowing in all his verse. This one departure from his principles apparently preyed upon his mind, for after he had finished the poem and after P had been transcribed he acknowledged his indebtedness by adding lines 62–65, whose couplets interrupt the linked rhymes of the terza rima.

59–61. Cf. OA **31**. 37, and lines 57–58 of Dyer's 'He that his mirth hath lost',

> O fraile unconstant kynd, and safe in trust to noe man,
> Noe woemen angels be, and loe, my mystris is a woeman.

60 *coi'de*, appeased or coaxed.

81–82. Professor R. W. Dent called to my attention Antipater's remark about the old orator Demades, that he was like an animal that had been eaten at a sacrificial feast, there was left only the belly and the tongue (Plutarch, *Moralia*, 183F, *Life of Phocion*, 741E).

101 *raynes*, reins or loins.

109 *way*, weigh.

121–30. Geron's prescriptions are similar to those of Sannazaro's Eugenio (lines 121 ff.), but are even closer to Ovid's *Remedia Amoris*, lines 315–16 and 178–210.

10

Geron, angered because Philisides does not accept his advice, sees his dogs
fighting and speaks to them 'as yf in them a man shoulde fynde more obaydience,
then in unbrydeled younge men'. His old acquaintance Mastix, who 'beheld no
body but with a mynde of mislike', joins him in berating youth; but Geron then
turns upon him also. Geron's speech contains a slight admixture of unusual
words, which appear to be intended, not as archaisms (though uncommon, most
of them were current in Elizabethan times), but as country speech, the real
language of a shepherd. 90 omitted this poem and 93 transferred it to the end
of the Second Eclogues.

   1 *Melampus*, the name of one of Actaeon's dogs (Ovid, *Met*. iii. 206).
   7 *Laelaps*, another of Actaeon's dogs (*Met*. iii. 211). Since Sidney's 'p' and
'x' look much alike, the scribe of T probably read his 'Lelaps' as 'Lelanx'.
   9 *jarle*, quarrel.
   10 *brim*, breme, fierce.
   19 *grewe*, Greek.
   20 *narr*, nearer.
   22 *snebb*, snub.
   23 *red*, advised.
   26 *saddest*, gravest. *out*, confused.
   33 *bonnet vaile*, take off the hat in token of respect.
   34 '*I con thee thanke*', (You say) 'I thank you.'
   47. 'Blowe point', &c., are children's games. The omission of 'els at' in the
manuscripts results from a scribal error in T.
   58 *cocklinges cockred*, young cocks (or pampered ones) pampered.
   60 *man-wood*, fierce as a man.
   73 *siker*, certainly.
   73–87. This etiological fable, similar in type to Ovid's story of why the raven
is black (*Met*. ii. 534 ff.), is probably Sidney's invention. Cf. OA 8.

11

Dorus (Musidorus), gazing at Pamela and accompanying himself on a lute,
sang these 'Eligiac' verses. His song repeats the laments that he and Pyrocles
had earlier expressed in prose: 'Alas what farther evill hathe fortune reserved
for us? what shall bee the ende of this oure tragicall pilgrimage? Shipwrackes,
Daily daungers, absence from oure Contry, have at lengthe broughte forthe this
Captiving of us within our selves, whiche hathe transformed the one in Sexe,
and the other in state, as muche as the uttermoste worcke of changeable fortune
can be extended unto' (iv. 39).
   At the end of the First Eclogues, Je and Qu contain a passage (deleted in the
later manuscripts, perhaps because its substance appeared in the *Defence of
Poesie*, iii. 44) in which Dicus and Lalus debate the relative merits of measured
and rhyming verse (I emend and punctuate; for a *literatim* text see *PQ* xxix
[1950], 72.)

Dicus said that since verses had ther chefe ornament, if not eand, in musike, those
which were just appropriated to musicke did best obtaine ther ende, or at lest were the

most adorned; but those must needes most agree with musicke, since musike standing principally upon the sound and the quantitie, to answere the sound they brought wordes, and to answer the quantity they brought measure. So that for every sem[i]brefe or minam, it had his silable matched unto it with a long foote or a short foote, wheron they drew on certaine names (as dactylus, spondeus, trocheas, etc.), and without wresting the word did as it were kindly accompanie the time, so that eyther by [the] tune a poet should strayght know how every word should be measured unto it, or by the verse as soone find out the full quantity of the musike. Besides that it hath in it self a kind (as a man may well call it) of secret musicke, since by the measure one may perceave some verses running with a high note fitt for great matters, some with a light foote fitt for no greater then amorous conceytes. Wher, sayd he, those rimes we comonly use, observing nothing but the number of sylables as to make it of viii, x, or xii feete (saving perchaunce that some have some care of the accent); the musicke, finding it confused, is forced somtime to make a quaver of that which is ruffe and heavy in the mouth, and at an other time to hould up in a long that which, being perchaunce but a light vowell, would be gone with a breath; and for all this comes at leng[t]h a hinc, inck, blirum and lirum for a riming recompence. . . .

Lalus on the other side would have denied his first proposition, and sayd that since musike brought a measured quantity with it, therfor the wordes lesse needed it, but as musicke brought tune and measure, so thes verses brought wordes and rime, which wer foure beawties for the other three. And yet to denye further the streng[t]h of his speach, he sayd Dicus did much abuse the dignitie of poetry to apply it to musicke, since rather musicke is a servaunt to poetry, for by [the one] the eare only, by the other the mind was pleased. And therfor what doth most adorne woordes, levelled within a proportion of number, to that musicke must bee implied; which if it cannot doe it well it is the musitions fault and not the poettes, since the poet is to looke but to beawtifie his wordes to the most delight, which no doubt is more had by the rime, especially to common eares to which the poet doth most direct his studies, and therfore is caled the popular philosopher. And yet in this the finest judgment shall have more pleasure, since he that rimes observes somthinge the measure but much the rime, wheras the other attendes only measure without all respect of rime; besides the accent, which the rimer regardeth of which the former hath litle or none.

The attempt to write vernacular verse in accordance with Latin quantitative principles was a preoccupation of a small number of renaissance humanists and learned poets. The earliest attempts appear to have been made at the end of the fifteenth century in France, where by 1562 they received the advocacy of Ramus in his *Gramere*. Baïf and Courville's Académie de Poésie et de Musique, founded at Paris in 1570, had as its main object the recital of *vers mesurés* to a musical accompaniment; while Baïf's *Etrènes de Poézie Fransoèze* (1574) contained examples of quantitative verse of his own composition in an adaptation of the phonetic alphabet devised by Ramus. In Italy the Accademia della Nuova Poesia, and Claudio Tolomei's *Versi e Regole della Nuova Poesia Toscana* (1539), sought to acclimatize quantitative metres. In England, Ascham in his *Scholemaster* told how he had discussed the application of the Latin quantitative system to English verse with Cheke and Watson at Cambridge in the early 1540's; though the only extant results of their discussions were a dozen lines by Watson and Ascham himself, printed in *Toxophilus* and the *Scholemaster*, and another dozen or so published by James Sandford and John Grange in 1576 and 1577.

The earliest reference to Sidney's experiments is in Spenser's letter to Harvey of October 1579, in which he said that Master Sidney and Master Dyer had proclaimed 'a general surceasing and silence of balde Rymers', and instead had 'prescribed certaine Lawes and rules of Quantities of English sillables for English Verse . . . and drawen mee to their faction'. Sidney may have heard of the experiments with measured verse during his youthful travels in France and Italy (the musical analogies he used in defending them suggest that he may have attended or heard of the recitals at Baïf's Académie); but his 'rules', Spenser reported, were 'the very same which M. Drant devised, but enlarged with M. Sidneys own judgement'. Thomas Drant had been at Cambridge shortly after the time of Watson and Ascham; so Sidney's main inspiration was probably of English origin, in direct line from Watson and Ascham through Drant. He probably began his classical experiments before Drant's death in April 1578.

The rhythmical pattern of Sidney's other verse is controlled by stress; but in his 'measured' experiments he imitates the patterns of Latin verse with a system of quantitatively long and short syllables. Therefore he ignores normal English stress where it conflicts with the quantitative pattern, though unfortunately he does not achieve the quantitative pattern itself without 'wresting the word', that is without arbitrarily assigning quantities to some syllables that are at variance with normal Elizabethan pronunciation. Sidney's rules for scansion, preserved only in a 'Nota' appended to OA 11 in the margin of St, are as follows (I emend and repunctuate the text for ease in reading).

The rules observed in thies Englishe measurde verses be thies:

[1] Consonant before consonant allwayes longe, except a mute and a liquide (as 'rĕfrayne') suche indiffrent.

[2] Single consonantes comonly shorte, but suche as have a dowble sownde (as 'lăck', 'will' 'till') or suche as the vowell before dothe produce longe (as 'hāte', 'debāte').

[3] Vowell before vowell or dipthonge before vowell allwayes shorte, except suche an exclamacon as 'ōh'; els the dipthonges allwayes longe and the single vowells short.

[4] Bicause our tonge being full of consonantes and monasillables, the vowell slydes awaye quicklier then in Greeke or Latin, which be full of vowells and longe wordes; yet are suche vowells longe as the pronounciacon makes longe (as 'glōry', 'lādy'), and suche like as seeame to have a dipthonge sownde (as 'shōw', 'blōw', 'dȳe', 'hȳe').

[5] Elisiones, when one vowell metes with another, used indifferently as thadvantaige of the verse best serves; for so in our ordinarie speache we do (for as well we saye 'thow art' as 'th'art'), and like scope dothe Petrarche take to hym self sometymes to use apostrophe sometymes not.

[6] For the wordes derived out of Latin and other Languages, they are measured as they are dennisinde in englishe and not as before they came over Sea (for we say not 'fortŭnate' tho the Latin saye 'fortūna', nor 'usŭry' but 'ūsury' in the first); so our language hath a speciall gifte in altringe theym and making theym our owne.

[7] Some wordes especially short.

[8] Particles used nowe long, nowe shorte (as 'bŭt', 'ŏr', 'nŏr', 'ŏn', 'tŏ').

[9] Some wordes, as they have divers pronounciacons, to be written dyversly (as some saye 'thōugh', some pronounce it 'thŏ').

[10] As for 'wĕe', 'thĕe', 'shĕe', thoughe they maye seeme to be a dowble vowell by the wronge orthographi, be heere shorte, being in deed no other then the greek iota; and the lik of our 'o', which some write dowble in this worde 'dŏo'.

Analysis of Sidney's 13 poems in measured verse indicates that he follows these 'rules' with fair consistency. Rule 1, the Latin rule of length by position overrides all others. Thus the syllable 'tune' in 'misfortŭne is' is naturally short, but in 'Fortūne Nature' it becomes long by position (in applying this principle the letter 'h' is not considered a consonant either alone or in combination—'ăs he ordrĕth hĭs heart'). Sidney follows this first rule meticulously (in the first hundred quantitative lines in the *Old Arcadia* there are only three places where he fails to count a syllable long by position—**11.** 18, **12.** 14, **13.** 30); but its application depends upon the eye only, for it is made to operate even when it distorts normal Elizabethan pronunciation ('trĭumph', 'shĭnĭng').

Rules 2 and 3 are also essentially visual devices. The combinations 'ck' and 'll' do not actually have a double sound, but by doubling or not doubling consonants Sidney produces longs and shorts at will ('infernāll', 'vassăl'); and in determining natural vowel length he is sometimes guided more by spelling than by his ear and so falls into strange contradictions ('dīē', 'bў'; 'wōe', 'lŏ'; 'mōōving', 'prŏve'). Elision (rule 5) is likewise more of a mechanical device for shaping a line to Latin feet than a rhythmical principle—thus **31.** 4 'Echo, aproche' is elided, even though the sense demands a strong pause between the words.

Rules 4 and 6 properly specify that the length of syllables should be determined by English pronunciation; but like his contemporary H. B., who in *Certen observacons for Latyne and English versyfyinge* (1589, A2) complained of 'the uncertaine and variable judgement of the eare', Sidney found it difficult to distinguish the natural quantity of English sounds. Thus he regularly wrote 'alās', 'ăs'; 'becōme', 'cŏme'; 'hēre', 'hĕrein'; 'hūmor', 'hŭmorists'; and 'whĭch', 'rĭches'. Other words, such as 'can', 'go', 'have', 'may', 'say', and 'they', he sometimes counted naturally long and at other times naturally short. In addition his rules 7, 8, and 9 allow many arbitrary variations. He does not specify the words 'especially short' according to rule 7, but inspection of his verses reveals more than fifty monosyllabic words which he regularly counts short by nature, though similar sounds when they occur in other words he counts long. Thus 'do', 'how', 'lo', 'made', and 'there' are always short; but 'you', 'thou', 'those', 'they', and 'their' are always long.

By applying Sidney's rules it is possible to scan his lines so that the eye perceives his syllables to fit the patterns of Latin metres; but when read aloud many of his lines do not sound like verse to English ears. This is because the rules themselves incongruously yoke contradictory principles. The quantities of syllables are determined first by their position, otherwise by their natural sound; but the Latin rule of position is not valid for determining the length of English syllables, and its mechanical application results in patterns of scansion that continually clash with Elizabethan pronunciation. Since Sidney measures his lines by artificial rules that are divorced from phonetic actualities, a passage such as CS **26.** 5–6,

$$- \;\; \smile\smile- \;\; \smile\; - \;\smile$$
With violence of heavn'ly

$$- \;\; \smile\smile- \;\; \smile\; - \;\smile$$
Beautie tied to vertue,

may have the appearance of, but cannot be read aloud to sound like verse.

But very few of his quantitative lines grate as harshly on the ear as these, and it must be remembered that all the *Old Arcadia* measured poems are described as being sung, sometimes to an instrumental accompaniment, and not as being recited by themselves. Dicus, in his defence of measured verse, pointed out that each syllable of a word should be matched to a long or short note of the music, so that by the tune of the music the poet or listener 'should strayght know how every word should be measured'. But unfortunately the effect of Sidney's verses when accompanied by music must remain a matter of theory only, for he never provided any notes of his own or any hint of the tunes which could be used. (See note to OA 34.)

Sidney himself was aware of the clash of his measures with normal English pronunciation, and though he never succeeded in writing truly quantitative verse in which the rhythmical pattern is determined by the natural quantity of English syllables rather than by arbitrary rules, in two of his poems (OA 32 and CS 5) he did succeed in so ordering his syllables that the artificial and natural quantitative patterns coincide, and in which in addition the quantitatively long syllables are also those that normally receive stress in English, so that the quantitative pattern produces a regular stress pattern. But he did not continue his experiments in this kind, and his Elizabethan followers practised only 'artificial versifying', which gave precedence to the Latin rule of position, despite its conflict with normal pronunciation. None of their work in this kind was truly successful as poetry. (See G. D. Willcock's excellent article, 'Passing Pitefull Hexameters', *MLR* xxix [1934], 1–19.)

The scansion model for OA 11 fails to indicate the allowable substitutions, for in the hexameter either a dactyl or spondee may appear in any of the first four feet and the last foot may end with a short syllable, and in the pentameter a dactyl or spondee may appear in either of the first two feet. The first distich should be scanned:

$$\text{Fortune, | Nature, | Love, long | have con|tended a|bout me,}$$

$$\text{Which should | most mise|ries, || cast on a | worme that I | am.}$$

In line 8 the original spelling may have been 'misshapps' to make the first syllable long; in line 14 the final syllable of 'agonies' is long by nature (cf. OA **13.** 89), and in line 18 'a' is counted short even though it is long by position. Sidney apparently at first considered the practice of measured verse a characteristically noble and courtly accomplishment, for in the *Old Arcadia* none of the ordinary shepherds use it, only the princes Pyrocles and Musidorus, and Philisides (who is Sidney himself); but by the time of composing the *New Arcadia* he may have changed his opinion; for he has the boorish Dametas write a hexameter (OP 2). The 90 editors did not share Sidney's enthusiasm for these experiments, and omitted all the quantitative poems except OA 12 and 31; but 93 restored them to the Eclogues.

9 *choller adusted*: when choler (one of the four humours of the body) becomes adusted (loses its moisture through heat), melancholy results. Cf. CS **17.** 52.

12 *Heraclitus*, of Ephesus (the Latin scansion is Hēraclĭtŭs), who bewailed 'the weakenesse of mankinde, and the wretchednesse of the world' (*Defence*, iii. 22). W. Blount quotes him as saying, 'Quis sit diuitiarum modus queris, primus habere quod necesse est proximus quod sat est.' He lived in the early fifth century B.C., so the reference to him is an anachronism in the *Arcadia*.

14 *a bewtye divine*, Pamela.

15 *left'st*, from P, is grammatically correct; 'lefte' derives from a scribal error in T.

12

When Dorus finished, Cleophila (Pyrocles) took up the lute and, gazing at Philoclea, 'sange these sapphickes, speaking as yt were to her [i.e. his] own hope'. His purpose is to express his affection for Philoclea without revealing to the other members of the assembly that his Amazonian costume is a disguise, and his hope is that Philoclea will penetrate his disguise; but she does not. The scansion model fails to indicate that the final syllable of each line may be either long or short. Greville (*Caelica* 6) has a set of rhymed quantitative sapphics; and cf. OA 59 and CS 5. Horace used the stanza in 25 of his odes.

2 *she*, Philoclea, and likewise in 20, 21, 26, and 27.

4 *we*, Pyrocles and his hope.

15 *thĕ mūte*, an emendation in 90-93, Ph, and Da to correct the metre; the omission of 'the' was probably a scribal error in T. St improperly emends to 'mūētt'.

13

The disguised Musidorus and Pyrocles together sing of their loves 'in a secrett maner', hoping that the 'partys intended' (Pamela and Philoclea) will understand their meaning; but they are no more successful than Shakespeare's Viola was when she addressed Orsino in similar fashion. The metre is hexameter (as in OA 31) and except for line 130, where 'high' is first considered short and then considered long, appears to be correct according to Sidney's own rules. Elisions or contractions not indicated graphically in the text are needed in lines 6, 16, 29, 34, 36, 50, 57, 63, 72, 77, 87, 97, 98, 110, and 115. 90 omits this poem. 93, taking its text from P, preserves the correct reading in lines 4 and 80 where the manuscripts descending from T are manifestly in error; 93 may also preserve readings of Sidney's first draft, that he later corrected or revised, in lines 12, 21, 32, 40, 76, 77, 82, and 121.

1 *Lady*, Pyrocles disguised as an Amazon.

8 *Worthy shepeheard*, the disguised Musidorus.

9 *sacred Muse*, Philoclea.

15 *Idea*, the Platonic 'Ĭdĕă' or Ideal, the 'fore conceit' of an artist's work (iii. 8); but Musidorus's 'Ĭdĕă' is a real woman, Pamela.

16 *manly affection*. The required elision throws the emphasis on 'man'—Musidorus, even though disguised, appears as a man and can express his love for a woman; Pyrocles, disguised as a woman, cannot.

19-20. Since 'soules' is the subject of the sentence, 'they do love' and 'their love' would be expected; Pyrocles's 'we' and 'our', which he continues through line 32, is intended to indicate that he too is 'vaild in a contrary subject', is disguised in the clothes of the opposite sex.

38 *Which*, who.

57 *gratefull*, pleasing.

64-68. W. Blount quotes Virgil (*Ecl.* i. 59-63):

Ante leves ergo pascentur in aethere cervi
et freta destituent nudos in litore piscis . .
quam nostro illius labatur pectore voltus.

72 *by*, in.

80 *rich*, an emendation by Cl and Le of an error in T; the correctness of the emendation is proved by line 78.

84 *puppet*, cf. 'Puppettes (whose motyons stoode onely upon her pleasure)' (iv. 107). *abuse*, deceive.

84–86. Poirier (*Études Anglaises*, xi [1958], 154) suggested that Sidney drew two of his three examples from Gosson's *Schoole of Abuse*, 1579 (ed. Arber, p. 58); but Sidney's phrasing is quite different, and the expressions are proverbial.

97 *to estates which still be adherent*, which always accompany high position.

105 *disgest*, digest.

113–40. Lists of this kind had been popular ever since Ovid, who in *Met*. x. 90 ff. named 11 of Sidney's 16 trees. Except for the hurtful shadow of the fig in line 125, the characteristics which Sidney assigns (some deriving ultimately from Pliny and Plutarch) were common knowledge in his time. The fig was usually referred to as having a sweet fruit and a bitter root (Plutarch, *Quaest. Conv.* v. ix).

121 *Ewe*, yew. *boy*, Cupid.

123 *barrein* refers to the tree. Plutarch (*Quaest. Conv.* II. vi) observes that though firs grow great, some bear no fruit at all.

THE SECOND BOOK OR ACT

14

Cleophila (Pyrocles), accompanying himself on a lute, sings of his love for Philoclea.

15

The elderly Basilius sings of his love for Cleophila, 'Love having renewed bothe his Invention and voyce'. For an amusing imitation of this poem see Rosenbach MS. 197 in the bibliography.

8 *honour*. 93 here consulted Cm and adopted its scribal error 'homage'.

16

Dorus (Musidorus), in order to gain access to Pamela, pretends to court her servant Mopsa. Accompanying himself on a harp, he sings this 'passyonate songe' really addressed to Pamela. His song is simply constructed on two schemes, the anaphora of 'since' and the anadiplosis of 'sight . . . sight', &c. The rhymes indicate two five-line stanzas, but all texts follow the sense and by spacing indicate a 4–4–2 division.

17

Dorus narrates the earlier adventures of Musidorus in such a way that Pamela understands that he is telling his own story. Noticing her interest, he takes up his harp and sings these 'verses'.

3 *On*, the reading of G, appears to be the preferable idiom; T's 'in' is probably a scribal error.

7 *whyle*, the reading of T, is the form   dney uses elsewhere.

18

Philoclea, before Pyrocles came to Arcadia, had found in a grove 'a fayre white Marble stone, that shoulde seeme had bene dedicated in auncyent tyme, to the Sylvan goddes', and had written these words upon it. W. Blount notes, as a similar situation, Dido's oath in *Aeneid* iv. 24–27.

19

Philoclea, after falling in love with Cleophila (Pyrocles), returns by moonlight to the marble stone, and finding the ink of her earlier writing worn and blotted, composes this 'retraction' of her former verses.

1 *blaze*, emblazon, picture.

4 *shame*. Six of the eleven copyists were led by the preceding plural 'Blots' to write 'shames'.

8 *store*, plenty.

20

Cleophila (Pyrocles), who is himself in love with Philoclea, but is receiving the amorous attentions of Basilius and Gynecia, laments his situation. His song is a heaping of contraries, a device which Sidney gently ridiculed in AS 6.

9–10. Cf. OA **8.** 9–10.

21

Cleophila (Pyrocles) 'tooke a Willow stick and wrote in a Sandy Bancke these verses'. This was set to music by Robert Jones, *The Second Booke of Songs* (1601), No. 11.

5 *watrie eyes*. An emendation by 90, St, and Cl of a d–e graphical error in T. Cf. OA **36.** 8.

22

Gynecia, in love with Cleophila (Pyrocles) and jealous of the attentions he is showing her daughter Philoclea, 'there came into her mynde, an oulde songe, whiche shee thoughte did well figure her fortune'. This is not a sonnet, but two stanzas of rhyme royal.

23

Dorus (Musidorus), in the fields with the shepherds and overjoyed at indications of Pamela's favour, sings a song continuing the imagery of OA 17. This and OA 24, the answer by Philisides, were omitted in the *New Arcadia* because the role of Philisides had been changed. The two poems were first printed (from Ph) by Bertram Dobell in *The Quarterly Review*, ccxi (1909), 96–97. They are not sonnets, but 12 lines of terza rima with a concluding couplet.

2 *sonne's approche*, the favour of Pamela.

24

Philisides (Sidney), 'as if Dorus joye had ben a remembrance to his sorrowe, tuninge his voyce in dolefull maner, Thus made answere unto hym, using the burdne of his owne wordes'. The writing of 'answers' or 'replies', which parallel the structure and in part the phrasing of another poem but reverse the sentiments, was a favourite device of both English and continental poets of the sixteenth century. There are examples in Tottel (Nos. 199 and 20, 243 and 26, &c.), the *Paradise of Dainty Devices* (Nos. 73 and 74), and elsewhere, the most successful being Ralegh's 'Reply' to Marlowe's 'Come live with me and be my love'. Sidney himself wrote an answer to a poem by Dyer (CS 16), and used the device again in OA 36 and 37, and variations of it in the responsive songs LM 2, OA 6, 7, 9, 27, 28, 29, and 71.

OA 23 and 24 are more elaborate than any 'answers' heretofore attempted in English, for they not only repeat the structure but also use the same rhyme words, a device possibly suggested by Gil Polo's two sonnets with identical rhyme words in Book III of the *Diana Enamorada*, though a less complex form had been used in English as early as 1548 in a pair of ballads on Stephen Gardiner. Sidney probably wrote OA 24 first and then patterned OA 23 upon it, for the rhyme word 'flowes' makes very little sense in OA **23. 4.**

1 *Leave of*, leave off, stop your feeding.

2 *My sonne is gon*, Mira has withdrawn her favour.

7 *filde*, field.

13 *Leave off my sheep*. OA 23 indicates that Sidney intended to repeat the same phrase at the beginning of lines 1, 4, 7, 10, and 13; 'Leave Leaving not' is a scribal error in T, from which all extant texts descend.

25

When the rebellious Phagonians attack the lodges, Dametas hides in a cave with Pamela. After the rioters have been quieted, he comes playing on a gittern, 'with no less lifted up Countenaunce, then yf hee had passed over the bellyes of all his enemyse: So wyse a poynte hee thoughte hee had performed in using the naturall strength of his cave'. 93 has adopted readings from Cm in lines 4 and 7.

4. Let the man who wishes to receive blows ('that bobs will have') be mocked ('be bob'd'). The reading 'bob'd' is correct because it continues the anaphora of lines 1–3; 'bold' results from misreading 'b' as 'l', letters which are easily confused in secretary hand.

8 *make brave lame shows* has a double meaning: 'make a gorgious-paltry exhibition', and 'show how their courage has lamed them'.

26

Basilius, thinking that by the quelling of the rebellion the terms of the oracle have been fulfilled, with his wife and daughters gives thanks to Apollo, the god of the oracle, in this 'Hymne'. The mythological details of the song are taken from Ovid's *Metamorphoses*, but its spirit is entirely Christian.

1. So Phaethon addressed his father:

> O lux immensi publica mundi,
> Phoebe pater'
>
> (*Met.* ii. 35–36.)

2 *little world*, the microcosm, the mind of man. *dost*, 'Apollo' is the subject here, and the antecedent of 'Which' in the following line.

5–6. After the flood which overwhelmed the world had receded, the huge serpent Python was born from the mud of the Nile and was killed by the young archer-god Apollo (*Met.* i. 434–44). W. Blount noted that 'Apollo' comes from 'the verbe ἀπολλυμ to kill because he consumd thos pestilent vapours left after the deluge causing putrefaction'. The fifteenth-century *Ovide Moralisé en Prose* (ed. C. de Boer, 1954, p. 64) interpreted Python as the devil and Apollo as Christ.

7–8. Latona (Leto) was prevented by the anger of Juno from remaining any-where at rest, and finally bore the twins Apollo and Diana on the floating island of Delos (*Met.* vi. 332–8).

8. Shows how difficult it is to learn what is good.

THE SECOND ECLOGUES

27

The Rude tumulte of the Phagonians gave occasyon to the honest Shepeheardes, to begin theyre Pastoralles this day with a Daunce whiche they called *The Skirmish betuixt Reason and Passyon*, For, Seaven Shepeardes whiche were named the *Reasonable* Shepe-heardes joyned them selves, fowre of them making a square and other twoo goyng a litle wyde of eyther syde, like winges of the Mayne battell, and the seaventh Man fore-moste lyke the forlorne hope, to begyn the skirmish. In like order came oute the Seaven *Passionate* Shepeheardes, all keeping the pace of theyre foote by theyre voyce, and sondry Consorted instrumentes they helde in theyre Armes: And first the foremoste of the *Reasonable* syde began to singe . . . . And the other that mett with him answered.

Their song announces the theme of the following poems, just as OA 6 did in the First Eclogues.

17. 'Then (as they approched nearer) Twoo of *Reasons* syde (as yf they shott att the other) thus sange.'

29. 'Then did the twoo Square Battells meete, and (in steade of feighting) embrace one an other, singing thus.'

28

'Dicus, that had in this tyme taken a greate lyking of Dorus [Musidorus] for the good partes hee found above his age in hym, had delighte to taste the fruites of his wittes: Thoughe in a Subject [love], whiche hee hym self moste of all other dyspysed, and so entered into speeche with hym in the maner of this followyng Eglogue.' The metrical pattern, in which terza rima alternates with lines con-taining medial rhyme (73–96, 102–8), is in part similar to that of OA 7. The authorial revisions in lines 39–45 and 81–90, made in T³, provide a better ordering of images and improve the rhymes. 93 in reprinting 90 corrected three of its errors (in lines 42, 85, 112) by conjecture, but allowed 20 others to stand.

9 *doubt*. An emendation by 90 of a scribal error in T.

35 *proofe*, experience.

45. Love's hands are bountifulness and could never have skill in frugality.

53 *framed*, disposed.

67 *mischiefes*, misfortunes.

72 *that's*. Metre requires the contraction indicated in 90–93 only.

29

When Dicus and Dorus finish their discussion of love, 'Owte startes a jolly yonker, his name was Nico: whose tungue had borne a very ytching silence all this whyle, and having spyed one Pas a Mate of his, as madd as hym self, both (in deede) Laddes to clyme up any Tree in the worlde, hee bestowed this maner of Salutatyon uppon hym, and was with like reverence requyted'. Their rustic flyting is a comic interlude, similar in function to the humorous fable of Cupid the hangman in the First Eclogues (OA 8), showing, as Sidney remarked of the pastoral singing match in his *Defence of Poesie* (iii. 22), 'that contentions for trifles, can get but a trifling victory'. It was printed after OA 28 by 90, but omitted by 93 and the later folios and not reprinted until Grosart's edition in 1873.

Sidney ordinarily treated the pastoral seriously, but he was fully aware of the thinness of the line dividing its artful simplicity from bathos, and in this poem by a process of deliberate coarsening he transformed the idyl into a vehicle for farce. Part of its humour arises from the contrast developed between the awkward rusticity of the shepherds and their pretensions to artistic skill, just as elsewhere in the *Arcadia* the affectations of Dametas and Mopsa provide matter for low comedy; but its most laughable effects are gained from its parody of Virgil's third Eclogue, whose lines every Elizabethan schoolboy would know almost by heart. Sidney's poem contains the conventional four parts: the preliminary banter of the shepherds (lines 1–26), the wager (lines 27–50), the singing match itself (lines 51–147), and the judgement (lines 148–50); but the situations which Virgil treats with dignity and grace, Sidney exaggerates for comic effect.

The mention of Dorcas (line 8), who is not elsewhere referred to in the *Old Arcadia* but who had appeared in the *Lady of May*, as had Lalus (line 14), suggests that this poem may have been written in 1578 or even earlier. I find no influence in either direction between Sidney's poem and Spenser's 'August'; nor do I find convincing the suggestion of M. Y. Hughes (*Virgil and Spenser*, 1929, pp. 271–86) that Sidney made use of Baïf's fourth eclogue. The first fifty lines are composed of six iambic feet, the accentual equivalent of Virgil's hexameters; the amoebaean lines of the singing match are in terza rima, which after Boccaccio's eclogues in the *Ameto* had become the standard verse form for Italian pastorals.

1–26. Virgil begins in similar fashion. I quote Abraham Fleming's awkwardly literal translation, published in 1575 'for the benefite of young learners', which is itself an unconscious burlesque of the original:

M[enalcas].　　Damoetas, tel's whose beasts be these, doth Melibey them owe?
D[amoetas].　　No sure, but Aegon, Aegon gave them me in grasse to goe.
M.　　　　　　O sheepe, alwaies unhappy beasts, whiles he Neaera trim,
Doth nourishe, fearing least that she should love me, more then him.
He is anothers herdman, twise an hower he mylkes the sheepe,
The juyce from Cattell, and from Lambs the milke is stolne to keepe.
D.　　　　　　That spareingly to men these things put forth must be well wat,
We know who lyk'te thee, when the gotes did looke awry thereat
And in what place, the gentle Nimphes dyd laugh perceiving that. . . .

9 *raged*. T's 'rayed' resulted from misreading Sidney's 'g' as 'y'.

10 *Cosma* (κόσμος, ornament), is so named only in 90-St-Bo. In the earlier manuscripts her name was Hyppa (ἴππη, mare).

12 *treene-dish*, wooden dish.

13 *crouch*, crutch.

14 *Lalus*, see OA **7**. 1 and note. *blesse*, wound.

15 *Menalcas*, the name of a shepherd in Theocritus and Virgil; see OA **4**.

22 *mate*, defeat (checkmate); in the next line Pas takes it to mean one of a pair.

27 *Dicus*, appeared in OA 8.

28 *whether*, which.

36 *espyes*, an emendation in Cl, Je, and Qu of a scribal error in T.

37 *thou . . . thou*, all scribes but St probably misread the abbreviation 'yᵘ' as 'you'.

45 *eft*, moreover.

47 *price*, prize.

49 *vaine*, vein.

57–58. The 90 readings are probably editorial emendations.

57 *he*, Pan—Syrinx, fleeing from him, was turned into a reed, on which he blew and so invented the shepherd's pipe (Ovid, *Met.* i. 689 ff.).

60 *he . . . her*, Apollo fell in love with Daphne, who fled from him and was transformed into a bay or laurel (Ovid, *Met.* i. 452 ff.).

70 *barlybreake*, a country game; see OP **4**. 208 ff.

76 *Leuca*, λευκός, white or fair.

81 *sive*, sieve, here meaning a net.

84–86. This is Skelton's 'sparow whyte as mylke' (*Philip Sparrow*, 213); cf. AS 83 and OP **4**. 83–104.

93–95. Cf. Spenser's 'April', 73–81.

103. Cf. OP **5**. 112.

105 *tine*, an eye rhyme for 'time'.

106 *fell*, skin (Grosart).

107. Cf. Greville's *Caelica*, 22. 26, 'Washing the water with her beauties, white'.

112 *babie*, reflection; cf. AS **11**. 10.

114–17. The image is from Montemayor, translated in CS **29**. 1–9.

136 *blea*, baa.

140. Cf. OA **7**. 7.

141–9. So Virgil concludes his eclogue with two riddles and the award of the prize:

Damoetas.　Tell's in what Land the heaven shewes no more but three elnes space
　　And thou shalt be to me therefore in wise Apollos place.
M[enalcus].　Tell's in what Land grow flowres wherein, are writ the names of Kings,
　　And Phillis faire possesse and take in whome great pleasure springs.
P[alemon].　Not your but our part 'tys, these brales t'appease and bring t'an end,
　　The cow thou hast deser'vde, and he, and who so doth contend.
　　Sweete love to dread, or else to trie love, bitter, sharpe, and roughe,
　　Ladds, stoppe the running rivers now, the fields have dronck enough.

Virgil's riddles contain learned literary allusions, Sidney's are of the simple nursery variety. The answer to Sidney's first may be a man on crutches wearing spectacles; I give up on the second.

30

After the eclogue between Nico and Pas had been acclaimed by the spectators as 'the Sportefullest they yet had heard', Cleophila (Pyrocles), 'whose hart better delighted in waylefull Dittyes', asked Histor to 'repeate the Lamentation some dayes before hee had tould them that hee had heard of a Straunger made to the wyse Bowlon'. In the prose of the First Eclogues Histor had told how Queen Erona (ἔρος, love), who was loved by Plangus, had been imprisoned and condemned to be burned at the stake after the lapse of two years unless Pyrocles and Musidorus presented themselves as her champions, and how Plangus, after searching in vain for the princes for more than a year, had recently arrived in Arcadia. Plangus laments the miseries that afflict humanity and the injustice of a world in which Erona is made to die; Boulon counsels moderation with essentially Biblical arguments. In the *New Arcadia* Erona's story is told in Book II, Histor and his opening and closing lines are omitted, and Basilius takes the place of Boulon. 93 emends 90 from P.

4 *refrayne*, restrain.

17. W. Blount quotes an unidentified ancient poet as saying that the gods 'homines quasi pilas habent'.

20. Sidney, though he defended poetry, agreed with Gosson's *Schoole of Abuse* in disapproving of the commercial acting companies and public theatres that had recently been established in London, for he said that comic drama had been 'justly made odious' by 'naughtie Play-makers and stage-keepers' (iii. 23).

24. 'And when I was borne, I receyved the common aire, and fell upon the earth, which is of like nature, crying and weeping at the first as all other do' (Wisdom vii. 3).

27–31. The four elements warring for mastery are the bases of the four bodily humours; only in a perfect man would they be in perfect equipoise.

33. Cf. Virgil's simile of the top (*Aeneid*, vii. 383) to which blows give life, 'Dant animos plagae'.

35 *stone*, the touchstone, used for testing the purity of metals.

38–41. John Ward, *The First Set of English Madrigals* (1613), No. 12, fashioned these lines into a five-line song with a setting for four voices.

58–59. John Hoskins (*Directions for Speech and Style*, ed. Husdon, p. 12) quotes these lines to illustrate the figure anadiplosis, 'a repetition in the end of the former sentence and beginning of the next'.

68–70. W. Blount cites Zeus's speech in the *Odyssey*, i. 32–34 ('Look you now, how ready mortals are to blame the gods. It is from us, they say, that evils come, but they even of themselves, through their own blind folly, have sorrows beyond that which is ordained').

71–76. The usual proof texts for the sweet uses of adversity (cited, for example, by St. Augustine, *De Patientia*, i. xiv) are Proverbs iii. 11–12 ('Refuse not the chastening of the Lord, neither be greived with his correction. For the Lord correcteth him, whome hee loveth, even as the father doeth the childe in whome he deliteth') and Wisdom iii. 4–6 ('And though they suffer paine before men, yet is their hope full of immortalitie ... for God proveth them, and findeth them meete for him selfe. He trieth them as the golde in the fornace').

86–88. Quoted by Fraunce (*Arcadian Rhetoricke*, I. iii) as an example of metonymy.

96 *myne*, see AS **2. 3**.

106 *Phaëton's damme*, Clymene, the mother of Phaethon by Phoebus the sun god (Ovid, *Met.* i. 756).

107–14. Vulcan the smith, husband of Venus, was made a cuckold ('witolde') by her amour with Mars (Ovid, *Met.* iv. 171 ff.).

129 *glasse*, see the reflection of.

130 *prove*, experience.

136 *baiting*, resting.

146 *she*, Erona.

154 *unlasing*, an Elizabethan anachronism; so Shakespeare's Cleopatra asks Charmian to cut her lace.

175 *spilled*, destroyed.

184. In Aesop's fable (ed. Chambry 275) the ass, trying to fawn like a dog upon its master, kicks him.

31

Philisides (Sidney himself), asked by Basilius to tell the story of his life, refused and instead 'began an Eglogue, betuixt hym self and the Eccho, framinge his voyce so in those Dezert places, as what wordes hee woulde have the Eccho reply unto, those hee would singe higher then the rest: And so kyndely framed a Disputatyon betuixt hym self and yt, with these Hexameters'. 90 assigns the poem to an unnamed 'young melancholy shepheard', but 93 reassigns it to Philisides.

The echo device was used by Ovid in his story of Narcissus and Echo (*Met.* iii. 379–92), by Erasmus in his colloquy *Echo et Juvenis*, and by many continental Latin and vernacular poets of the renaissance. Apparently the only English examples before Sidney are Gascoigne's verses for the Kenilworth entertainment of 1575, four poems in John Grange's *Golden Aphroditis*, 1577 (Brie, p. 244), and one in Henry Wotton's *Courtly Controversie*, 1578. Fraunce quoted Sidney's lines 8–9 and 29–35 in his discussion of 'conceited verses' (*Arcadian Rhetorike*, I. xxv), and they appear in Dousa's anthology of echo poems, 1638.

Metrically this poem (like OA 34) is exceedingly imperfect, which indicates that it is one of Sidney's earliest experiments in measured verse. He departs from his own rules in at least 14 places. Syllables long by position are counted short in 3 'do', 13 'enjoy', 20 'he', 29 'thy', 32 'be . . . be'; syllables regularly short are counted long in 5 'Echo', 7 'then it', 46 'Echo', 48 'is'; syllables regularly long are counted short in 18 'say', 36 'women', 45 'holy'; and in the fifth foot where a dactyl is always required a spondee is admitted in 42. The editor of 90 noticed the roughness of the metre and introduced a number of conjectural emendations to smooth it. He managed to make lines 36 and 43 scan correctly, but in trying to correct 13 and 42 he introduced new errors; and furthermore he unnecessarily changed correct readings in six lines, while allowing clear errors in nine lines to stand uncorrected. These changes are manifestly editorial and not authorial. Since 90 has here been so heavily corrupted by editorial tampering, I have used 93, which printed this poem from P, as copy text. 93 indicates all the elisions and contractions required by the metre except in lines 3, 7, 18, 34, 36, and 43.

9 *And what manner a* scans properly. T probably first wrote 'What maner of a' in error, and then corrected by adding 'And' and deleting 'of', which confused some of the copyists. *a vaine*, a vein.

13 *for to enjoy*. The first syllable of 'enjoy' is long by position, but is here arbitrarily counted short to produce the dactyl required in the fifth foot. 90 attempts to emend by reading 'for t' enioye', but in doing so improperly introduces a spondee.

14 *to enjoy*. Probably elided, making two long syllables; unless 'en' is arbitrarily counted short as in the preceding line.

24 *Aye*. The usual Elizabethan spelling is 'I', which appears in the majority of the manuscripts.

33 *recks*, reckons.

37 *woe-man*. Cf. OA **9. 61**.

42 *helde like* is a spondee, but a dactyl is required in the fifth foot. 90 attempts to correct by emending to 'helde uery', but falls into another error because the second syllable of 'uery' becomes long by position.

43 *th' hast narroly*. 93 has the correct reading from P, and 90 makes the correct conjectural emendation; 'neerly' was a scribal error in T. *pri'de*, pryed.

47 *matcht*, equalled.

32

Cleophila, who had a short time before (iv. 114) revealed to Philoclea that he was Pyrocles prince of Macedon, sings before her 'in Anacreons kynde of verses'. Sidney's metre is found in several of the *Anacreontis Teij odae*, a collection of love lyrics considerably later than the time of Anacreon and now known as *Anacreontea*, the Greek text of which was first printed with a Latin translation by Sidney's friend H. Stephanus in 1554. Sidney was, with Spenser and Watson, among the first Englishmen to make use of motifs from this collection. The scansion model fails to indicate that the last syllable may be long or short. The structure is not stanzaic, because the six sections, indicated by the repetition of the first line, vary in length from 8 to 11 lines. This and CS 5 are Sidney's only measured poems in which the quantitative and stress patterns coincide ('Vĕnŭs' in line 27 is the one exception); but he here achieves this union only by a monotonous march of monosyllables (the poem contains but one word of more than two syllables) and by departing from his own rules for quantity in lines 6, 49, and possibly 34. This and the two following quantitative poems were omitted by 90 but restored by 93.

2 *blase*, emblazon.

34 *therof* may have been written 'theroff' by Sidney to make the second syllable long.

41 *she*, Cleophila's muse.

47 *she*, Philoclea.

33

Cleophila (Pyrocles), asked by Basilius for another song, accompanies himself on a lyre and sings these 'Phaleuciackes' (used by Catullus). The last syllable may be either long or short, and the rules for quantity appear to be broken in lines 3, 11, 16, and possibly 29. Pyrocles, though ostensibly addressing the entire company, is telling Philoclea that her beauties have conquered his reason. The conceit of the lover as a walled town is a medieval and renaissance commonplace, and the analogy of the mistress's charms as a besieging army is incongruously elaborated. Sidney uses the siege image with much greater skill in AS 2.

27 *nature's Diamond*. Cf. OA **13.** 165.

34

Dorus, who had earlier (iv. 100) revealed to Pamela that he was Musidorus prince of Thessalia, sings before her these 'Asclepiadickes' (used by Horace). His song is an elaborate exercise in the use of polysyllables, arranged in three sonnet-like 14-line stanzas, which contrasts with the monosyllables of Pyrocles' OA 32. The metre is exceedingly imperfect, for the rules of quantity are broken in one or more places in 16 of the 42 lines, which indicates that this, like OA 31, is one of Sidney's early experiments in measured verse. The poem does not appear to have been originally written for this section of the *Arcadia*, for its praise of the retired country life, where no external danger or hidden treason exists, is inappropriate to the Second Eclogues, which take place immediately after the tranquillity of life in the rural lodges had been broken by the insurrection of the Phagonian villagers. The first two lines are used as the beginning of each of the four stanzas of song 10 in John Dowland's *Second Booke of Songs or Ayres* (1600); but Dowland's musical notes do not reflect the quantitative pattern of Sidney's syllables.

1. Miss Wilson (*Sidney*, p. 314) says that this line is a translation of Giovanni della Casa's 'O dolce selva solitaria, amica'; but the idea is a common one.

14 *if be not*, i.e. 'if it be not'.

20 *humorists' puddled opinions*, the unclear notions of those whose humours, or vital spirits, are disturbed.

33 *Cedar*. Cf. OA **13.** 140.

THE THIRD BOOK OR ACT

35

The day after the recital of the Second Eclogues, Dorus (Musidorus) and Cleophila (Pyrocles) retire to a secluded place and recount to one another 'theyre straunge Pilgrimage of passyons'. Dorus 'drewe oute a glove of Pamelas . . . and not without tender teares kissing yt hee putt yt ageane in his bosome, and sange these twoo staves'. This and the two following poems were omitted from the *New Arcadia*, because at this point in the revised narrative Dorus had not yet received any indication of love from Pamela. The three poems were first printed (from Ph) by Bertram Dobell in the *Quarterly Review*, ccxi (1909), 97–99.

9. Poirier, *Études Anglaises*, xi. 151, quotes Petrarch's sonnet 199. 9–11.

> Candido, leggiadretto e caro guanto,
> Che copria netto avorio e fresche rose,
> Chi vide al mondo mai si dolci spoglie?

36

Dorus (Musidorus) then played his shepherd's pipe, and afterwards 'sange these followyng'.

37

Cleophila (Pyrocles) replied to Dorus: 'Leste envyous fortune shoulde spyte at
the boasting of youre too muche blessednes I will mingle your Comycall tunes
with my longe used Tragicall notes, and will stayne a litle the fulnes of youre
hopes with the hanging on of my tedyous feares.' He thereupon sang 'with a
faynting kynde of voyce', using the same images and stanza form as Dorus
(see note to OA 24).

  5 *scoope*, scope.
  6 *loose*, lose.
  9 *so*, such.
  16 *prove*, find.

38

Basilius after his birthday devotions to Apollo (see OA 26), resumes his courtship
of Cleophila (Pyrocles). 'O Goddess (sayde hee) toward whome I have the
greatest feeling of Religion, bee not displeased at some shewe of Devotion I have
made to Apollo. Synce hee, (yf hee knewe any thinge) knowes that my harte
beares farr more and full reverence to youre self, then to any unseene Diety.'
He then kneels and presents her with 'certeyn verses' he had written. His ababb
stanza had been used by Wyatt and Alonso Perez.

  10 *still do prove*, always experience.
  14 *raste*, razed.

39

Cleophila (Pyrocles) takes leave of Basilius and, coming to the mouth of a dark
cave near the lodges, gives 'dolefull way' to his feelings in a 'Songe' in which he
acknowledges complete surrender to his passion for Philoclea. His sonnet, like
AS 89, has only two rhyme words, a device occasionally used by the Italian
Petrarchists (e.g. Petrarch's 18. 1–8, and Bembo's 'E cosa natural fuggir da
morte' in which all lines end with either 'morte' or 'vita').

  7 *windowes of my inward light*, my five senses.
  13 *this place*, the cave before which he sings.

40

From within the cave Cleophila (Pyrocles) hears a voice, accompanying itself
with a 'base Lyra', give forth this 'songe', which it follows with an 'Octave'
(OA 41). (The singer is Gynecia, lamenting her love for Pyrocles.)

  8 *Receipte*, reception.

42

Cleophila (Pyrocles) enters the cave and sees 'upon a stone a litle waxe lighte
sett, and under yt a peece of paper with these verses', which comprise a mono-
rhymed sonnet.

  1 *Sunn*, Pyrocles.
  5–8. Cf. AS 10.
  12 *Tyre on*, continue to rend (cf. AS **14. 2**).

43

'And hard under neathe the Sonett were these wordes written' (by Gynecia). This is correlative or reporting verse (*carmen correlativum*, *vers rapportés*) which became popular with neo-Latin and French vernacular poets in the second half of the sixteenth century. Scaliger (*Poetices*, II. xxv) defines it as a form in which 'uerba ipsa modo regunt: ubi inter se respondent'. An early approximation of the device is Wyatt's 'Disdain me not' (*Songes and Sonettes*, No. 79); the fully developed form appears in a sonnet by Sir George Bowes (*c.* 1560, printed in Wright and Halliwell's *Nugae Antiquae*, ii. 190); and the most successful early example is John Harington the Elder's 'Whence comes my love' (*c.* 1558–60). Richard Willes wrote a Latin poem in this form (*Poemata*, 1573, D8ᵛ). It became extremely popular in England in the closing decades of the sixteenth century (see H. H. Hudson, *The Epigram in the English Renaissance*, 1947, pp. 161–5; and J. G. Fucilla, *Studies in the Renaissance*, iii (1956), 23–48. OA 60 is an even more elaborate example; see also CS 3, 18, and 19, OP 5, and AS 43 and 100.

44

Dorus (Musidorus), in order to get rid of Dametas so that he can elope with Pamela, buries a box some miles away, and then tells Dametas that he had come upon 'a Boxe of Cypres with the name of the valyant Aristhomenes graven uppon yt: And within the Boxe hee founde certeyn verses which signifyed that some depthe ageane under that, all his treasures laye hidden, what tyme for the Discorde fell oute in Arcadia, hee lived banished'. Dametas departs to seek the treasure, unearths the box, and finds 'these verses written in yt'. The ten lines have only two rhyme sounds.

Brie (p. 206) suggested that Aristomenes is the Messenian hero who Pausanius (IV. xiii–xxiv) says led his countrymen in their second revolt against the Spartans in 685–668 B.C. But there is no good evidence that Sidney had read Pausanius and he here represents Aristomenes, not as a Messenian liberator, but as an Arcadian ruler who had been banished from his country as the result of an internal revolution. He more probably recollected the name from Alciati's emblem 'Signa fortium', the verses to which (translating Antipater of Sidon's epitaph in the Greek Anthology, vii. 161) praise Aristomenes as a great and brave man, but do not indicate his nationality.

10 *baite* has two meanings: (*a*) a halting place for rest and refreshment, and (*b*) food used to attract animals (cf. OA **56**. 2–10). Dametas expects to find gold that will give him ease, but finds only earth (see OA 68).

45

Dorus (Musidorus), in order to get Dametas's wife Miso out of the way also, tells her an invented tale of seeing her husband lying with his head in the lap of the shepherdess Charita while she sings this song to him and he replies with OA 46, and of hearing them make an assignation to meet that night in the Oudemian street (οὐ δῆμος, without people). Miso immediately departs to prevent their meeting. Sidney has framed one of his most exquisite lyrics in an episode of comic buffoonery, for the young shepherdess, 'of the fynest stamp of

Beuty', fondling ugly old Dametas is like Titania caressing the translated Bottom. These are *serpentina carmina* (see Ovid, *Fasti*, ii. 235, OA 72, and AS 24).

Puttenham (*Arte of English Poesie*, Bb 4ᵛ) quoted, as an example of 'linking verse', a ten-line version of this song consisting of the first two quatrains with the first line repeated as a refrain after each quatrain, which indicates that the text had been set to music before 1589. A later musical setting, probably of the early seventeenth century, is in British Museum MS. Additional 15117, f. 18ᵛ, and another for three voices in John Ward's *First Set of English Madrigals* (1613), Nos. 1 and 2.

46

Sidney deliberately contrasts the complex rhetorical structure and the simple rural images of this song, as Longus (i. 17) had done in his account of the shepherd Daphnis's description of Chloe. These are not really the words of Dametas, but of the courtly Musidorus playing a trick upon the ignorant Miso. This is correlative verse (see OA 43 and note); but the distributed terms (words, breath, tongue, voice, &c.), instead of being repeated at the end are summarized in the phrases 'First fower' and 'next fowr' in line 17, and 'you' in line 18.

8 *plum*, plump.

13 *cruddes*, curds.

14 *sleekestone-like*, in the manner of a stone used for polishing or smoothing (ironing).

18 *you*, 'skinne' and 'flesh' of lines 13 and 15.

47

Musidorus and Pamela, eloping from Arcadia, pause to rest in a pine grove. Pamela walks under the trees, and on the bark of one 'shee entrusted the Treasure of her thoughtes in these verses', and on the root wrote the following 'Couplett' (OA 48).

49

Musidorus 'made the Trees aswell beare the Badges of his passyons: As this Song engraved in them did Testify'.

1 *brave assent*, magnificent ascent.

50

Pamela, 'Making a Poesy of the fayre under growing Flowers', sings to Musidorus; 'her songe was this, and hys Reply followes'.

6 *outward glasse*, external appearance, which reflects her mind.

12 *borne*, born.

14. Referring to the myth of Icarus (Ovid, *Met.* viii. 183 ff.), usually interpreted as exemplifying the golden mean and the disaster that overtakes those who aspire too high (Natalis Conti, *Mythologiae Libri Decem*, VII. xvi).

51

Pamela, growing sleepy, laid her head in Musidorus's lap and 'was invited by hym to sleepe with these softly uttered verses'. His sonnet had only two rhyme

sounds (cf. OA 39 with only two rhyme words). A musical setting for five voices
was provided by Thomas Vautor, *Songs of divers Ayres* (1619–20), Nos. 8 and 9,
and another for four voices by Martin Peerson, *Private Musicke* (1620), No. 13.

52

Basilius, 'seeyng the Sunne what speede hee made to leave oure West, to doo
his office in the other Hemisphere, his Inwarde Muses made hym in his best
Musick singe this Madrigall' in which he expresses his love for Cleophila
(Pyrocles). The non-Petrarchan type of madrigal, a single stanza of long and
short lines and varying rhyme scheme, became popular in Italy as a literary
form in the early sixteenth century. This appears to be the earliest appearance
of the word and the type in English. Sidney's form, which he repeated in OA 55,
is longer than the ordinary madrigal.

6 *Sunne*, Cleophila.

15 *Disdainst*. 93 has the correct reading from P; 'disdaines' in the other texts
results from an error in T. *staind*, put to shame; cf. OA **29**. 93–95.

53

Basilius asks his daughter Philoclea to sing something to divert his thoughts,
and she, 'not unwilling to disburden her secrett passyon', sings of her love for
Pyrocles.

1 *subject*—in the political sense.

2 *unrefrain'd*, unchecked (not in the *OED*).

5 *Mine owne*. Pyrocles yielded himself as subject to Philoclea in OA 33.

6 *gripe*, the vulture that preyed on the vitals of Prometheus.

7 *Thy title*. Time's right of possession.

12 *occasion*, opportunity, usually personified as a young woman (see Alciati's
emblem 'In occasionem'), but described as a man in Phaedrus, v. viii.

54

Philoclea finds in her chamber a lute, 'upon the Belly of which Gynecia had
written this Songe', and reading it she realizes that her own mother is her rival
in love.

8 *ground*, surface, also musical accompaniment.

16 *stops*, frets.

55

Basilius, 'Looking still uppon Cleophila [Pyrocles], (whome nowe the Moone
did beutify with her shyning all moste at the full) as yf her eyes had beene his
Songebooke, hee did the Message of his mynde in singing these verses'. His
song duplicates the metrical form of his earlier madrigal (OA 52), and continues
its praise of Cleophila as a second sun.

56

Cleophila (Pyrocles), having lain awake all night wondering how to avoid the
attentions of Gynecia and Basilius and how to gain the love of Philoclea, 'was

offended with the dayes bolde entrie into her Chamber, as yf hee had now by Custome growne an assured bringer of evill Newes, whiche shee (taking a cittern to her) did lay to Auroras charge with these well songe verses'. The rhyme-word 'bait' in lines 2, 6, and 10 is used in three different senses: the bait of a trap, a stopping place for refreshment, and baiting a bear tied to a stake.

6 *in steede*, instead.

57

Cleophila (Pyrocles) decides to pretend to grant his favour to both Basilius and Gynecia who are in love with him. He accordingly dines with them, and '(first saluting the Muses with a Base vyoll honge hard by her) sent this Ambassade in versifyed Musick to bothe her yll Requited Lovers'. The first stanza is built upon the figure anadiplosis, one of Sidney's favourites (cf. OA 16, 53; AS 1, &c.). After this song, he separately makes an assignation to meet both Basilius and Gynecia at night in the same place at the same time.

58

Gynecia, preparing for her assignation with Cleophila (Pyrocles), takes with her a vial which she believes to contain a love potion, with this inscription.

59

Basilius, on his way to what he thinks is his assignation with Cleophila (Pyrocles), 'his harte coulde not chuse but yeelde this Songe, as a Fayring of his Content-ment'. His song is an imitation, in accentual iambics, of a sapphic stanza (see OA 12). He then in the dark continues to the meeting-place, where Gynecia is waiting; he does not recognize her, and fulfils the prophecy of the oracle by committing adultery with his wife.

60

Pyrocles, having got Basilius and Gynecia out of the way, goes to Philoclea's chamber, where he overhears her sing these 'verses' while accompanying herself on a lute. This sonnet is Sidney's most elaborate example of correlative verse (see notes to OA 43); Fraunce quoted it in full in his *Arcadian Rhetorike* (I. xxv), along with other examples in four languages.

61

Philoclea, believing that Pyrocles does not regard her, 'tooke ageane the Lute, and began to singe this Sonet which mighte serve as an explayning to the other'. Puttenham (*Arte of English Poesie*, Bb1) quoted the last two lines as an example of the figure *acclamatio*.

3 *role*, roll.

62

Pyrocles, gazing at Philoclea upon her bed, 'there came into his mynde, a Songe the Shepeheard Philisides had in his hearing sunge of the beutyes of his unkynde Mistris'. The song thus appears to have been first written as one of a group of

poems concerning Mira, of which AS v, which echoes it, was originally another.
In the *New Arcadia* the reference to Philisides is deleted, and the poem is transferred to Book II where Zelmane (Pyrocles) is said to have composed it when
he saw Philoclea bathing in the river Ladon.

Sidney worked over this poem more carefully than he did any of his other
pieces, for the considerable variations among the 13 substantive texts show that
he added to or revised it on at least four different occasions. It became a favourite
with his contemporaries, who copied or quoted it more frequently than any of
his other verses—it was transcribed in at least eight manuscript anthologies, was
printed in *Englands Parnassus*, and was quoted or imitated by Puttenham,
Marston, Weever, Burton, and others.

The poem is an unusually elaborate 'blason' praising a woman's beauty by
means of an orderly anatomical catalogue—down her front from head to foot,
then down her back from shoulders to fingers, with a final brief comment on the
inward beauty of her soul. The formula had been established by Geoffrey de
Vinsauf in the thirteenth century and followed by innumerable poets afterwards.
An anthology of French examples, *Les Blasons anatomiques du corps femenin,
ensemble les contreblasons*, was published in 1536 and frequently reprinted. In
English Sidney would have known Skelton's humorous commendation of Jane
Scrope (*Philip Sparrow*, 845-1266) and the description of Rosial in the *Court
of Love* (778-812, printed in Stowe's Chaucer, 1561). He used the device again
in OA 3, AS 9, and elsewhere.

A few of Sidney's images derive from stock comparisons such as 'hair like
golden wire' or 'whyte as whalles bone'; but most of his details are original
rather than conventional. His poem is highly ingenious for it uses a shock
technique which at first surprises by the exaggeration and apparent incongruity
of the images, and then delights when further consideration reveals their essential
appropriateness and unexpected relationships. Thus the lady's blond brows are
described as a crescent moon arching over the black stars that are her eyes, the
wink of whose lids 'ech bold attempt forbids'. This is an exaggerated visual
hyperbole, which nevertheless associates the lady with all the beauty of the
heavens; the oxymoron of 'blacke starres' is physically descriptive (Mira's eyes
are black); and the lowered lids, shutting out the improper gazes of lovers, do so
beneath the moon which represents the goddess of chastity. It is no wonder that
the later Elizabethans, who delighted in the new metaphysical style, also admired
the witty conceits of this poem.

10 *bowes*, so written for the rhyme, though grammatically it should be 'bow'.

16 *paire*, an emendation by 90 or a late correction by Sidney himself of T's
scribal error 'praise'. The line as corrected means, 'They are so perfect that even
praise will blemish them'.

57 *Lycoras* (reading of first version), liquorish, juicy.

60 *mylken name*, the Milky Way.

68–70. Quoted by Fraunce (*Arcadian Rhetorike*, I. ii) as an example of
metonymy.

97 *bought incav'd*, the inward-bent curve behind the knee.

103 *Atlas*, the muscle of her calf supporting the heavens of her body.

104 *whall*, an eye rhyme for whale.

107 *sent*, scent.

116 *hate-spott Ermelin*, ermine. In the *New Arcadia* Clitophon bore as his device 'the Ermion, with a speach that signified, "Rather dead then spotted" ' (i. 108).

126 *warme snow*. See Petrarch 30. 10, 57. 5, 157. 9; cf. AS v. 37.

127 *Saphir-coloured*, blue.

132 *amatists*, amethysts are purple or violet.

THE THIRD ECLOGUES

63

The Arcadian shepherds and the stranger Philisides meet alone, without any members of the court, to celebrate the marriage of Lalus and Kala. After the wedding banquet, Dicus sings this 'Songe', which is the first formal epithalamium in English. The structural pattern is a form of correlative verse (see note to OA 43): in the first six stanzas the favour of Earth, Heaven, the Muses, the Nymphs, Pan, and Virtue is requested for the newly married couple; in the next four stanzas Lust, Strife, Pride, and Jealousy are asked to keep far hence; and in the last stanza the ten requests are recapitulated. Sidney derived his stanza form from the 'Versos Franceses' sung by Arsileo at the marriage of Syreno and Diana in Book IV of Gil Polo's *Diana Enamorada*, a continuation of Montemayor, which begins:

> De flores matizadas se vista 'l verde prado,
>   retumbe el hueco bosque de bozes [i.e. voces] deleytosas
>   olor tengan mas fino las coloradas rosas,
>   floridos ramos mueva el viento sossegado:
> El rio apressurado
>   sus aquas acresciente.
>   y pues tan libre queda la fatigada gente
>   del congoxoso llanto,
>   moved hermosas Nymphas regozijado canto.

This was translated in 1583 by Bartholomew Yong (but not printed until 1598):

> Let now each meade with flowers be depainted,
>   Of sundrie colours sweetest odours glowing:
> Roses yeeld foorth your smels, so finely tainted,
>   Calme windes, the greene leaves moove with gentle blowing:
>   The christall rivers flowing
>   With waters be increased:
>   And since each one from sorrowes now hath ceased,
>   (From mournefull plaints and sadnes)
>   *Ring forth faire Nymphs, your joyfull songs for gladnes.*

Gil Polo's epithalamium consists of seven stanzas with a refrain that changes in the last stanza to 'Dad fin hermosas ninfas al deleitoso canto'. The only similarities in content are Sidney's opening line, and the subjects of his eighth and tenth stanzas which treat at greater length ideas in two lines of Gil Polo's last stanza:

> Concorde paz os tenga contentos muchos anos,
>   sin ser de la raviosa sospecha atormentados.

J. A. S. McPeek (*Catullus in . . . Britain*, 1939, pp. 156-9), who noted Sidney's
dependence on Gil Polo, also suggested that he drew upon the two epithalamiums
of Catullus (lxi and lxii); but aside from the commonplace elm and vine image
(line 15) there are no specific resemblances.

20 *Lalus*, changed to Thyrsis by the 93 editor (see note to OA **7.** 1).

75 *recklesness*, neglect.

64

Nico, taking up the reference to jealousy in the epithalamium, 'with a Mery
Mariage Looke hee sange this followynge Discourse'. Peter Heylyn (*Cyprianus
Anglicus*, 1668, p. 57) suggested that Nico's fabliau represents Lady Rich using
her husband as an unwitting go-between in her courtship of Sir Charles Blount,
which is, of course, impossible because Lady Rich was not married until 1581,
long after the poem had been written.

31 *chumpish*, blockish, sullen.

65

Pas replies to Nico's aspersions on women with this sonnet. Harington quoted
it in full from manuscript in a note to Book XI of his translation of *Orlando
Furioso* (1591, H3) as an 'excellent verse . . . worthie to be praised and followed,
to make a good and vertuous wife'. After this poem 93 inserts OP 5.

4 *one man still*, always remaining the same, maintaining the same course.

66

Dicus asks Philisides (Sidney himself) to sing one of his 'Contry Songes'; but
he, not wishing during the wedding festivities to recount his own misfortunes
in love, instead repeats a song that had been taught him one August on the banks
of the Ister by 'old Languet'. 90 assigned this poem to an anonymous 'young
shepherd' and transferred it to the First Eclogues; 93 restored it to its original
position and to Philisides, but inserted OP 5 before it. Its position in the *Old
Arcadia* is appropriate, for it discusses the best kind of government for a state,
just as the other marriage poems in the Third Eclogues discuss the best kind of
government for the family.

The Protestant statesman Hubert Languet had been Sidney's mentor during
his continental tour, and they had been together in Vienna on the Danube (Ister)
in August 1573 and again in August 1574. Languet's letters to Sidney, post-
humously published in 1633 as *Epistolae Politicae et Historicae*, give a detailed
account of European political affairs in the 1570's. His song (lines 43-154) is a
beast fable, a genre which in the renaissance was expected to have a political
application; so that we are led to inquire, as the Arcadian shepherds do when
Philisides finishes, 'what hee shoulde meane by yt?'

The song describes how monarchy began, and the steps by which it later was
transformed into tyranny. In the Golden Age order was maintained by an
aristocracy of the stronger beasts, who ruled without doing harm to others. 'This
thinke I well', says Philisides. Later the lesser beasts ask Jove to give them a
king. The wise owl, and Jove himself, counsel against this; but the beasts insist,
so Jove contributes a spark of his heavenly fire and requires each animal to

contribute his own special characteristic. Thus man was made, and the animals grant him the perpetual priviledge that 'no beast should freely speake, but onely he'. Man at first ruled for the benefit of his subjects, and acted as though he meant all to participate in the government; but later he established a despotism by fomenting factions. He began by favouring the 'weaker sort' (the commons); this angered the 'nobler beastes' (the aristocracy), who retired to deserts where, forced by hunger, they began to ravage. Then man made the weaker beasts his guarders against the depravations of the nobler beasts. The weaker beasts were at first delighted to see the nobler beasts killed; but as soon as the nobler ones were destroyed or made powerless, man enslaved the weaker beasts, exploited them to satisfy his own appetites, and even killed them for his sport. The fable may be meant to mirror the growth of despotism on the Continent, especially in France and Spain. Whatever the specific reference, the general moral is clear—a powerful aristocracy is the best safeguard of the common people against tyranny.

When Philisides ends, some of the shepherds praise 'his words fit to frame a pastorall stile'—a reference to the apparent archaisms in his vocabulary. Elsewhere in Sidney's verse archaisms almost never appear; there are a few rustic terms in OA 10 and 29, but almost 30 archaic forms in this poem. Philisides' song is a fable like Spenser's tale of the oak and briar in the 'February' eclogue and the fox and kid in 'May', and nearly half of his archaisms or pseudo-archaisms also appear in the *Shepheardes Calender* (couthe, for to bene, heard, mickle, ne, n'is, reed, stowers, swincke, thilke, tho, welkin, won'd). His song then may be a deliberate experiment in the Spenserian manner. If it is it probably was not composed earlier than the latter part of 1579, the year in which two of the most important sixteenth-century treatises advocating limitation of the power of monarchs were published—the anonymous *Vindiciae Contra Tyrannos* and Buchanan's *De Jure Regni Apud Scotos*. But Sidney made no further experiments in this kind of 'pastorall stile', and later in his *Defence of Poesie* (iii. 37) he said that he 'dare not allow' Spenser's 'framing of his style to an olde rusticke language . . . since neither Theocritus in Greeke, Virgill in Latine, nor Sanazara in Italian, did affect it'.

1–21. The localization of the action on the banks of the Danube may be meant as a safety measure to indicate that the political situation with which the song deals applies to conditions on the Continent rather than in England. The night-time setting (pastorals are usually sung during the day) serves to underline Sidney's apprehensions that the sheep, the common people, might be led astray in the darkness of their ignorance.

2 *couthe*, knew.

4 *gatt*, arrived at. Sidney's archaisms confused his copyists, who often modernized—see the variant readings to lines 20, 46, and 100. *boothe*, temporary dwelling.

24 *clerkly reed*, learned advice.

40 *Coredens* is also mentioned in the prose of the Third and Fourth Eclogues as a friend of Philisides who like him is a non-Arcadian shepherd hopelesssly in love with Mira (iv. 229, 318). Since the name clearly ends in 's' it is probably not a variant of the Virgilian shepherd-name Corydon; it may be a made-up compound, 'co-red[i]ens', meaning 'returning with'. In his *Defence of Poesie*

(iii. 3) Sidney mentions being at the Emperor's Court in Vienna with the 'right vertuous' Edward Wotton, who returned with him to England in the spring of 1575; and Languet frequently sent greetings to 'noster Wottonus' in his letters to Sidney. Wotton, Sidney's Kentish neighbor and some six years his senior, a 'young man of great learning and knowledge of languages', was employed by Queen Elizabeth on several delicate diplomatic missions, and had a place at Sidney's funeral as one of his four most intimate friends. Brie (pp. 277–8), followed by R. M. Sargent (*At the Court of Queen Elizabeth*, 1935, pp. 66–68), suggested that 'Coridon' is Sidney's friend Edward Dyer; but Dyer had never been on 'Ister bank' with Sidney, and Languet did not become acquainted with him until he himself visited England some four years after the 'giving o'er' had been accomplished.

43–54. Dr. W. J. Stuckey pointed out to me that this is a combination of the Golden Age described by Ovid (*Met*. i. 89–112) and the millennial kingdom prophesied by Isaiah (xi. 6–8)—'The wolfe also shall dwell with the lambe, and the leopard shal lie with the kid, and the calfe, and the lion, and the fat beast together. . . . And the sucking childe shall play upon the hole of the aspe.'

43 *n'ot*, know not.

45 *won'd*, inhabited.

50 *pollicie*, system of government.

55 *beasts with courage clad*, nobler beasts, aristocrats.

57–152. Dr. Stuckey also pointed out that this account of the origin of monarchy combines the late classical myth of Prometheus, who when he created man of earth gave him the characteristics of every creature, including the fury of the raging lion (Horace, *Carm*. 1. 16. 13–16), with the fable of the frogs who asked for a king—Jupiter first sent them a harmless log of wood, which they despised, and at their second request he sent them a heron (or water snake) which devoured them (Aesop ed. Chambry 66, Phaedrus, 1. ii).

66 *puing*, pewing, crying plaintively.

68 *seech*, an eye-rhyme for 'seek'.

89 *Ermion*—see note to OA **62. 116**.

97 *mowing*, grimacing.

112 *common*, shared by all alike.

133 *Tho*, then. *their foen of greatnes*, their foes the nobler beasts.

134 *they*, the nobler beasts.

136. The structure of government, unsupported by a strong aristocracy, crushes the common people.

139 *gentle*, meek.

154 *know your strengths*, be aware that the aristocrats are the protectors of the commons against tyranny. W. D. Briggs (*SP* xxviii [1931], 153), noting the arguments of some sixteenth-century theorists that in certain circumstances it may be lawful to rebel against a tyrant, says that the point of Sidney's poem, brought out by line 103 and this line, is 'that kings are the creation of the people, and that the people may overthrow them when they come to be tyrants'. Irving Ribner (*JHI* xiii [1952], 261), noting the Tudor doctrine that prohibited rebellion under any circumstances and prescribed absolute obedience even to a tyrant, says that ' "strength" [*sic*] may very reasonably be the power of God, rather than the power of armed rebellion against the state'. It seems to me, however,

that in this poem Sidney is dealing, not with the question of the lawfulness or unlawfulness of rebellion, but with the kind of government—a monarchy limited by a strong aristocracy—that will prevent the development of tyranny.

157 *stowers*, tumults.

67

Old Geron, who bore Philisides a grudge because he had ignored his advice when they sang together in OA 9, criticized him for telling 'a Tale of hee knewe not what Bestes' at a wedding banquet; and then invited Histor, who had himself been in love with Kala, 'and nowe prevented, was growen into a Destestation of Mariage', to sing with him. 90 transferred this poem to the First Eclogues, but 93 restored it to its original position.

4 *sample*, example.

21 *combrous*, troublesome.

31–33. Omitted by the transcriber of T, but restored or new lines supplied by Sidney himself in T³.

38 *fremb'd*, unfriendly.

43 *lucklest*, most unlucky (superlative of 'luckless').

44 *yet*, pronounced [jɪt] by Sidney.

48 *bywords*, epithets of scorn.

62–63. Our 'little world' is the microcosm, the individual man, which knows (acknowledges) its king (reason) by rationally choosing the good.

67–69. Cf. *Defence of Poesie* (iii. 31), 'With a swoord thou maist kill thy Father, and with a swoord thou maist defend thy Prince and Countrey.'

72 *drawne-out line*, line of descendants.

97–98. A reference to Histor's prose account, in the First Eclogues, of the miseries visited upon Erona for despising love (iv. 62–67).

118–20. Omitted in 90 because the poem had been transferred to the First Eclogues where there was no mention of a bride. 93, though it replaced the poem in the Third Eclogues, took its text from 90 and also omitted these lines; 13 restored them from an *Old Arcadia* manuscript.

THE FOURTH BOOK OR ACT

68

Dametas, digging for the treasure of Aristomenes (see OA 44 and note), 'founde no thinge but these twoo verses written uppon a broade peece of velume'.

69

Basilius, after sleeping with the woman he supposes is Cleophila, sings these 'verses' in praise of the night which had given him so much pleasure.

11 *Witnesse his wrong*, testify to his [Basilius's] suffering.

12 *desart places*, the country about the lodges and cave to which Basilius had retired from his court.

70

Basilius recognizes Gynecia as the woman with whom he had spent the night; feeling thirsty, drinks the potion she had brought; and collapses as though dead. The Arcadian shepherds find his body; lament the loss of their ruler; and ask one of their fellows, Agelastus, to make a 'Complaynte' for them, which he does in this 'sestine'. 93 transferred this poem from Book III to the Fourth Eclogues.

The sestina, invented by the troubadour Arnaut Daniel and used by several early Italian poets, consists of six six-line stanzas and a three-line conclusion, in which the same words ending the lines of the first stanza reappear in a different order, varying in accordance with a definite formula, as the end words of the lines of the succeeding stanzas. Sidney's form is the same as Petrarch's 142, 214, 237, and 239, and Montemayor's ii. 1, but differs slightly from Sannazaro's 7. He was the first Englishman to use the form, and also composed a double sestina (OA 71) and a rhyming sestina (OA 76). Spenser, probably inspired by Sidney's example, appended a sestina, with a different pattern of end words, to his 'August' eclogue. The monotonous sevenfold repetition of the same six words is appropriate to a song of mourning, though Puttenham (II. xi), the only Elizabethan critic to recognize the form, commented that 'to make the dittie sensible will try the makers cunning'.

1 *causefull*, well-grounded.

18. Basilius had been an inadequate ruler, but at his death 'favoure and pitty drewe all thinges nowe to the highest poynte' (iv. 264).

22 *impe's*, offspring's.

THE FOURTH ECLOGUES

71

After the supposed death of Basilius, the shepherds retire to the side of a hill, where the Arcadian shepherds lament the loss to their country and the 'stranger' (foreign) shepherds record their own private sorrows. Among the strangers are Strephon and his older friend Klaius, two gentlemen who had become shepherds because of their love for a maiden named Urania, 'thought a Shepeherdes Daughter, but in deede of farr greater byrthe'. She never returned their affection, and some months previously had departed from Arcadia, leaving orders that they should remain there until they received written instructions from her. They now express their grief at her absence in this 'Duble Sestine' and in the following OA 72. Sidney later, in OP 4, described how Strephon and Klaius first fell in love with Urania, and he opened the *New Arcadia* with a scene in which they lament her absence. Since they are, with Philisides and Coredens, the only non-Arcadian shepherds in the eclogues, they may be intended to represent two of Sidney's personal friends, but the details are not sufficiently specific to make identification certain (see notes to OP 4).

The arrangement of the end words in this double sestina (see notes to OA 70) is the same as in Petrarch's 332 and Sannazaro's 4, but slightly different from Montemayor's v. 1. 90 transferred the poem to the First Eclogues, where it was reported by Lamon, and 93 transferred it to the Second Eclogues, where it was reported by Histor and Damon. It has been analysed and praised by W. Empson (*Seven Types of Ambiguity*, 1930, pp. 45–50) and J. C. Ransom (*The New Criticism*, 1941, pp. 108–14).

25 *deadly Swannish*—the swan was supposed to sing only when at the point of death; cf. OA **10.** 73–87.

35. Sidney may have had in mind the myth of Acteon who was torn to pieces by his own dogs, which was often applied by renaissance poets to the lover tormented by his own thoughts.

42 *mortall serene*, deadly dew.

45 *sent*, scent.

61 *she*, Urania.

72

Strephon and Klaius continue to express their grief at the absence of Urania, Strephon beginning with a 'Dizaine', and Klaius answering 'in that kynde of verse which ys called the Crowne', in which succeeding stanzas have the same rhyme scheme and begin by repeating the final line of the preceding stanza (see L. L. Martz, *Poetry of Meditation*, 1954, p. 107). 90 and 93 transferred this poem to the Second Eclogues, where in 90 it was repeated by Lamon and in 93 by Histor and Damon. 93 reprinted the text of 90, but corrected errors in seven lines from P, though it left errors in seven other lines uncorrected.

19 *sent*, scent.

29 *haste*, hast.

37 *wast*, wasted—apocopated for the sake of rhyme.

48 *scope*, intended goal.

63 *Torpedo*, the electric ray or cramp fish, which when caught paralyses the angler (Pliny 32. 2). E. M. Denkinger (*SP* xxviii [1931], 162–83) cites numerous references from classical and renaissance sources.

70 *in chase*, while pursuing.

72 *Basiliske*, a fabulous monster that kills by its look (Pliny 8. 33), often referred to.

77 *loose*, lose.

80 *spent*, destroyed.

87 *hent*, seized.

93 *sell*—the correct reading, as shown by the rhyme word of line 97.

100. Klaius ends as Strephon began; the 'crown' has come full circle.

73

Philisides, at the request of Strephon and Klaius, tells his life story. Beginning in prose, he says he was born of a worthy family in Samothea; in early youth was educated in moral and scientific learning, and exercised in horsemanship and the practice of arms; in later youth travelled in foreign countries to ripen his judgement; and then returned to his native country where he was considered a young man of great promise. Continuing in verse (OA 73), he tells how in a dream he saw Mira, the gold-haired waiting nymph of Diana, and fell in love with her. And concluding in prose, he says that when he awoke his dream came true, for he met Mira herself, whom his friend Coredens also loved; he at first received 'some measure of favoure' from her, but was finally 'refused all Comfort' and left his country in despair.

The melancholy Philisides had appeared earlier, but only here is his full story given. In the First Eclogues Geron had engaged him in a singing match (OA 9); in Book II he had sung with Dorus (OA 24) and had helped him fight the rebellious Phagonians; in the Second Eclogues he had sung an echo song (OA 31); in Book III a song he had sung about the beauties of his unkind mistress (OA 62) had been recalled by Pyrocles as he gazed at Philoclea; and in the Third Eclogues he had repeated a fable (OA 66) which old Languet had taught him on the banks of the Danube before he returned to his own country with Coredens. He also has a place in two early poems not included in the *Old Arcadia*—AS v, originally written as an address of his to Mira, and OP 5, his lament for her absence.

Philisides is Sidney's fictionalized self-portrait. The name, meaning lover of a constellation or star, is made up of the beginning syllables of his own first and last names; and the account of Philisides' parentage, education, foreign travel, and friendship with Languet parallels the events of Sidney's own early life. The personal references are unmistakable and did not escape his contemporaries, who from Richard Latewar (*Peplus*, 1587, E1ᵛ) onwards often referred to Sidney as Philisides. The author's personal appearance in the narrative under an assumed name was a well-established tradition of the pastoral. Virgil appears as Tityrus in his *Eclogues*, Sannazaro as Sincero in his *Arcadia* (and like Philisides recites his autobiography in the seventh prose), and Spenser as Colin Clout in the *Shepheardes Calender*. Mira, meaning wonderful, if she represents a real person, may have been one of the attendants of Queen Elizabeth (Diana). I do not find tenable the arguments of Brie (p. 271) that she is Penelope Devereux, who did not begin attending the Queen until after the *Old Arcadia* was completed; or of R. M. Sargent (*At the Court of Queen Elizabeth*, 1935, pp. 68–69) that she is the Countess of Pembroke, Sidney's sister. The fact that Philisides first sees Mira in a dream may be meant to indicate that she is merely imaginary.

In the revised *New Arcadia* of 1584 Sidney radically altered his fictional self-portrait, for Philisides appears only once, in a new guise as an Iberian knight (see notes to OP 1). He deleted the episode in which Philisides sang OA 24 with Dorus and helped him against the Phagonians, and assigned three of his songs to other characters—OA 62 to Zelmane, OA 73 to Amphialus, and OA 74 to Dorus. This indicates that he intended either to omit or reassign all the Philisides poems, which the editors of 90 perceived, for they carefully excluded Philisides from the eclogues, and though they used OA 31 and 66 they assigned them to an anonymous young shepherd. But the editors of 93 replaced Philisides in the eclogues by printing OA 9 and OP 5 for the first time and by restoring his name to OA 31 and 66, which does not accord with Sidney's own plans for the revised version of his work.

Philisides' dream of Mira is an adaptation of the well-known story of the Judgement of Paris. See the epigram on the actress Ariadne in the Greek Anthology (v. 222), which says that if there were a new contest for beauty, Venus would lose because Paris would revise his judgement in favour of Ariadne. In the *New Arcadia* Sidney or the editors of 90 transfer this poem to the third book, where it is introduced as a dream Amphialus 'had seen the night before he fell in love' with Philoclea. Cm leaves two pages blank at this point, but does not transcribe the poem. 90 gives the poem in full, but retains the name Mira in lines 91 ff., which may indicate that G, if it specifically identified the poem to be inserted, contained only the incipit or first few lines—in which case 90 must have drawn the rest of its text from T⁵.

16 *hatch*, conceal.

30 *coarse*, corpse.

36 *Samothea*, an imaginary country representing England.

44 *ground*, the earth, which in the Ptolemaic system does not move.

76. A saying from Horace's *Ars Poet.* 139 which had become proverbial.

84 *mother*, mother of pearl. *seed*, tiny seed pearl.

115 *staye*, condition.

161 *Styx*, the usual oath of the Olympian gods (Ovid, *Met.* i. 189; Virgil, *Aeneid*, vi. 323–4). Cf. CS **17**. 6 and AS **74. 7**.

74

Philisides, continuing his story, says that before he left his native Samothea he sent these 'Elegiackes' to Mira, who had refused him. In the *New Arcadia* they become a verse epistle which Dorus (Musidorus) sends to Pamela. For the scansion see notes to OA 11.

3 *monument*, this verse epistle.

12 *deadly*, dying.

32 *monument*. The metre requires that this be made disyllabic by syncopation.

66 *Pedante*, schoolmaster (with Italian pronunciation; cf. 'pedanteria' iii. 3).

83 *recov'rie*, remedy.

75

After reciting his farewell to Mira, Philisides 'woulde have gon on in telling the rest of his unhappy adventures, and by what desperate worck of Fortune hee was become a Shepehearde'; but Dicus interrupted him to bewail the death of Basilius and 'rather cryed oute then sange this following Lamentation'. In the *New Arcadia* Sidney transferred this song to the third book where it becomes a lament for the death of Amphialus (Cm leaves a blank space for the verses, but 90 has the full text); 93 replaces it in the Fourth Eclogues.

This poem, and Spenser's lament for Dido in his 'November' eclogue, are the earliest examples of formal pastoral elegy in English. The genre had been established by Theocritus and further developed by Virgil, and after its revival by Petrarch and Boccaccio it became extremely popular with both vernacular and neo-Latin writers on the Continent. Sidney was probably acquainted with a number of classical and renaissance poems of this kind, but his immediate model was the eleventh eclogue of Sannazaro's *Arcadia*, which in turn owes much to the *Lament for Bion* attributed to Moschus. Like Sannazaro, Sidney uses terza rima and a recurring refrain; asks the trees, the earth, and flowers to weep for him; calls upon echo and Philomel; and laments that other growing things renew themselves but man dies. In the latter part of his poem Sidney departs from Sannazaro, because he is writing a lament by a pagan shepherd for a pagan ruler who did not have the consolations of Christian immortality.

1–3. Sannazaro's eleventh eclogue opens in similar fashion (text ed. M. Scherillo, 1888; translation by H. J. Leon):

> Poi che 'l soave stile e 'l dolce canto
> Sperar non lice più per questo bosco,
> Ricominciate, o Muse, il vostro pianto.

(Since that charming style and sweet song may no more be hoped for in this wood, *Once more, Muses, begin your lament.*)

Sidney's refrain is ingeniously devised to end with the cry of lamentation *ai*.

4–15 and 31–39. Elaborated from the hint provided by Sannazaro's lines 7–9 and 13–15.

> Piangete, faggi e quercie alpestre et dure,
> Et piangendo narrate ad questi sassi,
> Le nostre lacrimose aspre venture. . . .
> Et tu, che fra le selve occolta vivi,
> Echo mesta, rispondi ale parole,
> Et quant'io parlo per li tronchi scrivi.

(Weep, beech trees and rugged mountain oaks, and with weeping relate to these rocks our lamentable, harsh fate. . . . And you that live hidden among the woods, gloomy Echo, reply to my words and write on the tree trunks that which I speak.)

13 *Myrrhe*, a tree that exudes sap from its trunk and so appears to weep (Ovid, *Met.* x. 310; cf. OA **13**. 116).

16–30 Elaborated from Sannazaro's lines 16–18 and 25–33:

> Piangete, valli abandonate et sole;
> Et tu, terra, depingi nel tuo manto
> I gigli oscuri et nere le viole. . . .
> O herbe, o fior, ch'un tempo excelsi et magni
> Re foste al mondo et hor per aspra sorte
> Giacete per li fiumi et per li stagni,
> Venite tutti meco ad pregar Morte,
> Che, se esser può, finisca le mie doglie,
> Et gli rincresca il mio gridar sì forte.
> Piangi, Hyacintho, le tue belle spoglie,
> Et radoppiando le querele antiche,
> Descrivi i miei dolori in le tue foglie.

(Weep, you vales, abandoned and desolate; and you Earth, on your mantle paint the lilies dark and black the violets. . . . You grasses and flowers, which at one time were lofty and great kings in the world and now in harsh fate lie amid the rivers and pools, come all with me to pray Death that he should, if it can be, end my sorrows, and that he become wearied of my loud cries. Weep, Hyacinth, for your lovely spoils, and re-doubling your ancient laments, depict my sorrows in your leaves.)

16 *attaint*, condemn.
19 *coaly*, coal black.
23 *damme*, mother, the earth.
61–66. Compare Sannazaro, lines 46–54:

> O Philomena, che gli antichi guai
> Rinovi ogni anno, et con soavi accenti
> Da selve et da spelunche udir ti fai;

Et se tu, Progne, è ver ch'or ti lamenti,
  Nè con la forma ti fur tolti i sensi,
  Ma del tuo fallo anchor ti lagni et penti;
Lasciate, prego, i vostri gridi intensi,
  Et, finchè io nel mio dir diventi roco,
  Nessuna del suo mal ragione o pensi.

(Philomel, renewing each year your ancient woes and with sweet accents making your-self heard by the woods and the caves; and if it is true, Progne, that still you lament and that your senses were not taken from you with your shape, but that still you grieve and repent for your crime; leave off, I pray, your intense cries, and until I become hoarse with my speaking let neither of you tell or think of her own evil lot.) [See CS 4 and note.]

79–96. Sannazaro; lines 55–63:

Ai, ai, seccan le spine, et poi che un poco
  Son state ad ricoprar l'antica forza,
  Ciascuna torna e nasce al proprio loco;
Ma noi poi che una volta il Ciel ne sforza,
  Vento nè sol nè pioggia o primavera
  Basta ad tornarne in la terrena scorza.
E 'l sol, fuggendo anchor da mane ad sera,
  Ne mena i giorni e 'l viver nostro inseme,
  Et lui ritorna pur come prima era.

(Ah, the thorns dry up, and then when they have had a brief space to recover their former strength, each returns and grows in its own place; but with us, when once Heaven overpowers us, neither wind nor sun nor rain or spring avails to restore us to our earthly shell. And the sun, ever fleeing from morn till eve, leads on our days and our lives in his course, and he returns even as he was before.)

This sentiment recurs in the pastoral elegy from Moschus (iii. 99–104) onwards; cf. Spenser's 'November', 83–92.

97 *spilleth*, spoileth, marreth.

109 *refrayned*, held back.

111 *distrained*, a legal term meaning compelled by confiscation or seizure to perform an obligation.

113 *moisture*, vital spirits.

119 *conclusion*, a legal impediment or estoppel.

129 *Private . . . publike*, the citizens . . . the state.

76

When Dicus ended his elegy for Basilius, Agelastus 'thus meyntayned the Lamentation in this Rhyming Sestine: Having the Doleful tune of the other Shepeheardes pypes joyned unto him'. This is in the same form as Agelastus' first sestina (OA 70), with the added complication that the end words rhyme ababcc in the first strophe. The sestinas of Petrarch, Sannazaro, and Monte-mayor do not rhyme, but Pontus de Tyard has two sestinas rhyming abcbca in his *Erreurs Amoureuses* (1549).

8 *queint*, quenched.

THE FIFTH BOOK OR ACT

77

Musidorus and Pyrocles, in prison and expecting to be executed for their attempts upon the princesses, discuss in Plotinian terms the nature of the soul and the after life; whereupon Musidorus sings this 'Songe' containing five arguments against the fear of death.

CERTAIN SONNETS

(i) *Date of composition*. The 32 *Certain Sonnets* appear to be Sidney's own collection of the miscellaneous poems he had composed on a variety of occasions over a period of years. CS 5 was probably written when he first began to experiment with measured verse under the influence of Thomas Drant in 1577 or 1578, for it contains a larger number of false quantities than he was ever guilty of after he had established his principles and gained facility in quantitative versifying in the later poems of the *Old Arcadia*; and CS 28 and 29, translated from Montemayor, may have been done before the plan of the *Old Arcadia* had taken shape. CS 1 and 2, with their modified Italian sonnet forms, and CS 7, 26, and 27, with their trochaic measures, none of which appear in any of the *Old Arcadia* poems, were probably among the latest of the *Certain Sonnets* to be written. There is no specific evidence for dating the other poems, which were probably composed at various times in between. CS 3–32 appear at the end of Cl, a manuscript containing the third state of the *Old Arcadia* text that was probably transcribed in 1581; while the earliest texts of CS 1 and 2 are preserved in Bo, a manuscript containing the fourth state of the *Old Arcadia* text that was probably transcribed late in 1581 or in 1582. Thus it appears that all except the first two *Certain Sonnets* were written in 1581 or earlier, and that the first two were added to the collection late in 1581 or in 1582. Since *Astrophil and Stella* was probably composed in the summer of 1582, all, or all but two, of the *Certain Sonnets* must have been written before the latter work was undertaken.

This conclusion runs counter to opinions that have been generally accepted for the past hundred years. Sidney's nineteenth-century biographers, beginning with Mrs. Sarah M. Davis in 1859 and H. R. Fox Bourne in 1862, assumed, without any evidence beyond their own desires to have the later sequence end with 'Leave me ô Love, which reachest but to dust', that the *Certain Sonnets* were also concerned with Sidney's love for Lady Rich, and had been composed as a part of *Astrophil and Stella*. The editors followed the biographers; Grosart in 1873 printed CS 31 and 32 as sonnets 109 and 110 of *Astrophil and Stella*, and editors of that work since, from Pollard to Poirier, have printed anywhere from 2 to 14 of the *Certain Sonnets* as poems concerned with Stella. Only a few critics have demurred. Hallett Smith (*Elizabethan Poetry*, 1952, p. 155) argued that 'the course and tendency' of *Astrophil and Stella* 'in no way leads up to' the sonnets of renunciation, CS 31 and 32; and Karl M. Murphy (*PQ* xxxiv [1955], 349–52) pointed out that CS 32 is in the English or Surreyan form, which is 'out of keeping' with the Italianate forms of the *Astrophil and Stella* sonnets.

There are also other reasons, in addition to these arguments and the evidence of chronology, for believing that the *Certain Sonnets* are an independent collection with nothing whatever to do with the poems concerning Stella. In the first place, *Astrophil and Stella* is unified and complete with a clearly discernible three-part structure, and the textual evidence shows that the order of the songs and sonnets was determined by Sidney himself. He did not hesitate to use earlier material if he found it appropriate, for song **v** bears evident traces of having been originally composed for the Mira of the *Old Arcadia*. Therefore the fact that he did not include any of the *Certain Sonnets* in his own arrangement of the *Astrophil and Stella* poems shows that he did not intend them to be taken as a part of the later sequence. In the second place, one of the *Certain Sonnets* is a reply to a poem by Dyer, five are translations from Latin or Spanish, and none contain any details that connect them with Stella. In *Astrophil and Stella* her name appears on the average in every other poem; in the *Certain Sonnets* her name is never mentioned. Sidney was just as capable as any other poet of writing about a number of mistresses either real or imaginary. CS 8–11, 'made when his Ladie had paine in her face', concerns someone whose face bears 'cruell staines' and who suffers 'loath'd constraint', which a note in Ra identifies as a victim of the smallpox. If this is correct she could not be Lady Penelope, who had smallpox in 1597 (*HMC De L'Isle*, ii. 265, 268), for that disease once contracted cannot be caught again. The *Certain Sonnets* are appended to three manuscripts of the *Old Arcadia*, and in the 1598 folio the Countess of Pembroke printed them after the last three books of the *Old Arcadia* and before the *Defence of Poesie*. The evidence, it seems to me, indicates without a reasonable doubt that they were written during the years that Sidney was composing, but at intervals when he had tired of working on, his *Old Arcadia*; that is, between 1577 and 1581. The biographical evidence shows that Sidney would have had no opportunity of becoming acquainted with Penelope until the early months of 1581, by which time most of the *Certain Sonnets* had been written; so they could not have been addressed to her.

(ii) *The text.* Groups of from 1 to 31 of the *Certain Sonnets* are preserved in 30 early manuscripts and prints which are described in the Bibliography. Eleven of these appear to be copies of other extant manuscripts or prints, and so need not be considered in the construction of a critical text.[1] The 19 substantive sources are indicated by the following sigla, with the numbers of the poems or parts of poems they contain in parentheses.

MANUSCRIPTS

Ba (30)	Ha (16a, 23)
Bo (1–4, 6–24, 26–28, 31)	Hn (1, 3, 27, 30)
Cl (3–32)	Hy (3, 16a, 16, 19, 23, 30)
Cm (3)	Ma (15, 19, 22, 23)
Dd (3, 30)	Ra (3, 8–11, 16a, 16, 19, 21–23, 25)
Fo (16a, 16)	St (3, 5, 6, 19, 30)

PRINTED BOOKS

90 (3)	Di (1, 2, 8–11, 18, 20)
93 (3)	Fr (3)
98 (1–4, 6–32)	Pu (27)
Bn (3)	

---

[1] The derivative texts and the poems they contain are: Cambridge University MS. Kk. 5. 30 (32); British Museum MS. Additional 10309 (25); Bodleian MS. Engl. poet. d. 3 (32), and Rawl. poet. 148 (15); Folger MS. 1032. 2 (32); *Englands Helicon*, 1600 (4, 16a, 16, 18, 28, 30); *Englands Parnassus*, 1600 (8, 10); Bateson's *First Set*, 1604 (4); Jones's *Muses Gardin*, 1610 (27); Corkine's *Second Booke*, 1612 (3); and Ward's *First Set*, 1613 (16).

Cl, Bo, and St (the three *Old Arcadia* manuscripts with the *Certain Sonnets* appended), Ba (the scribal copy of CS 30 which Edward Bannister said that Sidney personally presented to him in 1584), and Ma (an anthology of courtly poetry) must derive from the copies of his miscellaneous poems that Sidney retained in his own possession. Cm and 90 derive from G, the manuscript of the *New Arcadia* that Sidney left with his friend Greville, which contained CS 3 only, hastily transcribed with about four errors. Fr, 93, and 98 derive from an excellent manuscript, complete except for CS 5, in the possession of the Countess of Pembroke. Hn contains corrupt texts of four *Certain Sonnets* transcribed by or for Sir John Harington whose numerous peculiarities and errors do not appear to be related to those of any other known exemplars. Dd, Di, Ha, and Pu derive from good originals whose exact provenance cannot be determined. Ra, Bn, Hy, and Fo, four poetical anthologies whose *Certain Sonnet* texts share a number of significant agreements in error (see the apparatus to 3, 16a, 16, 19, and 23), descend through two or more intermediaries from a corrupt common ancestor, perhaps a sheaf of 13 or more *Certain Sonnets* on separate sheets of paper which Sidney allowed to be copied by one of his friends who then further circulated them.

The most complete and most obviously accurate texts are 98, Cl, and Bo. 98 contains CS 1–4 and 6–32 in that order; Cl contains 3–32 in that order; and Bo originally contained 1, 2, 15–21, 31, 22–28, 3, 4, and 6–14 in that order. The damaged and incomplete collection appended to St, on different paper and in a different hand, contains 19, 6, 5, 3, and 30 in that order. The varied order of the poems in Bo and St indicates that Sidney kept his miscellaneous songs and sonnets in a portfolio on unbound separate sheets of paper that could easily be disarranged. But the similarity in the order of the contents of Cl and the original of 98, the second of which must have been transcribed several months after the first because it contains the later-written CS 1 and 2, indicates that he tried to maintain the poems in a preferred sequence. He could not provide the collection with a middle, but his overriding sense of structure at least led him to give it a beginning and an end, for as finally arranged it opens with 'I yeeld, ô Love, unto thy loathed yoke', and after playing a number of variations on the theme of unfulfilled desire it concludes with 'Leave me ô Love, which reachest but to dust'.

For three poems we have only two substantive witnesses to the text, but for the others we have three or more, and for more than a third we have between five and thirteen. More than half of the extant texts appear to have been copied, with considerable care and accuracy, either directly or at not more than a single remove from Sidney's originals. Whether these originals were his own holographs or scribal fair copies I have not been able to determine. The relatively few variants in the substantive texts appear to be due to the usual scribal and compositorial errors. I have found no evidence of authorial revisions in any of the poems.

Sidney's original wording of the *Certain Sonnets* has been exceptionally well preserved. 98, which is more complete and more accurate than the other prints and manuscripts, is the obvious choice for a copy text, and Cl is in most places almost equally dependable. Their amazingly few scribal and compositorial errors can easily be detected with the aid of the other substantive sources, so there are no textual problems of any complexity. Aside from a few revisions of possibly ambiguous spellings and marks of punctuation, I have found it necessary to emend only thirteen words in 98 (at **3**. 9, **3**. 21, **8**. 8, **12**. 2, **12**. 7, the heading of **13**, **13**. 4, **15**. 7, **15**. 11, **21**. 5, **22**. 6, **22**. 13, and **26**. 5), all but one of which (**15**. 7) have the support of other substantive texts. In CS 5, preserved only in Cl and St, I have found it necessary to introduce four conjectural emendations.

Title

Although 13 of the 32 poems in this collection are quatorzains, 'Sonets' in the title has the generalized meaning 'songs'; for eight (CS 3, 4, 6, 7, 23, 24, 26, and 27) are specifically designated as having been composed to existing tunes, a ninth (CS 30) is in song form, four (CS 3, 4, 16, and 27) were later given musical settings by English composers, and most are adaptable to singing.

I

1–7. Nine passages of oxymoron to illustrate the contrarious nature of love, in the tradition of Petrarch's earlier 'Pace non trovo, e non ho da far guerra' (134) and Romeo's later 'Feather of lead, bright smoke, cold fire, sick health' (I. i. 186).

3 *stopped eares*—like the men of Odysseus whose ears were plugged with wax so they would not hear the enticing songs of the Sirens.

13 *gratefull gardien*, pleasing gaoler.

2

2 *patterne*, an example.
6 *affectes*, emotions.
9 *mortall*, death dealing.
10 *of*, in.

3

Sidney later used this poem in the *New Arcadia*, III. xv, as a song composed by Amphialus for Philoclea, which was performed by a consort of 'five Violles, and as manie voyces'. The editor of 13, noticing that it appeared twice, removed it from the *Certain Sonnets*. I have not found the original tune on which the stanza was modelled, though in 1612 William Corkine composed a three-part setting for Sidney's words.

The four elements as ground of invention for a poem was a favourite device; cf. OA **13**. 29–32 and Shakespeare's Sonnets 44 and 45. The structure is that of correlative verse, recapitulated in line 20 (see OA 43 and note).

4 *earth*, the earth is the centre of the universe, and dull, dry earth, the heaviest of the elements, corresponds to the melancholy humour. Cf. *Lear*, II. iv. 58, 'Down thou climbing sorrow, Thy element's below'.

5 *blazed*, emblazoned.
24 *makes of*, considers.

4

Philomela was ravished by Tereus, who cut out her tongue to prevent her from revealing what he had done; she was afterwards metamorphosed into a bird

(Ovid, *Met.* vi. 424 ff.), later writers say into a nightingale. Classical poets and the Elizabethans frequently refer to her melancholy song; cf. OA **75.** 61, OP **4.** 473–4, and the *New Arcadia* (i. 13)—'the nightingales (striving one with the other which coulde in most dainty variety recount their wrong-caused sorrow)'. In 1604 Thomas Bateson set Sidney's words to music for three voices.

4 *a thorne her song-booke*, i.e. prick-song as opposed to plain-song; perhaps also with reference to the story that may have developed from the song 'By a bank as I lay', popular from early Tudor through Elizabethan times, in which the nightingale,

> She syngyth in the thyke
> And under hur brest a prike
> To kepe hur fro slepe

(British Museum MS. Royal Appendix 58, f. 8ᵛ)—cf. Gascoigne's *Master F. J.*, 1573 (*Works*, ed. Cunliffe, i. 449), where she 'singes with pricke against her brest'. See H. W. Garrod's essay, 'The Nightingale in Poetry', in *The Profession of Poetry* (1929), pp. 150–2.

5

These sapphics (see OA 12) are Sidney's only quantitative verses with rhyme. They were first printed in 1926 by Feuillerat (iv. 401) from Cl, where they follow CS 4 and precede CS 6; in the disordered St fragment they follow CS 6 and precede CS 30. The two extant texts are so obviously corrupt that I have conjecturally emended lines 9, 17, 21, and 25 to restore omissions and correct the metre. The false quantities in lines 12 'wee', 17 'bee', 18 'to', and 23 'betweene', which are long by position but ought to be short, appear to be Sidney's own errors.

9 *that a Sunne defaces*, an inversion, 'that defaces a sun'.

11 *movinges*, movements.

22 *for stay*, by absence.

6

Miss Isabel Pope informed me that there are half a dozen different settings of 'Basciami vita mia si dolcemente'—by Faigniant, Ferabosco, Ferretti, Rampallino, and anonymous composers—printed in numerous Italian and French music books between 1543 and 1589, any one of which might have been Sidney's model. Miss Wilson noted that Sidney used the same imagery again in OP **4.** 201–4; cf. AS **71.** 14.

3 *way*, away.

7

Miss Pope pointed out to me that this is a *villancico*, a popular Spanish form in the renaissance, though in Spanish the introductory refrain is usually rhymed abb or aba. I find no support for Gustav Ungerer's suggestion (*Anglo-Spanish Relations in Tudor Literature*, 1956, pp. 213–19) that it was based on Juan Vasquez's setting of 'Duélete de mí, Señora, Señora duélete de mí', for Vasquez and Sidney's wording and stanza forms are entirely different. This song, and CS 26 and 27, are notable for containing, aside from one isolated exception, the earliest true accentual trochaics in English.

8

Grosart suggested that the 'paine in her face' was a toothache; but the note added in Ra says it was the smallpox, which appears more likely in view of the 'cruell staines' of line 12 and the 'loath'd constraint' of **10. 1**.

10

2 *man's weakness foster-child*, an inversion, 'foster-child of man's weakness'.
5 *constraint*, a personification, the subject of the verb 'feare'.

11

5 *forbeares*, endures.

12

A compact and literal translation of *Carm*. ii. x, rendering each of Horace's sapphic stanzas in three lines of terza rima. There are three versions of Horace's poem in Tottel (Nos. 28, 194, 295), the last in aaa^{6}b^4 stanzas.
5 *of foreworne house*, 'obsoleti . . . tecti'.
6. Sidney, in the light of his own experience of the English court, slightly changes the meaning of Horace's 'caret invidenda sobrius aula'.
15 *and bow hath sometime sparde*, 'neque semper arcum tendit'.

13

Quantitative elegiacs (see OA 11) paraphrasing Catullus, lxx—his first appearance in English. The sixteenth-century texts of Catullus I have seen read 'quod dicit' in line 3 and 'et rapida . . . aqua' in line 4; but Sidney's '*or* water stream' shows he is following the Latin text he quotes. Cf. OA **9.** 53–55.

14

Another quantitative elegiac distich paraphrasing, as Grosart pointed out, Seneca's *Oedipus*, lines 705–6, which are hexameter. Sidney quoted the Latin again (iii. 23 and 59). In line 2 'they' is long, as it is in OA **13. 43**.

15

This is a poem upon an *impresa*, a simple illustration in black and white with a subjoined motto, worn on a shield or brooch and used in jousts or amorous services. The main rule in composing an *impresa* was that the meaning should only be evident from the illustration and the motto together and not be evident from either alone. 'Seeling' was part of the taming process in falconry, in which the eyes of a bird were kept closed by stitching the eyelids together with thread; the bird if freed would then have no sense of direction and would fly upwards until exhausted. Cf. *New Arcadia* (i. 96), 'a seeled Dove, who the blinder she was, the higher she strave'; and Bacon, 'Of Ambition', 'a seeled dove, that mounts and mounts because he cannot see about him'. The motto, 'He does not want me for his own, and does not release me from my trouble', is adapted from one of Petrarch's best-known sonnets (134), from which it becomes evident that Love is the tyrant:

> E non m'ancide Amore, e non mi sferra,
> Ne mi vuol vivo ne mi trae d'impaccio.

16a

1–8. A popular fable appearing in some sixteenth-century editions of Aesop and referred to by Lyly, Greville, Davies, and others. Cf. CS 25. 15–18.

6 *wood*, mad.

16

Sidney's answer (see note to OA 24) may have been suggested by Alciati's emblem 'In subitum terrorem', in which others are frightened by a horn blown by a Satyr. John Ward in 1613 composed a four-part musical setting for this sonnet.

17

A monologue by a rebellious lover.

6–7. Cf. OA 73. 161 and note.

9. Cf. AS 2. 9–12.

10 *then*, than.

16 *knotted straw*, a reference, as Grosart noted, to the proverb 'nodum in scirpo quaerere' (Terence, *Andria*, 941), to seek a knot in a bullrush, that is, to find a difficulty where none exists.

18. The wooden horse, by which the Greeks gained entrance to Troy.

19. The sacred tripod at Delphi from which the Pythian priestess recited her oracles, which were consulted before engaging in war.

20. Demosthenes' fable of the man who hired an ass to go a journey, but when in the heat of the day he wished to sit in the ass's shadow the driver argued that he had not hired the shadow (Plutarch, *Moralia*, 848A).

26–30. Cf. AS 54.

33–34. Cf. AS 15. 7–8.

34 *dumpe*, mournful song.

36–37. Cf. CS 12. 14–15.

38–40. Cf. AS 74.

45 *Thinke*, consider. *Hanniball*. Professor E. G. Fogel pointed out to me that Petrarch used this anecdote in similar fashion in his 102. 5–8:

> Et Anibál, quando a l'imperio afflitto
> Vide farsi fortuna sí molesta,
> Rise fra gente lagrimosa e mesta,
> Per isfogare il suo acerbo despitto.

47 *found*, base myself upon.

52 *Choler adust*, melancholy; cf. OA 11. 9.

18

Correlative verse, recapitulated in line 13. Cf. OP 5.

10 *assent*, ascent.

19

Another example of correlative verse, recapitulated in the last line.

22

As Poirier noted (*Études Anglaises*, xi. 151), the structure of this poem may have been suggested by Petrarch's 135, a canzone in which he compares himself in love to six things 'diversa e nova'—the Phoenix, the adamant, &c. Sidney's seven wonders of England, a number derived from the traditional seven wonders of the ancient world, appear to have been drawn as much from observation and conversation as from reading. 13 and all later folios insert PP 1 after this poem, probably because it also refers to Wilton.

1–4. Stonehenge, which Sidney would have seen on visits to his sister at Wilton. William Harrison (in Holinshed's *Chronicles*, 1577, p. 93) says the stones are 'very difficult to be numbered', and confesses that he cannot explain how they 'were brought thyther'.

11 *Bruertons*, apparently Sidney's spelling of Brereton, a family, members of which Sidney may have known, that had its seat at Brereton in Cheshire. Camden (*Britain*, trans. Holland, 1610, p. 609) says: 'A wonder it is that I shall tell you, and yet no other than I have heard verified upon the credit of many credible persons, and commonlie beleeved: That before any heire of this house of the *Breretons* dieth, there bee seene in a poole adjoining, bodies of trees swimming for certaine daies together.' The legend continued current into the nineteenth century, and Egerton Leigh wrote a poem upon it (*Ballads and Legends of Cheshire*, 1867, pp. 262–6).

16. So Narcissus 'Spectat humi positus geminum, sua lumina, sidus' (Ovid, *Met*. iii. 420, noted by Poirier, p. 151).

21 *fish*, the pike—see Drayton's *Poly-Olbion*, iii. 272.

27 *Anatomy*, dissection.

31–34. The cave in the Peak district designated in earlier times as one of the wonders of England is that at Castleton, which Camden says was called 'Diaboli Podex' but is now known more politely as Peak Cavern; however, this has an exceptionally wide entrance, as has Eldon Hole some three miles distant which Camden and other early writers also mention. Sidney more likely had in mind the cave now known as Poole's Hole, about a mile south-west of Buxton, which has a low entry that leads to a large limestone cavern containing white stalactites in grotesque shapes. The Earl of Leicester frequently visited Buxton to drink the waters, so Sidney may have heard of the cave from his uncle, or accompanied him and seen it for himself.

35 *streight*, narrow (or low) entrance.

41–44. 'Neere unto the place where Winburne monasterie sometimes stood, also not farre from Bath there is a faire wood, whereof if you take anie peece, and pitch it into the ground thereabouts, or throw it into the water, within twelve moneths it will turne into hard stone' (William Harrison, in Holinshed's *Chronicles*, 1587, p. 130—not in 1577 edition).

51–54. The 'bernekke' or barnacle goose, supposed to be hatched from barnacles on rotting hulks; frequently mentioned as a marvel from the thirteenth century onwards. Harrison in 1584 sought to test the story by examining barnacles in the Thames, and thought he observed the figures of embryonic fowls in the shells (Holinshed's *Chronicles*, 1587, p. 138).

23

'Wilhelmus van Nassouwe', the song of the House of Orange and now the national anthem of the Netherlands, was adopted from an earlier French tune and provided with Dutch words by Marnix van St. Aldegonde in 1572. Words and music of the oldest printed version, in *Een nieu Geusenliedenboecxken*, 1581, are given in Grove's *Dictionary of Music*. The words are:

> Wilhelmus van Nassouwe
> ben ick van Duytschen bloet,
> den Vaderlant ghetrouwe
> blijf ick tot inden doot:
> een Prince van Oraengien
> ben ick vrij onverveert,
> den Coninck van Hispaengien
> hab ick altigt ghe-eert.

Sidney follows the syllabic and rhyme pattern of this stanza precisely; he may have heard the song during his visit to the Prince of Orange in 1577.

24

It is unfortunate that the tune of 'The smokes of Melancholy' cannot be found, for Sidney's words need the music to give them metrical pattern. The verses are strictly syllabic, and appear to be cast in the form:

$$\cup - \cup - \cup\cup - \cup - \times 5$$
$$\cup - \cup - \cup - \cup - \cup - \times 2$$
$$\cup - \cup - \cup -$$
$$- \cup\cup - \cup -$$

24–25. According to the late medieval bestiaries, the eagle was the only bird capable of looking directly at the sun, and it was also supposed to renew its sight and feathers in the fire of the sun (F. Lauchert, *Geschichte des Physiologus*, 1889, pp. 9–10).

25

This is in the Aristophanic (or First Pherecratic) metre, used by Horace as the first element in the distichs of his *Carm.* I. viii, 'Lydia, dic, per omnes'.

15–17. Cf. CS 16a.
25–26. Cf. OP 4. 370.
30–34. British Museum MS. Additional 10309, f. 45ᵛ, of the second quarter of the seventeenth century, contains a version of these lines modelled upon the expanded text in Ra:

> Sweet I cannot be from you:
> ffor all my senses are on you:
> And what I thinke it is of you:
> That which I seeke it is in you:
> All that I doe shall be for you:
> Thus all that I am it is you.

27

The Italian villanella was an unaccompanied part-song of light rustic character
—this is the first appearance of the word and the form in English. Sidney's song
is structured on the triad 'sweetness—hair—words' (cf. LM 1), and his metre
is trochaic as it also is in CS 26. I have not identified the original tune; but later
Sidney's words were given a three-part setting by Robert Jones in 1610, and
were set as a glee for five voices by R. J. S. Stevens in 1799.

5–6. This nonsense refrain earlier had a sexual connotation—see 'the dery-
dan' in Dunbar's 'In secreit place' (lines 59–60), 'Than dyry cum dawn' (British
Museum MS. Royal Appendix 58, f. 8ᵛ), and 'dandirly dan under the levis
grene' (British Museum MS. Additional 5465, f. 99ᵛ).

39–40. Quoted by Puttenham (*Arte of English Poesie*, 1589, Z3) as an example
of *prosonomasia*.

28

A fairly close translation of the first song in Book I of the *Diana*. Sireno 'sacó
del seno un papel donde tenía embueltos unos cordones de seda verde y cabellos
. . . y començó a cantar lo siguiente':

> ¡ Cabellos, quánta mudança
> he visto después que os vi
> y quán mal parece ay
> essa color de esperança!
> Bien pensaba yo, cabellos,
> aunque con algún temor,
> que no fuera otro pastor
> digno de verse cabe ellos.
> ¡ Ay, cabellos, quántos días
> la mi Diana mirava
> si os traya o si os dexava
> y otras cien mil niñerías!
> Y quantas vezes llorando
> ¡ ay, lágrimas engañosas!
> pedía celos de cosas
> de que yo estava burlando.
> Los ojos que me matavan
> dezí, dorados cabellos
> ¿ qué culpa tuve en creellos
> pues ellos me asseguravan?
> ¿ No vistes vos que algún día
> mil lágrimas derramava
> hasta que yo le jurava
> que sus palabras creía?
> ¿ Quién vió tanta hermosura
> en tan mudable subjecto
> y en amador tan perfecto?
> ¿ Quién vió tanta desventura?
> O cabellos, ¿ no os corréis
> por venir a do venistes
> viéndome cómo me vistes
> en verme cómo me véis?

Sobre el arena sentada
de aquel río la vi yo
do, con el dedo escrivió:
antes muerta que mudada.
    Mira el amor lo que ordena
que os viene a hazer creer
cosas dichas por mujer
y escritas en el arena.

(Text ed. Francisco López Estrada, Madrid 1953, from the edition printed at Barcelona, 1561.) Bartholomew Yong's translation of the same poem, made in 1583, begins:

Haire in change what libertie,
Since I sawe you, haue I seene?
How vnseemely hath this greene
Bene a signe of hope to me?
Once I thought no Shepherd might
In these fieldes be found (O haire)
(Though I did it with some feare)
Worthy to come neere your sight.

Sidney's translation is more compact. He reduces Montemayor's octosyllabics to six syllables, and begins his stanzas abab instead of abba.

29

A line-by-line translation of the third song in Book I of the *Diana*. Sylvano tells Sireno that he saw him seated beside Diana while she combed her golden hair, 'y tú le estavas teniendo el espejo en que de quando en quando se mirava . . . y aún se me acuerda de los versos que tú le cantaste sobre averle tenido el espejo en quanto se peinava'.

De merced tan estremada
ninguna deuda me queda
pues en la misma moneda,
señora, quedáis pagada.

Que si gozé estando allí
viendo delante de mí
rostro y ojos soberanos,
vos tambièn viendo en mis manos
lo que en vuestros ojos vi.

Y esto no os paresca mal
que de vuestra hermosura
vistes sólo la figura
y yo vi lo natural.

Un pensamiento estremado
jamás de amor subjectado
mejor vee, que no el cativo
aunque el uno vea lo vivo
y el otro lo debuxado.

Bartholomew Yong's translation begins:

> For a fauour of such woorth
> In no doubt I doe remaine,
> Since with selfe same coyne againe
> (*Mistresse*) thou art paide right foorth.
> For if I enioy with free
> Pleasure, seeing before me
> Face and eies, where Cupid stands:
> So thou seeing in my hands,
> That which in thine eies I see.

30

An imitation of this song, attributed to Sidney (AT 21) and adapted to the praise of Queen Elizabeth, is printed above, pp. 357–8.

6 *faire scorne*, scorn from a fair lady.

8 *franzie*, an accepted Elizabethan pronunciation.

21 *Trentals*, a series of thirty masses designed to mitigate the pains of purgatory for the dead; in Sidney's day no longer accepted as a service by the Church of England.

31

D. G. Hoffman has commented on this sonnet in *Explicator*, viii (1950), item 29, bringing to bear what appear to me to be some irrelevant associations.

1 *marke*, target.

3 *Band*, swaddling band.

4 *web*, cloth in the process of being woven, suggesting Penelope's web.

32

Splendidis . . . nugis, John Lilliat (Bodleian MS. Rawl. poet. 148, f. 1) quoted Sidney's Latin and translated it:

> ffowle vanities, to you
> for evermore adiue.

This was only a temporary mood for Sidney, because he continued to work upon his *Old Arcadia* and some time afterward composed *Astrophil and Stella*.

ASTROPHIL AND STELLA

(i) *Occasion and date*. None of the surviving manuscripts of *Astrophil and Stella* appear to have been copied during Sidney's lifetime, and there are no datable references to the sequence until after his death;[1] but several items of evidence indicate that it was composed after the completion of the *Old Arcadia* and before the composition of the *New Arcadia*. The metrics and forms of the songs and sonnets of *Astrophil and Stella* mark an innovation in English poetry and in Sidney's own practice. The poems of the *Old Arcadia*, for all their variety, are, except for the quantitative experiments, all iambic, but six of the songs in *Astrophil and Stella* are trochaic, a rhythm unknown in Elizabethan verse until Sidney introduced it. The Italianate sonnet forms are also a new departure, for none of the 18 *Old Arcadia* sonnets are cast in any of the *Astrophil and Stella* rhyme schemes. Sidney used these sonnet forms elsewhere only in CS 1 and 2, which the evidence of the manuscripts shows were the latest of the *Certain Sonnets* to be written and were not added to the collection until late in 1581 or 1582.

Furthermore, several prose passages in the *New Arcadia*, which do not appear in the *Old*, contain striking images and conceits that closely parallel and appear to be recollections of the poems to Stella (see notes to AS 7, 12, 61, 98, and xi). Of even more significance are the changes in the character of Philisides, who is Sidney's fictional self-portrait. In the *Old Arcadia* Philisides speaks often and openly of his love for a nymph named Mira; he has nothing to hide and is melancholy only because his lady has refused him. But in the *New Arcadia* he appears only once as quite a different person, for the object of his affections has there become a lady whom he calls his 'Star', and he is in the grip of a secret passion which would be shameful if it were known (see notes to OP 1). Since the *Old Arcadia* was completed by the end of 1580, and the manuscript of the *New Arcadia* is dated 1584, *Astrophil and Stella* must have taken form sometime between, during the years 1581–3. An examination of the events referred to in the sequence itself will allow us to establish its date of composition with even more precision.

The sonnets and songs form a first-person narrative that tells the story of the love of the poet, Astrophil, for a beautiful black-eyed gold-haired lady, Stella. Astrophil is clearly identified as Sidney himself, for sonnet 30 refers to his father's governorship of Ireland and sonnet 65 describes his own coat of arms.

---

[1] Several poems in Fulke Greville's *Caelica*, 'written in his youth, and familiar exercise with Sir Philip Sidney', are modelled on or echo phrases from the poems to Stella; but as we have no precise evidence for dating Greville's work, the parallels afford us no help in dating Sidney's. Frances Yates (*John Florio*, 1934, pp. 104–7) assumes that Bruno's dedication to Sidney of *De gli eroici furori* in 1585, in which he attacks the woman worship of the Petrarchists, but excepts the women of England, who are goddesses 'E siete in terra quel ch' in ciel le stelle', contains a reference to Sidney's sonnets. But 'le stelle' is plural and Bruno is speaking of Englishwomen in general—calling women 'stars' was, of course, a commonplace of renaissance verse.

Stella also is identified. The 'roses gules . . . in silver field' of her cheeks in sonnet 13 resemble the Devereux arms; sonnets 24, 35, and 37 indicate that her name is Rich (she is possessed by a 'rich fool', Fame 'doth even grow rich, naming my Stella's name', and she 'hath no misfortune, but that Rich she is') and that she lives in the east of England ('toward Aurora's court'); and sonnet 78 and song viii say that she is married ('her fair neck a foul yoke bare'). The only young married woman named Rich who is known in the courtly circles of Sidney's time is Penelope Devereux, eldest daughter of the first Earl of Essex, who became the wife of Robert, third Baron Rich. The family seat of Lord Rich was at Leighs in Essex, one of the eastern counties. Henry Constable, who later was in the service of Lady Rich and carried her portrait to King James of Scotland, wrote sonnets praising her 'black sparkling eyes' and the 'waves of gold' that were her hair.[1]

As soon as the sonnets began to circulate after Sidney's death, a number of contemporaries identified Stella as Lady Rich, and in five of the seven books dedicated to her, between 1594 and 1606, the authors went out of their way to associate her with Astrophil, which shows that she was pleased with and accepted the identification. That Sidney intended, that contemporaries believed, and that Lady Rich herself accepted the identification is established by an overwhelming amount of evidence, as certainly as any historical fact can be.[2]

Sidney's biographers, who lacked some of the essential evidence set forth below, have been uncertain when Sidney first became acquainted with Penelope, and even the date of her marriage has only recently been ascertained. Her father, whose principal residence was at Chartley in Staffordshire, sought to win glory and fortune by military campaigns in Ireland. He therefore sought the friendship of the Sidneys; but Sir Henry, though he maintained an appearance of reserved cordiality, saw his own position as governor being weakened by the Earl's manœuvres to be made supreme military commander, and privately considered him as one of his most malicious enemies.[3]

Essex died in Ireland in September 1576. In his last illness he thought often of his impoverished estate and the future of his children, who would become royal wards. Four days before his death he expressed the wish that, 'yf god so move ther hartes' Philip Sidney 'myght matche with my daughter', and a month later his secretary wrote Sir Henry inquiring 'what will become of the Treaty betwene Mr. Phillip, and my Lady Penelope'.[4] It is obvious that the initiative for this proposal was taken by the Earl and his followers and that Sidney's family and friends did not look upon it with favour. Philip, who as the prospec-

---

[1] *Poems*, ed. Hazlitt, pp. 44 and 7.

[2] See H. H. Hudson's definitive study, 'Penelope Devereux as Sidney's Stella', *Huntington Library Bulletin*, vii (1935), 89–129, which effectively refutes J. M. Purcell's arguments (in *Sidney's Stella*, 1934) that the sonnets have no autobiographical basis. Sir John Harington in 1591 or earlier appears to have been the first Elizabethan to leave a record of the identification (see Hudson, and Ruth Hughey in *The Library*, 4th ser., xv. 433). Hudson cites a number of other early identifications; see also Kathrine Koller, *MLN* l (1935), 155–8, and Bodleian MS. Rawl. poet. 172 in the Bibliography.

[3] Arthur Collins, *Letters and Memorials of State*, i (1746), 88.

[4] British Museum MS. Cotton Vitellius C. xviii, f. 370ᵛ, and Collins, i. 147 (noted by Fox Bourne, *Sidney*, 1862, p. 129).

tive heir of his uncles, the childless earls of Leicester and Warwick, had extra-ordinary prospects for wealth and influence, was being much sought after by the matchmakers, and the Earl's proposal was only one of at least five that were made by various noble families, all of which were refused for political or financial reasons.[1] The Earl's deathbed statement shows that at that time the hearts of Philip, then almost 22, and the 13-year-old Penelope had not been moved; indeed, there is no reason to believe that they had ever seen one another.[2]

In September 1578 the Earl of Leicester secretly married Penelope's mother, the widowed Countess of Essex. Since Sidney was often in the company of his uncle, his biographers have assumed that from this time forward he would have frequently been in the presence of Penelope. But in the sixteenth century it was not the custom among noble families to maintain their children in the house-holds of their mothers. The Earl of Essex, before his eldest son Robert was eight years of age, wrote that it was 'time to draw him from his mother's wing', and requested that after his death Robert should be placed under the guardian-ship of Lord Burghley, which was done. He made similar provision for the separate bringing up of his other children. In the will he drew up before his departure for Ireland he assigned Penelope, Dorothy, and Walter to his cousin the Earl of Huntingdon 'for maintenance', and on his deathbed he wrote a special letter to his legal agents giving final instructions for their care:

> Provide that my Lord of Huntingdon be duly paid of the porcions appointed yerely for my doughters and for Wat my boy. I have assigned them to his Lordship and to my Lady and do assure myself they will not refuse them.[3]

Therefore it appears that Penelope, instead of remaining with her mother, after her father's death became a member of the household of the Earl and Countess of Huntingdon.

The seat of the Earl of Huntingdon was at Ashby de la Zouch in north-western Leicestershire, more than a hundred miles from London. But the Earl was also Lord President of the North, with headquarters at York, and during the period with which we are concerned the troubled relations with Scotland re-quired his continuous presence on the northern borders—he was even required to remain at his post during the sessions of Parliament and the annual Garter Feasts. Penelope, then, from the latter part of 1576 to the early part of 1581, was probably residing either at York or Ashby de la Zouch,[4] and Sidney, who during

---

[1] See D. E. Baughan, 'Sir Philip Sidney and the Matchmakers', *MLR* xxxiii (1938), 506–19.

[2] Fox Bourne (p. 108) and Sidney's later biographers have suggested that he may have seen Penelope while attending the Queen on the progress that stopped at Chartley on 5 and 6 Aug. 1575; but this is unlikely, because on the Queen's visits the younger members of the host's family were often removed to make room for the royal entourage —see John Nichols, *Progresses of Queen Elizabeth*, ii (1823), 412.

[3] A summary of the will (34 Carew) is in W. B. Devereux, *Lives of the Earls of Essex*, ii (1853), 485, and another summary, with Essex's letter to his legal agents, was pub-lished by H. E. Malden, *Camden Miscellany*, xiii (1923), 18 and 6.

[4] I have made an extensive search of contemporary records, which show that, except for a brief visit to London in 1579, the Earl remained continuously in the north from May 1576 until Nov. 1581. The Earl and Countess exchanged New Year's gifts with the Queen in 1578 and 1579 (the rolls are lacking for other years), but this indicates only

that period was attending the court near London or visiting his sister in Wiltshire, would have had no opportunity to meet or become acquainted with her.

The Countess of Huntingdon did not come to court until 1581, where she was graciously received by the Queen on 29 January.[1] The beautiful and vivacious Penelope, who was then about 18, was also received at court and made one of the Queen's attendants, while the Countess busily went in search of a husband for her young ward. On 27 February the second Lord Rich died, and his son Robert, then a few months short of 21, succeeded to his estates and title. Eleven days later the Earl of Huntingdon wrote from Newcastle to Lord Burghley, Master of the Court of Wards, and to Sir Francis Walsingham, the Queen's Principal Secretary, informing them that the Lord Rich 'hathe lefte to hys heyre a propper gentleman and one in yeares verry fytte for my ladye penelope devereux', and asking their assistance so that, 'withe the favor and lykyng of her majesty', a match might be arranged.[2]

The young Lord Rich, evidently enthusiastically in favour of the proposed marriage, in August made a special trip to Cambridge to ingratiate himself with Penelope's brother, the 14-year-old Earl of Essex, who wrote to him as one 'qui mihi multis de causis . . . est charissimus'.[3] Plans for the wedding went on apace. On 18 September Richard Brakinbury, a gentleman usher at court, wrote that 'my lady and mistress will be married about Allhallow tide to Lord Rich'; and on 29 October Lord North paid £11. 6s. for 'a cup to give to my Lady Penelope to her marriage'.[4] The ceremony was probably performed on 1 November, as Brakinbury said it would be.

Stella appears as a married woman throughout the sequence. In the first sonnet Astrophil is in love; in the second he says that when he first saw Stella he 'loved not', and only after a considerable lapse of time did his affection develop; in the fourth his love is a 'vaine love' opposed to 'vertue'; in the 24th he specifically identifies Stella as Lady Rich; in the 28th he joys in his love, 'though Nations count it shame'; in the 33rd he tells us that when he 'might' have possessed her he 'would not', and only after she could not be his (after her marriage), did he realize that he loved her. The poems therefore must have been arranged in order, and for the most part composed, after Penelope's marriage on 1 November 1581.

Attempts have been made to establish a *terminus ad quem* for the composition of *Astrophil and Stella* by analysing the apparent duration of its action. No unanimity has been attained by these methods, because the materials, being poems, are not susceptible to the same kind of analysis as are factual chronological narratives. We should always bear in mind Sidney's own distinction between history and poetry. The historian, he said, 'brings you images of true

---

that they were in the royal favour, not that they were present at court. For the strict puritanical education of the Huntingdon wards see *The Diary of Lady Margaret Hoby*, ed. D. M. Meads, 1930, pp. 5–9.

[1] Huntington Library MS. HA 13057, and Nichols, ii. 389.

[2] British Museum, MS. Lansdowne 31, f. 105 (noted by Fox Bourne, p. 287).

[3] British Museum, MS. Lansdowne 33, f. 20 (noted by Wallace, p. 247).

[4] *HMC Rutland*, i (1888), 128—noted by L. C. John, *PMLA* xlix (1934), 961–2; and Lord North's Household Book, quoted by Nichols, ii. 148—noted by J. M. Purcell, *MLN* xlv (1930), 310.

matters, such as indeed were done', and so is 'captived to the trueth of a foolish world'; but the poet makes 'things either better then nature bringeth foorth, or quite a new, formes such as never were in nature', and creates 'freely raunging within the Zodiack of his owne wit' (*Defence*, iii. 16, 18, and 8).

The poems, though they present a continuous narrative, are more concerned with states of feeling than with events; the action progresses, but its duration is left vague. There are only two apparent references to seasons. In sonnet 22 Stella rides forth with other ladies when the sun is 'in highest way of heav'n ... Progressing then from faire twinnes' gold'n place'; the other ladies, though they hide their faces with fans, are sunburned, Stella, without protection, is not. We can look up astronomical tables and find that the sun is highest, and passes from Gemini to Cancer, in June; but if we do only that we miss what Sidney is saying. He is here concerned, not with indicating the date of an event, but with indicating, by hyperbolical amplification, the surpassing beauty of Stella, a beauty so great that even the sun at its brightest and hottest (i.e. highest) cannot touch it.

The other seasonal reference occurs in the eighth and ninth songs, which are given a springtime setting ('May then yong his pide weedes showing'). Since May is the month conventionally associated with lovers' meetings, the question arises whether the seasonal indication refers to the time of an actual meeting, or whether it is used to enhance the tone of the episode. If we take these seasonal references as literal indications of the dates of actual events, we must refer sonnet 22 to June 1582, and songs viii and ix to May 1583 at the earliest, from which we should have to conclude that the entire collection was completed sometime after the latter date. I do not believe that the sonnets are susceptible to that kind of factual analysis. Sidney was composing a poem, not a calendar.

If the temporal span of the narrative cannot be exactly established, there nevertheless remains one sonnet whose date of composition can be determined with fair precision. This is sonnet 30, which is made up of a list of seven topical allusions, questions about international affairs 'now', asked by the politically-minded courtiers of Astrophil's acquaintance, which would only be appropriate, taken together, in the summer of 1582 (see notes). Sonnet 30 must therefore have been composed in the summer of 1582, for if Sidney had written it at an earlier or a later time his poetical structure would have demanded a different set of questions.

From what we know of Sidney's biography, between the date of Penelope's marriage and the summer of 1582 he would have had opportunities for seeing her only during a few weeks in 1581, from early November until mid-December, and the next year for only two or three months during the spring. The events of the sonnets could perfectly well have taken place during that time. The surviving records indicate that for most of 1581 Sidney was extraordinarily active in social and political affairs, but that after the spring of 1582 he retired from court and spent several months in apparent inactivity on the borders of Wales. The one sonnet (30) for whose date of composition we have clear evidence was composed in the summer of 1582, and there is no reason to suppose that the other sonnets were not also written during the same summer.

It is of course possible that the composition of the poems extended into the year 1583, and even later; but it is scarcely probable. Any close reading of the sequence shows that it was carefully planned. The flashbacks in sonnets 2 and 33, the integrated three-part structure, the repetition of themes which provide a series of contrasts between part and part, all show that when Sidney wrote the first few sonnets he knew perfectly well what the shape and conclusion of his work were going to be. The poems, so far as they are factual, were written retrospectively and form a unified whole. They have the appearance of being the result of a single creative impulse, and were probably composed within a relatively short span of time. The consensus of the evidence, it seems to me, indicates that the bulk of the poems were composed and the work was given its final form during the summer of 1582—

> Never season was more fit,
> Never roome more apt for it.

(ii) *Fact and fiction.* Sidney took considerable pains to indicate that the *Astrophil and Stella* poems were based upon personal experience. Many of his readers, Charles Lamb among them, have found this autobiographical element one of their main attractions—'They are full, material, and circumstantiated . . . an historical thread runs through them . . . marks the when and where they were written'.[1] Some of Sidney's more sentimental admirers were disturbed by the autobiography, because it did not conform to their notions of their hero as 'sublimely mild, a spirit without spot', and attempted to avoid the issue by claiming that the poet's love of a married woman, 'though there may have been in it some of the poetic passion that stirred Dante and Petrarch . . . was more playful than real'.[2] More recent critics have denied the autobiographical elements for somewhat different reasons. Professor C. S. Lewis, for example, asserts categorically that a sonnet sequence 'is not a way of telling a story. It is a form which exists for the sake of prolonged lyrical meditation', and therefore 'the narrative, still more the biographical, reading of a sonnet sequence may obscure its real qualities'.[3] But we cannot avoid the biography, as Hazlitt tried to avoid Spenser's allegory, by ignoring it; Sidney put it there, and if we ignore it we ignore one of the effects he intended. The legitimate critical procedure is, not to ignore the biography, but to find out what kind of biography it is. This can be done by comparing what is known of Sidney's activities during the years 1581 and 1582 with the story told by the sonnets.

In 1581, when Penelope first journeyed from the north to begin her regular attendance on the Queen, Sidney also returned to Court, after his previous year's retirement in Wiltshire, and began to take a more active part in social and state affairs than he had done at any time since his embassy in 1577. On New Year's Day he presented the Queen with a 'whip garnished with small diamonds' in token of his submission to her will in the matter of the Anjou marriage proposal, which he had joined his uncle in strongly opposing. On 22 January he took part in a tournament with the Earl of Arundel,[4] and from January into March he regularly attended the sessions of the House of Commons. In April and May he

---

[1] 'Some Sonnets of Sir Philip Sidney', in *Last Essays*, 1833.

[2] Fox Bourne, *Sidney*, 1891, p. 247.

[3] *English Literature in the Sixteenth Century*, 1954, p. 328.

[4] William Segar, *Honor Military, and Civill*, 1602, R 2. Sidney's best biographer, M. W. Wallace, 1915, pp. 260–87, gives a fairly full account of his activities during these years; I provide references only for details that supplement Wallace.

took part in the festivities for the French commissioners who had come to con-
duct negotiations for the proposed marriage of the Queen and the Duke of
Anjou. On 15–16 May he was one of the four challengers in the Fortress of
Perfect Beauty tournament, which celebrated the romantic beauty of the Queen.
From July onwards he was often in the company of the Earl of Angus, the titular
head of the pro-English faction in Scotland, who had fled to the protection of
Elizabeth's Court after the execution of his uncle Morton; Sidney read him his
recently completed *Arcadia*, and the Earl was delighted to listen to it.[1] Probably
from July, and certainly through the end of September, he was one of the
gentlemen assigned to entertain another important political visitor, Don
Antonio, the Pretender to the Portuguese throne.

During this year also an event occurred that seriously affected his future
prospects. He had always been considered the sole heir of his childless uncle the
Earl of Leicester; but sometime before July 1581 the Countess, Penelope's
mother, bore the Earl a son, who would be the inheritor of his estates and titles.[2]
Camden reported that on the next tilt day Sidney bore as his device 'SPERAVI,
thus dashed through, to shew his hope therein was dashed'.[3]

In addition to taking part in public affairs, he did many favours for others.
He wrote a friendly letter to Jean Hotman, a French Huguenot student at
Oxford who the following year became Leicester's secretary; he had an inter-
view with Sir Francis Walsingham to gain more favourable treatment for the
recusant Sir Thomas Cornwallis; he exerted himself on the behalf of Fulke
Greville for an office in Wales; and he supported Dr. Tobie Matthew, Vice-
Chancellor of Oxford, for appointment as Dean of Durham. Further indication
of the range of his interests at this time is afforded by the books dedicated to
him: William Blandy's *Castle . . . of pollicy*, showing the 'profession of a . . .
Souldier'; Nicholas Lichfield's translation of Gutierrez de la Vega's *De re
militari*; Abraham Fraunce's manuscript 'Comparison of Ramus his Logike
with that of Aristotle'; Henri Estienne's scholarly edition of the historian
Herodian; the Italian exile Scipio Gentili's *Paraphrasis aliquot Psalmorum
Davidi*; and the botanist Charles L'Ecluse's translation from the Spanish of
Monardes, *Simplicium Medicamentorum ex Novo Orbe Delatorum . . . Historia*.

On 1 November, the day set for the wedding of Penelope Devereux and Lord
Rich, the great public event was the arrival in London of Queen Elizabeth's
suitor the Duke of Anjou. At this time Sidney may have been staying at Bay-
nard's Castle, the city residence of his brother-in-law the Earl of Pembroke—
at least he wrote a letter from there two weeks later (iii. 137). It was during these
months, from late January through October 1581, when he was more active than
he had ever been before in political and courtly affairs, that he would have had
his first opportunity of becoming acquainted with Penelope. It was then, accord-
ing to the sonnets, that he 'saw and liked . . . but loved not'. During these months
Penelope was preparing for her marriage to the young Lord Rich. The persons

---

[1] David Hume of Godscroft, *History of . . . Douglas*, ii (1743), 290.

[2] Robert, Lord Denbigh, died 19 July 1584 'of the age of three years and somewhat
more' (John Stow, *Annales*, 1592, p. 1191). The deposition attesting Leicester's secret
marriage to Lady Lettice in 1578 was signed 13 Mar. 1581 (*Cal. SPD 1581–90*, p. 11),
probably in order to ensure the legitimacy of the newly born or expected heir.

[3] *Remaines*, 1605, p. 174.

most concerned in the negotiations were all either Sidney's relatives or close friends. Lady Huntingdon, Penelope's guardian, was Philip's aunt—in October she journeyed to Wilton to be godmother at the christening of his sister's daughter. The Earl of Leicester, Penelope's stepfather, was Philip's uncle and his chief guide and support in his career as a courtier. Sir Francis Walsingham, Principal Secretary and one of the intermediaries to the Queen in the negotiations for the marriage, was Philip's close personal friend and the English statesman whom he most highly admired. Sidney must have been aware, from the very beginning, of the preparations for the marriage; according to the sonnets he approved, and may even have had a hand in actively furthering them ('But to my selfe, my selfe did give the blow').

After the wedding Sidney remained in London and at Court for about a month and a half. On 17–18 November he ran against Sir Henry Lee in the Accession Day tournament in the tilt-yard at Whitehall while the Queen and her suitor the Duke of Anjou looked on from the gatehouse gallery. About the middle of December he retired from Court to spend the Christmas season with his sister in the country at Wilton. He probably remained away well into the following January, because he did not take part in the tournament held on New Year's day in which the Earl of Leicester and the Duke of Anjou were principal challengers. In 1582 he returned to Court in time to join the elaborate train under the Earl of Leicester that escorted the Duke of Anjou to Antwerp from the 1st of February until early March. The Duke was received with elaborate pageantry and assumed the overlordship of all the northern provinces except Holland and Zeeland, which would accept no leader except the Prince of Orange. Here at last was promise of support for the Netherlands against Spain. Sidney had devoted much of his energy to the cause of the Netherlands, but was chagrined that the needed aid should come from France rather than England.

We know very little of his whereabouts or activities during the remainder of the year. On 23 July he wrote a letter from Hereford on the borders of Wales; on 14 November he wrote a letter from Court about his father's affairs, in terms that indicate he had only recently returned to attend the Queen. Sir Henry apparently remained continuously at his post as Lord President of Wales throughout the year, and Philip probably spent the summer in his company— his letter from Hereford indicates some sort of visit to his father.

Sidney was now approaching 28, and was still unmarried. But his uncle, as soon as he had disposed of his eldest stepdaughter, Penelope, in marriage, began making plans for her younger sister, Dorothy. At the end of January 1582, before he departed for Antwerp, he drafted a will in which, after making provision for his recently born son, Lord Denbigh, he added, that as there had been 'some talk of marriage between my wellbeloved nephew Phillip Sidney and the Lady Dorothy Devereux', and as 'my hearty and earnest wish was and is that it be so, for the great good will and liking I have to each party . . . I do most heartily desire that such love and liking might be between them as might bring a marriage'; and he made provision for a two thousand pound dowry, over and above her father's bequest, and further provided for a yearly income for the couple.[1] But the 'love and liking' apparently did not develop, for a year

[1] Quoted by E. M. Tenison, *Elizabethan England*, v (1936), 70, from the Marquis of Bath's Dudley manuscripts at Longleat.

and a half later Dorothy married Sidney's friend, Sir Thomas Perrot, clandestinely and without the consent of the Queen and her guardians.

While these negotiations were going on, Sidney had still another string to his matrimonial bow. On 17 December 1581, while staying at Wilton with his sister, he wrote a friendly letter to Sir Francis Walsingham, which he concluded with 'humble salutacions . . . to yowr self, my good Ladi, and my ecceeding like to be good frend' (iii. 139). 'Friend' was a usual Elizabethan term for a lover or wife, so that, as Fox Bourne and later biographers point out, Sidney here appears to allude to his projected marriage to Walsingham's only daughter, Frances, who at that time was a little over 14. No more is heard of this proposal until February 1583, when references to it in the correspondence of Walsingham, Sir Henry Sidney, Lord Burghley and others become frequent. On Friday, 21 September 1583, 'the marriage of Sir Philip Sidney with Mistress Frances Walsingham' was solemnized.

This is all we know about Sidney's activities in the months before and during which *Astrophil and Stella* was written. To learn the character of Penelope and her husband we must draw upon later sources. All who knew her praised her surpassing beauty, of which she was self-consciously aware—once when invited to attend a christening with Lord Mountjoy she postponed the ceremony because she had a 'tetter' on her forehead and would not appear in public until it disappeared.[1] She possessed all the courtly graces and accomplishments. The number of dedications and poetical tributes she received indicate her interest in literature, and she acted parts in masques at court by Daniel and Ben Jonson. She read French, Italian, and Spanish, and King James 'commended much the fineness of her wit, the invention and well writing' of her letters.[2]

She also took a far more active part than other women of her time in the delicate and dangerous game of courtly intrigue and political manœuvring. In the 1590's her brother the Earl of Essex, to whom Sidney had bequeathed his best sword and who had married Sidney's widow, through his military exploits became a national hero and one of the most powerful noblemen in the kingdom. Lady Rich brought all her feminine accomplishments to bear in furthering his plans. When he fell into disgrace as a result of the failure of his Irish expedition, she wrote a spirited letter to the Queen in his defence, and when she was examined by the Council about it she maintained her position with vigour and denounced her brother's enemies.[3] She was courageous, loyal to her brother, and without scruple when what she thought his or her own advantage was at stake. She was at Essex House on the fatal Sunday when he rode into London attempting to rouse the citizens, and was instrumental in inciting him to his rash and treasonable rebellion. Essex, before his execution, in an orgy of self-abasement, made a full confession of his crimes and named his accomplices, especially 'my sister, who did continually urge me on with telling me how all my friends and followers thought me a coward, & that I had lost all my valour', adding that 'she must be looked to, for she had a proud spirit'.[4] But the Queen dealt leniently with her, and she escaped imprisonment.

---

[1] Collins, i. 385.
[2] *HMC Salis.* iii. 438.
[3] Huntington MS. HM 102, f. 15.
[4] Godfrey Goodman, *The Court of King James I*, ed. Brewer, i (1837), 17.

The surviving records indicate that she spent considerably more time either at Court, or in the London house of her brother, or in the country with her mother, than she did with her husband. Her marriage was not a happy one, as we know from several sources. In later years John Davies descanting on her name wrote:

> Yet to bee *rich* was to bee *Fortunate*,
> As *all* esteem'd, and yet though so *thou* art,
> Thou wast much more then most *unfortunate*,
> Though richly-well thou plaid'st *That* haplesse *part*.
> (*Microcosmos*, 1603, Nn1.)

She bore Lord Rich four children,[1] and then, in the winter of 1588–9, became the mistress of Sir Charles Blount, a young man who succeeded as Lord Mountjoy in 1594 and was created Earl of Devonshire in 1604. He had fought at Zutphen with Sidney, served against the Armada, and had become a favourite of the Queen, who in 1594 made him captain of Portsmouth, and in 1597 a Knight of the Garter. In October 1589 she bore him a daughter, Penelope;[2] thereafter she bore her husband a son, Henry, baptized 19 August 1590,[3] but all her subsequent children, three sons and a daughter, were acknowledged by Blount.[4] By 1590 their liaison was widely enough known to be mentioned in print. George Peele, describing the Accession Day tournament of that year wrote:

> Comes Sir Charles Blunt in Or and Azure dight,
> Rich in his colours, richer in his thoughts,
> Rich in his Fortune, Honor, Armes and Arte.[5]

But Lord Rich continued to maintain outwardly amicable relations with his wife, and acquiesced in her infidelity because it was to his advantage to do so—her brother the Earl of Essex, who was something of a philanderer himself, was considered the most influential nobleman in the kingdom.

Fifteen years later Blount, who by then had become Earl of Devonshire, wrote an apology for her actions and his:

A Lady of great Birth and virtue being in the power of her frends, was by them married against her Will unto one against whom she did protest at the very solemnity, and ever after: between whom from the first day there ensued continuall Discord, although the same ffears that forced her to marry constrain her to live with him.

---

[1] Lettice and Essex, born between 1582 and 1586; Robert, born 19 Mar. 1587; and a daughter, baptized 26 Nov. 1588, who died soon afterwards.

[2] Robert Thoroton, who was personally acquainted with Sir Gervase Clifton (*Antiquities of Nottinghamshire*, ed. John Throsby, i [1790], 108–10), said that Clifton's first wife was 'the beautiful Penelope, Daughter of Robert Earl of Warwick and Penelope his Wife, (Howbeit Ch. Blount Lord Mountjoy, Earl of Devonshire paid her Portion) . . . she died Oct. 26, 1613, aged 23 years'.

[3] G. E. C., *Complete Peerage*, vi (1926), 538.

[4] In his will, made 2 Apr. 1606 (PRO Wards 7/42/66), Blount named as his children by Penelope three sons (Mountjoy, St. John, and Charles) and two daughters (Penelope and Isabella).

[5] *Polyhymnia*, lines 134–7. Gervase Markham dedicated his *Tragedie of Sir Richard Grinvile* to Blount in 1595, which he prefaced with a poem 'To the fayrest', who must be Penelope since he addressed her in phrases quoted from AS 1.

Instead of a Comforter he did study in all things to torment Her, and by fear and fraud did practise to deceive her of her Dowry, and though he forbore to offer her any open wrong, restrained with the Awe of her Brothers powerfullness, yet as he had not in long time before in the chiefest duty of a Husband used her as his wife, so presently after his death [the Earl of Essex's in 1601] he did put her to a stipend, and abandoned her without pretence of any cause, but his own Desire to live without her. And after he had not for the space of twelve years enjoyd her He did by Persuasions and threatnings move her to consent unto a Divorce and to confess a fault with a nameless stranger without the which such a Divorce as he desired could not by the Laws in practise proceed.[1]

His apology was something less than ingenuous.

Lord Rich appears to have been a disagreeable person, but not so terrifying a monster as he has been painted. He was a little man who played things safe, and was willing to sacrifice self respect for advantage. He was given to bluster, but would retreat at any sign of opposition.[2] He had no part in decisions of state, no influence with people in power. When he wished a favour at court, his wife approached the holders of patronage; when a lawsuit threatened his estates, he sent for his wife to bring influence upon the judges.[3] In an age when every nobleman was expected to be a soldier he kept aloof from martial affairs. He was zealous in religion and affected the air of a Puritan, but like Malvolio he was more of a 'time-pleaser' than anything else. He became a lackey to the Earl of Essex, and subscribed himself humbly as 'Your Lordships poor brother to command, R. Rich'; but when Essex fell into disfavour, he dealt 'badly' with the Earl's followers and prudently retired to the background. He was morose and censorious, and certainly did not enjoy his situation; but because he did not have the courage to snarl he took refuge in sneers. Years after his wife and her lover were dead, he attained the dignity of an earldom, by a money payment; the wits wrote a poem for the occasion, dubbing him Cornucopia, the rich horn of cuckoldry.[4]

At the time of the Essex rebellion Blount was in Ireland, where he remained and pacified the country after so many others had failed; of all the Elizabethan noblemen he proved himself the most supremely competent general. After the execution of Essex, Lady Rich was released in the custody of her husband; but upon the accession of James, Blount returned to England a conquering hero, and the King showered honours and preferments upon him, and upon Lady Rich. About this time Lord and Lady Rich entered an action for divorce. The final decree, 14 November 1605, granted upon Lady Penelope's own confession of adultery with an unnamed correspondent, provided for a separation *a mensa et thoro*, but specifically prohibited the remarriage of either during the lifetime of the other.[5] But Blount was now in possession of an earldom which he wished

---

[1] British Museum MS. Lansdowne 885, f. 86ᵛ.

[2] See the controversy concerning his chaplain Robert Wright in Strype's *Aylmer* (1821), pp. 54–56, and in the *DNB*.

[3] British Museum MS. Lansdowne 57, arts. 45 and 51 (1588 wardship); *HMC Salis.* xv. 175–6 and 179 (1599 lawsuit).

[4] John Chamberlain, *Letters*, ed. McClure, ii (1939), 163.

[5] A summary of the proceedings is in British Museum MS. Additional 38170, ff. 82–84. The final judgement, entered in the Journal of the Consistory Court of the Bishop of London, f. 13ᵛ (preserved at Somerset House), specifically ordered both parties 'ne ipsi seu eorum alter altero vivente ad alias nuptias convolare ... sed ut caste et continenter vivant et vivat eorum uterque iuxta canones in ea parte editos sub pena iuris'.

to descend to his children, and on 26 December 1605 he married Lady Rich. The illegal ceremony was performed by his chaplain William Laud, later archbishop, who ever after kept the anniversary as a day of penance.[1] Neither the Earl of Devonshire nor the Lady Penelope were allowed to appear again at court. Their adultery could be countenanced, but not their illegal marriage.

The following April Blount died of a fever. A contemporary commented, 'Happy had he ben yf he had gon two or three yeares since, before the world was wearie of him, or that he had left that scandall behinde him'.[2] His last thoughts had been for Penelope, his last actions to provide for her and their children.[3] She did not long survive him. On 7 July 1607 'the Lady Rich fell sick, sent for Doctor Layfield, disclaimed her last marriage, sent her first husband to ask forgiveness, and died penitently'.[4]

It is hard to judge the Lady Penelope. Was she more sinned against than sinning? At a time when marriage was a business, she was sold to the first adequately financed buyer. If she had objected strongly to Lord Rich before their marriage, it is doubtful whether her powerful relatives and friends would have forced her to go through with it. Their differences more probably arose after the ceremony. Later she partly established her own household and had a liaison with a man who truly loved her. We are left partly admiring her courage, partly deprecating her departure from the moral standards of her day. At any event, the documentary records indicate that in later years the character of Lady Rich was quite different from that of Stella as pictured in the sonnets. She was only 19 when Sidney wrote, and had only recently left the pious household of the Countess of Huntingdon; she may still have been as demure and high-principled as Sidney thought she was, or he may have been deceived, either by her or by himself, as other lovers have been.[5] He may never have known her very well—all stars are distant and only dimly apprehensible.

[1] More than half a century later Peter Heylyn, in his *Cyprianus Anglicus* (1668), an apology for the career of the archbishop, attempted to find justification for Laud's illegal act in performing the marriage ceremony, by asserting that 'he found by the averment of the Parties, that some assurances of Marriage had passed between them, before she was espoused to *Rich*; which though they could not amount to a pre-Contract *in Foro Iudicii* . . . yet might satisfie himself in the truth thereof *in Foro Conscientiae*' (pp. 58–59). This is pure invention. Blount, in the elaborate *Defence of his Marriage* (see note 1 on p. 445) which he addressed to King James, sought every argument available to justify his course, but never once made mention of a pre-contract, which would have been a stronger justification than any he was able to find. J. Brownbill (*TLS*, 20 Sept. 1928, p. 667) and others have uncritically accepted Heylyn's unfounded statement.

[2] Chamberlain, *Letters*, i. 226.

[3] Professor Irving Ribner has shown me photostats of a lawsuit concerning the Earl of Devonshire's estates (James I, Star Chamber 8, Bundle 108, No. 10), in which Joseph Earth, the Earl's chief legal adviser who was present during his last illness, testified: 'That hee att the speciall requeste of the saide Earle, did fetche the saide Ladie [Penelope] to him in his sickenes, whose commynge to the saide Earle was verey acceptable and wellcome', and 'That the said Earll aswell before his sickenes whereof he dyed, as in all the tyme of his saide sickenes, was verey tender and carefull of the saide Ladie and of her children, and his greatest care was for theire advauncement and prefermente'.

[4] *HMC XII Report*, Appendix i (Cowper), i (1888), 63.

[5] Fulke Greville, whose *Caelica* 73–75 deal with the same situation as AS viii, attributes the lady's refusal to a prudential fear of scandal rather than higher considerations,

When we compare the known facts of Sidney's life during the years 1581–2 with the sonnets and songs of *Astrophil and Stella*, we are immediately struck with how much of his biography he left out of his poem. He tells us nothing about the disappointment of his hopes in being superseded as the Earl of Leicester's heir, nothing about his trip to Antwerp, nothing about his dominating interest in politics and international affairs—his friendship with the exiled Earl of Angus and the Portuguese pretender Don Antonio, and, most significant, nothing about his activities in opposition to the proposed marriage of the Duke of Anjou with the Queen. His sonnets concern courtship, and yet they do not contain a single hint of the attempts being made to marry him to Stella's sister, Dorothy Devereux, or of his own interest at the same time in Frances Walsingham.

Astrophil and Stella is in no sense a diary, for in it Sidney did not write about the full range of his interests and activities, but only about those directly connected with his love for Stella. His emotion may or may not have been recollected in tranquillity, but he was obviously in full command of himself and of his materials while he was writing. Everything in his poem is focused on his relations with Stella; everything in his experience during those months which did not directly relate to his central theme he ruthlessly excluded. Therefore, though the substance of his poem was autobiographical, mere fact was made subservient to the requirements of art.

(iii) *The text*. *Astrophil and Stella* (AS) is preserved, in whole or in part, in 26 manuscripts and early prints which are described in the Bibliography. Twelve of these are copies of other extant manuscripts or prints, and so need not be considered in the construction of a critical text.[1] The 14 substantive texts (seven manuscripts and seven prints) descend from a lost transcript (O) of Sidney's lost holograph original through one or another of three lost intermediaries (X, Y, or Z), as follows.

DESCENDANTS OF X

98 *Arcadia*, 1598. Complete (108 sonnets with 11 songs interspersed).

Bt British Museum MS. Additional 15232. 1–20, 105–8, viii, xi.

Fr Fraunce, *Arcadian Rhetorike*, [1588]. **1**. 1–5, **23**. 12–14, **44**. 1–4, **47**. 9–14, **54**. 14, **89**. 5–14, vii.

and also indicates that she did not really reciprocate the affection of her suitor. Lady Penelope, for lack of other idleness, was willing to play games. She later led Father Gerard to believe that she wished to become a Catholic, though there is no evidence aside from his own account of his interview with her that she had any leanings in that direction (Philip Caraman, *John Gerard the Autobiography of an Elizabethan* [1951], pp. 34–36).

[1] The 12 derivative texts, and the poems or fragments of poems they contain, are: British Museum MS. Additional 15117 (ii), MS. Additional 28635 (1, x), MS. Additional 29401–5 (vi, x), MS. Additional 31922 (vi, x); Bodleian MS. Rawl. poet. 172 (37); Lownes's edition of *Astrophel and Stella* (Q3, *c*. 1597–1600); the 1599 and later folio editions of the *Arcadia* (complete text); *Englands Helicon*, 1600 (5, 9, 22, 25, 32, 54, 78, 79, 88, v); Morley's *First Booke*, 1600 (xi); Youll's *Canzonets*, 1608 (iv); Robert Douland's *Musicall Banquet*, 1610 (viii, ix, x); and Ward's *First Set*, 1613 (x). There are also quotations in Drayton's *Ideas Mirrour*, 1594 (**74**. 8); Thomas Combe's *Anatomie of the Metamorphosed Aiax*, 1596 (**15**. 5–6); John Harington's *The Metamorphosis of Aiax*, 1596 (**63**. 1 and **63**. 14); Hoskyns's *Directions for Speech and Style*, *c*. 1599 (**15**. 5–6); Nashe's *Summers last will and Testament*, 1600 (**54**. 13); and Shakespeare's *Merrie Wives of Windsor*, 1602 (**ii**. 1).

DESCENDANTS OF Y

Dr Edinburgh University MS. De. 5. 96. 1–66, 87–108, i, ix–xi.

Q2 *Astrophel and Stella*, 1591. 1–36, 38–95 (substantive only in those passages which vary from Q1).

DESCENDANTS OF Z

Ho Arthur A. Houghton, Jr. MS. 1–23, 26–27, 29–34, 36, 38–39, 41–44, 47–108.

Hn Arundel Castle Harington MS. 1.

Hn Harington, *Orlando Furioso*, 1591. 18.

Q1 *Astrophel and Stella*, 1591. 1–36, 38–108, i–x (viii omits lines 69–100 and x omits lines 25–42).

DESCENDANTS OF O OR X OR Y

Bd Byrd, *Psalmes Sonets & songs*, 1588 [entered 1587]. vi.

Bd Byrd, *Songs of sundrie natures*, 1589. x. 1–18.

Dd Cambridge University MS. Dd. 5. 75. ix.

Ha British Museum MS. Harley 6910. viii.

Hn Arundel Castle Harington MS. x.

Ra Bodleian MS. Rawl. poet. 85. iv, viii, x.

Greville's *Caelica* (in Warwick Castle MS. E and Greville's *Workes* printed in 1633) contains occasional echoes of *Astrophil and Stella* that may be substantive, but are too distorted to be useful for textual purposes.

X

An important clue to the relationships of the extant texts is provided by their patterns of line indentation. Sidney did not, like Shakespeare, write all his sonnets in a single invariable form; for though he preferred an abbaabba octave and a cdcdee sestet, he introduced several variations and altogether used fourteen different rhyme schemes. In Dr, Ho, Hn, and Q1–2 variations in rhyme scheme from sonnet to sonnet are indicated by different patterns of indentation. In general the beginnings of quatrains and couplets are indented. Thus sonnets with abbaabba octaves usually have lines 2–3 and 6–7 indented, sonnets with cross-rhymed octaves usually have line 5 indented, sonnets with cdcdee sestets usually have lines 9 and 13–14 indented, and sonnets with ccdeed sestets usually have lines 9–10 and 12–13 indented. The indentations in this group of texts, then, are functional, and must derive from the author's holograph, for individual scribes would not take the time to analyse rhyme schemes to determine the different patterns of indentation.

But 98, Bt, and Fr reduce all the sonnets to a single standardized pattern in which lines 2–4, 6–8, 10–11, and 13–14 are indented. This was a common continental form, the one most frequently used in printed editions of Ronsard and Petrarch; but it is singularly inappropriate for most of Sidney's sonnets, because it divides the sestets three and three where rhyme and sense divide most of his sestets four and two. The standardized indentation of 98, Bt, and Fr sets them apart from the other texts, and suggests that they descend from a common ancestor which I designate X. Their common descent is also indicated by the similarity of their readings, by agreements in error, and by external evidence of their relationship.

98 is the only complete text and is with Bt the most accurate of the extant texts, for it has verbal errors in fewer than 90 of its 2,049 lines. It contains 108 numbered sonnets and the complete texts of 11 songs which are interspersed among the sonnets in the same order as in Bt, Fr, and Dr.

Bt contains sonnets numbered 1–20, songs numbered viii and xi, and sonnets numbered 105–8, in that order and with blank pages after sonnet 20 and song viii, which indicates that it was copied from an original that contained the same number of sonnets and songs arranged in the same order as 98. The text of Bt differs from 98 in only 33 single words, 14 of which are correct readings of passages in which 98 is in error, two of which are superior to 98 but like it still in error (**1.** 2, **12.** 2), and the remainder of which are errors on the part of the Bt scribe. These similarities, and the fact that Bt agrees in error with 98 against all other texts at **2.** 13 'mee self', **9.** 2 'choycest', **13.** 14 'scantly', and **14.** 5 'ye', show that it is a transcript of the same original from which 98 was printed.

Fr quotes only 47 lines, from six sonnets and one song, which are designated by the same numbers they bear in 98. It varies from 98 in only eight places, six of which are unique errors, and two of which (**1.** 2, **vii.** 3) are correct readings of passages in which 98 is in error. Fr agrees in error with 98 against all other texts at **47.** 12 'doo'. Thus Fr's quotations must have been taken from the same original from which 98 was printed.

Since the Countess of Pembroke patronized Fraunce and appears to have had a hand in the publication of 98, she probably owned X, the exclusive common ancestor of 98, Bt, and Fr. A number of 98-Bt variants indicate that X was in a secretary hand in which e-d, o-e, &c., could be confused (i.e. **2.** 3 'mine-mind', **9.** 13 'mind-myne', **7.** 7 'these-thos', &c.). Since both Sidney and his sister wrote Italian hands in which graphical ambiguities of this kind do not appear, X must have been a scribal transcript. But though X was not in the Countess of Pembroke's hand, it may have been executed under her direction. She preferred regularity to variety and admired invariant patterns, as can be seen in her rewriting of Sidney's partial stanzas in the Psalms to make them regular full stanzas; so the reduction of the line indentations of the sonnets to a standardized form in X may have been done at her suggestion.

X then, from which 98, Bt, and Fr descend, appears to have been a scribal transcript in secretary hand made in 1588 or earlier for the Countess of Pembroke. It contained all 108 sonnets with 11 songs interspersed, and standardized the indentations of the lines. It was executed with extreme care and had a factor of error of only 0·003, that is, on an average only about three words in a thousand were wrong.

Y

Dr, which is unfortunately defective in its central portion through loss of several of its gatherings after it had been transcribed, is also an excellent text only slightly less accurate than 98. It originally contained 108 sonnets and 11 songs interspersed among the sonnets in the same order as in 98. Its readings are very close to those of X, but its functional indentations are similar to Ho, Hn, and Q1-2. Dr differs from 98 in only 184 passages; 114 of these are errors peculiar to Dr, but most of the remaining 70 are clearly superior readings. Dr omits **52.** 12–14 (and indicates the omission by the numbers 1, 2, 3 in the margin), and

G g

leaves spaces for words omitted at **15.** 8, **20.** 6, **21.** 1, and **38.** 13. These blank spaces are especially revealing, for they indicate that Dr's original either lacked three lines at **52.** 12–14 or was illegible at that point, and that the Dr scribe could not decipher single words in the four other lines. Since none of the surviving texts, except the corrections in Q2, gives evidence of having difficulty at any of these places, Dr must have been copied from a separate lost original, which I designate Y. As several of Dr's errors are graphical confusions of a kind that commonly occur when reading secretary hand (**2.** 3 'mynde' for 'mine', **4.** 10 'least' for 'left', &c.), Y must have been a scribal copy rather than Sidney's holograph.

Further evidence for the existence of Y is provided by the corrections in Q2. The bulk of the text of Q2 merely reproduces Q1; indeed, similarity of spelling and punctuation and the reproduction of misprints (**v.** 14 'metamorphisde', **93.** 5 'brath', &c.) show that Q1 was used as printer's copy. But in sonnets 1–95 verbal changes have been introduced affecting 349 of the 1,316 lines of text. These changes appear to have been made by collating a copy of Q1 with a manuscript. A glance at these changes shows that they could not possibly have come from Ho or its ancestor Z, and that though they are quite similar to both X and Y, they share several special peculiarities with Y. Consider the following passages, for which I give the readings of all extant texts and indicate the correct readings by italics.

 15. 8 *denisend wit do* 98 Bt; ⟨ ⟩ witt to Dr, deuised wit do Q2; wytt devysing Ho, wit disguised Q1.

 20. 6 *secret* 98 Bt; Ho Q1-2; ⟨ ⟩ Dr.

 21. 1 *friend (right healthfull caustiks)* 98; Q2, frend right helthful ⟨ ⟩ Dr; frinds doth cawslesly me Ho, freends me causelessly do Q1.

 21. 6 yeeres 98; Ho Q1; geers Dr, *giers* Q2.

 25. 10 *tooke* 98; takes Dr Q2; take Q1.

 38. 2 *that vnbitted* 98; Dr; Ho; the vnbitted Q2, that my troubled Q1.

 38. 13 *Cald it* 98; Ho Q1; ⟨ ⟩ yt Dr, Conclude Q2.

 46. 8 *of* 98; Q1; on Dr Q2.

 48. 4 *growes one* 98; growes on Dr Q2; Ho, is linckt Q1.

 48. 7 *hel-driu'n* 98; held even Dr, driuen Q2; blyndfold Ho, blinded Q1.

 51. 13 *And is euen irkt that so sweet* 98; And ys even reck't that sweet Dr, And is euen woe that so sweet Q2; as pitty twas so sweete a Ho, As pittie tis so sweete a Q1.

 58. 10 The 98; Q1, *Th'* Dr Q2; Ho.

 87. 8 saddest 98; *sadded* Dr Q2; sayd did Ho, sad deare Q1.

 95. 2 left 98; *least* Dr Q2; Ho, best Q1.

In this list Q2 and Dr agree in error at **25.** 10 and **46.** 8; are the only texts to preserve the correct readings at **21.** 6 and **87.** 8; and agree together and with Ho in correct readings against the other texts at **58.** 10 and **95.** 2, which shows that Dr and the Q2 corrections have a common source. Furthermore, both had trouble in deciphering their original at points where the other texts give no evidence of graphical difficulties. In the four places where Dr left blank spaces we find that at **20.** 6 Q1 had the obviously correct reading, so Q2 did not have to make a change; that at **21**. 1 Q2 recovered the correct reading; but that at **15**. 8 and **38**. 13 Q2 had the same difficulties as Dr. At **15**. 8 Y probably had the form 'denised', in which a tilde above the second 'e' was omitted or illegible; Dr could not make sense of what he saw and left a blank, but Q2 transcribed what he thought he saw, misread 'n' as 'u', and printed the erroneous 'deuised'. At **38**. 13 Q1 had the correct reading 'Cald It'; Dr could not read the first word in Y and left a blank, but Q2, who could not read the word in Y either, guessed at it and improperly changed the correct Q1 reading to 'Conclude'. Another place where Dr and Q2 both had difficulty was at **51**. 13, where Dr transcribed 'reck't' and Q2 transcribed 'woe' for 'irkt'. These passages prove that the Q2 corrections could not come from Dr or any other extant text, but stem directly from Y itself.

The evidence of Dr indicates that the corrector of Q2 had in Y an almost perfect manuscript to work from, so he should have been able to produce a text as complete as, and even more accurate in its readings than, 98. His simplest procedure, in view of the excessively high error of Q1, would have been to hand Y over to the printer; but, apparently for the convenience of the compositor, who would prefer printed to manuscript copy, he instead collated Q1 with Y and wrote the corrections in the margins of the print. As has been indicated earlier, he introduced changes in wording affecting 349 lines of the text, but only carried his collation through sonnet 95.

The Q2 corrector worked in an exceedingly haphazard and slipshod fashion. He corrected some Q1 errors but allowed just as many others to stand, and often in the process of making corrections he introduced new errors. Thus he properly corrected Q1 **4**. 2 'loue and me' to 'will and wit', but he allowed Q1 **18**. 9 'wit doth waste' (which should be 'youth doth waste') to stand. He only partly corrected Q1 **23**. 12 'farre otherwise alas the case' (which should be 'or ouer-wise, alas the race') to Q2 'or ouer-wise, alas the case'; and while he corrected the improper inversion at Q1 **8**. 8 'himselfe he pearch'd', he introduced a new error in Q2 'he preach'd himselfe'.

The Q2 corrector did his work at something under 50 per cent. efficiency; which in textual matters is about as inaccurate as it is possible to get. Q2's errors and failures to make corrections were almost entirely the result of the collator's carelessness, for the evidence of Dr shows that almost all the necessary corrections were to be found in Y. Therefore since Q2 was printed from a copy of Q1 that had been only imperfectly collated with Y, the agreement of Q1 and Q2 provides no evidence for the readings of Y; only in those passages where Q2 varies from Q1 do we have testimony to the readings of Y, and even in those passages the testimony is imperfect because of the carelessness of the Q2 collator.

Y then, from which Dr and the Q2 corrections derive, was a scribal transcript in secretary hand, made sometime before 1591, that contained all 108 sonnets with 11 songs interspersed as in 98, but made the line indentations of the sonnets functional. It appears to have been executed with considerable care and contained only a small number of errors. It probably omitted **52**. 12–14.

Z

Ho, Q1, and the sonnets 1 and 18 in Hn, have functional indentations like Dr, but are considerably more corrupt. Ho has a factor of error of 0·058, the two Hn sonnets 0·045 and 0·102, and Q1 0·122 if the omitted lines are included in the calculation, and 0·081 even if the omitted lines are not included. Ho, the most accurate of this group of texts, contains an even 100 sonnets whose sequence has been deliberately disarranged by the transcriber. Q1 contains 107 sonnets in an order identical with that of 98 except for the omission of 37 and the reversal of 55 and 56. Ho and Q1 agree significantly in error in more than 190 lines, and both reverse the order of sonnets 55 and 56 and of the first two quatrains of sonnet 5. Ho omits **44.** 12, **80.** 13–14, and **85.** 13–14; Q1 omits **44.** 12 and **85.** 13–14 and has two obviously made-up lines at **80.** 13–14 which show that its original was also defective at this point.

Ho leaves blank spaces for words at **79.** 12, **87.** 4, **94.** 3, and **99.** 11. None of the texts descending from X and Y had any difficulty in these four places, for they all contain the manifestly correct words 'ostage' (Q2 'a stage'), 'iron', 'inbent', and 'floure'. But Q1 in the same places reads 'a pledge', 'Stellaes', 'euen mine', and 'heauen', which make sense of a sort but do not preserve what was obviously Sidney's meaning, and could not derive by any stretch of transcriptional probability from the correct readings. It is evident that the original of Q1, like that of Ho, was defective in these four passages, and that Newman merely invented words to fill the blanks. Therefore Q1 and Ho must have an exclusive common ancestor, which I designate Z.

Harington's copies of sonnets 1 and 18 (Hn) agree with Ho against all other texts at **1.** 1, **1.** 8, **1.** 9, **1.** 13, **18.** 3, and **18.** 11, which proves that they descend from Z. But they also agree in error with Ho against Q1 and all other texts at **1.** 11 'sute', **18.** 2 'recknings', and **18.** 11 'spoyled' (Q1 'the spoile'), which proves that Hn and Ho descend from Z via a common intermediary, which I designate Z¹. Q1 does not contain these errors, so it must descend from Z either directly or through an intermediary different from Z¹.

The 100 sonnets common to Ho and Q1 agree in 416 verbal errors, which gives a factor of error of 0·035 (3½ per cent.). This indicates that Z was either very carelessly transcribed, or that it descends from O through one or more intermediaries. Z¹ contains about 1 per cent. more error than Z, and Ho about 1 per cent. more error than Z¹, which indicates that both were carefully transcribed. But Q1 contains about 6 per cent. more error than Z, which indicates either that it was printed with almost unbelievable carelessness, or more probably that it descends from Z through one or more carelessly executed intermediaries.

Z is only imperfectly preserved by its surviving descendants, because none of them is complete, and Q1, the most nearly complete of the three, has introduced numerous additional corruptions. The combined evidence of Ho and Q1 indicates that Z reversed the order of sonnets 55 and 56 and of the first two quatrains of sonnet 5, and omitted lines at **44.** 12, **80.** 13–14, and **85.** 13–14. Ho and Q1 omit sonnet 37; Ho contains none of the songs, ten of which Q1 collected at the end, omitting all of song xi and lines 69–100 of viii and 25–42 of x. Not all of these omissions, however, are the result of deficiencies in Z, for Harington's quotations from Z¹ in *Orlando Furioso* (see Bibliography) include references to sonnet 37 and to lines 95–96 of song viii, which are omitted in Q1. Therefore Z¹, and also Z, contained sonnet 37 and a probably complete text of song viii; whether Z¹ and Z also contained a complete text of song x, and song xi which is omitted in Q1, and whether they interspersed the songs among the sonnets, we have no way of knowing.

Z then, from which Ho, Hn, and Q1 descend, was a scribal transcript with a considerable number of corruptions that was made before 1591. It contained all 108 sonnets, with functional indentations, and at least 10 of the songs. It omitted five lines from three sonnets, and reversed the first two quatrains of sonnet 5 and the order of sonnets 55 and 56. It may have omitted song xi and lines 25–42 of song x, and it may have collected the songs at the end rather than leaving them dispersed among the sonnets.

O or X or Y

The five songs (iv, vi, viii, ix, and x) appearing in Bd, Dd, Ha, Hn, and Ra present a separate textual problem. These songs all occur in or derive from courtly manuscript anthologies of the 1580's or later, and all but one of the texts are exceptionally inaccurate (their errors average over 13 per cent.), the result, as Byrd indicated, of their 'going abroad among divers, in untrue coppies'. Dd contains song ix with about 11 per cent. of errors not related to any other known text. Ra contains songs iv, viii, and x scattered at ff. 42, 34^v, and 107^v, in texts containing from 12 to 19 per cent. error; the readings of its song iv do not relate it to any other known texts, its song viii agrees in error with Ha in 14 passages, and its song x agrees in error with Hn in six passages. The first 18 lines of song x also appear in Bd (Byrd's *Songs* printed in 1589) with only 0·057 error, far more accurate than the others and not related to them by any peculiarities of reading. The other Bd text (song vi in Byrd's *Psalmes* entered in 1587) has 0·125 error, and is not related to any other known exemplar. The great difference in the accuracy of Byrd's two texts suggests that he drew them from different sources; and the scattered position and varied relationships of the three songs in Ra also suggest that each came from a different source.

All we can be certain of is that Ra and Ha viii and Ra and Hn x each have exclusive common ancestors; that song vi circulated at least as early as 1587, and that songs iv, viii, ix and x, but none of the sonnets, circulated shortly thereafter; and that, since these texts contain no clear traces of the peculiarities of Z as represented by Q1, they probably descend through one or more lost intermediaries from either O or X or Y. They may have been originally put into circulation, not together as a group, but separately on individual sheets of paper, which is the way that a number of the *Certain Sonnets* found in the manuscript anthologies were also circulated.

Though the originals of the texts containing the songs only cannot be precisely established, all extant texts containing the sonnets (98, Bt, Fr; Dr, Q2; Ho, Hn, Q1) clearly derive from three now-lost originals (X, Y, and Z) which are themselves scribal copies. When we reconstruct X and Y from their extant descendants (X from 98, Bt, and Fr, and Y from Dr and the corrections in Q2), we find that their readings are so nearly identical that they must have been copied directly from the same original, O. The few variants between X and Y affect only single letters or groups of letters—i.e. (I italicize the correct readings) **9.** 2 'choisest—*chiefest*', **12.** 2 *lockes*—lookes' **13.** 14 '*scarcely*—scantly', &c.—

all obvious graphical variants resulting from different interpretations of the same original in a secretary hand.

Z presents more of a problem, because about 5 per cent. of its text varies markedly from X and Y. We must decide whether these variants result from scribal corruption, or whether they represent an earlier or later version of the poems made by the author himself. Previous editors, who did not know of the existence of Dr and Ho and so were unable to determine the line of descent of Q1 and of the corrections in Q2, believed that the extreme variations between 98 (which descends from X) and Q1 (which descends from Z) could be attributed to revisions made by Sidney himself. Professor Flügel was so convinced of this that he attempted to produce a critical edition of what he considered to be Sidney's 'earliest' text by reprinting Q1 with only a few of its most obvious errors corrected from Q2 and 98. Grosart, though he purportedly based his own text on the 98 Folio, was certain that Q1 'furnishes admirable readings' and that its apparent errors are 'in the greater number of instances not errors, but variant readings from earlier MSS' (1. xxx). But he was singularly unfortunate in the examples he chose to illustrate Sidney's supposed revisions. He observed that 98's 'mine' at **2. 3** 'seems later' than Q1's 'tract'—but Ho, which descends from the same ancestor as Q1, here agrees with or approximates 98 against Q1; he noted that 98's 'darke' at **20.** 3 is a 'later change' of Q1's 'a'—but Ho here agrees with 98 against Q1; and so on.

Pollard suggested that 'at least two, if not three, different texts were in existence, with variations . . . that are undoubtedly beyond the ingenuity of any mere copyist or editor' (p. xxxvii). In his notes he observed that at **32.** 3 Q1's unique variant 'of hidden mysterie', for 98's 'and oft an historie', plainly represents 'an earlier draught' of the poem—but Ho here agrees with 98 against Q1; in sonnet 94 he specified 26 variant words in Q1 as 'earlier readings'—but a glance at the apparatus shows that Ho agrees with 98 against Q1 in 19 of these, agrees with Q1 in only three, leaves a blank space for one, and has unique readings in the remaining three; and so on. Obviously Pollard underestimated the ingenuity of mere copyists. In almost every case where editors have suggested evidence of revision on the basis of Q1 readings, they are contradicted by the more authoritative evidence of Ho. The variants in Q1, that to some have looked like inferior early readings that were later revised by Sidney, all turn out to be scribal corruptions.

Of course it is not in the variants of Q1, but in the variants of Z as reconstructed by the agreement of Q1 and Ho, that we should look for evidence of possible revision. When we make that reconstruction we find that Z varies in only some two hundred single words from X and Y, and varies in a way that is typical of the changes ordinarily made by scribes in the process of copying. Thus in the first sonnet Ho and Q1 both read 'my love in verse' for 'in verse my love', an inversion; 'shewr' and 'showre' for 'showers', a singular for a plural; 'out' for 'forth', a simple sense substitution; and 'tongue and pen' for 'trewand pen', a common graphical error. The only certain examples we have of Sidney's methods of revision are in the poems of the *Old Arcadia*. There, though he occasionally changed single words or phrases, which are the only kind of variants we find in Z, he more often rewrote whole stanzas or added or substituted entire lines, a type of variant never occurring in Z.

I therefore conclude that the verbal variants in Z result entirely from scribal corruption, and if the verbal variants are corruptions, the omissions and changes of order in the sonnets and songs must likewise be scribal and not authorial. Z then must be a corrupt descendant of O, and Sidney must have produced only a single version of *Astrophil and Stella* which he never subsequently revised. This conclusion is supported by a series of errors in Z which show it agreeing with X or Y as a result of misreading a similar secretary hand (for example, see **21.** 6 ZX 'yeeres' for Y *'giers'* and 'geers', **61.** 3 Z 'assaild' and X 'assaid' for Y *'assayll'*, **60.** 14 ZY 'Blest' for X *'Blist'*, **25.** 10 Z 'take' and Y 'takes' for X *'tooke'*, &c.). Furthermore, X, Y, and Z agree together in error in five passages (see **6.** 6 'Bordred' for 'Broadred', **12.** 3 'sweld' for 'swell', **66.** 6 'Fortunes' for 'Fortune', **ix.** 27 'Astrophel' for 'Astrophil', and **90.** 9 'I could' for 'could I'), which also indicates that they descend from an exclusive common ancestor.

The lines of descent of the extant texts are shown in the following diagram.

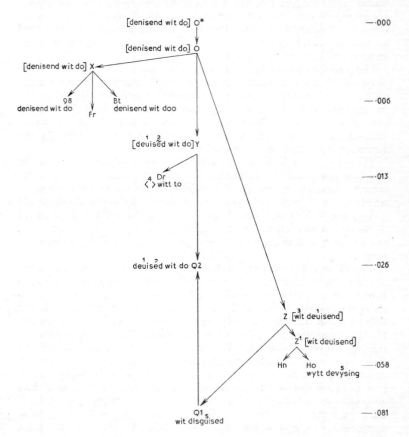

In order to illustrate the ways in which errors originate and proliferate, I have posted on the diagram the variants of **15**. 8, the correct form of which reads, 'With new-borne sighes and denisend wit do sing' (the line does not appear in Fr and Hn). The variants show how corruptions arise from the peculiarities of secretary hands and the transcriptional practices of different scribes: (1) in many secretary hands 'n' and 'u' look almost identical; (2) 'n' is frequently indicated by a macron or tilde over a preceding vowel, which if lightly stroked may not be noticed; (3) inversion and omission are among the commonest forms of scribal error; (4) careful scribes who cannot decipher or make sense of their original leave a blank space; and (5) less conscientious copyists who are puzzled by their originals invent readings of their own.

The result of this analysis, then, is that all extant texts of *Astrophil and Stella* derive from O, which is a scribal fair copy, probably made at Sidney's direction and possibly corrected in his own hand, of his holograph original O*. O* should be the ultimate object of a critical reconstruction; but since at least two lost transcripts (O and X or Y or Z) lie between the surviving texts and Sidney's lost holograph, we cannot expect to recover more than occasional traces of his original spelling and punctuation. On the other hand, the high average of verbal accuracy apparent in X and Y suggests that his original wording can be reconstructed with considerable precision.

The procedure for constructing a critical text is relatively simple. 98 is the obvious choice for a copy text, because it is the only complete text, because it is more accurate than any of the other texts except the fragmentary Bt, and because its accidents of spelling and punctuation accord with normal Elizabethan practice and present few difficulties to the twentieth-century reader. However, since 98's standardized line indentations are not authoritative, Sidney's own functional indentations have been reconstructed.

There are only 148 passages in which divergences of any consequence or questions concerning the correctness of a reading occur. In most cases the correct reading can be established by posting the variants on the stemma, for when any two of the three groups (X, Y, and Z) agree against the third, the odd group is usually in error. Where the stemma is divided equally, choice is guided by the relative accuracy of the surviving texts (a reading of X is preferred to Y, and a reading of Y to Z), transcriptional probability, and Sidney's customary usages.

Most of the text is supported by all three branches of the stemma; but sonnets 37 and 67–86 and songs ii, iii, and v are for the most part supported by only two branches. In sonnets 67–86, which have been lost from Dr, we have the testimony of 98 for the readings of X and of Ho and Q1 for the readings of Z, but only the occasional testimony of Q2 for the readings of Y. In these 20 sonnets Ho Q1-2 agree together against 98 in 26 passages; these may represent YZ readings, but since Q2 often failed to make corrections we cannot be certain that they represent anything other than the readings of Z. In three passages of these 20 sonnets 98 is demonstrably in error and I have accepted the Ho Q1-2 readings; in 16 passages the Ho Q1-2 readings are either clearly erroneous or there are positive grounds for preferring 98; but in seven passages (**67**. 5, **67**. 7, **69**. 2, **69**. 5, **79**. 6, **81**. 1, and **86**. 1) the Ho Q1-2 readings appear to be equally as appropriate as those of 98, but I have accepted the 98 readings because X has a higher average of accuracy than Z. Since in sonnets 67–86 the present critical text departs from 98 in only three passages, while in the 20 sonnets preceding it departs in 13 passages and in the 20 following in 22, it may be that several undetected corruptions of Sidney's original remain in this section. But 98 on occasion elsewhere achieves as high a level of accuracy as it appears to have here, for its seven sonnets from 37 to 43 contain only a single error and its five sonnets from 56 to 60 also contain only a single error. Elsewhere the reconstruction of the text appears to be based on solid foundations.

The first attempt to establish the text of *Astrophil and Stella* was made by Grosart in 1873 (reprinted with some new notes in 1877). He examined the Bright MS. (Bt), which he unfortunately dismissed as comparatively valueless, and also Q1 and Q2. He said (1. xxxiii) that he based his text upon 98, but the spelling of his edition shows that it actually was set up from 13. He was uncritically eclectic and departed from the wording of 98 in 143 passages; 98 of his emendations were from Q1, eight were from Q2, and 37 were merely conjectural. He was the first editor to provide any explanatory notes, a few of which are useful; but he did a great disservice to our understanding of Sidney's work by following Fox Bourne in assuming that the *Certain Sonnets* were also a part of the sequence to Stella and consequently printing CS 31 and 32 as AS 109 and 110, and by following the quartos in placing the songs after the sonnets.

In 1888 A. W. Pollard produced an edition based upon 98 with a few emendations from Q1 and Q2. His valuable notes have been the foundation of all subsequent commentaries, and his text, which departed from 98 in only 30 passages, was the most conservative and also the best of all the earlier editions. In 1889 Ewald Flügel published an edition with collations from Q2, 98, and Bt, which had been used by Grosart, and also from Fr, which had been brought to notice as a substantive text by Koeppel the preceding year. Flügel provided an unhappily inaccurate reprint of Q1, which he wrongly assumed represented the earliest state of Sidney's text, with some 90-odd emendations drawn from Q2 and 98. In 1922 Feuillerat, unfortunately following Flügel's mistaken notion of the textual relationships, printed a diplomatic transcript of Q1 with appended variant readings from Bt, Q2, 98, and all subsequent folios, but he provided no analysis of the significance of his variants.

In 1930 Mona Wilson published an edition based on 98, with 53 emendations from Q1, Q2, and Bt, and a useful introduction and notes containing some new material; but her method was eclectic, and her text is less close to Sidney's original than is Pollard's. The latest edition is that published at Paris in 1957 with a French translation by Michel Poirier. His notes contain some additional information on sources and analogues and his translation is a useful interpretation; but his text also is eclectic, containing 96 verbal departures from 98.

The present text is the first attempt at a truly critical reconstruction, and makes use of several important substantive sources (especially Dr and Ho) that were unknown to earlier editors. It critically corrects 98 in 88 passages. All but six of these corrections are supported by one or more substantive texts, and of the six conjectural emendations admitted all but one affect only a single letter (**36.** 2 'yelden' for 'golden', **iii.** 12 'birds . . . beasts' for 'beasts . . . birds', **v.** 71 'flee' for 'flie', **viii.** 73 'Astrophil' for 'Astrophel', **91.** 8 'jets' for 'gets', and **98.** 7 'gald' for 'gold').

Title

It is clear from the manuscripts and early references that Sidney provided no title for his work. Bt and Dr have no titles at all, Ho and Hn are headed only 'Sonnetts', and Fraunce in the quotations he printed in 1588 merely calls the poems 'Songs and Sonets'; but in 1591 Newman titled his first quarto 'Syr P. S. His Astrophel and Stella', which was taken over as 'Astrophel and Stella' in the 1598 folio. 'Astrophel', as Sidney's contemporaries perceived and as Grosart and Miss Wilson have pointed out, is meaningless as a proper name. It should be 'Astrophil', lover of the star, Stella, with a play upon Sidney's own first name, Philip, as in 'Philisides' of the *Old Arcadia*. Rabelais (IV. xviii) named an astronomer 'maistre Astrophile' (P. W. Long, *Nation* xci. 33). The name occurs only three times in Sidney's text: **viii.** 5, **viii.** 73, and **ix.** 27. Bt at **viii.** 5 and Dd at **ix.** 27 have 'Astrophil', though elsewhere the surviving texts read 'Astrophel', which probably results from misreading O's secretary hand 'i' as 'e', a confusion that also appears in some texts of AS **24.** 4, **60.** 14, **72.** 10, and elsewhere. Sidney in his many coined names in the *Old Arcadia* shows himself too well acquainted with Greek to have been guilty of the error. In all references before 1591 the name was spelled 'Astrophil'. Thus Matthew Roydon before 1589, and Thomas Watson in his *Italian Madrigalls* and *Meliboeus* in 1590, refer to Sidney as 'Astrophil'. After the appearance of Newman's quarto in 1591, usage was about evenly divided. Nashe, Daniel, Barnfield, Spenser, and Hall, all with a glance at Newman's edition, refer to 'Astrophel'; but Harvey, I. O., Harington, the author of *Zepheria*, N. Baxter, and Campion continue to refer to 'Astrophil'.

I

Sidney begins his work with a metrical innovation, a sonnet in twelve-syllable lines, possibly modelled on the Alexandrines of Antoine de Baïf and later French sonneteers (see also AS 6, 8, 76, 77, and 102). This introductory sonnet performs the double function of praising Stella as the ground of all poetical invention and of providing a brief essay on the proper method of writing love poetry. Sidney is considerably preoccupied with critical principles, especially in the earlier part of his sequence (see sonnets 3, 6, 15, 28, 34, 45, 50, 55, 58, 70, 74, and 90).

As Gascoigne had observed, 'The first and most necessarie point . . . meete to be considered in making of a delectable poeme is this, to grounde it upon some fine invention . . . some good and fine devise, shewing the quicke capacitie of a writer' (*Works*, ed. Cunliffe, i. 465). 'Invention', the discovery of ideas and subject matter, is the first of the three processes (*inventio, dispositio, elocutio*) prescribed by classical and renaissance theorists as necessary for producing any work of literature. Though the materials for invention are infinite, some hand-books, such as Cicero's *Topica*, tried to systematize the intellectual process (which as 'Nature's child' depends primarily upon the genius of the writer) by enumerating certain topics or places of invention, the most important being the intrinsic, which derive from the nature of the subject itself and include defini-tion, difference, adjuncts, comparison, &c. There was also another theory of composition, really opposed to the method of invention but widely practised in the renaissance, which advocated the imitation, not of nature, but of the writings of others (see Book II of Ascham's *Scholemaster*). Astrophil began in the wrong order with an inadequate method. He first sought words (*elocutio*) rather than matter, and tried to find words through imitation of others rather than by the proper processes of invention.

Sidney also criticized contemporary methods of imitation and elocution in his *Defence of Poesie* (iii. 41, cited by Pollard) by observing that the writings of many love poets, 'if I were a mistresse, would never perswade mee they were in love: so coldly they applie firie speeches, as men that had rather redde lover's writings, and so caught up certaine swelling Phrases . . . then that in truth they feele those passions, which easily as I thinke, may be bewraied by that same forcibleness or *Energia* (as the Greeks call it) of the writer'. ἐνέργεια, discussed by Aristotle (*Rhetoric*, III. xi. 1412ª) and Puttenham (III. iii) in their treatments of elocution, refers, not to the emotion felt by the writer, but to the effect that the sense of words, 'inwardly working a stirre to the mynde', has upon the reader.

1–5. Quoted by Fraunce (*Arcadian Rhetorike*, i. 18) as an example of the scheme climax (or *gradatio*).

7. Poirier cites Du Bellay's *Regrets*, 4, 'Je ne veulx feuilleter les exemplaires Grecs'.

8 *sunne-burn'd braine*, the intellect, whose capacity or vital moisture has been dried up by the flames of love.

11. 'Others' writings are alien to my purpose', with a play on 'feete' meaning (*a*) guides to be followed, and (*b*) metrical units—as Spenser said of Chaucer, 'I follow here the footing of thy feete' (*F.Q.* IV. ii. 34).

12 *throwes*, throes.

14. The most quoted and least understood line of all Sidney's poetry. 'Heart' refers to the mind in general, the seat of all the faculties. What the poet will see when he looks in his heart is the image of Stella (AS **4.** 12, **5.** 5–7, **32.** 13–14, **38.** 6, **39.** 14, **40.** 13–14, **43.** 13, **88.** 9–14, **105.** 4), which will give him all the material he needs for invention. AS 3 and 15 are variations on this same theme; see also Shakespeare's sonnet 38: 'How can my Muse want subject to invent, . . . When thou thyself dost give invention light?'

2

This second introductory sonnet, retrospectively recounting the slow development of Astrophil's love, is another declaration of independence from renaissance conventions, for most sonnet sequences from Petrarch onwards had dealt with love at first sight.

1 *dribbed*, ineffectual or at random, a variant of 'dribble'. The word was always used in a pejorative sense: Ascham referred to an unpractised bowman as 'a stark dribber or squirter', where 'stark' was ironical; Golding translated Ovid's 'rara per ignotos spargentem . . . tela' as 'dribling out his shafts among the Greekes'; and the Duke in *Measure for Measure* boasted, 'Believe not that the dribbling dart of love Can pierce a complete bosom'. I do not find satisfactory for this passage the definitions 'aimed high and dropping', 'short or wide of the mark', and 'indirect', given by Pollard, the *OED*, and Purcell (*PQ* xi. 403).

3 *mine*, tunnel dug in siege operations; cf. OA **30.** 96. Bt and Dr misread the

secretary hand 'e' of X and Y as 'd'; I am myself uncertain whether Ho has 'myne' or 'mynd'. *of time*, in course of time, slowly.

8 *partiall*, one-sided, favouring the lady only.

9 *footstep*, trace; cf. 'the Foote steppes of my over troden vertue' (iv. 172).

10–11. Cf. AS **47.** 3–4. The characteristic of the Russians most frequently noted in sixteenth-century accounts is that they enjoy slavery more than freedom (R. R. Cawley, *The Voyagers and Elizabethan Drama*, 1938, pp. 258–60, gives numerous references).

13 *my selfe*. 98's 'me selfe' derives from X (see **27.** 8, **x.** 7, and **93.** 11), which either preferred that spelling or misread O's 'mi' as 'me'; in Sidney's holographs the word is always spelled 'my selfe'.

14 *feeling*, cf. OA **30.** 126.

3

Sidney here reviews the chief literary movements of his time, both on the Continent and in England (the neo-Platonic cult of enthusiasm or inspiration, Pléiade imitations of the Greeks, rhetorical embellishers, and the Euphuists), in order to reiterate that he needs no art when he has Stella as his subject.

1–2. The ancient theory of *furor poeticus* was revived on the Continent in the sixteenth century and Spenser upheld the doctrine in his 'October' eclogue; but Sidney was sceptical. In the *Defence* (iii. 34) he said that Plato 'attributeth unto Poesie, more then my selfe do; namely, to be a verie inspiring of a divine force, farre above man's wit'; and in AS 74 he wrote:

> Some do I heare of Poets' furie tell,
> But (God wot) wot not what they meane by it.

1 *daintie wits*, delicate or weak intellects.

2 *bravely maskt*, gorgeously arrayed.

3–4. These lines describe precisely the procedure of the Hellenizers of the Pléiade, who carefully imitated the phrases and rhetorical devices ('flowers'), and even the ideas of the Greeks. Ronsard published his first volume of *Odes* in 1550 and proclaimed, as Miss Wilson noted,

> Le premier de France
> J'ai pindarizé. (II. ii. 36–37.)

5–6. Formal classical rhetoric, and especially that division of it dealing with style (*elocutio*) was assiduously cultivated in the later sixteenth century—one of the main characteristics distinguishing Sidney's own poetry from the earlier work of his countrymen is its complex rhetorical elaboration.

6 *Tropes*, rhetorical figures, specifically figures of thought. *problemes*, questions proposed for solution or discussion. The pseudo-Aristotelian *Problems* were popular in the Middle Ages, Erasmus devoted one of his *Colloquies* to the subject, and the handling of problems was a favourite device of the Petrarchists. In the *Defence* (iii. 24) Sidney pointed out, as the special praise of the lyric poet, the fact that he 'giveth morall preceptes and naturall Problemes'; and he himself deals with problems in AS 58 and vi.

7–8. These lines refer more to practices of prose writers than of poets; they specifically describe one aspect of the style called Euphuism that had been popularized by Lyly's *Euphues* in 1578. Gosson, another Euphuistic prose writer, dedicated his *Schoole of Abuse* to Sidney in 1579 and was, so Spenser reported, 'for his labor scorned'. In the *Defence* (iii. 42—noted by Pollard) Sidney said: 'now for similitudes in certain Printed discourses, I thinke all Herberists, all stories of beasts, foules, and fishes, are rifled up, that they may come in multitudes to waite upon any of our conceits, which certainly is as absurd a surfet to the eares as is possible.'

4

The struggle between will and wit (loosely, heart and head, desire and reason), is a major theme of the first part of the sequence (see especially sonnets 5, 10, 14, 18, 19, 21, 25, and 47, and R. L. Montgomery's excellent article in *Texas Studies in English*, xxxvi (1957), 127–40.

2 *bate*, debate or contention.

5 *old Catoe's*, Cato the Censor, who lived to the age of 85 and was known as 'a bitter punisher of faultes' (*Defence*, iii. 32).

5

1–4. In the *Old Arcadia* (iv. 16) Musidorus tries to persuade Pyrocles from love by arguing: 'The reasonable parte of youre sowle, ys to have absolute Comaundement, ageanst which yf any sensuall weykenes aryse, wee are to yeelde all oure sounde forces to the overthrowyng of so unnaturall a Rebellyon'.

2 *inward light*, reason, understanding (see AS **25.** 8 and **71.** 8).

5–8. This combines the common notion of renaissance psychology that, when the lover sees his lady, 'his eyes snatch that image and carrie it to the hart' (Castiglione, *Courtier*, Everyman ed., p. 313), with the medieval theme of worship of the lady. Shakespeare, in different fashion, made use of the same combination of ideas in his sonnet 105:

> Let not my love be call'd idolatry,
> Nor my beloved as an idol show.

Cf. OA 38, AS **4.** 13 and **40.** 12–14, and line 5 of Dyer's 'He that his'—'Whose harte the Aulter is, whose spirit the sacrifize'.

9–11. This is the Platonic theory that the form or idea of the Beautiful is also the Good; but physical beauty, which is produced by combination of the four elements in a living body, is only a shadow of the form of the Beautiful (*Symposium*, 204 and 210; Castiglione, ed. cit., pp. 306 and 317; Spenser, *Hymn to Beauty*, lines 64–140; &c.).

12–13. A common medieval notion—so Chaucer, *Knight's Tale*, i. 2847–8:

> This world nys but a thurghfare ful of wo,
> And we been pilgrymes, passynge to and fro—

and Sidney's statement in the *Defence* (iii. 11) that the end of all human learning is 'to know, and by knowledge to lift up the minde from the dungeon of the bodie, to the enjoying his owne divine essence'.

14. The poet asserts the conflict between the theories of philosophical ideal-
ism and his own experience, just as Romeo replied to the admonitions of Friar
Laurence with 'Hang up philosophy'. See also AS 21, 47, 71, and 72.

6

Sidney here refers in general terms to the most-used techniques in renaissance
love poetry: lines 1–4 oxymoron, 5–6 mythological references, 7–8 pastoral
disguise, 9 overuse of the word 'sweet', and 10–11 personification of emotions.
Examples of each can be paralleled in dozens of sixteenth-century poets, and
even Sidney himself used the devices in moderation—see AS **80.** 3, **82.** 1–4,
ix, 79. 1–2, and **102.** 12.

5–6. Jove wooed Europa, Leda, and Danae in the shape of a bull, a swan, and
a golden shower (Ovid, *Met.* vi. 103–13), a cluster of references often repeated
(by Turberville, ed. Chalmers, ii. 585—noted by Koeppel, p. 92; Greville, *Caelica*,
33. 9–11; &c.).

6 *Broadred* (in Dr only), meaning 'embroidered', carries out the clothes and
tapestry image. The most usual sixteenth-century spelling was 'brodered',
which the X Z scribes mistook for the more familiar but less appropriate
'bordered'.

8 *vaine*, vein.

7

Four reasons why Stella's eyes are black (Lady Rich had black eyes, see AS 9
and p. 436 above).

2 *wrapt*, included.

3–4. Sidney was greatly interested in the technical processes of painting (see
the report of his discussion with Hilliard, *Walpole Society*, i [1912], 27, and the
references collected by A. C. Judson, *Sidney's Appearance*, 1958, pp. 6 and 18–
22); he may have observed this new technique in pictures he saw in Italy.

5–11. Sidney used these two conceits again in the *New Arcadia* (i. 90—the
passage is not in the *Old Arcadia*) in Pyrocles' description of Philoclea: 'Her
black eyes; blacke indeed, whether nature so made them, that we might be the
more able to behold & bear their wonderfull shining, or that she, (goddesse like)
would work this miracle in her selfe, in giving blacknes the price above all
beauty.' Shakespeare, sonnet 127, said:

> In the old age black was not counted fair,
> Or if it were it bore not beauty's name;

and also used the mourning conceit of Sidney's lines 13–14. For backgrounds
of this commonplace see T. W. Baldwin, *Literary Genetics of Shakeseare's
Poems*, 1950, pp. 321–5. Miss Scott (p. 42) pointed out that Tasso praised the
black eyes of Lavinia de la Rovere with the same conceit as Sidney's lines 5–8
in a sonnet first printed in 1581.

6 *In*, with; cf. **viii.** 15–16.

8

This sonnet is an original combination of and variation on several conventional
themes. (*a*) The idea of Cupid as a runaway first appears in the first Idyl of

Moschus, and was popular in France from the time of Marot onwards; but Sidney's point that he fled because of the Turkish invasions (Pollard notes that Cyprus, the home of Cupid's mother Venus, was taken by the Turks in 1573) is original. (b) The most usual abode of love is in the lady's eyes or heart; only occasionally does he dwell in her face—see Guarini's' Dov' hai tu sede, Amore | Nel viso di Madonna o nel mio core?' (quoted by Ogle, *AJP* xxxiv. 142) and Shakespeare's sonnet 93—but Sidney's playful suggestion that he sought harbour there from the rigours of the English climate is again at least original in this context. (c) The conceit that Love remains in the lover's heart because he has lost his wings goes back to Propertius and the Greek Anthology; but apparently the earliest poet to say he burned his wings was Serafino Aquilano:

> Tennemi un tempo Amor per suo ricetto,
> fin che fe una fornace del mio core;
> ma come spesso per divin concetto
> de la sua opra un fraudolento more,
> volando un di dentro al mio ardente petto
> lui s'accesse, e non mai piu venne fore.
>
> (*Strambotto* 193, quoted by Koeppel, p. 95.)

There is no question of imitation here. Sidney made use of a few ideas or images that had become commonplaces; but he did not follow any one original, and he created anew quite as much as he took over from tradition. For discussion of the analogues see Miss Scott, pp. 32–33, and Miss John, p. 71.

2 *Turkish hardned hart*. The cruelty of the Turks was proverbial.

4 *our soft peace*. For the first twenty-odd years of her reign Queen Elizabeth avoided anything more than token entanglements in foreign wars, and her subjects' first praise was of the long peace she had given them; but there were some (Gosson, *Schoole of Abuse*, ed. Arber, pp. 34 and 50) who feared such inaction would weaken the moral fibre of the country, and Sidney in the *Defence* (iii. 36) complained of the 'over faint quietnesse' of the times.

9

Description of the lady by likening her, feature by feature, to various objects rich and strange had become a well-worn convention long before Petrarch (157) wrote 'La testa or fino, e calda neve il volto . . .'—see note to OA 62. The main distinction of Sidney's sonnet is the quadruple word-play at the end on 'touch', a glossy black stone which he apparently thought was a species of jet (in AS 91. 8 he calls Stella's eyes 'seeing jets'), a form of lignite that has the property of attracting light bodies when static electricity is induced by rubbing. The windows (Stella's black eyes) are made of 'touch' (glossy black stone) that without 'touch' (contact) doth 'touch' (affect with emotion); they are made of 'touch' (black lignite or jet) and I am their straw (irresistibly drawn to them).

Brian Twyne commented at length on this sonnet:

He likens his loves face to the court of vertue: the front built of Alabaster, the cover-ing of gold: her lips he likens to the doore made of redd Porphyre: her teeth to locks (for the doore) made of pearle: the porch (i.[e.]) the cheeks, made of red and whit marble: the windowes are her eyes made of touchstone, and therefore he likens himselfe to the strawe which it draweth: but this is improper for the touchstone doth not drawe strawe but iron: it hath no like sympathy with strawe: wherefore indeed this touchstone wanteth the touchstone of truth.

But Twyne confused the touchstone, used to test the purity of gold and silver, with the loadstone, a magnetic oxide that draws bits of iron to itself. Lyly (*Euphues*, ed. Bond, i. 228) made the correct distinction: 'Although the loadstone drawe yron, yet it cannot move golde, thoughe the Jette gather up the light strawe, yet can it not take up the pure steele.' Grosart, followed by Pollard, Miss Wilson, J. W. Lever (p. 77), and Poirier, assumed that 'touch' in line 14 refers to 'touchwood', an ignited match or tinder; but I believe that Sidney here is thinking of the magnetic rather than the inflammatory property of Stella's eyes. The *OED* cites the *Fayre Mayde of the Exchange* (1607): 'The drawing vertue of a sable jeat'. See also Max Putzel, *Explicator* xix. 25.

2 *chiefest*, supported by Y and Z, a common sixteenth-century superlative equivalent to 'best' (see AS **i.** 6). X's 'choisest', printed by all previous editors who use 98 as copy text, is a misreading of 'ief' as 'ois'; a similar graphical confusion occurs again at AS **10.** 4 and **43.** 4.

10 *over*. The rhythm demands Q2's 'ore'; but since none of the texts is consistent in indicating contractions and elisions (shown by spelling variants at **1.** 6, **1.** 8, **2.** 6, **2.** 9, **3.** 4, **3.** 5, &c., not listed in the selective apparatus), which may be a reflection of inconsistency on the part of Sidney himself, it is best to follow the reading indicated by the stemma.

12 *doth*. The Y Z 'do' may be an emendation made independently by both scribes on the assumption that the subject is 'windowes'; but the relative 'that' refers to the preceding 'touch'.

10

The debate between Reason and Love (see AS 4 and note) was a common theme of the amatory literature of the Middle Ages and renaissance. Miss Scott (pp. 35–36) quotes from Maurice Scève and Ronsard, and from Sperone Speroni's dialogue on love, in which one of the interlocutors compliments a lady by saying, 'Perhaps formerly I loved without reason, but in regard to you my dear lady, all my reason persuades me to love you'.

2 *brabling*, quarrelling or disputing. Bt and Dr's 'arguing' appears to be a sense substitution made independently by both scribes.

11 *fence*, action of fencing.

14. See OP **4.** 423–4.

11

5–8. Grosart (i. xxix) quotes Du Bartas, *Premier Jour de la première Sepmaine*, lines 155–60:

> Mais, tous tels que l'enfant, qui se paist dans l'eschole,
> Pour l'estude des arts, d'un estude frivole,
> Nostre veil admire tant ses marges peinturez,
> Son cuir fleur delizé, & ses bords sur-dorez:
> Que rien il ne nous chant d'apprendre la lecture
> De ce texte disert.

Sidney uses the comparison again in OP **4.** 180–4.

10 *lookst babies in her eyes*, looks at his reflection in her eyes (*pupula*, pupil of the eye, *pupulus*, little boy)—see K. Garvin, *TLS*, 5 December 1936, p. 1016.

11 *pitfould*, pitfall, a trap for birds.

12. Brian Twyne notes: 'Howe Cupid played at bopeepe in stellas eyes and brest'.

12

1–2. In Wiltshire larks were caught with 'day-nets' by attracting them with a brightly-shining lure made of small mirrors (Stella's eyes) and then capturing them with a net (her locks). Koeppel (*Anglia*, xiii. 467–8) quotes Pettie's *Petite Pallace* (1576, f. 59; ed. Hartman, p. 168): 'For as the Larketaker in his day Net hath a glasse whereon while the birdes sit and gaze, they are taken in the Net, so your face hath suche a glysteryng glasse of goodlynesse in it, that whyle I gazed thereon, I was caught in the snares of *Cupide*.' Miss Wilson and R. S. Kinsman (*Explicator*, viii. 56) quote seventeenth-century descriptions of this method of bird-catching. Sidney again makes use of line 2, and also AS **13**. 3–4, in Pyrocles' description of Philoclea in the *New Arcadia* (i. 90—the passage is not in the *Old Arcadia*): 'her haire (alas too poore a word, why should I not rather call them her beames) drawen up into a net, able to take *Jupiter* when he was in the forme of an Eagle'. See also OP **4**. 45–46. Petrarch may have originated the figure of the lady's hair as a net in his sonnet 253, but it was used by innumerable later renaissance poets (Ogle, *AJP* xxxiv. 128–30); see CS **27**. 2.

2 *That*, because (and also in lines 3–6 and 8). *lockes*. The Y Z 'lookes' is a graphical error resulting from misreading secretary hand 'c' as 'o'. *day-nets* (Q2 only), has been adopted by Grosart and all succeeding editors; the many variants result from improper attempts at emendation by scribes who were unfamiliar with the Wiltshire term.

3 *swell* (Ho only). Miss Wilson, without benefit of Ho, emended to 'swell' because the other seven clauses are in the present tense; Ho's reading is probably also an emendation. 'Sweld', the reading of the other substantive texts, probably results from X, Y, and Z misreading O's 'll' as 'ld', letters that are sometimes indistinguishable in secretary hands (see AS **61**. 3).

7 *speakes*, the indicative, supported by the stemma, is grammatically correct.

13

By the arms he gives them, Sidney portrays both Jove and Mars as unlawful lovers. When Jove burned with homosexual love for Ganymede, he took the form of an eagle, the only bird that could bear his thunderbolts, and carried the boy off to become his cupbearer (Ovid, *Met.* x. 155–61); Mars's adulterous amour with Venus was revealed by Phoebus to her wrathful husband Vulcan, who caught the lovers in his cunningly fashioned net (*Met.* iv. 171–89). Brian Twyne admired this sonnet as 'a fine conceit: for he makes Stellas face to be Cupids scutchin &c'. Sidney used the conceit again in OP **4**. 145–60.

11 *roses gueuls . . . in silver field*. Cupid's arms are the white and red of Stella's cheeks; but it also happens that the Devereux arms are *argent, a fesse, gules, in chief three torteaux*—three red disks, suggesting roses, in a silver field (R. B. Young, *Yale Studies in English*, cxxxviii [1958], 21). Constable (*Diana*, i. 10)

also described Lady Penelope in heraldic terms, but stressed the 'gules' and 'or' of the Rich arms. Sidney refers to his own arms in AS 65.

13 *blaze*, blazon. *these*. The stemma is evenly divided because Bt Ho Q1-2 read 'the'; but 98-Y is slightly more authoritative than Bt-Z, and 'these' fits the context better because it refers to Cupid's crest and shield, or to the roses and silver field of his shield.

14 *scarcely Gentlemen*, hardly entitled to a coat of arms. X's 'scantly' results from misreading O's 'rc' as 'nt' (see AS **104.** 6 where the same graphical error occurs in Z).

14

1 *friend*. The same person may be addressed again in AS 21 and 69 (and see 51 and 92).

2 *Gripe*, the vulture that rends with its beak ('doth tire') the vitals of Prometheus. The reference was a commonplace for describing the effects of love—thus Grimald translated Beza, 'By that gripes name he cleped love' (Tottel 129. 10). See also OA **53.** 6.

5 *Rubarb*, a bitter purgative drug (cf. AS **21.** 1).

6–13. Pollard calls attention to Musidorus and Pyrocles' discussion of love (*Old Arcadia*, iv. 15–21)—Musidorus argues that love will 'direct youre thoughtes from the way of goodnes', will 'overthrowe all the excellent thinges yow have done', and 'ronnes to infinite evills'; but Pyrocles replies that 'love hathe his worcking in a vertuous harte' and makes him 'sharpp witted'.

9 *maners*, moral character.

14. Cf. Angelo's 'To sin in loving virtue' (*Meas. for Meas.* II. ii. 183).

15

As Brian Twyne noted, this sonnet concerns 'diverse sorts of poets and Rimers'; it continues the criticisms, developed in AS 1, 3, and 6, of poets who mechanically imitate current fashions.

1–9. In his *Defence* (iii. 42—cited by Pollard) Sidney says of the diction of English poetry: 'So is that honey-flowing Matrone Eloquence, apparrelled, or rather disguised, in a Courtisanlike painted affectation. One time with so farre fet words, that many seeme monsters, but must seeme straungers to anie poore Englishman: an other time with coursing of a letter [alliteration], as if they were bound to follow the method of a Dictionary: an other time with figures and flowers [of rhetoric], extreamlie winter-starved.' T. Combe (*An Anatomie of the Metamorphosed Ajax*, 1596, L6ᵛ) observed that 'the incomparable Poet of our age, to give a most artificiall [i.e. artful] reproofe of following the letter too much, commits the same fault of purpose', and quoted lines 5–6; Hoskyns (*Directions for Speech and Style*, c. 1599, ed. Hudson, p. 15) made the same observation.

8 *denisend*, naturalized.

10 *inward tuch*, natural capacity.

11. Cf. AS **74.** 8.

16

9 *young Lyon*. A reference to the fable recorded by Aeschylus (*Agamemnon*, 717–36) to illustrate the harm that Helen caused to Troy—a shepherd brought up a lion cub which, while young, was a pet for his children, but when it grew up it destroyed all his flocks. Miss Wilson notes that the fable also appears in Erasmus's *Adagia*.

14. In the *Old Arcadia* the effects of love are described as a 'Cupp of poyson' (iv. 87); cf. OP **4.** 165.

17

4. To continue loving at the same rate as they did in the beginning.

6 *prove*, test or try.

14 *shrewd*, mischievous, injurious.

Miss Scott, pp. 33–34, suggested that this is a variation on the theme of Pontano's 'Exhausit pharetram Veneris puer: at Venus ignes | Extinxit . . .' (Love's quiver is empty and the torch of Venus extinguished; but the eyes of Stella my love provide thousands of arrows, and Venus lights her torch from the flames of my heart); but this provides no more than an analogue to line 11, which is a commonplace.

18

See *Orlando Furioso* in the Bibliography for Harington's comments on this sonnet.

1 *checkes*, reproofs. *shent*, shamed.

4 *hath*. The subject is 'heau'n', so the 98 Ho 'haue', accepted by previous editors, is an error.

9 *toyes*, useless trifles, his poems—see *Old Arcadia* dedication, p. 9 above.

19

10 *fare*. The stemma is split evenly with Bt Dr, which have the higher average of accuracy, reading 'fars'; but grammar requires the first person singular. *him*. Plato, *Theaetetus* 174A, tells how Thales fell into a well as he was looking at the stars; the anecdote became a commonplace—see the *Defence* (iii. 11), 'The Astronomer looking to the stars might fall in a ditch'.

12–13. Let me find some support for my young mind, which is not unfit by nature for producing the finest intellectual fruits.

14 *your*. Here again the stemma is split evenly with Bt Ho Q1, which have a slightly lower average of accuracy, reading 'thy'. Sidney used both forms indiscriminately, but had a four-to-one preference for 'thy'. We may consider the older pronoun 'thy' more appropriate to the older verb form 'saith', but there is no evidence that Sidney had enough knowledge of linguistic history to make a choice on such grounds—in the deliberately archaized OA 66 he used 'sayes' once, 'saith' not at all, 'your' three times, and 'thy' once. Where there is no other evidence upon which to base a decision, it is best to follow the mathematical odds of the stemma.

20

5 *Tyran*. An archaic spelling peculiar to X; it appears again in 98 and Bt at **viii.** 95, and in 98 at **v.** 57, 60, 61, and 85—all the other texts have 'tyrant'. Grosart guessed that 'tyran' was Sidney's own spelling; but I have not found the word in his holographs and so do not know how he spelled it.

6 *levell*, aim.

21

2 *windlas*, ambush, ensnare—figurative use of the hunting term meaning a circuit made to intercept game.

6 *coltish gyres*, youthful gyrations. Grosart and Pollard print 98's 'yeeres' but note that Q2's 'giers' is probably correct; Miss Wilson prints 'gires' and Poirier 'giers'. The 98 Ho Q1 'ye' probably results from X and Z's misreading of O's 'gi'. Miss Wilson suggests a verbal reminiscence of Plato's story of the charioteer and the two horses in *Phaedrus* 254, where the prancings of the black horse are denoted in Figliucci's translation by the verb 'girare'. Sidney may have had Plato's story in the back of his mind, but the Serranus translation of 1578, which we know he possessed, has only 'exultat impetuque abripitur' (Languet in a letter to Sidney on 24 September 1579 said a copy had been sent him three months before; and there appear to be a number of echoes of Serranus's introductions to the *Symposium* and *Ion* in the *Defence of Poesie*).

8 *Great expectation*. In the *Old Arcadia* (iv. 313) Philisides, upon his return like Sidney from foreign travel, was 'thought of good hope (for the worlde rarely bestowes a better Tytle uppon yowthe)'. But Sidney received no important public employment until he accompanied his uncle the Earl of Leicester to the Netherlands campaign, and even a few weeks before his death Edmund Molyneux still wrote of him as 'a gentleman of great hope, and exceeding expectation . . . if his good fortune . . . answer his noble deserts and woorthinesse' (Holinshed's *Chronicles*, uncensored 1587 edition, p. 1554).

22

2 *twinnes*'. The zodiacal sign of Gemini, from which the sun progresses in June. Sidney is not trying to date an event; but is saying that even when the sun is at its highest and hottest it will not burn Stella's face. Cf. OA **7.** 118.

23

7 *the Prince*, the sovereign (female sovereigns were regularly so referred to during Queen Elizabeth's reign). So far as is known, Sidney's 'service' in the latter part of 1581 and early 1582 consisted of no more than attending court functions and helping to entertain distinguished foreign visitors.

9. Cf. AS **27.** 11.

13 *hath* agrees with the subject 'race'; the Dr Z scribes, probably influenced by the preceding 'thoughts', improperly wrote 'have'.

24

The plays on the word 'rich' refer to Penelope's husband, Robert Lord Rich; see also AS **35.** 11 and 37. That she suffered 'abuse' from her husband Sidney asserts again in AS **viii.** 10, 'Her faire necke a foule yoke bare'. The phrasing of this sonnet is somewhat involved: Rich misers are fools because they hoard their possessions and deprive themselves in the midst of plenty, though even they have intelligence enough to recognize the value of the things they have and so to cherish them and keep them from harm; but let the rich fool, who by chance has come into possession of a great treasure and abuses it because he does not recognize its value, be deprived of joy and be rich in folly only.

25

1–2. The 'wisest scholler' is Plato, and the 'wight most wise' is Socrates, who had been adjudged the wisest of men by the Delphic oracle (*Apology* 21A). This characterization of Socrates became a commonplace as a result of its frequent repetition by Cicero and others—see the *Defence* (iii. 34), 'The Greeke Socrates, whome Apollo confirmed to bee the onely wise man'.

3–8. Miss Wilson noted that this derives ultimately from *Phaedrus* 250D, quoted by Cicero, *De Officiis*, i. 15, 'Formam quidem ipsam . . . et tamquam faciem honesti vides, "quae si oculis cerneretur, mirabiles amores", ut ait Plato, "excitaret sapientiae" ' (also in *De Finibus*, ii. 52). Plato is referring to φρόνησις (wisdom), which Cicero appears to equate with knowledge of the good, or virtue ('forma honesti'). That Sidney is following Cicero can be seen from the *Defence* (iii. 25): 'If the saying of Plato and Tully bee true, that who could see vertue, woulde bee woonderfullie ravished with the love of her bewtie.' Miss Scott, pp. 43–44, quotes verses by the minor French sonneteers De Buttet, Jamyn, and Blanchon, which begin with the same Platonic reference; but as there are no other resemblances, it is clear that all four writers were independently using the same renaissance commonplace.

5 *for*, because.

6 *While*. There is a three-way split in the stemma between 'while', 'whiles', and 'whilst'; in the sixteenth century the three forms were interchangeable. I have not noticed the word in Sidney's holographs; but at AS **2.** 2, **2.** 14, **6.** 10, **8.** 13, **16.** 9, and **19.** 4 the reading is clearly 'while'. *wayes*, the usual Elizabethan spelling of 'weighs'.

8 *inward sunne*, Reason.

9 *ster*, stir.

10 *takes*. 98's unique 'tooke' is attractive to modern ears because of the preceding 'of late' and following 'did see' (though to accept it we must assume that Y and Z misread O's secretary hand 'o' as 'a', which is a common graphical confusion); but 'takes' is acceptable Elizabethan usage and is supported by three of the four texts.

12 *It*. Plato's statement.

13 *prove*, experience.

26

1–11. These lines may have been suggested by Du Bartas, *Quatrième Jour de la Première Sepmaine*, 405–28:

> Ie ne croiray iamais que l'Ouurier Tout-puissant
> Ait peint de tant de feux le Ciel tousiours-glissant,

> Pour seruir seulement d'Vne vaine parade,
> Et de nuict amuser la champestre brigade.
> Ie ne croiray iamais que la moindre des fleurs,
> Que le moindre caillou, qu'en sa creuse matrice
> Recele auarement nostre mere-nourrice,
> Ait quelque vertu propre: & que tant de flambeaux
> Qui passent en grandeur & le terre, & les eaux,
> Luisent en vain au ciel, n'ayant point autre charge
> Que de se proumener par vn palais si large.

Many Elizabethans accepted the theories of astral influence, and Sidney took the subject seriously enough to have his horoscope cast (it is preserved in Bodleian MS. Ashmole 356, item 5).

1 *dustie*, earth-bound; cf. Harington, who calls carping critics 'the dusty wits of this ungratefull time' (*Epigrams*, ii. 64).

3 *wayes*, the paths followed by the stars in their circular dance. 98 Dr 'weighs' is an unusual spelling variant, though the opposite variant is common (see AS **25.** 6, **40.** 8, **63.** 12); Sidney did not distinguish the words by spelling and in his holographs has 'waies' for 'ways' and 'waied' for 'weighed'.

7 *brawle*, a dance in which men and women hold hands and move together in a circle.

28

7 *raines . . . slake*, reins . . . slack.

9. I do not ask for a topic to write about merely in order to show my rhetorical skill.

11 *quintessence*, the imperceptible fifth element, supposed to be latent in all things, which alchemists tried unsuccessfully to extract; cf. AS **77.** 8.

12–14. Poirier cites Du Bellay, *Regrets*, 4. 9–11:

> Je me contenteray de simplement escrire
> Ce que la passion seulement me fait dire,
> Sans rechercher ailleurs plus graves argumens.

29

13 *prospect*, situation, lookout.

30

The seven questions asked by 'busie wits', the politically-minded gentlemen of Astrophil's acquaintance, refer to the posture of international affairs at a particular time—'this yeare' and 'now' (lines 2 and 6); since all seven questions would have been topical only during the summer of 1582, Sidney must have written the sonnet at that time. The most thorough discussion of the allusions is that by L. C. John (*Elizabethan Sonnet Sequences*, 1938, pp. 189–93); E. L. Fogel (see note to line 6) provided the decisive evidence for dating.

1 *new-moone*, the standard of the Turks, who threatened Europe from the fifteenth until well into the seventeenth century. Miss John quotes news-letters written between March and June 1582 reporting that an attack on Spain by the Turkish fleet was believed imminent.

3–4. Stephen Bathory was crowned King of Poland in 1576 after an election contest in which the emperor Maximilian II was the other claimant, hence 'right king'. He invaded Muscovy in 1580, and in 1581 besieged Pskov until December. A treaty was negotiated at Zapoli on 15 January 1582, the terms of which were reported to Sidney's brother in London in a letter sent from Mentz on 28 March 1582 (*HMC De L'Isle*, ii. 99). Since letters often took many weeks to deliver, Sidney may not have heard of the treaty until early summer or later, and may not have considered it as marking more than a temporary cessation of hostilities.

3 *hoast*, refers (*a*) to the inhabitants of Muscovy, which Bathory had entered uninvited, and (*b*) to the Muscovite army which opposed him.

4 *ill-made fire*, Miss John suggests that this may refer to bombardment with red-hot cannon balls which Bathory used in siege operations.

5. Pollard notes that this alludes to the three French factions—the Catholics, the Huguenots, and the moderate Politiques—that struggled for power from 1575 until the accession of Henry IV in 1589.

6. E. G. Fogel, in a paper read before the Modern Language Association of America in 1952, pointed out that the word 'diet' was never used for parliaments of the Low Countries, and that 'Dutch' must refer, not to the people of the Netherlands, who are separately mentioned in the next line, but to the Germans; therefore the reference must be to the Diet of the Holy Roman Empire, the first since 1576, which was held at Augsburg from early July through September 1582, and whose proceedings were followed with great interest in England.

7-8. William of Orange was the accepted ruler of Holland and Zealand from 1576 until his death in 1584. Miss John notes that the Spanish general Parma in 1581 won Breda and Tournay, and in 1582 Oudenarde, Lier, and Ninove.

9-10. Sir Henry Sidney had been three times Governor of Ireland as Lord Deputy, his last term ending in 1578. He was considering a fourth term in 1582, for in April he drew up 'Certain special notes to be imparted to Mr. Philip Sidney' (Collins, i. 295-6), stipulating that he would accept another appointment only if Philip agreed to accompany and succeed him. His secretary Molyneux (in Holinshed's *Chronicles*, 1587, Ireland, p. 151) noted that his most praiseworthy achievement was in bringing the province of Ulster 'to the queenes peace and obedience'. Miss John points out that the 'golden bit' was the *cess*, an imposition levied on landowners, which Sir Henry revived and enforced to provide support for the troops needed to maintain order. Sidney's *Discourse on Irish Affairs*, *c*. 1577 (iii. 47-49), defended his father's handling of the cess.

11. The 'weltring', the rise and fall of political coalitions in Scotland, went on from 1568 to 1586. Pollard suggests that the line refers to the turbulent scenes which preceded the Raid of Ruthven on 22 August 1582, when the pro-English faction overthrew d'Aubigny and temporarily returned to power. Miss Wilson suggested that the 98 reading 'no weltring' (i.e. still staunch) was a deliberate editorial change designed to prevent offence to James VI, who in 1598 was expected to be the future King of England.

31

Mr. J. B. Leishman called to my attention, as a possible analogue, line 42 of the pseudo-Virgilian *Lydia*, 'Luna, dolor nosti quid sit: miserere dolentis' (O Moon, thou knowest what grief is: pity one who grieves).

14. Lamb, in 'Some Sonnets of Sir Philip Sidney', noted the transposition, which in normal order would read, 'Do they call ungratefulness there a virtue'? C. W. Lemmi (*MLN* xlii. 77–79) quotes Giovanni della Casa, Sonnet 40,

> Donna amar ch' Amor odia e i suoi desiri,
> Che sdegno e feritate onore appella,

and similar statements by Boccaccio (*Decameron*, i. 10) and Tasso (*Aminta*, iv. i).

32

1. Morpheus, the son of Somnus, has the special function of bringing dreams that appear in human shape (Ovid, *Met*. xi. 635); therefore 'lively' and 'deadly' mean 'life-like' and 'death-like'.

9 *of all acquaintance*. Here 'of' means 'for the sake of', but I do not know the idiomatic force of 'all'. It must have been a familiar locution, otherwise one or more of the four scribes would have emended to 'old acquaintance', an expression in common use since the early sixteenth century, for in some secretary hands 'all' and 'old' are practically indistinguishable. Miss Wilson suggests that it is analogous to Shakespeare's 'Speak, of all loves' (*MND* ii. ii. 154), the meaning of which is also obscure.

33

This is Astrophil's retrospective lament that he did not, while Stella was still unmarried, attempt to win her for himself (because, as AS 2 indicates, he had not yet fallen in love with her). Lines 9–11 imply that he even actively furthered her marriage to Lord Rich, which now, that he has become aware of the full noon-tide of her beauty, he bitterly regrets. I cannot agree with Grosart, Pollard, and others who suggest that the sonnet refers merely to an opportunity of seeing Stella which Astrophil had accidentally missed.

34

1–2. A common observation—i.e. Petrarch 23. 4, 'Perché cantando il duol si disacerba'.

4. 'As Aristotle saith [*Poetics* 1448^b], those things which in themselves are horrible, as cruel battailes, unnatural monsters, are made in poeticall imitation, delightful' (*Defence*, iii. 20).

7 *fond ware*, foolish trifles.

8 *close*, kept private, not allowed to circulate.

9 *hard*, heard.

35

4. Stella, though a product of finite nature, is goddess-like and therefore infinite.

11 *rich*, a second reference to Stella's married name (see AS 24 and 37).

36

2 *yelden* (Ho only), meaning 'yielded', an archaic past participle that confused the copyists. Pollard emended to 'yolden', but 'yelden' is Sidney's form—see OP 4. 529

5 *lies*, resides.

6 *forces*. Miss Wilson emended to 'fortress' because 'you cannot raze forces, or raise banners within them'; but forces can be 'razde', that is destroyed or swept away (*OED* 5), and the banners are 'raisd' within the castle of the lover's heart.

13–14. Even stones and trees, which do not have sense, are entranced by your voice.

37

Ho rearranged the order of the sonnets and omitted 24, 35 and 37 in order to remove the most obvious clues to Stella's identity; Q1 omitted 37 for the same reason, but with its usual carelessness retained the almost equally revealing 24 and 35. Sir John Harington was one of the earliest to solve the riddle and identify Stella as Lady Rich (see the Arundel-Harington MS. [Hn], and *Orlando Furioso*, 1591, in the Bibliography); see also Bodleian MS. Rawl. poet. 172, which contains an early transcript of this sonnet headed 'Ladie Rich'.

5 *Towardes*. The form Sidney uses in his holographs. *Aurora's Court*, the east—the family seat of Lord Rich was at Leighs in Essex, one of the eastern counties.

13 *make the patents*, comprise the grants.

14 *Rich*. Dr also reads 'Riche' with a capital.

38

2 *hatch*, close.

5 *error*, wandering.

7 *curious drought*, skilful draughtsmanship.

8. Stella's image shines like a star and produces the music of the spheres.

9–10 *closde up . . . opend sense*, sleeping . . . waking.

13 *it*, Stella's image.

14. That unkind guest (Stella's image) had slain her host Sleep.

39

5 *prease*, press, crowd.

9–11. Chaucer, *Book of the Duchess*, 250–61, promises he will give to Morpheus, or to anyone who will make him sleep, 'a fether-bed', 'many a pilowe', and 'al that falles To a chambre' (A. M. Lyles, *N & Q*, cxcviii. 99).

11 *A rosie garland*, the garland of silence or secrecy, *sub rosa*; Cupid dedicated the rose to Harpocrates, the god of silence, as a reward for his assistance in the intrigues of Venus. (Grosart, Pollard.)

40

4 *others* (Q1–2); 98 and Dr here read 'other', the plural form without 's'. Both forms were current in the sixteenth century; but Sidney preferred 'others', which is the reading of all texts elsewhere in *Astrophil and Stella*.

41

Attempts have been made, with little success, to identify this tournament. A tournament was a regular part of the entertainment provided for noble foreign visitors, and one was held annually on 17 November to celebrate the anniversary of the Queen's accession. From the position of Sidney's name in the chronological list of Elizabethan tilters printed by William Segar (*The Booke of Honor*, 1590, Nn3), it appears that he first took part in a tournament in company with Sir Walter Ralegh and Sir William Russell, who were both in England only between May 1579 and March 1580. No records of tournaments during these months survive, but there was probably an Accession Day tourney on 17 November 1579. Though probably more were held, records are extant of only seven tournaments during 1579–85, and Sidney is named as a participant in four of these: the challenge of the Earl of Arundel, 22 January 1581 (Segar, 1602, R2); the Fortress of Perfect Beauty tournament, 15–16 May 1581 (see notes to PP 4); the Accession Day tournament of 17 November 1581 (Bodleian MS. Ashmole 845, f. 165); and the tilt between the married men and the bachelors, 6 December 1584 (ibid., f. 168). The most important French visitors were the commissioners for whose entertainment the Fortress of Perfect Beauty was devised in May 1581; but M. de Simier was at court in November 1579, the Duke of Anjou accompanied the Queen to the jousts of November 1581, and spectators from France were doubtless present at all the Elizabethan tournaments. It would be futile to try to identify a particular tournament as the occasion of this sonnet, or of AS 53 or OP 1.

4 *sweet enemie*, a not unusual oxymoron; Poirier notes that Petrarch (146. 2) called his Laura 'dolce nemica'.

6 *daintier*, more precise.

7 *use*, practice.

9–10. Sidney's father and grandfather, and his maternal uncles the earls of Leicester and Warwick, had been frequent participants in tournaments in their younger years; the Earl of Leicester was a challenger with the Duke of Anjou in the royal combat of 1 January 1582 in which Sidney did not take part.

11 *man of armes*, technically a heavily armoured horseman.

12 *shoote* (Q1-2 only), the present tense was frequently spelled 'shot'.

43

Correlative verse—see AS 100 and note to OA 43.

2 *pray*, prey.

6 *by and by*, immediately.

44

1–4. Quoted by Fraunce (*Arcadian Rhetorike*, i. 18) as an example of the scheme climax.

5 *yet I no pitty* (Dr). 98 to be metrical requires an awkward elision of 'pitie I'; Dr and Z agree in all but one word, so I accept Dr because it is more authoritative and because its 'yet' is more emphatic.

7 *overthwart*, perverse, contrary.

45

3 *cannot skill*, is not able.

4. A confusing inversion that may be paraphrased 'even though she herself

knows the cause of my woe' or 'even though she knows that she herself is the cause of my woe'. Q2's partial correction of Q1 indicates that 'thereof the cause' appeared in Y, which thus agrees with X, though present-day readers may prefer 'the cause thereof'.

5–8. 'But how much it [tragedy] can move, Plutarch [*Life of Pelopidas*, 29] yieldeth a notable testimonie of the abhominable tyrant Alexander Pheræus, from whose eyes a Tragedie well made and represented, drew abundance of teares, who without all pittie had murthered infinite numbers, and some of his owne bloud: so as he that was not ashamed to make matters for tragedies, yet could not resist the sweete violence of a Tragedie' (*Defence*, iii. 23–24). T. B. Stroup (*PQ* xxix. 440–2) comments on Sidney's theories of art vs. actuality in this sonnet.

46

6 *Rogue*. 'All and everye persone and persones beynge whole and mightye in Body and able to labour, having not Land or Maister . . . shalbee taken adjudged and deemed Roges Vacaboundes and Sturdy Beggers' (*An Acte for punishement of Vacabonds*, 14 Eliz. [1572], cap. 5).

7–8. Pollard paraphrases, 'unless love learn to love and gaze without any further desire'.

13 *myche to desire*, be a truant from the school of virtue and give himself to desire.

14. Until you cease to be the fuel that causes his flames of love. Cf. Dyer's:

> As rare to heare as seldome to be seene,
> It can not be, nor ever yet hath beene,
> That fire should burne, with perfect heate and flame,
> Without some matter for to yeeld the same.

47

2 *burning markes*, brands indicating slavery.

9–11. Pollard quotes Musidorus's statement (*Old Arcadia*, iv. 16) that reason must overthrow rebellious passion: 'Wherein, how can wee want corage, synce wee are to dealle ageanst so weyke an Adversary, that in yt self, ys no thing but weykenes: Nay, wee are to resolve, that yf reason direct yt, wee must doo yt, and yf wee must doo yt, wee will doo yt. For, to say I can not, ys Chyldish, and I will not, womanish.'

48

4 *one*, Sidney's spelling of the ordinal; but the spelling 'on' was also current, so Y supports X.

7 *hel-driv'n*. The Q2 partial correction and the Dr partial error together show that Y supports X.

13 *sweet cruell shot*. Koeppel quotes Petrarch's 'dolce amaro Colpo' (296. 3–4), a common oxymoron.

14. Koeppel quotes Petrarch's 'Un modo di pietate, occider tosto' (207. 88).

49

Koeppel points out that Petrarch several times uses the figure of Love riding the lover (71. 9, 161. 9–11, 173. 8, &c.).

5 *raines* (Q1-2), required by the following 'are'.

7 *bosse*, metal knob adorning the bit.

50

1–4. 'But as I never desired the title [of poet], so have I neglected the meanes to come by it, onely over-mastered by some thoughts, I yeelded an inckie tribute unto them' (*Defence*, iii. 36).

9–11. Poirier cites Petrarch's *Trionfo d'Amore*, ii. 115–17:

> Da indi in qua cotante carte aspergo
> Di pensieri, di lagrime e d'inchiostro;
> Tante ne squarcio, n'apparecchio, e vergo.

51

5 *silly*, innocent.

13–14. Comedy presents the common affairs of daily life, usually love, in a plain style; it is a breach of decorum to introduce matters of gravity or to use a high style—the proper artist will not 'matche horne Pipes and Funeralls' (*Defence*, iii. 40).

52

Love asserts his right of possession ('title') to Stella by citing facts—that she outwardly wears his badge or livery; Virtue enters a demurrer—admits the facts but denies that they establish legal title, by raising the question whether the essential Stella is her inside or outside; this stops the action (stays the suit) until the court can decide the legal point.

53

7 *I would no lesse*. Grosart, Pollard, and Miss Wilson provide varying interpretations. I think Love speaks with conscious irony, 'I would give you no less (i.e. no higher) title than Sir *Fool*'; or the phrase may be a parenthetical comment by the poet which is meant to appear unconsciously ironic, 'I would accept (or, I deserve or desire) no less honourable a title than Sir Fool'.

10–14. The trumpet sounds for beginning the course and Astrophil sits motionless in his saddle, mawkishly gazing at Stella; his opponent, in another way just as oblivious to what is going on, charges to the middle of the lists and finds no one there—then in the last line farce becomes painful.

54

14. Fraunce (*Arcadian Rhetorike*, i. 22) quotes this as an example of *epanalepsis*. It is a rephrasing of a popular proverb; cf. Dyer's 'The lowest trees' lines 9–10:

> The firmest fayth is fownd in fewest woordes,
> The turtles doe not singe, and yet theye love.

55

1. Actually Sidney is sceptical of the theories of inspiration; he seldom addresses the Muses, and when he does so he is usually ironical. See CS **17**. 36–40, OP **4**. 5–8, and note to AS **3**. 1.

56

2 *learne it without booke*, memorize.
4 *large precepts misse*, forget your long lessons.
7 *lead'n*, heavy and dull.
11 *flegmatike*. Phlegm is the cold and moist humour.

57

4 *thorowest words*, words that will pass through or pierce.
7 *dainty rind*. Koeppel quotes Petrarch, 127. 35–37:

> E quella dolce leggiadretta scorza
> Che ricopria le pargolette membra
> Dove oggi alberga l'anima gentile.

58

1–4. Alciati's emblem, 'Eloquentia Fortitudine praestantior', pictures Hercules leading a crowd of people by a chain extending from his mouth; this is explained by Lucian in his *Heracles*, who says the Celts picture Heracles as an old man drawing a great crowd of people after him, all tethered by the ears with 'delicate chains fashioned of gold and amber' which are attached to the tip of his tongue, because he was 'a wise man who achieved everything by eloquence'. Puttenham (III. ii) also referred to Lucian's account.

5–8. In Cicero's *De Oratore* (iii. 223) Crassus asserts that *actio* (delivery, 'pronouncing grace') is the most important element in oratory. 'Delivery has most effect on the ignorant, on the mob, and on barbarians; for words influence nobody but the person allied to the speaker by sharing the same language, and clever ideas frequently outfly the understanding of people who are not clever, whereas delivery, which gives the emotion of the mind expression, influences everybody.' See also Quintilian, XI. iii. 2–4.

59

Comparisons of the lover to a dog were common. Koeppel quotes Serafino Aquilano, sonnet 12:

> O felice animal, felice dico
> Che godi di tal dea le labra e 'l fiato . . .
> Tu de sue braccia cinto, and io mendico . . .

Lee refers to Melin de St. Gelais's 'Ha petit chien', and Ronsard's *Amours*, i. 78; see also Tottel, No. 202, and Turberville, ed. Chalmers, ii. 609. About 1593–5 Antonio Pérez sent Lady Rich a present of a pair of gloves with a letter saying, 'De perro son, Señora, los guantes, aunque son de my, que por perro me tengo y me tenga Vuestra Señoria en la fee, y en amor à su serviçio', which he signed 'Perro dessollado de Vuestra Señoria' (*Obras y Relaciones*, 1654, p. 525). This is the popular 'eloquençia Cortesana' which Shakespeare satirized in Don Armado, and to which Sidney could give new life by his turn of wit at the end.

60

14 *Blist* (98 only). Though Y and Z have 'Blest', Sidney's custom of graphically indicating eye-rhymes suggests that he wrote 'Blist . . . blisse' to parallel the polyptoton of 'curse . . . cursed'; the Y Z scribes probably misread O's 'i' as 'e'.

61

3 *assayll.* Dr only, and an emendation made independently by Miss Wilson because it seems more likely that 'transcribers should be in error than that Sidney should have put a past and present tense in such jingling juxtaposition'. The X Z scribes probably misread O's 'll' as 'ld' (see note to AS **12.** 3).

5–14. Poirier (*Sidney*, p. 213) calls attention to the *New Arcadia* (i. 157–8) where Pamela tells Dorus that 'it becomes a true Love to have your harte more set upon her good then your owne, and to beare a tenderer respect to her honour, then your satisfaction', to which he replies, 'I find my love shalbe proved no love, without I leve to love'.

7 *selfnesse.* 'Apparently a coinage by Sidney, and a favourite of Greville's' (Miss Wilson).

12 *Doctor*, teacher, with specific reference to a Schoolman or teacher of logic.

13 *Angel's sophistrie*, the angelic Stella's sophistry, possibly with a play on the Scholastic method of St. Thomas Aquinas, who was called Doctor Angelicus.

62

5. A current expression—e.g. 'Thy silver is become dross, thy wine mixed with water' (Isaiah i. 22).

63

Astrophil's argument is doubly sophistical: (*a*) in the sixteenth century the double negative was a common and accepted English usage, so that his 'grammer rules' apply only to Latin and not to English; and (*b*) grammatically 'no, no' is a repetition for emphasis and not a double negative at all. Since 1762, when the grammarian Robert Lowth prescribed that 'two Negatives in English destroy one another, or are equivalent to an Affirmative', the quibble has lost its freshness and half of its sophistry; but it was frequently repeated by Brian Twyne, Shakespeare, and others.

9. The illustrative quotation for 'Io Paean' in Cooper's *Thesaurus* (1565) suggests that an Elizabethan might associate the exclamation with the opening of the second book of the *Ars Amatoria* where Ovid, having previously described how to win a mistress, exclaims in joy that the prey he sought has fallen into his toils:

> Dicite 'io Paean!' et 'io' bis dicite 'Paean!'
> Decidit in casses praeda petita meos.

12 *weighe* (Dr only), but the Ho Q1–2 'waye' is a common spelling variant.

i

Set as a 'Canzonet' by R. J. S. Stevens in 1798.

32. Probably an inversion: 'Only with you miracles are not wonders.'

65

Miss Scott (p. 34) traces the story of Cupid as a beggar given harbour by the lover to the *Anacreontea*, No. 33; Miss John (pp. 71–74) points out that this is the first appearance of the story in English, and notes that Greville (*Caelica* 12) plays with the same conceit but gives it a different turn.

4 *prize*, estimate the relative value of.

14. The Sidney arms are *or, a pheon azure* and a 'pheon', as Pollard noted, is an arrow-head.

66

6. The wheel of Fortune revolves slowly; i.e. my fortune remains the same, I have not yet obtained Stella's favour. The testimony of Dr indicates that Q2's 'Fortune' does not derive from Y and so must be a misprint or an emendation; nevertheless the Q2 reading must be correct. 'Fortunes' in the other texts must result from an error in O or a misreading by X, Y, and Z of O's 'e' as 's'.

8 *stilts*, crutches.

67

4. Pollard notes, ' "Time" is here rather "opportunitas" than "tempus": the sense is, "will she forestall my ruin".'

68

1. Stella is the only sun that gives me light. Miss Wilson conjecturally emends 'light' to 'night', thus destroying the anadiplosis in the first two lines.

70

4. Ganymede, beloved by Jove, was given the office of mingling the nectar and attending Jove's cups (Ovid, *Met.* x. 155–61); so Astrophil speaks of himself as a cup-bearer because he is loved by his goddess Stella (that Sidney held official appointment as cup-bearer to Queen Elizabeth does not appear to be relevant here).

9 *thou* (98 only). Ho Q1–2 read 'the'; but even though Q2 corrected the following word, the corrector worked so carelessly that we cannot assume that 'the' is the reading of Y. The rhythm requires that the word carry stress, so 'thou' is more appropriate.

71

1–4. Miss Scott (p. 39) compares Petrach 248. 1–2 and 9–11 (who wishes to see what Nature can do, let him look upon Laura . . . in her he shall see every virtue and every beauty perfectly joined in one body).

7 *night-birds*, vices (the owl, for example, is used variously to pictorialize avarice, envy, sloth, and gluttony).

14. Cf. CS 6.

72

8. Ovid (*Met*. i. 468–70) says that Cupid has two arrows, one of gold which kindles love, the other of lead which causes the person wounded to reject love. Sidney has changed the significance of the golden arrow.

ii

This describes the stealing of the kiss which is celebrated in sonnets 73, 74, and 79–82. The 'baiser' had been popularized as a poetic kind by the *Basia* of Johannes Secundus and Ronsard's adaptations; but I have not noticed that Sidney's sonnets anywhere specifically resemble these earlier works. This is his first poem entirely in accentual trochaic rhythm, though he had used the rhythm earlier in parts of CS 7, 26, and 27. A musical setting of about 1616 or earlier is in British Museum MS. Additional 15117, f. 19.

73

14 *Anger'*. Possessives without 's' occasionally occur (see AS **20**. 12, **iii.** 7, **v.** 32, and **103**. 14; PS **9**. 39, **10**. 12, and **29**. 17).

74

1–4. Miss Scott (pp. 44–45) points out that this was a frequently voiced protestation and cites analogous statements by Persius, Du Bellay, Ronsard, and others.

1 *Aganippe*, 'A fountayne in . . . Greece . . . which was dedicate unto the Muses, wherof they be called *Aganippides*' (Cooper, *Thesaurus*, 1565).

2 *Tempe*, the valley in Thessaly where Daphne, pursued by Apollo, was turned into a laurel tree (Ovid, *Met*. i. 452–570).

5–6. See AS **3**. 1–2 and note.

7 *brooke of hell*, the Styx; see OA **73**. 161 and note.

8. Brian Twyne entered this line in his notebook, and Drayton quoted it in the prefatory sonnet to his *Idea*. Sidney kept his oath and never merely copied from others; see note to OA **9**. 53.

75

1–8. Holinshed said that Edward IV was 'highly favored of the people', and More described him as 'a goodlye personage, and Princely to beholde'; but beyond saying that he was 'politique in counsell', the chroniclers did not credit him with exceptional learning or mental capacity. When his father the Duke of York was slain in battle against the Lancastrians, Edward usurped the throne and defeated his family's enemies, thus revenging his father and winning a kingdom. The earlier years of his reign were beset with civil broils, but the later years were tranquil and his rule 'juste and mercifull'.

9–11. In 1474 Edward marched into France (fleur-de-lis); but Louis XI persuaded him to withdraw by paying him 75,000 crowns. Scotland (red lion), though frequently at war with England, had before 1474 agreed to a long truce; therefore at this time France was not hedged, or protected, by Scotland.

12–14. Earlier in Edward's reign, while the Earl of Warwick was by his order negotiating a marriage for him in France, the King became infatuated with the widow, Lady Elizabeth Gray, and after she had 'denyed hym to be his paramour', secretly married her. Warwick took the King's marriage as a personal affront and drove him into exile, and Edward was only able to regain his throne by vigorous campaigning.

The chroniclers and poets of the sixteenth century, though they admitted Edward's popularity with the people, represented him as neither great nor admirable, and emphasized his violence and self-indulgence. The *Mirror for Magistrates* said he died of 'surfeting and untemperate life', and told at length the sad end of his favourite paramour, Shore's wife, and how he furthered the drowning of his own brother in a butt of malmsey. The usually non-committal Stow said he 'murdered' the rightfully crowned King Henry VI in the Tower, and 'slewe' Prince Edward after he had yielded himself prisoner. All the chroniclers stressed that he was 'greately given to fleshely wantonnesse'; Shakespeare called him 'lustfull Edward' and portrayed him 'lolling on a lewd day bed . . . dallying with a brace of courtesans'. Sidney knew, and knew that his readers would know, the unsavoury aspects of Edward's life and character; so he is being patently sophistical.

4 *impe*, engraft feathers in the wing of a falcon to improve its flight.

11 *wittie*, crafty.

13 *for*, because.

14 *faile*, lack, be without.

76

13 *walking*, with ideas in motion, agitated—cf. AS **viii**. 23.

14. Cf. AS **78**. 14.

77

8 *sublime*, extract.

14. Cf. OA **3**. 14.

78

8. See AS **24**. 11.

9–13. A description in the manner of the emblem books.

14 *hornes*, the badge of the cuckold. See H. S. Wilson, *Explicator* ii. 17.

79

3 *consort*, a harmonious combination of instruments.

4. Venus was traditionally represented as drawn in a chariot by doves (Ovid, *Met*. xiv. 597).

13. Brian Twyne noted, 'She was ye very breakefast of love: and ye highway to passion'.

80

1. Miss Scott (p. 29) quotes Tasso's sonnet on Signora Sanvitale (1579):

> Quel labbro che le rose han colorito
> Molle si sporge e tumidetto in fuore.

8 *graine*, the purple of political dignity.

81

5. 'A kisse may bi saide to bi rather a coupling together of the soule, than of the body . . . And therefore Plato the divine lover saith, that in kissing, his soule came as farre as his lippes to depart out of the bodie' (Castiglione, *Courtier*, Everyman ed., p. 315).

12 *peace*, be silent.

82

3–4. Narcissus, who died gazing at his own reflection, and Venus who appeared naked before Paris.

6. The golden apples of the Hesperides (*Aeneid*, iv. 483–8).

11 *bit*, bite.

14. 'Oscula mordenti' (Catullus, lxviii A, 87).

83

The sparrow was associated with lechery (OA **10.** 79). As Grosart noted, this is based on Jane Scrope's description in Skelton's *Philip Sparrow*, 115–42:

> It was so pretty a foole
> It wold syt on a stoole
> And learned after my scoole
> For to kepe his cut
> With Phillip kepe your cut.
> It had a velvet cap
> And wold syt upon my lap
> And seke after smal wormes
> And sometime white bread crommes
> And many times and ofte
> Betwene my brestes soft
> It wold lye and rest
> It was propre and prest
> Sometime he wold gaspe
> When he saw a waspe
> A flye or a gnat
> He would fly at that
> And pretely he would pant
> When he saw an ant
> Lord how he would pry
> After the butterfly
> Lord how he wold hop
> After the gressop
> And whan I, sayd, phyp phip
> Then he wold leape and skip
> And take me by the lip
> Alas it wyl me sloe
> That Philip is gone me fro.

For other references to Skelton's sparrow see OA **29.** 84 and OP **4.** 83–104.

3 *your cut to keepe*, act with propriety, maintain modest conduct. Commentators and the *OED* have been uncertain of the meaning, which is explained by Dudley Carleton's account of the carryings-on at a wedding in 1604: 'Many

great ladies were made shorter by the skirts, and were well served that they could keep cut no better'.

iii

1–4. These fables of Orpheus and Amphion were among the most common of commonplaces. See AS **68.** 6, OP **6.** 13–14, and the *Defence* (iii. 4), 'So as Amphion, was said to moove stones with his Poetry, to build Thebes, and Orpheus to be listened to by beasts'.

4 *which Amphyon's*. Miss Wilson omits 'which' in order to relieve Sidney of 'a shocking false quantity', and notes that he scans the name properly in AS **68.** 6; but both texts read 'which'.

7–10. Pollard points out that these stories are from Pliny's *Natural History*, viii. 61 and x. 18. Thoas an Arcadian was rescued from robbers by a dragon which he had nurtured, and an eagle, which a maid of Sestos had cared for, at her death flew into her funeral pyre and was consumed—the story of the eagle was also used by Lyly in *Euphues and his England*, 1580 (ed. Bond, ii. 77).

The three stanzas deal with hearing, sight, and reason. R. B. Young (*Yale Studies* xxxviii. 70), quotes Ficino's commentary on the Symposium (trans. S. R. Jayne, 1944, p. 130): 'Beauty pertains only to the mind, sight, and hearing. Love, therefore, is limited to these three, but desire which rises from the other senses is called, not love, but lust or madness.'

The song is structured on an elaborate chiasmic pattern. In the first stanza we are told of trees and stones, and in the last line have 'O stones, ô trees'. In the second stanza we are told of a beast and a bird, in line 10 'his . . . her' is set against 'her . . . his', and in line 12 we should have 'O birds, ô beasts' (both texts are in error here, perhaps because of an accidental inversion by the scribe of O). In the last stanza 'birds, beasts, stones and trees' is set against 'trees, nor stones' and 'beasts, nor birds'.

84

Miss Wilson suggests that, 'If . . . Sidney was riding to the Countess of Leicester's house at Wanstead . . . this highway was the Whitechapel Road'. She apparently assumes that Sidney would start his journey from London; but the sonnets have courtly life as their background, and throughout the spring of 1582 the Court was at Greenwich. Moreover, we do not know where the Countess of Leicester resided. She was forbidden the Queen's presence, so if she was at Wanstead when the Court came to nearby Greenwich, she may have removed to a greater distance, possibly to Langley which is west of London. Unless definite evidence is available, speculations of this sort are futile.

1. You are my way to poetry because you lead me to Stella.

3 *Tempers*, tunes.

6 *safeliest* (Ho Q1–2). 98 has the correct but confusing contracted form 'saflest'; but Gray, Grosart, and other editors adopt 13's 'safe-left', which is either a misprint resulting from foul case or a mistaken attempt at emendation. 'Safeliest' emphasizes the secrecy made necessary by Astrophil's adulterous courtship.

9–11. C. Dahl (*Explicator*, vi. 46) explains, perhaps unnecessarily, that the poet hopes that magistrates will prevent landowners from encroaching on the public right of way, that the road will be kept in good repair, and that no murders or robberies will be committed upon it.

14. A common conceit; so Petrarch asks the river Rhone to kiss Laura's foot and hand (208. 12).

85

13 *indentures*, a play upon (*a*) 'indentations', and (*b*) 'contracts'.

iv

Set to music by Henry Youll, *Canzonets*, 1608; and printed with music by Giovanni Giacomo Gastoldi in *Synopsis of Vocal Musick*, 1680. Bruce Pattison (*Music and Poetry of the English Renaissance*, 1948, pp. 175–6) says there is a note in an early hand in the John Rylands Library copy of *Englands Helicon* stating that this was sung to 'Shall I wrastel in disp.', and transcribes the seventeenth-century melody to which Wither's poem was sung.

28 *take time*. Miss Wilson observes that this has the meaning of Horace's *carpe diem*.

47. It is clear from the pattern of the poem that lines 5 and 6 of each stanza should be invariant until the last stanza.

86

4 *gripe*. See AS **14.** 2 and note.

5 *Ermine*. See OA **62.** 116 and note.

14 *one's* (Ho Q1-2), a reading accepted by Grosart and all subsequent editors, and clearly demanded by the sense.

v

Internal evidence indicates that this song was composed earlier than the *Astrophil and Stella* sonnets, and that the 'Stella' of line 31 was originally 'Mira'. (*a*) Lines 1 and 13 refer to a love affair in which the lady at first showed the poet favour but later became 'unkind' and rejected his advances. This is precisely the experience that Philisides had with Mira (see OA 73 and notes), but is the reverse of the situation in *Astrophil and Stella*, where Stella at first appears to be cold but later admits her love for Astrophil. This song, therefore, was probably originally written as part of the 'hasty Revenge' (OA **74.** 66) that Philisides said he took when Mira first disdained him, and of which OA 31 may have been another part. (*b*) As Poirier (*Sidney*, p. 180) pointed out, only a few of the phrases in lines 10–11 and 37–39 that the poet said he had formerly used to praise his lady can be approximated in *Astrophil and Stella*; but all (except 'thy voyce the Angels' lay' line 11) appear practically verbatim in OA 62, the *blason* composed by Philisides in praise of Mira. Three of these phrases (lines 10–11 and 37), which cannot be found in any form in *Astrophil and Stella*, clearly echo OA 62 (lines 60, 131, and 126).

R. B. Young (*Yale Studies*, cxxxviii, 75) quotes Ficino's commentary on the *Symposium* (trans. S. R. Jayne, p. 145): 'Anyone who is loved ought in very justice to love in return, and he who does not love his lover must bear the charge of homicide, nay rather, the triple charge of thief, homicide, and desecrator.'

4 *of*, on.

7. See OA **74.** 31, AS **8.** 12, and **21.** 14.

8. See OA **74.** 37; Koeppel (p. 93) quotes Petrarch's 'dolce veneno' (152. 8). *wert*. The reading of Q1, accepted by Grosart and all succeeding editors, parallels 'wert' in line 7.

10–11. See OA **62.** 15, **62.** 60, **62.** 131, and AS **vii.** 18.

22 *flewst*. The reading of Q1, accepted by Grosart, is required by the preceding 'thou'.

27 *hidnest*. The reading of 98 accepted by Miss Wilson and Poirier; the earliest *OED* entry (s.v. 'hidden') is 'hidnest corner' 1625. Gray, Grosart, and Pollard accept 13's unauthoritative emendation 'kindest'.

32 *Defiance*'. Grosart and Poirier assume this is a genitive, I believe rightly (see AS **73.** 14 and note).

36 *babies*, dolls. *shrewd*, shrewish.

37 *warme . . . snow*. See OA **62.** 126. Koeppel (p. 93) quotes Petrarch's 'calda neve' (157. 9, see also Petrarch's 30. 10 and 57. 4).

38–39. See OA 62, lines 61–66, 37–42, and 3–4.

49–50. Brian Twyne thought this worthy of comment: 'He likens Stella his love to an English theife'.

83 *refuse*, refusal.

vi

In order to settle their dispute concerning precedence, Stella's Voice and Face appear before the judge Common Sense in the court of True Delight. They engage Music and Beauty as lawyers to plead their respective causes, and bring Wonder and Love as character witnesses and the Ear and the Eye as technical witnesses. Common Sense finds the claim of each to be equal and cannot decide the case, so appeal is made to the sovereign Reason. Sidney started with a simple committee of arbitration and added to it some of the procedures of higher tribunals such as the Court of Common Pleas, a medley which may annoy some lawyers, but which William Byrd found sufficiently attractive to merit a musical setting in his *Psalmes Sonets, & songs*, entered in 1587.

5 *bate*, debate, controversy.

9 *oratours*, pleaders, the lawyers of line 14.

11. The Court before which they make their arguments.

14 *wage*, hire.

25 *loftly*, a syncopated form of 'loftily', though the *OED* gives 'loftly' a separate entry with this passage as the only example.

34 *Musick's*. An emendation by Gray and the reading of Q1 accepted by Grosart and all subsequent editors; 'Musike' may be a genitive without 's', but more probably is a misreading by 98 and Bd of final 's' as 'e'.

40 *The*. The reading of Q1 accepted by Miss Wilson and Poirier; 98 and Bd misread 'The' as 'Eye', which can easily be confused in secretary hand.

42 *exceptions*, legal objections.

43 *common sence*, the inward apprehending faculty of the sensible soul, which receives impressions from the five outward senses and transmits them to the

imagination, which in turn transmits images to the understanding and will of the rational soul.

44 *Arbiter*, arbitrator.

vii

Fraunce (*Arcadian Rhetorike*, i. 23) quotes this entire song as an example of 'epanodos' or regression, an iteration by parts of the whole that has been spoken before.

viii

See the Introduction, p. xlvi, for discussion of the use of the third person here. Greville's *Caelica* 76 is a companion poem to this; it uses the same metre, deals with a similar situation, and even echoes some of Sidney's phrases. Sidney's song was set by Robert Douland, *A Musicall Banquet*, 1610; and a medley of words made up from lines 29–46 and **x.** 1–2 was printed with music by Giovanni Giacomo Gastoldi in *A Synopsis of Vocal Musick*, 1680.

2 *wanton*, sportive, gay.

5 *Astrophil*. See note above to the Title.

19 *armes crost*. A sign of sorrow (Pollard).

21 *of*, for.

30 *of*, over.

55 *allowes my reason*, approves my argument.

73–74. 'Do not try to test my love by this display of passion' (Miss Wilson).

102 *so*. An emendation by Gray, and the reading of Bt (and Ha Ra) accepted by Miss Wilson and Poirier; 98's unique 'to' results from misreading 's' as 't'.

104 *broken*, cut off, brought to an end.

ix

See the Introduction, p. xlvi, for discussion of the use of the pastoral disguise here. This was set to music by Robert Douland, *A Musicall Banquet*, 1610, and there is another setting in Christ Church Oxford MS. 439, f. 9.

4 *From* (Q1 Dd). Probably O had 'Frõ' and X Y did not observe the tilde.

88

This with AS **91**, **97**, **xi.** 21–22, and **106** are on the *remedia amoris* theme of 'examine other beauties' to get over love.

3–4. Another woman who offers him an immediate reward.

8 *pray*, prey.

89

For sonnets with only two rhyme words see OA 39 and note. Miss Scott (p. 41) cites a sonnet by R. Fiorentino rhyming on 'giorno' and 'notte'—there is no other resemblance.

5–14. Quoted by Fraunce (*Arcadian Rhetorike*, i. 23) as an example of 'epanodos'.

13–14. Koeppel (p. 94) cites Petrarch's 150. 6 and 182. 5 for the common heat-cold contrary.

90

The point of this sonnet is similar to AS 1, 3, 6, and 15; it may have been composed with those and introduced here to add variety of another subject to the absence group (see also AS 74).

1. A common protestation. Koeppel (p. 94) cites Petrarch's assertion that during Laura's lifetime his object was to express his grief, not to gain fame (293. 9–11); and Poirier cites Desportes (*Diane*, i. 1), 'Et puis je n'escry pas pour gloire en acquérir'.

9 *could I*, the reading of Q1–2 accepted by Grosart and all subsequent editors, is an emendation but one clearly demanded by the sense. 'I could' was probably an inversion error by the scribe of O.

14. Cf. AS **28**. 14. Koeppel (p. 94) quotes Petrarch (151. 13–14),

> Ch'a parte a parte entro a' begli occhi leggo
> Quant' io parlo d'Amore, e quant' io scrivo;

and Poirier cites Desportes (*Diane*, 'Chant d'amour', line 7), 'Amour guide ma plume'.

91

8 *seeing jets*, pieces of jet that can see, black eyes; cf. AS **9**. 9–13.

11 *wood-globes*, wooden globes on which are depicted the arrangement of the constellations; since the heavenly bodies are merely painted or drawn on the globe, they lack the brilliance and magnitude of the real stars in the sky. (The *OED* does not enter 'wood-globe', and its earliest entry for a celestial 'globe' is 1592; but they were in use throughout the century—see E. L. Stevenson, *Terrestrial and Celestial Globes*, ii [1921], 201.)

92

1–2. Are your words so precious that you give me only a few?
3 *cutted*, concise, laconic.
5 *totall*, brief.

x

Set by William Byrd, *Songs of sundrie natures*, 1589, and by Robert Douland, *A Musicall Banquet*, 1610; lines 43–48 were also set by John Ward, *The First Set of English Madrigals*, 1613.

35 *prove*, make trial of.

93

There is no hint of the nature of this well-intentioned misdeed that harmed Stella.

4 *vexed*, made to suffer.
8 *misse*, go astray.
11 *quite*, acquit.

95

1. Poirier cites Ronsard, *Amours*, ii. 36, 'Mes souspirs, mes amis, vous m'estes agreables'.

8 *mate-in-arms* (Q1-2 only, accepted by Grosart and all subsequent editors); not in the *OED*, but clearly an Anglicization of the French 'compagnon d'armes'. Since the term was unfamiliar, X Y Z probably misread O's 'arms' as 'arme' and only Q1 emended properly.

96

2 *kind*, nature.
6 *holds one degree*, has the same station or rank.
9 *mazefull*, frightening.
10 *stur*, stir.
12 *fur*, Sidney's spelling of 'far', which he pronounced [fʌr].

97

1–4. Diana the huntress brings with her the stars, who in their hunting ('chace') take up a shooting position ('standing') in the sky, whence they cast their beams on human beings.

9 *Lady*. Unidentifiable; perhaps the same one who appeared in AS 88.

98

Addresses to the bed were frequent in renaissance love poetry. Koeppel refers to Petrarch 226. 8 and 234. 5–7; Lee (*Elizabethan Sonnets*, I. xlv) quotes Antonio Tebaldi, *Opera d'Amore*, 15, and Desportes, *Diane*, i. 7. Though the subject is conventional, Sidney's handling is, as usual, entirely original.

7 *gald*. 13's emendation, accepted by Grosart, Miss Wilson, and Poirier. X and Y misread secretary hand 'a' as 'o', and Z misread 'ga' as 'he'. Cf. 'Spurr'd, gall'd and tir'd by jauncing Bolingbroke' (*Rich. II*, v. v. 94), and 'Zelmane . . . (inflamed by Philoclea, watched by Gynecia, and tired by Basilius) . . . was like a horse, desirous to runne, and miserablie spurred, but so short rainde, as he cannot stirre forward' (*New Arcadia*, i. 95). Poirier cites Petrarch, 145. 1, 'Amor mi sprona in un tempo ed affrena'.

11 *marks* (Ho Q1, accepted by Gray and all subsequent editors). X and Y must have omitted 'r' in error, for 'makes' does not make sense.

13 *winke*, close.

99

3 *marke wanting*, lacking a target (a Sidneyan coinage not listed in the *OED*).
5 *windowes*, shutters, eyelids.
8 *mazde*, confused.
9 *charme*, chirm, sing in unison.

100

The structure is that of correlative verse; see OA 43 and note.

1. The much-used figure of *epanorthosis*; cf. Petrarch 161. 4, 'Oi occhi miei, occhi non gia, ma fonti!'

4 *gracefull* (98 only), favourable and attractive. Y Z's 'gratefull', which does not fit the context, is a graphical error resulting from misreading O's 'c' as 't'.

13 *prove annoy*, demonstrate sorrow.

101

The scribe of X or the 98 compositor must have fallen asleep over this sonnet, for he made five errors and is here no more trustworthy than Q1.

3 *conclusions tries*, undertakes experiments.

6 *white*, purity.

8 *in*, with.

9 *Love moves thy paine*. A typical Sidneyan inversion which would have been somewhat clearer if written 'Love thy pain moves'—'Love' is the object of 'moves' (and the subject of 'runs'). Editors from Grosart onwards have taken 'Love' as the subject and so have been forced to emend 'moves', the reading of all four texts, to 'mones'.

12 *with care sweates*, suffers with apprehension.

14 *heaven stuffe*, heavenly material, her bodily beauty.

102

2 *encrease*, heightening of colour, blush.

5 *vade*, fade.

6 *selfe engraind*, she herself dyed it in a fast colour.

9 *Gallein's adoptive sonnes*, followers of Galen, old-fashioned physicians unaware of the empirical methods of the new Paduan school.

10 *hackney on*, allow to proceed in stumbling fashion like a worn-out worthless horse.

11 *feeling proofe*, the evidence of my emotions.

103

A type of *prosopopoeia* that Sidney also used in his prose: 'But when she was imbarked, did you not marke how the windes whistled, and the seas daunst for joy, how the sailes did swel with pride, and all because they had Urania' (*New Arcadia*, i. 6).

9 *Æols' youthes*, sons of Aeolus, the winds.

104

8 *rigrows* (Ho), the only text to indicate the needed syncopation, unless 98's 'rigours' was also meant to be a syncopated form of 'rigorous'.

9–11. One of the few passages of Sidney's poetry where association of ideas interrupts the logical progression of the images. The parenthetical '(though but of empty glasse)', suggested by 'thirsty' and 'glad', refers back to window: 'If I pass Stella's window, which is "happy" (fortunate) because it belongs to her; if I wear stars on my armour; if I appear to be sick or thirsty or glad—glad even though I cannot see her (her glass is "empty" because she does not appear at the window). . . .'

10. Thomas Lant, in the engravings he made of Sidney's funeral procession, pictured his armour with stars upon it.

12 *morall notes*, allegorical interpretations—see Harvey (*Works*, ed. Grosart, ii. 54): 'My leisure will scarcely serve, to moralize Fables of Beares, Apes, and Foxes: (for some men can give a shrewd gesse at a courtly allegory).'

13 *prove* (Dr Ho)—the subject is 'notes'.

xi

Set by Thomas Morley, *The First Booke of Ayres*, 1600, and by R. J. S. Stevens, 'Dialogue & Duetto', *c.* 1798. Morley conjecturally corrected all three of 98's obvious errors (in lines 23, 40, and 43), 13 corrected none, and Gray corrected two.

18. Things change in time in accordance with their own natures (some grow weaker and some grow stronger—my love will grow stronger).

33–35. Sidney uses this image again in the *New Arcadia* (i. 115): 'But alas, well have I found, that Love to a yeelding hart is a king; but to a resisting, is a tyrant. The more with arguments I shaked the stake, which he had planted in the grounde of my harte, the deeper still it sanke into it.'

105

3 *Dead glasse*, eye. G. C. Moore Smith (*TLS*, 18 December 1930, p. 735) explains: 'In his mind's eye the poet still sees Stella when his bodily eye sees nothing'. Grosart interprets 'glasse' as a telescope, and Purcell (*PQ* x. 399) as tears; both I believe are mistaken.

6 *dazling race*, the flickering course of the beams of sight.

106

3 *Bare me in hand*, deceived me, promised me falsely.

10 *charme*, harmonious tone (cf. AS **99.** 9).

11 *mould*, earth, the heaviest of the four elements that compose the body.

107

7 *Lieftenancy*, delegated authority or command.

8 *this great cause*. Miss Wilson suggests that this refers to his father's proposal that Philip join him in the government of Ireland (see note to AS **30.** 9); but there is no evidence that such an appointment was in fact contemplated by the government. The 'great cause' more probably refers to public service in general, which requires 'use' (experience) and 'art' (knowledge of the principles of government and statesmanship). Astrophil took leave of Stella, turned from his affections to serve the world; but Philip Sidney received no public employment of consequence until his appointment as Governor of Flushing in November 1585.

108.

1–4. The flames of desire in the lover's heart were a favourite subject for poetical invention from Serafino Aquilano onwards. Gascoigne in 1573 wrote:

These sides enclose the forge, where sorrowe playes the smith,
And hote desire, hath kindled fire, to worke this mettall with.
The Anvile is my heart, my thoughtes they strike the stroake,
My lights and lunges like bellowes blow, and sighes ascend for smoake.
(*Works*, ed. Cunliffe, i. 37.)

Shakespeare's Venus, lamenting the dead Adonis, says:

Mine eyes are turn'd to fire, my heart to lead.
Heavy heart's lead, melt at mine eyes' red fire!
So shall I die by drops of hot desire.   (1072–4.)

The Elizabethans regularly indicate heightened emotion by exaggerated elaboration of conceit.

11 *iron doores.* Cf. the 'iron lawes of duty' of AS **87.** 4. But Astrophil does not cease to love, for 'yet alas how shall?'

OTHER POEMS

I

In the second book of the *New Arcadia* Pyrocles describes the jousts held to celebrate the wedding anniversary of Andromana, Queen of Asiatic Iberia. On the fourth day the Iberian Philisides entered the lists dressed as a shepherd, his *impresa* a sheep marked with pitch with the motto 'Spotted to be knowne', while among the ladies watching at the windows 'was one (they say) that was the *Star*, wherby his course was only directed'. His companions, also dressed as shepherds, played upon recorders while two of their number sang an eclogue in which they asked the cause of Philisides's 'sodaine growing a man of armes' and replied with these six verses, which are the only ones that Pyrocles remembers. Philisides then tilted against his friend Lelius, who deliberately lost to him because he had been commanded to do so by his mistress.

This is the only mention of Philisides in the *New Arcadia*. He is no longer the Samothean gentleman of the *Old Arcadia*, trained in learning and arms, who had become a shepherd because of his love for Mira, a love which he openly acknowledged; but has been transformed into an Iberian shepherd who became a man of arms because of his love for a 'Star', a love which would be shameful if it were known. Philisides has taken on the characteristics of Astrophil. The episode of the Iberian jousts combines several personal reminiscences. Brie (p. 293) pointed out that another contestant, the 'frosen Knight', had appeared in the Fortress of Perfect Beauty tournament of May 1581, in which Sidney also had a major part. Hanford and Watson (*MP* xxxii [1934], 1–10) identified Lelius as Sir Henry Lee, with whom Sidney jousted on 17 November 1581 in a tournament celebrating the anniversary of Queen Elizabeth's accession, and probably on other occasions. D. Coulman (*Journal of the Warburg and Courtauld Institutes*, xx [1957], 179–80) noted that Abraham Fraunce, in the manuscript of his *Symbolicae Philosophiae liber quartus* dedicated to Philip's brother Robert (after Robert's return from his European travels in February 1582 and before Philip was knighted in January 1583), listed among Philip's devices, 'Ovis Saturni [?] sidere notata' with the motto 'Maculat modo noceat'. W. Blount apparently did not know the real name of Sidney's 'Star', for in his manuscript annotations of 93 he merely quoted in the margin a Latin translation of Greek Anthology vii. 669: 'My star (Stella meus), while you look at the stars would that I myself might be the sky that I might gaze at you with many eyes.'

The verses refer to a tilt, in which two horsemen ride at one another and try to break their blunted spears (staves) upon the other's helmet or shield. If one misses, that is does not hit his opponent, he loses the course. A spear is 'well broke' if it is shattered by a direct blow of the tip, rather than by an oblique blow (across).

2 *where he most would hit*, the heart of his Star.

4 *crossely crost*, adversely thwarted.

5 *gaily*, showily, in appearance only.

2

In the third book of the *New Arcadia* the cowardly boaster Dametas is per-
suaded to challenge the equally cowardly Clinias to combat by assurances that
Clinias will not dare to meet him. He has his *impresa* painted, consisting of a
plough, a sword, dismembered arms and legs, and many pens, ink-horns, and
books, which he explains signify 'that he had lefte the plowe, to doo such bloudy
deedes with his swoorde, as many inkehornes and bookes should be employed
about the historifying of them'. Then remembering that his wife Miso 'would
not take it well at his returne, if he forgat his dutie to her, he caused about in
a border to be written' this line, which is a quantitative hexameter. 'Pigsnie'
(pig's eye) is a rustic term of endearment. Sidney may have lost his earlier
admiration for English quantitative verse, which in the *Old Arcadia* he used
only for the serious discourse of cultivated courtiers, but which he here makes
part of the burlesque device of a clownish countryman.

3

The heroic and sentimental devotion of Argalus (ἀργαλέος painful,) and his wife
Parthenia (παρθένος, maiden) is told in four episodes of the *New Arcadia* (I.
v–viii, xvi; III. xii, xvi). It was the most popular of Sidney's stories, for it pro-
vided material for several plays, was versified by Quarles, and later was made
into a chap-book. In the last episode Argalus, the champion of Basilius, meets
the mighty Amphialus and is slain. Parthenia, overcome with grief, disguises
herself as the Knight of the Tomb and challenges Amphialus, who chivalrously
attempts to spare his weak adversary; but she forces him to continue fighting
and dies, as she desired, by the same hand and sword that killed her husband.
Basilius has her buried beside her beloved Argalus, and upon their tomb 'caused
this Epitaphe to be written'. 93 is the earliest and sole substantive text, for both
Cm and 90 have only a blank space for the epitaph. In the Houghton and both
the Huntington copies of 90 it is written in by early hands, and there is a later
handwritten transcript on sig. A6ᵛ of an early printed *Pervula* (STC 19440,
Bodleian Douce B 238 [3]); but these probably derive from 93 or a later folio.
It is possible that Sidney did not himself compose this epitaph, and that it was
written by his sister to fill the lacuna, just as she completed his unfinished
metaphrase of the Psalms. But it is equally possible that he wrote it on a separate
sheet of paper that was overlooked by the editors of 90, and that later came to
the Countess of Pembroke's hands as did the obviously authentic OP 4 and 5.
The spelling 'hir' in line 6 (which Sidney, his sister, and the 93 compositor
normally spell 'her') provides a slight but very tenuous basis for suggesting that
the manuscript from which the epitaph was printed might have been copied by
the same scribe who copied OP 4.

4

This poem was inserted by the editor of 93 at the end of the First Eclogues,
immediately after OA 13. Zelmane (Pyrocles) desired 'to heare' Strephon and
Klaius 'for the fame of their frindly love, and to know them, for their kindenesse
towardes' Musidorus; but since they were not present, Basilius 'commaunded
on[e] Lamon, who had at large sett down their country pastimes and first love

to Urania to sing the whole discourse which he did in this manner'. In the *Old Arcadia* Strephon and Klaius appear only in the Fourth Eclogues, where they lament the absence of Urania in OA 71 and 72, and are mentioned briefly in the conclusion, where it is suggested that someone else tell 'the strange continuance' of their 'desire'. The *New Arcadia* opens with a scene on the coast of Laconia in which Strephon and Klaius, while lamenting the absence of Urania, who sometime previously had taken leave of them on that spot to sail to the nearby island of Cithara, rescue the shipwrecked Musidorus and lead him to their own country of Arcadia. They are not mentioned again in the narrative, and Urania is later referred to only once, at 1. xvi, where we are told that she is a poor shepherdess, and that 'a rich knight called Lacemon, farre in love with her', had upheld the pre-eminence of her beauty in a tournament against Phalantus and had been defeated.

Sidney must have begun the present poem, which is incomplete, after he had finished the *Old Arcadia*, for though Cosma (line 243) is mentioned as the beloved of Pas in the *Old Arcadia*, she is so named only in St-Bo and is called Hyppa in the earlier manuscripts (see OA **29**. 10). In the poem Urania is courted by Antaxius 'a heardman rich' (line 117), but in the prose of the *New Arcadia* she is loved by Lacemon 'a rich knight'; this may indicate that the poem was written some time before the *New Arcadia*, and that Sidney later changed the name of her suitor when he began his revision, or it may indicate no more than that he planned to give her two rich suitors to balance her two poor suitors Strephon and Klaius. The poem contains a few images repeated from the *Old Arcadia* (see line 107 and OA **7**. 84; 147–8, OA **62**. 130–1; 451, OA **62**. 21–22), and a considerable number that also appear in *Astrophil and Stella* (see line 7 and AS **3**. 1–2; 45–46, AS **12**. 2; 84–104, AS **83**; 139, AS **104**. 9; 145–60, AS **13**. 9–12; 165, AS **16**. 14; 180–4, AS **11**. 5–8; 360, AS **92**. 6; 423–4, AS **10**. 13–14; 430, AS **2**. 4; 435, AS **89**. 5–8; 442, AS **ix**. 30; 454, AS **20**). Several images from *Astrophil and Stella* also reappear in the prose of the *New Arcadia*, for Sidney had a retentive memory and was prone to repeat himself; but there is a far higher proportion of parallels in the poem than there is in the prose. These numerous similarities suggest proximity of composition, and give us a date either shortly before or shortly after *Astrophil and Stella*, that is sometime during the years 1581–3.

Though the poem was probably written near the time of composition of *Astrophil and Stella*, it tells an entirely different story about the love of two friends for the same woman, in which 'love-fellowship maintained friendship betweene rivals' (1. 8). The Countess of Pembroke apparently found the uncompleted poem among her brother's papers and inserted it at what she considered an appropriate location in the 1593 edition. Sidney, even if he had completed it, probably would not have included it in the *Arcadia*, because it is too obviously a poem of the contemporary Elizabethan rather than of the ancient Arcadian country-side. 93 was not printed from the holograph, but from a copy made by a scribe who used the spelling 'hir'. The 93 text contains ten manifest errors; 98 conjecturally corrected seven of these, but 13 made no further improvements.

1–2. The pastoral traditionally requires the low style, 'playne language' (Barclay, *Egloges*, Prologue 23).

3 *plaining*, mourning. *plaine-singing*, the simple melody of plain-song.

6 *seely*, pitiable.

16 *weygh*, consider.

25 *Epeirus*, Epirus, a country north-west of the Peloponnesus and south of Macedonia.

26 *Æole's land*, the island of Aeolus between Sicily and Sardinia, far to the west of Epirus.

43 *fourm*, lair.

47 *keels*, kayles, a game similar to ninepins.

53–55. Green was the colour of lovers, and May games were decried for the acts of immorality that often accompanied them.

56 *quintain*, tilting at a post, formerly an exclusively knightly exercise, had by Elizabethan times become a village game.

70 *Piller*, a favourite object in devices, used in one form or another by the Earl of Surrey, Edward Dyer, Sir Henry Lee, and others; cf. Wyatt's 'The pillar perisht is wherto I lent' (based upon Petrarch 269).

83 *a maid*, Urania (line 167), Muse of astronomy and representative of the stars and heavenly matters. Spenser called the Countess of Pembroke Urania in *Colin Clouts come home againe*; but in *Astrophel*, printed in the same volume, he called her Clorinda, and Thomas Moffet, who lived at Wilton, referred to her as Mira in his *Silkewormes and their Flies*, 1599, F8ᵛ. If there are any personal references in the Arcadia poems, it appears that, aside from Philisides and Languet, Sidney's contemporaries were unable to identify them.

84–104. Skelton's *Philip Sparrow* (lines 120–40 and 213) is white with a black cap and rests between his mistress's breasts.

94 *micher*, truant.

101 *bias*, nipple, 'the irregularity which was given to some "bowls" that they might move in a particular curve'; Puttenham in 1579 used the same image in describing breasts as 'balles of alabaster' in which 'Eche byas was a little cherrie' (Grosart).

102 *peeper*, chirper and looker.

116 *Antaxius*, ἀντάξιος, worth as much or no less.

119 *some such*, such a.

121 *Kindly*, properly.

127 *These*. 93 misread 'thes' as 'This'.

129–31. Cupid is so described in Petrarch's *Trionfo d'Amore*.

143 *Their*, Klaius and Strephon's.

189 *batefull*, contentious.

201–4. Cf. CS 6.

206. The sun enters the zodiacal sign of Leo about 21 July, so about two months have passed since Strephon first saw Urania.

208–416. In the country game of barley-break the two couples at either end of the field attempt to change partners without being caught by the couple in the middle (called hell). The couple in the middle must hold hands while chasing the others, and if they catch any one member of an opposing couple before they meet as partners, that pair must take their place in hell. The game Sidney describes is comic because Strephon and Pas are more interested in Urania and Cosma than in winning. In the first game Pas and Nous catch old

Geron as he attempts to reach Urania, but tumble over him in the process. In the second game Geron and Urania take their place in hell and Strephon is supposed to run to Nous; but instead he follows Urania and is caught, and Nous has to go to hell with him. In the third game Nous wants to go after slow old Geron, but Strephon insists upon pursuing the swift-footed Urania; when they cannot gain upon her together, Strephon breaks away from Nous, which is, of course, against the rules, and runs after Urania by himself. At the same time Klaius, who is only a spectator, also runs after Urania. The two friends catch her, and completely disrupt the game.

240 *fremb'd*, fremd, stranger.

244 *Nous*, νοῦς, mind or heart; she is the only one of the contestants who does not appear in the *Old Arcadia*.

259 *rake*, go forward quickly.

291–3. Pliny, 8. 50.

301 *Pursevants*, pursuivants, official messengers.

342–4. Ovid (*Met*. i. 532–8) describes Daphne pursued by Phoebus with a simile of a hare pursued by a hound (Poirier, *Études Anglaises*, xi [1958], 167). The 1613 editor, noticing the incongruity of a reference to Wilton in an Arcadian story, changed the name to Helis (a city west of Arcadia in the country of Elis).

349–51. The Tartars' trick of shooting backwards while retreating was frequently mentioned—by Marco Polo (ed. Yule, i. 262), Mandeville (chap. 76), and others.

357 *narr*, nearer.

362 *double-shining*, 'because both the sun and Urania were out' (Grosart).

370 *Girosol*, French 'girasol', the sunflower or heliotrope.

393–5. Cf. Ovid's 'Auctaque forma fuga est' (*Met*. i. 530; cited by Poirier, op. cit., p. 150).

396 *lustre*, become lustrous.

410 *Creon's child*, Creusa, whom the jealous Medea destroyed by sending her a poisoned robe and necklace (Seneca, *Medea*, 570 ff.).

5

This poem was inserted by the editor of 93 in the Third Eclogues between OA 65 and OA 66. Dicus, as in the *Old Arcadia*, asks Philisides (Sidney) to sing one of his 'country songes', and 93 adds that Philisides 'without further studie began to utter that, wherewith his thoughtes were then (as alwaies) most busied: and to shew what a straunger he was to himselfe, spake of himselfe as of a thirde person, in this sorte'. The poem was probably composed sometime during the period 1577–80, when the other Mira poems were written (see notes to OA 73). Brie (pp. 225–6), who misread line 106 and thought Philisides was described as being in Holland, mistakenly concluded that Sidney wrote the poem when he visited the Prince of Orange in the spring of 1577. But Philisides is imagined as tending his flocks on the eastern coast of England, perhaps in Suffolk or Norfolk; the wind blows 'in' from Holland (106) and continues 'westward' (125) across the 'hills' (96) that separate him from Mira. Sidney, perhaps because the setting is so obviously England, did not make the poem a part of his *Old Arcadia*. His sister probably later found it among his papers and inserted it in the Third Eclogues, a poor location because it is not appropriate to the 'marriage group'. However, we must thank the Countess of Pembroke for preserving one of her brother's most charming poems.

Philisides' song (stanzas 2–9) is a *canzone*, the first to be written in English, modelled on the third Eclogue of Sannazaro's *Arcadia*, which begins:

> Sovra una verde riva
>   Di chiare et lucide onde
>   In un bel boscho di fioretti adorno,
>   Vidi di bianca oliva
>   Ornato et d'altre fronde
>   Un pastor, che 'n su l'alba appiè d'un orno
>   Cantava il terzo giorno
>   Del mese innanzi aprile;
>   Ad cui li vaghi ucelli
>   Di sovra gli arbuscelli
>   Con voce rispondean dolce et gentile;
>   Et ey rivolto al sole,
>   Dicea queste parole.

Sannazaro's *canzone*, which is modelled on but differs slightly from Petrarch's 126, consists of six 13-line stanzas and a three-line *commiato* or envoy. Sidney has seven stanzas, in the same form as Sannazaro's except that he reverses the rhymes in the third and fourth lines, and his envoy (105–13) contains nine lines instead of three. Sidney's structural pattern (not in Sannazaro) is that of correlative verse (see notes to OA 43). 'Each thing' Philisides sees makes him think of Mira; he therefore devotes a stanza each to the earth, brook, flowers, pipe, lamb, and turtle dove, which are enumerated in the first stanza and recapitulated in line 92.

93, the only substantive text, preserves none of Sidney's characteristic spellings, and so was probably printed from a scribal copy. It contains eight obvious verbal errors (in lines 5, 6, 7, 39, 52, 62, 102, and 116), five of which were conjecturally corrected by the editor of 98 and two more by the editor of 13. I therefore list in the apparatus all verbal and punctuation variants found in 98 and 13, even though they are not substantive.

3 *to please*, that would please.

25 *Rogue*, vagabond.

42 *Make*, mate.

53 *seely*, innocent.

62 *liribliring*, onomatopoetic for sound of a pipe (not in *OED*).

78 *bea-waymenting*, lamenting by crying baa.

87 *lime*, glue used for catching small birds.

89 *prey*, the dove's mate caught by the bird-lime.

101 *Caban*, cabin, a poor hut.

105–9. In a somewhat similar situation, Chaucer's Troilus (v. 666–79) looks toward the Greek camp where Criseyde lies, and thinks that the wind blowing from her direction sighs, 'Allas, whi twynned be we tweyne'.

106 *Holland*. 13, noticing the impropriety of a wind blowing westward from

Holland in an Arcadian poem, arbitrarily changed the name to 'Ciprus', which is several hundred miles south-east of the Peloponnesus.

107 *leavell*, level, aim.

108 *but Kissing hit*, only touch lightly. Cf. i. 285 where Lelius made his lance come 'swimming close over the crest of the Helmet, as if he would represent the kisse, and not the stroke of Mars'.

109 *weights*, scales.

112. Mira combines the qualities of the moon (Diana) and the evening star (Venus)—see OA **73**. 170–8.

113 *willow's barke*, food of sorrow.

118 *plot*, map.

119 *tried*, experienced.

123 *proved*, strove.

6

These 'Two Pastoralls', Nos. 6 and 7, were printed as the first two poems in *A Poetical Rapsody*, 1602, an anthology compiled by Francis Davison, which is the only substantive text. Francis (born *c.* 1575), the eldest son of Sidney's friend and associate William Davison (1541?–1608), dedicated his volume to the 22-year-old William Herbert, Earl of Pembroke, eldest son of Sidney's sister, one of whose poems is also included. Davison was in a position to acquire manuscript copies of Sidney's poems, and since he dedicated his collection to a relative of Sidney's he must have had some assurance of their authenticity. The style and content of both poems are entirely in Sidney's manner, so they may be accepted as genuine beyond any reasonable doubt.

The two poems were probably composed after 1581, when Sidney first began to use trochaic metres. Dyer appears to have been Sidney's earliest close associate in the practice of 'singing skill'; Greville, though he had known Sidney since they had been schoolboys at Shrewsbury, was away from England for consider-able periods of time during the years 1579–81, and may not have become a member of the poetical 'Trinitie' until later. The 'Sir' before Dyer's name in the title was supplied by Davison or his printer, for Dyer was not knighted until 1596.

6. One of the great prevailing ideas from classical times onwards. Cf. iv. 159, OA 45, and, for numerous references, C. G. Smith, *Spenser's Theory of Friend-ship* (1935), pp. 37–42.

9 *prest*, prepared.

13–14. A frequently cited anecdote—Ovid, *Met.* xi. 2, &c.; cf. AS **iii**. 1–4.

58 *metamorphoz'd wonder*, the miracle that three should be changed into one.

7

6. Cf. AS **viii**. 3–4.

28 *arte of Love*, cf. AS 54.

44 *Oten Reedes*, the shepherd's pipe of oat straw, 'avena' (Virgil, *Ecl.* i. 2).

45. The only one of Sidney's poems written in competition with his friends that can be identified is CS 16, an answer to a sonnet by Dyer. Several of Greville's earlier *Caelica* poems, which he said were 'Written in his Youth, and

familiar Exercise with Sir Philip Sidney', echo or deal with themes treated in *Astrophil and Stella*.

51 *Junoe's birdes*, peacocks.

53 *blacke Swannes*, Juvenal's 'rara avis in terris, nigroque simillima cygno' (vi. 165), which had become proverbial.

61 side-note: Sir Edward Dyer and Master Fulke Greville.

71 *reflected*, turned or influenced.

(i) *Authorship and date of composition.* There are at least 14 known manuscripts of the metaphrase of the Psalms by Sidney and his sister, which are described in the bibliography and designated by the letters A–N. The work was frequently mentioned—by Daniel, Moffet, Harington, Jonson, Donne (who wrote a poem 'Upon the translation of the Psalmes by Sir Philip Sydney and the Countess of Pembroke'), and others; but no extant printing is recorded until the eighteenth century,[1] when one of the Countess of Pembroke's Psalms appeared in *Guardian* No. 18 in 1713 and seven more in Henry Harington's *Nugae Antiquae*, in 1775 and 1779. The first and only printing of the complete text, edited by S. W. Singer, was issued by the Chiswick Press in 1823. A was used as printer's copy, supplemented by C and collated with another manuscript in the collection of Dr. Henry Cotton; but the text was emended on eclectic rather than critical principles. Ruskin reprinted many of the Psalms from this edition, with extravagantly laudatory comments, in *Rock Honeycomb* (1877). In 1873 Gosart printed, with several inaccuracies and arbitrary emendations, Sidney's Psalms 1–43 from B. Feuillerat in 1923 printed Psalms 1–3 from B and 4–43 from A, and listed variant readings from B–I and the 1823 edition; but his variants are not complete and not entirely accurate. The present text is the first one to present Sidney's own version freed from the revisions later made by his sister.

The title of C states that the metrical version was 'begun' by Sidney and 'finished' by his sister; Greville, speaking in round numbers, said that Sidney had left '40' of the Psalms in manuscript (PRO SP 12/195/33); while notes in B, E, H, J, and N ('Hitherto [or Hactenus] S^r Ph. Sidney') show that at the time of his death he had only completed the first 43. Some of Sidney's earlier biographers supposed that his metaphrase was done in 1580 or before, and Theodore Spencer opened his critical discussion of Sidney's poetry with an account of the versification of the Psalms as his 'earliest important poetic task' (*ELH* xii. 254); but Wallace (p. 324) assumed, and the evidence available suggests, that Sidney began the work late in his career, perhaps not long before his departure for the Netherlands in 1585.

Stylistic tests are an uncertain guide to dating because the Psalms were either versified from English prose or translated from French metrical versions and therefore take on some of the qualities of their originals. Since Sidney's admiration for the Psalms is evident from his references in the *Defence of Poesie*, it

---

[1] An earlier lost edition of some of Sidney's Psalms is recorded in a memorandum by Drummond of Hawthornden: 'Their Names who haue composed some psalms of Dauid to the french Tunes, in Meter. S. Philip Sidney / Iosua syluester / Francis Dauison / ... 40. 41. 42 S. Phil. Sydney.... All the other psalmes by Io. Standish. / The Booke is printed for Iohn Standish / dwelling in St. Bartolomews neer Christ Church / in the Long Walk' (National Library of Scotland MS. 2060, f. 150). The only books printed for John Standish listed in the *Short Title Catalogue* are editions of Sir John Davies's *Hymnes of Astraea* and *Nosce Teipsum* between 1599 and 1608.

appears strange, if he had begun work on them early in his career, that he should have completed less than a third of the total number. Each of the Psalms is cast in a different stanza, and if they were early work we should expect Sidney to repeat some of his more successful effects in later poems; but only two of his 43 stanza forms appear in his other poems—the accentual Sapphics of Psalm 6 in OA 59, and the terza rima of Psalm 7 in the *Old Arcadia* and *Certain Sonnets*. His probable use of the 1580 London edition of Beza's *Psalmorum Davidis . . . vario carminum genere latine expressi* (see notes to PS 4 and 29) indicates that the Psalms were not among his earlier productions. Thomas Moffet, a member of the Pembroke household, stated that Sidney began his work on the Psalms after he had composed his *Stella* and *Arcadia* (*Nobilis*, ed. Heltzel and Hudson, 1940, p. 12). Five of the Psalms are in trochaic metres, a rhythm new to the Elizabethans which Sidney appears first to have mastered in the *Astrophil and Stella* songs of 1582. In September 1584 Scipio Gentili dedicated his *In XXV Davidis Psalmos Epicae Paraphrases* to Sidney, in which he praised him as a poet in general terms but said nothing of his work on the Psalms, though a reference to it would have been singularly appropriate in this context if Gentili had known it existed. It therefore appears that the metaphrase of the Psalms was not an early work of experimentation, but a later exhibition of virtuosity.

The Countess of Pembroke probably got possession of the manuscript of her brother's unfinished version of the Psalms after his death, and undertook to complete it. She worked carefully, revised repeatedly, and considered the finished collection to be her own most important contribution to literature— her portrait, painted by Simon Pass in 1618, represents her with a volume labelled 'Psalms' in her hand. About 1606 Sir John Harington observed that Gervase Babington 'was sometime chaplen to the late Earle of Pembroke, whose nobel Countess used this her chaplaen's advise, I suppose, for the translation of the psalms . . . for it was more than a woman's skill to expresse the sence so right as she hath done in her vearse' (*Nugae Antiquae*, ed. Park, ii [1804], 172). But his assumption is almost certainly wrong, because Babington was the Earl's chaplain only for about a year in 1581, and the Countess probably did not begin her own version until after her brother's death in 1586. She had begun and may have completed her first draft by the autumn of 1593, when Daniel mentioned her work in the dedication to his *Cleopatra*. She introduced various changes over a number of years. Her final revised version, preserved in A and J, was dedicated to Queen Elizabeth, who visited her at Wilton in 1599. Probably the date 1599 in J, even though it is added in a different early hand, indicates the year in which she finally completed her revision.

(ii) *Construction of the text*. As far as I have been able to determine, only J and PS 27–150 in F were copied from other now existing manuscripts; therefore, since the original of B and X itself are lost, all the extant manuscripts are substantive witnesses to the text, for even J, though it was copied from A, is partly substantive because A wants the preliminaries and first three Psalms. The clue to the relationships of the 14 known manuscripts is provided by B, a transcript made in 1695 by Samuel Woodford from a damaged original that contained numerous interlinear and marginal revisions. In the body of his text Woodford transcribed what he considered to be the readings finally intended by the author, and in the margins he carefully entered the earlier readings of his original as far as he could decipher them. Analysis of Woodford's marginal notes and of the variants in all the texts shows that the manuscripts fall into two groups: A B F I J K, transcripts descending from the original of B, which itself was revised on three different occasions; and C D E G H L M N, descendants of X, which was transcribed from the original of B after the first set of revisions had been made and was itself subjected to further independent revisions.[1] The relationships are shown in the following table,[2] which lists all changes affecting two or more lines in the first 43 Psalms (B⁰ indicates the first draft of the original of B, B¹ the first set of revisions, &c.).

Psalm and line	B⁰	B¹	B²	X	B³	
		K FI (1–26)	C D N EHL G M		A	B
					F (27–150) J	
1. 13–22	B⁰–1	KFI–1	C [D] EGHLMN–1		[A] J–2 B–1	
16. 37–44	B⁰–1	KFI–omit	C [D] EGHLMN–2		AJB–2	
22. 73–78	B⁰–1	KFI–omit	CDEGHLMN–omit		AJB–2	
23. 19–27	B⁰–1	KFI–1	CDEGHLMN–1		AJB–2	
25. 71–72	B⁰–1	KFI–1	C–2 DEHLN–1 GM–3		AJB–1	
25. 77–78	B⁰–1	KFI–1	C–2 DEHLN–1 G–3 M–4		AJB–1	
26. 31–39	B⁰–1	KFI–1	CDEGHLMN–2		AJB–3	
27. 33–34	B⁰–1	K–1	CDEGHLMN–2		AFJB–1	
29. 25–29	B⁰–1	K–1	CDEGHLMN–1		AFJB–2	
31. 64–69	B⁰–1	K–1	CDEHLN–1 G–2 M–3		AFJB–4	
32. 10–11	B⁰–1	K–1	CDN–1 EGHLM–2		AFJB–1	
42. 53–56	B⁰–1	K–1	C–2 D–1 EHLN–3 G–4 M–5		AFJB–1	

Analysis of the single word and phrase variants in PS 1–43, and of sample collations from PS 44–150, reveals the same pattern of relationships.

Evidently the Countess of Pembroke was an inveterate tinkerer who found it difficult to make up her mind. In composing her first draft she groped for words and made many false starts. For example, Woodford notes that **49.** 7 was originally written (1) 'Why should I fearfull be in the evill day', and then successively rewritten as (2) 'Why should yᵉ time of evill my face affray', (3) 'Why should yᵉ time of evill work my dismay', and (4) 'The times of Evill why should they me dismay'. Only the fourth version appears in the other manuscripts. But even after the Countess had completed her first draft, she returned to her work time and again and made numerous further changes. Thus there are five

---

[1] The existence of X is proved by the agreement of C D E G H L M N against A B F I J K in single words or phrases at **7.** 26 theire—the, **10.** 65 that—the, **12.** 4 they with vaine mates—with uaine mates they, **21.** 7 to aske—to craue, **26.** 12 I neuer will—will not, **27.** 63 glad—cladd, **31.** 5 with—in, **34.** 67 his true—his, **35.** 24 soules—spoiles, **37.** 12 shall—will, **41.** 41 did'st—do'st, &c., and in longer passages at **26.** 31–39, **27.** 33–34, &c.

[2] In addition, 31 Psalms appear in earlier or variant versions as follows: in B only 44, 46, 50, 53, 58, 60, 62, 63, 64, 69, 71, 80, 86, 105, 108, and 117; in BEHIL 122; in BI 68; in BIKN 75; in BKX sections g, h, s, w of 119; in GM 120–7; in I only 89 and 113; and in N only 131. CM agree against the other texts at **22.** 7–8; C has unique variants at **25.** 15–16 and **25.** 47–48, J at **1.** 13–22, K at **16.** 31–32, and M at **31.** 59–60.

different versions of the conclusion to PS 42, three entirely separate versions in different stanza forms of PS 122, and two distinct versions of 30 other Psalms, besides hundreds of lesser changes.

The Countess apparently had two working copies, the original of B, and X, one of which she probably kept in her country residence at Wilton and the other in her London residence at Baynard's Castle. The chronological sequence of her revisions can easily be plotted from the table of major variants. For example, the conclusions to PS 16 and 22 were crossed out before K was copied; a revised conclusion was provided for 16 before X was copied, but none was provided for 22 until after X had been copied. Frequently revisions made in X, such as the conclusion to PS 27, were never transferred to the original of B at all. In addition, as the Countess allowed copies of her work to be made, she sometimes provided further revisions for single transcripts which she did not enter in either of her working copies. Thus C, G, and M each contain a few unique passages, and I contains a unique version of PS 113.

With such heavily revised and interlined copy, the scribes were sometimes uncertain about which reading to select and on occasion inadvertently wrote down the earlier rather than the later reading. Woodford notes 25 revisions of single words or phrases in the first 43 Psalms; the other manuscripts usually contain the revised readings, but ten of the earlier readings reappear in one or more of the later transcripts. That John Davies of Hereford, who copied A from the original of B after its third revision, was frequently at a loss is shown by his interlinear and marginal additions; variation in the colour of ink in several of his stanzas indicates that he sometimes left blank spaces and filled them in later, probably after receiving instructions from the Countess herself.

Some of the longer revisions must have been entered on separate slips of paper which had fallen out by the time Woodford made his transcript. Woodford notes that the conclusion to PS 1 was marked for revision in his original, but he does not give the revised version preserved in J (the leaf containing PS 1 is wanting in A), which indicates that the revision was made on a separate slip of paper after X had been copied, and that the slip had been lost by the time the original of B came to Woodford's hands. Woodford's versions of 16 Psalms are unique, which indicates that the slips containing the revised versions appearing in other manuscripts were lost after A had been copied. K notes opposite PS 68, 75, 89, and 122 'this is otherwise translated', and I contains a version of 68 otherwise found only in B and two different versions of 75, 89, and 122.

Since the Countess of Pembroke revised her brother's work as well as her own, and since none of the manuscripts as they now stand are entirely free from her revisions, the words that Sidney himself wrote can only be ascertained by reconstructing the wording of the unrevised state of the original of B. For this we have three primary authorities—B itself, from which the unrevised original of B can be approximately reconstructed by transferring Woodford's marginal notes of the earlier readings to the body of the text; K and F I 1–26 which derive from the original of B after the Countess had completed her first set of revisions; and A, which was copied from the original of B after the Countess had completed her third and last set of revisions. F I 1–26 are closely related to K, but thereafter F was transcribed from A and I wants PS 27–50; their readings are not so dependable as those of B, K, and A, because they share a number of agreements in error, which proves that they descend from the original of B through an intermediary (Y) rather than directly.[1] The descendants of X (C D E G H L M N) can be disregarded in constructing Sidney's text, because they contain still further revisions by the Countess of Pembroke and are so affected by scribal corruption that their readings are untrustworthy. Indeed, a number of agreements in error in the groups E H L and G M indicates that they in turn descend from X through intermediaries rather than directly, which makes them too far removed from Sidney's original to be of any dependable textual authority.

The Countess of Pembroke's major revisions, most of which were made to eliminate Sidney's partial stanzas at the end of seven of the Psalms, are easily identified because they were made after K was copied from the original of B. But 27 other changes indicated by Woodford's notes present more of a problem, because all but one (**19.** 35) were made before K was copied. Two inversions of phrasing (**9.** 36, **10.** 22), indicated in the body of the text instead of by marginal notes, may have been errors of transcription made by Woodford himself and immediately corrected. Eight other changes (**5.** 8; **10.** 13; **11.** 5; **12.** 14; **18.** 24; **24.** 12, 34, 33–48) are corrections of demonstrable errors, which were probably made by the copyist of the original of B, and may have been immediately corrected, or conjecturally corrected later by the Countess. But most of the remaining 17 changes are deliberate revisions of perfectly acceptable readings, and revisions similar in kind to those that the Countess of Pembroke made in her own versions of the Psalms. Her trial-and-error attempts at improvement are illustrated at **7.** 34 where 'Therefore thou' is changed to 'Then dost thou', and then changed again to 'For him thou'; and her preference for elegant variation at **12.** 12, where 'bold emboldned' is changed to 'brave emboldned'. Some of the changes were made by mechanically collating Sidney's text with the prose Psalter; thus **32.** 1 'Bless'ed is the man' is changed to 'Blessed is He' because the latter is the phrasing of the Psalter, and Psalm 14 is marked with a 'Quære' because it omits verses 5–7 of the Psalter—though an analysis of Sidney's sources shows that he here was following, not the Psalter, but the Geneva version which also omits this passage. It therefore appears fairly certain that all the changes noted by Woodford were made by the Countess of Pembroke. In consequence, even when these changes are corrections of demonstrable errors, they must be considered as conjectural emendations rather than as substantive readings.

The original of B could not have been Sidney's holograph, for even before it was revised by the Countess of Pembroke it contained all 150 Psalms, of which Sidney had versified only the first 43, and Woodford did not note any change in the handwriting of his original. Since it was a scribal copy, it inevitably contained a few transcriptional errors (**5.** 8, **12.** 14, **33.** 7, &c.). Woodford apparently made his own copy, B itself, with moderate care; but the testimony of K and A

---

[1] In PS 1–26 F and I agree in error in more than 30 places against all other texts—**2.** 1 heathen rage; **4.** 35 safest rest; **5.** 3 that calls, 20 thine holynesse . . . **22.** 33 wax are heated, 35 tride, 53 who feares, 65 remoted, 69 to god the crowne; **24.** 13 the god; **25.** 23 *om.* grave, 24 *om.* have, 55 myne eyes, 59 o looke help, 77 in tyme. They also agree together in error with K in about 16 places (**1.** 13 blessing, **3.** 6 strengthes, &c.), but they do *not* reproduce some ten other K errors (**5.** 14 shall, **9.** 38 straie, &c.).

shows that he omitted **36.** 5 and introduced verbal errors at **1.** 3, **1.** 10, 4. 23, 4. 24, **5.** 18, &c.

I have therefore chosen B as copy text (K has several lacunae and A is overlaid with later revisions), and have emended it to correct scribal errors and to delete the Countess of Pembroke's revisions. I have constructed the critical text from materials provided by complete collations of PS 1–43 in all 14 extant manuscripts; but in the apparatus, except for a few readings of particular interest, I have cited only variants occurring in K and A, because they are the transcripts descending most directly from the original of B. The citation of variants from F I and C D E G H L M N, which descend from the original of B through one or more intermediaries, though it would establish more precisely the successive steps by which the Countess of Pembroke made her revisions, would otherwise only record a mass of scribal errors, and would make no significant contribution toward establishing the wording of Sidney's own text. Except for emendations recorded in the apparatus, I reproduce the copy text literatim. Since B is a copy of a copy of Sidney's holograph, it at best preserves no more than a slight trace of his spelling and punctuation.

Sources

In Sidney's time the most widely known English metrical version of the Psalms was *The Whole Book of Psalms* (1562) by Thomas Sternhold, John Hopkins, and others which, set to music, was regularly printed after the prose Psalter in the Book of Common Prayer. Its thumping fourteener couplets made it easily adaptable for singing to a small number of interchangeable tunes, but the best that its most sympathetic students have been able to say for it artistically is that it 'occasionally rises to the verge of the poetic'. Sidney, who considered the Psalms to be the most excellent and very highest kind of poetry (iii. 9), decided to provide them with an English dress more suitable to the nature of their originals than the versions currently available. He therefore attempted a new poetical rendering, but not a new translation.

He did not consult the original Hebrew text, which he was unable to read; he ignored the Vulgate; and there is no evidence that he made use of the standard Protestant Latin version by Tremellius, whose *Quinque Libri Poetici* he had quoted in his *Defence of Poesie*. For his artistic model he used *Les CL. Pseaumes de David, mis en rime Françoise* (1562), containing metrical versions by Clement Marot and Theodore Beza set to music by Claude Goudimel. For his phrasing he went to the English prose Psalter appended to the Book of Common Prayer, whose text was that of the Great Bible prepared by Coverdale in 1539. He probably knew this version almost by heart, for he would hear its sonorous phrases in the services of the church and would use it in his own private devotions. But like any other educated Elizabethan he would know that its translation left something to be desired in the way of accuracy, and he therefore also consulted the most scholarly English translation available, the Geneva Bible of 1560. He probably also made some use of one of the best recent commentaries, *Psalmorum Davidis et Aliorum Prophetarum Libri Quinque, Argumentis & Latina Paraphrasi illustrati*, by Theodore Beza, the Latin version of which, and an English translation by Anthony Gilbie, were published in London in 1580, dedicated to Sidney's uncle and aunt, the Earl and Countess of Huntingdon. I have examined more than fifty sixteenth-century versions of the Psalms, but I have found no clear evidence that Sidney made direct use of any texts other than these four.[1]

Sidney's main object was to alter the dress of the Psalms from prose to verse; but though he changed the cut, he used the same material. Much of the vocabulary and even phrasing of his own version preserves that of his sources. He omitted nothing from his originals, never wittingly changed the sense, and only occasionally allowed himself the poetical licence of heightening the imagery. Though he wished to produce an artistic metrical version of the Psalms, he also strove to make it as accurate as possible. He probably had the English prose Psalter, the Geneva version, the Marot–Beza French metrical Psalter, and Beza's *Paraphrasis* open before him, and read each Psalm through carefully in all four texts before making his own metaphrase.

In everything affecting the meaning and interpretation of his own version, he gave precedence to the Geneva version. Thus at **6.** 10 where the Psalter reads 'punish' and Geneva 'delay', Sidney follows the latter, and at **14.** 12–13, where Geneva omits three verses of the Psalter as spurious, Sidney also omits the passage. In his earlier Psalms the influence of the Psalter is all-pervasive on his phrasing, but in his later ones its influence is overshadowed by that of the Geneva version; thus the phrasing of PS 1–5, 7–9, 11–13, 15, and 17–18 comes primarily from the Psalter, that of most of the later Psalms primarily from the Geneva version. But usually he combines the wording of both texts; for example, his **2.** 21 'With Iron scepter bruse thou shalt', combines Geneva's 'Thou shalt crush them with a *scepter* of yron' and the Psalter's 'Thou shalt *bruyse* them with a rodde of iron'. The influence of the Marot–Beza metrical Psalter is mainly evident in his versification, though he appears to have translated PS 16, 34, 41, and 42 directly from the French, and to have been influenced by its phrasing in half a dozen other Psalms. He made only occasional use of Beza's *Paraphrasis* (see notes to PS 4 and 29).

Sidney usually followed his originals closely and even reproduced their phrasing as accurately as the exigencies of metre allowed. His **5.** 1–8,

> Ponder the words, O lord, that I do say,
>   Consider what I meditate in me:
> O, hearken to my voice, which calls on Thee,
>   My King, my God for I to thee will pray.
> So shall my voice clime to thyne eares betime:
>   For unto Thee I will my prayer send,
>   With earliest entry of the Morning prime,
>   And will my waiting eyes to thee ward bend,

follows the wording of the Psalter—

---

[1] Teut Riese, *Die Englische Psalmdichtung im Sechzehnten Jahrhundert* (Münster, 1937), p. 104, assumed that Sidney's main source was the Geneva Bible; but the passage he used to demonstrate his assumption (**18.** 15–21) is actually closer in phrasing to the prose Psalter than to the Geneva version. Waldo S. Pratt, *The Music of the French Psalter of 1562* (New York, 1939), pp. 30 and 81 ff., pointed out the similarity of some of Sidney's verse forms to those of Marot and Beza.

Ponder my woordes, O Lord: consyder my meditation.
O hearken thou unto the voyce of my callyng, my king and my God:
for unto thee wyl I make my prayer.
My voyce shalt thou heare betimes, O Lord: early in the mornying wyl I
direct my prayer unto thee, and wyl looke up.

His PS 24 is an extremely literal rendering of the Geneva version, in which he
uses only 200 words of verse to render his original's 182 words of prose.

At other times he elaborates his original, though he never distorts the sense
of a passage. Only rarely is he verbose, as in **37. 73–76**. Usually his elaborations
make more effective the latent imagery of a passage. Thus in PS 6 he renders
Geneva's 'Mine eye is dimmed for despite, & sunke in because of all mine
enemies', and the Psalter's 'My beautie is gone for verie trouble: & worne away
bicause of all mine enimies', as

> Woe, lyke a moth, my face's beauty eates
> And age pull'd on with paines all freshness fretteth:
> The while a swarm of foes with vexing feates
> My life besetteth.

But his main contribution, and evidently his primary aim, was effective versi-
fication, and even there he had a model. There were two traditions of versifying
the Psalms in the sixteenth century. The one, represented by the earlier English
versions of Wyatt, Robert Crowley (1549), William Hunnis (1550), Sternhold
and Hopkins (1562), and the Latin versions of Eobanus Hesse (1547) and
Sidney's friend Scipio Gentili (1584), for the most part used only a single verse
form—usually fourteener couplets or poulter's measure in English, and hexa-
meters in Latin. The other, represented by the versions of Archbishop Parker
(c. 1557) and the Scottish Metrical Psalter (1564) in English, the Marot–Beza
French Psalter (1562), and the Latin paraphrases by George Buchanan (1566)
and Theodore Beza (1579), employ a variety of verse forms—Buchanan (whose
version Sidney knew as early as 1574—see iii. 90) carefully catalogued at the
end of his volume the thirty different metres he had used. Sidney followed the
second tradition, and employed as his immediate model the French metrical
Psalter by Marot and Beza, which his friend Melissus had also imitated when
he prepared the new German Psalter for Frederick III in 1572.

This French Psalter uses 110 different metres, which combined with varia-
tions in rhyme scheme result in individual stanza forms for almost each one of
the Psalms. Most of the measures are iambic, but 15 appear from the music to
be trochaic. The stanzas vary in length from 4 to 12 lines, and the lines them-
selves from 4 to 13 syllables. About 30 of the Psalms end with a half-stanza,
which require a tune that is correspondingly divisible. Some of the happiest
effects are gained by careful patterning of masculine and feminine rhymes.
Sidney's verse follows the general characteristics of the French. He devised a
different stanza for each of the 43 Psalms he translated, his stanzas varying in
length from 2 to 12 lines, and his lines from 3 to 14 syllables. Five of his
measures are trochaic, the rest iambic; more than a third of his stanzas contain
patterns of feminine rhyme. Eight of his Psalms conclude with a partial stanza
(a couplet, triplet, or quatrain), which, however, are usually not half-stanzas
like those of Marot and Beza and thus are not adaptable for singing. **Sidney**

appears to have regarded only the words, and not the music of the French
Psalter.

Eight of Sidney's Psalms (1, 3, 19, 34, 39–42) duplicate in whole or in part
the metre and rhyme scheme of the corresponding French Psalm;[1] but though
he got the general idea for his versification from the Marot–Beza Psalter, he
imitated it in fewer than a third of his Psalms, and worked independently in
devising his remaining verse forms. He even worked independently of his own
earlier practice, for only two of his 43 stanza forms can be found in his other
poems.[2]

The following abbreviations are used for the sources cited in the notes:

Beza's *Paraphrasis. Psalmorum Davidis . . . Argumentis & Latina Paraphrasi
illustrati, ac etiam vario carminum genere latine expressi . . . Theodore Beza
Vezelio Auctore* [1st ed., 1579], London, 1580.

Beza or Marot. *Les CL. Pseaumes de David, Mis en rime Françoise par Clement
Marot, & Theodore de Beze. Auec la prose en marge, comme elle est en la
Bible* [1st ed., 1562], Lyon, 1564.

Geneva. *The Bible. Translated according to the Ebrew and Greeke* [Geneva
Bible, 1st ed., 1560], London, 1581.

Psalter. *The Psalter, or Psalmes of Dauid, after the translation of the great
Bible* [Prayer-Book Psalter, text of 1539], London, 1576.

In Sidney's text the Psalms are numbered according to the usual sixteenth-
century Protestant system, which derives from the Hebrew and makes two
separate Psalms of the Vulgate's ninth. The Latin headings, which are the
incipits of the Vulgate version, had become established as titles; they appear
in the Psalter, Beza–Marot, Sternhold and Hopkins, and most of the Latin and
vernacular metrical versions of the sixteenth century. The Biblical verse numbers
in the margin are from Geneva (and correspond with those of the present
Authorized Version). They were probably added later, as they are found only in
MS. B and there only in Psalms 1–115. MS. K contains a different set of verse
numbers taken from the Psalter; none of the other manuscripts contain verse
numbers.

The copy text, B, has light internal punctuation, and end-of-line marks of
punctuation only at **1.** 2–14, 16–18, 22; **2.** 2–13, 14–18, 20, 22–28, 31–32;
3. 20–30, 32–36; **4.** 2–6, 9–10, 12, 14–19, 22–25, 27, 30, 32–35; **5.** 1–8, 10–14,
18, 20, 22–23, 25–28, 32–35, 38, 40; **6.** 1–2, 4, 8, 10, 13, 16–20, 22, 26, 29, 32;
7. 2, 4, 8–10, 13–15, 18, 21–22, 24, 29–30, 34, 37–38, 41, 45, 48; **8.** 2, 4–5, 8,
13–14, 16, 34; **9.** 1–5, 7–8, 11–13, 17–18, 20, 22, 25, 27–28, 33–34, 35–36, 38–40,
42, 45, 47, 52, 57, 63, 65; **10.** 4, 6, 8, 10–12, 17–18, 26, 38, 44–45, 48, 52, 54, 56,
66, 74, 76, 78; **11.** 10–11, 14–16; **12.** 9, 27; **13.** 2, 4, 6, 8, 10, 12, 20; **14.** 6, 12,

---

[1] Six others used the metre and rhyme scheme of different French Psalms (8–9;
14–114 and 115; 21–91; 22–28; 32–36 and 68; 37–17, 54, 63, and 70)—though some if
not all of these correspondences are probably fortuitous. My analyses differ somewhat
from those of Pratt, op. cit., pp. 81–200.

[2] Sidney's achievement has been well assessed by Hallett Smith, 'English Metrical
Psalms in the Sixteenth Century and their Literary Significance', *HLQ* ix (1946),
268–71. The later influence of his and his sister's work is discussed by Philipp von
Rohr-Sauer, *English Metrical Psalms from 1600 to 1660* (Freiburg, 1938).

18, 21, 24; **15.** 1–3, 6, 13; **16.** 6, 17–18, 22, 26, 32, 36, 44; **17.** 24, 36, 40, 44, 48; **18.** 7, 14, 21, 70, 74, 77, 84, 91; **19.** 4, 12, 28, 32, 42, 50, 64; **20.** 10, 15, 25, 30, 35; **21.** 32, 40, 52; **22.** 1, 3, 36, 48, 52, 56, 70, 72, 78; **23.** 6, 12, 27; **24.** 1, 4, 20, 24; **25.** 6, 12, 18, 36, 47–48, 54, 56, 58, 60, 66, 78; **26.** 6, 12, 18, 24, 30, 39; **27.** 6, 30, 42, 66; **28.** 5; **29.** 29; **30.** 24, 30, 39; **31.** 30, 36, 48, 54, 60, 66, 69; **32.** 6, 12, 24, 42; **33.** 6, 12, 24, 30, 48, 60, 66, 72, 84; **34.** 8, 16, 49, 65, 73; **35.** 10, 30, 36, 38, 55–56, 60, 72; **36.** 8, 14, 18, 21, 24, 30, 36; **37.** 16, 24, 32, 40, 56, 64, 72; **38.** 18, 30; **39.** 28, 30, 33, 42; **40.** 20, 40, 50, 70; **41.** 8, 16, 48; **42.** 24, 32, 48; **43.** 5–6. All other end-of-line punctuation is editorial and is not separately noted in the apparatus. But each emendation of the existing punctuation of the copy text and all punctuation added within the lines is indicated in the apparatus.

To the Angell spirit

This tribute to her brother by the Countess of Pembroke is preserved only in J, a copy of her finally revised version of the Psalms prepared for presentation to Queen Elizabeth which also contains a 12-stanza dedicatory poem to the Queen. Another version of this poem in 11 stanzas (in the order 1–3, two different stanzas, 4–7, 11, and 13) was printed in error as Daniel's in the posthumously published *Whole Workes of Samuel Daniel*, 1623, M7ᵛ–8ᵛ. The present text is printed from the only known manuscript by generous permission of the owner, Dr. B. E. Juel-Jensen.

1

Except for the concluding partial stanza, the metre and rhyme scheme are the same as Marot's Psalm 1, which contains four six-line stanzas; though Sidney's phrasing is from the Psalter, with two words from Geneva.

1 *loosely*, carelessly, immorally.

16 *Consist*, remain, abide.

20 *proceeding*, conduct of affairs.

2

8 *yoakes*. Marot has 'le joug', the Psalter and Geneva 'cordes'.

11 *bravely*, an effective reading, meaning in magnificent fashion or with splendour, preserved only in Woodford's note and I. The Countess of Pembroke probably emended on the basis of the Psalter's '*Then* shal he speake unto them in his wrath'.

18 *yt*. 'To' is an unnecessary emendation; Geneva reads, 'Aske of mee, and I shall give thee the heathen for thine inheritance, and the endes of the earth for thy possession'.

3

The stanzaic pattern is similar to half of Marot's 12-line stanza in his Psalm 3, though Marot does not have feminine rhyme in his third and sixth lines.

17–18. The later revisions are not improvements. The Psalter and Geneva read, 'I layde me downe and slept, and rose up agayne: for the Lorde susteyned me'.

4

19 *when your chamber you do close*. The Psalter has, 'in your chamber'; Marot, 'Dessus vos licts en chambre close'.

21 *sacrifices sacrify*. The 'Interpretatio' in Beza's *Paraphrasis* notes, 'Sacrificate sacrificia iusticiae, *id est*, *rite*, & confidite in Domino' (p. 10).

23 *in that lord*. The scribes may have had difficulty in deciding whether the abbreviation in the original was 'yᵗ' or 'yᵉ'. B's 'the lord' could be correct, for the Psalter and Geneva have, 'Put your trust in the Lorde'.

24 *folkes*. Both the singular and plural forms were current, but Sidney appears to have preferred the plural—it is a rhyme word in PS **32.** 37.

34 *whose*. Since 'power' is disyllabic, the addition of 'Owne' is unnecessary.

5

8 *waiting*. Though Sidney otherwise follows the Psalter closely in this Psalm, 'waiting' was suggested by Geneva's 'in the morning will I direct me unto thee, and I will wait', or Marot's 'attendant grace'; there is nothing in the Psalm to suggest 'wayling', which is a graphical error.

19 *knees of my heart will fold*. The Psalter and Geneva have 'worship', Marot 'adorer'; but Sidney's expression was common—see the Wedderburns' popular pre-Elizabethan *Spirituall Sangis* (ed. Mitchell, *STS* xxxix. 51):

> The kneis of my hart sall I bow
> And sing that rycht Balulalow.

26 *fowl sinns* expresses the original better than 'Mischeif'—the Psalter reads 'their inward partes are verie wickednesse', Geneva, 'within they are very corruption'.

33 *bend*, fasten. The Psalter and Geneva read, 'put their trust in thee'.

37 *thou blessest*, an emendation in G which I follow Grosart in accepting; 'they blessed', which does not make sense, is a scribal error that several later copyists tried to correct. The Psalter reads, 'For thou Lorde wylt geve thy blessyng unto the righteous'.

7

20 *Thy throne*. It is tempting to retain B's 'Thy self', since the Psalter reads, 'therefore lyft up thy selfe agayne'; but the testimony of 13 other manuscripts cannot be controverted.

32–34. The revisions are unnecessary. The Psalter reads, 'God is a righteous judge, strong and patient: and God is provoked every day. If a man wyll not turne, he wyl whet his sword: he hath bent his bowe, and made it redy.'

8

The stanza, aa₈bb₉, is used by Marot in his ninth Psalm. The repetition of the first two lines at the end of the Psalm is also in the prose of the Psalter.

12 *life no life*. Woodford's suggested emendation also occurred to the copyist of X, but it is unnecessary because 'life' here means 'duration' (cf. 'Essence' in line 10). The Psalter reads, 'For I wyl consyder the heavens, even the woorkes of thy fyngers: the Moone and the Starres which thou hast ordeyned'.

29–32. The Psalter reads, 'The foules of the ayre, and the fyshes of the sea: and whatsoever walketh through the pathes of the seas'.

9

36 *mercie, mercie lord*. The inverted order in B, corrected by the superscript numbers, may have been an error by Woodford which he immediately corrected. If it had been a reading of his original that was later revised, he probably would have listed it in a marginal note.

39 *Death' gates*. See note to AS **73.** 14 for possessives without 's'.

10

13 *is his*—'hee is' is a manifest scribal error.

22 *themselves to him*. The inverted order in B, corrected by the superscript numbers, was probably an error by Woodford. See note to PS **9.** 36 above.

11

5 *Behold*. 'Perhaps' is a demonstrable error in the original of B emended by the Countess of Pembroke. The Psalter reads, '*For loe*, the ungodly bende their bowe', and contains nothing to suggest doubt.

16 *peyse*, peise, usually meaning 'weigh', but here 'judge'.

12

12 *bold emboldned*. The Countess of Pembroke's emendation 'braue' destroys the polyptoton.

14 *quell*. An emendation required by the rhyme.

18 *their force*. An acceptable reading. The Psalter has only, 'and wyl set them at rest'.

13

The stanza form was suggested by the opening words of the Psalter: 'Howe long wylt thou forget me (O Lorde) for ever: howe long wylt thou hyde thy face from mee.'

15 *troublous*, causing me grief.

14

The stanza form is similar to that of Marot's Psalms 114 and 115.

The Countess of Pembroke marked this Psalm for revision and the scribe of K noted that some verses were 'wanting', because they noticed that verses 5–7 of the Psalter had been omitted; but Sidney was here following the more accurate Geneva text, which like Marot also omitted this passage. Geneva reads for Sidney's lines 10–16: '3 All are gone out of the way: they are all corrupt: there is none that doeth good, no not one. 4 Do not all the workers of iniquitie know that they eate up my people, as they eate bread? they call not upon the Lord.'

15

9 *word to neighbour* reflects the Psalter's, 'He that sweareth unto his neighbour and disapoynteth hym not'.

16

This is translated from Beza, but does not use his stanza form.

18 *partage*, a portion or share. Beza has 'mon partage', Geneva, 'a faire heritage'.

37–44. The Countess of Pembroke's revision, first made in her second working copy (X) and not transferred to the original of B until sometime later, but before A had been copied, eliminates Sidney's final partial stanza. Beza's conclusion reads:

> Plustost, Seigneur, me mettras au sentier,
> Qui me conduise à vie plus heureuse:
> Car à vray dire, on n'a plaisir entier,
> Qu'en regardant ta face glorieuse:
> Et dans ta main est, & sera sans cesse
> Le comble vray de joye & de liesse.

17

9 *When.* An emendation, in C E G H L M and independently suggested by Woodford, of the graphical error 'where'. The Psalter and Geneva read, 'Thou hast proved and visited myne hart in the nyght season' (Geneva omits 'season').

18

22 *Cherubins* is the sixteenth-century form, 'Cherubyms' was introduced later.

24 *hee.* As Woodford notes, 'high' is an obvious scribal error.

26 *disclos'd*, exposed to view.

67 *plants*, soles of the feet, or footsteps. Cf. PS **25**. 42.

19

Sidney probably took his rhyme scheme from the first half of Marot's 12-line stanza in his Psalm 19, which begins aabccb$_6$.

12 *conceived*, understood.

27 *Rea'ms*, realms.

35 *it gives.* 'As give' is a late emendation made after X but before A was copied.

37–38. Geneva reads, 'The feare of the Lord is cleane, and endureth for ever.'

20

27 *chivalry.* The Psalter and Geneva read 'horses', Beza 'chevaux'.

21

The stanza form is the same as the first half of Marot's Psalm 91.

9 *prevent'st*, anticipatedst.

31–32. Geneva has only, 'Thou shalt make them like a firie oven in time of thine anger.' 32 *amated*, overwhelmed.

46 *pointed*, appointed.

22

7–8. The revisions in C and M eliminate the imperfect 'plaint—lent' rhyme.

10 *lawdes*. Geneva reads 'praises'.

11 *in*. Geneva reads, 'Our fathers trusted in thee'.

20 *lust*, pleasure, delight.

42 *rehearsed*, enumerated.

73–78. The Countess of Pembroke's revision, not made until after K F I X had been copied, eliminates Sidney's final half-stanza. Geneva reads: 'All they that be fat in the earth, shall eate and worship: all they that go downe into the dust, shall bow before him, even he that cann not quicken his owne soule. Their seede shall serve him: it shall be counted unto the Lord for a generation. They shall come, and shall declare his righteousnes unto a people that shall be borne, because he hath done it.'

23

19–27. The Countess of Pembroke's revision eliminates Sidney's half-stanza. Geneva reads: 'Thou doest anoint mine head with oyle, and my cup runneth over. Doubtles kindenesse and mercy shall followe me all the dayes of my life, and I shall remaine a long season in the house of the Lord.'

24

12 *falsly*. 'Safely' is a graphical error. Geneva reads, 'nor sworne deceytfully'.

15. Geneva, 'This is the generation of them that seeke him'.

25

4 *quite*, completely. Geneva, 'Let me not be confounded'.

42 *plant*, establish oneself in position.

60 *left*. Geneva, 'For I am *desolate* and poore'.

26

12. This line wants two syllables, which may have been the fault of the scribe of the original of B, or of Sidney himself. K emends the sense and metre by reading 'I would not once' and X by reading 'I neuer will', for 'will not'. Geneva reads, 'For thy loving kindnesse is before mine eyes: therefore have I walked in thy trueth'.

30 *bloodseeker's*. Geneva reads 'the bloody men', the Psalter 'the blood-thirstie', and Beza 'les meurtriers'.

31–39. Sidney follows Geneva, 'In whose hands is wickednes, and their right hand is full of bribes. But I will walke in mine innocencie: redeeme me therefore, and be merciful unto me. My foote standeth in uprightnes: I will praise thee, O Lord, in the Congregations.' The Countess of Pembroke eliminated

Sidney's partial stanza, and probably revised with an eye on the Psalter, which reads 'gyftes' for 'bribes'.

39 *prest*, impressed, forced.

27

17–18. Geneva reads, 'I will trust in this,' and explains 'this' by a side note: 'That God wil deliver me, and give my faith the victorie.' To be intelligible Sidney's lines require the Geneva side note.

28

11–15. Sidney's images of the 'chain' and 'spotted thoughts' are not in his sources. Geneva reads, 'Draw me not away with the wicked, and with the workers of iniquitie: which speak friendly to their neighbours, when malice is in their hearts'.

29

16–18. This is imperfectly expressed; reference to the Psalter shows that the meaning intended is: He made Liban (Lebanon) skip like a calf, and Shirion skip like a unicorn.

20 *try'd*, had experience of.

21. The Psalter and Geneva have only 'the wildernesse of Cades'; the 'Arabs' may come from Beza's *Paraphrasis*, 'Vox Iehouae horrenda deserta & Arabum tesqua succutit' (p. 100).

23 *makes bald*. Geneva, 'discovereth'.

25–29. Sidney's phrasing appears to be closer to Beza than to Geneva or the Psalter:

> Dieu preside comme Juge
> Dessus les eaux du deluge:
> Et sans aucun jour ne terme
> Dure son royaume ferme
>   Parquoy le Seigneur tout fort,
> Des siens sera le support:
> Puis en paix les mourrira
> Des biens qu'il leur donnera.

30

8 *score*, record or account.

15. A typical Sidneyan inversion: 'Doth fill life [with] joyes.'

28 *dust*. Emended to 'earth' by the Countess of Pembroke, probably because 'dust' is used again in line 30.

35 *sack*. Geneva has 'sacke', the Psalter 'sackecloth'.

31

6 *forteress*. The spelling indicates the rhythm and rhyme.

36 *broken pott*. Geneva and the Psalter have 'broken vessel', Beza, 'un pot cassé'.

42 *my bane to bake*, to prepare my destruction.

61–69. The Countess of Pembroke's revision eliminates Sidney's half stanza. Geneva reads: 'Though I sayd in mine haste, I am cast out of thy sight, yet thou heardest the voice of my prayer, when I cryed unto thee. Love ye the Lord all his Saints: for the Lord preserveth the faythful, and rewardeth abundantly the proude doer. All ye that trust in the Lord, be strong, and he shall establish your heart.'

32

The stanza is similar to the first half of Marot's Psalm 36 and Beza's Psalm 68.

1 *Bless'ed is the man*, a perfectly acceptable reading because 'bless'ed' is a monosyllable. The Countess of Pembroke may have emended on the basis of the Psalter's 'Blessed is he'.

33

7 *harp*. An emendation by K of a scribal error in the original of B. Geneva reads, 'Praise the Lord with harpe: sing unto him with viole and instrument of ten strings.'

34

The metre and rhyme scheme are the same as Beza's Psalm 34, but Sidney does not have the concluding half stanza.

33–48. Since Sidney in this Psalm translates Beza almost line for line, the reversal of lines 33–40 and 41–48 must have been a scribal error in the original of B.

67 *And will save whom his sight cleere*. A word was omitted, probably in error by the scribe of the original of B, leaving the line one syllable short. The scribe of X emended to restore the rhythm by reading 'his *true* sight'. Something of the sort is required, but Sidney's wording is irrecoverable. Beza reads 'A ceux volontiers il subvient | Qui sont les plus foulez', which suggests that the line may have begun, 'And willing saves . . .'.

35

25–30. Sidney probably depended upon eye-rhymes (imperfectly preserved by the scribes) to maintain his aababb pattern. In line 25 the eye-rhyme 'beare' (bore) would ordinarily have been spelled 'bare' as in line 29. 'Weare' (were) in line 26 is Sidney's spelling in his holographs and indicates his pronunciation. That 'ware' (wore) in line 30 is a past tense is indicated by Geneva's 'Yet I, when they were sicke, I *was clothed* with a sacke'.

48 *lawdes*. Geneva, 'I will praise thee among much people.'

50 *fleere*. Geneva reads 'winke with the eye', but has a side note, 'In token of contempt and mocking'.

37

Sidney's stanza is similar to the first half of Beza's Psalms 17 and 63.

73–76. Sidney is here merely wordy. Geneva reads simply, 'The righteous men shall inherit the land, and dwell therein for ever'.

90 *laurell*. Geneva reads 'a greene baye tree', Marot 'un laurier'; elsewhere in this Psalm Sidney follows Geneva closely.

38

51 *orethwart*, unfriendly, hostile.

39

Sidney's stanza is the same as Beza's Psalm 39, but his phrasing is from Geneva, except possibly for hints from Beza in lines 3 and 28.

32 *thy handy stroakes*, strokes given by your hands.

40 *baiting*, halting for refreshment on a journey. Cf. AS **39.** 2.

40

The stanza is from Beza's Psalm 40, but not the wording.

41

The stanza is from Beza's Psalm 41, and the words are translated from Beza with some reference to Geneva.

42

Sidney took his rhyme scheme (though not his pattern of feminine rhymes), and possibly his trochaic metre, from Beza's Psalm 42, and his phrasing follows Beza stanza for stanza and almost line for line. Compare his fourth stanza with Beza's:

> Car j'ai de toy souvenance,
> Depuis outre le Jordain,
> Et la froide demeurance
> De Hermon pays hautain,
>   Et de Misar autre mont.
> Un gouffre l'autre semond,
> Lors que tonnent sur ma teste
> Les torrens de ta tempeste.

Geneva reads: 'Because I remember thee, from the land of Jordén, and Hermoním, and from the mount Mizár. One depe calleth another depe by the noise of thy water spoutes.'

1 *chafed*, heated.

53–56. The four different revisions in C, E H L N, G, and M were made to avoid repetition of the same rhyme sound in lines 52–54.

I

This was first printed between CS 22 and CS 23 in the 1613 *Arcadia*, the only substantive text. The poem is in poulter's measure, with heavy alliteration and fixed caesura, an old-fashioned metre that Sidney otherwise used only once in the burlesque OA 3; but its rudeness, which deliberately reproduces the crudities of earlier poetry, is appropriate to a country 'pastorall shew'. The interlocutors, Will and Dick, appear nowhere else in Sidney's writings; but Dick's mistress has black eyes (line 28), for which Sidney had a special partiality (Mira, Philoclea, and Stella all have black eyes). Sidney paid frequent visits to his sister at Wilton, and a letter from Sir Arthur Basset, dated February 1583/4 (printed in Butler's *Sidneiana*, p. 81), shows that he had a hand in arranging entertainments nearby. Pastoral shows continued to be presented at Wilton, for in *A Poetical Rapsody* (1602, B5–6) there is 'A Dialogue betweene two shepheards, Thenot, and Piers, in praise of Astrea, made by the excellent Lady, the Lady Mary Countesse of Pembrook, at the Queenes Majesties being at her house at [Wilton] Anno [1599]'. The Countess of Pembroke does not appear to have been personally concerned with the publication of the 1613 edition; but the anonymous editor, whoever he was, had an exceptional regard for accuracy, and at one point consulted an *Old Arcadia* manuscript to perfect the text. He or the publisher may also have made inquiries among members of the Sidney circle for any additional literary remains of his still extant. In 1613 Sidney's brother Robert, his sister the Countess of Pembroke, and his friend Fulke Greville were still alive. The fact that this poem was reprinted in all subsequent folio editions of the *Arcadia* indicates that his family and friends took no action to suppress it, and so possibly accepted it as genuine.

10 *stoolball*, a country game resembling cricket played chiefly by young women and children.

2

This is subscribed 'S P S' in Bodleian MS. Rawl. poet. 85, where it is preceded by OA 51 and followed by CS 3, which are also subscribed 'S P S'; but another transcript, in British Museum MS. Harley 7392, is anonymous. MS. Rawl. poet. 85 is a poetical anthology of courtly and academic verse of the 1570's and 1580's that was compiled in the late 1580's and early 1590's by a man who had been a student at Cambridge. It contains 143 poems, 23 of which are certainly by Sidney; 11 of these are properly attributed to him by name or initials, nine are unsigned, CS 22 is subscribed 'Incertus author', CS 21 is attributed to 'Mr Nowell', and AS x to 'Britton'. Another poem, 'At my harte there is a payne', subscribed 'S P S', also appears in British Museum MS. 34064 in a collection of poems that are probably all by Breton. The attributions of all but two of the 51 other poems that have the names or initials of their authors subscribed are accurate as far as they can be checked. The compiler collected his materials from a variety of sources; the fact that many of his texts are quite corrupt indicates that he often drew from other manuscript anthologies rather than from the author's own manuscripts.

The present poem is a species of correlative verse similar to OA 60, which Sidney was among the earliest to write in English; but he was soon followed by others, and the most popular poem of this type was 'Her face Her tongue Her wytt' by Sir Arthur Gorges. There is nothing against this attribution to Sidney; but since the compiler sometimes made mistakes, we cannot be certain that the poem is his.

3

Printed by A. C. Judson, *Sidney's Appearance*, 1958, p. 51. Copied by Drummond in Dn at f. 9ᵛ, headed 'S. P. S. on his picture', and again at f. 48ᵛ without a heading and reading 'all the' for 'all' in the first line:

> Take this thou who makest all virtues live,
> Who gives himself may well his picture give.

4

The Earl of Arundel, Lord Windsor, Philip Sidney, and Fulke Greville, calling themselves the Four Foster Children of Desire, were the challengers in a tournament devised to entertain the French ambassadors who had come to treat of the proposed marriage of Queen Elizabeth to the Duke of Anjou. On Whit Monday, 15 May 1581, they entered the tiltyard adjoining Whitehall with a canvas-covered 'Rowling trench' concealing musicians, and proceeded to the gallery at the end where Queen Elizabeth sat, which they called the Fortress of Perfect Beauty. A boy declared in a set speech that the Fortress would be assaulted, whereupon 'the musike played verie pleasauntly, and one of the Boyes being then accompanied with Cornets, summoned the Fortresse with this song' (PP 4). 'When that was ended, another Boye turning himselfe to the Foster children and their retinue, sung this Allarme' (PP 5). Then 22 defendants entered and each ran six courses against one of the challengers. The next day the challengers fought at tourney and barriers against the defenders; but in the evening they acknowledged that they had been overcome by the Queen's virtue, and vowed to be 'slaves to this Fortresse for ever'.

These two sonnets were first printed by Henry Goldwel in his *Briefe declaration*, 1581, describing the tournament and reporting the speeches of the contestants, which is the only substantive text. Goldwel did not name the author of the sonnets, but Professor E. G. Fogel, *MLN* lxxv (1960), 389–94, argued that Sidney was the most likely person to have written them for the following reasons. (*a*) Goldwel implies that the contestants had a hand in the composition of the triumph. (*b*) Lord Windsor is not known to be a poet, and the style of the two sonnets is quite unlike the known work of the Earl of Arundel and Greville. (*c*) In 1581 Sidney was the only living Englishman known to have had any considerable practice in the writing of sonnets. (*d*) The style of the two sonnets is Sidneyan, and their intricately devised patterns of repetition (the second is a line-by-line reply to the first) are remarkably similar to Sidney's answer poems, especially to OA 25 and OA 26. These are persuasive arguments, and I fully agree with Professor Fogel's cautious conclusion that the two sonnets are possibly by Sidney. If they are his, they were the first of his poems to be printed, and the only products of his pen to appear in print during his lifetime.

5

8 *no force*, it is of no avail.
12 *much may*, we may win much praise.

BIBLIOGRAPHY

BIBLIOGRAPHY

THE OLD ARCADIA

Je	Le
Qu	As
Da	St
Ph	Bo
Cl	

THE NEW ARCADIA

Cm	98 Rptd. 1599, 1605, 1613, 1621–2–3,
Penshurst 'History of Arcadia' MS.	1627–9, 1633, 1638, 1655, 1662,
90	1674, 1725–4, 1739, 1907, 1921.
93	13

ASTROPHIL AND STELLA

Bt	Q1
Dr	Q2
Ho	[Q3]

THE PSALMS OF DAVID

A	H
B	I
C	J‖
D	K
E	L
F	M
G	N

POEMS IN MANUSCRIPTS

Hn Arundel-Harington
Dd Camb. Dd. 5. 75.
Cambr. Kk. 5. 30.
BM Add. 10309
BM Add. 12515
BM Add. 21433—nothing
BM Add. 27406
Ba BM Add. 28253
BM Add. 34064
Eg BM Eg. 2421

BM Eg. 2877
BM Harl. 3511
Ha BM Harl. 6910
Hy BM Harl. 7392
BM Sl. 1925
Bodl. Eng. poet. d. 3
Ra Bodl. Rawl. poet. 85
Bodl. Rawl. poet. 142
Bodl. Rawl. poet. 148
Bodl. Rawl. poet. 172

CCC Ox. 328
Ma Marsh's Dublin
Natl. Lib. Scot. 2059
Dn Natl. Lib. Scot. 2060
Rosenbach 197

Fo Folger 1. 112
Folger 452. 4
Folger 1302. 2
Fl Folger 2071. 7

POEMS IN PRINTED BOOKS

Go Henry Goldwel, *A briefe de-
claration*, [1581]
Bd Wm Byrd, *Psalmes, Sonets, &
songs*, 1588
Fr Abraham Fraunce, *The Ar-
cadian Rhetorike*, [1588]
Pu [George Puttenham], *The Arte
of English Poesie*, 1589
Bd Wm Byrd, *Songs of sundrie
natures*, 1589
Hn John Harington, *Orlando
Furioso*, 1591
Di H. C[onstable & others],

Diana, [1592–7]
Bn N. B[reton & others], *The
Arbor of amorous Devises*, 1597
[1st ed., 1594]
Englands Helicon, 1600
*Bel-vedére or The Garden of the
Muses*, 1600
Englands Parnassus, 1600
Dv F. Davison, *A Poetical Rap-
sody*, 1602
Theodore Dousa, *Lusus Imaginis
Iocosae sive Echus*, 1638

MUSICAL SETTINGS

BM Add. 15117
BM Add. 31723—also ptd. n.d.
BM Add. 31810
BM Loan 35
CC Ox. 439
Bd Byrd, *Psalmes*, 1588—copied
BM Add. 31992, BM Add. 29401–5
Pu Puttenham, *Arte of English Poesie*,
1589—no music but quoted as song
Bd Byrd, *Songs*, 1589—copied BM
Add. 31992, BM Add. 29401–4,
BM Add. 23636
J. Dowland, *Second Booke*, 1600—
words copied Bodl. Douce 280
T. Morley, *First Booke*, 1600

R. Jones, *Second Booke*, 1601
T. Bateson, *First set*, 1604
H. Youll, *Canzonets*, 1608
T. Ravenscroft, *Pammelia*, 1609—
copied Melvill 1612
R. Douland, *Musicall Banquet*, 1610
R. Jones, *Muses Gardin*, 1610
W. Corkine, *Second Booke*, 1612
J. Ward, *First Set*, 1613
T. Vautor, *First Set*, 1619–20
M. Peerson, *Private Musicke*, 1620
F. Pilkington, *Second Set*, 1624.
A. B., *Synopsis of Vocal Musick*,
1680—copied J. Forbes, *Songs and
Fancies*, 1682

THE OLD ARCADIA

*[Je] Jesus College, Oxford, MS. 150. [*Old Arcadia*—title wanting.]

187 ff. The text, ff. 6–146, in a single small late sixteenth-century hand, is paged with some errors 11–285 (should be 11–292). Inside the front cover in a single hand different from the text is written, 'Edward Thelwall Anne Thelwalls brother Sidnay Thelwall Simone Thelw[all]'; on f. 1ʳ the first names 'Owen, Robert, Anne, Elisabeth, Dorothy'; and on f. 1ᵛ 'Anne Myddelton'. The watermark of the original leaves is the royal arms within a garter, not in Briquet, Churchill, or Heawood (cf. Cl). Not listed in *Coxe's Catalogue*, 1852; first reported by Miss Margaret Beese, *TLS*, 4 May 1940, p. 224, who noted that Edward Thelwall of the Denbighshire family was the brother of Sir Eubule Thelwall (1562–1630), principal of Jesus.

Probably originally contained the complete text of the *Old Arcadia*, but ff. 1–5, 12–16, 64–65, 75–77, 88–89, 124, and 147–87 are blank inserts of different paper with a pot watermark, so that the text corresponding to Feuillerat's iv. 1. 1–12. 4, 27. 19–40. 2, 156. 38–161. 17, 186. 33–195. 23, 225. 4–230. 22, 317. 26–319. 16, and 377. 22–389. 19 is wanting, causing the loss of OA **1**; **3.** 5–14; **4**; **33.** 13–30; **34**; **35**; **36.** 1–6; **47**; **48**; **49**; **50**; **51**; **62.** 87–146; **63.** 1–31; **73.** 165–86; and **74.** 1–28. Lines are also omitted at **30.** 164–6; **31.** 25; **32.** 27–28, **62.** 25–26, 29–36, 69–70; **67.** 31–33; and **73.** 135–6. Agrees in error with Qu in omitting OA **31.** 25 and **67.** 31–33 and in an average of about two verbal errors per page—e.g. in the prose at the beginning of the First Eclogues Je-Qu read in error 'bodies' (iv. 52. 5), 'imploy all' (52. 16), 'princes disguised' (52. 34), 'his other side' (53. 7), 'continually' (53. 10), &c.— clear proof that both were copied from the same faulty original. The Je scribe also introduced many unique errors of his own, so that his text is only slightly better than that of Qu, the most inaccurate of the nine manuscripts.

Contains the earliest form of the *Old Arcadia*, with the unrevised text of OA 28, a short and unrevised form of OA 62, and the discussion of quantitative verse at the end of the First Eclogues (printed in *PQ* xxix [1950], 70–74).

*[Qu] The Queen's College, Oxford, MS. 301. [*Old Arcadia*— untitled]

vii+142+ii ff., in 25 gatherings; ff. 1–5ᵛ in a single late sixteenth-century hand, ff. 6–142ᵛ in several different hands or variants of a second hand. On f. i is the draft of a letter dated 1636 concerning Adrian Bubbe or Tho. Baude who had been in the service of Lord Berkeley or Lord Savoy; f. vii contains a watermark which Briquet (No. 1882) dates 1586; ff. 1–142 contain three watermarks, one of which Briquet (No. 8079) dates 1564–96 and another (No. 13194) 1581–1603. Listed in *Coxe's Catalogue*, 1852, and described by Zandvoort, pp. 9–12.

Contains the complete text of the earliest form of the *Old Arcadia*, though lines of poems are omitted at **7.** 179; **13.** 46; **31.** 25; **52.** 11; **62.** 25–26, 29–36,

71–92; **67.** 31–33; and **73.** 28, 110. The First Eclogues conclude with a discussion of quantitative verse found elsewhere only in Je, and OA 28 and 62 are in their earliest unrevised form. Agrees in error with Je in several hundred passages, which shows that both were transcribed from the same inaccurate original; but also contains many unique errors of its own, which makes it by far the most inaccurate of the nine *Old Arcadia* manuscripts.

Feuillerat printed its text of OA **30.** 1–4 and 185–90 (i. 563); OA **9.** 62–63 and 138–41 (ii. 368); and OA 23, 24, 35, 36, and 37 (ii. 238–40). Zandvoort, pp. 11–12, printed the discussion of quantitative verse.

*[Da] British Museum MS. Additional 41204 (Davies MS.). [*Old Arcadia*—untitled.]

ii + 190 ff. in 19 gatherings of ten leaves, written in a single late sixteenth-century hand. Belonged to the antiquary Thomas Martin (1697–1771); bought by Charles Brietzcke in 1774; and presented to the British Museum by Miss M. E. Davies in 1925. Described by Zandvoort, pp. 13–14, and in the British Museum *Catalogue of Additions* (1950).

Contains the complete text of the *Old Arcadia* in its second state, though lines are omitted in the poems at **30.** 33–35, **46.** 1–6, **62.** 25–26, and **67.** 31–33. In the margin of OA 62 is an alternative version of lines 69–70 which later appear in the text of St-Bo. Agrees with Ph-Je-Qu in omitting OA **67.** 31–33 and in containing the unrevised form of OA 28. The conclusion of the First Eclogues is in a state related to Ph, intermediate between the earlier Je-Qu and later Cl-As versions (see p. 368, n. 1).

The text is fairly accurate, though slightly inferior to St, Bo, and As.

*[Ph] British Museum MS. Additional 38892 (Phillipps MS.). *A treatis made by Sr Phillip Sydney Knyght of certeyn accidents in Arcadia. made in the yeer 1580 and emparted to some few of his frends. in his lyfe tyme and to more sence his vnfortunat deceasse.*

i + 202 ff. in 25 gatherings of eight leaves plus an imperfect gathering of two leaves at the end. Transcribed after 1586 in a late sixteenth-century hand that changes slightly after ff. 96^v and 110^v. Listed as lot 1171 in Thorpe's catalogue of 1836, became Phillipps MS. 9610, purchased by Dobell in 1908, and by the British Museum in 1914. Identified as the *Old Arcadia* by Bertram Dobell, *Quarterly Review*, ccxi (1909), 74–100; described in the British Museum *Catalogue of Additions* (1925), and by Zandvoort, p. 8.

Contains the text of the *Old Arcadia* in its second state, complete except for blanks at the bottom of ff. 90 and 90^v–91^r (causing the omission of iv. 170. 1–171. 28, including OA 40, 41, and 42), and a leaf of text missing at the end (causing the loss of iv. 387. 31–389. 19). Lines are also omitted in the poems at **2.** 13–14; **7.** 166; **11.** 17–19; **28.** 100–1; **35.** 5; **62.** 25–26, 29–36, 77–92; **66.** 130; **67.** 31–33; and **77.** 13–14. Another hand has made several corrections and additons to OA 62 and occasional corrections in other poems, but the readings (especially 'her thyes' in OA **62.** 88) show that these were taken from 93 or a later printed edition. The conclusion of the First Eclogues is related to Da, and it agrees with Da-Je-Qu in omitting OA **67.** 31–33 and in containing the unrevised form of OA 28. The scribe was both careless and inventive, and had no compunction about writing nonsense, though some of his errors were due to a faulty original. It is only slightly superior to Je and Qu, and thus is one of the threemost inaccurate *Old Arcadia* manuscripts.

Dobell published from this manuscript the previously unprinted OA 23, 24, 35, 36, and 37 in his *Quarterly Review* article, pp. 96–99.

*[Cl] Folger Library MS. 4009. 03 (Clifford MS.). *The Countess of Pembrokes Arcadia.*

229 ff., 3–228 numbered 1–226, in a single fine late sixteenth-century professional hand, on paper having a watermark of the royal arms within a garter surmounted by a crown, not in Briquet or Heawood (cf. Je). On the first leaf are scribbled the names 'davide Morgan' and 'Iohn lluid'; on the second 'Iohne Morgan', 'Arthur Trogmorton', 'Alexander Clifford', and 'Iohn lloid'; and on the last 'Willm Clyforde' and 'Mountgomrey'. Purchased by Bertram Dobell in 1907, who mentioned it in his 1909 *Quarterly Review* article; passed to W. A. White before 1926; and acquired by the Folger in 1940. Described by Feuillerat, iv. vi–vii, and by Zandvoort, pp. 12–13.

Contains, ff. 2–216, the third state of the *Old Arcadia* text. Lines are omitted in the poems at **34.** 23; **62.** 25–26, 29–36, 83–84; and **74.** 38–39; and several phrases or sentences are also omitted in the prose. Agrees with As and St-Bo in having a revised form of OA 28, and with Le-As and the earlier manuscripts in having the unrevised form of OA 62. Agrees with Le in omitting **34.** 23 and in verbal errors in 22 lines of the poems, and agrees in error with Le and As in 17 lines of the poems; but since most of these few agreements in error originate from mistakes in single letters or groups of letters only, they are more likely the result of chance independent variations than evidence of descent from a similarly defective original. A moderately good text by Elizabethan standards, but slightly less accurate than As and Le.

On ff. 216^v–226^v, in the same hand, are 30 'Dyuers and sondry Sonett*es*' in the order 3–32. The complete *Old Arcadia* text and CS 5, which also had not previously been printed, were published by Feuillerat in 1926.

*[Le] British Museum MS. Additional 41498 (Lee MS.). [Poems from the *Old Arcadia*—untitled.]

38 ff. in a single late sixteenth-century hand. Upside down on the back parchment cover is written, 'Sir Henry Lee delivered being champean to the qwene delivered to my lor^d cwmberla[n]d deli by willeam simons', which must refer, as Chambers (*Sir Henry Lee*, 1936, p. 268) pointed out, to Lee's surrender of his office as Queen's champion in the Accession Day tournaments to the Earl of Cumberland in 1590. But the unrevised form of OA 62 indicates that the manuscript was transcribed before 1582. Presented to the British Museum by Viscount Dillon in 1927 and described the same year in the *British Museum Quarterly*, ii. 69–70.

Contains 66 poems in the order in which they appear in the *Old Arcadia*, and two short passages of prose from Book II (iv. 94. 14–95. 3, 95. 14–101. 40). OA 5, 6, 9, 10, 25, 26, 28, 29, 58, 68, and 77 are omitted, and lines are omitted at **30.** 1–4, 185–9; **34.** 23, 35; **62.** 25–26, 29–36; and **66.** 89. On f. 38, otherwise blank, are two lines of music in lute tablature, which Mr. D. S. Hoffman, jr., identified as a version of 'Watkin's Ale' (see W. Chappell, *Popular Music of the Olden Times*, i. 137). The text is similar to, and in point of accuracy stands midway between, As and Cl.

*[As] Huntington Library MS. HM 162 (Ashburnham MS.). *The Counties of Pembrokes Archadia* [title, wanting at the beginning, supplied from the end of the First Eclogues].

183 ff. numbered 7–189, in several late sixteenth-century hands. On f. 86ᵛ is the name Robert Walker, Treasurer to Sir Henry Sidney from 1575 until about 1581 and who appears in Sidney family records until 1583. Belonged to the Earl of Ashburnham in 1897; bought by Dobell in 1907, who first identified it as the *Old Arcadia* in the *Athenaeum*, 7 Sept. 1907, p. 272; passed to W. A. White before 1914; and purchased from his estate by the Huntington. Described by Zandvoort, p. 13, and listed by de Ricci.

Contains the third state of the *Old Arcadia* text, similar to Cl and Le. Six leaves are wanting at the beginning causing the loss of iv. **1.** 1–11. 28, including OA 1. OA 7 and 8 are omitted without any break in the text; and lines are omitted in the poems at **13.** 9–10; **62.** 25–26, 29–36, 77–92; **72.** 44; and **75.** 32–34. After the first quantitative poem, OA 11, is a note, 'write these rules', and the following page (40ʳ) is blank—the rules appear in St. At the end of Book II (f. 68ᵛ) is a detached couplet:

> Could the starres that bredd such wytt
> in fors no longer fixed sytte.

Different portions of the manuscript vary in accuracy, but in general the text of the poems is slightly superior to Cl and Le.

*[St] St. John's College, Cambridge, MS. I. 7 (James 308). [*The*] *Countes of Pembro*[*okes*] *Arca*[*dia*].

250 ff. in a single hand. Probably transcribed late in 1581 or slightly afterwards, for it contains the same revisions in OA 29 and 62 that appear in Bo. In 1588 Fraunce drew quotations in his *Arcadian Rhetorike* from this manuscript. In 1633 it was purchased by William Walker of Chiswick from the estate of Sir Edmund Scory (born 1575). Sir Edmund's father, Sylvanus Scory of Hereford (d. 1617), had been on friendly terms with Sidney but received an angry letter from him in July 1583 (*HMC De L'Isle*, ii. 98). Later the manuscript passed from Thomas Wagstaffe (d. 1712) to Thomas Baker, who presented it to St. John's. It was listed in the St. John's handwritten catalogue of *c.* 1717 and in the printed catalogues of 1842 and 1913; otherwise it was first mentioned by Mona Wilson, *Sidney* (1931), p. 302.

Contains, ff. 3–239, the fourth state of the *Old Arcadia* text, similar to Bo, with the poems complete except for the omission of OA **7.** 156. In the margin opposite OA 11 (f. 40ᵛ) is a 'Nota' containing rules for determining the quantities of syllables; this does not appear in any other text, but a blank space is left for it in As. OA 62 contains 146 lines, 19 of which are revisions; and there are also a few slight revisions of phrase in the prose. A different hand has changed the original reading of OA **13**. 32 'in lickor can coole' to 'no lyckor cooles', **13**. 34 'avancement' to 'advancement', **23**. 4 'flowers' to 'flowes', **25**. 4 'bould' to 'bobde', and **71**. 68 'from' to 'from the', and has added opposite Cleophila's name on f. 235ᵛ 'or Zelmane'; these changes appear to have been made by reference to 93 or a later print. The manuscript was executed with extreme care, and its text is the most accurate of all the sources for the *Old Arcadia* poems.

At the end, ff. 241–2, in a different hand and on different paper which obviously was not part of the original manuscript, are five untitled poems: CS 19, 6, 5, 3, and 30. The 'Nota' is printed above in the notes to OA 11, and was printed earlier in *PQ* xxix (1950), 70–74. St is used as copy text in this edition for OA 23, 24, 35, 36, 37, and CS 5.

*[Bo] Bodleian MS. e Museo 37 (formerly Museo 141, *Summary Catalogue* 3607). *The Countes of Pembrookes Arcadia.*

i+247 ff. in 16 gatherings, foliated 1–36 and (in a later hand) 36–246; ff. 1–96 have the same watermark (Briquet No. 11055) as a holograph letter of Sidney's written from Salisbury on 28 December 1581; the remaining leaves contain a watermark similar to Briquet's No. 12775, which he dates 1557. Written in a single hand except for the Fourth Eclogues, which are in a different hand. On f. 246ᵛ are written in different hands, none of which resemble Sidney's own, 'Phillipus Sydney', 'R. M.', 'Sydney', and 'C R'. Acquired by the Bodleian between 1655 and 1660; listed in *Bernard's Catalogue* (1697), p. 172; and described by Zandvoort, p. 9.

Contains ff. 1–236ᵛ, the fourth state of the *Old Arcadia* text, similar to but slightly less accurate than St, with the poems complete except for the omission of OA **7**. 156. On ff. 237–46, in the same hand as the preceding *Arcadia* text, are 27 'Certein lowse Sonnett*es* and songes', originally in the order 1–2, 15–21, 31, 22–28, 3–4, and 6–14; but a leaf has been lost after f. 241 with the result that CS **24**. 17–27, all of **25**, and **26**. 1–6 are wanting.

THE NEW ARCADIA

*[Cm] Cambridge University Library MS. Kk. 1. 5 (2). [*New Arcadia*—untitled.]

210 ff.; 5–210 numbered, with some errors, 5–208. Contains the date 1584, in the same hand and ink as the text, in the upper left margin of f. 1. Written in a single elaborate Italian hand. Begins, 'It was in the time that . . .', ends, '. . . hauing receiued his masters commandement and' (i. 504. 20). Acquired from the library of Richard Holdsworth (1590–1645). Though it was listed in the University's printed *Catalogue of the Manuscripts*, iii (1858), 559, it has been unaccountably overlooked by students of the *New Arcadia*. When I first examined it in 1947, I thought I was the first person to be aware of its significance;

but I subsequently learned that Professor B. M. Wagner was engaged on a study of its contents. I therefore restrict my own account of it as much as possible to a discussion of the textual characteristics of the poems.

The earliest reference to a manuscript of Sidney's *New Arcadia* is in Fulke Greville's letter to Sir Francis Walsingham endorsed 'november 1586' (first printed by J. P. Collier, *Gentleman's Magazine*, N.S., xxxiii [1850], 371–2) which I here transcribe from the holograph in the Public Record Office, SP 12/195/33.

Sir this day one ponsonby a booke bynder in poles church yard, came to me, and told me that ther was one in hand to print, Sir philip sydneys old arcadia asking me yf it were done, with yor honors co[n]s[ent] or any other of his frends, I told him to m[y] knowledge no, then he advised me to give w[ar]ning of it, ether to the archebishope or doctor Cosen, who haue as he says a copy of it to pervse to that end/ Sir I am lothe to reneu his memori vnto you, but yeat in this I might presume, for I haue sent my lady yor daughter [Sidney's widow] at her request, a correction of that old one don 4 or 5 years since which he left in trust with me wherof ther is no more copies, & fitter to be printed then that first which is so common, notwithstanding euen that to be amended by a direction sett doun vndre his own hand how & why, so as in many respects espetially ye care of printing it i[s] to be don with more deliberation,—besydes he hathe most excellently translated among diu[ers] other notable workes monsieur du plessis book agains[t] Atheisme, which is since don by an other, so as bothe in respect of the loue betwen plessis & h[im] besyds other affinities in ther courses but espetially Sir philips uncomparable Iudgement, I think fit ther be made a stei of that mercenary book to [i.e. so] that Sir philip might haue all thos religous honors which ar worthelj dew to his ljfe and death, many other works as bartas his semayne, 40 of the spalm[s] translated into myter &c which requyre the care of his frends, not to amend for I think it fales within the reache of no man liuing, but only to see to the paper and other common errors of mercenary printing Gayn ther wilbe no doubt to be disposed by you, let it helpe the poorest of his seruants, I desyre only care to be had of his honor who I fear hathe caried the honor of thes latter ages with him . . . Sir I had wayted on you my selfe for aunswer because I am Ielous of tyme in it, but in trothe I am nothing well Good Sir think of it
ffoulk Greuill

Ponsonby published an edition of the incomplete *New Arcadia* in 1590, with a text evidently based upon the unique manuscript referred to by Greville. Cm cannot be that manuscript, for it wants some 15 pages of text at the end and omits several other passages that are found in 90. It must therefore be a transcript, perhaps made shortly after 1586, of the manuscript Sidney left with Greville. The date 1584 on the first page must refer to the date of composition; it cannot be the date of transcription if Greville was correct in saying that in 1586 there was only one manuscript in existence.

Cm is written continuously without book or chapter divisions of any kind, though three pages are left blank after f. 149, the point where the prose of Book II ends in 90. In the early part of the manuscript, where the proper names of the *Old Arcadia* characters are changed, the original name is first written and then scored through and the new name is written above it; in the latter part of the manuscript blank spaces are left for many of the proper names. There is no trace of either the prose or verse of the eclogues, though the narrative promises 'pastorall pastymes' of some sort at ff. 65 and 149, the positions occupied by the First and Second Eclogues in 90. The prose text contains or provides blank spaces for 26 poems in the following order: OA 3, 2, 4, 5, 14, 15, 16, 17, 18 (blank), 19 (blank), 62 (lines 1–8 only), 30 (lines 5–37 only), 8 (incipit only), 20, 21, OP 1, OA 22, 25, 1 (blank), 26 (lines 1–4 only), 74 (lines 1–6 only), 73 (blank), OP 2, CS 3 (incipit only), OP 3 (blank), and OA 75 (blank).

The scribe apparently mechanically copied what was set before him, and did not attempt in any way to improve or correct his original. He left blank spaces for the description of *impresas* at f. 33 (i. 64. 1), f. 99 (i. 216. 25–27), and f. 127ᵛ (i. 284. 36–37); at f. 168ᵛ (i. 399. 22), where he left a blank page for OA 73, he also omitted a sentence of the following prose; and at f. 191 (i. 449. 17) he left a blank space for the epitaph of Argalus and Parthenia (OP 3). These must represent lacunas in the original, for 90 also leaves blank spaces at these points.

Though the scribe copied mechanically, he also worked rapidly and made numerous errors of transcription on every page. Many of these are obvious slips of the pen as f. 1 'eye' for 'eyes' (i. 5. 16) or f. 149 'besought' for 'bethought' (i. 337. 36); others are common scribal substitutions as f. 1 'ouer' for 'on' (i. 5. 10) or f. 65 'mortallitye' for 'mortally' (i. 145. 11). In several places he omitted a phrase or a whole line that appears in 90—f. 44 (i. 83. 4–5), f. 66ᵛ (i. 147. 34–36), f. 91 (i. 198. 31–32), f. 172ᵛ (i. 408. 18–21). But he also preserved the correct reading in many places where 90 is in error (see p. 373); so Cm is a substantive source almost as important as 90 for a critical reconstruction of the text of the *New Arcadia*.

Penshurst Place, Kent. Viscount De L'Isle and Dudley MS. *The History of Arcadia.*

255 ff. in a single seventeenth-century hand. An epitome of Books I–III of the *New Arcadia*, omitting the eclogues and all but ten of the poems, and pruning the narrative to about a third of its original length. Peculiarities of wording show that it was compiled from the 1627 edition.

*[90] *The Covntesse Of Pembrokes Arcadia, Written By Sir Philippe Sidnei.* [Cut of Sidney arms] *London Printed by Iohn Windet for william Ponsonbie. Anno Domini, 1590.* [All copies known except Huntington 69442, Trinity College Cambridge, Pforzheimer, and Crocker have the imprint, 'Printed for William Ponsonbie'.]

364 leaves, A4, B–Zz8; B1–Zz8 foliated 1–360. STC 22539a and 22539; entered by Ponsonby 23 October 1588. Facsimile of British Museum G. 10440 ed. H. O. Sommer, 1891, and a reprint of the same copy ed. A. Feuillerat, 1912 (with variant readings of the twelve folio editions issued from 1593 to 1674). There are at least thirteen copies in institutional libraries—British Museum (two), Trinity College Cambridge, Keble College Oxford, Chapin Library, Huntington (two), Morgan, New York Public, Newberry, Pforzheimer, University of Indiana, and University of Texas—and seven in private hands.

Contents: A1 blank; A2 title-page, verso blank; A3–4 'To My Deare Ladie And Sister'; A4ᵛ note by the 'ouer-seer of the print' (the original A4ᵛ is blank in Huntington 69442, but a second A4 leaf containing this note on its verso has been tipped in from another copy); B1–Zz8ᵛ 'The Covntesse of Pembrokes Arcadia' in three books. The note on A4ᵛ reads:

The diuision and summing of the Chapters was not of Sir *Philip Sidneis* dooing, but aduentured by the ouer-seer of the print, for the more ease of the Readers. He therfore submits himselfe to their iudgement, and if his labour answere not the worthines of the booke, desireth pardon for it. As also if any defect be found in the Eclogues, which although they were of Sir *Phillip Sidneis* writing, yet were they not perused by him, but left till the worke had bene finished, that then choise should haue bene made, which should haue bene taken, and in what manner brought in. At this time they haue bene chosen and disposed as the ouer-seer thought best.

Ponsonby's report to Greville in November 1586, that another publisher proposed to print the *Old Arcadia*, apparently resulted in the suppression of that proposed edition and the acquisition of the rights to publication of the *New Arcadia* by Ponsonby himself. Ponsonby entered it on the Stationers' Register two years later and offered the printed volume for sale in the spring of 1590 at a price of 5*s.*, apparently for unbound, and 6*s.* 6*d.* for bound copies (see below and Collier's *Bibliographical and Critical Account*, ii [1865], 350).

Contemporary references indicate that the work was edited by Greville himself with the assistance of Dr. Matthew Gwinne. An anonymous dedication to Greville of *De Caede et Interitu . . . Henrici Tertii*, about August 1589 or somewhat later, begins, 'Dum tu Sidnaei regale poema recudis' (Hudson, *HLQ* ii [1939], 216); and Thomas Wilson's dedication to Greville of his manuscript translation of Montemayor mentions Sidney's *Arcadia*, 'which by your noble vertue the world so hapily enjoyes' (British Museum MS. Additional 18638, f. 4ᵛ, quoted by Greg, *Pastoral Poetry and Pastoral Drama*, 1906, p. 148). On a preliminary leaf of the Huntington 69441 copy of 90 there is written in a contemporary hand, 'May .29. 1590. pr[etium]: vˢ. published by D. Guin, Doctor in physick, fellow of S Iohns in Oxon.' A note by a former owner of the Huntington 69442 copy of 90 states that its title-page, before it was cleaned, contained Gwinne's autograph (this copy also has manuscript corrections of OA **31.** 50 'where' to 'in', OA **74.** 19 'that I do' to 'that do', and CS **3.** 4 'turneth' to 'keepeth'). Gwinne's association with Greville is attested by his presence at the Ash Wednesday supper at Greville's house in 1584 described by Bruno, and by his poem in the 1587 Oxford *Exequiae*, D2ᵛ–3ᵛ. Frances Yates (*John Florio*, 1934, pp. 203–6) suggested that the learned words and quibbles in the chapter headings added by the editors were similar to the style of Florio; but they are just as typical of the style of Gwinne, who in a poem to Queen Anne described her as 'of worth / A wondrous Anacephalaiosis; / A None-pareil, Sans parallel'.

The editors divided the work into three books, divided each book into chapters with headings summarizing the narrative, and added eclogues after the First and Second Books. The text of the Third Book breaks off in the middle of a sentence. The volume contains 36 poems, with a blank space for a 37th: CS 3; OA 1–8, 12, 14–22, 25–31, 62, 67, 71–75; OP 1–2 (3 blank). They are arranged in the following order: Book I—OA 3, 2, 4, 5; First Eclogues—OA 6, 7, 66, 67, 71, 12; Book II—OA 14–19, 62, 30, 8, 20, 21, OP 1, OA 22, 25, 1, 26; Second Eclogues—OA 27–29, 72, 31; Book III—OA 74, 73, OP 2, CS 3, (blank space for OP 3), OA 75.

The narrative portion of the text was taken from the manuscript of the *New Arcadia* (G) that Sidney had left in trust with Greville, and the Eclogues and poems or parts of poems not in G were taken from Sidney's own manuscript working copy of his *Old Arcadia* (T⁵). Greville and Gwinne appear to have done their editorial work intelligently and on the whole carefully, and the volume was fairly well printed—verbal errors appear on the average only about once in every eight or ten lines of text, which is not below usual Elizabethan standards. Collation of the poems in (1) Huntington 69442, (2) Huntington 69441, (3) British Museum G. 10440, and (4) British Museum C. 30. d. 22 reveals a few minor spelling differences and only half a dozen verbal variants:

		Corrected	*Uncorrected*
3. 5 and 9	C4ᵛ	[*indented*] (2, 4)	[*not indented*] (1, 3)
3. 6	C4ᵛ	smooth (2, 4)	smothe (1, 3)
62. 146	V8ᵛ	dwell. (2)	dwel.l (1, 3, 4)
30. 111	X5ᵛ	flames (1)	flame (2, 3, 4)
28. 109	Hh5	Barr'd (2, 3)	Barred (1, 4)
31. 35	Ii3ᵛ	stormes (3)	scornes (1, 2, 4)
31. 50	Ii3ᵛ	in hell where (3)	where hell if (1, 2, 4)
74. 54	Ii7	eu'n (1, 3)	euen (2, 4)
74. 59	Ii7	onel' habitaco'n (1)	onel' habitacion (2, 3, 4)
73. 22	Nn1	top doth downeward (3, 4)	top downeward (1, 2)
73. 33	Nn1	with freer (3, 4)	with cleere (1, 2)
73. 102	Nn2ᵛ	mou'd (3)	moude (1, 2, 4)
73. 130	Nn2ᵛ	contentions (3)	contentious (1, 2, 4)

Huntington 69442 has been used as copy text for all poems in 90 except OA 31 and CS 3; but readings of the corrected formes listed above have been substituted in its uncorrected formes, and in the few places where an 'e' is obviously intended but looks like a 'c' because of faulty type an 'e' has been printed in the critical text without a note in the apparatus.

*[93] *The Covntesse Of Pembrokes Arcadia. Written By Sir Philip Sidney Knight. Now Since The First Edition augmented and ended. London. Printed [by John Windet] for William Ponsonbie. Anno Domini. 1593.* [Within an engraved border, McKerrow and Ferguson No. 212.]

248 leaves, ¶4, A–Rr6, Ss4; A1–Ss3 foliated 1–243. STC 22540. The added Books III–V and the poems in the earlier books not printed in 90 were reprinted by Feuillerat in 1922 (ii. 1–238), with variant readings from the eleven folio editions issued from 1598 to 1674. Copies are in the British Museum, Cambridge University, Folger, Harvard, Haverford, Huntington, Morgan, New York Public, and Wellesley College Libraries, and five others are in private hands. The Folger copy contains the contemporary autograph of W. Blount and many marginal annotations in his hand indicating parallels in classical authors. I have cited some of his references in my notes to the poems. The printer was identified by G. W. Williams, *The Library*, 5th ser., xii (1957), 274–5. The title-page

border contains at the top the porcupine statant of the Sidney arms, to the left and right Musidorus disguised as a shepherd and Pyrocles as an Amazon, and below a pig smelling a marjoram bush with the motto *non tibi spiro*—devised by Hugh Sanford to indicate that 'the wortheles Reader can never worthely esteeme of so worthye a writing' (see R. L. Eagle, *The Library*, 5th ser., iv [1949], 68–71).

Contents: ¶1 probably blank; ¶2 title-page, verso blank; ¶3ʳ⁻ᵛ 'To My Deare Lady and Sister'; ¶4ʳ⁻ᵛ 'To the Reader' signed 'H[ugh]. S[anford].'; A1–Ss3ᵛ 'The Covntesse of Pembrokes Arcadia'; Ss4 blank. That Hugh Sanford, tutor and secretary in the Pembroke household, was the Countess of Pembroke's assistant in editing the volume is indicated by a note in John Hoskyn's *Directions for Speech and Style*, *c.* 1599 (ed. Hudson, 1935, p. 1 and note). Sanford's address 'To the Reader' begins:

> The disfigured face, gentle Reader, wherewith this worke not long since appeared to the common view, moued that noble Lady, to whose Honour consecrated, to whose protection it was committed, to take in hand the wiping away those spottes wherewith the beauties therof were vnworthely blemished. But as often in repairing a ruinous house, the mending of some olde part occasioneth the making of some new, so here her honourable labour begonne in correcting the faults, ended in supplying the defectes; by the view of what was ill done guided to the consideration of what was not done. Which part with what aduise entred into, with what successe it hath beene passed through, most by her doing, all by her directing, if they may be entreated not to define, which are vnfurnisht of meanes to discerne, the rest (it is hoped) will fauourably censure. But this they shall, for theyr better satisfaction, vnderstand, that though they finde not here what might be expected, they may finde neuerthelesse as much as was intended, the conclusion, not the perfection of *Arcadia*: and that no further then the Authours own writings, or knowen determinations could direct. . . .

A1–Ff3 reprint the incomplete *New Arcadia* from 90, but without the chapter headings, and with some rearrangement of the eclogues and minor changes in the text. At the point where 90 breaks off in the middle of a sentence the following note is printed:

> How this combate ended, how the Ladies by the comming of the discouered forces were deliuered, and restored to *Basilius*, and how *Dorus* againe returned to his old master *Damœtas*, is altogether vnknowne. What afterward chaunced, out of the Authors owne writings and conceits hath bene supplied, as foloweth.

Ff3–Ss3ᵛ contain the complete text of Books III–V of the *Old Arcadia*, with the proper names changed and some minor alterations made in the narrative to conform with the *New Arcadia*, and some rearrangement of the eclogues.

The volume contains 77 poems (CS 3; OA 1–22, 25–28, 30–34, 38–77; OP 1–5) in the following order: Book I—OA 3, 2, 4, 5; First Eclogues—OA 6, 7, 11, 12, 13, OP 4; Book II—OA 14–19, 62, 30, 8, 20–21, OP 1, OA 22, 25, 1, 26; Second Eclogues—OA 27–28, 71–72, 9–10, 31–34; Book III—OA 74, 73, OP 2, CS 3, OP 3, OA 38–61; Third Eclogues—OA 63–65, OP 5, OA 66–67; Book IV—OA 68–69; Fourth Eclogues—OA 70, 75–76; Book V—OA 77. Of these poems, 34 are reprinted from 90 (all the poems in 90 except OA 29, which 93 omits, and OA 31, which 93 prints from manuscript). OP 3, for which a blank space was left in 90 and Cm, and OP 4 and 5 are printed from now-lost manuscripts and are unique substantive texts. All the other poems not in 90 were printed from the Countess of Pembroke's *Old Arcadia* manuscript (P) and are also substantive texts. The Huntington 69478 copy of 93 is used as copy text in this edition for OA 9–11, 13, 31–34, 38–61, 63–65, 68–70, 76–77, and OP 3–5.

*[98] *The Covntesse Of Pembrokes Arcadia. Written By Sir Philip Sidney Knight. Now The Third Time published, with sundry new additions of the same Author. London Imprinted [by Richard Field] for William Ponsonbie. Anno Domini. 1598.* [Within the engraved border cut for 93.]

292 leaves, ¶4, A–Bbb6; A1–Bbb6ᵛ paged 1–576. STC 22541. Ponsonby, who had earlier entered the *Arcadia* and *Defence*, entered 'Astrophell and Stella' on 23 October 1598, which may indicate that the present volume was published about that date, unless the entry is somehow connected with Lownes' edition of Q 3. H. R. Plomer (*The Library*, N.S., i [1900], 195) identified the printer and noted that the volume sold for 9s. (see *HMC Rutland*, ii. 352). Reprinted 1599, 1605, 1613, Dublin, 1621 (reissued London, 1622 and 1623), 1627 (reissued 1629), 1633, 1638, 1655, 1662, 1674, 1725–4, 1739, and (*Arcadia* only) 1907 and 1921. Feuillerat (ii. 301–22 and 329–38) reprinted 98's texts of CS and LM. There are 20 or more copies extant.

Contents: ¶1 blank; ¶2 title-page, verso blank; ¶3ʳ⁻ᵛ 'To My Deare Lady And Sister'; ¶4ʳ⁻ᵛ 'To the Reader' signed 'H[ugh]. S[anford].'; A1–Rr2ᵛ 'The Covntesse of Pembrokes Arcadia'; Rr2ᵛ–Ss5ᵛ 'Certaine Sonets Written By Sir Philip Sidney: Neuer before printed'; Ss6–Xx1ᵛ 'The Defence Of Poesie'; Xx2–Bbb3 'Astrophel and Stella, Written By The Noble Knight Sir Philip Sidney'; Bbb3ᵛ–Bbb6ᵛ 'Her Most Excellent Maiestie Walking In Wansteed Garden, . . .' [the untitled *Lady of May*].

This is the first collected edition of Sidney's writings, and was evidently issued with the approval of his family. Rowland White, a confidential family agent, writing to Sir Philip's brother Robert the following year, called it 'the best Edition' (Arthur Collins, *Letters and Memorials*, ii [1746], 119). The *Arcadia*, with Sidney's dedication and the preface by H. S., is a reprint of 93; the *Defence of Poesie* is a reprint of Ponsonby's 1595 edition; while CS, AS, and LM are new texts from manuscripts probably supplied by the Countess of Pembroke. Ten years earlier Abraham Fraunce, a retainer of Sidney and his sister, in his *Arcadian Rhetorike* had quoted from the same manuscripts of CS and AS that were used by the 98 printer.

The text of the 93 *Arcadia* is reproduced with the usual new errors and occasional conjectural emendations that we expect from an Elizabethan printer. For example, in OP 5 five obvious errors of 93 are corrected, three others are allowed to remain, and one new error is introduced; but in OA 72 one error of 93 is corrected, another obvious error is allowed to stand, and three new errors are introduced. However, the three new items printed from manuscript are all excellent texts. CS contains only about a dozen errors in its 32 poems, AS contains only about 80 errors in its 119 poems, and LM, the only substantive text, appears to be accurate except for a few verbal errors and the designation of speakers in the third poem.

Though the wording of the 98 texts is quite accurate, their accidents of spelling and punctuation differ more widely from Sidney's originals than do those of some of the inferior prints and manuscripts, because Richard Field the printer rigorously imposed his own standards of spelling and punctuation on his copy (for his procedure in printing from manuscript see Sir Walter Greg, *The Library*, 4th ser., iv [1924], 102–18). My own copy of 98 (formerly William Wordsworth's) is used as copy text in this edition for LM, CS, and AS.

The 1599 edition, 'Edinburgh. Printed By Robert walde-graue, Printer to the Kings Maiestie. Cum priuilegio Regis', reprinted the *Arcadia* directly from 93 and the other items from 98. This was a piratical venture sponsored by a syndicate of English booksellers who sold their copies for 3s. under Ponsonby's price. Ponsonby brought suit against them in November 1599 and collected damages (see H. R. Plomer, *The Library*, N.S., i [1900], 195–205, and C. B. Judge, *Elizabethan Book-Pirates* [1934], pp. 101–11). The title was transferred to Simon Waterson on 3 September, and to Waterson and Mathew Lownes on 5 November 1604. The 1605 edition, printed by George Elde and Humphrey Lownes (see W. A. Jackson, *Pforzheimer Catalogue* [1940], p. 966), is a paginary reprint of 98. The 1613 edition deserves separate notice.

*[13] *The Covntesse Of Pembrokes Arcadia. Written By Sir Philip Sidney Knight. Now the Fovrth Time published, with some new Additions. London Imprinted by H[umphrey]. L[ownes]. for Simon Waterson 1613.* [Within the engraved border cut for 93. Some copies have the imprint 'for Mathew Lownes, 1613.']

292 leaves, *2, A–Bbb6 (after Ee5 an unpaged insert signed Ee5, and after Ss1 an unpaged insert signed Ss II); A–Bbb6 paged 1–576. STC 22544–44a. This is actually the fifth authorized edition. Three of the 12 copies of 13 that I have examined contain, instead of the insert sheet Ee5, a ten-leaf supplement by Sir William Alexander that bridges the hiatus in the narrative. This was entered by William Barret on 31 August 1616, and appears in three different states in copies of 13 and 21–22–23. State A is found in the Harvard 14457. 23. 8. 7 F* copy of 13 and in the British Museum and Huntington copies of 23; state B is found in the Shrewsbury School and University of Chicago copies of 13, in the British Museum and Newberry Library copies of 22, and in my copy without title-page of 21-22-23; and state C is found in the British Museum and Huntington copies of 21. Evidently when the 21–22–23 edition was printed some sheets of the 13 edition remained in stock, and for some reason Alexander's supplement was set up in three settings of type—state A designed for the remainder sheets of 13, and states C and B designed for the 21–22–23 sheets printed for sale in Dublin and London; but when the sheets were actually bound, states A and B were inserted indiscriminately in the remainder sheets of 13 and the new sheets of 22–23. There appears no reason to assume that any of the three states of Alexander's supplement were printed before 1621.

The Harvard 14457. 23. 8. 7 F* copy of 13 has the chapter headings from 90 and a few comments inserted in an early hand which a bookseller's note calls 'Gabriel Harvey's autograph', but it is quite unlike Harvey's. The Harvard

Widener Collection copy of 13 has written on its title-page, 'This was the Countess of pembrokes owne booke given me by the Countess of Montgomery her daughter 1635', and below in a different hand, 'Ancram'. Hazlitt's quotation of this inscription led Grosart (i. xxxiii) to say, 'We attach much weight to the folio of 1613, as it is the only edition known to have been in the library of the Countess of Pembroke', and to conclude that 13 gives us 'the best text of the whole Writings of Sidney'. But Professor W. A. Jackson pointed out, in a lecture delivered 9 October 1946, that the binding had originally been made for a smaller book and that the signature 'is quite unlike any of the signatures of Ancram'; the volume is sophisticated and the inscription is probably a fabrication. It is unlikely that the Countess of Pembroke had any hand in the preparation of this edition, for it is the only folio edition to omit Sanford's 'To the Reader' which said that the editing of the *Arcadia* had been 'most by her doing, all by her directing'.

13 is a paginary reprint of 98, with a few changes and corrections and three small additions. Sanford's 'To the Reader' with its ill-natured attack on the editors of 90 is omitted, and in its place a brief note, explaining that the 'revised' version was incomplete and that the rest of the story had been pieced out from the 'first written Arcadia', is added, at the point where the incomplete *New Arcadia* narrative ends, on the insert sheet Ee5. Sanford, whose own editing of 93 had been severely criticized, had died in 1607. Three lines are added to OA 67. CS 3, which also appears in the *Arcadia* portion of the text, is dropped from the *Certaine Sonets*, and an entirely new poem, 'A Dialogue betweene two Shepherds' (PP 1), is added after CS 22 on the insert sheet signed Ss II. The running titles and catchwords show that the two insert sheets were not after-thoughts, but were set up in type at the same time as the gatherings in which they appear. They are the compositor's device for keeping the endings of his pages even with 98 in places where he was instructed to make additions to the text.

The volume gives evidence of the attention of an intelligent and perceptive editor, who did not work in the printing house, and of a faithful but unperceptive printer, who followed his copy mechanically. The editor carefully read through a volume of 98 which was used by the 13 printer as copy and wrote a number of verbal corrections in the margins. In OP 5, for example, he corrected one error 98 had introduced and two others found in 93 which 98 had overlooked; and at line 106 he noticed the inappropriateness, in an Arcadian song, of a wind blowing from 'holland', and corrected the geography by substituting 'Ciprus'.

Only twice, so far as I am aware, did the 13 editor refer to another text in order to make a correction. He noticed that a line was missing from 98 at the top of Ee1, and restored it correctly, possibly from a copy of 90 or 93 (in the Huntington copy of 98 this line is added in an early hand). There is no other indication of his having referred to an earlier print. In reading OA 67 he noticed that in line 5 of the poem and in the prose introduction Histor's rival is named Lalus, but that in the prose at the end he is referred to as Thyrsis. He accordingly consulted a manuscript of the *Old Arcadia*, and changed Thyrsis to Lalus. As he looked at the end of OA 67 in this manuscript he noticed that in line 94 it read 'are' for 98's 'be' and contained three extra lines. He accordingly made the correction and added the three lines. His *Old Arcadia* manuscript was similar to Cl, Le, and As; it could not have been St, Bo, Da, Ph, Je, or Qu. There is no evidence that he consulted it at any other point.

Elsewhere in the *Arcadia*, and in CS, AS, and LM, the 13 editor read 98 with care, but referred to no other text as a source for his corrections. In AS **16.** 9, for example, he noticed that the line lacked a syllable in 98, and so emended it to read, 'But while I (*fool*) thus with this Lyon plaid'; but the correct reading in all other substantive texts is, 'But while I thus with this *young* Lyon plaid'. Though he worked almost entirely by conjecture, the 13 editor used considerable care and intelligence in making his corrections. The 1609, 1611, and 1617 editions of the *Faerie Queene* were also 'Printed by H. L. for Mathew Lownes', and Spenser's text shows evidence of having received the same kind of careful emendation as 13.

13 is substantive only for the new poem PP 1 and possibly for the three lines added to OA 67; but though the other poems are merely reprints of 98, the emendations of the 13 editor deserve consideration. I have used my own copy of 13 as copy text for PP 1 in this edition.

The later folios all derive from 13, and so have no independent textual authority.

ASTROPHIL AND STELLA

*[Bt] British Museum MS. Additional 15232 (the Bright MS.).

42 ff. in four gatherings of 8, 8, 12, and 14 leaves, damaged at the top by damp. A collection of prose and verse written, probably in the late 1580's, in what appear to be nine different hands. Contains: ff. 1–7, hand A, Latin astronomical definitions; ff. 7ᵛ–19, hands B–H, 18 anonymous poems not found elsewhere, some with what appear to be author's revisions; ff. 20–42, hand I (a careful but somewhat laboured Italian script), AS 1–20, viii, xi, 105–8, untitled and unattributed but correctly numbered. After sonnet 20 twelve pages and after song viii two pages are blank, though the copyist would have needed 66 and 22 pages to complete the transcript. The AS poems begin on the fourth leaf of the third gathering, and the blanks occur within the fourth gathering, so no leaves have been lost.

The watermark, a shield with initials 'P S' (Briquet 9665), occurs in continental documents dated 1580–4. Bound in stiff green-surfaced paper, contained in but not attached to a calf binding stamped with the arms of a Baron Montague of Boughton. Inside the front cover is the name 'Iohn woper', inside the back cover the partly obliterated name 'ffraunces Berington' (Flügel read it as 'B[ington]'). Edward Montague, created first Baron Montague in 1621, was the grandson of Lucy Sidney, Sir Philip's aunt. B. H. Bright, a former owner, inserted a holograph letter, dated 1590, from the Countess of Pembroke, and in appended notes suggested that the volume was written by Sidney and his sister, and possibly Samuel Daniel; but none of the hands in the manuscript corresponds with those of either of these writers. Two of the anonymous poems, 'In a greene woode thicke of shade' f. 11 and 'All mi sensecs weare bereaved' f. 14, may have been inspired by AS viii and CS 26.

Purchased by the British Museum in 1844 at the Bright sale, lot 240. Described by Grosart, i, xxxix–xlviii, who wrongly pronounced it 'comparatively valueless'; and by Flügel, pp. lxvii–lxxiv, who saw that it derived from the same original as 98. The text is clearly an independent transcript of X, from which 98 was printed, and is slightly superior to 98 in accuracy.

*[Dr] University of Edinburgh MS. De. 5. 96 (the Drummond MS.).

60 ff. Originally untitled and containing *Astrophil and Stella* complete, written in secretary hand by or for Sir Edward Dymoke (the hand is slightly different after f. 41ᵛ). In the 1820's the manuscript was bound in tan leather stamped with the Drummond Collection device, by which time it had lost 21 leaves after f. 37. Contents: f. 1ᵛ the motto 'Strepit [*sic*] Anser inter olores', in an Italian hand; ff. 2–3 three sonnets praising (but not naming) Sidney and lamenting his death, signed 'Ed. Dymoke' (autograph); f. 3ᵛ originally blank; ff. 4–53ᵛ AS 1–63, i, 64–66, ix, 87–92, x, 93–104, xi, 105–108, in that order and correctly numbered, except 87–108 which are numbered 86–107; ff. 54–60ᵛ originally blank.

Several leaves of the original have been lost between the present ff. 37 and 38, which accounts for the omission of the 20 sonnets and eight songs between sonnet 66 and song ix. The missing poems, if written with the same spacing used in the rest of the volume, would precisely fill the recto and verso of 21 leaves. The watermarks indicate that f. 37, after which the break in the text occurs, is the third leaf of a quarto gathering, and that f. 38, on which song ix begins, is the first leaf of another quarto gathering with a different watermark; thus the last leaf of one gathering and all the leaves of five following gatherings have been lost. If only 19 sonnets had been included in the missing section, the present f. 38 would have begun with line 16 of song ix; but as it begins with line one, the misnumbering of the sonnets must result from an error in numbering in the missing section and not from the omission of a sonnet. Therefore Dr in its original state contained all 108 sonnets and eleven songs arranged in the same order in which they are printed in 98.

William Drummond of Hawthornden recorded his gift of the manuscript to the University of Edinburgh in his *Auctarium Bibliothecae Edinburgenae* (1627), F2. I owe thanks to Dr. William H. Bond for calling this volume to my attention, which led me to inquire at the University of Edinburgh and so learn of the existence of the manuscript. I later found that E. Koeppel (*Anglia*, x [1888], 530) had referred in tantalizingly vague fashion to a 'noch nicht benutzte edinburgher handschrift des cyklus', and that L. E. Kastner (*Poetical Works of Drummond*, i [1913], p. xxix) had mentioned 'a copy in Drummond's hand of *Astrophel and Stella* among the books which he presented to the University of Edinburgh'. The manuscript is not in Drummond's hand, but he has made some additions to it. He has written on f. 1 'Astrophel and Stella written by Sʳ Philip Sidny Knight Giuen to the Colledge of Edenb. by W. D.'; on f. 3ᵛ 'S. P: Sidneys Astrophell and Stella'; at the top of f. 4 'The first Sonnet', over the first line 'my loue' (omitted by the original scribe), and over the phrase 'the deare She' in the second line 'she (deare She)'; and on f. 60 'This is Sʳ Phil.

Sidneys Astrophell and Stella'. These additions are taken from 98 or a later folio, probably the 1599 Edinburgh edition, which are the only texts with the reading 'she (deare She)' in AS **1. 2**.

Sir Edward Dymoke (*c.* 1559–1624), of Scrivelsby and Kyme, Lincolnshire, hereditary King's Champion who officiated at the coronation of James I, was admitted to Gray's Inn in 1577, was knighted in 1584, and from then until after Sidney's death was Sheriff and Deputy Lieutenant of the county of Lincoln. Except that both Sidney and Dymoke were members of the Parliament that met from November 1584 to March 1585, I have not found evidence that they were either connected or acquainted. However, as early as 1584 Dymoke became a patron of Samuel Daniel; they were in Italy together in 1590 and 1591, and in 1592, when he published *Delia*, Daniel was a member of Dymoke's household in Lincoln (see Mark Eccles, *SP* xxxiv [1937], 148–67; Leslie Hotson, *Trans. of the Royal Society of Literature*, N.S., xvii [1938], 58). In the dedication of *Delia* Daniel indicated that he was acquainted with a text of AS that was better than the first printed edition which had appeared the preceding year. Daniel was also an early protégé of Sidney's friend and literary executor Fulke Greville, whom he acknowledged in *Musophilus* as the one

> By whose mild grace, and gentle hand at first
> My Infant Muse was brought in open sight.

If Dymoke did not get the original of his transcript directly from Sidney himself, he may have got it from Greville through Daniel.

Dymoke's transcript could have been made any time after October 1586, when news of Sidney's death reached England, and 1624 when Dymoke himself died; but the balance of probabilities favours an early date. The paper bears two watermarks, one a tower similar to Briquet 15940, which is found in documents dated 1576–99, and the other an eagle and shield, similar to Briquet 940, which is found in documents dated 1581–1617. How the manuscript came into Drummond's possession is problematical, since there is no evidence of any connexion between him and Dymoke. However, Drummond's uncle, William Fowler (1560–1612), exchanged verses with Dymoke in Padua in 1591 or 1592 (National Library of Scotland MS. 2065, ff. 5 and 13); so it is possible that Dymoke gave his transcript to Fowler, and that Drummond inherited it with the other papers of his uncle. If this is so, the transcript was probably made in the late 1580's or very early 1590's. Its text was copied from Y, the same original from which the Q2 corrections were taken in 1591.

Dr omits **52**. 12–14 (and indicates the omission by the numbers 1, 2, 3 in the margin), and leaves spaces for words omitted at **15**. 8, **20**. 6, **21**. 1, and **38**. 13. It also omits, probably inadvertently, **x**. 44 and words in **1**. 1, **88**. 4, **99**. 5, **102**. 6, and **108**. 8. Dr was copied with considerable care and has a factor of error of only 0·013, which makes it only slightly less dependable than 98.

*[Ho] Wye Plantation, Maryland, Arthur A. Houghton, jr. MS.

120 ff. A collection of prose and verse compiled by William Briton of Kelston in Somerset. Purchased in 1950 from Quaritch's, who acquired it in 1932 or earlier and listed it in their *One Hundredth Anniversary Catalogue* (1947), item

198. Contains, on ff. 91–103, 'Sonnetts wrytten by Sr Phillipp Sydney Knight', an even hundred AS sonnets in the order 1, 6–8, 10, 22, 31–32, 34, 38, 44, 47; 3–4, 49–54, 56, 55, 57–108; 2, 5, 9, 11–21, 23, 26–27, 29–30, 33, 36, 39, 41–43, and 48.

At one end of the volume are memoranda in the hand of William's father, John Briton, dated from 1564 to 1571, followed by two pages in William's hand concerning trees grafted 'in Kelston orchard' in January 1588[9] and January 1589[90]. The volume was then turned upside down and, beginning at the opposite end, William made entries on ff. 1–115 as follows: (*a*) ff. 1–53^v Legal forms and notes, some of which refer to William's own affairs and none of which are dated later than 1586. (*b*) ff. 54–61^v 'Rules of Husbandry', translations of parts of Virgil's *Georgics* with other observations 'proved by experyenc'; additions and marginalia in different ink are dated from 1594 to 1602. ff. 62–76^v blank. (*c*) ff. 77–90^v 'Pithie Sentences and wise sayinges', beginning with 'Emblemata Andreae Alciati', and followed by untitled extracts from Baldwin's *Treatice of Morall Philosophy* (1547), Googe's translation of Palingenius (1560), Chaloner's translation of *The praise of Folie* (1549), Blennerhasset's *Seconde part of the Mirrour for Magistrates* (1578), and Norton and Sackville's *Tragedie of Gorboduc* (from the first edition of *c.* 1565); at the bottom of f. 87^v is a single line of verse in different ink, AS **23.** 4. (*d*) ff. 91–103 Sidney's 'Sonnetts'; ff. 103^v–4 are blank, and between them are stubs of four leaves that have been torn out. (*e*) ff. 104^v–9 Another set of 'Rules of husbandry', dated 1596, partly repeating and rearranging the material of the earlier set; marginalia in different ink are dated from 1594 to 1605; ff. 109^v–12^v blank. (*f*) ff. 113–15 Miscellaneous jottings with dates 1599 and 1593[4], including notes on ancient deeds concerning Kelston manor with a memorandum that 'Io. Bryton delyu*er*ed to M^r Io: harrington thyounger one oth*er* Copy . . . of all the Scite and demaines of Kelston'.

The will of John Briton of Kelston (34 Spenser) was proved in 1587. According to the manuscript his son William was born at Cirencester in 1564. The Kelston parish registers record the birth of William's two sons and seven daughters between 1591 and 1607 and his burial in 1637; his will (Goare 128) was proved in the same year. The dates in the manuscript indicate that William began making entries shortly before or after the death of his father in 1587 and continued until 1605. If the items were written seriatim, Sidney's sonnets were transcribed sometime between 1586 and 1596, and more probably between 1594 and 1596; but since the 'Pithie Sentences' and Sidney's 'Sonnetts' are preceded and followed by blank leaves, we cannot be certain of the order of transcription.

The manuscript indicates that the Britons had business dealings with John Harington (who in 1599 became Sir John), whose principal residence was at Kelston from the time of his marriage in 1583 until his death in 1612. At least as early as 1591 Harington owned or had access to an apparently complete manuscript of AS which has since been lost (Z^1), from which he transcribed the first sonnet into his own manuscript miscellany (now at Arundel Castle) and quoted the eighteenth in the notes to his translation of *Orlando Furioso* in 1591. Comparison of the texts of Harington's two sonnets with Briton's proves conclusively that both derive from the same original. Harington had deduced the identity of Stella from the three sonnets playing on the name 'Rich', and had revealed his knowledge in the notes to *Orlando Furioso*, though in terms which only other people who were also in on the secret would understand. But Briton removed all clues to Stella's identity by omitting sonnets 24, 35, and 37, and obscured the love story by omitting the songs and jumbling the order of the remaining sonnets.

Ho agrees with Q1 in reversing the order of sonnets 55 and 56 and the first two quatrains of sonnet five, and omits **44.** 12, **80.** 13–14, and **85.** 13–14. It also leaves blank spaces for words undecipherable in its original at **79.** 12, **87.** 4, **94.** 3, and **99.** 11. Though its text contains many corruptions, it is considerably more accurate than Q1, for in the 100 sonnets both have in common Ho has a factor of error of 0·058 and Q1 a factor of error of 0·090.

*[Q1] *Syr P. S. His Astrophel and Stella. Wherein the excellence of sweete Poesie is concluded. To the end of which are added, sundry other rare Sonnets of diuers Noble men and Gentlemen. At London, Printed for Thomas Newman. Anno. Domini. 1591.*

44 leaves, A–L4; B–L4ᵛ paged 1–80. STC 22536; not entered by Newman. Only two copies extant: British Museum G. 11543 (Grenville, Caldecott); and Trinity College Cambridge VI. 7. 51 (gift of Beaupré Bell, 1730), wants A2–4. Reprinted, without the poems of 'other . . . Gentlemen', by Ewald Flügel, Halle 1889, with a few corrections introduced from Q2 and 98, and by Feuillerat, ii (1922), 241–99, 369–71, with a list of variants from Q 2 and 98–74. A modernized text of the poems of 'other . . . Gentlemen' was printed by Edward Arber, *An English Garner*, i (1877), 580–600.

Contents: A1 title-page, verso blank. A2ʳ⁻ᵛ 'To the worshipfull and his very good Freende, Ma. Frauncis Flower Esquire', signed 'Tho: Newman'. A3–4ᵛ 'Somewhat to reade for them that list', signed 'Tho: Nashe'. B1–I3 'Sir P. S. His Astrophel And Stella'—107 unnumbered sonnets, followed by ten songs titled 'Other Sonnets of variable verse' and headed respectively 'First Sonnet . . . The tenth Sonnet'. I3ᵛ–L4ᵛ 'Poems and Sonets of sundrie other Noble men and Gentlemen'. These consist of 28 sonnets signed 'Daniell', 24 of which appeared the next year in *Delia* with greatly improved texts; five songs signed 'Content', by Thomas Campion (identified by G. C. Moore Smith in his edition of *Victoria* [1906], p. xxxviii); a poem beginning 'Faction that euer dwelles', signed 'E[arl of]. O[xford].' but actually Greville's *Caelica* No. 28; and a 12-line anonymous poem beginning 'If flouds of teares'—attributed to Nashe by Collier in his edition of *Pierce Penilesse* (1842), p. xxi, a mere guess rejected by McKerrow in his edition of Nashe, v (1905), 139–40.

The text of AS contains 107 sonnets and ten songs in the order 1–36, 38–54, 56, 55, 57–108, i–x. All of sonnet 37 and song xi and lines **19.** 8, **30.** 8–9, **44.** 12, **63.** 9, **85.** 13–14, **viii.** 69–100, and **x.** 25–42 are omitted, and the first two quatrains of sonnet 5 are reversed. Q1 is exceedingly corrupt, for even without taking the omissions into account, more than 8 per cent. of its words are wrong. The evidence is overwhelming that it derives from Z, which is also the ancestor of Ho.

If readers did not identify the initials 'Syr P. S.' on the title-page, they would learn the author's full name from the running title on F1ᵛ and F3ᵛ ('Syr Phillip

Sidneys'), and from Nashe's statement on A4 that the author was the Countess of Pembroke's brother. Francis Flower, the dedicatee, was a member of Gray's Inn, a Gentleman Pensioner to the Queen, a follower of Sir Christopher Hatton, and in 1587 had collaborated in writing *The Misfortunes of Arthur*; I have found no evidence to connect him with the Sidney circle. Thomas Nashe, who supplied the preface, had left his studies at Cambridge in 1588 to make his way as a writer in London, and had probably been engaged to introduce AS by Newman. Since he was primarily a prose writer and at this time had never printed rhyme in his life, it is unlikely that he had any hand in emending the text of Sidney's sonnets.

Thomas Newman issued 15 titles between 1586 and 1592 by Fraunce, Greene, and others. AS was by far his most important publication, and was certainly the most significant literary event of the year in which it was issued, for in addition to presenting for the first time an almost complete though corrupt text of Sidney's sonnets, it marked the first appearance in print of the poetry of Campion, Daniel, and Greville.

I have not identified the printer of Q1, who had good reason to keep his name and device from the title-page, for Newman had not obtained a licence for publication, nor had he received the authorization of Sidney's family or of the three living poets whose work he also included. An ordinary author had no recourse against a piratical publisher, but persons in high position could bring pressure to bear through members of the Privy Council or other court officials. That action was taken against Newman is shown by the accounts of the wardens of the Stationers' Company for 1591 (ed. Arber, i. 555):

Item paid the xviij[th] of September for carryeinge of Newmans bookes to the hall. iiij[d].

And after one intervening entry:

Item paid to John Wolf [the company beadle] when he ryd with an answere to my Lord treasurer [Burghley] beinge with her maiestie in progress for the takinge in of bookes intituled Sir P: S: *Astrophell and stella*. xv[s].

Since the Queen was on progress from the beginning of August until the end of September, it is probable that Q1 appeared in the late summer of 1591, that some person of influence lodged a complaint after a few copies had been sold, that a government order was issued for the suppression of the remainder of the edition, and that before the end of September the Stationers' representative Wolf rode to discuss the matter with Lord Burghley. We know how at least one of the living authors felt about Newman's unauthorized publication, for in the following February Daniel issued a corrected edition of his sonnets to Delia, and in his dedication to the Countess of Pembroke complained:

Although I rather desired to keep in the private passions of my youth, from the multitude, as things utterd to my selfe, and consecrated to silence: yet seeing I was betraide by the indiscretion of a greedie Printer, and had some of my secrets bewraide to the world, uncorrected: doubting the like of the rest, I am forced to publish that which I never ment. But this wrong was not onely doone to mee, but to him whose unmatchable lines have indured the like misfortune; Ignorance sparing not to commit sacriledge upon so holy reliques. Yet *Astrophel* flying with the wings of his own fame, a higher pitch then the gross-sighted can discerne, hath registred his owne name in the annals of eternitie, and cannot be disgraced, howsoever disguised.

Newman in his dedication said that it had been his 'fortune . . . not many daies since, to light upon' a manuscript of AS. His text derives from Z, from which Harington's Z¹ was copied. In the summer of 1591 Harington was writing notes for his *Orlando Furioso* while it was printing. He knew that AS had been or was going to be printed, for in a note to Book XVI he referred to Sidney's 'sonets of *Stella* . . . which many I am sure have read'. But since Z¹ contained errors not in Z, and since Q1 descends from Z through a different corrupt intermediary, Newman probably did not get his manuscript from Harington.

Newman said of his manuscript, 'I have beene very carefull in the Printing of it, and whereas being spred abroade in written Coppies, it had gathered much corruption by ill Writers: I have used their helpe and advice in correcting and restoring it to his first dignitie, that I knowe were of skill and experience in those matters'. It is obvious that the manuscript from which he printed was corrupt; but his text does not bear out his claim to have taken pains in the printing, nor does he appear to have made more than perfunctory attempts at emendation. Q1 contains a dozen or more obvious typographical errors (**93.** 5 brath, **v.** 14 metamorphisde, &c.), and omits at least one line (**19.** 8) that the catchword shows was present in the printer's copy. Newman was also singularly unsuccessful in detecting and emending the errors of his original. For example, at **26.** 7 he allowed the erroneous 'braue within' to stand where the correct reading should be 'brawle which in', at **86.** 4 he printed 'eyes' (a rhyme word) for 'eye', and at **105.** 10 'therefore your necklace' for 'thereof your Nectar'. Evidently it did not bother him to print nonsense.

Q1 is a 'bad quarto', for its publication was unauthorized and its text is extremely corrupt; but there is no need to construct improbable theories of memorial reconstruction or reporting to explain its errors. They are the usual corruptions that would be introduced by the eyes and hands of careless scribes and compositors during as few as three or four removes from the author's holograph 'foul papers'. We should never underestimate the capacity of Elizabethan copyists for perverting their texts.

*[Q2] *Sir P. S. His Astrophel And Stella. Wherein the excellence of sweete Poesie is concluded. At London, Printed for Thomas Newman. Anno Domini. 1591.*

32 leaves, A–H4; A2–H4 paged 1–61. STC 22537. Four copies extant: British Museum f. 39. c. 34 (with autograph, 'Ant a Wood'); British Museum G. 11544 (Grenville); Representative Church Body, Ireland, Cashel X. 7 (wants H1 and H4)—at one time deposited in Marsh's Library; Huntington 69457 (Huth, Corser, Bright).

Contents: A1 title-page, verso blank. A2–H4 'Sir P. S. His Astrophel and Stella'—107 unnumbered sonnets, followed by ten songs titled 'Other Sonnets of variable verse', in the same order as in Q1. This is a corrected second edition of Q1, omitting Newman's dedication, Nashe's preface, and the 'Sundry other rare Sonnets of divers Noblemen and Gentlemen'. The similarity of spelling, punctuation, and indentation, and the reproduction of misprints (**93.** 5 brath, **v.** 14 metamorphisde, &c.) show that Q1 was used as printer's copy; but the first two quatrains of sonnet 5 are rearranged in correct order, the seven lines omitted from the sonnets are restored, and verbal changes are introduced affecting 349 lines of sonnets 1–95. However, sonnet 37 is still omitted, sonnets 56 and 55 remain in that order, and the songs are still collected at the end precisely as they stood in Q1, with **viii.** 69–100, **x.** 25–42, and all of song xi omitted.

The corrections in Q2 were made by collating a copy of Q1 with Y; but the collations were made in an exceedingly haphazard and slipshod fashion, and were only carried through sonnet 95. Though some Q1 errors were corrected, just as many others were allowed to stand, and in the process of making corrections new errors were often introduced. Why Q2 should be so poor a text when the publisher had in Y an almost perfect manuscript to work with is hardly understandable, unless we assume that Newman deliberately scanted editorial duties which he had undertaken only on compulsion.

The records concerning the 'takinge in' of Newman's AS in September probably refer only to Q1. We have no direct evidence of the attitude of Sidney's brother and sister to this unauthorized publication. In 1598 there was published, probably with the assistance of the Countess of Pembroke, an excellent and complete text of AS in the first collected edition of Sidney's writings; but this was done only after the appearance of Spenser's *Astrophel* in which, possibly at the suggestion of the Countess, the sonnets to Stella were interpreted as having been addressed to the lady who became Sidney's wife (see H. H. Hudson, *HLB*, vii [1935], 116–20). Sidney's close friend Greville always maintained a discreet silence concerning Stella, and did not mention the sonnets either in his letter of November 1586 enumerating his friend's works or in his later *Life of Sidney*. But Greville's acquaintance Daniel complained that he had been 'betraide by the indiscretion of a greedie Printer', who not only made public his 'private passions' but printed them in a corrupt text, and lamented that Sidney had 'indured the like misfortune'. Other friends of Sidney may also have objected both to the revelation of the love story that the sonnets told and to the badness of the text.

But Q1 had made the story of Stella public, for some copies had been sold before the edition was called in (two still survive), and Harington was already hinting in his *Orlando Furioso* that Stella was the wife of Lord Rich. Members of the Sidney circle had had earlier experience of the ineffectiveness of censorship, for when in 1584 the government authorities attempted to suppress *The Copie of a Leter*, a libellous attack on Sidney's uncle the Earl of Leicester, the confiscation of the printed volumes resulted only in the proliferation of manuscript copies. So it is likely that Sidney's friends decided that total suppression of AS would be useless, and that the best service to Sidney's reputation would be to insist that a corrected text of his work be issued. If this supposition is valid, we may suppose that after the unsold copies of Q1 had been impounded, Newman as a punishment for his indiscretion was ordered to publish at his own cost a corrected text of AS, for which Sidney's friends provided an excellent manuscript, Y. This was the same original from which Dr, Sir Edward Dymoke's transcript, was made. Since Daniel had been Dymoke's travelling companion in Italy during part of 1590–1 and was still a member of his household in March 1592 (see M. Eccles, *SP* xxxiv [1937], 161–7), he may have acted as an agent in the negotiations with Newman, and so have come into possession of the manuscript from which his patron copied. In 1592 Daniel himself issued a complete and correct version of his *Delia*; but Newman, when he reissued Sidney's sonnets, did so as cheaply as possible and so spent very little time in partially correcting the text.

[Q3] *Syr P. S. His Astrophel and Stella. Wherein the excellence of sweete Poesie is concluded. To the end of which are added, sundry other rare Sonnets of diuers Noble men and Gentlemen.* [Device of Felix Kingston, McKerrow 167B] *At London Printed for Matthew Lownes.* [*1597–1600.*]

40 leaves, A–K4; unpaged. STC 22538; not entered by Lownes. Copies: Bodleian Malone 617(6); Arthur A. Houghton, jr. (from Rosenbach, sold at Sotheby's 1901); Huntington 13689 (Britwell, Bright)—title-page is a pen facsimile made by A. A. Burt in 1875.

Contents: A1 title-page, verso blank. A2–H3 'Sir P. S. His Astrophel and Stella'. H3^v–K4^v 'Poems and Sonnets of sundrie other Noblemen and Gentlemen'. Except for the omission of Newman's dedication and Nashe's preface, this is an almost *literatim* reprint of Q1. There are only 39 verbal variants from Q1, all printer's errors or attempted emendations.

Q3 is undated (Grosart, I. xxvii, says he was informed that the Britwell copy was dated 1591, but at the time he wrote that copy lacked a title-page). Matthew Lownes' first dated publication appeared in 1596; Felix Kingston is not known to have been in business before 1597 and printed his earliest dated book for Lownes in 1598; and in 1600 John Dowland published two of the poems of 'sundrie other Noblemen and Gentlemen' in his *Second Booke of Songs or Ayres* (Nos. 11 and 18), while in the same year *Bel-vedére*, *Englands Helicon*, and *Englands Parnassus* appeared with selections from AS containing Quarto readings. The texts of Q1 and Q3 are identical in the passages they quote, but it is more probable that they drew from the recently published rather than from the earlier volume—in 1610 Robert Douland definitely used Q3.

Ponsonby separately entered AS on 23 October 1598, and issued an excellent text in his 1598 Folio. Newman had not entered his copy, and since there is no evidence (such as we have for Waldegrave's 1599 *Arcadia*) that Q3 was a piracy, Lownes may have published his edition before Ponsonby's entry.

THE PSALMS OF DAVID

*[A]. Penshurst, Kent. Viscount De L'Isle and Dudley MS. [*The Psalms of David*—title wanting.]

ii+135+iv ff. Colophon f. 135: Iohn Dauies of the City of Hereford handwriter hereof (Davies was a dependant of the Countess of Pembroke). Ff. 2^v–38^v (where Psalm 43 ends) paged irregularly 8–82. In a probably later blind-stamped leather binding. Written in a single beautiful Italian hand with the capitals, and loops of the other letters, in gold. A slip is pasted over a passage on f. 45ᵛ, there are marginal additions on ff. 41 and 48, and the final stanzas of Psalms 16, 22, 23, and 26, and numerous interlinear corrections, are in different ink. Contains, in its present mutilated state, Psalms 4–150. Probably originally had eight more leaves at the beginning, consisting of a preliminary blank leaf, a title-page, four leaves containing the dedicatory poem to Queen Elizabeth and 'To the Angell spirit of . . . Sʳ Phillip Sidney' preserved in J, and two leaves containing Psalms 1–3 with the new conclusion to Psalm 1 preserved in J. The text was carefully transcribed from the original of B, which was the Countess of Pembroke's own working copy, after she had made her final revisions in her own and her brother's text of the Psalms. The interlineations and passages in different ink indicate that Davies was often uncertain about which version of a passage to copy from his original, and probably consulted the Countess herself for instructions.

The manuscript was probably originally prepared for presentation to Queen Elizabeth, but was not presented because the many corrections made in the process of copying marred its appearance. John Aubrey, who visited Wilton in 1652, said the library contained 'a manuscript very elegantly written, viz. all the Psalmes of David translated by Sir Philip Sydney, curiously bound in crimson velvet' (*Brief Lives*, ed. Clark, i. 109), and later he reported that the manuscript of the Psalms, 'writt curiously, and bound in crimson velvet and gilt', had been sold, with the other books and pictures at Wilton, by the fifth Earl of Pembroke (*Memoires of . . . the County of Wilts*, ed. J. Britton, 1847, p. 86). It is probable, as an earlier unidentified owner suggested in a note on f. ii, that this is the very manuscript described by Aubrey. In 1823, by which time it had already lost the leaves containing the preliminaries and first three Psalms, it was used as printer's copy for the Chiswick Press edition (the pencilled printer's marks are still visible), and in 1844 was sold as part of the collection of B. H. Bright). On f. iiᵛ is the signature 'Wylimot De Marisco, Banchor: Monach:' dated 1845, with a note suggesting that the corrections are in the hands of the authors (though they are obviously in Davies' hand), and stating, probably wrongly, 'This MS was at Penshurst the Antient and Modern Seat of the Sidneys, till a few years ago.' Grosart (ii. 202) said that it 'passed from the Bright Sale to Penshurst'. In 1923 Feuillerat printed its Psalms 4–43.

*[B]. Bodleian MS. Rawlinson poet. 25 (*Summary Catalogue* 14519). [*The Psalms of David*—title wanting.]

vii + 156 ff. Contains Psalms 1–87 (after 43 'hitherto Sʳ Ph. Sidney') and 102–130, transcribed in 1695 by Samuel Woodford from a damaged original that contained numerous interlineations, strike outs, and marginal corrections, and which must have been the Countess of Pembroke's own working copy. Woodford copied in the body of his text what he considered to be the final readings intended by the authors, and carefully entered the earlier crossed-out readings in the margin of his transcript. He noted that Psalms 44, 46, 53, 58, 60, 62, 63, 64, 68, 69, 71, 75, 80, 86, 105, 108, 117, sections g h s w of 119, and 122 were marked with a cross for later revision, and these and Psalm 50 are entirely different from the versions in most of the other manuscripts. The

Countess, in addition to making many interlinear and marginal changes, must have inserted new versions of these Psalms on separate slips of paper, and the slips must have fallen out before her damaged original reached Woodford's hands. This is the most valuable of all the known manuscripts of the Psalms, because it preserves the readings of the original draft of the Countess of Pembroke's version of the entire Psalter, which included her brother's versions of the first 43 Psalms, and also records a large proportion of her later revisions. The sequence of her revisions can be traced through K, X, and A, which are successive transcripts made from the original of B. Woodford copied his original with moderate care, but he occasionally omitted a word and once omitted a whole line (**36.** 5), and fairly frequently made verbal errors (**1.** 3, **1.** 10, **4.** 23, **4.** 24, **5.** 18, **6.** 14, **7.** 12, &c.).

Woodford noted on f. ii, 'The Originall Copy is by me Given me by my Brother Mr. John Woodford who bought it among other broken books to putt up Coffee pouder as I remember'; on f. 82ᵛ (after Psalm 87) 'But here all the leaues are torn off, to the 23 verse of the C II. Psalms, . . . Sam: Woodforde:' and on f. 131ᵛ (after Psalm 130) 'But from this place to the end my copy is defectiue the leaues being torn off Ita testatur Sam: Woodforde Who for Sʳ Philip Sidnys Sake, and to preserue such a remaine of him undertook this tiresome task of transcribing. 169⅘.' It is a pity that the original from which Woodford made his transcript was either destroyed or remains untraced. As it is, the editor of Sidney must reconstruct that original by transferring Woodford's marginal notes to the text, and must collate the other manuscripts to detect Woodford's own errors of transcription.

In 1873 Grosart, who like Woodford mistakenly believed that the original of B was 'copied under the superintendence of Sir Philip Sidney himself' (ii. 203), printed Psalms 1–43 from B, with eclectic emendations from G, and with several verbal and many spelling errors.

*[C] Bodleian MS. Rawlinson poet. 24 (*Summary Catalogue* 14518). *The Psalmes of Dauid translated into diuers & sundry Kindes of verse, more rare, & excellent, for the method & varietie then euer yet hath bene don in English: begun by the noble & learned gent. Sʳ P: Sidney Kᵗ, & finished by the R: honnorable the Countesse of Pembroke, his Sister, & by her dirrection & appointment.—Verbum Dei manet in æternum.*

114 ff. Contains Psalms 1–150 in a single early seventeenth-century hand. Descends from X and is most closely related to D and N. The conjugate ff. 2–3 have a watermark similar to Heawood No. 1768, of *c.* 1616, also found in J; ff. 4–87 have a watermark similar to Briquet No. 2291 of 1587–1601. On the title-page, f. 2, is the eighteenth-century signature 'W. Barkwith'. The 1823 edition took its title from C.

*[D] Wadham College, Oxford, MS. 25. [*The Psalms of David—* title wanting.]

74 ff. Pasted on f. 1 is a note: '(The old Title) A Translation of the Book of Psalms into English Verse By the most noble & virtuous Gentleman Sir Philip Sidney Knight NB. 16 Psalms are wanting in this MSS.' ff. 2–22 are blank, and ff. 23–74 contain PS 17–150 carefully written in a single seventeenth-century hand. The text descends from X with C E G H L M N, but it is most closely related to C and N and is probably earlier than E H L and G M.

Inside the front cover is written: 'Richard Warner 1738 Bought at the Auction of Sʳ Joseph Jekyll's MSS &c collected by the late Ld Somers.' Lord Somers (d. 1716) bequeathed his books to Sir Joseph Jekyll, and Richard Warner (d. 1775) bequeathed his books to Wadham. When I first inquired for this manuscript it could not be found, but it has since been located and I was able to examine a microfilm kindly sent by Mr. J. C. A. Rathmell.

*[E] The Queen's College, Oxford, MS. 341. *The Psalmes of Dauid done into English verse By yᵉ most noble & vertuous gent: Sʳ Phillip: Sydney knight.*

216 ff. Contains 150 Psalms (after Psalm 43 'Hactenus Sʳ Phillip Sydney') in a single early seventeenth-century hand. A descendant of X through the same original as H and L. On f. 2, 'Queens College Library Oxon 1697'.

*[F] Trinity College, Cambridge, MS. O. 1. 51 (James 1075). *The Psalms of David Translated Into English Verse By That Noble and Virtuous Gent: Sʳ Philip Sydney.*

i+172+i ff. Contains 150 Psalms in a single late sixteenth-century hand, with some corrections in a different hand and ink. PS 1–26 descend with I from B¹ through Y (see p. 504, note 1) and are closely related to K. PS 27–150 were copied from A and are not substantive.

Presented by Roger Gale in 1738. Thomas Zouch printed Psalms 93 and 137 from this manuscript in the second edition of his *Memoirs of . . . Sidney* (1809), pp. 398–400.

*[G] Trinity College, Cambridge, MS. R. 3. 16 (James 596). *The Psalmes of Dauid metaphrased into sundry Kindes of verse, By the noble & famous gent: Sir Philip Sidney Knight.*

ii+152+ii ff. Contains 150 Psalms in a single early seventeenth-century hand, with the title in a different and later hand. The text belongs to the C D E G H L M N group, but it agrees with M against all other texts in PS 120–7 and at 25. 71–72, and contains unique versions of 25. 77–78, 31. 63–68, and 42. 53–56. Presented by W. Lynnet in 1664.

*[H] British Museum MS. Additional 12048. *The Psalmes of Dauid done into English verse By the moste noble and vertuous gentellman Sʳ Phillipp Sidney Knight.*

vi+148+v ff. Contains 150 Psalms (after Psalm 43 'Hactenus Sʳ Phillip

Sydney') in a single early seventeenth-century hand, with a few corrections in different ink. A descendant of X through the same original as E and L. Sold at Dr. Taylor's sale in 1793; belonged to Richard Heber in 1804 and later to Samuel Butler, Bishop of Lichfield, from whose estate it was acquired by the British Museum in 1841.

*[I] British Museum MS. Additional 12047. [*The Psalms of David*, untitled.]

iv+94+ii ff. Contains a blank page for the wanting title, and 81 Psalms (with two different versions of PS 75, 89, and 122) in the order 1–26, 51, 69, 104, 70–71, 75–76, 80, 83, 86, 89 (two versions), 91, 93, 96, 98–100, 105, 108, 110, 112, 117, 120–1, 122 (two versions), 124–7, 129–34, 138, 147, 149, 58, 85, 123, 73–74, a second version of 75, 68, 109, 142, 77, 88, 84, 102, 111, 143, 150, 78, 113, and 137, in a single late sixteenth-century hand. A second early hand has labelled some of the Psalms for morning and evening prayer according to the days prescribed in the Book of Common Prayer, though in the manuscript they are not copied in the prescribed order. The texts of 68, and the second versions of 75 and 122, are those of the original version preserved in B; the second version of 89 differs from the other texts but may be the original version which is wanting in the damaged surviving transcript which is B; while 113 is unique. PS 1–26 descend with F from B¹ through Y. I have not determined the textual relationships of the later Psalms.

Formerly owned by Joseph Haslewood (d. 1833), and Bishop Butler (d. 1839), from whose estate it was acquired by the British Museum in 1841. Haslewood wrongly thought that Sir John Harington was the author of this version; and Bishop Butler suggested that Harington was the transcriber, though the British Museum cataloguer disagreed with this identification of the hand. The manuscript, however, probably descends from a Harington source, for its text of Psalm 69 agrees in error with the text printed from family papers by Henry Harington in *Nugae Antiquae* (Harington could not have printed from I itself because he also printed Psalm 128 which is wanting in I). In *Sidneiana* (Roxburghe Club, 1837, pp. 57–66), Bishop Butler printed the versions of 68, 75, 89, 113, and 122 that differ from the texts of A printed in 1823.

*[J] Headington, Oxford, Dr. B. E. Juel-Jensen MS. *The Psalmes of David translated into diuers and sundry kindes of verse, more Rare and Excellent for the Method and Varietie than euer yet hath been done in English. Begun by the Noble and Learned gent. Sʳ Phillip Sidney knight. and finished by the Right Honorable the Countess of Pembroke his Sister. (1599.)*

ii+145 ff. In a contemporary vellum binding tooled with gold stamps. Written, except for the title-page, in an early seventeenth-century Italian hand. The title-page, on f. ii, of different paper stock and in a later hand, was probably copied from the 1823 edition, with the date 1599 taken from the end of the following poem. On ff. 1–2 (numbered in a later hand iii–iv) is a dedicatory poem to Queen Elizabeth of 12 eight-line stanzas beginning 'E'uen now that Care wch on thy Crowne attends'—lines 77–78, 'The very windes did on thy partie blowe, | and rocks in armes thy foe men eft defie', appear to refer to the Armada. At the end of this poem, added in a seventeenth-century hand different from the text and the rest of the manuscript, is the date '1599'. On ff. 3–4^v (numbered v–vi) is another poem of 13 seven-line stanzas beginning, 'To thee pure sprite, to thee alone's addres't', titled 'To the Angell spirit of the most excellent Sr Phillip Sidney', and signed at the end, 'By the Sister of that Incomporable Sidney'. Another version of this poem, in 11 seven-line stanzas and similarly titled, was printed in the posthumous *Whole Workes of Samuel Daniel*, 1623, ²M7^v–8^v— probably from an early draft of the Countess of Pembroke's poem found among Daniel's papers by his brother and erroneously attributed to him. On ff. 5–142 (numbered 1–137) are Psalms 1–150 (at the end of Psalm 43 'Hitherto Sr Phillipp Sidney'), followed by an alphabetical list of the Latin incipits.

This appears to be a careful and accurate direct transcript of A because, except for a few trifling scribal errors and some intelligent scribal emendations, it follows the text of A exactly and agrees in error with A against all or almost all other texts at 4. 29 'haruests', 8. 8 'ouer-hating', 9. 38 'do stray', 9. 42 'sound', 9. 56 'But on', 10.16 'the name', 10. 20 'can them not', 10. 47 'hud-winck', 10. 69 'o lord', &c. Since A is defective and wants the preliminaries and Psalms 1–3, J is the most important substantive text for the Countess of Pembroke's final version of these poems. It is the only manuscript to preserve her revised conclusion to the first Psalm.

Ff. i–ii (f. ii is the title-page), of different paper stock, contain part of a watermark, the Roman capitals 'NCE', possibly the mark of Thomas or Edmund Valence who manufactured from 1781 to 1816. All the other leaves have a watermark similar to Heawood's No. 1768, of *c.* 1616—a similar watermark appears in C. Contains bookplate of Laurence W. Hodson, but no other marks of early ownership. Purchased at Sotheby's, 8 April 1957, by Dr. Juel-Jensen.

*[K] British Museum MS. Additional 46372. [*The Psalms of David*—untitled.]

110 ff. Originally contained Psalms 1–150 in a single late sixteenth-century hand, but leaves torn out or damaged have caused the loss of 6. 29–8. 16, 10. 18–24 and 61–64, 21. 17–22. 36, 103. 65–96, and all after 148. 16. A different early hand has made a few interlinear corrections, has added in the margin lines omitted by the original scribe in Psalms 141 and 145, has noted at the head of some of the Psalms 'Evening prayer', 'Morning prayer. 2', &c.; has numbered the verses in the margin according to their order in the Psalter of the Book of Common Prayer; and has noted opposite Psalms 68, 75, 89, and 122 'This is otherwise translated'.

This appears to be a descendant of the original of B, copied after the Countess of Pembroke had completed her first set of revisions but before she made her later revisions found in X and A. It therefore comes after B as the second most important manuscript for determining the original readings of Sidney's version. Like B and X it contains the original version of sections g h s w of 119, and contains a version of 75 found elsewhere only in B, I, and N; otherwise its texts of Psalms 44, 46, 50, &c., are the Countess of Pembroke's revised versions. It has a number of agreements in error with FI 1–26 (see p. 504, note 1) and also shares a few readings with C, D, and N.

This is the seventh volume of a collection of Harington family papers acquired by the British Museum in 1947. Sir John Harington in 1610 noted that he possessed 'Countess of Pembr: psalms: 2 copies' (British Museum MS. Additional 27632, f. 30) of which this manuscript is doubtless one.

*[L] H. E. Huntington Library MS., HM 100. *The Psalmes of Dauid done into English Verse by the Most Noble & Vertuous gent: Sʳ Phillipp Sidney Knᵗ.*

ii+164+ii ff. 150 Psalms in a single early seventeenth-century hand. A descendant of X through the same original as E and H. Its version of Psalm 122 appears elsewhere only in B, E, H, and I. Contains pencilled note: 'W. A. White April 10, 1922'.

*[M] H. E. Huntington Library MS. HM 117. *The Psalmes of David metaphrased into verse by the noble, learned, & famous gent Sʳ Philip Sidney Knight.*

ii+163+ii ff. 150 Psalms in a single early seventeenth-century hand. A descendant of X related to G. Has versions of PS 120–7 found elsewhere only in G, and unique final stanzas in 31 and 42. Belonged to William Hayley, 1789; B. H. Bright, 1844; Thomas Corser, 1870; A. H. Huth, 1871–1917.

*[N] Bibliothèque de l'Université de France MS. 1110. *The Psalmes of David: donne Into English Verse, by The most noble and vertuous Gentleman Sʳ Philip Sydney knight.*

199 ff. 150 Psalms in a single early seventeenth-century hand; after Psalm 43, 'Hactenus, Sʳ P. Sidney'. A descendant of X related to C and D. Contains a second version of PS 75 (also in BIK) and 131 (unique). Inscribed 'Vacate et videte Kenelme Dig[by]'. First noticed by A. W. Osborn in 1932.

POEMS IN MANUSCRIPTS

*[Hn] Arundel Castle, His Grace the Duke of Norfolk. 'Harrington MS. Temp. Eliz.' (G. F. Nott's 'Harrington MS. No. II').

A poetical miscellany compiled by John Harington the elder (d. 1582) and his son Sir John (d. 1612) which contains, in its present mutilated state, 324 poems by authors ranging from Wyatt and Surrey to writers of the 1590's. Written in several hands over a period of years. Described by Ruth Hughey in *The Library*, 4th ser., xv (1935), 388–444, and in her edition of the complete text (1960).

When I first began work on Sidney, and before I had examined the original at Arundel Castle, Miss Hughey generously gave me access to her transcripts and notes. G. F. Nott made a paginary transcript on paper watermarked 1808, which is now British Museum MS. Additional 28635.

Contains eight poems by Sidney, five of which are anonymous: OA 51 (f. 145) and 74 (ff. 157–8ᵛ); CS 1 (f. 130), 3 (f. 34) subscribed 'Ph. S.', 27 (f. 145), and 30 (f. 146); and AS 1 (f. 155) headed 'Sonnetts of Sʳ Phillip Sydneys to ~~vppon~~ yᵉ Lady Ritch', and x (f. 36ᵛ) subscribed 'Sʳ Phillip Syd: to the bewty of the worlde'. Sir John copied OA 74, CS 3, and AS 1 and x, a secretary copied the others.

Sir John Harington had apparently made a fairly complete manuscript collection of Sidney's writings before any of them appeared in print. In his *Orlando Furioso*, 1591, he quoted the *Defence of Poesie*, which was not printed until 1595; quoted OA 65 from the 'first *Arcadia*', which was not printed until 1926; and quoted AS 18 in a text different from the two quartos of 1591 and the folio of 1598. In a memorandum of 1610 (British Museum MS. Additional 27632, f. 30) he noted that he owned two manuscripts of the metaphrase of the Psalms by Sidney and his sister, which was not printed until 1823.

Harington's texts of OA 51 and 74 have only 13 minor errors in their 100 lines. They were probably carefully transcribed from his own manuscript of the *Old Arcadia*, which must have been a very good text but is not identifiable with any of the nine extant manuscripts. But his four *Certain Sonnets* are extremely inaccurate, having verbal errors that are not related to those of any other known texts in 49 of their 98 lines. They may derive from copies of the separate poems that were handed about in courtly circles.

His text of AS x, which is separated from his transcript of AS 1 by 119 following leaves, may have been transcribed earlier and certainly comes from an original different from that of his source for AS 1. AS x contains 20 per cent. error, which makes it by far the most inaccurate of the six extant substantive texts. Eighteen of its errors are unique, but six agree strikingly with Ra (lines 23, 28, 44, 45, 46, and 47), which is clear evidence that both derive from a common original. Hn agrees in error with Q1 in three places, in two of which Ra has the correct reading (line 8 'absence' for 'parting', 43 'thoughts' for 'thought', and 44 'yowr' for 'Thy'—Ra 'These'); but these are common substitutions made independently by Hn and Q1 that provide no acceptable evidence for relationship, especially since none of the other characteristic readings of Q1 (in lines 2, 13, 45, and 47) appear in either Hn or Ra. Harington obviously got his text of AS x from a source similar to that of Ra, probably a group of AS songs that was circulated among the compilers of manuscript anthologies. Hn-Ra and Q1 have entirely different lines of descent.

At the time of transcribing AS x Harington apparently did not know the identity of Stella, for he designated the lady only as 'the bewty of the worlde' (a phrase also applied to Philoclea in the *Old Arcadia*, iv. 6. 35). But when he transcribed AS 1 in the latter part of his volume, he specifically stated that it was addressed 'to yᵉ Lady Ritch'. He probably derived this information from a complete manuscript of the sequence to which he had access by 1591, for in the introductory remarks to his quotations of AS 18 in *Orlando Furioso* he paraphrased sonnet 37 and indicated that he knew that Sidney called his lady 'rich'. Several characteristic readings prove that Harington's texts of both AS 1 and

AS 18 derive from Z¹, the same original from which his Kelston neighbour William Briton copied Ho.

*[Dd] Cambridge University Library MS. Dd. 5. 75 (2). A poetical miscellany compiled in the early seventeenth century. At the beginning and end are some youthful pieces by William Lord Paget (1571–1629), George Lord Berkeley (1601–58), and H. Stanford dated between 1581 and 1612. The central portion, ff. 25–47 (three gatherings with one leaf missing after f. 45), is headed 'Poems' and appears to be a separate item, an anthology of verse composed by Breton, Dyer, Gorges, Ralegh, Sidney, Spenser, and others, though their names are not given—most of these verses appear to have been composed in the 1580's, but one poem on f. 46 is dated 1598.

Contains 11 poems by Sidney, none of which has an author's name attached: OA 2 (f. 38), 3 (f. 37ᵛ), 35 (f. 36ᵛ), 41 (f. 26ᵛ), 42 (f. 26ᵛ), 48 (f. 26ᵛ), 51 (f. 26), and 62 (lines 1–2 f. 26, complete ff. 36ᵛ–37); CS 3 (f. 27) and 30 (f. 27); and AS ix (f. 47ʳ⁻ᵛ, written in the margin beside another poem). The *Old Arcadia* poems were probably copied from another manuscript miscellany descending ultimately from an original with characteristics similar to but not identical with St. CS 30, which contains only a single error, and CS 3, which has unique errors in nine lines, follow one another in that order on the same page; they probably derive from different sources, perhaps copies of the poems on single sheets that were distributed by Sidney himself (such as the one he gave his friend Bannister in 1584). AS ix appears to have been added as an afterthought, for it is crowded onto the margin of the last leaf of this section beside another poem. It contains errors in 23 of its 50 lines, which indicates manuscript transmission at least two or three removes from Sidney's original. None of its variants provides acceptable evidence to relate it to any extant text. All the Sidney texts are substantive.

Cambridge University MS. Kk. 5. 30 (II). Twenty-nine poems transcribed by Sir James Murray of Tibbermure, c. 1612.

Contains CS 32 (ff. 71ᵛ–72) with no indication of authorship. The text, except for two unique errors, is the same as 98–05.

British Museum MS. Additional 10309. Extracts of prose and verse in a single hand, second quarter of the seventeenth century.

Contains a six-line paraphrase of CS **25**. 30–34 (f. 45ᵛ), printed above, p. 431; and a poem 'vpon Sydneis Arcadia sent to his m*istress*' of seven six-line stanzas beginning 'Goe happie booke, the fates to workes the blisse'.

British Museum MS. Additional 12515. A collection of extracts, mainly prose, made in the mid-seventeenth century.

Contains, ff. 17–24, a series of extracts drawn from 98 or a later folio, including (f. 22) the first six lines (damaged) of OA 77.

British Museum MS. Additional 21433. Various poems transcribed about the middle of the seventeenth century. The British Museum *Catalogue of Additions* (1875), p. 382, misled by a note in a later hand on f. 187, wrongly states that this contains poems by Sidney; there is nothing by or attributed to him in the manuscript.

British Museum MS. Additional 27406. Poems on separate sheets of paper in different hands, mostly of late seventeenth and early eighteenth century.

OA 62. 1–4 (f. 117), probably from a folio edition of the *Arcadia*.

*[Ba] British Museum MS. Additional 28253. Miscellaneous poems on separate sheets of paper in a variety of hands, late sixteenth to eighteenth century. Ff. 1–13 contain verses collected by Edward Bannister between 1583 and 1603 (identified by handwriting).

Contains CS 30 (f. 3ʳ⁻ᵛ) in the hand of a scribe, endorsed by Bannister, 'A Dyttye mad by Sʳ phillip sydnye gevene me Att pvttenye In svrrye Decembris xᵒ Annᵒ 1584' and the name of the donor, 'Sʳ phillyppe Sydnye'. The text contains eight verbal errors in its 167 words, or 5 per cent. error. Bannister, a Catholic recusant, had in 1583 leased a house in Putney near Barn Elms, where Sidney resided with his father-in-law Sir Francis Walsingham. In 1582 he had persuaded his friend Bartholomew Yong to translate Montemayor's *Diana*, and shortly after 1587 he married Mary Southwell, sister of the Jesuit poet Robert Southwell. His will indicates that he was a collector of books, musical instruments, paintings, and statuary.

British Museum MS. Additional 34064 (Cosens MS.). Transcripts of poems by Breton, Sidney, Spenser, and others, made *c.* 1596. The manuscript was used by Grosart in his edition of Breton (1879), and described by P. M. Buck, jr., *MLN* xxii (1907), 41–47, neither of whom recognized the poems by Sidney.

Contains OA 27, 15, 16, 2, 14, 21, 47, and 62 (ff. 27–31) without indication of authorship. Fifteen agreements in error prove that they were copied from 93.

*[Eg] British Museum MS. Egerton 2421. Poetical miscellany of the mid-seventeenth century.

Contains, f. 46ᵛ, OA 62. 143–6 written upside down, incomplete because the leaves containing the preceding lines have been torn out. The readings 'perfection' in line 145 and 'pens' in line 146 show it was transcribed from a manuscript of the *Old Arcadia*, possibly similar to As.

British Museum MS. Egerton 2877. Miscellany of prose and verse compiled by Gilbert Frevile, *c.* 1630.

Contains OA 77 (f. 105), 'Verses ag*ainst* feare of Death: made by S*ir* ph: sidney'. Copied from 93 or a later print.

British Museum MS. Harley 3511. Poetical miscellany of the mid-seventeenth century.

Contains OA 21 (ff. 74^v–5). The reading 'my tales' in line 15 shows that it was copied from one of the prints; on f. 71 is 'Sr Philip Sidney's epitaph', which was printed in the 1655 and later editions of the *Arcadia*.

*[Ha] British Museum MS. Harley 6910. An anthology of 222 poems copied in a single professional hand about 1601. A few of the items, such as Spenser's *Complaints*, Chapman's *Shadow of Night*, and extracts from the *Mirror for Magistrates*, were transcribed from printed editions; but most of the rest derive from a variety of manuscript sources. More than half of the texts appear to be unique.

Contains six poems by or attributed to Sidney, three apparently signed with his initials and three anonymous: OA 3 (f. 145^v), OA **15.** 1–8 and 13–14 (f. 154^v), OA 64 (ff. 173^v–5) subscribed 'P. S.', CS **23.** 1–32 (f. 149), AS viii (ff. 171–2^v) subscribed 'P. [S?]', and AT 14 (ff. 169^v–70) subscribed 'P. [S?]', a unique text probably by an imitator of Sidney (printed by Grosart, iii. 65, by Feuillerat, ii. 343–4, and above, p. 355). All of these are substantive.

The Sidney poems are scattered in the manuscript and were evidently copied from a variety of sources. OA 3 and 15 could have been copied directly from an *Old Arcadia* manuscript, but the corruption of OA 64 indicates that it is several removes from Sidney's original. CS 23 has five unique errors and three that agree with Ra or Ma, but these may be independent errors rather than indications of relationships. AS viii contains errors in 48 lines, 14 of which agree with Ra, which is clear evidence of descent from a common ancestor.

The textual relationships of other poems in this manuscript show that the manuscript miscellanies, even when they have a number of poems in common, frequently draw them independently from widely differing sources. For example, Ha contains two poems, 'A day a night' and 'Yf floodes of teares', which may have been copied directly, or in the case of the second poem possibly through an intermediary, from the Newman or Lownes *Astrophel and Stella* (Q1 or Q3); but its text of AS viii descends from the same original as that of Ra, which bears no relation whatever to the Quartos. Ha and Ra also both contain Dyer's 'Prometheus' (CS 16a); but though the Ha text might derive from Cl (it agrees in error with Cl in line 3 'the light'), the Ra text comes from an entirely different source which is also the original of Hy and Fo (Ra, Hy, and Fo agree in error in line 5 'outward', line 12 'rest and runne', and line 14 'time'). Therefore even when two or more manuscript miscellanies have a number of poems in common, we cannot assume that they drew them from the same originals; but must make a separate textual analysis for each poem.

*[Hy] British Museum MS. Harley 7392 (2). An anthology of 153 poems, compiled by St. Loe Kniveton between about 1584 and 1600, 44 of which also appear in Ra.

Contains nine poems certainly of Sidney's authorship, six attributed to him by name and three anonymous: OA 3 (f. 75), OA 45 (f. 68), OA 51 (f. 38ᵛ), and OA 60 (f. 66); CS 3 (f. 39), CS 16a (by Dyer) and 16 (f. 25), CS 19 (f. 38ᵛ), CS 23 (f. 70ᵛ), and CS 30 (f. 35). It also contains an anonymous text of PP 2 (f. 66); and it subscribes Sidney's name or initials, probably in error, to three other poems—AT 19 (f. 48ᵛ), AT 21 (f. 37ᵛ), and AT 25 (f. 63ᵛ)—printed by B. M. Wagner, *PMLA* liii (1938), 118–24, and the first two only, above pp. 356–8. The texts are fairly inaccurate, with errors in every second or third line.

Most of the errors in the four *Old Arcadia* poems are unique, so they cannot be specifically related to any other extant texts. But the texts of CS 3, 16a, 16, 19, and 23 also appear in Ra and agree with it in error in 24 passages, which indicates that they descend from a similar lost original. Since the text of CS 3 in the *Arbor of amorous Devises* [1594], and the texts of CS 16a and 16 in Fo are also related to Hy-Ra, the *Certain Sonnet* poems must derive from a body of texts that circulated in the manuscript miscellanies of the 1580's and 1590's. Hy's *Old Arcadia* and *Certain Sonnet* texts, though fairly corrupt, are all substantive.

British Museum MS. Sloane 1925. Extracts in prose and verse, mid-seventeenth century.

Contains (ff. 13–14) OA 20, 17, and 62 (lines 35–36, 95–96, 125–6, 123–4, 73–76, 65–66, 37–38, 21–22), preceded by prose extracts from one of the printed editions of the *Arcadia*.

Bodleian MS. Eng. poet. d. 3 (*Summary Catalogue* 30049). Extracts of verse and prose transcribed by Edward Pudsey in 1616 or earlier.

Contains CS 32 (f. 1) and sentences from the *Defence of Poesie* (f. 73ʳ⁻ᵛ), probably from 98 or a later folio.

*[Ra] Bodleian MS. Rawlinson poet. 85 (*Summary Catalogue* 14579). An anthology of 144 poems, by Breton, Dyer, Robert Mills, the Earl of Oxford, Ralegh, James Reshoulde, Sidney, and others, compiled in the late 1580's by a Cambridge student or graduate.

Contains 25 poems by or attributed to Sidney, a far larger number than by any other author: OA 7. 152–6 (f. 65ᵛ); OA 13. 113–39, 141–4, 146–54 (f. 22ʳ⁻ᵛ); OA 21 (f. 23ᵛ); OA 22 (f. 23); OA 33 (f. 24); OA 38 (f. 5ᵛ); OA 41 (f. 21ᵛ); OA 51 (f. 9); and OA 71 (ff. 20–21ᵛ); CS 3 (f. 9ᵛ); CS 8–11 (f. 55ʳ⁻ᵛ); CS 16 (f. 8ᵛ); CS 19 (f. 11ᵛ); CS 21 (f. 12); CS 22 (ff. 102–3ᵛ); CS 23 (ff. 12ᵛ–13); and CS 25. 27–34 (f. 65ᵛ); AS iv (f. 42ʳ⁻ᵛ); AS viii. 1–36, 41–104 (ff. 34ᵛ–36ᵛ); and AS x. 1–30, 37–54 (ff. 107ᵛ–8); and two poems, PP 2 (f. 9) and AT 5 (ff. 25ᵛ–26), which are subscribed 'S. P. S.' A note on f. 85 indicates that the manuscript also originally contained OA 31 on a leaf near the beginning which is now missing. Philip Bliss printed from this manuscript OA 41, CS 10, 11, and 16, and PP 2, in *Bibliographical Miscellanies*, Oxford, 1813, pp. 62–65; and lines 9–36 of AT 5 in his edition of *Athenae Oxonienses*, i (1813), 525 (see above, p. 354). The entire manuscript has been edited by Dr. L. A. Cummings (typescript in Washington University Library), who suggests that it was compiled in his younger years by Sir John Finett (1571–1641).

Fourteen poems (including AT 5 and PP 2) are signed with Sidney's name or initials, nine are anonymous (OA 7, 13, 22, 33, and 41; and CS 19, 22, 23, and 25), and two are wrongly attributed (CS 21 to 'Mr Nowell', and AS x to 'Britton'). The scattered location of the poems, the corruption of their texts, and the uncertainty in attribution indicate that they were copied from other anthologies rather than directly from complete manuscripts of the *Old Arcadia*, *Certain Sonnets*, and *Astrophil and Stella*.

The nine *Old Arcadia* poems contain numerous errors, none of which provides evidence for relating them to any other extant text. The eleven *Certain Sonnets* also contain numerous errors; four of them (CS 3, 16, 19, 23) and Dyer's 'Prometheus' (CS 16a) also appear in Hy with texts that agree significantly in error. AS iv contains variants in 30 of its 54 lines, but does not appear to be related to any other known text; AS viii has 14 significant agreements in error with Ha; and AS x has six significant agreements in error with Hn.

Bodleian MS. Rawlinson poet. 142 (*Summary Catalogue* 14636). Extracts, mid-seventeenth century.

Contains OA 3 (f. 26^v), from one of the printed editions of the *Arcadia*.

Bodleian MS. Rawlinson poet. 148 (*Summary Catalogue* 15366). Poems collected by John Lilliat between 1589 and 1599.

Contains CS 15 (f. 86), OA 21 (ff. 99^v–100), and OA 68 (f. 5^v), transcribed from the 1598 folio. On f. 69^{r-v} are two sonnets by D. E. 'On the Lady Riche', describing her attack of smallpox in 1597, when 'moalhills' appeared upon 'that rose and lilie playne *Riche* bewties seat'.

Bodleian MS. Rawlinson poet. 172 (*Summary Catalogue* 14664). A miscellaneous collection of poems, in different hands and on separate sheets of paper, composed from the late sixteenth to the early eighteenth centuries.

Contains OA 15 (f. 6) and AS **37.** 5–9 and 12–14 (f. 15^v) without indication of authorship; probably transcribed early in the seventeenth century. OA 15 varies in 11 words from the critical text; though its reading 'brauest' in line 7 agrees in error with Je, it contains no trace of Je's erroneous readings in line 12, and its reading 'honor' in line 8 shows that it could not derive from any print other than 90. AS 37 contains eight unique variants in its eight lines. The degree of corruption of both poems indicates manuscript transmission; so the present copies were probably made immediately from manuscript sources, which may ultimately have derived from earlier prints.

AS 37 is the first item in a collection of 'Epitaphes' and is headed 'Ladie Rich:' It is followed immediately by:

> Heare lyeth Penelope or my ladie Rich
> or my ladie of Deuonshire I know not w^ch
> she shuffled, shee cutt she dealt & plaid
> she died neither weife vidowe nor maid
> One stone containes her this death can doe
> which in her life was not content with two.

The latter piece became one of the most widely circulated poems of the earlier seventeenth century—I have noted it in versions of from two to six lines in more than a dozen manuscripts, printed in the 1640 *Wits Recreations* and the 1674 Camden's *Remains*, and translated into Latin in British Museum MS. Additional 15227, f. 24ᵛ. A related poem in Huntington MS. HM 116, p. 65, is headed:

> On yᵉ L[ady] Rich & Earle of Devonshire
> The Divell men say is dead in devonshire Late
> Of Late did devonshire live in rich estate
> Till Rich wth toyes did devonshire bewitch
> That Devonshire died & left yᵉ Divell rich.

Another copy of this is in British Museum MS. Additional 25303, f. 98.

Corpus Christi College, Oxford, MS. 328. A collection of poems compiled in the second quarter of the seventeenth century.

Contains OA 62 (ff. 85–86ᵛ) titled 'In commendation of a beautifull lady'; copied from 93 or a later print.

*[Ma] Marsh's Library, Dublin, MS. Z 3. 5. 21 (formerly V 3. 5. 37). A miscellany of verse and prose in several hands, containing items composed 1572–1615.

Most of the verse is in earlier hands and probably was transcribed in the 1590's. Inside the front cover is the name 'Robert Thornton' (Thomas Thornton of Christ Church, later master of Ledbury Hospital in Herefordshire, was Sidney's tutor at Oxford); inside the back cover, 'Wm Sheridan'. The manuscript has probably been in Marsh's Library since its foundation in 1705, and may have been one of Bishop Stillingfleet's books. Described by Edward Dowden, *Modern Quarterly of Language and Literature*, i (1898), 3–4.

Contains 57 English poems by Constable, Dyer, Sir Henry Goodyer, Francis Kinwelmarsh, the Earl of Oxford, Ralegh, James Reshoulde, Sidney, and unidentified authors; most of these also appear in other manuscripts or early prints (12 in Ra, 11 in Hy, &c.), but all appear to be substantive texts.

On ff. 17ᵛ–19ᵛ are five poems by Sidney with no indication of authorship: CS 15, OA 17, CS 23, CS 22, and CS 19. The texts are quite accurate and could not come from any of the prints. Lines 3 and 7 of OA 17 show that it descends from T through the same intermediary from which Fl also descends. The four *Certain Sonnets* derive from an original similar to but not the same as Cl (Ma and Cl are the only extant texts that preserve the heading to CS 15, but Ma does not have the Cl errors at CS **15.** 6, **19.** 3, &c.); they are substantive texts equal in authority to 98, Cl, and Bo.

National Library of Scotland MS. 2059 (Drummond MS., Vol. VII). Extracts in prose and verse by William Drummond of Hawthornden, early seventeenth century.

Contains 144 pages of extracts (ff. 6ᵛ, 36–42, 166, 236ᵛ–99ᵛ) in prose and verse from Sidney's *Lady of May*, *Arcadia*, and *Certain Sonnets*, copied from one of the folio editions, probably 1599 (on f. 381 Drummond listed among his books an *Arcadia* for which he had paid 6s. 3d., approximately the price of the 1599 edition).

*[Dn] National Library of Scotland MS. 2060 (Drummond MS., Vol. VIII). 'Democritie', a collection of prose jests and other items collected by William Drummond of Hawthornden, early seventeenth century.

Contains a version of PP 3 headed 'S. P. S. on his picture' f. 9ᵛ and the same lines without a heading on f. 48ᵛ.

A. S. W. Rosenbach MS. 197 (Cosens–Ellsworth). A mid-seventeenth-century miscellany. Present location unknown.

Contains a 15-line poem imitating and partly made up from OA 15 (p. 81), noted as taken from 'An old paper of my coz. Burrows'. The readings 'doe' from line 5 and 'honour' from line 8 of the original indicate that the poem was imitated from 90.

*[Fo] Folger Shakespeare Library MS. 1. 112 (Cornwallis–Lysons MS.). An anthology of 33 poems probably compiled by Anne Cornwaleys in the 1590's. Described by W. H. Bond in the *Adams Memorial Studies* (1948), pp. 683–93. A transcript made by George Steevens before 1800 is bound at the end of a printed copy of Thomas Watson's *Ekatompathia* [1582] now in the Harvard Library.

Contains CS 16a and 16 (ff. 13–14), properly attributed to 'Dier' and 'Sydney', in texts related to Hy and Ra.

Folger MS. 452. 4. A poetical miscellany of the mid-seventeenth century.

Contains OA 62 (ff. 93–96ᵛ), copied from 1621 or a later print.

Folger MS. 1302. 2. A miscellany of prose and verse of the late seventeenth and early eighteenth centuries.

Contains an inaccurate transcript of CS 32 (f. 7), headed 'By Sir ffrancis Bacon'. Probably taken from a late manuscript miscellany ultimately derived from a print.

*[Fl] Folger MS. 2071. 7. A miscellany of prose and verse compiled by Joseph Hall in the seventeenth century.

Contains OA 17 (f. 187), subscribed 'T. L.' Line 7 'I' for 'they' shows that the text derives from an original similar to the original of Ma.

POEMS IN PRINTED BOOKS

*[Go] *A briefe declaration of the shews, deuices, speeches, and inuentions, done & performed before the Queenes Maiestie, & the French Ambassadours . . . on the Munday and Tuesday in Whitson weeke last, Anno 1581 Collected . . . by Henry Goldwel, Gen. Imprinted at London, by Robert Waldegraue, . . . [1581].*

STC 11990; entered 1 July 1581. Reprinted in Holinshed's *Chronicles*, iii (1587), 1316–21, and in John Nichols, *Progresses . . . of Queen Elizabeth*, ii (1788), 121–42. Contains PP 4 and 5 (A8ᵛ–B1). Copy used: Huntington 59975.

*[Bd] *Psalmes, Sonets, & songs of sadnes and pietie, made into Musicke of fiue parts: wherof, some of them going abroad among diuers, in vntrue coppies, are heare truely corrected, and th'other being Songs very rare and newly composed, are heere published, . . . By William Byrd, . . . 1588.*

STC 4253; entered 6 November 1587. Reprinted [1590?]. Ed. E. H. Fellowes, *The English Madrigal School*, xiv (1920). Words and music of 35 songs by various unnamed writers; the last two ('Come to me grief . . .' and 'O that most rare brest . . .') are titled, 'The funerall songs of that honorable Gent. Syr Phillip Sidney Knight'.

Contains AS vi (No. 16), anonymous and untitled, in an extremely corrupt text whose readings provide no acceptable evidence for relating it to any other known text.

*[Fr] *The Arcadian Rhetorike: Or The Praecepts of Rhetorike made plaine by examples, . . . out of Homers Ilias, and Odissea, Virgils Æglogs, Georgikes, and Æneis, Sir Philip Sydneis Arcadia, Songs and Sonets, Torquato Tassoes Goffredo, Aminta, Torrismondo, Salust his*

Iudith, and both his Semaines, Boscan and Garcillassoes Sonets and Æglogs. By Abraham Fraunce. At London, Printed by Thomas Orwin [*1588*].

STC 11338; entered 11 June 1588. Ed. Ethel Seaton, 1950. A handbook of rhetoric for the most part translated from Talaeus, dedicated to the Countess of Pembroke, with quotations illustrating the rhetorical figures drawn from the authors named on the title-page and others. Contains, in addition to numerous extracts from the prose of the *Old Arcadia*, 199 lines from 31 *Old Arcadia* poems; CS 3; and AS **1.** 1–5, **23.** 12–14, **44.** 1–4, **47.** 9–14, **54.** 14, **89.** 5–14, and song vii entire. E. Koeppel (*Anglia*, x [1888], 522–30) first noticed the extracts and saw that they came from manuscript sources; Flügel (p. lxxii) pointed out the resemblance of the AS quotations to 98. The AS quotations are actually from the manuscript (X) used by the 98 printer, and CS 3 is also from the manuscript used by the 98 printer; but the *Arcadia* quotations are from St and so are not substantive.

Fraunce could not have drawn from the *New Arcadia* because he calls Pyrocles Cleophila rather than Zelmane, and quotes OA 35 which appears only in the *Old Arcadia*. His manuscript of the *Old Arcadia* must have been of the St-Bo type, because only in those two manuscripts does the name Cosma, which he mentions, appear in OA 29. But he could not have used Bo, because in 17 places where Bo is in error he has the correct reading. However, he varies from St in only 26 of the 199 lines of verse he quotes; two of these (**4.** 10 and **71.** 3) are corrections of obvious errors in St, and the rest are errors he himself made in the process of copying. He also agrees in error with St in three passages: at **12.** 11, where the correct reading is 'So becomes our losse', Fr reads 'So become our losses', an attempt to emend the obviously wrong reading of St 'so becomes our losses'; at **30.** 108 Fr and St read 'virgins' for 'virgin'; and at **71.** 2 Fr and St read 'which hunt' for 'that haunt'. Fraunce clearly drew his *Old Arcadia* quotations from St itself.

Fraunce was a native of Shrewsbury, studied at Cambridge from 1576 until he received his M.A. in 1583, and was a member of Gray's Inn from the latter year until he was called to the bar in February 1588; by the summer of 1590 he was practising as a barrister in the Court of the Marches at Ludlow, the headquarters of the Earl of Pembroke who had succeeded Sir Henry Sidney as Lord President. He 'first came in presence of' Sidney in the spring of 1581, and during that year and the next sought his patronage by dedicating to him manuscript treatises on logic and impresas and a Latin translation of an Italian play. He said he had been 'bred up' at Cambridge partly by the assistance of Sidney, whom he called his 'Master and Patron', and at his funeral walked in the procession among his gentlemen and yeomen servants. After Sidney's death he sought and received the patronage of the surviving members of his family, especially the Countess of Pembroke.

Since in his dedications of 1581 and 1582 Fraunce gave no indication of knowing that his patron was himself a man of letters, he may not have gained access to manuscript copies of Sidney's writings until after his death. He was probably given access to St by his Herefordshire neighbour Sylvanus Scory, and to the manuscripts of CS and AS by the Countess of Pembroke.

*[Pu] *The Arte Of English Poesie.* [*By George Puttenham*] . . .
Printed by Richard Field, . . . *1589.*

STC 20519. Entered to T. Orwin 9 November 1588 and to R. Field 7 April
1589. Ed. Gladys D. Willcock and Alice Walker, 1936. Quotes CS **27**. 39–40
(Z3), OA **45**. 1–8 (Bb4ᵛ)—arranged as a ten-line song, and OA **61**. 13–14
(Bb1), from manuscript sources.

*[Bd] *Songs of sundrie natures, some of grauitie, and others of myrth,*
fit for all companies and voyces. Lately made and composed into Musicke
of 3. 4. 5. and 6. parts . . . By William Byrd, . . . *1589.*

STC 4256; entered 6 December 1596. Reprinted 1610. Ed. E. H. Fellowes,
The English Madrigal School, xv (1920). Words and music of 33 songs by various
unnamed writers.

Contains AS **x**. 1–18 (No. 33), anonymous and untitled, in a corrupt text
containing no readings relating it directly to any other extant text.

*[Hn] *Orlando Fvrioso In English Heroical Verse, By Iohn Harington*
[*1591*].

STC 746; entered 26 February 1591 (title-page portrait dated 1 August 1591
and colophon dated 1591). Reprinted 1607, 1634. Harington probably wrote the
preface and notes during the summer of 1591 as he was seeing his work through
the press.

Quotes seven rhyme words from OA **7**. 1–15 ('Preface',¶ 8ᵛ) and OA 65 entire
(notes to Bk. XI, H3), also quotes AS 18 entire and paraphrases AS 37 and
viii. 95–96 (notes to Bk. XVI, L4ᵛ). Harington introduced OA 65 as 'that
excellent verse of *Sir Philip Sidney* in his first *Arcadia* (which I know not by
what mishap is left out in the printed booke)', which shows that he quoted from
an *Old Arcadia* manuscript. He introduced AS 18 by saying:

Petrarke . . . in the midst of all his lamentation, still had this comfort, that his love
was placed on a worthie Ladie: and our English *Petrarke, Sir Philip Sidney,* or (as
Sir Walter Raulegh in his Epitaph worthely calleth him) the *Scipio* and the *Petrarke* of
our time, often comforteth him selfe in his sonets of *Stella*, though dispairing to attaine
his desire, and (though that tyrant honor still refused) yet the nobilitie, the beautie,
the worth, the graciousnesse, and those her other perfections, as made him both count
her, and call her inestimably rich, makes him in the midst of those his mones, rejoyce
even in his owne greatest losses, as in his eighteenth sonet which many I am sure have
read.

His phrase 'though that tyrant honor still refused' is a quotation of AS **viii**. 95–96
('Tyran honour doth thus use thee, / Stella's selfe might not refuse thee'), and
his following words paraphrase AS 37 which tells us that Stella's name is
Rich. His quotations and references were taken from Zⁱ, a manuscript of
Astrophil and Stella in his own possession, from which Ho was also copied.

*[Di] *Diana. Or, The excellent conceitful Sonnets of H[enry]. C[onstable]. Augmented with diuers Quatorzains of honorable and lerned personages . . . Printed by Iames Roberts for Richard Smith.* [*1594–97*].

STC 5638. Not entered. There are two editions, one represented by the British Museum copy, the other by the Bodleian and Huntington copies, both printed between 1594 and 1597. An anthology of 77 sonnets, including all but one of the 23 sonnets of Constable's *Diana* printed in 1592, eight by Sidney, one by Richard Smith, and 46 by unknown authors.

Contains CS 1–2, 8–11, 18, and 20 (C3ᵛ–6ᵛ, D4), printed from a manuscript having characteristics almost identical with the one used by the editor of 98. I have collated the British Museum and Huntington copies, which in the Sidney sonnets differ from one another only in a few spellings.

*[Bn] *The Arbor Of amorous Deuises. Wherin, young Gentlemen may reade many plesant fancies, and fine deuises: . . . By N[icholas]. B[reton]. Gent. Imprinted at London by Richard Iohnes, . . . 1597.*

STC 3631. Entered 7 January 1594, in which year an edition was printed but no copy survives. Facsimile ed. H. E. Rollins, 1936. An anthology of 44 poems, few if any of which are actually by Breton. Contains CS 3 (B3ᵛ–4), printed from a manuscript similar to the original of Hy.

Englands Helicon . . . Printed by I. R[oberts]. for Iohn Flasket, . . . 1600.

STC 3191; entered 4 August 1600. Reprinted with additions, 1614. Ed. H. E. Rollins, 1935. An anthology of 150 pastoral poems by about 30 Elizabethan authors, planned by John Bodenham and probably edited by N[icholas] L[ing] with the assistance of A. B.

Contains 14 poems by Sidney, all attributed to him by name: LM 2 (lines 7–32 only); OA 4, 6, 17, 60; CS 4, 16a (by Dyer), 16, 18, 28, 30; AS iii, iv, viii, and ix. A poem by Sidney opens the anthology, and he is represented by a larger number of selections than any other contributor except the translator Bartholomew Yong—Spenser is represented by three poems and Shakespeare by one. Professor Rollins pointed out (ii. 33) that all Sidney's texts are from 98, and in his notes gives a complete list of variant readings. However, AS ix differs from the other texts in that it was originally transcribed from one of the Quartos (probably Q 3) and then partly corrected by collation with 98.

To the editor of *Englands Helicon* Sidney was always Astrophel, and he therefore entitled CS 4 'Another of *Astrophell*' and CS 30 '*Astrophels* Loue is dead'. He at first wrongly attributed 'Faire in a morne' to Sidney and titled it '*Astrophell* his Song of *Phillida* and *Coridon*', though later by a cancel slip he correctly changed the attribution to N. Breton. The second edition of 1614 reprinted the 14 poems by Sidney and added OP 2, the text of which was taken, as Professor Rollins has shown, from the 1611 edition of *A Poetical Rapsody*.

Bel-vedére Or The Garden Of The Mvses . . . Imprinted at London by F. K[ingston]. for H. Astley, 1600.

STC 3189; entered 11 August and 3 November 1600. Reprinted 1610. Ed. James Crossley, for the Spenser Society, 1875. A collection of 'sentences', verse quotations of one or two lines each arranged under topical headings, planned and in part collected by John Bodenham and edited by A[nthony] M[undy]. The preface states that the quotations were taken 'out of sundry things extant, and many in priuat', by noble and gentleman poets including 'Sir Philip Sidney'. No authors' names are attached to the extracts, and Charles Crawford (*Englische Studien*, xliii [1911], 206) was able to identify only six quotations from Sidney, one from the prose of the *Arcadia* and five from *Astrophil and Stella*. The extracts have been heavily altered by the editor and are of no textual value. The reading 'dare not' in AS **54.** 14 shows that it was drawn from one of the Quartos (probably Q3); there is no reason to assume that manuscript sources were used.

Englands Parnassus: Or The choysest Flowers of our Moderne Poets, with their Poeticall comparisons . . . Imprinted at London for N. L[ing]. C. B[urby]. and T. H[ayes]. 1600.

STC 378–80 (listed as three issues); entered 2 October 1600. Ed. Charles Crawford, 1913. A collection of quotations from various English poets, gathered and arranged under topical headings by Robert Allott. The author's name is given with each extract, and though attributions are sometimes wrong, Mr. Crawford has traced almost all the quotations to their sources.

Contains 57 selections from Sidney, including 413 lines from 36 poems in the *Arcadia*, *Certain Sonnets*, and *Astrophil and Stella* (see Crawford's index, p. 380). All but one of the 24 OA poems quoted are drawn from 98; OA 65 is taken from Harington's *Orlando Furioso*. CS **7.** 1–2 and **9.** 1–4 are signed 'H. C.' and are taken from Constable's *Diana . . . Augmented*. Eight of the ten AS poems quoted are definitely copied from Q1 or Q3 (the two Quartos do not vary from one another in the lines quoted); AS 32 is from 98, and AS 79 appears to be from 99. There is no evidence to indicate that any of the selections are substantive.

*[Dv] A Poetical Rapsody Containing, Diuerse . . . Poesies [by Francis Davison and others], . . . Printed at London by V. S[immes]. for Iohn Baily, . . . 1602.

STC 6373. Entered 28 May 1602. Reprinted 1608, 1611, and 1621. Ed. H. E. Rollins, 1931–2. An anthology of 176 poems by various authors, edited by Francis Davison. The first two items in the volume are OP 6 and 7, headed 'Two Pastoralls, made by Sir Philip Sidney, neuer yet published'. This, the only substantive text, appears to be a careful printing of an authentic manuscript.

Lusus Imaginis Iocosae sive Echus A Variis Poetis, variis linguis & numeris exculti. Ex Bibliotheca Theodori Dousae . . . [Utrecht] 1638.

An anthology of echo poems in various languages, first collected by the

Netherlands poet Johan van der Does the younger (1571–1596). Contains OA 31 'Out of the countesse of Pembrokes Arcadia'. Miss Jean Robertson informs me that Sidney's poem did not appear in the first edition of the anthology in 1608 and that its text is from a 1621 or later printed *Arcadia*.

MUSICAL SETTINGS

British Museum MS. Additional 15117 (*c.* 1616). OA 45 (f. 18ᵛ), and AS ii (f. 19). The words of OA 45 (which is a sonnet, but is set as three quatrains with the final couplet used as a refrain after each quatrain) are from one of the 93-13 folios, the words of AS ii are probably from Q 3. The music for AS ii was printed by J. P. Cutts, *SQ* xi (1960), 91.

British Museum MS. Additional 31723 (1798). AS i (ff. 38–39ᵛ), 'Canzonett. The Poetry from Sir Philip Sidney'; and AS xi (ff. 36–37ᵛ) 'Dialogue & Duetto. Poetry Sir Philip Sidney'. Both with music by R. J. S. Stevens (1757–1837). The second was also 'Printed for the Author, Charterhouse', without date.

British Museum MS. Additional 31810 (1799). CS 27 (ff. 101ᵛ–5) 'Glee for five Voices', music by R. J. S. Stevens.

British Museum MS. Loan 35. OA 34 (f. 9ᵛ), and OA 54 (f. 1ᵛ). Reported by J. P. Cutts, *RN* xi (1958), 184.

Christ Church, Oxford, MS. 439. AS ix (f. 9). Reported by J. P. Cutts, *RN* xi (1958), 184.

William Byrd, *Psalmes, Sonets, & songs of sadnes and pietie*, 1588. AS vi with music in five parts. See Bd above. Byrd's music was copied *c.* 1611 in British Museum MS. Additional 31992, f. 37ᵛ, and after 1613 in British Museum MS. Additional 29401–5, ff. 8ᵛ–9.

[George Puttenham], *The Arte of English Poesie*, 1589. OA 45—no music, but the sonnet is quoted as a ten-line song. See Pu above.

William Byrd, *Songs of sundrie natures*, 1589. AS x with music in five parts. See Bd above. Byrd's music was copied *c.* 1611 in British Museum MS. Additional 31992, f. 36; after 1613 in British Museum MS. Additional 29401–5, ff. 3ᵛ–4; and in the eighteenth century in British Museum MS. Additional 23626, f. 73.

John Dowland, *The Second Booke of Songs or Ayres*, 1600. OA **34.** 1–2 (No. 10) with four-part setting; Sidney's lines are used as the opening of each of the song's four eight-line stanzas. The words of Dowland's first stanza were copied in Bodleian MS. Douce 280, f. 69; and the words of all four stanzas were re-printed, without the music, by E. H. Fellowes, *English Madrigal Verse* (1920), p. 42.

Thomas Morley, *The First Booke of Ayres*, 1600. AS xi (No. 7), with two-part setting; words almost certainly from 98. Words and music ed. E. H. Fellowes, *English School of Lutenist Song Writers*, 1st series, xvii (1932).

Robert Jones, *The Second Booke Of Songs And Ayres*, 1601. OA 21 (No. 11) with three-part setting; words from 90–99. Words and music ed. E. H. Fellowes, *The English School of Lutenist Song Writers*, v (1926).

Thomas Bateson, *The first set of English Madrigales*, 1604. CS 4. 1–7 (No. 3) with music for three voices; words from *Englands Helicon*. Words and music ed. E. H. Fellowes, *The English Madrigal School*, xxi (1922).

Henry Youll, *Canzonets To Three Voyces*, 1608. AS **iv.** 1–6 (No. 6); words identical with 98–05. Words and music ed. E. H. Fellowes, *The English Madrigal School*, xxviii (1923).

[Thomas Ravenscroft], *Pammelia. Musicks Miscellanie*, 1609. OA **5.** 1–6 (No. 95) set as a round for six voices; words from 93–05. Words and music ed. Peter Warlock, 1928. Ravenscroft's music and his version of Sidney's words were transcribed in 'Ane buik of roundells . . . Collected and notted by dauid meluill. 1612' (No. 68), manuscript edited by Granville Bantock and H. Orsmond Anderton for the Roxburghe Club, 1916. J. P. Cutts, *RN* xi (1958), 183–8, prints Ravenscroft's music and Melvill's copy.

Robert Douland, *A Musicall Banquet*, 1610. AS viii (No. 7), AS ix (No. 4), and AS x (No. 5), each with three-part setting; words from Q 3. Douland dedicated his anthology to Sir Philip's brother, Sir Robert Sidney Viscount Lisle. The music for AS ix and x is anonymous, but that for AS viii is by 'Tesseir' (Charles Tessier, who dedicated his *Premier Livre de Chansons et Airs* to Lady Rich in 1597). The words only were reprinted by E. H. Fellowes, *English Madrigal Verse* (1920), pp. 454–9.

Robert Jones, *The Muses Gardin for Delights*, 1610. CS 27 (No. 17) with three-part setting; words from 98–05. Words and music ed. E. H. Fellowes, *The English School of Lutenist Song Writers*, 2nd series, xv (1927).

William Corkine, *The Second Booke Of Ayres*, 1612. CS 3 (No. 9) with three-part setting; words from 90. Words and music ed. E. H. Fellowes, *The English School of Lutenist Song Writers*, 2nd series, xiii (1927).

John Ward, *The First Set of English Madrigals*, 1613. OA **30.** 38–41 expanded to five lines (No. 12) with four-part setting, OA 45 (Nos. 1 and 2) with three-part setting, CS **16.** 1–4 (No. 7) with four-part setting, and AS **x.** 43–48 (No. 8) with four-part setting; words from 98-13. Words and music ed. E. H. Fellowes, *The English Madrigal School*, xix (1922).

Thomas Vautor, *The First Set: Beeing Songs of diuers Ayres and Natures*, 1619–20. OA 51 (Nos. 8 and 9) with setting for five voices; words from 93-13. Words and music ed. E. H. Fellowes, *The English Madrigal School*, xxxiv (1924).

Martin Peerson, *Private Musicke*, 1620. OA 51 (No. 13) with music for four voices; words probably from 93-13. Words only reprinted E. H. Fellowes, *English Madrigal Verse* (1920), p. 163.

Francis Pilkington, *The Second Set Of Madrigals, and Pastorals*, 1624. OA **4.** 5–10 (No. 14) with music for five voices; words probably from 90-23. Words and music ed. E. H. Fellowes, *The English Madrigal School*, xxvi (1923).

A. B. Philo-Mus., *Synopsis of Vocal Musick*, 1680. AS iv (pp. 124–5), words from *Englands Helicon*; and a medley made up from AS **viii.** 29–46 and **x.** 1–2 (pp. 126–7), words probably from an earlier print—both with three-part musical setting by Giovanni Giacomo Castoldi [i.e. Gastoldi] da Carravaggio (d. 1622?). The words and music from the medley made up from AS viii and x were reprinted in the third edition of John Forbes's *Songs and Fancies*, Aberdeen, 1682, as item No. 6 in an added section titled 'Severall of the Choisest Italian Songs Composed by Giovanni Giacomo Castoldi da Carravaggio'.

There are eight or more nineteenth and twentieth-century settings of OA 45 (see S. A. Tannenbaum, *Sidney: a Concise Bibliography*, 1941, items 314–24).

TABLE OF VERSE FORMS

Sidney's verse forms are here listed in order according to their rhythm, number of lines to the unit, order of rhymes, and line length. Capital letters indicate refrains; subscript numbers syllables per line; numbers in parentheses the total lines in the poem, or if separated by a hyphen the lines of a polymetric poem containing the form in question. Poems whose structure can be variously analysed have their components cross listed (i.e. the first entry below indicates that OA **42**, which is listed as a 14-line poem, can also be considered as monorhyme); but final couplets in stanzaic poems and concluding partial stanzas in the *Psalms*, though they are noted in the main entry, are not separately cross listed.

ACCENTUAL IAMBIC

1 a_{10} monorhyme. See OA 42:14.

1 a_{12} monorhyme. PS 15 (13).

2 aa_8. OA 6 (8), 62 (146); OP 3 (8).

2 $a_{10}a_4$ pentameter lines in which end of first line rhymes to fourth syllable of next. OA 7 (115–46), 9 (1–25), 28 (73–96 and 101–8).

2 aa_{10}. OA 27 (42), 48 (2), 58 (2), 68 (2); PP 3 (2).

2 $a_{12}a_6$. PS 2 (32).

2 aa_{12}. OA 26 (16), 29 (1–50), 73 (186); OP 1 (6).

2 $a_{12}a_{14}$ poulter's measure. OA 3 (14); PP 1 (48).

3 aaa_8. PS 29 (29) ends aa.

3 aaa_{10}. See OA 1:10.

3 aba_8 terza rima. PS 30 (39) ends yzz.

3 aba_{10} terza rima. OA 7 (1–114 and 167–79) ends wywyzyz, 9 (32–61 and 66–141) ends z, 10 (98) ends zz, 23 (14) ends zz, 24 (14) same rhyme words as 23, 28 (1–72 and 96–101 and 108–26) ends z, 29 (51–149) ends yzz, 30 (5–190) ends yzz, 67 (120) ends yzz, 75 (75) with refrain; CS 12 (18); PS 7 (48) ends yzz.

4 $aa_{11}B_{10}A_{11}$. AS i (36).

4 $aabb_8$. OA 30 (1–4).

4 aa_8bb_9. PS 8 (34) ends aa.

4 $aa_{10}bb_8$. PS 17 (48).

4 $aabb_{10}$. OA 9 (62–65).

4 $aa_{11}bb_{10}$. PS 22 (78) ends aa.

4 $a_8b_7c_8b_7$ with first and third lines rhymed internally. PS 19 (64).

4 $a_{10}b_5a_{10}b_3$. PS 13 (20).

4 $abab_{10}$. OA 72 (101–4). See OA 1:10, 49:18, 72:10.

4 $a_{10}b_{11}a_{10}b_5$ accentual Sapphic. OA 59 (16); PS 6 (32).

5 $a_6a_{10}bc_8b_{10}$ next stanza begins with c rhyme. PS 20 (35) last stanza ends bbb.

5 $abaab_{10}$. CS 17 (52) ends aa.

5 $ababb_8$. PS 4 (35).

5 $abab_{10}b_4$. PS 9 (65).

5 $ababb_{10}$. See OA 16:10, 38:17, 50:22.

5 $a_{10}b_6c_{10}c_6d_{10}$ last line repeated as first line of next stanza. OA 7 (147–66).

6 sestina. See OA 70:39, 71:75, 76:39.

6 $aababb_{10}$. PS 35 (72).

6 $a_{10}a_8b_{10}b_8c_{10}c_8$. PS 39 (42).

6 $aa_{10}bb_{11}cc_{10}$. PS 1 (22) ends aabb.

6 $aabb_{12}cc_{11}$. AS iii (18).

6 $aabbcc_{12}$. OP 1 (6).

6 aabbcc$_{14}$. AS vii (18).

6 a$_6$a$_4$bc$_6$c$_4$b$_6$. PS 33 (84).

6 aa$_6$b$_7$cc$_6$b$_7$. PS 3 (36).

6 aa$_6$b$_{10}$cc$_6$b$_{10}$. PS 26 (39) ends aaa.

6 aa$_8$b$_7$cc$_8$b$_7$. PS 32 (42).

6 aa$_{10}$b$_7$cc$_{10}$b$_7$. PS 14 (24).

6 aabccb$_{10}$. PS 31 (69) ends aaa.

6 aa$_{12}$b$_{13}$cc$_{12}$b$_{13}$. AS v (90).

6 abaabb$_{10}$. OA 19 (12).

6 ababab$_8$. PS 36 (36).

6 ababcc$_6$. AS vi (54).

6 abab$_6$cc$_8$. PS 25 (78).

6 a$_6$b$_7$a$_6$b$_7$CC$_8$. OP 6 (60).

6 abab$_8$cc$_4$. PS 27 (66).

6 ababCC$_8$. OA 5 (12), 25 (12).

6 ababcc$_{10}$. LM 1 (12), 2 (32) ends aa, 3 (18); OA 8 (48), 9 (26–31), 18 (18), 21 (18), 36 (18), 37 (18), 46 (18), 64 (126); CS 19 (18).

6 a$_8$b$_6$b$_4$a$_8$c$_6$c$_4$. PS 23 (27) ends aaa.

7 ababbcc$_{10}$ rhyme royal. OA 22 (14), 66 (161).

7 ababbcc$_{12}$. PS 18 (91).

8 aaa$_8$b$_7$ccc$_8$b$_7$. PS 11 (24).

8 aabb$_6$ccdd$_8$. PS 10 (80).

8 aabbccdd$_8$. See OA 6:2; OP 3:2.

8 a$_{10}$a$_6$b$_{10}$b$_6$c$_{10}$c$_6$d$_{10}$d$_6$. PS 41 (48).

8 ababaabb$_{10}$. OA 41 (8).

8 abababcc$_{10}$ ottava rima. OA 35 (16), 54 (16) same rhymes in second stanza; OP 4 (544).

8 ababbcbc$_{10}$. See OA 4:10.

8 ababccdd$_{10}$. OA 17 (8).

8 ab$_6$a$_8$bcd$_6$c$_8$d$_6$. CS 28 (40).

8 a$_7$b$_6$a$_7$b$_6$c$_7$d$_6$c$_7$d$_6$. CS 23 (36) ends abab.

8 a$_8$b$_7$a$_8$b$_7$c$_8$d$_7$c$_8$d$_7$. PS 21 (52) ends abab.

8 abbacdcd$_{10}$. PS 5 (40).

8 a$_6$bb$_8$ac$_6$dd$_8$c$_6$. PS 34 (80).

8 a$_8$bb$_9$ac$_8$dd$_9$c$_8$. PS 37 (104).

8 abcabcdd$_{10}$. OA 43 (8).

9 abab$_{10}$bc$_6$c$_{10}$d$_6$D$_{10}$. OA 63 (99).

9 abab$_8$ccddc$_9$. CS 29 (18).

9 a$_6$ba$_{10}$cc$_6$d$_{10}$d$_6$ee$_{10}$. OP 5 (105–13) envoy.

9 abbabbabb$_{11}$. CS 6 (9).

9 abcabcabc$_{10}$. PS 12 (27).

10 a$_{10}$a$_4$b$_7$c$_6$b$_7$c$_6$DD$_7$EE$_6$. CS 30 (40).

10 ababbababb$_{10}$. OA 44 (10).

10 ababbcacdd_{10} crown. OA 72 (1–100).

10 ababbcbcdd$_{10}$. OA 4 (10).

10 ababbcdcdd$_{10}$. See OA 16:5.

10 ababcccddd$_{10}$. OA 1 (10).

10 abbaabababcc$_{10}$. CS 22 (70).

10 a$_{10}$bb$_8$a$_{10}$cc$_7$deed$_6$. PS 40 (70).

12 abaabbcdccdd$_{10}$. See OA 19:6.

12 ababbabaccdd$_{10}$. See OA 50 (11–22).

12 ababccdedeff$_8$. See OA 5:6, 25:6.

12 ababccdedeff$_{10}$. See LM 1:6.

12 abab$_{11}$cdc$_7$def$_{11}$e$_7$f$_{11}$. CS 3 (24), 4 (24).

12 a$_{13}$b$_8$a$_{13}$b$_8$c$_{13}$d$_8$c$_{13}$d$_8$e$_{13}$f$_8$e$_{13}$f$_8$. PS 24 (24).

13 ab$_6$a$_{10}$cb$_6$c$_{10}$cdee$_6$d$_{10}$f$_6$f$_{10}$. OP 5 (1–104 and 114–26) framed canzone with 9-line envoy.

SONNETS

14 aaaaaaaa aaaaaa$_{10}$. OA 42.

14 abababab ababcc$_{10}$. OA 56.

14 abababab ccdccd$_{10}$. AS 4, 62.

14 abababab ccdeed$_{10}$. AS 3, 61, 73, 88.

14 abababab cdcdcd$_{10}$. OA 53.

14 abababab cdcdee$_{10}$. CS 15, 20; AS 7, 20, 24, 25, 26, 33, 36, 39, 42, 50, 65, 66, 70, 74, 101, 103.

14 abababab cdcdee$_{12}$. AS 1, 77.

14 abababab cddcee$_{10}$. AS 35.

14 ababbaba ababab$_{10}$. OA 39 with two rhyme words 'dark' and 'night'.

14 ababbaba abbabb$_{10}$. OA 51.

14 ababbaba accacc$_{10}$. OA 47.

14 ababbaba bccbcc$_{10}$. CS 31.
14 ababbaba ccdeed$_{10}$. AS 81, 87.
14 ababbaba ccdeed$_{12}$. AS 6.
14 ababbaba cdcdcc$_{10}$. OA 40.
14 ababbaba cdcdee$_{10}$. AS 5, 10, 43, 75.
14 ababbaba cdcd$_{10}$ee$_{11}$. CS 11.

14 ababcbcb dbdbbb$_{10}$. PP 4, 5.
14 ababcdcd efefaa$_{10}$. OA 15, 45.
14 ababcdcd efefdd$_{10}$. CS 21.
14 ababcdcd efefgg$_{10}$. OA 2, 14, 20, 60, 61, 65, 77; CS 8, 9, 10, 16, 18, 32; PP 2.
14 a$_{10}$b$_{11}$a$_{10}$b$_{11}$c$_{10}$d$_{11}$c$_{10}$d$_{11}$e$_{10}$f$_{11}$e$_{10}$f$_{11}$gg$_{10}$. OA 57.

14 abbaabba ababab$_{10}$. AS 89 with two rhyme words 'night' and 'day'.
14 abbaabba ccdccd$_{10}$. AS 40.
14 abbaabba ccdeed$_{10}$. AS 15, 48, 58, 63, 78, 80, 98, 100, 106.
14 abbaabba ccdeed$_{12}$. AS 102.
14 abbaabba cdcdcd$_{10}$. AS 94.
14 abbaabba cdcdee$_{10}$. CS 1, 2; AS 2, 9, 11, 12, 14, 16, 17, 18, 19, 21, 23, 27, 28, 30, 31, 32, 34, 37, 38, 41, 44, 45, 46, 47, 49, 51, 52, 53, 54, 55, 56, 57, 59, 60, 64, 67, 68, 69, 71, 72, 79, 82, 83, 84, 85, 86, 90, 91, 92, 93, 95, 96, 97, 99, 104, 105, 107, 108.
14 abbaabba cdcdee$_{12}$. AS 8, 76.
14 abbaabba cddcee$_{10}$. AS 22.
14 abbaabba cddece$_{10}$. AS 29.
14 abbaabba cdcde$_{11}$. OA 69.
14 abbabaab cddcee$_{10}$. AS 13.
See also the 14-line OA 3:2 poulter's measure, 22:7 rhyme royal, 23:3 and 24:3 terza rima.

15 a$_6$a$_{10}$b$_6$c$_{10}$c$_6$b$_{10}$b$_6$d$_{10}$d$_6$ee$_{10}$d$_6$eff$_{10}$. OA 52 (15), 55 (15).

17 ababb bcbcc dedeeff$_{10}$. OA 38 (17).

18 abab abab baba cacacc$_{10}$. OA 49 (18).
18. See LM 3:6; OA 18:6, 21:6, 36:6, 37:6, 46:6; CS 19:6.

22 ababb cdcdd dede eded ffgg$_{10}$. OA 50 (22).

39 abcdef &c. sestina. OA 70 (39), 76 (39) rhymed.

75 abcdef &c. double sestina. OA 71 (75).

ACCENTUAL TROCHAIC

4 aa$_7$bb$_8$. AS viii (104).
4 a$_8$bb$_7$a$_8$. AS ii (28).
5 a$_7$b$_8$a$_7$b$_8$a$_7$. AS xi (45).
5 a$_7$b$_8$a$_7$bb$_8$. AS ix (50).
5 abbaa$_7$. PS 28 (35).
6 aabb$_7$CC$_8$. AS iv (54) lines 5–6 iambic.
6 aabb$_7$cc$_8$. OP 7 (78).
6 aa$_5$b$_6$cc$_5$b$_6$. PS 43 (36).
6 a$_7$a$_3$bc$_7$c$_3$b$_7$. PS 38 (66).
6 aabccb$_7$. PS 16 (44) ends aa.

6 aa$_7$b$_8$cc$_7$b$_8$. AS x (48).
8 aabb$_8$C$_{12}$D$_{11}$ee$_8$. CS 27 (40) line 5 rhymed internally and lines 5–8 iambic.
8 a$_8$b$_7$a$_8$bcc$_7$dd$_8$. PS 42 (56).
10 A$_{10}$A$_8$Ab$_7$cc$_8$b$_7$c$_8$aA$_7$. CS 7 (40) lines 1–2 iambic.
11 A$_{10}$BBC$_6$d$_8$d$_4$e$_8$e$_4$f$_8$f$_4$A$_{11}$. CS 26 (33) lines 1 and 11 rhymed internally and lines 1–4 iambic.

ACCENTUAL UNCLASSIFIED

9 aabbb$_9$cc$_{12}$dd$_8$. CS 24 (27) see Commentary for rhythmic pattern.

QUANTITATIVE

Anacreontic. OA 32 (57).

Aristophanic. CS 25 (39).

Asclepiadic. OA 34 (42).

Elegiac. OA 11 (20), 74 (86); CS 13 (4), 14 (2).

Hexameter. OA 13 (175), 31 (50) echo; OP 2 (1).

Phaleuciac. OA 33 (30).

Sapphic. OA 12 (28); CS 5 (28) rhymed abab.

POEMS CONTAINING FEMININE RHYMES

OA 6, 7, 9, 27, 28, 30, 57, 59, 62, 64, 66, 67, 69, 70, 71, 72, 73, 75, 76.

CS 3, 4, 5, 6, 7, 11, 23, 26, 27, 29, 30.

AS i, ii, iii, iv, v, viii, ix, x, xi.

OP 5, 6, 7.

PS 1, 3, 6, 8, 11, 13, 14, 16, 19, 21, 22, 24, 28, 32, 37, 38, 40, 42, 43.

There are trisyllabic rhymes in the terza rima of OA 7, 28, 30, 75.

INDEX OF FIRST LINES

(Wrongly attributed poems are listed by first line on pp. 349-53)

PRINTED IN GREAT BRITAIN
AT THE UNIVERSITY PRESS, OXFORD
BY VIVIAN RIDLER
PRINTER TO THE UNIVERSITY